Philip E

BOOK

The Philip E. Lilienthal imprint
honors special books
in commemoration of a man whose work
at University of California Press from 1954 to 1979
was marked by dedication to young authors
and to high standards in the field of Asian Studies.
Friends, family, authors, and foundations have together
endowed the Lilienthal Fund, which enables UC Press
to publish under this imprint selected books
in a way that reflects the taste and judgment
of a great and beloved editor.

The publisher gratefully acknowledges the generous support of the Philip E. Lilienthal Asian Studies Endowment Fund of the University of California Press Foundation, which was established by a major gift from Sally Lilienthal.

The Saint in the Banyan Tree

THE ANTHROPOLOGY OF CHRISTIANITY

Edited by Joel Robbins

1. *Christian Moderns: Freedom and Fetish in the Mission Encounter,* by Webb Keane
2. *A Problem of Presence: Beyond Scripture in an African Church,* by Matthew Engelke
3. *Reason to Believe: Cultural Agency in Latin American Evangelicalism,* by David Smilde
4. *Chanting Down the New Jerusalem: Calypso, Christianity, and Capitalism in the Caribbean,* by Francio Guadeloupe
5. *In God's Image: The Metaculture of Fijian Christianity,* by Matt Tomlinson
6. *Converting Words: Maya in the Age of the Cross,* by William F. Hanks
7. *City of God: Christian Citizenship in Postwar Guatemala,* by Kevin O'Neill
8. *Death in a Church of Life: Moral Passion during Botswana's Time of AIDS,* by Frederick Klaits
9. *Eastern Christians in Anthropological Perspective,* edited by Chris Hann and Hermann Goltz
10. *Studying Global Pentecostalism: Theories and Methods,* by Allan Anderson, Michael Bergunder, Andre Droogers, and Cornelis van der Laan
11. *Holy Hustlers, Schism, and Prophecy: Apostolic Reformation in Botswana,* by Richard Werbner
12. *Moral Ambition: Mobilization and Social Outreach in Evangelical Megachurches,* by Omri Elisha
13. *Spirits of Protestantism: Medicine, Healing, and Liberal Christianity,* by Pamela E. Klassen
14. *The Saint in the Banyan Tree: Christianity and Caste Society in India,* by David Mosse

The Saint in the Banyan Tree

Christianity and Caste Society in India

David Mosse

UNIVERSITY OF CALIFORNIA PRESS
Berkeley Los Angeles London

University of California Press, one of the most distinguished university presses in the United States, enriches lives around the world by advancing scholarship in the humanities, social sciences, and natural sciences. Its activities are supported by the UC Press Foundation and by philanthropic contributions from individuals and institutions. For more information, visit www.ucpress.edu.

University of California Press
Berkeley and Los Angeles, California

University of California Press, Ltd.
London, England

Library of Congress Cataloging-in-Publication Data

Mosse, David.
The saint in the banyan tree : Christianity and caste society in India / David Mosse.
p. cm. — (The anthropology of Christianity ; 14)
Includes bibliographical references (p.) and index.
ISBN 978-0-520-25316-2 (cloth : alk. paper) — ISBN 978-0-520-27349-8 (pbk. : alk. paper) — ISBN 978-0-520-95397-0 (ebook)
1. Christianity—India, South. 2. Tamil (Indic people)—Religion. 3. Christianity and other religions. 4. Social classes—India, South—Religious aspects. 5. Caste—Religious aspects—Christianity. I. Title.
BR1156.I54M67 2012
275.4'0808694—dc23 2012021913

Manufactured in the United States of America

22 21 20 19 18 17 16 15 14 13
10 9 8 7 6 5 4 3 2 1

In keeping with a commitment to support environmentally responsible and sustainable printing practices, UC Press has printed this book on fifty-pound Enterprise, a 30 percent post-consumer-waste, recycled, deinked fiber that is processed chlorine-free. It is acid-free and meets all ANSI/NISO (Z 39.48) requirements.

CONTENTS

ILLUSTRATIONS

FIGURES

MAPS

TABLES

PREFACE

Anywhere between 2.3 and 6 percent of the Indian population are Christian, 24 to 68 million people.[1] Around two-thirds are Roman Catholic, and over 40 percent live in the two southernmost states of Kerala and Tamil Nadu, where their proportion of the population varies across regions and districts. Behind these figures is a chronicle of Christianity that is fragmented over different missions, regions, and periods. From a complex mosaic, this book draws out one tradition that is of particular importance. It began in the early seventeenth century with a remarkable Jesuit missionary experiment, which by the twenty-first century had been turned to radical social and theological ends. Researched over three decades, this is a historical project with anthropological objectives (cf. Peel 2000). Its first ethnographic and historical subjects are the inheritors of the Jesuit tradition in one particular region and community on the southern plains of present-day Tamil Nadu state (map 1). This locality offers up some of its history through a rich archive of letters, diaries, and notebooks from generations of mostly Jesuit priests who worked there from the early eighteenth century, including the parish priests who lived in the village of what I shall call Alapuram, where I stayed in 1982–84 and to which I have often returned since.

Alapuram, meaning "village of the banyan tree," is the pseudonym I have invented (to preserve anonymity for present-day informants and to ensure consistency with other published research) for a settlement first mentioned in Jesuit letters of the 1730s as the site of a popular pilgrimage focusing on the miracle-working tree of Santiyākappar, or Saint James the Greater. The saint had been brought from a coastal shrine to this interior village several decades earlier by four brothers, ancestors of the subordinated Paḷḷar caste (long treated as

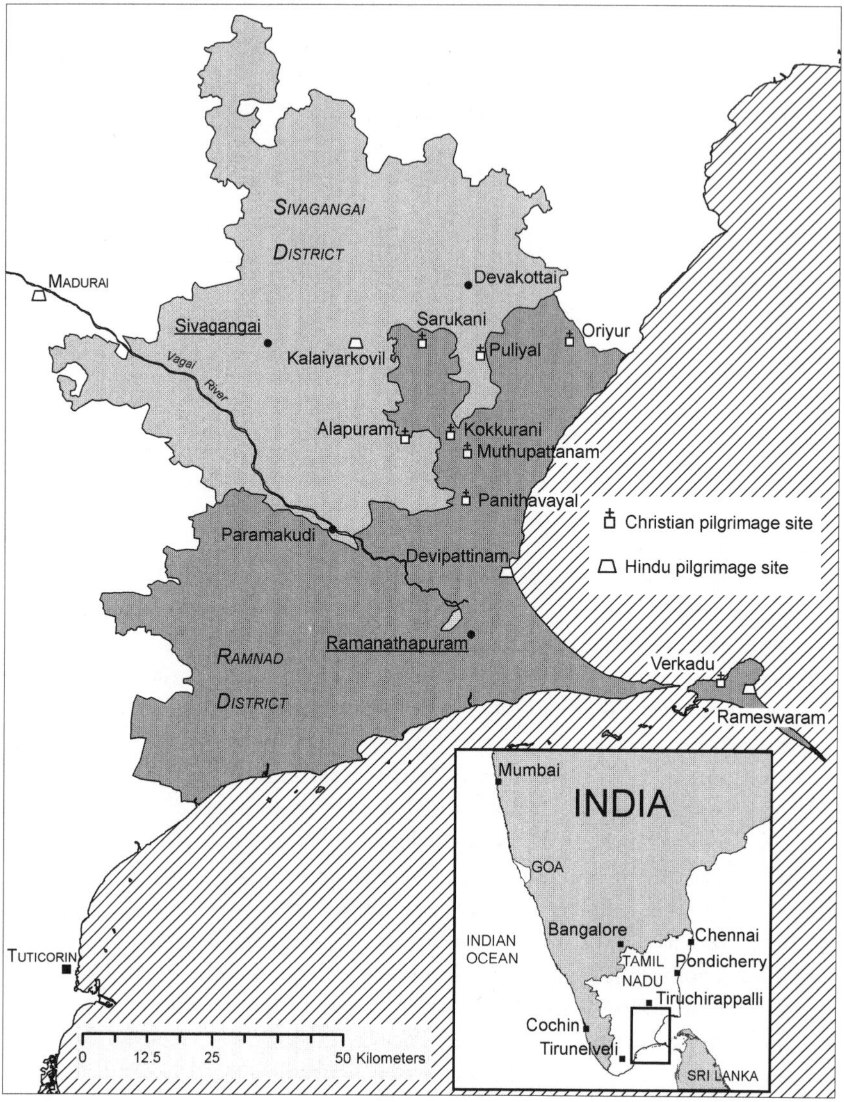

MAP 1. Ramnad and Sivagangai districts (Tamil Nadu), showing Christian and Hindu centers.

"untouchable"), in the form of a cutting from a sacred banyan tree by which the same saint had healed their crippled sister. This legend and its central image—the saint in the banyan tree—invokes the central problematic of this book—the relationship between Christianity and culture, and between the Catholic Church and Tamil society—while pointing to broader questions concerning religious pluralism in India.

The banyan tree (*Ficus benghalensis* or *Ficus indica*) is a pervasive metaphor of (and within) what has come be known as Hinduism. Commonly divinized, taken to represent eternal life, or used as an image of the all-encompassing mantle of Hinduism by today's religious nationalists, the banyan tree was also a favored motif in the colonial and orientalist imagination. It signaled "difference as well as fecundity and complexity." Growing "up, out and down at the same time," its "swirling lateral growths" indicated the "tangled web of otherness" of the East. It stood as a symbol of the inscrutable depths of Indian spirituality, the interlocked lattice of caste, and bafflement to Western rationality (Pinney 1992, 171–72, in Lipner 2006, 96–97). The overarching theme of this book, however, is *not* Christianity trapped and timeless in the syncretic, polycentric unity-in-diversity banyan tree of Hinduism—certainly not that only. Rather, it is the history of missionization, political struggle, and caste politics that begins with, and centers on, an actual tree shrine through which a domain of Indian Catholic religion was worked-out locally by missionaries and missionized alike in tension with Tamil society. Christianity is here conceived neither as inescapably merged into indigenous religious life nor as a purely external force confronting "indigenous" culture (van der Veer 2002, 176). Instead, the religious, institutional, and social distinctiveness of Christianity and the separateness of "culture" are to be regarded as the *outcome* and not the starting point of a historical process that has to be traced within south Indian society.

The Saint in the Banyan Tree is concerned with the relationship between the Christian religion and Tamil culture, but its more fundamental objective is to show how and with what consequences the very categories of "religion" and "culture" are produced in historically and locally specific ways. One strand of the study will explain how Jesuit missionaries who found themselves operating within an existing religious-political system only gradually succeeded in making themselves agents within a distinct sphere of Catholic religion. The book traces the processes and events that separated Christian from "pagan," religious affiliation from political loyalty, and purified categories of action in a dangerously hybridized world of saints and spirits, kings and caste. A second strand will show how from the early seventeenth century the claimed universalism of Christian missionaries provincialized Tamil traditions as "culture." It will become apparent that Jesuit missionary religion produced the "secular"—the realm of caste, politics, and culture—even before the colonial secular produced the modern category of "religion" as we understand it today (as a scholarly consensus holds).

While the book traces missionary involvement in the reciprocal production of domains of religion and culture, a third strand examines Christianization as the root of a kind of political awareness and social activism with significant, sometimes transformative effects on south Indian society. We will see, for instance, how a Jesuit "secularizing" view of the social order of caste as *adiaphora*—"indifferent things" beyond moral law (Županov 1999, 97–101)—coupled with the idea of Christian truth and salvation as *beyond the social*, transmitted a critical understanding that relativized and denaturalized caste society. Whatever its (complex) effects on Tamil religious life, Catholic mission opened space for a certain form of social self-awareness among converts. This would come to be acted upon by subordinated groups in Tamil society implicitly drawing on a notion of society "as a system of power and constraint" on individuals that is at once Christian and sociological (Sahlins 1996, 404).

This story of Christianity is not, however, one of cultural displacement or social rupture among convert communities—far from it. It will become apparent just how embedded in Tamil sociocultural orders Jesuit Catholicism remained for centuries and how, from the first, Jesuits secularized the institution of caste *in order* that it could be tolerated among converts—that is, as civil rather than "pagan" practice. The book's long-term perspective shows that it took centuries for a "new ethical or political charge" afforded by Christianity (Bialecki, Haynes, and Robbins 2008, 1144) to be turned, by some, to the radical goal of challenging forms of cultural domination. The tension between the emphasis on cultural continuity and on discontinuity thrown up by a relatively new anthropology of Christianity can be resolved by examining the cultural effects of Christianity through specific social histories. These histories explore the circumstances in which Christian religion comes to be (or fails to be) a socially meaningful category and ask not only what Christianity is, but also what it *does*—in this case, within south Indian history.

Recent scholarship presents equally profound questions concerning the relationship between Christianity and anthropology itself, and particularly raises a mirror awareness of "the Christianity of anthropology"—that is, the way in which some presuppositions of social enquiry have their origin in, or are aligned to, Western Christian tradition and the difficulty of grasping Christianity itself *as* culture (Cannell 2005, 2006; Robbins 2003; Sahlins 1996). There is a now well-acknowledged intimacy between anthropological and missionary enterprises. It is not difficult, for instance, to see that the seventeenth-century Jesuit missionary project that wrought "culture" as a category out of the encounter between universal faith and other peoples finds its counterpart in the claimed universalism of anthropology as a discipline for the comparative description of culture with its own relativizing analytic.

This means that an anthropological analysis such as this one, which traces the discourse of the missionaries and their subaltern converts, also mimics that which it describes. But in recognizing this, my attention will turn less to the "hindrance to proper concept formation in anthropology" that Christianity presents (Bialecki, Haynes, and Robbins 2008, 1143), which is the point of arguments made by Asad (1993) and Sahlins (1996), and more to the above-mentioned significance of Christianity in producing "the reflexivity and sociological perception that stand at the heart of anthropology" (Bialecki, Haynes, and Robbins 2008, 1143, referencing Burridge 1973) *and* to exploring this as an effect on subaltern groups who have turned such awareness to cultural critique.

This, then, is a historical anthropology of Christianization at different levels. It is anthropological in that it is concerned with the associations, relations, and ecclesiastical structures of Tamil Christian practice as much as with religious talk. But above all it is anthropological in that it draws on the direct encounters of fieldwork in a community that I have come to know well. In August 1982, I traveled to south India with Julia Cleves, my first wife. By early 1983 we had made our home in rented space with a Catholic farming family in Alapuram village, where I stayed until May 1984, sharing house and food. This half-Hindu, half-Christian (80 percent Roman Catholic) village stood in the center of the ancient Jesuit mission field, in a district (Ramanathapuram or Ramnad) whose scarcity-prone agro-ecology I have written about elsewhere (Mosse 2003).

Serendipity rather than science leads most anthropologists to their field sites. Following kin connections from a low-income Catholic neighborhood in the city of Madurai in which we had settled in order better to learn Tamil, Julia and I were led to the dauntingly hot, flat, and dry Ramnad plains. And it was Jesuit activists of PALMERA (People's Action for Liberation Movement in Eastern Ramnad), working in this poorest of districts, who in 1982 directed us to Alapuram as a village in which we might stay. Within a few weeks we were off-loading our bicycles from atop a local bus, sharing living space with food aid sacks of bulgur wheat (labeled "Gift from the People of America") in the disused village dispensary, and negotiating entry into a village whose diverse inhabitants were in general benignly puzzled by our presence. Having moved to the shared house in an upper-caste Catholic street (which, as a thoroughfare to the village "tank" from where women drew water, brought many to our door), I began to explore the village and its surroundings: getting to know people in different quarters, undertaking a household survey, drawing up genealogies, bicycling to surrounding villages, and following our neighbors to the important saint shrines and festivals of the region (map 1). Alapuram itself was a fairly large (328 households) and socially diverse village, with nineteen different castes, including four groups historically subordinated as "untouchables" (today's *dalits*), whose members together made up 40 percent of the village. Three-quarters of Alapuram's dalits were

Christian—mostly Catholic, but some Protestant (Church of South India) or Pentecostal. It was this association between Christianity and the lives of those subordinated within hierarchies of caste that had initially inspired this research.

I have become familiar with this village over many years. After my fieldwork in 1983–84, I made short visits while working for Oxfam in Bangalore (1987–91), stayed for a period in 1992–94 during research on water-harvesting systems, and after several years returned to Alapuram for a few months with each of my two sons—with Jake in 2004 and Oliver in 2009. By that time my location in the village had shifted from an upper-caste street to the dalit "colony," where I stayed with my research assistant and dear friend M. Sivan. Without Sivan, research in this village would have been very different and altogether shallower. As a repatriate to his native Alapuram from Sri Lanka, where he worked on a tea estate, Sivan had acquired the sociological perception of an outsider-insider. As a dalit, for long periods without assets and dependent upon his labor to support a large family, he had a biographical understanding of subordination and patronage. His talent for undertaking surveys and his skill in facilitating and conducting interviews, dealing with sensitive subjects, and helping me interpret the significance of what people said (based on a permanent resident's knowledge of *who* spoke) were invaluable. Sivan's knowledge of English, spoken and written, acquired on the tea estates—a skill that few in the village knew he possessed and that, unusually, did not mark a class difference—was always superior to mine of Tamil, which without extended formal training has remained rather rustic and rudimentary. During my 1980s fieldwork in Alapuram I did not (as I do today) make much use of recording devices. Instead I would spend long hours in the evenings writing up my notepad jottings from events and interviews on carbon-copied foolscap sheets and, with Sivan, exchanging and verifying recall and carefully transcribing and translating important statements and conversation fragments (or occasionally longer tape-recorded dialogue).

The narrations of my interlocutors began to reveal a rich social and mission history that made archival work essential, drawing me from the village to the cool tranquillity of the Jesuit Madurai Mission Archives in hill-station Sacred Heart College at Shembaganur. The diaries of Jesuit parish priests resident in Alapuram from the 1850s, and (copies of) letters from a century earlier along with miscellaneous notebooks (in a mixture of Latin, French, and English with Tamil), were a real discovery and a remarkable resource.

In preparation for the writing of this book, I returned to Alapuram (as mentioned) in late 2004 and again in early 2009, to a village much changed in the intervening quarter century or so. Aggressive Hindu nationalism and militant dalit activism had placed Christianity in quite a different context. These two issues were interlinked in that dalit (and tribal) protest from the margins in the 1990s has been interpreted as "Christian aggression" arising from internationally orchestrated proselytism by Hindu nationalists who vilified the Christian minority as colonial, foreign, and antinational. In its delocalized form—Catholic or Pentecostal—Christianity manifested its own form of fundamentalism alongside Hindu or caste extremism, all threatening social rupture and violence. I wanted to make sense of these changes, not only in the village where I sat with old acquaintances, youth activists, teachers, or Pentecostal leaders, but also beyond in the wider Jesuit and Tamil Catholic world. And so I began a varied set of interviews with Jesuit priests, lawyers, and dalit theologians, dalit activists, diocesan priests, bishops, nuns (and ex-nuns), the heads of institutions, leaders of social movements, writers, and mavericks in order to profile the various pressures and priorities of the contemporary Church. There were visits to earlier-studied centers of pilgrimage, healing, or exorcism, and to new centers of Jesuit theology, research, or social activism. I was hosted by many Jesuit houses, and invited to meetings with students and seminarians. I gained accompaniment from Jesuit philosopher and dalit activist Fr. Selvaraj Arulnathan, whose personal narratives gave depth to my understanding of the subjective experience of caste discrimination, religious vocation, and social activism.

In addition to revisiting earlier questions on the role of Christianity in the transformation of caste, and in the articulation of alternative social and political identities, these encounters raised new questions about the part played by Christianity in dalit struggles for rights, justice, development resources, political power and in processes of cultural re-imagining. It was clear that the missiological and theological dilemmas of Indian Christianity increasingly took shape within a framework of "dalitness" and social justice that had to be taken account of, and that the 1990s and 2000s had added an important chapter to a remarkable four-hundred-year engagement of the Society of Jesus with Tamil society. This was a history that had to be told through further tacking back and forth between Jesuit thought and the social relationships of the village.

ACKNOWLEDGMENTS

During the thirty years over which this book has been researched, I have gathered a small army of people to whom I am indebted. During recent fieldwork, priests, bishops, and social activists generously shared experiences and insights. I would rather not present a limited list, but I cannot resist the impulse to name some of the many who have opened their lives to my enquiry, including Fr. Xavier Arulraj; Fr. Arulselvam; Fr. Joe Arun, SJ; Fr. Jabamalairaja Irudayaraj, SJ; Fr. L. Yesumarian, SJ; Fr. S. Jeyapathi, SJ; Fr. Prakash Louis, SJ; Fr. Aphonse Manickam, SJ; Fr. Mark Stephen, SJ; Dr. Mary John; Fr. Michaelraj, SJ; Rev. Jeyakaram; Fr. Anthony Raj, SJ; Fr. Vincent; Fr. Francis Xavier, SJ; and especially Fr. Anthony Packianathan and Fr. A. Selvaraj, SJ. I was warmly received and hosted by many Jesuit houses and centers, including the Jesuit Archives at Shembaganur by Fr. Edward Jeganathan, SJ. Among my older debts to members of the clergy, I must mention Fr. S. Ponnad, SJ, who awakened my interest in rural Ramnad; Fr. Arulanandar, parish priest of "Alapuram" in the 1980s; and Fr. Aloysius Irudayam, SJ, who first directed me to that village.

Some part of this work began long ago with doctoral research supervised by N. J. Allen at Oxford University's Institute of Social Anthropology. When trying to organize fieldwork in Bangalore, Dick and Molly Taylor offered a steadying hand and Charles Ryerson gave useful pointers. While I was in Madurai, Dr. J. C. B. Abraham, V. P. Sundaram, Eleanor Jackson, and the Gorringe family offered care, Dr. K. Paramamsivan taught me Tamil, and Jane and Jyoti Sahi were always there for me. In Alapuram village my greatest and enduring debt is to Mr. M. Sivan, village resident, research assistant, and good friend over many years, as well as to his wife, Sandanamma, and daughter, Revathi, who have offered me a home and family in the village. I am immeasurably grateful to all those in Alapuram who have been willing to be enrolled onto my research project in large or small ways.

Among the many who have accompanied me on this particular intellectual journey, I would like to thank Susan Bayly, Tony Good, John Harriss, Robert Frykenberg, Chris Fuller, Pamela Price, and Jock Sirrat, who lent support over many years, and S. Anandhi, Hugo Gorringe, Rajan Krishnan, and M. S. S. Pandian, who have done so more recently. I thank Ines Županov and Caroline Osella for reading the manuscript and for editorial suggestions, and Paolo Aranha for advising with expert historical interpretations. I am grateful to my colleagues and students at SOAS for their encouragement during the book's preparation, and to Giulia Battaglia, who worked on the bibliography. My intellectual debt to the many whose work I admire and learn from is contained in the list of references.

I would like to thank CISRS (Christian Institute for the Study of Religion and Society), IDEAS (Institute of Development Education, Action and Study, Madurai), IDCR (Institute of Dialogue with Cultures and Religions, Loyola College, Chennai), and MIDS (Madras Institute for Development Studies, Chennai) for institutional affiliation at various times. This project has benefitted from various research grants that have given me time to work on it, including doctoral research funding from the Social Science Research Council (1981–84), a grant from the Leverhulme Trust Research Fellowship (2004–5), from the Arts and Humanities Research Council (AHRC)/Economic and Social Research Council (ESRC) in 2008–9 (grant no. AH/F007523/1 titled "Religion, Development and the Rights of Subordinated People"); and an ongoing ESRC grant in 2009–2011 (no. RES-062-23-2227, titled "Caste Out of Development").

Some chapters draw on material published in preliminary form elsewhere. Chapter 2 uses "Catholic Saints and the Hindu Village Pantheon," *Man* 28, no. 2 (1994); and "Possession and Confession: Affliction and Sacred Power in Colonial and Contemporary Catholic South India," in *The Anthropology of Christianity*, edited by Fenella Cannell (Duke University Press, 2006). Chapter 3 draws on "South Indian Christians, Purity/Impurity, and the Caste System: Death Ritual in a Tamil Roman Catholic Community," *Journal of the Royal Anthropological Institute* 2, no. 3 (1996). Chapter 4 draws on "Honour, Caste and Conflict: The Ethnohistory of a Catholic Festival in Rural Tamil Nadu (1730–1990)," in *Altérité et identité: Islam et christianisme en Inde*, edited by J. Assayag and Tarabout (Ecole des Hautes Etudes en Sciences Sociales, Paris, 1997). Chapter 5 borrows from "Idioms of Subordination and Styles of Protest among Christian and Hindu Harijan Castes in Tamil Nadu," *Contributions to Indian Sociology* 28, no. 1 (1994), and chapter 6 from "Dalit Christian Activism in Contemporary Tamil

Nadu," in *Ethnic Activism and Civil Society in South Asia,* edited by David Gellner (Sage, 2009).

I would like to thank Joel Robbins for inviting my contribution to the University of California Press Anthropology of Christianity Series, anonymous reviewers for suggestions, and Reed Malcolm, my commissioning editor, for understanding and support. I am grateful to Carl Walesa for his meticulous copy-editing, to Pablo de Roulet for producing the maps, and to Oli Mosse, who improved the photographs.

With this book I remember my parents, Charles and Veronica Mosse; Julia, with whom I set out on this project what seems a lifetime ago, who shared in a youthful adventure, and who trusted that it would have meaning despite the ordeals; and my darling Jake who lives in my heart. Oli inspires me with his extraordinary courage and creativity, and Siobhan has woven love around the writing of this book and the North London home in which it finally took shape.

Note on Transliteration

Transliteration and the use of diacritical marks generally follows the conventions of the Madras University *Tamil Lexicon* (1982), although I retain the commonly accepted usage of certain terms such as *puja, bhakti, panchayat, sanniyasi,* and *varna.* Non-English words are italicized and given diacritical marks on their first appearance. Proper names are not italicized, and diacritical marks are generally omitted from them, whether presented in their Tamil or common-usage forms, except in the case of the first appearance of caste names. Where not dictionary verified (mostly in Fabricius 1972), the spelling is that provided by my interlocutors. In addition, a nonitalicized letter *s* has been suffixed to denote plurals, and proper names have been given initial capital letters.

Introduction

On 17 March 2009, the archbishop of Chennai (Dr. M. Chinnappa, SVD) stood before an audience of priests and theologians to proclaim passionately that the Catholic Church in Tamil Nadu had to make a public confession for the sin of caste committed historically. "We have done this injustice to thousands and thousands of our own people," he proclaimed. "We have damaged a community." The occasion was the launch of another two volumes in a new series of *dalit* commentaries on the books of the Bible at a Jesuit center of theology. *Dalit* is a word of Sanskrit origin meaning "broken" or "crushed" and stands for the identity of those inferiorized communities who are today struggling from the humiliation and oppression of untouchability, and who in significant numbers had earlier turned to Christianity in various moves to reject inferiority and build an alternative future for themselves.[1] Indeed, in the Tamil country, a conversion history stretching over four centuries produced a dalit majority among the four million members of the Christian churches in the state. However, pressure to find institutional or theological expression for this demographic is only now gathering momentum.

A few days before the event launching these dalit Bible commentaries, across his desk in Chennai's prestigious Loyola College, Francis Xavier, the former head of the Jesuit Province of Madurai, was telling me that "being a dalit is more than original sin because baptismal water is able to wash original sin but cannot remove the stigma of being a dalit. You say all human beings are made in the image and likeness of God, [but] is there a dalit God? You bury the dead separately; is there going to be a dalit heaven and a non-dalit heaven? Or do we need a messiah who should be born as a dalit? . . . My question is, When a dalit priest celebrates Mass, is a dalit Christ coming or a regular Christ? Because some people do not want to receive Communion from a dalit priest." Both the archbishop and the Jesuit provincial are dalit Christians who despite senior ecclesiastical rank find themselves inescapably tied to the stigmatized identity of "untouchable," but equally wedded to a project of social and self-emancipation.

A year previously, in March 2008, dalit Catholics of Eraiyur village, seeking liberation from continuing discrimination in the life of the Church, had demanded a separate parish from their bishop. They had been refused the honor of reading scripture, serving at the altar, or joining the choir in the parish church. They had endured separate seating at Mass, separate funeral biers, and separate cemeteries, and were denied access to the church street for their funeral and wedding processions. They followed other dalit Catholics who had begun to withdraw to separate churches with their own festivals, often dedicated to St. Sebastian, whose tortured figure tied to a tree and pierced by arrows was a fitting image of dalit suffering. Their demand for the consecration of a parish church in their quarter triggered a headline-grabbing assault on dalit persons and property by upper-caste Catholics. Dalit priests in the diocese responded by locking their churches and replacing the Holy Week celebrations with black flags and hunger strikes.

These events and the sentiments of the dalit clergy are symptomatic of an unresolved tension between Christianity and the culture of caste, which has been central to Tamil Catholicism for centuries. It dominated my conversations with clerics, bishops, and the religious more than ever in the spring of 2009, when I returned to Tamil Nadu to conduct a round of interviews twenty-seven years after first beginning this study of Tamil Catholicism. Anthropologists of Christianity are familiar with the strain between the universal demands of faith, including fidelity to the Bible, and the particularities of the cultural situation in which converts live and in which they have social investments (Robbins 2010). The particularities that are to be overcome may even be regarded as defining and animating the universal stance, making the Christian convert one who struggles against sin and the old order in an endless process of becoming a new subject (ibid.). Even those who regard Christian conversion in the most disjunctive terms (Joel Robbins and others who work on Pentecostal-charismatic forms) acknowledge that the break with the past is always incomplete. Christian self-making is an ongoing work inexorably tied to the past, to what is regarded as the propensity to sin, to the particular as the necessary ground for any social life (ibid.). Commonly, this is imagined as the struggle of individual Christians caught in a particular postconversion moment. But the question of the relationship between Christianity and culture—which is at the heart of this book—can also be framed in institutional, societal, and historical terms. This at any rate is what is required to make sense of the complex juncture between Christianity and caste society in south India—a relationship that will be traced over four centuries and has recently turned into political struggle.

Christianity is a world religion that, not having its own sacred language, holds every language as potentially sacred (Frykenberg 2003, 3), at least theologically.[2] Its claimed universals have to be lived through particular cultural forms. This has produced a great proliferation of Christian centers, cultures, and languages from the time of St. Paul's preaching to the Gentiles—although it might better be said, as Coleman (2006, 3) does of Pentecostalism, that missionary Christianity "constitute[s] 'part-cultures,' presenting worldviews meant for export but often in tension with the values of any given host society." In fact, we have to go further, to show how the encounters that came with the global spread of Christianity required new reflection—by both missionaries and the missionized—on the universal and the particular, from which the very categories of "religion" and "culture" were themselves formed (Keane 2007, 84).

It is now accepted that the division of the social world into the "religious" and the "secular" is historically contingent, and many argue that "religion" as a distinct category is itself a modern Christian idea (or born out of European historical circumstances) subsequently "attributed to all the peoples of the world" (Daniel 2000, 171). "Given the way global power relations have worked over the past thousand years," Daniel continues, "the 'conquered' in their turn have clamored to prove that they too, not just the conquerors, have 'religion'" in the Christian sense (ibid.). The reasoning for India suggests more specifically that "the modern category of religion [as in "Hindu" religion] was constructed in imperial encounters" (van der Veer 2002, 178), not only through assumptions about religion developed in the work of colonial Orientalists and Indologists, but also paradoxically by the self-representation of the colonial state as *secular* (or religiously neutral). This left the public sphere open to Christian missionary activity and lobbying (from the mid-1800s), which in turn prompted resistance among non-Christian groups who for this purpose now organized themselves in mirror fashion as institutional religion (ibid., 177–78). Bate (2005), for example, shows how, by mimicking the Protestant Sunday sermon and liturgical rationalization, Tamil Saivism, hitherto without any "institutionalized realm of the metapragmatic," became a "religion" with the transformation of older practices emphasizing affect and aesthetic into those regulated by stipulations modeled explicitly on Christian practices.

Christianity here is commonly seen as a rationalizing world religion, tied up in the march toward enlightenment—its revelation and redemptive vision firmly linked to crisis or reform in the surrounding indigenous traditions (Weber 1956; Bellah 1964; Hefner 1993). Such a narrative of Christian modernity has been deepened and made more sophisticated with recent ventures in the anthropology of Christianity (Robbins 2004a; Keane 2007). But the common focus on colonial power relations, Protestant missions, and Christian modernity (for example, in British India) has drawn attention away from other histories in which Christianity was not tied up with the rupture of colonial modernity: Christian cross-regional encounters that preceded and helped produce the separate category of "religion," and where Christianity was itself profoundly shaped by indigenous traditions. In early missionary encounters with other peoples, Europeans may have imagined they were bringing faith or truth to lands where none had been before (or where the devil had turned ignorance to superstition and idolatry).[3] Here the modern separation of the "religious" and the "secular" was preceded by a triadic distinction between true Christian *faith; idolatry,* which was to be destroyed; and a further category of idolatry-free *civic* custom, which was necessary so that Christianity could be communicated into local "culture" (cf. Balaganghadara 2010). This book begins with a seventeenth-century Jesuit missionary project in south India worked out around these categorizations of faith, idolatry, and culture—a project of cultural "accommodation" (*accommodatio*) with profound implications for the social history of Christianity in the region, as well as for the categories of Western scholarship on India.[4]

RELIGION AND CULTURE IN CHRISTIAN TAMIL COUNTRY

Jesuit converts in the south Indian Tamil hinterland (away from the trading ports) were relative latecomers to Christianity. The presence of ancient Christian communities on the western Indian coast tracing their ancestry to the arrival of the Apostle Thomas in 52 C.E., and the eastern movement of the Syriac Church from Persia and Syria from the fourth century, quite independent of Rome, remind us how mistaken it is to regard Christianity as Western in origin or colonial in transmission to India (Frykenberg 2003, 2008; on "Thomas Christians," see Brown 1982). But of course the region's diverse Christian populations *do* also reflect, and socially mark, a series of Western encounters. Thus the elite upper-caste Syrian Christians always regarded themselves as quite distinct from the low-ranking fishing and boat-handling castes Christianized by the Portuguese trading power on the Konkan and Coromandal coasts in the fifteenth and sixteenth centuries under Padroado—"the sword accompanying the cross in the quest for spices" (Robinson 2003, 289). Here, Christianization demanded radical separation from the culture of paganism and involved an assault on temples and superstitious belief that was backed by colonial power and the instrument of the Inquisition.[5]

It was precisely to break with the European cultural captivity of Christian faith that the Italian Jesuit Roberto Nobili in 1606 began experiments in "accommodation" in the Tamil cultural center of Madurai.[6] Choosing to live under the patronage of a "Hindu" sovereign, Nobili developed a radical approach to mission that sought not the extraction of Christian souls from the grip of paganism, but the conversion of a great civilization itself. His approach to Indians or "heathens"[7] and their traditions drew on Thomas Aquinas's *Summa contra Gentiles* and particularly the distinction drawn there between, on the one hand, truths that the human mind can know through reason and experience—that is, the "natural law" evidenced in the wisdom of learned Brahmans including their knowledge of the existence of God as creator—and on the other hand, truth beyond, known only by revelation and faith: the incarnation and salvation through Christ alone. This was the "true Veda" (*cattiya vētam*) that transcended human reason and set out a universal morality of right action necessary to achieve salvation and avoid damnation.[8]

Upon this Thomist dualism, Nobili built a distinction between the abstract discourse of truth, salvation, and morality (a revelation)—that is to say, "religion"—and the languages and cultures in which it could be implanted (the relativity of civil customs). Since universal truth could be separated from particular linguistic form, Christian religion could through analogy be embodied in a language (Tamil or Sanskrit) that was shaped by "gentile" traditions instead of the Latin or Portuguese mandatorily retained elsewhere.[9] Nobili's mission was premised on a particular "semiotic ideology," to borrow Webb Keane's term denoting specific beliefs about (or reflexive awareness of) signifying practices (2007, 16–21). In this instance, words were vessels that could be hollowed out of pagan significance and filled with Christian meaning. Indeed, using heathen vocabulary for Christian truth could be a kind of "linguistic exorcism," "beating the devil out of Tamil speech" (Županov 1999, 163, 104).

The signifier and the signified were not, however, always detachable in this way. Not all Tamil knowledge anticipated Christ, and not all Tamil words or symbols could be separated from their pagan referents. Words, objects, gestures, and other semiotic forms that were indissolubly bound to pagan meaning—including priestly knowledge, false beliefs, and idolatrous practice having no part in natural law—had to be expunged.[10] Thus in order for Christian faith to be accommodated to native customs, Tamil life had to be separated into those elements that were neutral, merely practical, or civil ("the cultural") and could be joined to Christian faith and retained by converts, and into those that were grounded in idolatry and superstition. Nobili's distinction between "religion" and "culture" thus depended upon the theologically defined third category of "idolatry" (bad religion), designated for destruction. Wherever actions of everyday necessity or civil distinction had been overlaid with "incantations or rites of a superstitious character," these had to be stripped away, so that the substance of the act could be retained; but, Nobili writes, "wherever in the customs of this country we find anything that has no relation to civil adornment, anything that does not serve as a sign of social distinction, anything that is not adapted to common human usage [food, clothing, etc.], but is exclusively oriented by idolaters towards the veneration and worship of an idol, such a thing can in no way be permitted to Christians . . . unless perchance the Church has introduced some suitable alteration and transferred [those practices] to the field of Christian piety" (Nobili [1613] 2005, 201–3).

Separating the civil and the superstitious invoked both semiotics and function. First, the "cultural" was the realm in which the relationship between signifier and signified was contingent and changeable; whereas idolatry involved the fusion of meaning and semiotic form. With more than one semiotic ideology at work, Nobili and his converts had to negotiate a dual "representational economy" (Keane 2007, 18–21). Second, since function, including status distinction, was central to defining customs as "civil," ranked caste became a necessary mediator between idolatry and culture.

The borderlands of idolatry were in fact negotiable. Even "nonfunctional" practices such as marking the forehead or wearing sandal paste could be retained where Christian meanings could be substituted for "pagan" ones—for example, *poṅkal* rice[11] offerings at the foot of the cross, blessed by a priest. At the same time, various "functional replacements," such as the cross for an idol, inserted Christian signifiers into existing procedures (Županov 1999, 121; Keane 2007, 141). Like the early Fathers of the Church, to whose decisions he appealed, Nobili insisted that "practices, which [are] gradually and in the course of time to be eliminated[,] should at first be tolerated, and . . . for the sake of suavity a good many could be transformed from superstitious ritual into sacred rites of a Christian tenor and complexion" (cited in Clooney 2007, 162). Stripped of idolatrous elements, Tamil culture became for Nobili "a tree of signs primarily in need of correct interpretation" (Županov 1999, 104).

This tolerance did not, it should be emphasized, arise from any attempt actually to understand or concede to indigenous reasoning (for example, on the relationship between the material and the immaterial in different forms of worship [Amaladass and Clooney 2005, 16, 18]). Indeed, learning from another religious tradition was not only inadmissible but also inconceivable given the vocabulary of the time (ibid.).[12] Rather, Nobili stood out among his missionary peers as a pragmatic rationalist. The residual world of idolatry and superstition he regarded primarily as a failure of reason—"a forgetfulness that got out of hand and led to intellectual confusion and moral depravity" (Clooney 1999, 408). Nobili conjectured that Indians had begun to worship images instead of that which they symbolically represented (the kind of "fetishism" of which Protestant missionaries routinely accused Catholics [Keane 2007]).[13] Whereas natural reason would promote worship of the creator God, Indians had begun to worship created things of human design, man-made idols and divinized humans, and to honor the immoral acts of gods, which were all "fruit[s] of the mind diminished by original sin" (Rubiés 2005, 258). Paganism with its idolatrous semiotic, as Županov notes, was not so much a different religion as a demonic corrupting force (1999, 204).

Nobili's method of "reconstruct[ing] the shreds of the divinely bestowed truth from degenerated, local texts and practices" (Županov 1999, 133) thus involved a Thomist separation of the rational from the irrational, as well as revelation from reason, universal truth from particular semiotic forms, and Christian from idolatrous representation.[14] Such insistence on the transcendence of religion and its separation from language, culture, and the material is often regarded as a distinctively Protestant achievement, at least when linked to the sharpening of a range of categories and distinctions of social life that today we take as self-evident (sign/signified, religion/culture, mind/matter, spirit/substance), and as a quintessentially modern project associated with the historical processes that separated Church from state and religion from science in Europe and the United States. Studying a Calvinist mission encounter in nineteenth-century Indonesia, Keane (2007), for example, sees the underlying separation of belief from language and of words from things as preparing the way for notions of individual agency and emancipation for "Christian moderns."

Nobili's mission cannot, however, simply be enrolled onto the teleological narrative of Christian modernity as an anticipatory project. This Jesuit separation of faith and culture, the religious from the civil, might of course have a bearing on the later historical process of secularization as well as on the contemporary political question of "where Indian culture ends and Hindu religion begins" (Amaladass and Clooney 2005, 46), on subsequent efforts at Christian "inculturation," or more broadly on the categorization of actions, opinions, practices, and associations as "religious" as opposed to "secular" with juridical and political implications in any society (Keane 2007, 87; Fitzgerald 2007).[15] But, in its time, Nobili's separation of religion and culture served a more pragmatic missiological purpose. It was first a *social* project to affirm the prestige of Christian practices, without which his faith and his mission would be consigned to the impure periphery of outcasts, fisherfolk, and foreigners.

SECULARIZING BRAHMANISM; BRAHMANIZING CHRISTIANITY

Around 1619, Nobili wrote to Pope Paul V to say that, in Madurai, "all the efforts to bring the heathens to Christ had been in vain . . . my efforts were fruitless because with a sort of barbarous stolidity they turned away from the manners and customs of the Portuguese and refused to put aside the badges of their ancestral nobility."[16] Fundamental to recruiting beyond the enclaves of Portuguese power was the principle that becoming Christian did not require discarding the primary social identification of caste. Conceiving a world of culture as "indifferent external things" open to Christianization—and Brahmanism as a social system rather than pagan idolatry (Županov 1999)—Nobili "secularized" caste in order that it could be tolerated among converts. He set caste apart as a worldly matter of etiquette—as a cultural ranking of occupations and a hereditary division of labor and social honor. "Indian society differs from foreign societies particularly in this," he wrote in his *Report,* "that here men are sorted out precisely on the basis of the functions they fulfill, and that their respective social rank is attributed not to merit but to a class superiority transmitted by generation. It follows from this that in India we find as many distinct clans or tribes as there are distinct classes of occupations or civic functions, and that their respective nobility or lack of it is proportioned to the respective superiority of the functions they discharge" ([1613] 2005, 58).

Converts could retain the "civil" caste codes of diet, practices of purification, or marks of distinction such as the sacred thread—all of which were understood as neutral with regard to sin, merit, and ultimate salvation (except insofar as attention to these displaced moral matters such as honesty or sexual conduct) (Clooney 1999, 2007). Only on this basis could Nobili write in his palm-leaf public manifesto in 1611: "The holy and spiritual law which holds this doctrine of mine does not make anyone lose his caste or pass into another, nor does it induce anyone to do anything detrimental to the honour of his family."[17] Moreover, those who supplied Nobili with the codes of this social ordering and by whose rules Christian social practice was to be elevated—the priestly Brahmans—had themselves to be secularized as "learned doctors" (Nobili 2005; cf. Županov 1999, 121).

Rather than driving a project of Christian modernity, Nobili's separation of the religious and the cultural was a method for "traditionalizing" Christianity as Brahmanic practice with the immediate purpose of argumentation with Brahman scholars and defense against his critics in Rome and Goa, and within the Society of Jesus. In fact, his approach outraged his missionary adversaries and seemed to have confused rather than converted his Brahman interlocutors.[18] Moreover, although the "thought work" of Nobili and other Jesuits did not exactly cut the way to Christian modernity, it did prepare for a modern sociological incorporation of Brahmanical conceptions of "traditional" India as the basis of Western scholarship, colonial administration, and later anthropological writing. Many of the issues that preoccupied orientalist scholars[19] had long before been Jesuit missionary conjecture on religion and Indian cultural history, some of it by French Jesuits whose knowledge was marginalized with the eclipse of French power by the British in India (Trautmann 1997, 37).[20] Jesuits were quite entangled in Brahmanical conceptions. Francis Clooney, himself a Jesuit, describes the seventeenth- and eighteenth-century encounter between the Brahman and the Jesuit in terms of "a mutually dependent pair" (2006, 166). There was a deep ambivalence in Jesuit attitudes to Brahmans. They were the worst and the best—both arrogant obstacles to the Gospel and the "essential guardians of a culture that with a little correction would flourish as a Christian culture" (ibid.).[21] This ambivalence produced a tradition of Jesuit proto-ethnographic description, exemplified by men such as Father J.V. Bouchet (1655–1732) and Father G.L. Coeurdoux (1691–1779).[22] These descriptions, directed at European debates on Christianity and the downfall of paganism, were also intended to produce knowledge on native culture for missionizing ends (ibid., 167). They characterized the moral flaws of Brahmans, who as religious counterparts and competitors were to be challenged and defeated, while proffering appropriate cultural idioms for Christian adaptations and Jesuit "spiritual entrepreneurship" (Clooney 2006, 158, 166, 169; Županov 2004, 2007).[23]

Nobili's Thomist distinctions between natural reason and the irrational corruptions of idolatry set a "high tradition" of the reflective few apart from a "low tradition" of the unreflective masses. This ensured a division between, on the one hand, an authentic Brahmanical scriptural tradition (later codified as "Hindu religion" with the help of orientalists such as Max Müller; cf. M.S.S. Pandian 2007, 45–51) and, on the other, inauthentic popular tradition that was a corrupted version mixed with superstition and survivals of primitive tribal rites—a division that endures in colonial ethnography and contemporary religious studies. If sense could be made of village religion, it was only by its imperfect reference to the scriptural tradition (Dumont and Pocock 1959). Other practices such as trance, possession, sorcery, and magic were excluded from the realm of Tamil "religion" altogether (Clark-Decès 2007). Meanwhile, Nobili's ontological separation of "the religious" and "the civil" (or political), the transcendent sacred and the relegated profane, would reappear in different guise in the highly Brahmanical twentieth-century anthropology of Louis Dumont (1980) and his notion of the encompassing religious ideas of purity and impurity, and the nonreligious "encompassed" aspect of social life. Jesuits did first what colonial officers and anthropologists would do later—that is, construct knowledge through an "intercultural mimesis," coming to knowledge about India through a relationship with Brahmans and their view of society—not a Brahman point of view per se, but an imitation of Brahman theorizing, as Burghart (1990) argues.

JESUIT "SUBSTITUTION" AND THE CULTURE OF TAMIL CATHOLICISM

Nobili's separation of transcendent Christian faith and the secularized Brahmanic order of caste was a key moment in the making of Tamil Catholicism. But his mission's Brahmanic mode of apprehending Tamil society was ill equipped to deal with the "non-Brahman" rural populations from where the majority of converts would actually come (and whose descendants feature in this book).

Unlike the Brahmans to whom Jesuits allowed a wisdom in natural law and readiness to receive the light of Christian revelation, these unlettered "gentiles" were subject to more standard forms of cultural "othering." They were denied the character of rationality or moral judgment, imagined as ruled by family and caste, by emotionalism, "enhanced sensuality[,] and oversexed bodily functions," and subject to the "pulleys and axles" of the "mindless and diabolic machine (*máquina*) of paganism" (Županov 2005, 173–74, 179, 309n34). Instead of learned dialogue on the truth and morals of the Christian Veda, the "sacred theater" of missionary life in the Tamil countryside narrated in the Jesuit letters from the seventeenth century revolved around a battle between the Christian and the demonic, the struggle to "expurgate the demon . . . the creator of delusion" who had reconquered India (Županov 1999, 133). Apostolically framed writing (and performances in Jesuit colleges) portrayed exemplary dramas of conversion, miraculous healing, treachery, persecution, endurance, and the victory of Christians intruding on the devil's domain (ibid.).

If the Jesuits' Brahmanical project was one of *rationalization,* erasing paganism as an irrational accretion, their project with non-Brahmans was one of *substitution*—that is, the redirection of popular Tamil religiosity to Christian ends, replacing "demonic paganism" with Catholic devotions so as to, as Fr. Saint Cyr later put it in 1841, "faire rendre au Seigneur du ciel les hommages qui, jusque là, n'avaient été rendus qu'au prince des ténèbres" (in Bertrand 1865, 274). Rather than extending the dialogical relationship with Brahmans to others—for example, by translating the Bible and Christian thought into everyday idiomatic Tamil so as to "convince and convert," as the Protestants did (M. S. S. Pandian 2007, 18, 119)—Jesuits put in place Catholicism as a "high tradition" while adapting to forms of indigenous religiosity.

The high tradition's emphasis on the transcendent and faith in God did not, however, depend upon rejection of the efficacy of sacred substances, actions, or words. Jesuits denounced the idolatry of paganism but never sought to *dematerialize* belief in the way that Protestant missionaries and reformers so commonly have by emphasizing the transcendent *against* and in rejection of mediations that displace the agency of sincere individuals.[24] For one thing, Jesuits were products of the Counter-Reformation in Europe, which refused such moves (Keane 2007, 62–63) and where, Ditchfield argues, an emphasis on devotion to the Eucharist and the cult of saints, supported by the "almost ceaseless processing of relics, images, and sacred bodies (as well as the pilgrimages which this activity encouraged)," provided a "visible badge differentiating Roman Catholicism from Protestant confessions" (2009, 575). For another, the Jesuit strategy of "substitution" involved the *rematerialization* of faith as Christianized Tamil religiosity. This encouraged veneration at holy shrines, statues, sacred trees, tombs of saints, and relics, so as to mark out the provenance of Catholicism amid other sects in India, while "binding together the faithful in a mobile medley of devotions" (ibid., 575). The "flood of words—spoken and printed—unleashed" by Protestant missionaries in the nineteenth century (M. S. S. Pandian 2007, 19) was preceded by a Catholic flood of images and objects a century earlier. In fact, great material displays at festivals of the saints were, as Županov (2004) notes (of Christianization under Padroado), a means to win converts; to recruit people to spiritual instruction, confession, and baptism; and "to entertain, amuse, edify and in some cases terrify the population," sometimes using the "proselytising potential of exorcism" (Clark-Decès 2007, 66; Županov 2008) in dramatizing victory of the Christian over the pagan.

Underlying this missionary practice was a still-relevant theology of the immanence of God, who has a continuing and active presence in all aspects of the material world He created. Catholic theologian David Tracy (1981) identifies a tradition from Aquinas in which theology is the work of "analogical imagination" aiming to find a harmony of meaning between God and the world, standing in contrast to the Protestant "dialectical imagination," which finds disjuncture between transcendent God's word and the world, and human reason. In more popular terms, Greeley writes of a "Catholic imagination" that accepts both the presence of God in the world and the "metaphorical nature of creation," which means that God is disclosed by the world and that ordinary objects, events, and persons "hint at the nature of God" and make God present to and among us (2001, 6–7).[25]

Correspondingly, Catholicism has always allowed a partially independent agency for words and things. The Catholic Mass is not so much a medium for making propositions as a medium for efficacious action, for changing moral persons. Like other ritual speech, Catholic liturgy (until the 1960s, in the foreign Latin language) involves what Keane (2007, 68–69; 2008) refers to as the "decontextualisation of language" that effects an "absence" of the actual speaker (present only as officiate) and the sense that the words come from elsewhere, which produces an ontological gap that signals the *presence* of the divine. This gives words the agency to materialize this presence in the consecrated Eucharist, which is accomplished regardless of the moral status of the priest so long as he is ordained.[26] The precise opposite is of course the Christian reformers' insistence on "sincere" speech as the real-time outer expression of the inner self—that is, a "recontextualisation" of speech in the speaker that refuses agency to words or substances beyond the individual actor (Keane 2007, 183–85).[27]

The Catholic theology of immanence—explicit in the doctrines on the sacraments and the "real presence" of Christ in the Eucharist[28]—has always built a bridge to popular practice, in Europe and elsewhere, including the many cults around miraculous objects, images, and relics, tombs of the holy dead, pilgrimages, and processions. In these practices, however, "hints of presence" often become actual presence, the metaphoric or analogical tends toward an "indexicality" in which the sign and the object of signification possess a real connection—juxtapositional or causal (Keane 2007, 22). Such a tendency toward materialization of sacred power was (and is) pervasive in the popular devotional practice that took root in Catholic south India, confounding Nobili's separation of the Christian from the idolatrous.

A representational ambiguity has long allowed movement between analogy and materiality, symbol and substance. Material signs are infused with divine power to which they lend physical properties. In the form of a banyan tree, the power of St. James is multiplied and relocated as a cutting. Divine power can be imagined as material flow, being drawn to and used by people. The tendency of sacred earth or water to require physical replenishment is then transferred to immaterial power. Thus the image of the Sacred Heart brought to south Indian fisherfolk houses becomes a repository of protective power, which can also be "used up" through family petitions and so requires annual reconsecration (a practice with Hindu parallels) (Busby 2006, 87–92). Words, too—written or spoken—acquire independent agency and materiality, providing bodily protection when attached as talismans as well as effecting moral transformation in rites of mass, baptism, or confession (ibid., 91–92). The Tamil recitation of the rosary (*japamālai* or "prayer garland") is a materialization—no longer just words but substances, flowers "fresh with feeling" worn by Mary (Bloomer 2008, 195–97). Later chapters will introduce several Catholic tombs, trees, water sources, statues, or special places that become repositories of power or blessing transferred directly by ingestion, wafting, inhalation, touch or gaze (as a "kind of touching" [Eck 1981, 9]), scraping, rubbing, or through mediation of substances "transvalued" through contact with divinity, whether water or dripping oil, salt, leaves, dust, or sand that work against the substances of evil, bad actions, sorcery, or spirits (Mines 2005, 31).

The transferability and physical incorporability of divine power so common in popular Catholicism draws on a pervasive Tamil mode of signification. Valentine Daniel (1984) explains how, in this semiotic, the moral and the physical intersect; qualities such as kindness and meanness are understood partly in terms of substances capable of being transmitted to other people through transactions.[29] Likewise, "[t]he character of the man who works in the steel mills is seen as likely to be strong and unbending, taking his qualities from the material he works with" (Busby 2006, 86, citing Osella 1993, 283). The idea underlies a theory of caste: people are morally and bodily different by virtue of their caste and its work and have to maintain separation or compatibility through guarded exchanges involving food, sex, or services when charged substances become part of the transactors themselves (Marriot and Inden 1977). There is *nonduality* between actor and act, bodily substance and moral code, occupation and caste, human and divine. Given the tendency for abstract qualities to take material form and the notion that people and divinity are substantially interconnected, it is not difficult for Tamils to make sense of the Eucharist in these terms—relating to God through the ingestion of God's substance (Busby 2006, 87)—or the veneration of a saint as incorporation of the holy personage's qualities through substances transferred in worship.[30]

Jesuit strategies of substitution allowed Catholic practice to settle into existing forms of religiosity; the "functional replacement" (Keane 2007, 141) of "pagan" images, substances, or ceremonial procedures with Christian ones went along with the persistence of practices, meanings, and modes of signification from which Christianity could not be isolated. In the seventeenth- and eighteenth-century Tamil countryside Christianity was anyway perforce transmitted semi-autonomously. Shrine- and cult-focused practice expanded faster than the structure of a partially itinerant Jesuit priesthood whose ecclesiastical intervention in popular pilgrimages was intermittent (Bayly 1989, 380). Christianity took root not as a conserved religious tradition but through innovation beyond the mission center involving the search for the miraculous and creative inference from basic mission teaching (cf. Keane 2008). Some innovations would have failed; others, being socially relevant, became public. Reports of miracles spread: dreams became shrines, shrines attracted pilgrims, pilgrimages required priests and were drawn into (not sent out from) the structure of mission, articulating with Catholic teaching (ibid.). As the story of the banyan tree of St. James illustrates, the development of a regional cult of saints and sacred geography could not but be informed by indigenous notions of sacred power.

Županov (2005) uses the term *tropicality* (both trope and tropical) to capture the indeterminacy of Catholic conversion in the seventeenth century. She points to an "endless conversion of meanings and relations of things" as preconversion beliefs and practices "returned to weave together and reinterpret Christianity in unpredictable ways" (2005, 25, 27). This arose out of Nobili's "adaptationist palimpsest strategy . . . [that] targeted alternatively either the signifier or the signified" (Županov 2005, 24) and from the inherent ambiguity of material forms, which could (and can) correspond to very different experiences and interpretations (Keane 2008). By the time systematic records resumed with the "new" Jesuit mission under a colonial power in the mid-nineteenth century, a major preoccupation was dealing with undisciplined substitution and semiotics so as to demarcate proper Catholic devotion apart from heterodox or pagan idolatry among rural converts (see chapter 2). But the Jesuit project of filling existing semiotic forms with Christian meaning—at least those not overcommitted to pagan usage—still underestimated the extent to which meaning lay not in the Christian content, but in the semiotic *form* itself. Meanwhile the sharply differentiated semiotic forms that missionaries introduced—including Gothic churches and saint statues shipped from Europe—were organized according to notions of power or grace, ritual processes, and a symbolic logic shared with non-Christians, who themselves drew Christian figures (saints) into their own pantheon. The interdefinition of saints and deities or the Virgin and the goddess, and the tensions between missionary meanings and Tamil cultural forms, will be explored in later chapters.

Was this Tamil Catholicism syncretistic? It depends what is meant by the term. Stewart and Shaw (1994) describe syncretism as a diversity of religious practice subject to politically shaped discourses of authorization or prohibition—a definition so general as to apply to any religious practice. From another viewpoint, syncretism is a mode of resistance to religious authority, especially to Christianization as a colonial project (ibid., 20–21). It is true that some of the "heterodox" practices that Jesuits tried to discipline could be seen as a response to new Church authority under colonialism (see chapter 2). But in the main, popular forms of Tamil Catholic religiosity were shaped by political projects and forms of domination (of kings and castes) ahead of colonial rule. If anything, Christianization was itself a mode of resistance in south India: anticaste rather than anticolonial, and taking the form of dalit conversion movements or protests against caste-tolerant "Hinduized" Catholicism. Third, syncretism has been defined as the coexistence of elements of different religions traditions but indicative of *competition* rather than cooperation between religious groups (Hayden 2002). Tamil Catholicism has, in fact, never been syncretistic in this sense. Catholics may adopt "Hindu" ritual and aesthetic forms (but not images) along with shared attitudes to sacred power; but elements from clearly distinct provenance are not mixed (for reasons that will become clear). Hindus readily incorporate Catholic divinity into their practice, but Hindus worshipping at Catholic shrines (or visiting them for exorcism) do not try to give Christian saints Hindu identities or bring their own ritualists to mediate. Instead, at Catholic shrines Hindus find complementary qualities of divinity. Hayden's idea that syncretism (as defined above) is indicative of negative rather than positive tolerance between coexisting religious groups fits in the sense that the historical *absence* of syncretistic forms corresponds to a lack of segregation, political competition, or hostility between Tamil Christians and Hindus—indeed, the absence of *religious communities* properly speaking. (It was only the passing influence of Hindu nationalism in the 1990s that brought Hindu symbols [tridents] into the sacred space of the church of St. James in Alapuram village; see chapter 7). All this means that it will be more useful to speak here of religious *synthesis* than of syncretism (Hayden 2002).

The success of the Jesuit Madurai mission in the rural periphery (in contrast to its failure in Brahman centers) evidently had much to do with the way Catholicism was articulated through an indigenous religiosity; but more important still was its adaptation to existing caste-political forms. Catholic missionary encounters with the non-Brahman majority did little to alter their Brahmanic social perspective. Caste was not only tolerated, but regarded by some as a necessary "Hindu legislation," restraining unruly passion and idolatry. Thus after a lifetime of arduous but largely unsuccessful missionary work, the Abbé (Jean-Antoine) Dubois (1765–1848), himself a sort of refugee from the French Revolution, writes:

> I believe caste division to be in many respects the chef-d'oeuvre, the happiest effort, of Hindu legislation. I am persuaded that it is simply and solely due to the distribution of people into castes that India did not lapse into a state of barbarism, and that she perfected the arts and sciences of civilization whilst most other nations of the earth remained in a state of barbarism [. . .] caste regulations counteract to a great extent the evil effects which would otherwise be produced on the national character by a religion that encourages the most unlicensed depravity of morals, as well in the decorations of its temples as in its dogmas and ritual. (Dubois 1906, 28–33, quoted in Dirks 2001, 24–25)

But if Jesuit missions made a virtue of caste, it was also because they could do little else. In Tamil plains areas such as Ramnad, Catholicism took root through its entanglement with a precolonial caste-political order. While Jesuits "secularized" caste, Christianity was here politicized. Christian conversion is always "a matter of belief and social structure, of faith and affiliation" (Hefner 1993, 17). In seventeenth-century Ramnad, being Christian was a matter of sect affiliation, loyalty to a charismatic spiritual guru (Jesuit teachers), a rite of initiation (baptism), and sect-specific practices. Such affiliation was inseparable from political allegiance, itself a collective identification signaling protection from the particular local warrior chief or king under whose patronage the gurus of the Christian "sect" fell (chapter 1).[31] But why was Christianity a popular alternative religious affiliation in this political system?

In influential articles on the rationality of African conversion, Robin Horton (1971, 1975) argued that it was often the "dissolution of microcosmic boundaries" that encouraged a turn to the more universal doctrines of world religions better corresponding to a now expanded social sphere (1975, 381, in Hefner 1993, 22). On the Tamil plains, too, in the late 1600s, rulers of previously peripheral regions sought affiliation to status-enhancing cults with overarching cosmologies in place of localized clan deities to legitimize their expanding power within larger state systems (see Baker 1984; Dirks 1987). If Catholicism was among such cults, it was only because the Brahmanizing Jesuit cultural work had made it possible for Christian centers to authorize kingly rule and to receive patronage alongside Brahmans and Hindu temples. With its rites, centers of sacred power, and systems of ceremonial honor, Catholicism would be consolidated as another ritual form through which caste-political relations could be organized. Whatever the initial processes of conversion, Catholicism spread in Tamil south India through its flexible capacity simultaneously to "Brahmanize," to popularize in cultic form, to attract royal patronage, and to enact systems of caste ranking. Rather than disrupting existing authority and social investments, Christianity provided another means for their reproduction.

The first three chapters of this book examine the processes of localization of Christianity within existing social and representational structures to produce a Tamil Catholic religiosity and caste order. But Christianity was not merely a "thin veil[s] over an underlying autochthonous South Indian 'folk religion'" (Stirrat 1992, 196). The Jesuit mission introduced alternative practices, ideas of person and of God, and modes of signification that would have a major impact in themselves. At the same time, it was the Jesuit notion of faith *apart* from society and culture that allowed a distinctive religious synthesis to develop.

CHRISTIAN FAITH BEYOND THE SOCIAL

Nobili was not interested in "accommodating" Christianity to Tamil culture and society so much as preparing the basis for Tamils to engage with "Catholic religion" *beyond* the social. His separation of revelation and reason, religion and culture, Christianity and caste, was founded upon a notion of faith as a matter of individual conscience and choice. A tradition of Jesuit spirituality founded by Ignatius of Loyola (1491–1556) placed emphasis on the inner Christian life, on prayer, discernment of spirits, the examination of conscience, repentance, and contrition, particularly that following from Ignatius's *Spiritual Exercises*—a recursive reflection on the experience of reflection, which lies at the center of Jesuit formation (Endean 2008). Missionary teaching brought a notion of personal interiority as a target for moral evaluation following from the need to consider the fate of the individual soul, inculcated through the work of the sacraments of confession and the Eucharist (cf. Cannell 2006, 15; Robbins 2004a, 218).

Even while some shared Abbé Dubois's enthusiasm for caste as a social order, Jesuits might have also seen the caste collective as a restriction on the sphere of personal action and responsibility and on the individuality and rationality required of the Christian person (Županov 2005, 174). Christian faith, truth, and the individual soul's fate lay beyond the cage of caste. This is not to suggest, however, that Jesuits brought with them individualism as a *social* value.[32] Rather, the Christian individual and the Christian fellowship that flowed from it were ultimately located *beyond* the social world of caste, whose honors and obligations were accepted as lesser matters belonging to a subordinate nonsacred (civil) realm.

Jesuit thought here anticipates Louis Dumont's thesis (1982, 3) that in "holistic society," absolute universalism and individualism such as that contained in the fundamental conception of man that flowed from the teachings of Christ can exist only "outside" the social order: "[a]s Troeltsch said, man is an *individual-in-relation-to-God* . . . in essence an 'outworldly individual'" (original emphasis). Dumont's mentor Marcel Mauss, in his essay on the "category of the person," had already identified individual interiority and moral personhood as a particular historical effect of Christianity, the Christian individual arising from the notion of the oneness of God that came out of controversies of the doctrine of the Trinity, from which developed the "metaphysical entity of the "moral person" (*personne morale*)" (Mauss 1985 [1938], 358, cited in Cannell 2006, 18, 19). This historical particularity of the valued individual was central to Dumont's own conception of India's holism and hierarchy as a world of relations in which the particular, the individual, existed empirically but had no conceptual reality (Dumont 1965a, 1965b; Biardeau 1965; Pocock 1964).[33] Dumont found the "encompassed" value of individuality in the institution of the renouncer or *sanniyāsi*, an "individual-outside-society" in relation to whom the world of caste, the householder, or the "man-in-the-world" was insubstantial and relativized. He then saw something similar to Mauss's Christian person in the special circumstance of the Indian devotional sect or "religion of choice" founded by and infused with the thought of the renouncer, and joined through voluntary initiation. As Dumont puts it:

> Here the divine is no longer a multiplicity of gods as in ordinary religion it is the unique personal God, the Lord, Ishvara, with whom the devotee may identify himself, in whom he may participate . . . . This is a revolutionary doctrine since it transcends both caste and renunciation and opens an easy road to salvation for all without distinction. . . . This religion of love supposes two perfectly individualised terms; in order to conceive of a personal Lord there must also be a believer who sees himself as an individual. (1980, 282)

Dumont's idea of the outworldly individual and the devotional sect that he (or occasionally she) inspired maps onto the Jesuit missionary conception of religiosity—the ultimate apartness of individual Christian faith. Both Nobili's Jesuits and Dumont find the Christian individual in the renouncer beyond society.

As a sociological model, there are now well-known problems with Dumont's characterization of Indian holism: the absence of individuals, the structural opposition between renouncer and householder or between "sect" and caste.[34] But if we accept Burghart's important insight that "Dumont's theory of renunciation in Indian society is not a theory about renouncers but an observation about Brahmanical theorising" (1983, 641), it is possible to see early Jesuit missionary reasoning about their own identity as renouncer-teachers (*sanniyāsis*) of the *cattiya vētam* (true religion), and their rationalization of Christianity as transcending a relativized (insignificant) world of caste, as a parallel (or anticipatory) case of Brahmanic theorizing—one that significantly influenced the social form of

Tamil Catholicism.[35] It will become clear that a basic dual model compartmentalizing absolute religion on the one hand, and the (subordinated) relational-political world of caste on the other, took root. This was not dislodged despite the fact that in the eighteenth century Jesuits were as often ritualists of *kōvils* (temples/churches) who transacted the very signs of royal rule and caste power (chapter 1), and that by the mid-nineteenth century they had themselves become "little kings" endowing shrines and fusing the functions of rule and renunciation (chapter 4), or that in the twentieth century Jesuits mediated access to prestige education and professions (chapter 6).

Jesuit bifurcation of reality into a transcendent realm of Christian truth, individual conscience, and salvation on the one hand, and the (encompassed) world of caste rules and relations on the other (cf. Cannell 2006, 13)—between spiritual *individuals* and social *persons* of caste (Burridge 1979)—was not so foreign. First, it settled into or mimicked a preexisting model found within Indian religion, allowing Catholicism a place as a devotional *bhakti* order based on the teachings of Jesuit renouncer-gurus. Through this the Church allowed for converts' continued participation in the subordinated world of caste without the development of a critical social ethics (Dumont 1992, 26). Catholicism did not offer a new noncaste identity—and tendencies toward religious identity formation are still inhibited—but a different route to salvation, the *kiricittu mārkkam* or Christian path.[36] In this scheme, the world of caste was not denied, but deprived of its value centrality by a superior spiritual morality.[37] We can say at least that the Jesuit relativizing of culture and caste in relation to the transcendent found a parallel within an existing Tamil religious imaginary. Second, this Jesuit "dual morality" fitted with a more general indeterminacy in Tamil moral tradition between "particularistic and universalistic tendencies," between action appropriate to particular social contexts, castes, genders, or bodily states and universal morality-defining virtues claimed irrespective of identity, condition, or context—existing, for example, as a dispersed tradition of the moral self, the interior, the heart (*maṉacu*) as "a critical locus of reflective engagement with the self" that offered space for a Catholic ethics of self (A. Pandian 2008, 473, 478n10).

Of course there are numerous ways to conceive of Christians existing "discontinuously" *within* cultural continuity. I will for instance show how Catholics differentiate ritual contexts of Christian ("outworldly") exclusivism or individuality apart from the everyday ("inwordly") relationality of Tamil social and religious life.[38] My argument will be that the potential contradictions between the caste collective and individual faith, or an unjust order and Christian equality, was for centuries stabilized by implicit reference to an existing Jesuit-Brahmanical model around which rural Catholics innovated (and priests tolerated) ritual practices that in various ways separated out complementary domains of village social order and Catholic religion.

The ethnographic focus of first part of the book is therefore not simply on "localization," but on the dual Christian embedding in, *and* transcendence of, Tamil social forms, and on the various modes of reconciliation between Christian expectations and the social world that make Christian life in community possible without loss of honor and without demonizing the gods of non-Christian neighbors. Another way of looking at this duality is to say that Christian social actors are involved in constituting themselves as persons in Tamil village society *and* in participating in Catholic religion, and that these are partly inconsistent processes. This allows for variability in individual resolutions while avoiding problematic actor categories such as "Indian Catholics" or the "Catholic community." However, in order to go beyond a static nondescriptive dual model that separates Christian faith and social life, we need to look more closely at what it means to participate in Catholic religion, at how this relates to rites of Tamil social belonging, and at the *effect* of Catholic experience in village social life.

BEING CATHOLIC AND BEING A PERSON IN TAMIL VILLAGE SOCIETY

Among the array of contemporary Catholic practices, a distinction can be drawn between those that connect to authorizing theologies and meanings, and those that do not. Even within the first category, there are varying ways in which Christian significance arises. From one point of view, to participate in Catholic religion is to participate in a realm of explicit meaning. As a historically specific, Christian-derived category, "religion" itself, Daniel suggests, "is an exercise in aboutness" (2000, 175). But it would be a mistake to regard Catholic practice primarily as the outer expression of doctrine, abstract thought, belief, or inner conviction—as "meaning imprisoned in action" (Evans-Pritchard 1937, 81, in Daniel 2000, 175).[39] Religion is a realm of *practice* (Armstrong 2009). Indeed, the pragmatist view that experience precedes and produces theory or belief is consistent with a Catholic tradition in which the outer practices of religion are understood as a means to exert agency over or transform the inner life (Keane 2008; Rothfork 2006). Repeating forms of liturgy, confession, public devotion, or pilgrimage can be regarded as a kind of "learned grammar" that cultivates apt behavior, sensibility, and attitude (Asad 2008). The Catholic Church has always elicited faith by guiding practical action (ritual or ethical) and the shaping of imaginations as much as by the transmission of theology—by "inundating people with [Christian] stories" (Greeley 2001, 34). Narratives and architecture, image and movement, scent in ceremony produce religious imaginaries, shaping the prereflective assumptions through which to construe experience and practice, and underpin belief (Taylor 2004; Asad 2008).[40]

Catholic dispositions (or beliefs) may also be the effect of power—not just the disciplinary activities of church or school, catechism and cane, but the divine sanctions, stories of hell, and the terrifying images of the Devil that, instilled in childhood, remain underlying into adulthood, alongside the comforting images of Christ, the Virgin, and protector saints. Attitudes or beliefs are certainly the consequence of the acquisition of knowledge—for instance, on the conditions and effects of confession or on the lives of the saints—but, drawing on Mauss (1973 [1934]), Asad also points out that they arise from disciplines of the body (2008, 2002). In other words, body techniques—think of the rosary—are a means to produce religious attitudes such that one might say that the inability to enter into communion with God "or the inability to revere words and things or persons associated with Him may be a function of inexperienced bodies, or bodies for which certain kinds of experience have been made difficult if not impossible" (2008). Asad's point is that ritual forms and techniques of the body are not external coercions but are part of the developing self, at the center of moral potentialities.

Here is the notion that Catholic practices, images, and procedures can inculcate attitudes and imaginaries without being treated simply as meaning-bearing symbols. As Asad (2002, 120) puts it, "[D]iscourse involved in practice is not the same as that involved in speaking about practice. It is a modern idea that a practitioner cannot know how to live religiously without being able to articulate that knowledge."[41] But there is a second category of Tamil Catholic practice that does not present itself as Christian symbolic action or ritual at all—especially where that practice involves "Hindu" rites, or interactions with non-Christian divinity, which have no legitimate mode of construal, and refuse interpretation. Tamil Catholic rituals of protection, separation, or transition at puberty or death (see chapter 3) involve actions, objects, and procedures that resist any "speaking about practice." These are rites where "mood" is more important than meaning, but also ones in which, as Daniel puts it, people are themselves signs. "What one has here," he writes,

> is not a cogito or an agent in a world of representations or signs, decoding, interpreting, and explaining them, but rather, men and women who are themselves signs and therefore immersed in a semeiotic ontology, a semeiotic being-in-the-world. In such a world, what is important is not how well one makes mental representations of what is "really going on," but rather how one as a sign among signs finds one's niche, one's place, one's angle of repose or the direction of flow. [I]t calls for knowing the world through a more comprehensive being-in-the-world, which the very notion of religion can only partially accommodate. (2000, 181–82)

Missionaries themselves drew a distinction between the practices of converts with, and without, explicit meaning. The latter were often described in terms of Christians' attachment to irrational or meaningless superstitions, which, being continuous with the practices of non-Christians, were cultural "hangovers" frozen in time, as missionary ethnographer Gustav Diehl (1965) wrote of the persistence of "Hindu" practices among Lutheran converts. These actions and objects were regarded as cut adrift from proper Hindu meaning and existed (as Nobili intended they should be) as a sort of nonreligious residue explained in terms of *social* obligations and pressure from dominant groups (1965, 39, 40–41, 45–52, 80).

Rather than centering Christian religious meaning and residualizing other practices, in this book I will suggest framing Tamil Catholicism in terms of the relationship between participation in the realm of Catholic religion and the Tamil modes of "being in the world" that are enacted through village rites of life crisis and rituals of agriculture or house building, in the ways of dealing with misfortune and of seeking reconciliation with the divine, and in the search for cures or caste distinction. These involve a language of practice mutually interchangeable among Christians and non-Christians. It remains the case that procedures that make a person Roman Catholic and those that are essential to the Tamil "semiotic being in the world" articulate only imperfectly. Hence ritual improvisation is constantly required. Baptism and puberty ceremonies as well as marriage and widow purification, as examples, awkwardly straddle the distinction, while funerary rites come to be organized into two complementary parts (see chapter 3). The difficulty for the Church has always been that fundamental cultural identifications defined by kinship, caste, and place are socially prior to Christian religious identification defined by participation in the Church. If caste identity is trivialized in the domain of religion, religious affiliation is rendered unimportant in the world of caste, which is why there are few obstacles to marriages between Catholics and Hindus within the same caste, yet alliance between Catholics of different castes even in 2011 was unthinkable.

CHRISTIAN SOCIAL EFFECTS

While the social life of Tamil Catholics might have been imagined so as to keep the demands of the Church and the obligations of caste apart, the spiritual and the social were not separable spheres as Nobili schemed. In reality, Jesuit priests were not renouncers and Catholic congregations were inexactly Dumont's *bhakti* sects. On the one hand, the Tamil villagers with whom I lived participated in Catholic religion as members of endogamous castes. Caste-structured Catholic ritual, even the Eucharist, produced hierarchized and humiliated caste persons alongside Christian individuals (cf. Burridge 1979). But, on the other hand, converts participated in village society *as Christians*, bringing aspects of their religion to bear on social relations as a source of innovation, reflection, and critique. Religious life brought new perspectives on social obligations and oppressions.

Jesuit interventions, from the start, rested upon certain theological, semiological, and sociological innovations (none perhaps entirely without precedent in Tamil culture) that over two or three centuries had effects of their own. Already mentioned is the separation itself of the transcendent realm of faith from the mundane social order. As Cannell says of Bicolano Catholics in the Philippines, "[F]our centuries of Roman Catholicism have rendered familiar the idea of 'religion' as a separate sphere of life" (2006, 27), which involved partly discordant cultural orientations, modes of signification, conceptions of the person, and ethics. The very idea of a "religious" sphere sacralized Christianity and desacralized indigenous social order for Catholic villagers as well as for Jesuit missionaries, rendering the relationship between the sacred and the social "intrinsically oppositional" (Mosko 2010, 232–23).[42]

Caste in Catholic form was (as Nobili has insisted) progressively "secularized" as an external thing, a display of public honor and social order, and as such became the focus of deliberative contests, especially at saint festivals at which caste was a public performance of social order (chapter 4). Caste inequality and servitude had no *religious* sanction—all people were alike in their prior servitude to God (Williams 2008)—and people's core identities were not fused to their particular occupations or services.[43] Even while the Church tolerated or helped reproduce hierarchical orders of caste, participation in Christian religion (a realm that tutored explicit meaning and symbolic association) inculcated capacities for the manipulation of symbolic meanings or transactions that would be used (alongside political action) by subaltern groups. The Jesuit semiotic that held signs as readily detachable from referents in the social realm was a departure from the idea of a pervasive Indian "nonduality." Christianity provided a context in which dalits could view their exclusion as "polluted" persons as an arbitrary *symbolic* representation of their subordination as tied laborers, rather than as an "index" of their person and substance. This allowed a range of symbolic innovations, especially by lower castes, that delinked identity from occupation, action, and substance, and would lead to larger-scale experiments in resignification that turned signs of polluted identities into symbols of liberation, displayed in public performances of dalit arts (as later chapters will explain). It is not necessary to regard these as exclusively Christian processes to recognize that it was in fact Christian seminaries that became centers of south Indian dalit cultural production. At any rate the meaning making of dalit theologians and activists that honor an "outcast culture" will be found to be as significant for contemporary Catholicism as was Nobili's cultural production of Brahmanical Catholicism four hundred years earlier.[44]

While scholars have paid attention to the important influence of Christian mission in south India, especially in shaping the public sphere and in the emergence of religious identity or education policy (Dirks 2001; van de Veer 2002; M. S. S. Pandian 2007), few have examined the long-term cultural effects of Catholic Christianity, including at the village level (see chapters 3 and 4). Four hundred years of Catholic missionization can certainly be seen as a significant influence altering the production of caste as a form of Indian civil society and in the dynamic politics of change alongside the usually emphasized role of the colonial state (Dirks 2001).

THE INSTITUTIONALIZATION OF CATHOLIC RELIGION

The long-term process of missionary engagement with Tamil society also established and gradually expanded Catholic religion as a domain separate from caste and politics. We will see that the consolidation of ecclesiastical authority within the legal framework of British colonial rule was a critical moment in this history. It allowed French Jesuits of the "new" Madurai mission (from the 1830s) to divide evermore sharply Christian from pagan, religion from heresy/schism, or church from village. It put in place an unstable dual system of Catholic public worship: one part within the domain of the Holy Church (*tiruccapai*) and its sacraments under clerical authority; the other part involving rites, services, and honors inseparable from caste society and focused on the church as *kōvil* (Tam. *kō-il:* royal-place, palace, temple), a source of political authority and caste power. The struggle between these two, which itself involved shifts in the line between what was construed as "religious" and what was "civil," defined a key social dynamic traced at the village level over 150 years. Through a series of interventions the Church overruled the *kōvil,* successively excluding caste division from the Eucharist, from seating arrangements, from ceremonies and festivals, cemeteries, schools, colleges, and beyond. Paradoxically, as an institutionalized domain of *religion,* the Church became important in opening space for dalit *politics,* which began in the twentieth century as the assertion of rights as Christians.

During that century, the Nobilian perspective was progressively marginalized. On the one hand, as foreign missionary priests were replaced by men of caste, the Church was perceived less as a "corporate organisation with its own esprit de corps" (Ram 1995, 295) independent of dominant social groups, and more as a body, like others, divided by caste, with competition for resources and upward mobility. On the other hand, Tamil Catholic clergy interacted with wider anti-Brahman and anticaste ideologies developed out of Protestant proto-Dravidianism (Ram 1995). The domain of Catholic religion had expanded and was progressively disembedded from caste society, but at the same time the dual moral complementarity between Christian faith and caste collapsed (especially in the 1980s and 1990s) to expose a structure of caste *within* the Church, no longer made invisible by the category of "religion." This change radicalized a humiliated dalit priesthood and generated novel forms of social action, protest, and cultural and theological innovation that will be shown to have made an important contribution to secular dalit movements and politics.

Dalit Jesuits rejected Nobili's Brahmanism and his religion–society dichotomy. Their movements and dalit theology (inspired by liberation theology) reframed caste as evil rather than profane, and religion as a sphere of social struggle. Caste was a sinful, idolatrous practice, and Jesus an inworldly revolutionary (outcast as dalit). Focusing on the person of the historical Jesus, dalit Christianity did not relativize caste obligations, but organized militancy against them, prominently claiming "dalitness"—simultaneously an assertion *of* and *against* caste—as Christianity's core. At the same time the transcendent "religious" was itself called into question by the particularism of caste that infected the clergy and the religious orders.[45] A significant split in Catholic theology is opened up by the dalit movement, between an order-affirming "analogical imagination" finding continuity with the divine, and a more disjunctive Protestant "dialectical imagination" that involves a radical negation or critique of the world, the evil of power, and oppression—a theology of judgment and promise in which divine "manifestation" is revealed in the struggle for justice (Tracy 1981; Greeley 2001, 141).

However conceived theologically, the prior construction of the Christian self as a caste self has today become the principal social problem of the Catholic Church in Tamil Nadu. Caste is once again the mediator between "idolatry" and culture. Thus dalit theology now repudiates the post-Independence and post–Second Vatican Council Church's "Indianization" through adoption of certain Sanksritic semiotic forms previously prohibited as "pagan" (Hindu), by rejecting these as acts of Brahmanic cultural domination. Some dalit Christians go further to recover formerly prohibited folk practice, now construed as "pre-Hindu" rather than pre-Christian, as autochthonic dalit religion rather than "pagan." This contemporary "dalitizing" of Christianity, like Nobili's Brahmanizing, is, we see, linked to wider political agendas and speaks to international as well local audiences.

AN ANTHROPOLOGY OF TAMIL CATHOLICISM

Through tracing the long historical outworking of the contradictions of a particular Jesuit mission, this book contributes an approach to the anthropology of Christianity. Its object of enquiry—Catholicism—like religion in general, is not approached as a "transhistorical essence" or translocal cultural regime with agency of its own, but as an emergent field of debate and practice, the product of particular regional histories (Asad 1993; 2002, 118). The inquiry does not address Catholicism as a stable entity or agent. As has been said of other institutions—whether the economy, law, or property—Catholic religion in India was not a preformed conceptual structure imposed from outside but was "worked out through compromise and contingent action[s] in a variety of areas . . . which wrought change not by their own logic but through the rupture and contradictions they effected in the existing social and political systems" (Mitchell 2002, 77). Catholic missionaries had to work hard at making themselves external agents acting from within a distinctive religious domain separate from the politics and culture in which that domain was embedded. This was an accomplishment, not the premise, of missionization. Tamil Catholicism itself is a matter of participating in a set of events, practices (ritual and ethical), and relationships brought together as "complexes" or "assemblages" productive of certain imaginaries, dispositions, or attitudes, partly contiguous with those of non-Christian Tamils, and sanctioned (or not) by wider theological ideas. In short, Tamil Catholicism will better be understood by "analysing practices" than by "reading symbols" (Asad 2002, 120), and by understanding struggles of power and authority that shape these practices.

Religious authority is of central importance in Christianity. It concerns kinds of mediation and representation (figurative or literal) that are thinkable in different traditions by which the absent divine is made present. After all, the central Christian paradox is that God is simultaneously present and absent—absent first as creator apart from his creation, and second by virtue of the Fall and expulsion from Eden. Although re-presented in Christ, his presence becomes "conditioned by absence," marked by pathos and uncertainty (Engelke 2007, 12–14). In the Roman Catholic tradition, the uniqueness of the Incarnation, the centrality of the sacraments, and mediation by the hierarchy of an ordained priesthood define exclusivity in mediation between humans and divine power. To be Catholic is not so much to hold particular beliefs as to be part of a tradition through submission to authority within a structure that invokes a lineage of teachers and Fathers of the Church, back to the Apostles and Jesus Christ (Clooney 2004; Asad 2002, 124).

What distinguished Catholics from Hindus in Tamil villages was their relationship with religious authority. But this authority had to be wrought in struggles with others—Hindu rulers, missionary competitors, colonial officers, dalit movements. There have been repeated challenges to authority from different kinds of direct mediation (cf. Leach 1972), ranging from heterodox saint cults, holy personages, sacred tombs, and charismatic healing centers to contemporary mobilization in the name of Jesus as social revolutionary that sacralizes social struggle as the true presence and the means to salvation. But claims to religious authority also depended crucially on historically contingent distinctions between the religious and the sociopolitical.

It should be obvious, therefore, why an ethnographic account of Catholicism cannot be confined to the study of "Catholic religion" but has to deal with the political systems and modes of representation within which this category developed and today strives to exist as a distinctive arena of meaning and practice. So this is not a book about the religious life of Christian Tamils—still less an account of Catholic "folk religion." It is a study of the historical relationship between modes of Tamil "being in the world" (of caste, kinship, and place) and a domain of Catholic religion. It examines the cultural models of reconciliation of social being and religious commitment, as well as their instability and collapse, which turned tensions between faith and culture into an engine of social transformation. It asks questions about the effects at different moments of participation in, and loyalty to, Catholic religion—its ideas of person, modes of signification, and conceptions of divinity and social ethics—and examines the Catholic parish as a political institution.

Too often explanations of Christian missionary encounters oscillate between one or the other of two opposed anthropological perspectives. In the first, the emphasis is on the persistence of "indigenous" cultural forms and the transformation of Christianity by convert societies. This itself is a challenge to the assumption that modernizing and culturally dominant colonial Christianity would supplant local religious and cultural systems. The latter assumption also lies behind the concern of national churches that Christians are alienated by the legacy of missionary paternalism, and therefore that there is need for "inculturation." The anthropological interest in "localization"—the resistance that "the local" provides to Christianity—and the ecclesiastical concern for "inculturation"—the "incarnation of the Christian life and of the Christian message in a particular cultural context"[46]—are indeed mirror opposites (Keane 2007, 91). Rewriting mission history from the point of view of the missionized themselves replaces the modernist-nationalist image of the passive proselyte with an anthropological view of converts as themselves active creators, manipulators of symbolic and ritual systems that served indigenous social and political ends, and of missionaries as being unwittingly drawn into rather than displacing these systems (Comaroff 1985; S. B. Bayly 1989).

The second anthropological perspective makes Christianity itself rather than "local culture" the focus of analytical description and emphasizes its disjunctive and transformative effects. As Robbins, drawing on Peel, puts it: "Christianity moves from being a 'dependent variable' governed by a 'social situation' that determines its uses and expression, to an 'independent' one, 'modifying the behaviour of individuals' and creating new social situations of its own" (2004, 123; Peel 1968, 288). This perspective, advanced by Robbins among others, and calling for an anthropology of Christianity's culture, is itself a response to what is regarded as the discipline's in-built orientation toward cultural continuity, and its failure therefore to grasp the rupture and discontinuity that are often uppermost in Christians' views of themselves (2003, 2007; Cannell 2006).

Clearly something must be drawn from each of these perspectives without regarding them as alternatives. This study of Catholicism in the Tamil countryside must avoid the presumptions of "continuity thinking" without developing an overattachment to an imposed "theory of modernity" (Robbins 2007; Cannell 2006, 45). It offers three orientations to help with this. The first is "to explore the complex ways in which continuity and rupture are combined in the production of cultural forms" (Peel 2007, 27). The argument will be that in south India, the question of Christian cultural continuity or discontinuity has been mediated by a cultural politics of caste that reveals the conflicting perspectives and interests *within* convert communities who use Christian rites for opposed social purposes.

The second orientation is to develop a historical perspective that shows how the tensions within cultural forms unfold *through* a dynamic of change. The relationship of Christianity to culture has to be examined over time without resort to foreshortened characterizations of "Christian culture." Looking toward radicalized dalit Christians in contemporary Tamil Nadu, one might argue with Robbins (2007) that Christianity is "'good to think' about change, being itself founded on the idea of radical change" (Cannell 2007, 19); but then at other historical moments Christianity has been good to stabilize and reproduce social hierarchy. Christianity was not introduced in rural south India as part of "a great transformation" (Hefner 1993), but in the 1990s it became a critical ingredient in radical anticaste politics. The scholarly challenge is to give importance to the various contingent and contextual factors (of Tamil society and missionary strategy) without ignoring "the distinctive cultural dynamics of the world religions themselves, which produce real effects even where their initial adoption has a strongly local rationale" (Peel 2000, 4; cf. Robbins 2007, Cannell 2006). Conversion itself has to be viewed in the long term as a historical process rather than within a conventional narrative of rupture (Hann 2008, 390). Centrally, the social dilemmas of convert communities are not produced at some originary moment of conversion. Rather, it is in its historical unfolding that Christianity provides a means to "reimagine local cultural sensibilities" (Bialecki et al. 2008, 1144), and that conversion becomes a powerful trope in countercultural discourses, even among south Indian communities that did not experience conversion as rupture (Kim 2003; G. Viswanathan 1998; Menon 2002). The "continuity-rupture" debate has been distorted by a bias toward short-time-frame ethnographies of Protestant and Pentecostal forms of Christianity and their "moral narrative[s] of modernity" (Hann 2007, 391) and has largely excluded noncharismatic Catholic or Orthodox traditions that do not valorize discontinuity or modernity.[47] This historical anthropology of Catholicism tries to redress the balance.

Finally, by drawing attention to Christianity-in-relation-to-culture as a matter of power, where recent writing has been overly "idealist" in its analysis (Hann 2007), I want to show how the experience of being Christian is preconditioned by processes of authority and protest that produce Catholic religion in south India. Religious thought has no agency beyond the social conditions of its expression, and it cannot be assumed that convert groups necessarily graduate from instrumental motivations to those grounded in truth claims and morality (Keane 2006a, 233). Matters of power and matters of religion do not separate in this way. Indeed, this book shows how Indian Christianity continues to be linked to struggles of power, and perhaps becomes increasingly defined by them. In other words, Tamil Catholicism has to be treated as an institutional whole, interlinking priests and politics, sacraments and schools, festivals and farming. The tension between "the religious" and "the social" itself provides a continuing locus of power returning us repeatedly to the dynamic challenges of caste, which, being central to the cultural construction of power and the politics of culture, mediates the assimilations and the transformations of Tamil Catholicism. Cultural continuity and discontinuity retain significance by being drawn into a politics of caste: on the one hand, Christianity provides a refuge for a Tamil culture of caste; on the other, dalits turn Christian disjuncture into an anticaste countercultural politics of the "outcast."

The plan of the book: the central theme of this book is that, while profoundly localized into existing social and representational structures, Christianity nonetheless becomes a source of distinctive forms of thought, action, and modes of signification that are potentially transformative and (as the bishop and Jesuit provincial insisted) demand new forms of institutional repentance and vigilance within Christian living. But while Tamil Catholicism implied cultural critique, for centuries it stabilized rather than challenged existing social orders. The question is, What were the particular historical circumstances of cultural continuity or critique?

Chapter 1 provides the historical context, explaining how a "Brahmanized" Jesuit mission was incorporated into a precolonial political system in the plains area of Ramnad. As Catholic saints were worshipped through Tamil temple forms, missionary priests became crucial mediators of political honors. This chapter traces the ecclesiastical controversies and transformations brought along with British colonial rule, and the mass conversion movements of "untouchable" castes that changed the profile both of Christianity and of caste in south India. Chapter 2 turns historical and ethnographic attention to a localized Catholic imaginary and popular practice described as a dynamic social field (not a stable religious synthesis). It examines the way in which incompatible missionary and indigenous conceptions of divinity or misfortune are handled by priests and people, and turns finally to the implications for contemporary Christian trends in inculturation, piety, and Pentecostalism.

Chapter 3 focuses on the Catholic caste order of Alapuram village. It examines the distinctive negotiability, changeability, and politicization of caste as a historical effect of Christianity, but also the kinds of ritual improvisation required (for example, in life-crisis rites) to reconcile the demands of Catholic religion and those of being a person in a Tamil village. Chapter 4 turns to forms of public Catholic worship and traces the history of the Santiyakappar festival in order to show how a domain of Catholic religion was gradually institutionalized by priests while they contended with the political projects of others focused on the shrine, whether ecclesiastical rivals, kings, village heads, or caste groups. I examine how religious change created political space for dalits but also separated Christian and Hindu in new ways.

Chapters 5 turns to the postmissionary, post-Independence context, providing an account of mobility and immobility among different (Catholic and Protestant) dalit castes. It reveals the contrasting ways in which Christianity has been drawn into dalit social projects, while also arguing that the social meaning of Christianity was itself altered by an emerging dalit politics. This is taken further in chapter 6, where it is made clear that a rising stream of anti-Christian Hindu nationalism in 1990s Indian politics intersects the Tamil politics of caste and of religion in ways that influence dalit theological-cultural work to produce a contemporary dalitization of Catholicism every bit as significant (and international) as Nobili's Brahmanization, which it opposes. Christian truth would now have to pass through the suffering and culture of the dalits.

Chapter 7 asks how this changed field of caste and Christianity has influenced social relations and religious practices in Alapuram village in the quarter century or so since my first stay. It also looks at how a long history of moving between incompatible meaning, morals, and modes of signification allows a diffusion of the tension and conflict that might have arisen from the new politics of caste and religious extremism when Christianity itself has become socially disembedded, diversified, and globalized. The Conclusion summarizes the main arguments of the book and connects it to a wider and comparative discussion of Christianization, ethics, and social change, while indicating a path for the anthropology of Christianity beyond cultural continuity/discontinuity or models that rest on the presumed stability and ahistoricity of the categories of both culture and Christianity.

1

A Jesuit Mission in History

The experience of religious conversion is always caught within a "matrix of motives and representations" (Hanretta 2005, 490). Whatever the inner experience, conversion to Christianity in Tamil history was an irreducibly social process that involved change of allegiance given significance by prevailing social relations. Yet regardless of its political import, new Christian affiliation came to be narrated within missionary discourses that construed the change as a matter of spiritual transformation. Inevitably, then, the history of Christian conversion is an account of the incompatible logics and mutual effects of missionary intentions and the exigencies produced by the intentions of others (cf. Hefner 1993).[1] The Tamil convert communities who are the subject of this book were brought into existence in such circumstances. The message of missionaries was assimilated into existing categories of understanding and relating (Robbins 2004a), although south Indian history shows just how diversely Christianity was communicated—and how different was its reception, for instance, by Brahman philosophers, warrior kings, and "untouchables." There is also no doubt that Christian practices and agents altered existing arrangements, but since the social or religious disjunctures involved were defined by existing categories and sets of relations, it makes little sense to talk of Christian conversion as rupture per se. Christian conversion, as argued in the Introduction, is a long-term historical and institutional process of continuity and discontinuity.

The aim of this chapter is to explain in broad terms the historical conditions that shaped Catholicism in a particular Tamil region up to the twentieth century, and so to set the scene for later chapters.[2] I begin by returning to the circumstances—south Indian and European—of Roberto Nobili's mission in the early seventeenth century, drawing a contrast between his Brahmanic perspective and the kingly politics through which Catholicism (mission, churches, affiliations) was actually drawn into Tamil society. The chapter shows how Christian centers were party to processes of precolonial state formation, and how Tamil socio-political relations became constitutive of the character of the Christian sacred. Indeed, while Nobili tried to separate Christianity from empire, the logics of mission and of rule were again intertwined, albeit in indigenous form within Tamil strategies of statecraft. I turn then to the external impacts on this politically and culturally assimilated Christianity: first, that of the Roman Church, which eventually suppressed the Jesuit order; and second, that of British rule in south India, which helped institutionalize religion apart from indigenous politics. It will become clear how the changed arrangements of power under colonialism brought new conflicts and new opportunities for a Jesuit mission reconsolidated in the mid-nineteenth century. Among the most significant conflicts were those with Hindu rulers and rival missions—Padroado and Protestant—which intersected in interesting ways with local caste politics. The chapter turns finally to what was the most dramatic turn of events for a mission that had sought Brahmanic emulation and eschewed the dishonor of association with inferior castes—namely, mass conversions to Christianity by subordinated dalits. We will see how the missionary response—Catholic and Protestant—to this social movement profoundly rearranged the language of caste and its position astride the social and the spiritual by putting in place the modern notion of caste as a Hindu religious institution and conversion as a religious rather than a political-economic act.

THE JESUIT MADURAI MISSION

When in 1606 young Roberto Nobili (1577–1656) settled in Madurai, center of the ancient Tamil Pandyan kingdom, as an "ambassador" under the protection of the Nayak ruler, he signaled a change in the course of Roman Catholicism in the region (Županov 2005, 233). As noted in the Introduction, Nobili imagined Christian mission to the Tamils less as a spiritual conquest than as the restoration of a lost truth—the fourth veda of salvation—and he viewed indigenous theological texts not as heathen religion but as a sort of defective Catholicism.[3] His mission would "'sacrilize' Tamil society in the Augustinian sense of giving a visible form, the Catholic Church, to the invisible grace of God" (Županov 1999, 115, 133, 154).

The Pandyan kingdom (fourth century B.C.E.–fifteenth century C.E.) had been the site of earlier Christian encounters, being the transit ("mahbar") between the ancient Christian centers of Kottayam (Kerala) and the tomb of the Apostle Thomas at Mylapore (Chennai). But at the start of the seventeenth century,

Christianity was largely confined to low-status Portuguese-protected fishing and pearl-diving castes baptized by Francis Xavier (see S.B. Bayly 1981, 1989; Frykenberg 2008). Christian identity was fused to European culture, and to social inferiority. In the eyes of the elite groups that Nobili hoped to influence, baptism meant joining the ritually impure community of *parangis* (firangi, aliens, or Westerners) whose social and bodily practices (meat eating, alcohol drinking, alleged lax bodily cleanliness) were judged morally inferior, and whose Eucharist ritual involved the use of polluting wine and an interpretation—eating blood and flesh—that "would suggest to the agamic thought the bloody and polluting 'pariah' rites of darkness" (Hudson 2004, 215; cf. Neill 1984; S. B. Bayly 1989, 389–92; Irschick 2003).

Nobili sought to redefine and render honorable the Christian faith, while at the same time revising the European view of Indian paganism. This was to be accomplished by carving out a mediating space for "culture" in the mutual confrontations of civilization and barbarism (cf. Eagleton 2009), beginning with cultural work on himself. Nobili dissociated himself from the Portuguese. He devoted his mind to the study of Sanskrit and Tamil sacred texts, while expecting that his "body covered in the right signs" would be the "passport into the world of the other" (Županov 1999, 126). He dressed in layers of ochre robes, wore the sacred thread, separated himself from polluting substances and persons, and lived in a simple thatched hut. He combined behavioral codes of the Brahman with renunciation of the *sanniyāsi* to test a culturally acceptable Tamil model of Christian holiness, while drawing on the devotional and epic traditions of Saivism to develop a Tamil Christian vocabulary (1999, 3, 25–27, 116–17). Nobili presented himself as a Brahman renouncer of royal (Kshatriya) birth, the guru of a devotional tradition "based on privileged knowledge (*ñāṇam*) as a way of approaching and understanding the transcendent" (1999, 161). He likened himself to St. Paul, becoming Brahman in order to convert Brahmans, following Jesuit founder St. Ignatius of Loyola's injunction "to enter by the door of the others in order to make them come out" (1999, 126).[4]

At a time when pagans and Christians were regarded as absolutely different and Christian doctrine hardly translatable into pagan languages (Županov 2005, 232 et seq.), Nobili framed the relationship between Tamil culture and Christianity as "form" and "content," signifier and signified. As Županov (1996, 1203–5) puts it, he replaced a theological articulation (of Brahmanism) with a sociological one. His was an *ethnographic* perception: where superstition and paganism had hitherto been seen, he discovered Hinduism as a universe of social practice onto which Christianity would graft the light of true religion.

Nobili's innovations were forged not in the abstract, but through contests within a specific social and ecclesiastical context; his ideas were conceived in order to contradict opponents and to persuade and enroll supporters, whether in

Cochin, Goa, or Rome, and it was to them (rather than to Tamils) that his arguments were first communicated. There was more than one ecclesiastical conflict into which the controversy over Nobili's methods was drawn, but as Županov's brilliant analysis of Jesuit correspondence argues, the most immediate foil for Nobili's peculiar mix of ethnographic argument and inquisitorial investigation (1999, 84) was an older Portuguese missionary, Gonçalo Fernandes, who served the small enclave of Paravar and European Christians in Madurai. Folded into and shaping an epistolary contest between these two missionaries were frictions of class, national rivalries, and a tension between the Holy See and the Portuguese royal Padroado (patronage), which itself revealed the struggle of the time between the papacy and rising nation states (Županov 1999, 114; Wright 2004, 56). Nobili was a highly educated self-fashioned Italian aristocrat well connected in Rome, while Fernandes was a lower-class, locally recruited ex-military man, loyal to Padroado and resentful of Nobili's anti-Portuguese elitism and Brahmanic claims, which would have recalled for him precisely the kind of social hierarchy from which his career as a Jesuit had promised escape (1999, 34, 54). Typical of European subaltern agents, insecure in their social position and threatened by alterity, Fernandes's letters adopt what Županov calls a *proto-etic* approach—that is, a descriptive ethnology that positioned him firmly outside the object of study in order to enumerate and classify observed diversity and to record a rejected outer world of pagan idolatry. Nobili's approach, on the other hand, involved a *proto-emic* "participant observation" concern with the inner hidden world, an ideal Brahmanical textual order that was generative of the manifest world (its imperfect residue) open to theological speculation and reinterpretation with the "eyes of the soul" (Županov 1999, passim).[5]

The significant social implication of Nobili's position was not only that converts could retain caste identities and separations, but also that parallel divisions were required among missionaries themselves in order to minister to those of different rank in separate churches. The Brahmanic Jesuit sanniyasis distanced themselves from the priests serving lower castes, restricting contact and commensality, and from c. 1640 a second category of Jesuits, known as *paṇṭāracāmis* (from *paṇṭāram,* a low-caste Saivite mendicant and ascetic), was created to work among non-Brahmans (Ponnad 1983, 5; Dumont 1972, 250–51, 272 n102g). The only way Jesuits imagined they could preach to the most inferiorized "Pariahs" without jeopardizing the whole mission was covertly, at night, in separate locations, without visible churches.[6] Even then this provoked violent reactions: the demolition of converts' shrines and the arrest of priests (Manickam 2001).

The Brahmanic necessities of Nobili's mission might seem strange in the light of recent scholarship suggesting that rigid rules of caste became prevalent only in the nineteenth century as the *result of* British colonial rule and the unprecedented prominence it gave to Brahmans and their codes (Dirks 2001; Inden

1990). However, Nobili's missionaries worked at a time when south Indian society was already becoming more susceptible to Brahman influence and more "castelike" in a manner that would, for sure, be intensified under British rule. As S.B. Bayly (1999) argues, in the seventeenth century caste identity and rank became a strategic asset. Self-made warrior rulers of successor states thrown up as the Mogul polity fragmented invoked caste norms, idioms of purity-pollution, exalted blood ancestry, and courtly styles and titles to legitimize their rule and to forge upward links and downward domination. And Brahmans (and other literate groups) themselves gained social power with the growing importance of trade and revenue systems as "men of pen, lamp and ledger" (S. B. Bayly 1999, 66).

Nobili's sociology may not have been mere Brahman fantasy (although the centrality of caste rank and regulations was likely exaggerated to serve the end of defending his mission in Europe), but his goal of winning over the intelligentsia in the expectation that the rest of society would follow in a process of "global conversion" was doomed by the elitist failure to accept the heterogeneity of Tamil society (Županov 1999, 175). By the 1630s there were still very few Brahman converts. Jesuits were losing trust in Sanskrit as a missionary tool for recreating sacred texts, and by 1673 the missionary model of Brahmanic dialogue was probably abandoned (ibid., 235), leaving the Madurai mission to expand through the work of its pantaracamis who catalyzed large-scale conversions, not so much among exteriorized "Pariahs" (for whom a third category of missionaries was appointed [Rajamanickam 1972, 49–50]), but rather among the politically high-profile warrior castes (such as Maṟavars), especially in the southeastern coastal plains known as "Maravar country" (*maṟavar nāṭu*)—that is, the kingdoms of Ramnad and Sivagangai.

WARRIOR CONVERSION AND PLAINS POLITICS[7]

The mid-seventeenth century is widely regarded by historians as a period of considerable social upheaval in south India. Population movements and political competition accompanied the often unsuccessful attempts to resist invading Mogul armies after the 1565 Battle of Talikota. With the militarization of the southern region, the kingdom of Ramnad itself gained importance as a source of troops and military supplies for Nayak rulers of Madurai (viceroys of the Vijayanagar emperor), who "exploited a pre-existing system of decentralised Maravar martial-political authority, obliging a set of auxiliary powers or *pāḷaiyakkārars* ('poligars' or chiefs of a *pāḷaiyam* 'fort') to build garrisons, organize levies and push forward cultivation in return for regional political autonomy" (Baker 1984, 36). The ruling Maravar Cētupatis ("lords of the causeway" to the pan-Indian pilgrimage of Rameswaram) maintained a degree of independence from the Nayak overlords. This was jealously guarded against the constant threats from Dutch and Portuguese powers on the coast, and assertions by lesser chieftains within this loosely structured and decentralized polity.

This was a time of shifting power, secessionism, and royal succession disputes that opened up spaces for new forms of religious leadership offering legitimacy and status to competing warrior chiefs aspiring to become sovereign rulers. Christianity took root in Ramnad as a dissident but not markedly foreign "Brahmanic" sect, spreading through caste and kinship networks, accelerated by the baptism of members of the royal lineage and those with high office in the army (S. B. Bayly 1989, 394, 398; Županov 1999, 74). Between 1640 and 1690 the Jesuits Antão de Proença (Paramandarswami) and then João (John) de Britto (Arulanandaswami) claimed tens of thousands of converts often arranged through mass baptism ceremonies. Baptism signified affiliation to a sect that allowed an ambitious but culturally marginal caste or lineage to enhance its standing. Warrior clans had already promoted the cults of their own non-Sanskritic goddesses and warrior deities that dramatized martial power and honor. Thus Christian religion, Bayly suggests, was easily incorporated into the caste lifestyle of the martial Maravars, facilitated by the existence of two well-known soldier groups who were Christian: the Syrian Christians; and the Eurasian Christians or "Topasses," commonly recruited into the armies of the south Indian "poligars" (S. B. Bayly 1989, 395).

Christian affiliation also helped build constituencies or demarcate autonomous domains. Conversion, Bayly argues, was "conceived and understood as an act of statecraft" through which political alliances were forged or fissured. This might involve a "strategic tightening of the ruler's open-ended alliance system," but it could equally dramatize political challenge as individual "poligars" joined Christian churches "to define and stabilise their [own] domains" and to mark these off from the ruling Cetupati (S. B. Bayly 1989, 396–97, 400–401; cf. Dirks 1987, 48). For example, late-seventeenth-century challengers to ruling Raghunatha Tevar ("Kilavan") Cetupati—including influential Maravar chiefs and village headmen, kinsmen of the ruler, members of his court, and contenders for the throne—regularly turned to the Jesuit mission along with their dependents and followers, some perhaps expecting links via the missionaries to the foreign coastal powers.

The Portuguese Jesuit João de Britto, who moved into the Ramnad kingdom in 1685, missionized amid such turbulent politics. Regarded as a political or military threat by the Cetupati, he was arrested later that same year allegedly after interception of correspondence with a missionary linked to the Dutch (Nevett 1980, 1969–70). He was imprisoned and tortured, first at the temple town of Kalaiyarkovil and then at Ramnad before being deported. Much about de Britto remains contested and in need of further research, but the emphasis in the various hagiographic narratives of the saint's life is then focused on his return to

Maravar country as a fugitive in 1691. He lives in the forests and is protected by *pāḷaiyakkārar*s opposed to the Cetupati. One of these, Tadaiya Tevar of Siruvalli and rival to the throne, converts to Christianity in 1692 after a miraculous cure. Conversions follow among his retinue and dependents and en masse in the villages of his domain. Britto insists that on being baptized Tadaiya Tevar keep only his first wife, divorcing all others including Kadalai, his youngest spouse and Kilavan Cetupati's niece. Enraged by this dishonor to his kin, Kilavan rearrests Britto and banishes him to the frontier fort of Oriyur with execution instructions, sealed to avoid the uprising that the preacher's public death might provoke among the considerable Christian population. De Britto was indeed beheaded on 4 February 1693 and his body impaled on a stake—like his Lord, tortured and murdered as a political criminal.

The martyr became incorporated into the regional pantheon as a warrior embattled with the demonic in a way that overflows this political analysis (see chapter 2), and Britto would likely have seen his own vocation within the contemporaneous Jesuit narrative of mission as suffering on distant shores for the salvation of others' souls, and through martyrdom winning the prize of sainthood (Wright 2004, 73). The Brahmans meanwhile considered the Christian practice Britto was propagating as socially and ritually degrading as well as politically dangerous. As competing "professional ideology makers" (Županov 1999, 20), they offered intense opposition, spreading suspicion of Christians' unclean association with Parangis, accusing them of the heinous act of trading cows for slaughter and advising the ostracism of converts to *cēri*s (untouchable settlements) (Nevett 1980, 151; Manickam 2001, 197–98, 200–201).

Immediately following Britto's execution, Christians were in fact repressed, their houses and churches burned, and their rites outlawed; but within ten years the faith had become politically tolerated and more widely adopted.[8] Christian affiliation still signaled challenge to the Cetupati (as when his brother Thiruvalavar Tevar was baptized), enacted insubordination (as when Christian soldiers escorting the Cetupati's Rameswaram pilgrimage refused sacred ash), or marked opposing alliances, such as when between 1708 and 1711 twenty Maravar headmen (*ampalakkārar*s) around the village of Ponnalikkottai came to Pierre Martin for baptism (Hambye 1997, 162; Ponnad 1983, 137). Read as a political act, Christian conversion still provoked attacks on missionaries and churches. But after 1729–30, when the new Cetupati, Kattaya Tevar became a supporter and patron of the Jesuit mission, Catholicism ceased to be only a cult of dissidents. In the following decades, rulers constructed churches in what remain the key Catholic centers of Ramnad, and granted land and other rights to their Jesuit gurus, as well as to powerful Christian Maravar chiefs with influence over Maravar and non-Maravar Christians (Khadirvel 1977). In 1734, Kattaya Tevar built a shrine at the site of de Britto's martyrdom, which was by then a popular pilgrimage, and in 1770 another was established at the place where his body had been impaled (which today preserves a two-foot length of the stake).[9]

The royal patronage of Christian centers followed a regional political and economic logic that I turn to later on. But compared with temples, Brahman communities (*brahmatēyas*), or pilgrim houses (*cattirams*), the political position of Christian centers was nonetheless precarious. They remained a focus for insurrection. For example, it was to gain support from dissident Christian members of the royal family settled in the village of Sarukani (below) that contenders to the Ramnad throne made grants of land to the local church in 1710 and again in 1762 (Kadhirvel 1977, 53, 143). The patronage of Christian shrines represented competitive bids for scarce demographic, agricultural, or trade resources, or threatened links (via missionaries) to foreign coastal powers. As such they continued to attract acts of persecution in what amounted to a reversal of royal patronage: intimidation, the confiscation of lands, or the transfer of land grants (*māṉiyams*) to Brahmans, for example, from the churches of Oriyur, Pulial, and Tiruvadanai in 1721 (ibid., 52n85). One thing is clear: Christianity on the Tamil plains was not faith "assimilating" to some stable Brahmanic social order. Christian affiliation had become *part of* a set of political-religious relations and was being drawn into a globalizing economic system in the late precolonial context of instability, warfare, and large-scale internal displacements (cf. Waghorne 2004).

In this political mélange, Jesuit missionaries were not just objects of patronage mimicking Brahmans or temples but were themselves power-holding "big men," building domains and attracting endowments from royal overlords (Županov 1999, 220).[10] The Church developed here as a personalized institution around individual Jesuit gurus as heads of communities with networks of followers expanding or contracting according to a missionary's charisma and his ability to distribute honors (see below) and "integrate local communities into a larger, galactic Hindu polity" (ibid., 220). To sustain their domains, these Jesuits needed money, mobility, a territorial basis, vertical linkages, and divine authorization (ibid., 182); and they were always at risk of according themselves "more sovereignty than [local opponents] thought appropriate" (ibid., 180). In any case, with few missionaries, weak institutionalization, and limited dissemination of formal Christian knowledge or liturgy, these followings could fragment after the death of the guru (ibid., 29). The patronage of rulers and local overlords was crucial to success. In general, however, Jesuit domains were diffuse. Missionary letters suggest a spiritual leadership as renouncer-teachers, recruiting through conversion, administering the sacraments, presiding over ceremonies (Correia-Afonso 1997), and giving primary agency to the Jesuit-appointed catechists, as recorded in a significant body of Tamil Christian literature (S. B. Bayly 1989, 385). As visiting functionaries or ritualists, they could not assert much authority over the churches and their festivals, in which regional chiefs, local headmen, or serving caste groups and catechists held recognized rights. What they did control, however, was access to ritual honors, and from this they acquired a significant role in local politics (see chapter 4).

The Jesuit annual letters of the eighteenth century give a vivid picture of the alternating political fortunes of Ramnad mission centers; but sacred power, too, is woven through these "theatrical mode" narratives of miraculous and spectacular manifestations of a superior Christian divine (Županov 1999), over which, for Protestant mission historian Stephen Neill, there "hangs an atmosphere of cloying piety" (1984, 301). More significantly, however, these narratives were constructed out of local legends and involved, as Županov (1999, 165) puts it, "dialogic bridges between Tamil oral and Jesuit written history." Christianity became a successful social project in Ramnad not primarily through the preaching of a handful of Jesuit priests, but through incorporation into the mission structure of existing popular devotional saint cults that had filtered inland following networks and nodes of trade and pilgrimage from established Coromandel coastline Catholic communities (S. B. Bayly 1989, 380). Such cults and pilgrimages, some initiated by low-caste devotional leaders with limited exposure to Christian doctrine or liturgy, were attracting large and diverse followings and thence political patronage (1989, 389). The cult focused on the sacred tree of Santiyakappar (St. James) at Alapuram was one such.

It was in the late 1600s that Santiyakappar, an established tutelary of the Paravar fishing caste (ibid., 382), was brought to the village in the form of a miraculous banyan-tree cutting from his shrine at Verkatu. From the 1730s onward Jesuit annual letters blend folklore into the accounts of the Santiyakappar cult at Alapuram, "where every Friday crowds of people [pagans and Christians] come . . . to fulfill some vows in return for favors asked or to ask for new ones." They describe tremendous "prodigies" at the shrine, brought about by the sacred tree and its leaves, prominent among them being the saint's punishment of perjurers making false oaths (*poy cattiyam*) in front of his statue.[11] The Jesuits tried to make Alapuram the focus of their mission in the Maravar country under the patronage of Cetupati Kattaya Tevar, but were overtaken by political events when the area was annexed to the Maratha king of Thanjavur (who first granted then withdrew land for the saint).[12] Instead they centered on Sarukani village (see below) under the patronage of Nallukkotai Utaiyan Tevar, raja of Sivagangai (a kingdom independent from Ramnad after 1730). Jesuit priests traveled from Sarukani to Alapuram to minister the sacraments and preside over the annual Santiyakappar festival, which by the 1740s attracted large crowds and a considerable income. A church was constructed in 1731 under the protection of the new raja of Sivagangai (who the letters tell us received a miraculous cure[13]). However, it was local Maravar headmen (*ampalams*) or chiefs of the *nāṭu* microregions (*nāṭṭampalams*)[14]—including one Yagappa ("St. James") recalled as the powerful chief of the Mankalam Natu—who would have become protectors or trustees of the shrine, receiving first "honors" from the priest at the annual festival. It was they who erected a new church for a miraculous statue of St. James in the 1770s,[15] although in 1792 the shrine again received royal patronage in the form of a land grant (*māṉiyam*) from the Cetupati Mutturamalingam (Ponnad 1983, 200).

The rationales of popular religiosity, Jesuit mission, and Maravar statecraft intersected at such Christian shrines. They attracted royal patronage because they were centers of power, recognizable within the region's sacred geography (S. B. Bayly 1989, 9). At the same time, mission building created ritual systems that enabled popular shrines to be incorporated into the regional political system. This produced equivalence between Catholic and Hindu divinity in signifying and validating political orders. Sovereignty became constitutive of the character of saints such as Santiyakappar, making their shrines the focus of political and social struggle (see chapter 4). There was an underlying conception of divine power as localized, material, and not clearly distinguished from the secular power of the king, a power that is focused on the *kōvil*—the deity's "seat," shrine, or royal palace (Ludden 1985, 30–31; S. B. Bayly 1989, 48). It is not difficult to see how the cult of the miraculous banyan tree of St. James, himself portrayed as divine warrior and protector (in fact, slayer of the "Moors"), was compatible with prevailing notions of power among gods and men. I return to the cultural definition of "warrior" saints in the next chapter, but first the role of Catholic churches in the political order of the region in the eighteenth and into the nineteenth century needs further exploration.

HINDU TEMPLES, CATHOLIC CHURCHES, AND POLITICAL ORDER

Historians agree that religious institutions, specifically temples, had a key role in integrating and extending the loose domains of authoritative control of the little kings and warrior chiefs of plains areas such as Ramnad in the precolonial period. A system of pyramidal political patronage gave autonomy to regional chiefs and village headmen who organized local systems of production and redistribution, while ensuring an upward flow of resources and recruits to rulers like the Ramnad Cetupati as their political and military head (Baker 1984, 45). Power at every level resided in the capacity to direct ritual and material systems of distribution rather than on outright domination, resource control, or collecting taxes. In practice this meant the capacity to allocate both shares in agricultural produce and rights to various insignia—titles and honors that conferred both status and legitimate authority. It is here that religious centers had a critical role. There was, as Appadurai (1981, 64) puts it, an exchange in which rulers gave material resources to the temples and in return received not only ritual honors but also political constituencies from the religious leaders who "were crucial intermediaries for the introduction, extension and legitimation of warrior control."

Practically, the royal gift involved the transfer of the overlord's fiscal share of the produce of whole villages as an endowment often to religious institutions. In fact, by the nineteenth century over half of the villages of the old Ramnad kingdom were recorded as so gifted, 85 percent endowed to temple establishments, to priests and ritualists, for the support of communities of Brahmans, pilgrim rest houses, monastic institutions, and other charitable gifts. The patronage of Christian churches and their missionary priests fell within this system of gifting as a "mode of statecraft" (Dirks 1987). *Politically* it forged alliances and built constituencies by integrating socially diverse and immigrant groups, some of whom were already Catholic—Pallar agricultural laborers, Shanar (Nadar) palmyra workers from the south, and (Utaiyar) peasant cultivators from regions to the north. *Economically,* endowing churches and settling productive groups opened up new areas for dry-land or irrigated cultivation. Churches, like temples, were a way of incorporating social groups into an expanding surplus-generating economic system that established "charters of entitlement" for cultivators, artisans, and others as well as a fiscal grain share for the royal overlord (see Mosse 2003, Breckenridge 1985).

Consider the case of Sarukani, the Jesuit mission center of "the Maravar" in the eighteenth century. In the 1790s Marudu Pandiyan (one of two Cervai caste brothers and ministers of the kingdom of Sivagangai who had become de facto rulers) advanced his royal standing by granting the resources of the village of Sarukani to support the Catholic priest and to maintain cults and festivals of the church, especially the major "temple car" processions that culminated the Easter celebration. Ultimately, the Marudu brothers were unsuccessful in their efforts to claim the throne (being executed as rebels by the British in 1801). The royal gift to the church was nonetheless confirmed by Periya Vodaya Tevar (a Maravar), who assumed rajaship in 1792 as British control took hold. The copper plate inscribing the gift closely paralleled royal grants to Brahmans. The same term (*carvamāṉiyam*) was used, and there was a similar emphasis on the merit attached to the king in protecting the shrine and its presiding divinity (cf. Dirks 1987, 121). The inscription states that the village of Sarukani, including rights to the king's "upper share" (*mēlvāram*) of the produce of the village, is granted to "the manager for the time being of Carvēcuraṉ kovil—'temple of the supreme being':

> for lighting, incensing and other such religious worship forever and ever, to the end of the world (until the extinction of the sun, moon . . . so long as stone and water, grass and land exist), let all the rights and properties mentioned above be fully possessed and enjoyed. To those who protect this donation more and more, let there be as much merit as those who help with free gifts the marriage of [a] thousand crores

> and lakhs of Brahmans, who light crores of sacred lamps in one hundred thousand temples. Should anyone dare damage or destroy this donation, let him be guilty of the heinous crime of killing the sacred black cow, the mother, the Guru on the bank of the Ganges. May God help.[16]

As holder of the granted land or *iṉām,* the priest (the *iṉāmtār*) took the part of the ruler in overseeing a local system of agricultural production and controlled the distribution of shares both in material produce and in the symbolic resources of the church. The first included hereditary rights to grain shares of the harvest held by village cultivators, officers, artisans, and village servants (see chapter 3) that were linked to obligations in relation to village common property (irrigation systems) and church ritual, especially the preparation and dragging of the great festival chariot (*tēr*). Shares also included honorary "gifts" of grain (*kaipiccai* or *makamai*) received by the serving catechists on behalf of the church (kovil) and the revenue half-share of the inamtar overlord (the priest/deity) himself.[17] Second were the shares in symbolic resources: essentially, caste-specific privileges in the worship of the church—ritual services and publicly allocated "church honors" (*kōvil mariyātai*) at the magnificent annual festivals including St. Xavier's feast, Easter, and the feast of the Holy Sacrament. Such church honors, summing up and expressing rights and rank, became central to forming and contesting caste orders throughout the nineteenth and twentieth centuries (see chapter 4).

There are two points to stress here. The first is that this redistributive system integrated diverse social groups; including Christians and Hindus; different specialist castes; and incoming migrant groups, from the village and its microregion into a publicly enacted hierarchical social order. The "rituals of unity" (Spencer 1990) involved were necessary precisely because of the highly fluid, incoherent, and conflict-ridden social situations that they disguised. Second, while overseen by the missionaries, the system was instituted by and made explicit reference to the king as chief patron of the church. From the eighteenth century and well after their demise in the twentieth, the (Hindu) rajas of Sivagangai (or their representatives—the "palace people," *araṇmaṉaikkārars*) arranged the final Easter procession of the image of the risen Christ in a huge ceremonial "car." The raja was paraded to the festival at its climax with the Maravar regional chiefs to receive "first honor" marked by prestations of cloth and betel nut from the hand of the presiding Catholic priest.[18] Important churches—the seats (*stala*) of powerful divinities—were thus shaped into pivotal institutions that, like Hindu temples, symbolized political connections *upward* to the chiefs and king, and *downward* to the putative village caste social order. Like Muslim cult centers (S. B. Bayly 1989), Catholic churches were integrated into a Tamil political-religious system. They were incorporated into the geography of regional temples, and their honors mapped the reach of chiefly domains. Powerful or aspiring Maravar big men could hardly afford not to be recognized in the honors of popular churches and saint shrines.

Jesuit mission building in eighteenth-century Ramnad revealed a politics of culture and caste quite foreign to that conveyed to Nobili by his Brahman interpreters of Tamil tradition. It involved power articulated through rights and honors in Christian divinity, worshipped (like local gods) as the paradigmatic sovereign. The shape of the mission reflected the political circumstances in which Jesuit pantaracamis operated, which *required* their participation in an existing economy of exchanges between religious leaders and warrior overlords. They received protection and resources in return for public "honors" in Christian festival systems that signified legitimate political power, and in relation to convert groups, the Jesuits established the same link "between *recruitment* to the sect and the *rewards* for new recruits in the form of shares of some sort of temple service and temple honours," as Appadurai describes for medieval sectarian leaders (1981, 77 [author's emphasis]).

Missionary collusion in the prevailing system also involved adopting its ritual and aesthetic (Bate 2009) forms. In Ramnad, the festival of Dasara (Tam. *navarāttiri*, or "nine nights") was the principal occasion for the ceremonial "great gift" (*mahādāna*) from the king to the deity as ultimate sovereign with whom the ruler was identified (Dirks 1987, 37–41). This ritual form rooted in the devotional tradition of Puranic Hinduism was merged with the Catholic "novena" (nine-day devotion) to provide a model for public worship, reproducing the role of the king (or local headman) as principal donor-devotee. Symbols of Tamil royal power were carved alongside Gospel themes into the wooden processional chariots, just as eighteenth-century churches adopted architectural details of the regional royal palaces (Waghorne 2002, 22).

At the time when Nobili's Indianizing method of theological reinterpretation, dialogue, and reasoned cultural mimesis was collapsing under growing pressure from Rome (and from difficulty in raising funds for this most expensive of experiments; Županov 1999), Catholicism in regions such as Ramnad was becoming tactically embedded within the existing social order as a politically effective and emotionally satisfying form of popular religiosity, "whose external pomp and shew," Abbé Dubois considered, was "so well suited to the genius and dispositions of the natives" (1977, 10).

Implanting Christianity within a regional culture of power—human and divine—rested on, but also breached, the Jesuit separation of "the religious" and "the secular" in a way that "worked to undermine the Jesuit project of global conversion as envisaged by Nobili" (Županov 1999, 29). By acting on ritual form as much as content, converts turned Christian rites and spaces to their own political ends, making Christian churches into political institutions (see chapter 4). But such political incorporation of Christianity was not stable, either, because the pragmatic effort of missionaries to reinstate a separation between "the religious" and "the political" always unsettled the arrangements of power around their churches. This ambiguity and dynamic gave Catholic centers a particular salience as sites of challenge or resistance to domination and gave their socioreligious orders a distinctive contestability. This was especially so as the relationship between the religious and the political—between Christian priests and Hindu kings—was altered by the circumstances of colonial rule. Just as the British power was consolidating in south India, however, the Jesuit mission faced a more immediate challenge from within the Church.

THE MALABAR RITES CONTROVERSY AND SUPPRESSION OF THE SOCIETY OF JESUS

Nobili's cultural experiment had always been controversial. It was approved by Pope Gregory XV in 1623 only through a papal bull that permitted rites such as wearing the sacred thread, applying sandalwood paste to the forehead, ablution before Mass, and various distinctions of caste. Of course, delayed communication and local reinterpretation of orders gave Nobili and others considerable latitude in allowing local practices in their churches, but they also felt caught between innovation and obedience (Bugge 1994, 48; Županov 1999, 12; Wright 2004, 54–56).

At the beginning of the eighteenth century various complaints came to Rome against the method followed by the Jesuits in their missions of Madurai, Mysore, and the Carnatic. In 1704 the papal legate Carlo Tomaso Maillard de Tournon issued a decree that tried to "restandardize" mission practice by restricting the list of permitted indigenous customs. These were later known as Malabar Rites and were repeatedly condemned by following popes, and definitively in Benedict XIV's papal bull of 1744, the *Omnium sollicitudinum,* which was the first major move taken against Jesuit overseas missions (Ballhatchet 1998, 8; Bugge 1994, 49). Among the everyday Tamil Catholic practices that were forbidden were puberty ceremonies, "pagan" forms in weddings and festivals, and drumming (by converts) at temple festivals. Remarkably, missionaries themselves were now forbidden from reading books on heathen religion without special permission, and certain Catholic rites that were offensive to converts, such as the use of salt, saliva, and insufflation by priests in the pre-baptism exorcism of demons, or the admission of women to the sacraments during menses, *had* to be observed (1994, 49; Hambye 1997, 214).[19]

Jesuits went to Rome to defend the Malabar rites, made appeals, sought exceptions or time extensions, and played on ambiguities in the letter of the decree or in the words of papal audience (*viva voce oraculum).* The Catholic hierarchy's focus on "rites" of course entirely overlooked the way in which Catholic identity and practice was being incorporated wholesale into indigenous socioreligious orders. Meanwhile, for converts the form of this or that rite was of minor concern, but the expectation that priests enter the dwellings of "Pariahs," or that "Catholics whatever their birth should hear Mass and receive communion in the same church and at the same time" was an entirely different matter (Ballhatchet 1998, 8; Hambye 1997, 218–19).

In the area of caste, Jesuits had to work out practical compromises: the provision of separate entrances in the same church for "upper" and "lower" castes, or walls erected to keep them apart while still being included in the sacraments.[20] In some cases Jesuits equivocated, saying that they came close to "Pariah" houses "in a moral sense" without entering them (Hambye 1997, 218–19). The provision of missionaries exclusively for the "Pariahs" itself was actually an order contained in the *Omnium sollicitudinum.* As one nineteenth-century writer imagined the scene: "One missioner would be seen moving on horseback or in a palanquin, eating rice dressed by Brahmans, and saluting no one as he went along; another, covered with rags, walked on foot, surrounded by beggars, and prostrated himself as his brother missioner passed, covering his mouth, lest his breath should infect the teacher of the great" (Strickland and Marshall 1865, 57–58). At the time, the revolt of upper-caste Catholics against gestures made toward Pariahs only confirmed a view that breaking caste barriers would entirely ruin the mission (Hambye 1997, 231–33; Ballhatchet 1998, 8).

The Indian Malabar rites controversy caught a rising tide against the Jesuits in Europe, culminating in the suppression of the Society of Jesus by Pope Clement XIV in 1773 and the expulsion of their priests from India, clapped in irons if within reach of a Portuguese official (Strickland and Marshall 1865, 59–60; Wright 2004, 15). To their critics, the Jesuit "all-things-to-all-men" mutability amounted to lax moral theology, the error of aggrandizing human will over divine grace, and the indulgence in "baser instincts" that turned worship into carnival (Wright 2004, 146, 160–62). However, the Society of Jesus was really a victim of changes in Europe that (differently in France, Spain, and Portugal) set secular national governments against Rome as "a rival hub of power in their domains" (2004, 201; 2008). Jesuits were an obvious target for anti-Rome sentiment, stereotyped as "designing political agents," disloyal, masters of disguise and intrigue (2004, 229). Wright concludes that Clement XIV *had* to destroy the Society of Jesus "because the secular powers of Catholic Europe left him with little choice" (2004, 204). But beyond dynastic politics were changes in the status of the Catholic Church itself within a new culture of secular modernity—one that Jesuits, in particular, had actually helped to create through their mission work, their enlightened account of other cultures, their observational empiricism, optimism about human nature, their emphasis on free will, the power of education, and, of course, the separation of human life into "social" and "religious" aspects (2004, 184).

Disbanding the Society of Jesus meant that the "fragile system of authority which the Madurai Jesuits had only just installed was suddenly deprived of its focus" (S. B. Bayly 1989, 421). Unlike eighteenth-century Protestant missions, Jesuits had not developed an indigenous priesthood. All 122 Jesuits who worked in the Madurai mission between 1606 and 1759 were Europeans (Rajamanickam 1987; Manickam 2001, 261). The ex-Jesuit priests who continued to work in the area came under the ecclesiastical jurisdiction of the See of Goa, and from the late 1770s until the return of the Jesuits in the 1830s it was the Padroado priests—apparently mostly Goans of Brahman origin (Hambye 1997, 168–69, 180–85)—who administered the churches of Ramnad. However, missionary resources were scarce (and made scarcer by the French Revolution), and pastoral care irregular in remote rural parishes (Strickland 1852). It was a popular Catholicism focusing on shrines, pilgrimage centers, and festivals that thrived under so-called Goanese jurisdiction, as it had under the Jesuits. In 1788, a bull of Pius VI transferred the Madurai Mission to the French Vicar Apostolic of Pondicherry, although the "Goanese" priests holding keys to centers such as Sarukani organized resistance to attempts by the French Propaganda Fide clerics of Pondicherry to enter the area.[21] Then in 1814 the Society of Jesus was reestablished by Pius VII. In 1836 after a papal bull that entrusted the (New) Madurai Mission entirely to the Jesuit Province of Lyon, French Jesuits arrived in the Tamil country, and in Ramnad. Here these Propaganda Fide Jesuits were truly appalled at the condition of the old Padroado Jesuits parishes under Goa. In 1838, mission superior Joseph Bertrand camped in the tiny village of Calladitidel (near Alapuram) and began a "guerrilla" war to recover parishes where, he reported, no confessions had been heard for decades, no catechism given, where apostasy was widespread and the new threat of Protestant "heresy" was growing.

JESUITS, KINGS, AND ECCLESIASTICAL COMPETITION UNDER COLONIAL RULE

The suppression of the Jesuits coincided with the consolidation of British power in the Tamil country. In 1792, British military successes left the Maravar kings and palaiyakkarars disarmed, and facing punitive tribute demands. From 1803, under a "permanent settlement," rulers of kingdoms became gentleman landlords (Zamindars) of estates defined by eighteenth-century British ideas of landholding under the authority of the civil government of the East India Company. Channeling segmentary political relations of warrior states into "the new domain of proprietary law" under the British Raj (Dirks 1986, 313) had important implications for the field of Catholic mission. This was not because there was a radical break with indigenous political life, but because (as chapter 4 will explain) British rule reallocated power, causing changes within. Catholic festival systems were still a language of power and rank—perhaps even more so since they were able to articulate the shifting economic, political, and caste relations brought about by colonial rule. Indeed, churches were the focus of intense conflicts in the nineteenth century when the struggle between the old and new orders, as Dirks puts it, "took place in the old regime form in temples over honours" (1987, 373).

This continuity of ritual forms disguised important changes in the political functioning of religious institutions, both Hindu and Catholic, brought under British rule. Hindu temple systems in Ramnad as elsewhere gradually came under the control of the bureaucracy (Presler 1988). The Devastanam Department (a branch of the revenue bureaucracy) replaced the rajas as the arbiter of religious disputes over honors, although it struggled (and failed) to apply consistent principles (Price 1996; Dirks 1987; Appadurai 1981). The administrative and judicial systems that weakened Maravar royal control over temple systems (Price 1996, 114; Mosse 2006b, 83) also gave power to the French Jesuits who returned the Society of Jesus to Ramnad in the 1840s, enabling them to wrest control of Catholic shrines from rajas, local chiefs, and village headmen. French priests slowly acquired an ecclesiastical realm and took up the functions of state that, in the case of Hindu temples, had passed to the bureaucracy. (The British regarded Hinduism as insufficiently "religious"—by comparison with Christianity—to comprise a separate and self-governing domain). During the second half of the nineteenth century Catholic priests set about erasing "royal" claims, rights, and honors in Catholic churches, and to this end occasionally even demolished old church buildings (cf. S. B. Bayly 1989, 430–31). They merged within themselves the sacred and the political in order to forge the Catholic Church as a separate realm of religious governance demarcated within Tamil society.[22] In particular they appropriated the royal functions of endowing shrines, patronizing key festival processions, receiving first respects, and becoming the arbiters of caste rank—all of which brought them into conflict with elements of the old political order.

These contests bring to light quite different understandings around particular Catholic churches. For example, the raja of Sivagangai held that the royal grant had been made to the kovil at Sarukani as the "seat" of the divinity (Carvēcuraṉ). The government's Inam Commission of 1864, however, recorded the grant as made to the Catholic priest in charge of the church. What the raja understood as a royal gift to support the ceremony and ritualists of the kovil (a political-religious institution), the missionaries had taken to be their appointment as sole managers of the shrine, its property, and associated rights under exclusive control of the Catholic Church. In a series of court cases (in 1811, 1829, 1845, and 1849) the raja challenged the Catholic priest's right to the overlord's "upper share" of the harvest that should be consecrated to the church and its festivals under separate management save 5 percent for the priest (*Cramam*, p. 7). The raja also challenged the priest's right to interfere in matters concerning the hereditary rights of village servants, to make or terminate the appointment of village officers such as the headman, or to arbitrate disputes over festival honors. To the raja, the Catholic priests were—as old Jesuit pantaracamis had been—serving ritualists, not "little kings." On this matter, however, the British court in Madurai consistently ruled against the raja and in favor of the missionary priests, confirming the latter as de facto rulers (if not bureaucratic managers) of their Catholic domains. In asserting their control over a religious realm separate from politics, the new Jesuits began to prize church honors and obligations of service from the bundle of rights that, under the old regime, had been linked to the overarching political authority. But this did not make Catholic festival honors socially irrelevant. As Dirks (1987) argues for honors in nearby Hindu temples, once separated from their political context, they became "fetishized" objects of intensified competition (Dirks 1987, 359,369, 378).

Despite these colonial transformations, until the last quarter of the nineteenth century the power of Jesuit missionaries was in practice limited, and they were often forced to operate within the parameters of the existing political-religious system. Jesuits were thin on the ground, faced mission rivals and a state power with an ambivalent attitude to mission. In the early years of the new Jesuit mission, foreign priests covered large areas, traveling frequently between scattered congregations to preach, hear confessions, and administer sacraments. Conditions were so harsh that in the first ten years after 1837, twenty-one out of sixty-four priests died, most before the age of thirty-five (Strickland 1852). However, the constraint on their agency most forcefully portrayed in their letters and diaries was their battle over jurisdiction of Ramnad parishes with the sitting Padroado "Goanese" priests. In chapter 4 it will become clear how conflict between these Catholic mission agencies came to a head in 1850s ceremonial confrontations at major saint festivals that intersected with caste politics. By the end of the nineteenth century, Jesuits in Ramnad had successfully consolidated their religious domains against both political elites and ecclesiastical rivals. However, they had won the allegiance of local Catholics at the cost of being deeply implicated as actors within a local socio-ritual system. We will see how over several decades priests strove to assert what locally was a quite novel kind of religious authority that involved new attempts to discipline popular religious practice and caste honor, and thereby brought about significant social and religious changes.

Although Jesuit priests' religious authority was made possible by the conditions of colonial rule, the attitude of the British administration to their mission was equivocal—simultaneously supportive and distancing. Roman Catholic missions had been regarded as part of the environment into which the East India Company had settled. At times they were patronized as an extension of support to indigenous (Hindu) religious institutions (whose endowments the company protected [Kooiman 1989; Waghorne 2004]), or in order to maintain relations with Portugal, as well as to provide priests for their own soldiers (Ballhatchet 1998, 13–22). The mostly non-British Catholic missions were in any case largely confined to the fringes of the company's territories (Kooiman 1989, 27–28; Oddie 1991, 40–46). It was the evangelistic Protestants rather than the pastoral Catholics that preoccupied the minds of company officers as a threat to the social order necessary for commercial interests. The distancing was mutual. Still worried about maintaining their status in indigenous society, Jesuits kept apart from "parangi" British officers and their "Pariah" servants.

THE JESUITS OF THE NEW MADURAI MISSION AND CASTE

Despite a sense of mission continuity, the French priests who arrived in Tamil country in the 1830s were themselves quite different from their seventeenth- and eighteenth-century forebears. Coming from the Jesuit province of Lyon (or Toulouse after its separation in 1852), these men were of a Europe much changed by events. When the Society of Jesus was reinstated in 1814, the Roman Church was under siege, not just from the immediate secularism and anticlericalism of the French Revolution, but also from a barrage of godless enlightenment ideas—liberalism, rationalism, capitalism, democracy, and pluralism (Wright 2004, 212–30). The postrevolutionary crisis facing the Church was institutional as well as ideological. At the start of a century that would see disestablishment in Europe, the Catholic Church was already experiencing exclusion from some of its traditional areas of control such as education and marriage (2004, 184). Its centralized hierarchy was being questioned, the pope was rapidly losing temporal power, and the wedge between church and state had thickened. Rather than accommodate liberalism and modernity, Rome's response was to challenge the modern, revive Catholic devotionalism and papal authority, and "rivet medievalism on the neck of the Church" (2004, 238). Jesuits, Wright shows, were central players in this turn against the modern world (2004, 241–43), nowhere more clearly than in the field of Indian mission.

For the postsuppression Jesuits, the mission in south India recalled their glorious past. When they arrived there, they did so in a spirit of restoration rather than experimentation, in an effort to put everything "back to the point it was before the disasters of the late-eighteenth century fell on the church" (Neill 1984, 306). Influenced by a post-Napoleonic feudal-monarchical reaction to the revolution, missionary societies were conservative, evangelical, and under a supervision and control from Europe that was "detailed and harassing" (ibid.). Parish administration, liturgy, and worship were to be "carried out in Roman fashion" (ibid.). While Nobili's adventures into Brahmanism were now somewhat out of place, Jesuits had not lost their admiration for hierarchy and found no reason to launch an attack on caste as a way of organizing society.

The highly conservative priests from rural southern France who landed in Pondicherry in the 1830s were less disturbed by the extreme social inequalities of the peasantry than they were to find themselves, as Europeans, judged as socially inferior by the upper castes of the town.[23] They quickly set about building their status by linking with upper castes and royals (using horses and palanquins) as well as distancing themselves from the beef-eating English officers served at table by the "Pariah," and especially from these "low" castes themselves. While Nobili aimed at honor by association with Brahmans, these French Jesuits did so by *dis-association* from Pariahs, neither mixing with nor being served by them; avoiding their settlements; or conducting Mass in their chapels, which were invariably built outside of towns and villages (Manickam 2001, 278).

These nineteenth-century missionaries emulated their Jesuit predecessors in approving of caste and reviling Pariahs. "We can picture what would become of the Hindus," wrote Abbé Dubois, "if they were not kept within the bounds of duty by the rules and penalties of caste by looking at the position of the Pariahs, or outcastes of India, who, checked by no moral restraint, abandon themselves to their natural propensities [. . .] a state consisting entirely of such inhabitants would not long endure and would not fail to lapse before long into a condition of barbarism" (Dubois 1906, 29). French Jesuit correspondence adopted such exteriorizing and racializing language, typifying "Pariahs" as obstinate "*hommes sauvages*" to whom preaching would be a waste of time, in relation to whom the French peasants were "angels of light," and who could easily be bought for money by the (now growing) Protestant missions (Manickam 2001, 275, 280). Indeed, Jesuit criticism of the upsurge in Protestant conversions (see below) and their degradation of "the Pariahs" were linked. For Jesuits of the time, "Pariah" conversions, like the people themselves, were inferior and of little value: Protestants would be judged by the social standing of their converts (Manickam 2001, 280–81). Unlike the Irish Catholics, French missionaries "thought it was quite proper that low castes would be excluded from any seminary and from schools for that matter" (Ballhatchet 1998, 9–10), long after the British had made schools open to all. Where they were admitted, they faced separation and discrimination. The same was true in Tamil convents, first formed to deal with the problem of widows socially prohibited from remarriage (Manickam 2001, 299). Even the slightest infringement of the ubiquitous caste separation of washing or dining arrangements in seminaries or boarding schools provoked protest and led to the periodic closure of institutions, reminding Jesuits of the inescapability of caste (Manickam 2001).

The new Jesuits assumed that preserving caste etiquette was necessary to attracting a better caste of convert—above all Brahman. They hoped to win access to Zamindaris and Princely States where Brahmans now held administrative influence, or at least to win elite groups back from the Padroado mission. In consequence, "low castes" were not to be given significant roles in the churches: they could not join choirs, take readings or prayers, or approach the altar. When low-ranking Shanars (Nadar or Nāṭār) brought candles for the Virgin Mary at Vadakkankulam, they had to be given to Veḷḷāḷar (upper-caste) choristers to place on the altar (Manickam 2001, 288–89). But Jesuits did not wish low-caste converts to be excluded from worship entirely. The compromises between inclusion and exclusion produced some extraordinary architectural and social arrangements in new or enlarged churches where Christians of different castes were installed in different places according to rank. These included the cathedral of Tiruchirappalli with its caste-dividing wall and the "trousers church" at Vadakkankulam with its two separate naves meeting at a shared altar. It was common in cruciform churches for low castes to be seated apart in the transepts, and not unusual for "Pariahs" to hear Mass only from outside, at the door, or under an exterior *maṇṭapam* (veranda), exactly as in a Hindu temples (ibid.).

The organization of space, level (height, plane), and time were used to differentiate access to the sacred—to the altar, the Eucharist, or scripture—and yet if the Superior General in Rome raised queries about the mission's policy, he was assured that these were simply *social* distinctions akin to those between nobles and peasants in Europe.[24] Mission Superior Father Bertrand claimed that "deference to high castes [was] essential in view of their influence over Indian society as a whole," and that any attempt to fuse castes together would spell the end of the mission. Perhaps more to the point, caste provided "an ordered social hierarchy very different from the disorder of revolutionary France," which had threatened religion itself (Ballhatchet 1998, 10). This position of local bishops and Madurai mission Jesuits on caste would not be changed by pressure coming from the Vatican with its history of conservative views on race or slavery, for example, but rather as a result of ideological innovation from within Tamil society in the late nineteenth and early twentieth centuries. One important factor influencing the course of an unfolding anti-untouchability social critique was the presence of Protestant evangelical missionaries in southern India.

When they returned to the Tamil country after 1836, Jesuits found their opposite in the highly visible Protestant missions, whose approach to Indian religion and society could not have been more different from their own. Evangelical Protestants generally regarded Brahmanic Hinduism and its spawn, the caste system, as the principal obstacle rather than the means to Christian conversion. To create a space for Tamil Christianity they set out not to emulate but to break the hold they imagined the Brahman priesthood had on Indian society (Dirks 2001; Washbrook 2009). Even theories of civilization were opposed. Roberto Nobili's Brahmanical "golden age" model of Tamil society found its contrary in the Anglican missionary Robert Caldwell's Dravidian "golden age" theory in which an original Tamil race would rediscover its greatness by being released from the oppressive and decivilizing impact of the Aryans represented by Brahmanic ritualism and caste (Dirks 2001). Caldwell's theorizing in fact grew out of mission experience that gave him the notion that the vastly greater numbers of low-caste converts (and the very few Brahman ones) were a demonstration of the weaker hold of Brahmanic values on these Dravidian peoples (Dirks 2001, 135–36).

Jesuits not only considered Protestants foolish to devalue the "cultural capital" of upper-caste converts; they also took an immediate dislike to Protestant missionary style—"the irreverent gesture and vehement language" of their street preaching, the mass distribution of Bibles and tracts, and above all their ignorance of how to conduct oneself in Tamil society (Strickland and Marshall 1865, 148). Jesuits regarded direct attacks on pagan divinity and scripture, without having first won "respect from the heathen" and "before they have sown the seeds of Christianity in the heart," as a dangerous folly (ibid.). They also resented Protestant use of power and money for proselytizing, and their misinformed condemnation of "Romanism" as "on a level with Paganism" (1865, 63). Catholic defenders claimed that "the festivals of [Catholic] religion [are] attended by multitudes of the heathen, who proclaim aloud that here indeed God is truly worshipped, and men who assert that they would deem themselves defiled if the shadow of a Protestant minister fell upon them, daily stretch forth their hands to touch with reverence the robe of the Catholic apostle whose life of prayer, penance, and charity excites their honest admiration" (1865, 215). What did worry, impress, and influence the Jesuits, however, was the proliferation of Protestant schools.

The Evangelical revival in England, which was deeply critical of the East India Company's involvement in Hindu religious affairs and its opposition to missions, gradually won the British government over to the value of Christian education in India (Oddie 1991, 46). In 1792, Charles Grant, former Bengal civil servant, MP, and chairman of the East India Company's Court of Directors, advanced the view that missionizing was a necessary means to create orderly subjects freed from the influence of degenerate Hindu values and superstition (Kooiman 1989, 28). By the mid–nineteenth century Christianization had become part of the colonial enterprise, captured in Lord Macaulay's policy of extending Christian influence to wider society through education and promoting a pro-British mediating Christian administrative elite: "a class of person Indian in blood and colour, but English in taste, in opinions, in morals and in intellect,"[25] as he famously put it (Forrester 1980, 28–33, 57–59).

Jesuit missionaries developed an educational policy in the space opened up by these Protestant debates (see Dirks 2001, 131–32). An "education method" that

Christianized an upper-caste elite, and through them the wider "conversion" of society, seemed a worthy inheritor of Nobili's historic mission, suited to the new circumstances of British India. First, novitiates and seminaries were founded that came eventually to produce more (Indian-trained but globally present) Jesuit priests and scholars than virtually anywhere else in the world. Tamil or Malayali priests began to have a presence in rural Ramnad from the 1930s and 1940s, and largely replaced Europeans in the 1950s. Second, prestigious Jesuit colleges and schools were founded in towns and cities that would produce a body of influential Catholic citizens, and in time a network of primary schools would spread into the remote parishes of regions such as Ramnad, where the emphasis was on literacy and training pupils for higher education, for government employment, or perhaps for religious vocations (Houtart et al. n.d., 73). Jesuits appealed to the government for grants commensurate with the Protestant institutions with which they competed, pointing (in the aftermath of the 1857 rebellion) to the "exemplary conduct of Catholic natives" and soldiers as well as favorably comparing the benefits of Catholic schooling with the secularizing effect of an Anglo-Protestant education (Strickland and Marshall 1865, 184 et seq.). While the divergent mission strategies of Catholics and Protestants came together in educational policy, something altogether different was happening on the ground.

MASS CONVERSIONS AND "LOW"-CASTE CHRISTIANS

In the later nineteenth century, throughout south India and across all denominations, a new form of Christian conversion was occurring: large scale, group rather than individual, and by members of "low" and especially "untouchable" castes (or dalits). Between 1851 and 1871 the number of Protestant Christians in the Madras Presidency increased from 74,000 to 300,000 largely as a result of group conversions from these groups (Richter 1908, 201), and Roman Catholic missions experienced similar increases with the Jesuit Madurai mission—for example, growing from 169,000 to 260,000 members from 1880 to 1901 (Bugge 1994, 143). Between 1871 and 1901 the population of the Madras Presidency rose by 22.2 percent, but that of Christians by 90.6 percent, largely as a result of dalit rural "mass" conversions. As Oddie notes, "[W]hat had been a multicaste [Christian] community in 1800 had become increasingly Paraiyar dominated by the 1890s" (1991, 153, 155). Such large-scale conversions continued in all Tamil districts and throughout India until Independence, such that of the 11 million Christians given in the 1961 census, over 62 percent were dalits from the southern states.

The nature of these conversion movements is a matter of unresolved historical debate,[26] but there is some consensus that, regardless of the particular doctrines of the various denominations, for the low-caste converts themselves becoming

Christian had something to do with the rejection of social inferiority and the affirmation of a positive social and religious identity. It involved self-betterment and self-respect through affiliation to missionary religion that gave previously denied access to sacred rites and texts, places of worship of their own—brick mission chapels standing amid crowded thatched huts—and eventually schooling. The dominant caste-class attacks against low-caste neophytes suggest that Christian conversion was indeed taken as a challenge to servitude, if not a mark of upward mobility. As Terry Eagleton (2009) says of faith in general, Christian conversion was performative rather than propositional; it was not a matter of signing up to new belief or an alternative description of reality, but of new allegiance and commitment that might make a difference to a desperate situation. Christian conversion was the hope for better patrons and protection at a time of crisis—particularly the crises brought on by the complex effects of British rule and the rupture and contradictions this produced within existing political and economic systems. These included deepening insecurity associated with agrestic servitude, manifest most acutely in widespread famine that targeted assetless dalits (Washbrook 1993; Hjejle 1967).[27] Christianity might offer alliance with powerful people who alluded racially to the ruling government and had better access to power and resources.[28] But mass conversion could be other things, too.

As Henrietta Bugge (1994) demonstrates, mass conversions were localized social movements that occurred in quite different ways in different contexts. Bugge compares the mass conversion to the Danish Missionary Society (DMS) of enslaved laboring Paraiyar communities in highly polarized wet-zone villages of Arcot with the similarly large-scale conversion of independent cultivating Paraiyars in the adjacent dryland area, this time to the French Catholic Société des Missions Etrangères de Paris (MEP). In the first case, the conversion of indebted (or bonded) laborers bereft of the partial protection of the old "moral economy" involved a transfer of allegiance to the missionaries as their new material and spiritual masters. Conversion did not express desired independence or upward mobility, even if through education this was the eventual outcome. In the second case, by contrast, dryland-cultivating Paraiyars with increased bargaining power from expanding groundnut cash-cropping did not convert to Christianity within an existing order of patronage, but as part of a modernizing means to get out of this order. These divergent responses to missions were amplified by opposed missionary styles. While the Danish Protestant missionaries' spiritual view of conversion made them poor patrons, unwilling to interfere in the social system and resistant to demands for temporal aid (famine relief, seed, loans, legal support), the MEP Catholic missionaries encouraged such support via their catechists. These French Catholic missionaries also fulfilled their *rāja dharma,* the duty of royal personages, through ritual and ceremonial honor or the grandeur of the bishop's visit, offering opportunities for social mobility to new Christians who could see themselves as belonging to "a larger network of spiritual authority" (Bugge 1994, 174).[29]

Albeit in opposed ways, both Danish and French, Protestant and Catholic missionaries catalyzed mass conversions *within* rather than against existing moral and social orders, producing Christian identities that were both part of, and yet separate from, the old village order (Bugge 1994, 171). In the villages of the southern plains region of Ramnad, low-caste group conversions had in fact taken place as early as the seventeenth century. Some converted as part of the retinue and dependents of upper-caste Catholics; others were missionized through fringe and clandestine engagements that reinscribed "low born" Pariahs as an exteriorized and subordinated category. Rather than invoking new relationships, dalit Catholics found their servitude ritualized in the church order. Protestant missions were slower to penetrate this heartland of Catholic mission, but by the early twentieth century many Ramnad villages contained small communities of new Protestant dalit converts alongside ancient Catholic ones. The different ways in which Christianity was incorporated into projects of self-respect by these two groups, and the complex interaction of caste and denominational (Caplan 1980b) and interreligious (Christian–Hindu) rivalry underpinning strategies of social mobility, is the subject of chapter 5. The mass conversions of dalits also brought about a broader "conversion of caste" (Dirks 2001) that has to be explained. They had the effect of stabilizing a policy view of caste, not as a condition of socioeconomic servitude, but as a form of spiritual slavery—a Hindu religious system that Christian conversion would cut at its roots.

MAKING CASTE RELIGIOUS

By the end of the nineteenth century, many Protestant missionaries had come to attribute "mass movements" to their own strict policy against the Hindu caste system, and to see conversion as a struggle for freedom by the "outcaste," the "Panchama" or excluded "fifth *varna*." By the 1850s, Protestant missions in India (excepting Lutherans) had reached a broad consensus on the relationship between caste and Christianity very different from earlier pre-evangelical Protestant missions (Dutch, Danish, or English).[30] Caste was a *religious* institution, and therefore fundamentally incompatible with the Christian gospel. As the conclusion to an enquiry by the bishop of Madras in 1845 put it, "[T]he distinctions [of caste] are unquestionably religious distinctions, originating in, and maintained by, the operation of Hindu idolatry," and as such, "caste is utterly incompatible with the very principle of Christian morals" (cited in Forrester 1980, 39). Conversion required the utter rejection of caste identity and practice. In areas of mass conversion, Protestant missions could look back at the effect of their stand against caste and deduce that while it had reduced or reversed the small trickle of individual "high"-caste converts, it marked the start of a dalit religious movement.

However, these conversions may in fact have had very little to do with missionary policy—Protestant or Catholic. Certainly those seeking conversion did not discriminate between missions with very different policies, and the evangelizing missionaries themselves neither expected nor desired mass group conversion. Their mission model, in which teaching led to personal conviction and then conversion, could hardly deal with conversion by caste panchayat, spread through kinship networks, or begun in areas where they were not even active.[31] It was not a little disconcerting for Protestant and Catholic missionaries alike to discover that those to whom they had preached (the upper castes) rejected them, while all those whom they had ignored—the "Pariahs"—actively sought conversion (Viswanath 2010, 127; Manickam 2001). These conversions were unsettling in another way, too.

Mass movements again revealed conversion as a matter of affiliation and identity rather than belief. Moreover, as Viswanath (2008, 10; 2010) points out, the "Pariah" appeal for transformation presented the misery of the body and of the spirit as one. This undermined the missionaries' own bifurcation of the world into spirit and matter, since they saw that poverty made it almost impossible for Pariahs to convert only for reasons of conscience. This raised anxieties (and accusations) about "inauthentic conversions" or "rice Christians" (a missionary phrase later adopted against them) (Viswanath 2008, 10). The very lack of a separation between the spiritual and the material among converts made this distinction crucial to the missionaries themselves. Whatever the complex circumstances of conversion, Protestant missionaries were obliged to construe their actions and effects as spiritual (Viswanath 2008, 2010). That is to say, while they clearly intervened in local power relations as allies of dependent and subjugated Pariahs in ways that had economic effects (freedom from debt bondage or the acquisition of land), this action was represented as *religious* in ways that effectively denied significance to material change in favor of "the improvement of souls" (Viswanath 2008, 4). Religion was necessarily central either as consequence or as cause: on the one hand, meeting Pariahs' material needs ultimately had spiritual effects (perhaps a precondition for spiritual transformation); on the other, the social benefits (economic improvement) were the effects of Christian religion (Viswanath 2008, 12). A consequence of the Protestant *response* to mass conversions, then, was that caste itself—always a political-economic matter of agrarian servitude (see chapter 3)—came to be reconceived primarily in *religious* terms as a matter of moral degradation or "spiritual slavery."

Caste and "untouchability" thus entered political debate and colonial policy making as a Hindu institution and the target of missionary attack and religious conversion. While Oddie (1979) argues that new Protestant theological understandings in Europe had broadened spiritual interpretation of the gospels to a more world-affirming conception of Christianity that encouraged social action, the context of mass conversion movements demanded a "spiritualization" of social change. Viswanath's point is that regardless of the political-economic nature of missionary engagements, the construal of this action within missionary discourse contributed definitively to abstracting and ritualizing caste so that its connection to economic relations became incidental (2010, 131).

Missionaries' motivations were surely as varied as those of their converts. A few missionaries were radicalized into social work and advocacy—for example, on land rights—by a people's movement of which their missions had become a part,[32] but mostly, as Viswanath points out, their aim was to "raise [the Pariah] in his social state, not *out* of it."[33] And Cederlöf shows that while missionaries might have repaid laborers' debts or supported them in court cases, they made a point of assuring the converts' landlords that they did not intend to provoke their laborers against them (2003, 349). Because caste became understood as spiritual servitude, the need was to alter mental attitudes or maybe habits rather than bringing about a structural change in socioeconomic relations (Viswanath 2008, 12, 19). The "Hindu excrescence" of caste could be stripped to leave a "rational core" of class. Even those within its system of relations would come to emphasize symbolic action or religious gestures, or to recall as most significant their freedom from religious obligations such as at Hindu temples (2010, 145).

Taken more widely, the mass conversion movements had an important impact on Protestant missionaries and government alike. Within the missionary movement, otherwise conservative men were transformed into fearless radicals and public campaigners, using the media to influence British public opinion and provoke public debate on the question of "untouchability" in the House of Commons (Oddie 1979, 249). The British government, despite a formal policy of noninterference in religious matters, in practice moved closer to the Evangelical view of Indian society as morally degenerate and profoundly corrupted by Hinduism (Oddie 2006). Adopting "the moral charter of Christian proselytization" in secular form (Dirks 2001, 150) then provided justification for British rule as a civilizing project to which Evangelicals, even more than administrators or businessmen, would acquire an intense moral commitment (Beidelman 1982, 6; Oddie 1991, 40–63; Kooiman 1989, 28). It was missionary discourse on untouchability and the disadvantages of "the Pariah" that drew attention to conditions of slavery from which officials had persuaded themselves India was exempt (Viswanath 2008). Moreover, it was through this missionary debate that subaltern groups (dalits) themselves gained access to the public realm, and eventually that interventions on behalf of the "weaker sections" were translated into an enduring state welfare regime (Viswanath 2008, 13). But having been framed by the "public problem" of conversion, public debate on untouchability consolidated caste as a matter of *reli-*

gion—of ritual subordination, exclusion from temples, and so forth—rather than as a question of economic relations, landlessness, or exploitation (Viswanath 2008).

It was in these terms that the Arya Samaj and other Hindu reform movements contending with Christian conversions set about projects for modernizing caste and offering Sanskritized Hindu identities and purificatory "reconversion" (*suddhi*) rituals to dalits (Heimsath 1964; Jordens 1977, 1981). These programs exemplify a shift in the public perception of Christian conversion from being a threat to dominant caste interests (for example, to their economic power/status by the removal of biddable labor) to conversion as a threat to "Hindu religion" that came from Hindu activists' appropriation of the Protestant theological norm of "authentic religious conversion" (Viswanath 2008, 15). In consequence, Viswanath points out, various conflicting interests get translated into religious differences, even though religion has rarely been important in defining relations across Tamil castes. We return to this theme in chapter 6; and before that, in chapter 5, it will become clear how the spiritualizing of caste by Protestants as much as its secularization by Jesuits impaired the social impact of mass conversion movements. Freed by conversion from spiritual servitude, dalit Christians remained an economic underclass. The post-Independence consolidation of Protestant church structures, the disappearance of the "away-from-home" radicalism of the foreign missionaries, and the reassertion of patterns of rural dominance left a scattering of Protestant chapels adorning the very poorest streets in the villages of Ramnad.

CONCLUSION

Jesuits and later Protestant missionaries had this much in common: in various ways they engaged with the sociopolitical order of which they were a part, but at the same time they narrativized their work and accomplishments as spiritual struggles. Jesuits, both before and after the suppression, brought the sacraments of Catholic faith into the structures of Tamil ritual and social life so as to make them accessible. Building a domain of Catholic religion from within a secularized caste order involved contradictions—most glaringly, having to pay for the societal acceptability of Christianity with the coin of untouchability; and yet this did not slow large-scale Catholic conversions in the late nineteenth century. Mass conversions of "untouchables" was no more the result of Protestant than of Catholic mission strategy. All missionaries were taken by surprise. The Protestant response to this social movement prompted the construal of caste as a form of spiritual slavery. This imposed a distinction between the material and the spiritual onto dalit conversions, rendering economic struggle as spiritual redemption. In the long run this turned conversion movements into a chapter in the history of Christianity—the key narrative being the "Pariah" acceptance of the Christian ideal of equality abstracted from their struggles with upper-caste landlords—and institutionalized a separation of "mission history" from "economic history" in the academy (Viswanath 2008).

Consolidated into official social policy through public debates on the evil of "untouchability," this missionary construction of caste as *religious* not only contributed to the systematic concealment of the economic characteristics of caste inequality and the caste character of unequal access to resources (Viswanath 2010, 145; Mosse 2003), but also led to non-Hindus being denied eligibility to state concessions established for "Scheduled Castes," being those whose (Hindu) religion subjects them to deprivation. This will be explained in chapter 5, and in chapter 6 we will see how the persistent discrimination of dalits, now perceived as religious, within the Catholic Church would ignite another mass movement for social liberation and equality in relation to the church and state.

While Protestants framed caste as spiritual slavery, Jesuits secularized caste. For the one, spiritual release from the grip of caste was essential; for the other, caste was ultimately irrelevant to eternal salvation. The secular space in which Jesuits contained caste so that it would not be an obstacle to the saving of souls also accommodated interventions on the side of dalits by nineteenth-century missionary priests, in part influenced by antislavery campaigns and the Church's response to the rights of the poor and the laboring classes in Europe. While this social action accelerated conversions, it was not considered relevant to salvation. It was only in the late twentieth century that the Jesuit Madurai mission began to promote an agenda of social justice (see chapter 6). A century earlier the view was rather that, as the bishop of Tiruchirappalli observed, low-caste converts who in earlier times had accepted exclusion as "natural" now made legitimate claims to equality in the church that could not be ignored.[34] He expressed a Jesuit opinion that was still not keen to abolish caste, preferring to preserve these "social distinctions" purged of "extreme customs." The shifting boundary between religious rights and social honors would be central to the unfolding of social struggles around Catholic churches for the next century. The Catholic Church (its rituals and festivals) had emerged as a space for more equal recognition *within* (rather than beyond) hierarchical village society. The way in which this then made the Tamil Catholic Church a powerful venue for "low"-caste converts to affirm new social aspirations and have them publicly recognized, and hence a focus of caste politics long before such struggle became part of the Church's own social ethics, will be described in chapter 4.

2

A Culture of Popular Catholicism

Missionary Christianity of all varieties brings distinctive notions of divinity and new monopolies of mediation that demand a radical reorganization of existing religiosity. As they consolidated their mission in nineteenth-century colonial southern India, Jesuits brought new religious symbols, a plethora of divine beings including the saints, and complex notions of worship.[1] They also tried to discipline religious boundaries in an unprecedented way. But rigorous prohibitions and punishments could not possibly isolate Tamil Catholics from existing modes of religious thought and feeling. Lived Catholicism would involve imaginaries, dispositions, attitudes, and modes of signification continuous with non-Christian neighbors. Where Church interpretations of sin or suffering, sacramental religion, or the priestly monopoly of divine mediation were inadequate to the range of religious needs, there would be conceptual, semeiotic, or ritual adaptation or innovation. This chapter examines several ways in which Catholic practice was informed by indigenous semiotics and reasoning. Devotional or healing practices, for example, allude to hybridized concepts of divinity and a tendency to shift from a metaphorical to an indexical relationship between sacred ideas/qualities and material things, from symbol to substance, analogy to materiality. These mark a resistance to the separation of the religious and the cultural in Nobili's treatises so as to Brahmanize Christianity, and a departure from modern-day Catholic "inculturation," which locates culture in the adaptable signifier rather than the mode of signification. At the same time, innovation and creativity driven by varied urgent social projects of healing, protection, or recognition defy any singular ethnographic representation of Tamil Catholic tradition.

While a strong Tamil cultural thread interwoven with European Catholic traditions speaks of "continuity" in Robbins's (2007) terms, Jesuit Catholicism (especially from the nineteenth century) was forcefully disjunctive. Missionaries communicated radical change: new moral codes—in Foucault's (1990, 1977) terms, new "modes of subjection" and "self-forming activity" and a new "telos" (Robbins 2004a, 216–19)—and the denunciation of non-Christian religion. The challenge is to see how these demands were conceived in indigenous as much as missionary terms—that is, to identify the ways in which Catholic converts both represented and reconciled the tension between their experience as inheritors of a cultural tradition and the demands of global Catholicism.

The structure of this chapter is given by two problematics. The first is the historical question of how and with what consequences Jesuit missionaries communicated their version of Catholicism in rural Tamil Nadu. The chapter begins with an account of the French priests in the late nineteenth century and the ideas of Christian religion, moral personhood, and interiority that they sought to impose, and the type of authority they tried to deploy. This involves looking at the "boundary work" through which these missionaries attempted to consolidate the realm of Tamil Catholicism against the pitfalls of surrounding paganism and superstition. The chapter will argue that Jesuit missionary religious discipline not only challenged existing notions of person and agency, but also provoked resistance manifest as popular heterodox cults with their *own* distinctive synthesis of Christian and Tamil modes of religiosity. These mostly focused on spirit possession—which, I argue, provides a counterpart to the missionary discipline of confession. We will see in particular how a Jesuit discourse on confession and Communion that stressed autonomous moral persons whose eternal future is shaped by the internal struggle with sin (see Mauss 1985) existed alongside a quite different concept of persons, agency, sin, and ways of dealing with misfortune that was enacted in the peripheral discourse of possession-exorcism at certain saint shrines. These involved a south Indian conception of the person-body with fluid boundaries, invaded by social, spiritual, and environmental forces that come to be objectified within the body (Osella and Osella 1996, 1999; Daniel 1984). In order to further understand these cults, the chapter turns to contemporary Catholic cults of possession, where, I will argue, the missionary teachings on pagan religion and on the dangers of human passion are still found in mimetic parallel. The tension between confession and possession will be introduced, then, as one dynamic in the historical production of Tamil Catholicism (cf. Županov 2008).

The second problematic concerns how exogenous religious figures—including the saints and the Virgin Mary—introduced by Jesuits and redirecting popular religiosity to Christian rather than pagan objects were organized by an existing structure of representations. Catholic saints and sainthood will be viewed in relation to *both* Tamil conceptions of death and posthumous power in different contexts *and* the ambivalent powers of Tamil village gods and goddesses; and some of the ways (including contemporary Pentecostal ones) in which the tension between Catholicism and Tamil village religion are represented and dealt with in indigenous terms will be described.

RELIGIOUS AUTHORITY AND CATHOLIC PRACTICE UNDER THE NEW MADURAI MISSION

When the French Jesuit father superior visited Alapuram village in January 1895, he exhorted the parishioners to remember that "the priest is father, teacher, judge, and doctor."[2] His missionaries did indeed sermonize and discipline their parishioners, arbitrate their disputes, and dispense medicines at times of cholera and smallpox[3] (or more often extreme unction) with a paternalistic authority quite impossible for their pantaracami forebears. They insisted particularly on the exclusive nature of Christian creed and sacraments, set rules of conduct, and drew boundaries between true religion and pagan idolatry. It was the transgression of these boundaries that brought the greatest scorn on their spiritual children: the faithless or foolish, the stupid "buffalo with a human face" discovered attending pagan dramas, worshipping pagan gods, removing "sorcery" (*cuṉiyam*), or observing astrological impediments (*cūlam*). Miscreants faced public humiliation. Sometimes they were made to circumambulate the church on their knees, to wear a crown of thorns during Mass, to swear an oath, touching a crucifix or standing before a statue of the saint, that they would "not attend pagan worship or secure things offered to the devil";[4] they paid fines or were whipped or excluded from the sacraments. And when misfortune struck, priests were ready to explain it as retribution for the "abominable villainy and deceit" of "witchcraft," taken broadly as any non-Christian religious practice.[5] For its contemporary Protestant critics, nineteenth-century Jesuitism was defined by an impulse to "absolute domination over the spirits of men," "crystallized and shining on its surface and mathematical in its figure," which was the nearest thing to a "spiritual polity" the church had produced (Taylor 1849). Meanwhile in the villages of Ramnad, a rich folk tradition attributed to missionaries the sorcerous powers they condemned: angered priests cursed (*cāpam*) villages with drought or famine, turned the water in village tanks to blood, or withheld the divine blessing assured by punitively curtailing festivals.

Jesuit diaries disclose the missionaries' thoroughly otherworldly pietistic form of religion and their singular focus on the fate of the eternal soul. Holding to the principles of St. Ignatius Loyola, priests considered that (to quote from the *Spiritual Exercises*)

> [m]an was created for this end, that he might praise and reverence the Lord his God, and, serving Him, at length be saved. But the other things which are placed on the earth were created for man's sake, that they might assist him in pursuing the end of his creation: whence it follows, that they are to be used or abstained from in proportion as they profit or hinder him in pursuing that end. Wherefore we ought to be indifferent towards all created things (in so far as they are subject to the liberty of our will, and not prohibited) so that (to the best of our power) we seek not health more than sickness, nor prefer riches to poverty, honour to contempt, a long life to a short one. But it is fitting, out of all, to choose and desire those things only which lead to the end. (Seager 1847, 16)

The priests were less concerned to avert suffering and misfortune in this world—which, after all, were the result of the Fall—than to bring to mind their consequences for the condition of the eternal soul—by way of prayer, searching conscience, and confession, redirecting present anxiety to anxiety about future eternity. (Meanwhile villagers themselves might treat confession as a kind of "offering" to bring rain or some other reward.) At times of crisis they were advised to fast and make their confession. One priest noted that "nearly all the villagers confess in the morning in the hope of getting some showers of rain," another that "cholera is a good preacher."[6] Despite the collective nature of such anxiety, for the Jesuits, religion was ultimately an individual matter. Spiritual development was through disciplined prayer and a moral personal and family life (Parish diaries, passim). This involved constant struggle against the passions of our fallen nature (Strickland 1852, 177); and Tamil villagers seemed to missionaries excessively subject to the passions and in need of moral self-possession through confession.

In practice the new Madurai mission Jesuits found a path of compromise between placing demands on the inner life and accepting the value of the judicious use of exterior means of awakening piety in the soul for "minds too rude and weak to do without material and palpable objects of adoration" (Strickland 1852, 4, 178). Like their predecessors, they sought not the suppression of Tamil religiosity but its redirection to Christian objects, and did not try to sort motives in devotion that fell "substantially within the boundary that distinguished Catholicism from paganism" (Greeley 2001, 38). So while missionaries elsewhere grappled with the dilemma of converts eating flesh sacrificed to idols (Keane 1996, 150), Jesuits ensured it was the saints who were the recipients of such sacrifices, the "outer rejoicings" of pagans being preserved so as to more easily share in the "inner rejoicings" of worship.[7] Cults to saints were indeed elaborated and multiplied. They were linked to special places, needs, and occasions. A rich festival calendar directed public worship and offerings to particular saints alongside those performed at times of private misfortune or public crisis (Parish diaries 1890s–1946, passim). During cholera epidemics, for example, novenas for

St. Sebastian, the Virgin, or other saints were inaugurated with processions and blessings with the statue, or a Way of the Cross undertaken. In 1898, one village was advised "to pray to the Sacred Heart and St. Joseph" as a means to overcome the tyranny of a pagan headman.[8]

The firm rejection of all things pagan was the impetus for the elaboration of a complex of Catholic divinity and ritual that would nonetheless be worked on by religious imaginations informed by Tamil tradition. Sharply demarcated Christian images and architecture went along with the replication of recognizably Hindu forms of worship.[9] However, the culturally specific ("Western") distinction between the object and the process of worship was itself hard to transmit. While Jesuits taught that saints were intercessors who would bring strength and moral fortitude to the suffering faithful, they were manifestly treated as power divinities who would intervene in the world on behalf of villagers (Hindu and Christian), to reward, punish, or defend against the demonic. And as will become clear below, in the process saints took on more of the pagan gods than Jesuit missionaries cared to acknowledge.

French Jesuit priests worked hard on their Tamil parishioners to get them to separate the Christian from the pagan, the eternal from the everyday, the interior from the exterior, faith from fantasy, spirit from body. Drawing on their own apartness from the social world—living in presbyteries behind compound walls, communicating through catechists, and clothed in full clerical dress[10]—an enduring metonym of austerity on the scorching Ramnad plains—missionaries tried to draw to themselves an authority that could discipline these separations. At the same time, submission to their authority and thereby in principle to bishop and pope was made the means to Christian salvation though the sacrificial cross, ensured through confession and Communion. However, the delineations of Tamil Catholicism and Christian identity did not arise from the imposition of a preexisting order of religion, but were shaped through contact with other local discourses, practices, and events (Linton 2003, 3, cited in Bloomer 2008, 21). As this book argues, the apparent coherence, universality, and authority of missionary Christianity was (and still is) produced through struggle and contingent action, which succeeded in forging a separate realm of Christian religion only by concealing these messy processes and constitutive exclusions (cf. Mitchell 2002).

Much of the time Jesuit missionaries had rather little capacity to defend Catholic religion from corruption. When all they could really defend in practice was their physical property, this itself acquired symbolic importance. The misuse of church property rather than mistaken doctrine or ritual practice—cutting ditches or threshing grain on church land, rather than worshipping pagan gods—was a reason for refusing parishioners' offerings or the denial of sacraments or last rites, even excommunication.[11] Jesuit authority failed in two obvious ways. First, missionary apartness left room for ritual action of a more direct and pragmatic kind through a range of non-Christian diviners, astrologers, and exorcists who helped manage misfortune by dealing with the array of potentially malevolent beings and forces that Jesuits dismissed as "devilry," but which converts could not ignore. Second, and relatedly, there were many heterodox popular Christian cults that evaded Church control. These cults were the particular concern of Jesuit parish diarists in the late nineteenth century.[12]

UNRULY SAINTS: INDEPENDENT SAINT CULTS IN THE NINETEENTH CENTURY

In July 1873, Father Favreux, the priest of Alapuram, wrote that he was dismayed that the "vast majority" of people were abandoning the important festival of St. James (Santiyakappar) and taking themselves to an unauthorized cult of Arulanandar (the as yet uncanonized John de Britto) at the site of his martyrdom at Oriyur. Favreux was particularly shocked by invocations of the saint's power here by the exorcist "Mandalacotei" Utaiyan, who,

> installed in a chair in front of the *kallaṟai* (martyr's tomb) without troubling himself to hear Mass[,] receives numberless so-called possessed . . . the majority of low caste, hair disarranged, breasts uncovered, on their knees submitting to an interrogation on the name, the number and quality of the demons, to the blows of a whip. Having cut a bunch of hair[,] [they were sent] to the tank to bathe and other indecencies practiced by this man and in view of all the world and the [Goan schismatic] priest approving, and this not only at the festival but again on all Wednesdays. Those possessed come in greater numbers than ever. A practice until this day unheard of in the church and at festivals even under the Goanese and which carries away by misfortune many of our Christians. Is there not need to refer to the bishop? (APD Favreux, 8 September 1872, translated)

In the 180 years since his death in 1693, de Britto's shrine had grown in popularity, attracting thousands. Above all it had become a special place for demonic exorcism, the processes of which fascinated as much as they repelled the Jesuits who described them—often and at length (see Mosse 2006a, 103–4). But Oriyur was only the most striking of a large number of popular saint cults in Ramnad that appear suddenly in the Jesuit records of the late nineteenth century. Most involved charismatic intermediaries of processes of exorcism and healing. For example, in 1877 Father Faseneille describes a crowd-drawing miraculous crucifix found in the "Forest of Vanattu Cinnappar" (St. Paul the Hermit) and brought from Colombo by a Catholic Pallar man. The crucifix appeared in a dream, refusing common shelter with St. Xavier, in whose chapel it had been placed before it was nailed to a massive cross outside where, as the object of offerings, it was "all running with butter, and oil like the Poulliers [Ganesh statues]." "The Pallen

[Pallar] has above all an unbelievable power for chasing the devil," Faseneille explains. "For this he obliged those possessed to stay for a long time in front of the crucifix. All at once, the poor devil uttered some great cries. He complained that he was being consumed by flames inside and out, and implored that he be left to leave. . . . The Pallen exorcist then ordered the demon to the end of a tuft of hair on the head and cutting this the demon departed."[13]

French Jesuits documented these and many other exorcism cults, saint trees, and miraculous crosses in their efforts to separate approved devotions from illegitimate "diableries," some of which focused on the same popular centers and tree shrines where an earlier generation of Jesuits had celebrated the thaumaturgical power of saints and missionary martyrs (not least de Britto) as signs to the unconverted of Christian divine power.[14] But in the 1870s to 1890s, claiming sacred power beyond Church authority was at best "foolery," at worst diabolical, and to do so in the name of the saints was "blasphemy and insolence." Jesuits also recorded these "diableries" as proof of the lax and corrupt administration of their mission rivals, the poorly educated Goan "schism," who tolerated the likes of the Mandalacotei exorcist "impostor," who also appropriated a quarter of the offerings of the church for the big men of his (Utaiyar) caste, who claimed rights in the shrine.[15] As Bloomer (2008, 398) argues from research on a present-day heterodox Tamil Marian center, these cults were actually necessary to the establishment of the Jesuit mission that was asserted against them—their challenge being the opportunity for new forms of authority. But the popularity of possession and exorcism cults themselves in the late nineteenth century may have a different explanation, as a *reaction* to the effects of the new disciplining pastoral Catholicism. They thrived at a time of transition, when a sharper line was being drawn between Catholic religion and other ritual practice, and when new prohibitions were being imposed on everyday ways of dealing with misfortune.

Jesuits preached an internal battle against sin and desire with eternal consequences and invoked a punitive Catholic divinity. Only through sacraments authorized by the Church could Christians find protection from evil, solace from personal affliction, forgiveness for sins, and ultimately salvation. The saints might be invoked, but only moral action and humble confession and Communion of the contrite individual would secure true benefits in this life and the next. The impress of this missionary teaching was evident among the Alapuram Catholic villagers with whom I stayed in the 1980s. While I was told that affliction could have external causes—astrological "bad time" (*keṭṭa kirakam*) or attack by demonic agents—fundamentally it was inseparable from the moral state of the individual person. Suffering might be sent by God to test individuals (demons might even be deployed to this end), but the more common explanations of misfortune related to sin. The struggle against sinfulness was made terrifying by the specter of the sharp-horned Devil with notebook tally of accumulated sins transmitted to children who entered the foreboding darkness of the church to perform their penances (as Tamil novelist Bama vividly recollects [2000, 70–75]). Some spoke as if unconfessed sin could accumulate and bring (bodily) sickness and affliction (see Introduction).[16] The Virgin might appear in dreams to diagnose such peril, or to help deal with it.[17]

Negotiation of the Church's demand for interiorization involved compromise with existing Tamil conceptions that "substantialized" or exteriorized inner emotions and moral processes.[18] Teaching on the effects of unconfessed sin (or its local interpretation) resonated with the Tamil karmic notion that "one's acts 'stick' to the person, altering their capacity for future action" (Mines 2005, 111). With this comes the idea that the effects of action can be transmitted to family members or across generations, while disease or the lack of rain could be the material consequences of collective sin. At the very least, a lapse in regular prayer and confession could interrupt the protection of Jesus or Mary and render a family vulnerable to mystical attack manifest as a run of misfortune (cf. Still 2007, 220), while seeking the renewal of the Eucharist with unconfessed sin or harboring hatred, guilt, or secret crimes was to invite the punishment of God. The various associated "techniques of self" of villager converts produced hybridized Catholic selves that both doubled and disturbed missionary or Church authority in a manner that often characterizes the global condition of religion (Bloomer 2008, 193, citing Bhabha 1994; Csordas 2007, 299).

POSSESSION AND CONFESSION

The internal drama of confession, repentance, and absolution found a more distinct counterpart in the "externalized" drama of possession and practices of exorcism that denied Catholic priesthood exclusive mediation of the divine. It was partly through encounters with possession, and its very different concept of agency, that Jesuit missionaries in the Tamil countryside put in place their idea of the Christian moral person. Take the case of Father Gnanaprakasam,[19] who describes his efforts over five days in August 1896 to bring a young woman (known only as Jeronym's wife) back to her moral self—to confession "in a most sensible manner" and to receive Communion—by subordinating a popular interpretation of affliction as torment by spirit agents. The reality of these agents and the charms of sorcerers are displaced, and personal affliction is made ultimately inseparable from personal sin through an "interiorization" of guilt (Taylor 1985; for details see Mosse 2006a).

The process is one in which the missionary effects separations of being and agency within a dangerously hybridized world of sorcerers, saints, and spirits, of feeling and fantasy, in order to stabilize this woman as a Christian moral person—a "purification" of agency and moral responsibility from unwanted actors and things. Keane (2007, 23–24) uses this concept of "purification" (borrowed from Latour 1993) to describe the way Calvinist reformers worked to recall all agency to the individual. However, unlike them, Father Gnanaprakasam (and other Jesuits) effected the separations that rehabilitated this young woman to her Christian self with the aid of various spirit-object hybrids of their own, whether prayer recitations, blessings with holy images or water, the crucifix or medals of the saints pressed to her body, or statues and images upon which to gaze. But it is clear from his description that Gnanaprakasam gave these things a circumscribed agency. They were applied to the afflicted as analgesics to quiet, to alleviate pain, or to bring sleep—not to battle with the spirits, but to prepare the way for sincere and contrite confession and Communion, which were the true means by which the woman would take possession of herself and return to ordinary social behavior (see Mosse 2006a). The Jesuit attitude to villagers' belief in spirits (and sorcery) was ambivalent. At times it was viewed as the diversionary work of the Devil, but more commonly it was derided as "foolery," to be replaced with the true struggle against evil as a matter of individual responsibility and personal guilt (cf. Caplan 1989, 61). To better understand what might have been involved in these Jesuit encounters with possession cults of the nineteenth century, let me turn to some more recent practice.

THE DRAMA OF POSSESSION

Although by the 1960s, under closer ecclesiastical regulation, exorcism gradually disappeared from Britto's shrine in Oriyur, other Catholic cults of exorcism thrived—both well-known centers such as St. Anthony's at Puliyampatti (Sébastia 2007, 2008) and smaller shrines in ecclesiastical backwaters such as St. Anthony (the Hermit)'s at Muthupattanam near Alapuram. The practices that I witnessed at the latter in 1983–84 (described with cases in Mosse 1986, 465–98; 2006a) conform to a characteristic pattern of Tamil Catholic possession-exorcism (Sébastia 2008; Deliège 1999; Ram 1991).

As in the cults described by the French Jesuits, demonic agents (*pēy-picācu*), which include inferior Hindu deities and malevolent spirits of the dead, are exposed to holy power through the medium of prayers, the crucifix or rosary, holy water, or extended stay at the shrine, and especially the force of the saint through the gaze of his statue. The victim's body, turned into a place of torture (Sébastia 2007), begins to "dance" (*āṭu*) with characteristically extreme, repetitive, and violent gestures until under interrogation (and assaults) from the catechist-exorcist the spirits—sometimes several in one person—are forced to identify themselves and the reason for their attack before being removed in a lock of the victim's hair. This thoroughly embodied rite of removal dramatizes the separation of a person from their afflictions and restores them to normal social life. It concludes what can be a long war of attrition between saints and demons and is only the final moment in an extended diagnostic process in which the subjective experience of the afflicted (predominantly young women)[20] becomes objectified as demonic through a public process that draws on conventional idioms of demonic agency and human susceptibility to construct a plausible narration of demonic attack (Mosse 2006a, 117). Autonomous persons become, temporarily, public spaces in which accounts of how and why an individual became possessed draw in various actors—including other family members (alive and dead), Hindu demons, gods and goddesses, and ritual specialists. That is to say, the state of possession is not defined by the victim herself; rather it is a group representation of a problem or set of problems.[21] Possession is not a matter of personal sin or infringement of moral order; it is a blameless condition of external attack or inadvertent infringement of the ritual order perhaps of Hindu gods—for instance, by walking near their shrines when menstruating (Deliège 1999). In fact, a range of issues including disrupted relationships and frustrated desires, as well as a large cast of actors, is involved. The self as bounded moral agent is replaced by a more fluid person, constituted and acted upon by the desires of others (alive and dead) and their spirit agents (Spencer 1997); and these effect substantial changes in the bodies of those they inhabit.[22]

The possession stories and spectacles of Ramnad Catholics whom I spoke with in the 1980s seemed above all to constitute a discourse on the objective dangers of extreme emotional states, especially fear (*payam*) that strips the self of its natural "command" (Nabokov 2000, 46). Possession is a discourse on the susceptibility of the superstitious or the less educated (Still 2007. 227), and on female vulnerability and weakness especially.[23] While uncontained female emotion and sexuality is a pervasive idiom of demonic possession, the female body is construed as the point of entry of demonic disorder (cf. Kapferer 1983, 100–101, 105). The sterile sexuality of the possessing demon Munis, who sleep with their victims, perfectly opposes the virginal fertility of Our Lady (see below). If sexuality is demonized, demons can take the place of sin and guilt. But perhaps most important of all, the exteriorizing discourse of demonic possession (whether originating in spirits or sorcery) allows a family collective publicly to recover honor and reputation following humiliating and damaging episodes, whether sexual indiscretion, elopement, failed marriages, or mental illness (Sébastia 2007; Still 2007, 214 et seq.), something denied in the Church confessional.

Paying attention to the public discourse of possession avoids a naive psychologizing; but it risks ignoring the way personal history *is* woven into these narratives. While no longer conventional subjects of their own actions, the possessed nonetheless use public representations of demonic agency to act out their problems, either in movement (as detailed by Stirrat [1992]) or narrative (Nabokov [1997]), even if the authoritatively controlled possession drama ultimately disciplines the afflicted individuals, as Nabokov argues in her aptly titled article "Expel the Lover, Recover the Wife." Possession episodes at the shrines of Catholic saints are also linked to romantic failure and sexual control (see cases in Mosse 2006a, 131–32). But my evidence suggests that these possessions refer to desires and passions wider than sexual longing, and a nexus of relationships of power and authority beyond marital ties. At St. Anthony's shrine, *pēys* are not in the main "spirits of young men craving intimacy" (Nabokov 1997, 300) but the spirits of those who in *different* ways remain dangerously attached to the world after death. It is true that *pēy* are attracted to their victims by love (*aṉpu*) more often than anger, but this is explicitly the fondness (*piriyam*) or jealousy of relatives, the "bond of blood" (*rattappācam*) as much as lust (*ācai*). The possessed have close relations or bonds (*pācam*) with their spirits; they are their intimates.

However you look at it, possession by *pēy-picācu* has always been "about" unbridled desire and attachment, passion, and the dangerous (destabilizing, heating) but "infinite capacity of human beings to want what cannot be had, a capacity which turns rancid with frustration" and which lingers perilously after death (Ram 1991, 84). And this relates to the allied danger of covetousness: the unintended harm of the emotion-laden envious glance at a newborn baby, a new house, or a fine pile of rice—the effect of *kaṇ tiruṣṭi,* poorly translated as "evil eye" (Mines 2005, 67).[24] Ultimately, desires and attachments and their power are to be trivialized in the face of the saint, and removed. Before departure, possessing ghosts and demon deities make requests, usually for trivial items indicative of the hold that desire has over them: a comb or mirror for a *kuratti* gypsy ghost, a hen with egg (*muṭṭaikōḻi*) for the goddess Kali, toddy (palm wine) or a rooster for a Muni demon-god. The demonic is cut from the victim's body as knotted strands of hair and discarded in the *kāṭu* (forest, or here the reservoir) just as the late-nineteenth-century Jesuits recorded.

As these missionaries strove to convey a particular notion of interiority and to enforce a discipline of confession and Communion in their Tamil parishes, the tension between two approaches to suffering and affliction and two conceptions of personhood and agency—possession and confession—sharpened in opposition. The Jesuits' own boundary making and letter writing may have made exorcism cults more visible and more diabolical; but at the same time their teaching on suffering and affliction bore down unbearably on the individual sinner in ways that might have opened up space for the expansion of these saint-exorcism cults, giving focus to the subjugated logic of possession so dramatically manifest at places such as Oriyur. As Michel de Certeau suggests in *The Possession at Loudun* (2000), this threat of possession occurred when inner uncertainties articulated with shifts in ideas and control of sacred power as a challenge to belief systems, when experience became unconstrained (or was not yet constrained) in authorized clerical language.

FIGURE 1. Burning incense in front of family lithographs of the saints. Photo by author.

THE RELIGIOUS CULTURE OF TAMIL CATHOLICISM

I have begun to introduce spirit possession here as a way of describing one historical dynamic in the cultural production of Tamil Catholicism in rural Ramnad. This culture making involves navigation not only between the authorized and the unauthorized, but also between the subjective and the social, "state of mind" and "cultural formation" (Ortner 2005, in Napolitano and Pratten 2007, 4). An ethnographic description of Catholicism that inevitably privileges the public and the shared always risks loss of the ambiguity, plurality, and provisionality of meaning in individual experience—the danger of apportioning too much or too little meaning (Napolitano and Pratten 2007, 4, learning from de Certeau). Catholic doctrine has of course always been subject to individual inference and elaboration beyond the authorizing/deauthorizing discourses of the Church, linked to personal projects and ideas that remain in the realm of private symbols or circulate within the restricted field of intimate relations. Such are the dreams (*kaṉavu*), visions (*kāṭci, taricaṉam;* Sk. *darsan*), or other revelations, often at moments of personal crisis (cf. Nabokov 2000, 20), with reference to which villagers speak to an enquirer such as myself about the saints, or the Virgin or Jesus, whose venerated images are at the center of the home (figure 1).

For the pregnant woman fearful for the health of her unborn child, the

FIGURE 2. Santiyakappar (St. James the Greater) statue in Alapuram church. Photo by author.

FIGURE 3. Man and son pray to Arulanandar (St. John de Britto) after fulfilling a tonsure vow. Photo by author.

Virgin appears on a lotus flower, throwing her not only a petal but also an areca nut that lands by a tree, signaling for her some sin, blemish, or fault (*paḻutu*). The Virgin summons another woman to her shrine at Velankanni through the sudden matting of her hair.[25] For a man in the grip of "smallpox," Santiyakappar (St. James) appears as a horseman chasing away a young woman in saffron (the pox-manifesting goddess) in a direction (east or west) that foretells the severity and course of his illness (figure 2). For the Hindu village official who refused land to raise the festival flagpole, that same horseman is a terrifying nightmare crushing his neck underfoot, prompting regular family offerings at the Alapuram church. Through dreams or signs—even sickness or misfortune—the saints, like Hindu deities, "initiate their own worship" (Nabokov 2000, 117). Sometimes their agency is known through answers to prayer: the recovery from illness, the birth of a child, good rain or harvest. Their dangerous power may be invoked against wrongdoers, as a threat or reflected in the cries of a tormented possessing spirit.

Falling between the private world of dreams and public forms of festival worship are vows (*nērtikkaṭaṉ*). These are another way in which internal desires or dilemmas can be externally acted upon in a direct and unmediated manner that allows public display (Raj and Harman 2006, 3; Christian 1981, 31–33). Inner promises become outer actions, from pilgrimages to promissory notes (*muṟikkai*).[26] These are reciprocal transactions between an individual and the saint.[27] Offerings or penances anticipate or give thanks for the saint's grace (*aruḷ*) and blessing (*ācīrvātam*). Chosen to suit the character of the saint (flour lamps for St. Sebastian, ponkal rice for St. Anthony) or of the desire of the petitioner, *offerings* are made of money, candles, grain, coconut saplings, cooked rice, goats, roosters, or hens. Meanwhile, *penances* involve, for example, circumambulation of the shrine (on knees, carrying coconut saplings for fertility, or sugarcane cradles—*karumpu toṭṭi*—with the prayed-for child) or burning rice-flour lamps (*māviḷakku*) on healed parts of the body. Penances include devotional or sacrificial tonsure (*moṭṭai*) performed equally as a rite of thanksgiving, petition, or dedication of a young child for the protection of the saint[28] (figure 3) (cf. Raj 2002, 94–99); and of course the journey by pilgrims themselves, on foot over days, by bullock cart or today by public bus, in the saffron or blue clothes of ascetics.[29] Consecrating animals (usually goats) to a saint, sacrificing them at the shrine, cooking and sharing the meat (with poor pilgrims as well as those protected by the saint) are acts ambiguously placed between propitiation, communion, and commensality.[30] Here the killing of animals is sanctified. They are first raised in a saint's name, adorned, and blessed with holy water or the sign of the cross, sometimes in front of the saint's statue, or by a priest. The prize cuts of meat are then placed by the altar along with the skin and offered to the priest.

THE SAINTS IN TAMIL IMAGINATION

So who are the personages at the center of such acts of worship? The question is complicated not only by ambiguous personal meanings, but also by overlapping Christian and Hindu religious imaginaries. Drawing out some of the shared representations revealed in local myths on the founding of particular churches, in narratives of intercession, rewards, oaths, or punishments, as well in the implicit orderings of religious practices, will help to delineate a popular discourse on Catholic divinity. This can be discerned as a historical effect of Catholic mission in relation to Tamil society, "a fetishized product of previous activity, the work of other lives . . . the sedimented world of ancestral acts and forgone conclusions" (Jackson 1998, 27, cited in Mines 2005, 20), and particularly as the product of encounters across religious boundaries. These localized encounters recorded from the interactions of village-level fieldwork in the 1980s do not, of course, claim to stand for some global Tamil Catholicism.[31]

The first point to make is that in the religious imaginations of both Hindus and Catholics, the multiple forms of divinity have powers and dominion that are circumscribed to different degrees. It is the localized, differentiated, particularistic, and specialist village gods or Catholic saints who are closest to humans and approachable for pragmatic concerns, while transcendent figures—the Christian or Hindu trinities—concern salvation or cosmic order.[32] Second, the "lower down" these divine orders, the more religious cultures interpenetrate, and the more Hindus and Christians have the same or formally similar ritual forms. The Christian Trinity and rites of the Catholic priest on the one hand, and the great Hindu deities and Brahmanical rites on the other, are clearly separate, and mutual ritual participation at this level is rare and usually prohibited. But when it comes to the Catholic saints and the Virgin, and village gods and goddesses, there are complex interreligious exchanges. These are asymmetrical. While Hindus participate directly and openly in cults to the Catholic saints (readily incorporated within their pantheon), Catholics interact with Hindu village deities only covertly, making offerings by proxy through Hindus. A few Catholic families I knew made regular offerings to a goddess such as Kali as their protector deity, or included themselves in the community of worshippers of a deity close to their fields to ensure good crops, and rather more sought protection or propitiation from/to potentially malevolent demon deities at times or places of vulnerability; but there was no means to construe such practice. This disposition surprised Jesuit Father Darrieutort, who in 1876 wrote of a woman who had decided to convert, telling him: "Here I am ready Swami; I have arranged everything to be baptized this morning. You see, all my life I have been a strong devotee of [Siva's son] Subramanium. In order not to irritate him too much by my desertion, I have these past days bought a quantity of fine cocks. While you baptize me they will be immolated. I hope that he will be content" (Darrieutort 1876, 5–6 [translated]). Finally, in relation to inferior demonic, ghostly or sorcerous supernatural agents of misfortune, Hindus and Christians shared a common culture of evil manifest in the possession cults.

DEATH AND SAINTHOOD

Let me begin this consideration of the relationship between saints and deities with Tamil Catholic concepts of sainthood that I encountered. The saints are those who died a "good death" (*nalla maraṇam*)—that is, without attachment, "leaving neither material nor moral debt behind" (Pocock 1973, 40).[33] Tamil Catholic funeral rites can themselves be seen as dealing with sin and worldly attachment and as symbolically transforming an ordinary death (a de facto misfortune) into an idealized sacrificial death, which—as the death of the saints and martyrs (and Indian sadhus) illustrate—is a source of benevolent power, regeneration, and blessing for the living (cf. Bloch and Parry 1982; Parry 1982). The explicit contrary is the "death with attachment": the mother in childbirth, the suicide with frustrated desire, who return to haunt the living as troublesome ghosts. Although the Catholic Church stresses the importance of rites *before* rather than after death—the extreme unction rather than the funeral rites—in practice Tamil Catholic funerals are rites of transition that convey the soul from this world to the next, separate the dead from the living, and inhibit their return as haunting spirits. The overall ritual structure that effects this transition and deals with the consequent states of danger (for participants and the dead) borrows from Hindu practice: preparing the deceased for the next world by purifying and removing worldly desires; crossing boundaries on a symbolic journey; and dealing with the "heat" and danger generated by transition (see Mosse 1996 for details). There is of course nothing uniquely Indian about this ritual structure (see Douglas 1966).

The beautification and adornment of the dead, the libations and offerings that characterize Tamil Catholic funerals, were usually explained to me as the need to honor the deceased, to satisfy their desires; and troubling spirits typically complained of an inadequate funeral. But if the dead are to become like the saints, the worldly wealth and honor that the funeral itself bestows have to be removed at the grave. The body is stripped of its flower garlands and finery, a married woman of her *tali* and jewelry—all removed by the village barber, for "as they were born, they need to be sent" (*piṟantamātari aṉuppa vēṇṭum*). Later (chapter 3) we will see how the positive and negative forces of worldly life are captured and removed in a socially significant way. For now, it is enough to understand their ritual disposal as necessary to accomplish the transformation of the ordinary into the ideal death; and when the body is carried to the church in the same bier as the statue of the dead Christ during the Good Friday procession, accompanied by the lament of Mary for her dead son, the individual death becomes identified with the sacrificial atoning death of Christ, from which comes the assurance of resurrection (cf. Cannell 1995, 380–84). Death, signaling life elsewhere, is a reenactment of the drama of redemption (Menon 2002, 1665).

Of course the transition to sacrificial death and saintliness is uncertain and incomplete. Lamp offerings for heaven's journey (*mōṭcaviḷakku*), Masses for the soul's peace (*ātmacānti pūcai*), and offerings at the grave continue to help the soul's progress, peace, and partition from the living. In being so transformed, the dead become a source of benevolent power for the living, mediating between the human and the divine. When on occasions such as All Souls (figure 4), before a marriage, or at the start of a pilgrimage families light candles, burn incense, or cook food as "alms rice" (*tarma cōr* or *piccai cōr*) in honor of the dead, they hope to obtain the blessing of their dead, who may have appeared in dreams with advice, predictions, or warnings (or reminders of their own needs). As the monsoon was delayed in 1983, I joined a family preparing ritual *poṅkal* rice beside the graves of their departed in an appeal for rain. Such offerings revealed an incompleteness in the shift of Catholicization from a focus on the dead in the lives of the living to a concern with changing the condition of the dead themselves—their passage to the afterlife, perhaps through purgatory. But they also signaled an underlying conception of the power of sainthood, which begins with the grave.

Some graves or tombs acquire wider powers. On 31 October 1983, during the same parched waiting, I found myself among a large crowd sheltering from a sudden cloudburst. We had gathered to make offerings and to pray for the forgiveness of sins, and for the rain this might release, at the tomb shrine of a saintly woman. It had been built some years earlier by a Nadar man whose wife had given birth following the appearance in her dream of this *mātā*—*mātā* being a generic term for a female saint as well as the Virgin Mary. This particular *mātā*, Saveriyayi, was apparently a foreigner (of unknown caste), married into a Hindu Maravar family, who converted to Christianity and lived a deeply spiritual life despite being tormented for her faith in a marriage that was never consummated. At death she had requested burial in an open public (*potu*) place outside her village where her blessing was accessible, beyond a restricted kin group, to all. She was honored in an annual cult in Purattaci, the month of goddess festivals, and her blessing transmitted through flower petals consumed or the ash from her tomb rubbed onto the bodies of the many mothers and young children who gathered to offer garlands, candles, raw rice, and sugar amid the din of drumming and "radio" music.

Tombs of the holy dead have long been a Tamil Catholic focus for healing power.[34] They were foci for many heterodox "diableries" as well as sites at which Jesuit missionaries themselves became sources of miraculous power. Among the popular cults recorded by the Jesuit Favreux in just one year (1874) were

FIGURE 4. All Souls festival, Alapuram, 1983. Photo by author.

those at the tombs of women—one of "low" Cakkiliyar caste, one of "une mendiante de très basse caste, passant pour vierge et moitie homme," and another of an "ill-famed" woman—at the tomb of a "vagabond" and of a Nadar child "named as the Infant Jesus."[35] A cult centered on a miraculous tamarind "tree of Arulanandar" (de Britto) was located over the tomb of a Christian woman who had hung from it (indicating the motif of self-sacrifice rather than suicide).[36] These all focus on individuals who were peripheral in Tamil village society in one sense or another—women, low castes, mendicants, foreigners, vagabonds, or children—and whose social marginality equated with renunciation. Their tombs are located, without exception, in the "wilderness" or *kāṭu,* away from other cemeteries, where they are attributed divinity as "common deities" (*potu cāmi*s).[37] Saveriyayi *mātā* (above) further recalls for us that physical and emotional suffering in the world is also a kind of renunciation (cf. Stirrat 1992; Dempsey 2001).[38]

By convention, the pious and austere Jesuit missionaries of Ramnad lived long, and had miraculous powers—to heal, bring rain, or drive away pests. Their regenerative sanctity continued after death. Inadvertently disinterred from his grave in Sarukani (after devotees gradually removed all the earth for its healing properties), the body of Father Leveil, an especially renowned miracle-working French missionary, was found to be incorrupt and to emit a sweet smell.[39] The special places of the Christian dead mediate life and death, the altar and the grave. Here the world beyond is manifest on earth. Time, death, and the forces of natural decay are suspended (cf. Brown 1981, 71, 75–78; Shulman 1980, 40–41; Turner 1973). Moreover, while the dead are normally denied individuality, being eulogized in Tamil funeral laments into the cultural shape of any good relative (Nabokov 2000, 117) or anonymized in cemeteries, the tombs of Christian persons such as Leveil remain "still heavy with the fullness of a beloved person" (Brown 1981, 11).

The theme of asceticism and sacrificial death as a source of regenerative power is nowhere clearer than in the saint as martyr. In Ramnad, St. Sebastian, represented with pierced body tied to a miraculously blooming dead tree, was a vital source of healing, particularly during epidemics, when his statue was taken in procession through village streets. At the festival of his local shrine in Kokkurani in the 1980s, pilgrims still fulfilled vows by burning rice-flour lamps (otherwise associated with the Hindu goddess) on the recovered parts of their bodies. But the exemplar of regenerative death was surely that of John de Britto, Jesuit renouncer-king and the martyr of Ramnad (see Nevett 1980; Saulière 1947), whose hagiographic representation in word, figure, and folk drama bears all the markings of the martyrs of Christian antiquity. Pain, endurance, "the miraculous suppression of suffering," and above all his violent death provide the imaginative focus for the saint's supernatural power (Brown 1981, 80). The death itself marks unnatural or regenerative events: on decapitation his body leapt back instead of slumping forward, it radiated beautiful light, and eight unseasonal days of rain followed the execution—scattering the body parts, as the saint had requested be its fate. It is the site and instruments of death (the impaling stake) that particularly channel the saint's posthumous power linked to the shedding of blood as *ratta cāṭci* ("blood testimony") or martyrdom (see Nevett 1980, 225, 228; Saulière 1947, 478). Tradition holds that a drop of the saint's blood fell into the blind eye of his executor, restoring sight, and that earth turned red by the saint's blood is a continuing source of regeneration, collected by pilgrims, applied to sick and infertile bodies or parched ground, and to the heads of the possessed as a torture to demons (Darrieutort 1876).

Here, Tamil mythic themes of blood as "the source of life, a substance imbued with power . . . a locus of sacred forces . . . [and] a conventional symbol of sanctity" (Shulman 1980, 105, 107) are aligned with sacrificial blood as a central Christian symbol. To Jesuit missionaries, the Tamil association of blood, fertility, and sanctity was threatening, Županov suggests, "precisely because the equation was 'correct' from their point of view, except that fertility, ideally, led to abundance in the celestial, not in the terrestrial, world" (2005, 180). At the same time, as deified heroes Catholic saints incorporate (or were incorporated into) a Tamil tradition in which tormented and slaughtered warriors (*vīraṉ*) are deified, and gods are worshipped as warriors, their fierce power rooted in their violent heroic death becoming a source of protection (Mines 2005, 133, 185; Blackburn 1985; Shulman 1980).

In sharp contrast to the public cults to the holy dead at tombs often outside the village and officiated by men are the private rituals conducted by women inside the house. These are oriented toward a different category of deified dead, ritually incorporated as household deities or *vīṭṭu cāmi*s and honored by Catholics alongside the saints whose illuminated lithographs adorn family shrines (see figure 1). Vittu camis are often female relatives who lived long, satisfied (fertile), and holy lives as married women and had a "good death" (cf. Reiniche 1979, 60, 68; Moffatt 1979, 226–28). However, the vittu cami par excellence is a girl who died before attaining puberty, a *kaṉṉi* or virgin (particularly among the cases I knew, the sister of a woman's husband or his father's or mother's sister) who resides as a source of protecting help for the family. Savariyammal told me how she was suffering from a run of misfortune, family illness, and domestic violence. She consulted a fortune teller (*kuṭukuṭuppakāran*) to discover the source of the problem. He told her to make a shrine in the west of the house and daily burn incense. Her *periyammā* (father-in-law's elder sister), who died at the age of twelve having "only worked in the house," appeared in a dream, after which, she insisted, the kanni has been looking after the family and things began to improve.

Here again, Catholics implicitly draw on cross-religion Tamil idioms. Several goddess shrines in Alapuram also originated in the spirit of a girl who died before puberty (see Mosse 1986, 434–35). As Nabokov (2000, 116–17) notes, those who die young become cool (*kuḷir*); and they unite with the goddess in the other world. Catholics explained the kanni as a girl who died in a state of absolute sexual purity, sometimes a girl killed or sacrificed while protecting this purity and therefore without *pāvatōṣam*—meaning in this context the blemish of both sin and, euphemistically, sex. A female death before puberty is a form of renunciation, arguably the ideal of *female* renunciation, which is not the (active) ascetic control of sexuality but rather a (passive) condition of asexual purity and absolution from original sin.[40] If the male saints were exemplars of the first sacrificial death, the Virgin Mary (*mātā*) provided a model for death-defeating sexual purity, which was the kanni's power. Given the equally strong identification of Mary with motherhood, the wider Catholic paradoxical ideal of the virgin mother was also reproduced locally.

AMBIVALENT POWERS

The imaginative association of sacrificial death and female sexual purity with regenerative power had both European and Indian roots, but what Catholics derived from their Tamil context was the notion that divine power associated with the violence of sacrifice is also profoundly dangerous. The power of popular male Catholic saints in particular is ambivalent. While saints were generally characterized as having sanctity (the word *saint* translates as *arcciyaciṣṭar,* from *arcciyam* or "sanctity"), those popular locally such as Santiyakappar (St. James), St. Sebastian, or St. Anthony the hermit were also associated with violent and dangerous aspects of divine power, such as the direct punishment of the guilty and battling with demons, or as God's vigilantes enforcing moral right or protecting church property. From eighteenth-century Jesuit letters, and the local tradition they inscribe, we find descriptions of saints including Arulanandar (de Britto) at the site and on the day (Wednesdays) of his martyrdom meting out violent punishment—such as paralysis, vomiting blood, or choking to death—to a variety of evildoers.[41] At their major shrines, the saints' violent punitive power was institutionalized through the practice of settling disputes through formal oath taking *(cattiyam)* in front of their statues, the saints' gaze (like the Hindu gods') being the source of terrifying discerning power as well as blessing.[42] Going publicly to a saint's shrine to invoke punishment on an enemy or one suspected of sorcery with a warning—Santiyakappar *kēppār* (St. James will "ask")—was enough to bring a confession or to halt the witchcraft, while a prolonged stay at a shrine would surely identify the wrongdoers through dreams if not inflicted punishment. Clark-Decès (2007, 79–80) makes an important point when, having asked, "why Tamil devotees would want to discover their gods in dynamics of aggression," she notes that "[t]he violence consists in shaming the self into better being. . . . [It] is concerned with self-transformation," which provides a better view of shared Catholic-Hindu popular religiosity focused on the saints than the missionary "obsession with bloodthirsty demons worshipped with violent rites" (ibid.).

Saints are differentiated by character but also as specified village deities (*kirāma teyvam*), each a guardian of the land and prosperity of a particular place. Like his counterpart the god Aiyanar, with whom he is paired as brother, Santiyakappar's village shrine is located by the tank embankment, and he is portrayed as a boundary-protecting divine warrior (*pōrvīraṉ*) riding on a horse trampling enemies underfoot (who in the representations are the Moors in Christian Spain). The differentiated identities of the male saints, and their ambivalent power localized in territory, shrine, or tree, contrasts the merged identity and benevolent healing/mothering power of *mātā*. Mata is the Virgin Mary in her various manifestations such as Arokkiyamata ("Our Lady of Health") and Ataikkalamata ("Our Lady of Refuge") as well as other imprecisely differentiated female saints (as above).[43] The contrast in local imagination between male saints and the Virgin has other dimensions. While the power of popular male saints is rooted in violence (suffered or inflicted) and symbolized by the spilling of blood (the martyr's or the Moors'), the Virgin was never wounded; her power is unimplicated in violence. While her relation to blood is sorrow and compassion, local myths associate her appearances with the spilling or overflowing of milk—in particular, that of the shepherd boy to whom (as the mata of Velankanni) she revealed herself.[44] In Tamil conceptions blood is a dangerous "heating" substance, whereas milk is purifying and cooling. Furthermore, whereas roosters and goats were sacrificed in honor of male saints, the offerings made at Mata shrines were, to my knowledge, exclusively "vegetarian." Indeed, at Oriyur, Arulanandar (de Britto) and Mata appeared to occupy different ritual spaces. Violent exorcisms focused on the saint's power at the place and time of violence (on Wednesdays at the site of impalement), where large numbers of goats and chickens were killed; but at the shrine dedicated to the Virgin (the first one built before de Britto had been canonized, on the site of his beheading), pilgrims fulfilled vows for health and fertility—the fruits of sacrifice—with offerings of sprouted coconuts.

This local Catholic ordering of saints and the Virgin was assembled through an indigenous symbolic logic. Here divine power, having its source in violence, is itself violent; and blood is an appropriately ambivalent symbol of both power and danger. A further connection is suggested between the violent source and nature of warrior saints' power and the kind of offerings made—namely, the life of animals. As one Catholic Alapuram man explained the practice of honoring Arulanandar with the sacrifice of animals: "[B]y blood sacrifice they killed [him]; blood sacrifice they give [to him]" (*rattappaliyil koṉṟārkaḷ rattappali kotuttārkaḷ*). Then, as David Shulman (1980, 131) explains, in Tamil mythology "the power rooted in violence and symbolised by the blood of the offering is also by nature polluting" and associated with inferior divine beings (Fuller 1992, 89 et seq.). In Ramnad, Catholics share with Hindus an ambivalent attitude toward killing and animal sacrifice at saint shrines, and the Church certainly disapproves of such practices.[45] There is a distinction between animal life and "vegetarian" offerings that points to others familiar from Hindu practice—between violent power and benign power, or blood and milk—that are hierarchical (Dumont 1959; Fuller 1992). That is to say, in relation to the Virgin Mary, the violent power of the saints, symbolized by blood and associated with animal killing, is conceived of as inferior.

Of course, the power of the saints *is* understood as of a lower order. It is power delegated from Christ or maybe the Virgin. In the received myth of Santiago, Christians of Spain prayed to the Virgin for assistance, whereupon St. James was dispatched to defeat the Moors. Male saints have power to act within a restricted realm of disease, infertility, exorcism, or punishment, to protect a defined territory—perhaps that enclosed by the boundary of the village or parish. In relation to Christ (and the Virgin), the saints were often described as ministers and warriors serving the king—the same metaphor describing the relationship between the god Aiyanar and the inferior guardian deities. And just as the highly differentiated forms of Hindu village divinity contrast the "great" gods of Siva or Vishnu, the multiplicity of male saint identities is itself indicative of localized powers contrasting the universal power of Mata and Jesus. But the point here is also that superior Catholic divinity (Christ and the Virgin) was separated from violent and inferior manifestations of power, and that this distinction was at least in part symbolically marked through a logic that Catholics shared with Hindus.[46]

Saints such as Santiyakappar did not, however, cease to be pure and holy. My reflections on saints as caught in a paradox of holiness and the contamination of power might have ended here were it not for a local story that appeared not only to acknowledge this paradox, but to attempt a resolution.

> One day the Catholic priest was traveling by horse to Alapuram from Sarukani to the north. On the way his party passed some people conducting a cult (*cāmi kumpiṭu*) to the Hindu god Muniaiyar. The priest sent his *kōvilpiḷḷai* (Vellalar-caste catechist) to see what they were doing, and the latter came away with some of the meat offering. As the priest proceeded on his way to Alapuram there was a heavy rainstorm during which Muniaiyar, appearing as a man with an umbrella, offered to protect the priest. When they arrived in the village, Muniaiyar said to the priest, "Now, what will you do for me? I have no place to stay." The priest replied, "You can stay to the [inauspicious] south of the church in a tree. If anybody comes and makes a false oath in the church you will avenge them."[47]

Thus, some say Muniaiyar resides by the south door of the church. He has long hair tied in a bun (*kontai*), brandishes a big knife, and there performs the violent punishments of Santiyakappar's judgments, and is more generally held responsible for the saint's violent manifestations. When a person walked from the north to the south door, having made a false oath, it was the Hindu god and not the saint who inflicted the grievous punishment.

RELATIONAL IDENTITY: HINDU DEITIES AND CATHOLIC SAINTS

Muniaiyar is, in fact, one of the serving or guarding deities (*kāval cāmis*) whose statues are located in the outer courtyard of the village temple of their lord, Aiyanar, from whom they are differentiated and inferiorized by their acceptance of animal sacrifices (Fuller 1992, 90). It was Louis Dumont's insight that Hindu divinity is *relational,* the variable characteristics of gods being defied by context-specific relations with each other, rather than in terms of a fixed set of attributes. Muniaiyar may be a subordinate meat-eating guardian deity in the village temple, but when he is the focus of a separate hamlet-lineage cult, he is worshipped as a superior "vegetarian deity" (*caiva cāmi*), while sacrifices are offered to an overlapping set of inferior gods whom he commands, including the lowest Conaiyar, the "lame god" (*nonticāmi*), crippled lest his violent strength destroyed the world.

The superiority of the higher deity derives here from the relegation of inferior attributes such as violence onto subordinate ones. Indeed, the condition for the exercise of fierce divine power is subordination within a structure of hierarchical relations (beyond which it is palpably demonic), much as local dominants have power delegated from the sovereign. Indeed, at the level of religious constructs *and* political relations, legitimate power is delegated power (Reiniche 1979, 224; cf. Dumont 1959). Not only is the domain of an inferior deity incorporated in that of a superior one, but in a sense the inferior deity is him- or herself included within the *being* of the superior one (cf. Reiniche 1979, 132). When possessing a victim, "Muniaiyar *is* Siva coming in an angry mood." As Kapferer puts it, "[D]eities conceived of as superior incorporate lower orders in their beings" (1983, 124). My point is that the relationship of a Catholic saint like Santiyakappar with Hindu village deities was imagined in the same hierarchical and relational terms as that between different forms of Hindu divinity. Having been delegated limited aggressive power, Santiyakappar retained superiority and sanctity through the further devolution of his own inferior qualities onto the subordinate Hindu deity Muniaiyar, whose domain is included within that of the greater divinity *(periya cāmi)*. The relationship between the Christian and Hindu dimensions of divine power was resolved, for village Catholics, through hierarchical incorporation or, in Dumont's apt phrase, the "encompassing of the contrary" (1980, 239–45). From the Catholic point of view, the authority of St. James within his territory is absolute; Hindu deities are either subordinated or excluded—fleeing, we are told, to establish their realms in neighboring territories, beyond the sound of the church bell.[48]

Dumont (1959) argued that such hierarchical relations of divinity also symbolized the relations of caste society. The next chapter will revise this conception of the relationship between religion and caste. More presently pertinent is the argument that it is in relation to the sacrifice that the pantheon of village deities is ordered and hierarchized (Reiniche 1979; Shulman 1980; Fuller 1992, chap. 4). Put simply, the sacrifice is bivalent: its beneficial consequences (renewed life) are indissolubly linked to the danger and impurity of death. Yet Tamil Hinduism succeeds up to a point in conceptually and ritually distinguishing these two aspects through a system of complementary oppositions (Reiniche 1979, 217; Biardeau 1976); its mythology constantly attempts "to remove the deity from the arena of sacrifice without relinquishing the fundamental symbolism of the sacrifice" (Shulman 1980, 131). This conceptual trick is inscribed on the conception of Hindu divinity: Siva delegates a part of himself "to fertilize" the sacrifice by destruction, in the form of the violent inferior demon god. But this separation of the positive from the negative itself demands the consecration of the negative pole—that is, through the blood sacrifice that the inferior deity receives (Reiniche 1979, 207, 212).

In the Paschal Lamb, Catholicism brought a quite different Judeo-Christian tradition of sacrifice to Ramnad villages;[49] nonetheless, many of the basic hierarchical discriminations— nonviolent/violent, vegetarian/nonvegetarian, superior/inferior—came into play in ordering the pluralistic pantheon so as to isolate the superior Catholic divine from the "contamination of power," as well as to include forms of Hindu divinity as complementary but inferior powers. Alapuram Catholics implicitly ordered divinity in a way that admitted both continued interaction with Hindu deities and the reality of socially inclusive relations with Hindu neighbors.[50] If village gods are not contrary to the saints but included and controlled in their domains, what of the Hindu goddesses and the Virgin Mary, whom scholars often culturally and theologically interrelate (e.g., Clooney 2005)?

THE VIRGIN AND THE GODDESS

If you fear the father go to the son. If you fear the son, go to the mother. —GREELEY 2001, 101

Tamil mythology conceives of the goddess as a source of ambivalent power that, like the sacrifice, contains both the positive forces of life and fertility and the negative, dark elements of disorder and death from which they emerge (Shulman 1980, 141–42, 224). These elements are separated in local tradition and village festivals by splitting the goddess into her two aspects—the violent, hot, destructive (and usually ascetic virgin) form, and the benign, cool, regenerative (married) one (Shulman 1980, 267–94). In many Tamil villages (Alapuram included) the goddess exists in a dynamic state between these two forms, one located outside the settlement (or on its boundary), the other at its center. During annual festivals, the goddess in powerful virginal form (receiver of sacrifices and identified with Durga or Kali) is brought into the village in procession from "outside" in the shape of ritual pots (*karakam*) containing milk that are said to "boil over" with her power (*sakti*). As the festival concludes, the goddess transforms herself from hot independence to cool wifehood as Siva's consort (Beck 1981; Moffatt 1979, 246–70; Reiniche 1979, 151).

In Tamil Catholic imagination, the Virgin Mary has characteristics that resemble those of the ascetic goddess. Both have their mythic origin in, or are associated with, water and the "forest" (*kāṭu*)—places beyond the pounding sound of rice mortars (*ural cattam*), an index of village life and metaphor for sexual intercourse.[51] The Virgin, like the goddess, reveals herself through symbols of asceticism such as the matting of hair (*caṭai*), is manifest in the boiling over of milk (or *poṅkal* rice), and is attributed power over the rains (Mosse 1986, 445–46; cf. Mines 2005, 152).[52] And yet Mary has none of this goddess's heat or violence. Her power is quite definitely cool and absolutely benevolent. Her compassion and care of health and childbirth places her at the very center of family life, reaching to the intimate needs of women (Busby 2006, 83). Since Mary's spiritual power derives from the absence of sexuality rather than its ascetic control, she lacks the erotic energy associated with the virgin goddess. Imagined as a kanni, Mary is a perpetual prepubescent who never "flowered" (*pūkkavē illai*), who was denied sexuality and ultimately any part in the physical processes of female reproduction.[53]

Catholicism in Ramnad *does* retain the indigenous notion of the ambivalence of female power—fertility and life dependent upon dangerous and destructive sexuality—but, rather than resolving the paradox through the bivalent goddess, split into her dangerous erotic and benign married forms, it isolates the positive (health, life giving, fertility, and motherhood) in the form of the Virgin Mary from its negative underpinnings (dangerous sexuality, violence, and death).[54] The positive pole of the relational pairs is, in Dumont's terms, "substantialized." The virgin birth, the virgin mother of God (*teyva mātā*), and the celibate (holy) family stand at the heart of the paradoxical ideal of fertility without sexuality, life without death. The forces of sexuality (without fertility), on the other hand, are demonized and banished in the form of the serpent upon which Mata as the Immaculate Conception stands and, in some Tamil contexts, projected onto the Hindu goddess (Ram 1991, 63). In effect, the Virgin stands beyond relational identity and manifests a universal transcendent Catholic spiritual power, perhaps most especially at her east-coast shrine at Velankanni.[55] Here Alapuram pilgrims leave behind their localized imaginaries to participate in a global Catholicism and encounter the Virgin Mary shorn of identification with the goddess.[56]

Meibohm (2004) suggests that the softening of the image of Mata, the suppression of exorcism rites, and the purification, unification, and standardization of her representation can all be seen as the result of a historical process, driven by the Church and "modernity," that erased an earlier warrior narrative of the Virgin embattled with the goddess whose seat (kovil) she overtook (see S. B. Bayly 1989). If Catholics took Mata away from the ambivalent goddess, some Hindus took their virgin goddess toward the Christian Mata. The virgin goddess of a major katu temple outside a village near Alapuram, for example, is now known as Piracavappattiṉi Karumeniyammāḷ ("chaste goddess of childbirth"). The theme of spilling milk and of childbirth in her unusual origin myth parallels Velankanni Mata's.[57] The goddess is characteristically cool and indulgent; she turns the burning coals on which her devotees walk in fulfilling their vows into flower petals, and is tolerant of reproductive pollution that ordinarily angers ascetic goddesses of the exterior. Even the goddess's name, Karumeni, deriving from the *karumavani* beads worn by girls before puberty, suggests the kanni's absence of sexuality rather than its ascetic control. Whatever the particular path of cultural influence here, the Catholic Virgin and the Hindu goddess appear to incorporate the opposed "other" as aspects of themselves.

SAINTS AND THE FOREST: NONRELATIONAL DIVINITY

Saints as well as the Virgin have acquired nonrelational, absolute or "substantialized" identities. These often come from an association with the exterior or the katu (forest). An alternative conception of Santiyakappar, for example, locates his terrible dimension not in the figure of a subordinated Hindu god but in the saint's association with a world outside. Santiyakappar, it will be recalled, was brought to Alapuram in the form of a banyan tree from an exterior place—the shore-land (*kaṭal kāṭu*) shrine of Verkadu, where a golden statue of the saint had been rescued from the stormy sea by local Christians (Besse 1914, 298).[58] Planted by the village tank, the tree became the locus of the saint's awesome power. During the annual festival, Santiyakappar was imagined as reenacting this ritual journey from the wilderness to the village, his arrival on his horse proven by the hoof marks seen on the fresh sand once placed at the door of the church. This horizontal transition between the two valued spaces of "village" and "forest" is, Good suggests, in Tamil representations often equivalent to movement on the vertical plane of the axis mundi linking heaven and earth, which the tree also signifies (1991, 203–5; Malamoud 1976). The festival, like others, is inaugurated with the raising of a *koṭimaram* or "flag tree" that marks both the arrival of the terrible "saint of the forest" in the village and the movement of the saint from "inside" the church to his royal presence "outside" with his people (see chapter 4; Reiniche 1979, 93–95). In Hindu tradition, the kotimaram is itself understood as a tree deriving from the forest and associated with dangerous divine power (Reiniche 1979, 208ff), and at several Tamil Catholic shrines (including de Britto at Oriyur, St. Anthony at Puliyampatti) the flag post is both barrier to evil spirits and the focus of the exorcising power of the saints. The possessed begin to shake or "dance" as they approach the kotimaram (Sébastia 2008).

The village shrine and the forest, respectively "inside" and "outside," are then associated with two dimensions of the saint's power, the benign and the dangerous. It is the tree outside rather than the statue inside the church that (while still standing) was associated with Santiyakappar's fearsome power. During his street processions, the statue of the saint as "dharmic ruler" should not be fixed straight on his chariot but askew, since to confront the fullness of the his power "outside" would be to court danger. These polarities—inside/outside, village/forest, and statue/tree—find close parallel with conceptions of village deities (Reiniche 1979), but as we will see, they are also used to oppose Hindu divinity.

The Tamil katu—the open space of the territory, as opposed to the social space of the village—is not only the source of dangerous divine power but also the place of demons and, Mines (2005) argues, the location of disposed evil and the harmful residues of former actions and desires. The katu is furthermore the source of transcendence, where divinities manifest their "yogic," ascetic, or absolute dimension (Reiniche 1979, 220).[59] No longer a relationally defined combination of sanctity and power, here Catholic saints are absolutely good and powerful; and the equivalent manifestation of Hindu deities is as illusions, demons, or undifferentiated evil with which the saints are at war. It is the ascetic or hermit saints of the forest (*vaṉam*)—forest St. Anthony (Vanattu Antoniar), St. Paul the first hermit (Vanattu Cinnappar)—who are at the center of practices of exorcism. Their shrines are of the "forest," not in their location in the physical wilderness, but in being exterior for those who make the pilgrimages to meet the saints unbound by the protection of particular territory or interests (cf. Stirrat 1982, 401–6).[60] In the nineteenth century, the "forest" shrine of the martyr Arulanandar at Oriyur was the exemplar "sacred periphery" (Turner and Turner 1978, 254)—a border fort, the place of execution of criminals, a cemetery and tomb of a foreigner.

The ascetic saints of the forest—austere, self-controlled, and detached from desire—are suited to defeating possessing passions. Their regenerative abstinence contrasts the barren eroticism of the demons they defeat. The saint of exorcism is a superperson, a figure who, like Christ, demonstrates personhood enduring beyond death and dismemberment; the more disfigured and divisible the body, the more resilient and impermeable the sinless saintly inner person and soul. The saint, whole person in divided body, becomes a fitting figure to reestablish the self of the possessed—unstable, changeable, and multiply invaded by passion and paganism: whole in body but divided in person.[61]

Preeminently it is the martyr Arulanandar who turned power from endured suffering and violent death at the hands of Hindu persecutors against demonic forces. The site and instruments of his death became the focus of this power: the impaling stake was a locus of exorcism, and the executioner's sword, according to legend, had the power to drive out demons (*picācus*) (Saulière 1947, 477). At his shrine, Arulanandar is represented not only as holy ascetic (with wooden staff and crucifix) and tortured martyr (being beheaded), but also as embattled warrior with sword to hand. In fact, the dangerous and violent power of warrior saints battling with demons comes close to the disorder manifest by the demon deities themselves and whose attributes they take on by receiving animal sacrifices or (in some cases) possessing their devotees.[62]

This antagonism between Christian saints and Hindu deities in which figures such as Muniaiyar and Kali are confronted as demonic intrusions is the contrary of the hierarchical control and complementarity of the village. At exorcism centers, saints expose demon gods' power as false and illusory. Possessing agents claiming the identity of Aiyanar, Muniaiyar, or Kali, or adopting yogic postures as Siva, are ridiculed by the saint and forced to leave their victims, returning the possessed to their Christian selves. These Catholic centers and their saints also make this mode of dealing with malicious affliction caused by fierce gods (*pollata cāmis*) available to Hindus—to those who might otherwise have resolved affliction traced to offended deities by inaugurating a regular proprietary cult so as to turn a deity that is "exterior" to the group—dangerous and associated with the wilderness—into one that is their "own" (*contam*) and in relation to which they would accept subordination in return for protection (Reiniche 1979, 183–86, 193; see examples in Mosse 1986).[63] In other words, exorcising Catholic saints are incorporated by Hindus as a conception of divine good embattled with absolute evil, along with Western idioms of demonic possession—the naming of spirits or their cries of burning when confronting holiness. These characteristics then reappear in Hindu exorcism rites (Clark-Decès 2007).

At their forest shrines, de Britto and St. Anthony are figures in which the Jesuit missionary opposition to the darkness of all pagan "idolatry" came to be represented. De Britto's life was a struggle against Hindu power, a neutralization of the "sorcery of Brahmans" directed against him. According to one nineteenth-century legend, the Hindu temple in which he once spent a night was "miraculously cleft asunder" (Besse 1914, 296). After his death, de Britto became a warrior king and protector of the Christians of Maravarnadu; but the historical and legendary conflict between the saint and Hindu power (the king and pagan religion) was transformed into a battle against demonic threat so that Hindus as well as Christians were able to participate in the benefits of the saint's blessing. From the sacred periphery Arulanandar provided a spiritual rule protecting the Ramnad country from pēy picācu, in counterpoint to the rule of the Maravar king at the "mundane center"—the palace in the town of Ramnad.

We have then two polarities at work: first, for the possessed victim, in moving from the home/village to the saint's shrine there is a transition from the stable moral person of everyday life to the unstable multiple person controlled by externalized desires and beings most clearly evident when exposed to the power of the saint (and then back again following exorcism); second, in the conception of the Catholic saints, there is the opposite shift from the saint in "the village," defined by a hierarchical set of relations in which Catholic saints and Hindu deities exist as unequal but complementary powers, to the saint "in the forest," conceived in singular, absolutist oppositional terms, and in relation to whom Hindu deities can exist only as demons or illusions.

CONCLUSIONS AND IMPLICATIONS

From the seventeenth century, Tamil Catholicism took root by drawing on existing popular practice to produce a complex religious imagination adapted to the continuing ritual demands of caste, kinship, and the management of misfortune in rural Ramnad, while also incorporating a keen sense of the universal and exclusive nature of missionary Catholicism. I have first examined the interface of missionary disciplines and local religiosity in term of a tension between opposed notions of personhood, interiority, and affliction manifest historically in practices of confession and possession. Second, I identified a particular mode of reconciliation between Catholic universalism and Tamil cultural particularities in which converts dealing with a complex and confusing religious situation involving relations with Hindu deities, household or lineage gods, and pey-picacus alongside Christian faith discovered at certain saint shrines "the liberating precision of exorcism" (Brown 1981, 110), in which Hindus, too, could participate.

It is now possible to link the analysis of conceptions of divinity with a particular historical transition. The first point is that the centers of "diableries" that missionaries so disparaged dramatized the very absolutist and universalistic teachings that the Jesuits themselves were imposing in the late nineteenth century. Exorcism cults were not simply resistance to the missionary focus on sin, guilt, and confession. They dealt precisely with the Jesuits' twin dangers to the soul—pagan religion and human passions. The saints did directly and dramatically what priests achieved only imperfectly (and in burdensome manner)—the purging of inner sin, desire, and passion from body and soul. The saints' shrines were places where sin and suffering could be objectified as demonic (not as personal failure) and be visibly defeated. In this sense possession can be seen as confession's parallel, not its opposite.[64] If, borrowing from Foucault (1976, 61–79), we see confession as bringing something hidden to light and removing it as a form of offering, then possession is a "mode of confession"; both are "techniques of truth." One could go further and, following Taussig (1993), suggest that possession cults involved a type of mimesis.[65] The saints mimic the preaching and practices of the missionaries (whose deified persons they sometimes are), vividly reproducing the Christian experience of struggle against passion and pagan religion while radically reformulating it into a more immediate, this-worldly, embodied form.

Catholics in Ramnad from the late nineteenth century also had to reconcile an uncompromising missionary teaching with the social reality of coexistence with non-Christians. Arguably, the popular saint cults of exorcism helped in this reconciliation. The gods of their Hindu neighbors could be demonized, but only "in the forest." In the world of the village, Catholics would not allow the everyday battle between good and evil to be conceptualized as a battle between Christian and Hindu divinity. They would not (as coastal communities of Catholics in south India and Sri Lanka did) "posit Hinduism as an evil and invasive force responsible for sickness, misfortune and suffering" (Ram 1991, 62, 71; see Stirrat 1992). Moving in the other direction (as it were, from "village" to "forest"), the shift from thinking in terms of relations to thinking in terms of essences was also a shift from the particular to the universal that allowed accommodation of the concepts and values of missionary Catholicism or Tamil religious traditions. Catholics, I suggest, had two different ways of thinking about divinity—relational and essentialist—corresponding to two moral worlds—specifically, the relational, hierarchical world of "the village" and its opposite, the world of essences, absolutes, and transcendent values associated with "the forest."

Ramnad Christians, then, inhabited a dual moral world. On the one hand, Hindu village deities are controlled by the saints, and Hindu neighbors are incorporated into Catholic village festivals. On the other, Christian religion employs absolute identities and distinctions—for example, when villagers make distinctions between God (*kaṭavuḷ*), Jesus (*iyēcu*), and possibly Mata on the one hand, and all created beings (*paṭaippu*), including saints, angels, Hindu deities, and demons, on the other; and within this latter category separate off self-active beings (*akaṅkarikaḷ*)—that is, those with willfulness and caprice (*akaṅkaram*, Sk. *ahamkara*)—that are fierce or arrogant and have lost their power from God and been sent to hell (*narakam*). Here we find Satan, the fallen angels (*tuṉmaṉacukaḷ*, opp. *cammaṉacukaḷ*), and the harmful ghosts of the dead (cf. Deliège 1988). The term *cattan* (Satan) is sometimes used to embrace all of these, reassembling the different demons into a single figure. But it is hard to sustain such a religious discourse "in the village." Few if any Christians I knew consistently argued that the deities of their Hindu neighbors were "fallen angels" or forms of Satan. But while saints are imagined alternatively in relational and essential terms, God (*kaṭavuḷ*) and Jesus (*iyēcu*) participate entirely in the world of the Christian absolute.

In the category katu as the geometric space of the transcendent and "outside," Nobili's conception of Catholic religion as beyond the Tamil social world is worked out locally. Equally, Dumont's notion of the "outworldly" space of renunciation (*saṃnyāsa*) and devotion (*bhakti*) as the structural location of the absolutism of Christian devotion, faith, and fellowship as a "religion of choice" superimposed on the relational world of village society is now expressed metaphorically as the relationship between the *ūr* and the katu (village and forest). Village Catholics admit relations with Hindu divinity, but only within a restricted and subordinate domain. The values of complementary inclusion are, however, denied ultimate validity in a hierarchy of values that Dumont (1980) captured in his idea of "encompassment."

RECENT TRANSFORMATIONS IN TAMIL CATHOLICISM'S CULTURE

As the Catholic Church became institutionalized in Tamil society in the twentieth century, it had to respond to the contradictory post-Independence, post-

Vatican II demands to modernize and democratize, Indianize and Catholicize; to "inculturate" and to abandon cultural accommodations. The complex and still unfolding set of changes involved can only be alluded to here. First, there is the fact that although the Church in postcolonial India replaced its denunciation of "Hindu culture" with programs of inculturation and interfaith dialogue, Catholicism in rural Ramnad had by the 1980s become increasingly disconnected from popular Tamil religious culture (see chapter 4). There is a double paradox here. In the nineteenth century, the manifestly European churches, Latin liturgy, and foreign missionary priests of the New Madurai Mission, together with the emphasis on conversion and rejection of other religions that followed from the doctrine of *extra ecclesiam nulla salus* (no salvation outside the church), in fact went along with a deep, albeit disguised, interreligious cultural practice. Yet the late-twentieth-century move to indigenize that began with the 1969 Catholic bishops' conference approval of twelve points of Indianization, such as the use of local gestures or oil lamps and extended to Indian forms of art, music, architecture, and liturgy (Houtart et al. n.d., 300–301), occurred at a time when the Church articulated a fundamentally distinct pattern of Christian belief and social ethics, and when the religious lives of Christians and Hindus in rural Ramnad were in practice separating to an unprecedented degree.

I will not dwell on the inculturation movement that developed after Vatican II, since it was fairly marginal to the lives of Catholics in rural areas such as Ramnad.[66] In some respects the newly theologized "meeting point" of Christianity and Indian-Brahmanic culture was a reinvocation of Nobili, whether in the form of the sanniyasi tradition and Christian ashram movement of the Benedictine monks Henri Le Saux and Bede Griffiths, the "fulfilment theory" of Panikkar's *The Unknown Christ of Hinduism* (1964), or Brahmabandhab Upadhyay's notion of being Hindu-Catholic (see Kim 2003, 111). Inculturation involved the same Thomist-Nobili distinctions between revelation and reason, the unmanifest and the manifest, and faith and culture. But it also added different, Gandhian modes of spirituality, incorporating service and communal living, that refused the spiritual/temporal dichotomy (Clémentin-Ojha 1997). It also implicitly provincialized Hinduism in ways that Hindus took exception to (see Kim 2003, 117–18). But in practice the Church retained Roman form and aesthetics, tending to adopt the different view of culture of Joseph Ratzinger (Pope Benedict XVI) as an "ordering of values," so that "the church *per se* and the life of the 'People of God' are 'a culture' and a 'cultural agent,' that 'faith is a culture'" (Collins 2007, 8–9, citing Ratzinger 2004, 67). It was within this mode of culture that dalit theology would later be worked out as a critique of culture in the 1990s (chapter 6).

At the time of my first fieldwork in 1982–84, parish priests (Jesuit or diocesan) mostly deemphasized that realm of practical religion where shared Catholic-Hindu religious imaginaries had developed. Exorcism cults were suppressed because they were regarded as backward, uncouth, and superstitious rather than diabolical. The focus was on salvation and the social-justice aspects of modern Catholicism, on Christ and the sacraments, rather than on popular devotions and the saints. Saints were themselves now presented as exemplars of Christian life rather than as divine mediators, still less as miracle-working, demon-defeating power divinities. Their festivals were encouraged because they brought people to confession or as opportunities for social and moral education, not as celebrations of saintly power and territorial protection (see chapter 4; Houtart n.d.). In short, post–Vatican II movements of liberation and inculturation left little space for innovations in folk tradition and further decoupled institutional religion from village religion with its focus on tangible sacred power.

In some parts of the Catholic world this decoupling has led to a lapse from sacramental practice and a weakening of "Catholic culture" (Barnes 1982 for Indonesia), in others to a postcolonial second Catholic upsurge of thaumaturgical saint cults (Stirrat 1992 for Sri Lanka). Late-twentieth-century Catholic Ramnad witnessed neither of these. After the 1960s, participation in local cults and village festivals declined, although pilgrimages to regional Catholic shrines such as Velankanni grew along with the rise in major Hindu pilgrimages, whose devotional styles were often emulated—for example, the use of saffron dress and beads, blessings before the journey, and returning with transformed substances (oil, water, earth, salt, icons).

Instead, Pentecostal and charismatic forms of Christianity (Catholic and Protestant) became more prevalent and provided a new context in which sin and misfortune conceived in demonic terms could be directly confronted.[67] As Caplan (1983, 30) argues, Pentecostalism "provide[s] a Christian context for popular modes of explaining misfortune as well as a Christian means of dealing with it," where the Church is less and less able to do so. In these terms, the growth of Pentecostalism is viewed as an indigenous reaction against the liberal theologies of the mainline churches and their imported post-Enlightenment worldview, alien to both local cultural practice and biblical Christianity. Thus Hwa (2005, 51) argues that "[i]n moving to Pentecostal-charismatic versions of Christianity" people are "laying claim to a recovery of their own indigenous Asian world view which takes the supernatural seriously." Here the "inculturation paradox" is that while explicitly rejecting the theology of contextualization, Pentecostalism is a "most powerful contextualizing force for churches in the non-western world" (Hwa 2005, 53; Bergunder 2008, 249).

In the late 1980s, the Tamil Catholic Church appeared to be on the verge of a major transformation in which Christians would turn en masse from the rational but emotionally cold liturgical practice and social gospel to vibrant charismatic centers of certainty and healing. In the 1980s and 1990s self-labeled, locally supported, but internationally connected "Pentecostal" churches founded small congregations in villages such as Alapuram (see chapters 5 and 7). They shared a religious praxis that included a regime of daily Bible reading, fasting, healing prayer, and spontaneous experimental "spirit-centered" devotion and "eye-crying prayer" in which the role of the pastor is to elicit expressions of the heart (Bergunder 2005, 189; Still 2007, 65; Robbins 2004b, 126).[68] Doctrinally, such congregations are biblical fundamentalists who give central importance to faith, divine grace, and the presence of, or baptism in, the Holy Spirit (*paricutta āvi*), evidenced by prophesy, healing, and to a lesser extent speaking in tongues. They are led by pastors with considerably less education than the Catholic priests, but they give more importance to spiritual inspiration than credentials. They emphasize member participation over authority and depend upon local donations rather than institutional support (cf. Robbins 2004b, 130). These churches define themselves against the Catholic Church from which they attract members, rejecting sacerdotal authority, the rules and ritualism of liturgy, confession or Communion, and especially the celebration of festivals and the veneration of saint statues that contravene Christ's first commandment. One pastor told me, "[Roman Catholicism] is *religion;* this [Pentecostalism] is the *path.*" (*atu matam itu mārkkam*). But perhaps most striking is the emphasis on the personal, on linking faith to testimony, and on suffering and healing through direct divine intervention including exorcism, especially at large-scale gatherings.

Early in 1984, I cycled with an Alapuram friend to a shrine of Arulanandar (de Britto) in the dalit (Pallar) village of Pannitavayal to witness, amid a largely female crowd of several hundred, a process of exorcism quite different from that of the older saint cults. The event was congregational and focused not on the saint's statue but on Jesus. People were told to remove all amulets or other protection against demons, to open small bottles of coconut oil, and, holding these in their right hands, to tell their suffering to Jesus. Intermittently speaking in tongues, the prayer leader stated that God would change the oil into his own blood and that on hearing Jesus's name the *picācus* (demons) would run. As the devotional chorus gained momentum, many women in the crowd began to sway arhythmically, shrieking with hair loosened. Male Pentecostal leaders moved through the crowd, grabbing the possessed women by their hair and pressing crosses onto their foreheads, or aspersing holy water, threatening the demons, and saying that this is not water but the blood of Jesus. Over several hours the session transitioned from ordered preaching and prayer to a frenzied climax before order returned and many *pēy-picācu* had been driven out.

The Catholic parish priest tried to assert some control over this cult and its *sanniyāsi*-styled charismatic healer-exorcist by forming an oversight committee and requiring parishioners seeking exorcism first to obtain a letter of permission from him. By the 1990s, however, the cult had anyway been superseded by the larger healing ministry of a charismatic ex–Catholic priest, Fr. S. J. Berchmans, whose *jepatōṭṭam* (Prayer Garden) of the "Church of Truth and the Spirit" drew thousands of Christians and Hindus to healing events for some years before it, too, declined in popularity.[69] Berchmans's guiding principle—"worship in spirit and truth" (John 4: 24)—emphasized devotion, healing, and the power of the Spirit and erased all signs of Catholic or Hindu ritualism, recasting church sacraments in a radical Protestant form that emphasized personal salvation and spirituality.

Such centers notwithstanding, the anticipated Pentecostal transformation never quite happened in rural Ramnad. The Catholic Church did not overall hemorrhage members to new churches. Chapter 7 will explain the nature of the small congregations that did take root in Alapuram village and their part in various religious and social projects, but for now the point is that for most villagers Pentecostalism was conceptually contained within the exterior space of the "forest saints." Pentecostal participation was externalized from village society. The members of these churches in Alapuram were mostly outsiders, coming from other villages as individual believers (*vicuvācikaḷ*), perhaps seeking relief from anxiety, ill health, or relationship problems away from home. Attending meetings, but avoiding conversion or baptism, prevented jeopardizing family relations, marriage prospects, or access to education and other Catholic Church benefits.[70] The radical rupture and antifamily ascetic codes that some of the Pentecostal churches in the village enjoined (Robbins 2004b, 127) not only widened the gap between pastors and people, but placed these churches beyond the village as an external spiritual space.

At the same time Tamil Catholic churches have given place to charismatic practices *within* as part of the global Catholic charismatic movement, influential in India from the 1970s (Csordas 2007). The Church now embraces a diversity of religious styles, adapting the Mass to accommodate Pentecostal forms, organizing healing conventions, and embracing the "born-again" spirituality of a "personal relationship" with Jesus and inspiration through "spiritual gifts" or "charisms" (ibid., 297).

In Ramnad, Pentecostal styles combine with conventional Catholic piety. A few priests buck the trend against orthodox Catholic devotions and place themselves in the tradition of miracle-working missionaries. Father Selvaraj (pseudonym), parish priest in Alapuram at the turn of the millennium, for example, cultivated a capacity for visions (especially of the Virgin Mary), healing and driving out spirits through prayer and the power of his "consecrated" (*apiṣēkam*) hands (experienced as prickling heat). He occupied a world made open to the living God through devotion and discipline—especially prolonged fasting, prayer, and recitations, or being in the presence of the Eucharist—and revealed through divine tests and proofs. When I met him, he narrated the time when the village rice crop was saved from severe drought after he organized fasting, confession, and a prolonged adoration of the Eucharist by parishioners. He recalled making a pilgrimage to the Virgin at Velankanni on this occasion, then spending the entire afternoon in front of the Eucharist appealing to Jesus: "[I]f you are alive in the Eucharist truly send me rain before 3 P.M." (the moment Jesus was taken from the cross, Fr. Selvaraj explains, when "grace is flowing" to grant requests); then challenging St. James, that if he was really there he must with Mother Mary intercede.

> I was praying; at 2:52, I opened my eyes and saw through the half-opened door it was drizzling without sound . . . Is it true or is it a dream? . . . I fell down like St. Thomas, "My Lord," I told God, "it is not enough, it should be heavy rain" . . . [then] not heavy rain, but *very* heavy rain [came]. You know the glass in the roof . . . water fell over me from the church roof. I surrendered myself to God. I deeply got faith . . . At 3 P.M. I came out. I play[ed] the shuttlecock . . . I stood in the rain. I did not want to forget this [moment] forever. (Interview, November 2004)

Fr. Selvaraj later commissioned new statues of Mary and Jesus to be placed at the entrances of the church compound to commemorate the rainstorm miracle. Indeed, he had a passion for memorializing charisma and building new churches, often with overseas aid, as a testament to faith. For Fr. Selvaraj, the saints were still intercessors of the healing power of Jesus, but there was no direct harnessing of their ambivalent power defined and transmitted in Tamil cultural terms through substance or sacrifice. Rather, the saints were contained within a global Catholicism, their statues encased behind glass, interrupting the popular worship by touch (*toṭṭu kumpiṭuṟatu*), as part of Fr. Selvaraj's project to redecorate old churches, sweeping away the sacred grime of popular worship—the dripping oil, the wax, salt, and incense—to create the clean and shining surfaces that provide, as he put it, "the right spiritual atmosphere for prayer . . . and [to] feel the presence of God."

3

Christians in Village Society

Caste, Place, and the Ritualization of Power

More than anything, the relationship between Christianity and culture in south India has revolved around caste. Nobili's mediating space of "culture" between Christian and pagan was itself carved in the shape of the customs and distinctions of caste, and in regions such as Ramnad, Catholic practices were elaborated around the frame of caste. But what is caste, and what is it to Tamil Christians?

It is hard to answer the general question without rehearsing complex arguments that have preoccupied anthropologists and historians (not to mention politicians, social reformers, and activists) for a century or more, and missionaries for a lot longer, but have not produced any widely accepted theory. There are of course differently positioned representations of caste—Brahmanic, royal, colonial-administrative, Protestant, Catholic, and Marxist—and contingent historical processes have produced modern caste in different forms: as rank, division of labor, religion, or race.[1] What is taken as caste or *jāti* (Tam. *cāti*) defies both structural definition as "caste system" and revisionist characterization as "colonial invention."[2] It is regionally variable and has been profoundly shaped by ideological currents and social-political (and religious) movements. Caste reappears in modern institutions (such as the Catholic priesthood) in the absence of any of its putative ideological underpinnings, and is subject to endless creative elaborations, manipulations, and reassociations. Indeed, caste is often best understood as attachment, performance, or "composition" rather than as a sui generis entity, the caste names that recur in this book as networks of attachments bringing about action—"actor networks"—rather than essential or substantial identities (Latour 2005, 217).[3] Cāti is a matter of self as well as association; it is personal as well as political—relevant as family, as village, as the connections around church or temple, and as an affiliation in regional politics (Mines 2005, 55). Caste is both a mode of domination and a means to challenge that domination; a discourse of rank but also of rights. Perhaps caste can best be understood, following Mines, as a living sign—concept as much as material reality—whose meaning is "refracted . . . through different social lenses and existential orientations" (2005, 55).

These themes will be addressed in the chapters that follow, but one specific question needs immediate attention—namely, What is caste for Christians? Of course, the question itself is significant only if caste is seen as in some way religious. The image of caste as a Hindu religious institution if not actually part of Hinduism was, as we saw in chapter 1, produced in part by the exigency and discourse of Protestant missions in the nineteenth century. During the twentieth century this solidified into administration and theory as the dominant view of caste. It was held, albeit in opposed variants, by Mohandas K. Gandhi and by his political opponent Dr. Bhimrao R. Ambedkar, who eventually came to regard religious conversion as a precondition for dalit emancipation; and the Indian state's idea of caste as Hindu underlies the continued exclusion of Christian or Muslim converts from statutory concessions as "Scheduled Castes" (see chapter 5). For over half a century, scholars have worked under the influence of the anthropologist Louis Dumont, whose paradigm-setting *Homo Hierarchicus* (1980) was emphatic that the ideological basis of caste was to be found in the Indian religious ideas of purity and impurity, in terms of which the system as a whole was ordered and made sense to those within it. Dumont rested his idealist view of caste on an ontological separation of *religion,* which gives society its form and meaning, and *politics,* a secondary, ordered, and "encompassed" realm of cause and power. The distinction is itself ideological and represented classically in the hierarchical relationship between priest and king, Brahman and Kshatriya, purity and power. The partition of sacred religion and residual politics of course corresponds with Nobili's discourse, although crucially the Jesuits gave purity a functional rather than a cosmological significance, making it a matter *of,* not over, power. The difference is crucial, moreover, because Dumont's idealist formulation made the existence of caste among non-Hindus a sociological problem, just as it had become a missiological problem for Protestant churches (and would become a subject of policy debate around reservations in post-Independence India).

A consequence of framing caste as religious is that the associated practices among convert groups are regarded as residual "hangovers" from a Hindu environment (Dumont 1980, 203). As Caplan, working on Tamil Protestants, concluded, Christians may have caste, but there is no caste system among them. The ideas, metaphors, or practices of impurity are purely vestigial (Caplan 1987, 151).[4] Fuller (1976), working among Kerala Christians in the 1970s, gave this kind of position greater conceptual clarity. He drew a distinction between "orthopraxy" or the "set of rules concerning caste and pollution" that Christians shared with Hindus, and their "theologies," which diverged (and in between was a common "caste ideology" interlinking status and power). There is no place, Fuller points out, among Kerala Christians for impurity either as a notion of bodily pollution or in relations between *Christian* castes. In Nobilian fashion, caste is divorced from religious ideas and relegated to the realm of politics.

Much culturally Western scholarship on Christianity and caste assumes that religious affiliation is the primary mode of social identification when in fact kinship, kind (jati), and place (*ūr*) can easily be taken as prior to religion in making Tamil persons. As determinants of caste, we may add residence and occupation; but socially speaking, which god a person worships or believes in has never been considered a criterion determining caste identity (Krishnan 2011). Despite "communal" legal-political constructions and an elite Christian discourse (Mallampalli 2004), the Church in south India failed to engender separate social-political identities except among coastal fishing communities, where Catholic religion and caste became mutually defining (S. B. Bayly 1981; Ram 1991). The "imagined community" of Christians lived alongside other religionists within villages integrated through the ritual-material exchanges of caste. And within particular castes (in the 1980s) "Hindu" and "Christian" existed as (mostly) nonintermarrying subgroups. Religious affiliation reinforced prevailing rules of subcaste endogamy or introduced another one.[5] But while caste endogamy was rarely broken, cross-religion marriage was not uncommon, a woman usually adopting the religion of her husband (converting prior to marriage).[6] Marriage across religion reproduced both the stability of the subcaste category and the patrilineage village as the matrix of faith.

Of course, making religious identity critical to the analysis of caste, or even, conversely, insisting on caste over religion as the primary identity, mistakenly suggests that the key problem to solve is "which grouping [religion or caste] is *preferable* to start a social enquiry" (Latour 2005, 28 [original emphasis]). The difficulty is that adopting one identity as real renders the other(s) artificial or irrelevant, when life is full of overlapping identities and affiliations historically shaped by various institutions, whether kings, kovils, census records, or reservation lists. The central concern of this chapter would be better stated as the Christian influence on the experience of caste. The Jesuits' ecclesiastical question of how Christianity can "accommodate" caste has become the ethnographic one of how caste has "accommodated" Christianity as part of its "fabrication mechanism" (Latour 2005, 31). Instead of viewing caste as a cultural residuum undissolved by Christian conversion, I ask how Christian ritual contexts have become part of the way in which an indigenous social order is produced and changed.

To understand the shifting relationships and identities assembled and contested as *cati,* and to explore the tension between the social "being in the world" that foregrounds such sociality on the one hand, and the demands of Christian religion on the other, I need to return to my time in the Christian-Hindu village, or *ūr,* of Alapuram.

A CHRISTIAN TAMIL *ŪR* AND ITS PEOPLE

Studying Indian villages has rather gone out of anthropological fashion in recent years (Gupta 2005). With deeper historical engagement, scholars rightly regard foundational ideas of their discipline—traditional India and its "village republics"—as significantly a product of colonial imagination, administrative reordering, and the legitimizing discourse of British rule.[7] Feminist anthropologists, moreover, point out that in patrilineal society, villages provide an overly male-centered perspective on social life (Lambert 1996; Raheja and Gold 1994). There are, however, good reasons to return to villages, not to discover "traditional India," but to grasp key dynamics of social reproduction and change. Even those who have long ago migrated to distant urban centers come to be "placed" in Tamil social reckoning (by their interlocutors) with reference to their "native village" (*conta ūr*)—geographical placement being the interrogatory means to identify a person's (caste) identity. Both place and caste remain central to the conceptualization of belonging and the effects of power in Tamil society. Turning, then, to Alapuram as a site for the cultural production of caste and power, let me begin with what I discovered of its historical coming into being.

In December 1982, Julia and I arrived in Alapuram from Madurai via the ancient Catholic center of Sarukani to the north, on a crowded bus that lurched along a particularly pitted and many times repaired road, passing the Christian shrines and burial grounds that interspersed village temples—reminders of the statistic that 15 percent of the district's population were Christian. But nothing quite prepared me for the far-off sight of the dome of the Church of St. James (Santiyakappar), modeled on St Peter's in Rome, rising out of the brilliant green sea of paddy fields and marking the place of the cult of the miraculous banyan tree so extravagantly described in Jesuit letters of the 1730s.

It was Catholic Pallars who narrated the legend (chapter 1) in which members of their founding lineage brought the saint in this form to Alapuram from his coastal shrine at Verkadu. One descendant, Arulappa, told me how four brothers of the Koilan *vamcam* (family) had carried their crippled sister on a bed to Santiyakappar's shrine in search of healing. With a mile to go, they rested beside a tank under a banyan tree. When the brothers returned from relieving themselves they found the girl up, washed, and ready with a meal. "Come, brothers, let's eat," she called. Astonished, they continued their pilgrimage. A European priest told them to stay at the shrine for ten days to receive Christian instruction.

On leaving for Alapuram, the priest allowed them to take one cutting from the tree (when they cut a second, it died), which they planted beside the village tank, erecting a thatched hut for the rosary and the saint's statue they also brought.

The incorporation of this popular shrine into the Jesuit mission, and its patronage by Ramnad rulers, were explained in chapter 1.[8] It was the Maravar caste village headmen, not the shrine's subordinated dalit (Pallar) founders, who became its protectors and trustees and were linked politically through festival honors (below) to their co-caste political overlords, even when by 1800 Maravars generally were no longer Catholic.[9]

In the eighteenth century, Alapuram's Pallars were dryland farmers or de facto cultivators of tank-irrigated land over which Maravars held superior rights. Another Catholic group over whom Maravars exercised control locally were Nadar (Naṭar) palmyra workers, who around the time of de Britto in the late seventeenth century converted along with Pallars, possibly as dependent clients of Christian Maravars. Evidently Maravar cultural forms and religious affiliations had influence, and even now the internal caste organization of these subordinate groups—their arrangement into exogamous matrilineal clans (*kiḷai*, "branch")—reproduces the structure of the ruling caste (cf. Good 1981).[10] As Alapuram grew through immigration during the eighteenth century, its social makeup diversified. Pastoralist Kōṉārs began to settle (putatively escaping the tyranny of a Ramnad ruler); high-ranking Veḷḷāḷars were appointed to the office of village accountant (*karṇam* or *kaṇakkupiḷḷai*); and Catholic Vellalars, who had converted in the seventeenth century, arrived from old Christian centers in the west to take up the caste-specific office of *kōvilpiḷḷai* (catechist)—*piḷḷai* being an epithet for the Vellalar caste.

As we sat on the tank embankment while he sharpened his carpenter's adze, "Tile House" Arulappa Pallar told me how just as his caste had lost political control of the Santiyakappar shrine to Maravars, they had lost sacerdotal power to Vellalars:

> An old Pallar woman Muccala used to come every evening to ring a "bell" made from an eating bowl (*vaṭṭi*) as worship (*pūcai*) for the saint by the banyan tree. One day a young Vellalar widow traveling north to Thajavur to escape male suitors stopped under the tree. Seeing Muccala's pucai, she called her and asked, "Why are you not worshipping the saint properly with the correct prayers (*mantiram*)?" Muccala asked how it should be done and said to the Vellalar that since she knew how to worship the *cāmi* she should stay in the village. Pallars built her a house, gave her land, and provided her with rice, in return for which she conducted the daily worship for Santiyakappar.

This story, narrated in the context of Pallar political assertiveness in the 1980s (see chapter 5), also captures the way in which the incorporation of Alapuram into the Jesuit mission (by 1800) involved the promotion of Vellalars as transmitters of proper Christian worship.

During the nineteenth century Alapuram, like other Tamil villages, took on a more caste-differentiated and hierarchized form as it also attracted artisan groups such as Catholic Ācāri carpenters, and low-status service castes. The latter included barbers, washermen, and oil pressers (Vāṇiya Ceṭṭiyār), "untouchable" Paṟaiyar weavers and drummers (converted by Anglican SPG missionaries in the 1940s), and Cakkiliyar leatherworkers. Some of these were dependent groups "settled" by upper-caste patrons with whom in the 1980s they retained relationships marked by the use of fictive kin terms.[11] But most significant for the unfolding structure of this and other villages in the area was the arrival of skilled Catholic Uṭaiyār cultivators displaced by war north of the Cauvery River, who were granted rights to cultivate tracts of highly productive black-soil land by Ramnad kings.[12] Their commercial success would drive significant social change in the nineteenth century (see below).

The Utaiyar oral historical interpretations of their settlement stressed the superiority of their agricultural knowledge over that of local Pallar cultivators,[13] while the latter emphasized to me their own naive generosity to incomers in narratives of dispossession through trickery. Not only did the mythic Pallar matriarch Muccala give Vellalars their ritual authority, but her largesse in property made Utaiyars into the landlords who would later enslave Pallars. These tales gloss a historical process that saw rising populations, expanding cultivation, and new relations of landlordism, tenancy, and agrarian servitude consolidated in nineteenth-century Ramnad under British rule (Mosse 2003). The arrival of further subdivisions of Alapuram's main castes swelled the village to a recorded 775 people in 1881, increased to 1,106 in 1961. The Alapuram I surveyed in 1984 had a resident population of 1,704 (328 households), half Christian and half Hindu, distributed through no less than nineteen different castes (table 1; for comparison with 1994, see Mosse 2003, 186).[14]

While Alapuram was an agricultural community for most of its history, in the last thirty-five years the village has grown as a commercial center, serving hinterland villages and connecting to local market towns. It had a church-run school from the 1920s, a bus service from 1965, and a weekly market from the late 1990s. A cluster of roadside provisions stores and teashops, grain traders, tailors, and cycle-repair and vegetable stalls spread from the hub of the bus stop, where we unaccountably stepped into Alapuram life at the start of the fieldwork in 1982.[15]

Like many outsiders coming to Tamil villages, I was first introduced to Alapuram through the social geography of its streets and lanes (map 2). Between the sacred and public center—the church and its compound, the convent school, and the encircling procession and commercial street—and the cultivated fields lie caste-segregated streets, trailing off from the church or fanning out from the

TABLE 1 Population and caste composition of Alapuram Village, 1983–84

Jati (subcaste)	Caste-ascribed occupation (*toḻil*)	Religion* (number of households)	Number of households	Resident population	Percentage of resident population
Paḷḷar	laborers/cultivators		83	447	26.2
Āyyā		R.C. (1)			
Āmmā		Hindu (14), R.C. (62), Pentecostal (6)			
Uṭaiyār	cultivators	Hindu (27), R.C. (35)	62	325	19.0
Kōṉār	shepherds	Hindu	43	250	14.7
Nāṭār (Nadar)	toddy tappers	R.C. (21), Protestant (4)	25	111	6.5
Maṟavar	headmen	Hindu	16	104	6.1
Veḷḷāḷar			23	102	6.0
Kārkaṭṭu (Vīrakoṭi)	accountants	Hindu (8)			
Cōḻi	"betel cultivators"	R.C. (4)			
Koṭikka	catechists	R.C. (11)			
Tōṭṭi Paṟaiyar	drummers	Protestant	23	99	5.8
Necavar Paṟaiyar	weavers	Hindu	21	86	5.0
Paṇṭāram	priests/florists	Hindu	5	30	1.8
Cērvārar	watchmen	Hindu	5	29	1.7
Ācāri	carpenters	R.C.	4	23	1.3
Vaṇṇar	dhobi or washermen/washerwomen	Hindu	3	19	1.1
Vāṇiya Ceṭṭiyār	oil pressers	Hindu	3	17	1.0
Ceṭṭiyār	merchants	Hindu	4	13	0.8
Poṭera Vaṇṇar	(dalit) dhobi/barber	Hindu	1	14	0.8
Ampaṭṭar	barbers	Hindu	1	10	0.6
Rāvuttar	merchants	Muslim	2	10	0.6
Cakkiliyar	leatherworkers	Hindu	2	8	0.5
Muslim-R.C. Nadar**			1	6	0.4
TOTAL			357	1,670	99.9

* R.C. = Roman Catholic.

** Mixed-marriage category without caste-ascribed occupation.

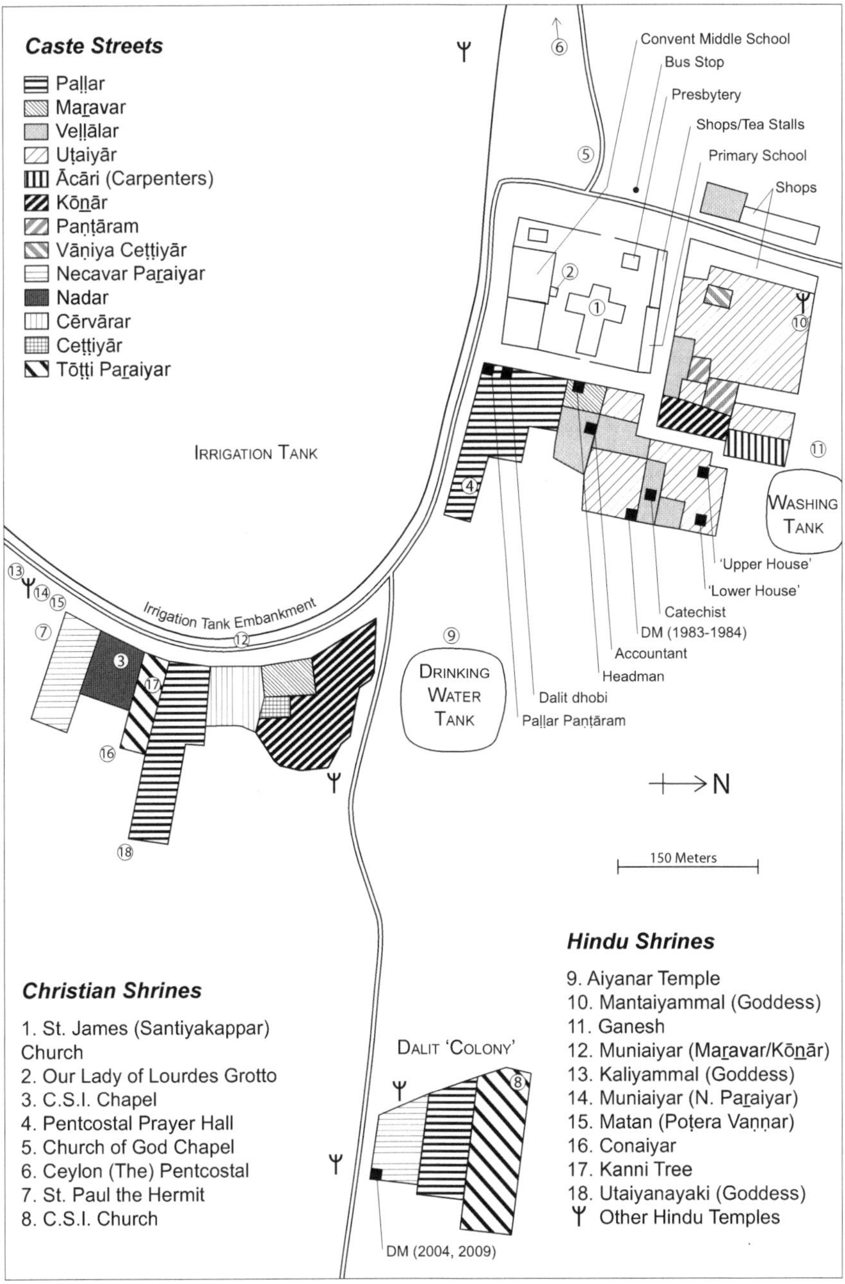

MAP 2. Sketch map of Alapuram showing caste streets, churches, and temples. ("DM" indicates the author's fieldwork residences.)

FIGURE 5. The "upper house" in Alapuram village, 1983. Photo by author.

embankment of the great irrigation tank. The main village comprised two residential areas. To the north and east of the church were the upper-caste Utaiyar and Vellalar streets (Catholic and Hindu) and clusters of the households that offered them services: carpenters, oil pressers, dhobis, temple priests. Towering above others were the houses of two Catholic Utaiyar landlord families—the "upper house" and the "lower house" (*mēlvīṭu* and *kīḻvīṭu*) (figure 5). Both were built to impress: one from the profits of extensive sharecropped land (the residence in 1983–84 of the village's largest landowner, "BA"—so named as the village's first graduate); the other from labor contracting on rice-growing estates in 1930s Burma, from where teak beams and columns were brought to uphold these mansions.[16] Modest in comparison were the still-grand houses nearby of the old elite, the former hereditary village officials: Maravar *ampaḷam* (headman) and Vellalar accountant or *karṇam*.[17]

To the south, separated by a small gap and thorn bushes, were the distinctly poorer Catholic Pallar streets, some sixty houses plus their separate specialists—dhobi and Pantaram catechist. In the 1980s, the more common palmyra thatch had only recently been replaced by tiled roofs, "Tile House" Arulappa's being the first. Farther down the cart track running along the tank embankment was Alapuram's second settlement. The northern section clustered houses of the shepherds (Konar), the Maravar Panchayat president and kin, and the Cērvārars

FIGURE 6. Children in Paraiyar (dalit caste) street in Alapuram, 1983. Photo by author.

(holders of the old watchman office or *kāval*).[18] To the south was another Pallar street (Catholic and Hindu), then the cramped thatched housing of two Paraiyar "untouchable" castes (Protestant Tōṭṭis and Hindu Necavars) (figure 6). Between them stretched the street of the Catholic/Protestant Nadar toddy tappers—to whom, playing on stereotypes, were attributed the business sense to have placed themselves amid their low-caste customers. Here also were two leatherworker (Hindu) Cakkiliyar houses. In 1983–84, Paraiyar families were resettling to the east with government grants, creating anew the spatial segregation of the "untouchable (dalit) colony" that is stereotypic of Tamil villages. Then truly "outside" (but within my village study) were the twenty or so families of Nari ("fox") Kuṟuvar "gypsies," who for three to four months after harvest made Alapuram their base for an itinerant trade in knife sharpening, trading trinkets or treatments (see Mosse 1986 for details on this group).

This imaginary walk through the village produces an ideal sociospatial order that was a recognizable public representation of caste order long before it was an ethnographic objectification. Indeed, for all important affairs the village would be assembled through representatives as a sociogeography of caste streets. But the street itself revealed caste as a matter of family and neighborhood, and of shared living. Houses with inner kitchens but open verandas were packed into often narrow lanes, allowing mutual arrangements for the care of children; for the chores of collecting water, fuel, or manure; and for grazing cattle, stacking straw, sun-drying chilies, or parboiling paddy rice in the open spaces. Belonging to their street and sharing their house for eighteen months made me part of a Catholic Utaiyar joint farming family who also ran a small teashop at the end of the street in front of the church. Our porch (*tiṇṇai*) was a shared space for winnowing grain, depositing infants, chatting, or dozing during the summer "fire-star" (*akkiṉi naṭcattiram*) days when life slowed to the meditative pace of the rice-straw-chewing bullocks gradually diminishing the stack in front of our house. In one direction we looked out across the paddy fields to the Pallar streets, and in another to the *urani,* the village drinking-water pond onto which women converged, returning along the narrow field ridges precariously balancing clay water pots on their heads. The cloudy suspension from this pond was the sole domestic water supply. It was separated from a second pond for bathing and for cattle. Both were filled from the intense monsoon runoff in November and thereafter accumulated and concentrated the impurities that caused so much gastric ill health, including my own. Caste "street corners" were public places for men or youth, but also spaces of exclusion and discrimination of caste "others" (below).

Hindus in Alapuram marked their residential belonging through annual collections for neighborhood cults to gods and goddesses. As caste collectives they also gathered paraphernalia for the worship of their separate, fiercer deities at rarely noticed shrines of trees, stones, or tridents, outside the settlement in fields, by the roadside or tank "bund," either annually or when misfortune intruded as a reminder of neglected divine guardians (cf. Mines 2005). Then, as members of regionally dispersed clans, they traveled long distances to the temples of their lineage gods (*kula tēyvam*), tracing in reverse the patterns of migration made to the village by earlier generations, so as to perpetuate a substantial connection to their soil of origin (Daniel 1984).[19] Others had brought their clan gods closer by carrying soil (*piṭimaṇ*) from these shrines and creating replica temples in the village. Hindus of the village also came together to worship the village deity Aiyanar, although by 1983–84 this caste-integrating festival had been attenuated and fragmented by defections arising from disputes over ranked temple honors.

Christianity, on the face of it, had the social effect of reducing such clan and territorial belonging (evident in ill-remembered rules of clan exogamy) and weakening the link between worship, kinship, and place. A few Christian families retained cults to preconversion lineage deities, some villages in the parish had caste-segregated churches, and several Catholic kin groups were affiliated with pilgrimage centers or formed communities of worship around local protector saints, especially Vanattu Cinnappar (St. Paul the hermit), who came closest to a kin-territory protector deity. After the birth of a child that rewarded a vow to this saint, for example, Philomena's family brought soil from de Britto's Oriyur shrine and planted a cross for Cinnappar at the edge of their rice field. Annually or at moments of collective need such as drought, her neighbors and kin joined together to honor the protector saint. This was but a weak echo of the shared substance and place involved in Hindu kula teyvam cults.

Alapuram Catholics did not, however, fail to imagine social belonging in sacred terms. Rather, they did so through affiliation with Santiyakappar (St. James), who as a kind of universalized kula teyvam integrated different Christian castes into the idealized "vertical" continuity of an ancestrally/divinely founded lineage/place.[20] The saint not only replaced clan or caste deities, but was the primary village deity (kirama teyvam) for both Christians *and* Hindus, defining belonging and interrelatedness in a distinctive way. To use the Tamil distinction that Daniel (1984) draws our attention to, Santiyakappar defined Alapuram not as an administrative village (*kirāmam*) with a mapped boundary, but as an *ūr*— a ritual center with a frontier, marked if at all by shrines at points of vulnerability. But his kovil did not just represent the village symbolically; it shared a quality of Tamil deities/temples by standing for the village metonymically as "a part which suffuses the whole village" (Mines 2005, 32). It was as if the localizing substantial connection between divinity and group, suppressed at the level of the lineage or caste, reappeared at the village (ur) level, indexed by the saint tree rooted to the village, his church and its compound materially connected to the protected territory (cf. Beck 1972, 121). We see this evident and encouraged by missionaries such as Father Gnanaprakasam, who in 1806 notes in his diary that, "having had no rain that year nor water even to drink, [the villagers] had a meeting in order to decide upon what is to be done in order to obtain rain. It was resolved that they should at once rebuild the ruined wall that surrounded the church compound. As the bricks were ready they at once set to work. Scarcely was the wall finished when a heavy rain fell on the country and gave them a plentiful supply of water for the fields and for drinking."

In particular, the ur was "a community of co-sharers" in the worship of the saint and corecipients of divine protection (as Stein [1980, 454] notes of the Hindu temple context). The saint's annual festival in the seed-sowing month of Āṭi[21] was for centuries a "meta-social event" (Mines 2005, 100) involving the self-representation of the village (according to those in power) as an order of ranked castes, as well as the principal occasion for contestations that remade this order (see chapter 4). Imagine: on 25 July of any year from the 1730s until the 1930s, at the climax of the festival after the great chariot procession with the statue of Santiyakappar has returned to the church, amid a jostling crowd of many thousands and against the din of drumming and shouting, the village gathers to receive the blessing of the saint and various marks of distinction or honor (*mariyātai*). Here a well-understood enactment of social ranking takes place in which each section of village society is honored with prestations of betel, sandalwood paste, and garlands of cloth—grace-conveying substances of status-related quantity/quality. First honors are announced for the kovil (the church), represented by the Vellalar catechist or kovilpillai, and for the rulers (Maravar chiefs and representatives of the king), heralding the village as a protectorate of God and of the sovereign. Then the village as an administrative kirāmam is presented through its set of hereditary caste-linked office holders—the Maravar village head, the Vellalar accountant, the head of the Konar shepherd caste or *mukkantar,* and the Cervarar watchman.

Next, the village is announced as ur—cosharers in the worship of the saint. Here it is the upper-caste donors of the festival—Vellalar and Utaiyar Christians or the *ūḷḷūr* ("inside ur")—who receive betel honors inside the church, standing as devotees in the place of all recipients of the saint's protection. Lower-caste Pallar Christians, not until 1924 admitted as donors and therefore cosharers, are included only as village servants along with other *kuṭimakkaḷ* or "sons of the village," an idiom of subordinate inclusion marked by the receipt of betel honors after the ullur Christians and *outside* the church or standing on its steps.[22] Kutimakkal included representatives of the Acari carpenters/blacksmiths (who alone of the village servants received betel *inside* the church) along with the village washerman and barber, the Pallar grain measurer/water turner, Paraiyar drummers, and Cakkiliyar leatherworkers.

These festival honors (and their spatial ordering) indexed a series of distinctions—ruler–ruled, center–periphery, inside–outside—that were hierarchical in Dumont's (1980) sense of the superior/center "incorporating" or metonymically standing for the inferior, as upper-caste people of the *ūr* stood for the *whole* village, encompassing the "outer" Pallars and kutimakal who served them (as Mines described the social logic of Tamil temple worship [2005, 56]). But we can also see these honors as having been a kind of "political talk" (Latour 2003), essential to the changing definition and interrelationship of social groups and, as the next chapter shows, the focus of contestation. Before that, let me explain the way that caste as relationship, service, and division of labor was encoded and enacted in Alapuram.

CASTE SERVICE AND THE IMAGINED ROYAL ORDER

The anthropologist A. M. Hocart first described caste as a matter of service, an arrangement of officers, ritual specialists, and menial servants that was a necessary provision for ordered village society. This was idealized in a royal idiom such that "the king's state is reproduced in miniature by his vassals: a farmer has his court consisting of the personages most essential to the ritual, and so present even in the smallest community, the barber, the washerman, the drummers" (1950, 66). Hocart regarded the hierarchy of ritual specialists and menial servants as required, in the first instance, to serve the deities in the shrines protected by the ruler, and so stressed the religious nature of service. Chapter 4 returns to the idea of caste as a ritual order serving a Catholic saint as sovereign enthroned in his kovil. Let me first explain a recurring model of caste as a set of services, rights, and titles granted by the king and organized into a system of economic production and redistribution.

From precolonial times right up until Independence in 1947, production and revenue in Ramnad was structured around a system of shares—for the ruler (often subject to religious gift), for cultivators, for the church/temple, for a set of caste-specific village officers (headman, accountant, etc.), for artisans (carpenter, blacksmith, etc.), for barber and washerman, and for "untouchable" servants—Pallar water turners (*nīrpācci*), grain measurers (*kuṭumpaṉ*), woodcutters and gravediggers (*veṭṭiyan*); Paraiyar drummers and funeral servants (*tōṭṭi*); and Cakkiliyar leatherworkers (*pakaṭai*). To these were allocated quantities of grain on the threshing floor, threshed or in the sheaf, from each harvested field.[23]

The details of this system do not matter here, although in 1983–84 it remained a well-etched social memory in Alapuram among those who had been its key players. (I recall, for instance, the glee with which Susai the old Pallar grain measurer explained how with the connivance of the village head he managed even under the watchful eye of revenue officials to cheat the estate of its full share, shoveling grain into a pit concealed under the threshing floor.) In essence, the share system dramatized the presence in village-level production of the major stakeholders in Ramnad village society—the royal or Zamindar overlord, the temples/churches, the village heads, pastoralists, and dependent service groups. The shares (*vāram*) had an expressive effect that became a mode of religious legitimation by reference to the saint's festival. Honorary shares for the cultivators (*kuṭi cutantaram*) were, I was told, held in recognition of their obligation to pull the saint's chariot, the carpenters' to repair it, the washerman's to provide ceremonial cloth, and so forth (see also *Cramam*). The share system publicly enacted the same graduated caste rights and associated ceremonial offices as the Santiyakappar festival, encoding the status of recipients (who as office holders stood for their group) through the grain-share quantity, form (threshed or in the sheaf), or mode of allocation (solicited/unsolicited)—the Pallar measurer receiving paddy in his straw cushion, the washerman on a winnowing fan, the leatherworker in the sheaf. And this referenced other acts of public sharing such as the apportionment of sacrificed animals: for the priest/church or headman, the thigh; for the washerman, the head; for Pallars, the "large guts"; for Paraiyars, the "small guts"; and so forth. The transactions of the village threshing floors and saints' festivals together highlighted a caste organization of agricultural production that assigned a hierarchy of entitlements to all sources of village wealth (land, water, produce).

The representation of the caste order as a royally instituted division of labor and graded rights was further dramatized through presentations made by caste representatives at the palace in Ramnad during the annual festival of Navarattiri. This order was summarized in the ideal-typical nine offices or *kuttuvakaiyār*, who constituted the village establishment. The old Alapuram village accountant recalled assembling such a group to travel from the village to the palace. It comprised the Velar potter with a bundle of pots filled with rice carried by a Pallar man; the Acari carpenter with coconut shell spoons, cutters, and buttermilk whisks; a Nadar with palm leaves for manuscripts; the village Pallar kutumpan carrying firewood and a pumpkin; a Totti Paraiyar with palm leave baskets and fans; and the Cakkiliyar leatherworker with fish skin and cowhide sandals. The group was led by the mukkantar head of the shepherd caste with goat and ghee. A similar ritual of social (re)presentation was made by Sarukani villagers (chapter 1) for their "lord," the Catholic priest (holder of the royal gift and king's representative), at the Christian New Year. Each caste representative received cloth, sandal paste, and betel "honors" from the palace or the presbytery as they made their *cantippu* (a presentation to a great personage [Fabricius 1972, 339]).

These were set pieces in a theater of power acted out at village, church, temple, or palace. As such the caste order they represented was also markedly divorced from actual social reality. A complex economy that by the mid-1800s involved private property and regional markets was publicly paraded as a system of rights in productive resources defined by caste and political-royal connections (Ludden 1985, 165–69; cf. Parry 1979, 82–83).[24] The Santiyakappar church (kovil) would have an important role in working out the contradictions between representations and reality generated by the shifting patterns of economic and social power in the village. Two changes were especially significant: first, the rising economic power of Catholic Utaiyar cultivators contending with Maravar-controlled village governance in the nineteenth century; and second, the struggle for economic independence of (dalit) Catholic Pallars in the twentieth century.

Catholic Utaiyar incomers made a success of dryland cotton and groundnut cultivation on black soil, benefiting from secure property rights and new markets encouraged under British rule. Their economic power challenged a pattern of Maravar political dominance (see Mosse 2003). Since fixed rents on dryland crops evaded the caste-controlled share system, Utaiyar cash-cropping simplified economic relations and weakened links tying the village to the Maravar ruler-Zamindar in Ramnad. The biggest Utaiyar landlords in Alapuram privatized control of common property, labor, and village services (ibid., 205–6) and by the 1930s had taken possession of large tracts of Maravar and Vellalar wetland, some acquired through litigation in lieu of debts. "Ranked economic rights revolving around Maravar caste power gradually became absolute economic rights" (ibid., 208). At any rate, late-nineteenth-century missionary diaries record an uneasy balance in Alapuram between Maravar political dominance, Utaiyar economic power, and the status of Vellalars as holders of the prestige offices of accountant and catechist.

By the time of the first post-Independence revenue survey of 1958, Utaiyars (20 percent of the population) owned a third of village's wet land and 60 percent of its dry land. Agricultural and nonagricultural resources had became concentrated in the hands of a few families within this and other dominant castes, their influence increased and extended to co-caste members through privileged links with the bureaucracy, politicians, and the market, by which they were able to exert a measure of control over access to essential inputs for agriculture, education, urban employment, and other scarce resources (ibid., 204 et seq.).[25] In this context, the distinction so evident in 1983–84 between "upper caste" (*mēl cāti*)—also including Konar shepherds and Ceṭṭiyār merchants—and "lower caste" (*kīḻ cāti*)—Pallars and Paraiyars, the principal dalit castes of the village—acquired its meaning as an ordering underpinned by economics and opportunity. Only after Independence would this as a structure of economic order be changed by Catholic Pallar mobility (chapter 5).

The point is that when my elderly interlocutors set out for me the system of grain shares they had experienced in the 1940s, they described what had long been changed from a redistributive village system into dyadic transactions between upper-caste landlords and their serving barbers, washermen, or carpenters—the kutimakkal (cf. Mayer 1993). In other words, a set of relationships actually driven by economic change, class division, and land-based patronage was still (well into the 1960s) articulated and recognized through the "old order" idioms of royal authority, shares, and generalized village service, explicitly referencing caste identity and rank. Landlords expected kingly tribute (cantippu) in the form of caste-typed gifts, from their laborer and tenant clients: woven mats from Paraiyars, firewood or pumpkins from Pallars, for example, at the harvest festival of St. Anthony, when dependents received shares from the landlord's ceremonial ponkal rice pot. And tied Totti Paraiyar households were expected to carry out funeral service, to drum when accompanying family members fulfilling vows at saints' shrines, and to dispose of the carcasses of dead cattle (women singing laments over the dead animal), which were flayed and passed to leatherworkers. The mythic redistributive order was repeated and repeated: in the shares apportioned on the communal threshing floor; in the gifts and receipts for village headmen or accountants at the festival of Ponkal; in the presentations at the palace; and above all in the duties and honors at the Santiyakappar festival, where ceremonial caste offices and insignia passed between serving lineages.[26]

Economic power became social dominance through the invocation of a long-gone royal-political order, using the template of its caste identities, occupations, asymmetrical transactions, substances, and gestures. And it was the inexact mapping of actual socioeconomic relations onto the public representations of power that created a particular cultural politics of caste, above all at the festivals of the Catholic saints.

CASTE, OCCUPATION, AND SERVITUDE

In Alapuram in the 1980s, when Utaiyar and other patrons gave carpenters, blacksmiths, or dalit caste servants their annual grain-share entitlements, known as *cutantaram* (or *cuvantaram*), they were not only paying a salary (*campaḷam*) for work done, but indicating the hereditary right (*urimai*) and the caste-specific qualities of the actor in fulfilling their particular role (Good 1982).[27] Caste was an occupational identity. As a village carpenter, one of four Catholic Acari caste brothers, Rayappar received twenty-four measures of paddy for every pair of plowing bullocks owned by his farmer patrons as a matter of right, irrespective of the amount of work he actually did. In 1984, this cutantaram covered only essential maintenance work on plows and other farm implements (*vivacāyam āyitam*). But when, as often, I stopped by his house on my way to the washing pond, invariably he would be working on a door frame, a table, or a new plow, which he described, using the English word, as "private" work, paid for separately in cash (*tāṉikkācu*). Any carpentry done for farmers from *outside* the village or for the few dalits who in 1983–84 owned draft cattle was also paid for in cash (or with a rooster and one day's free plowing labor in the case of Pallar cultivators). Evidently, certain kinds of work, and work for certain *kinds of people,* fell outside of the purview of *cutantaram.*

As a village Acari (the carpenter caste), Rayappar was also caste-qualified to conduct house-building rituals that marked the key moments of laying the foundation and raising the door frames. These divined and dealt with forces of good or ill fortune—through embedding items such as a margosa stake or a little gold, the breaking of coconuts, the lighting of candles, and signing crosses with sandal paste.[28] In recognition of this ritual service at the door-frame ceremony of one Antonymuttu Utaiyar, Rayappar was handed new cloth, betel, and raw food items used in the ritual along with a live rooster—all referred to as *taccaṇi* (or *taṭcaṇai,* Sk. *dakṣiṇā*), which denoted a gift transaction modeled on that between patrons and prestigious ritualists such as Brahman priests, who are *not bound* by obligation to serve their employers (see below).

Village artisans and servants (barbers, washermen, drummers), too, had *cutantaram* entitlements. They could also claim caste-coded *unmeasured* "handouts" (*kaipiccai*)[29] on the threshing floor of their patrons. The Pallar measurer (kutumpan) could scoop grain from the pile he was measuring into a straw cushion (*vaṇṭu*) on which he rested his knee, and receive (on request) a quantity of paddy in the *marakkāḷ* measure that symbolized his office. Barbers, washermen, and others could also solicit such *kaḷattupaṭi nellu* or "threshing-floor-measure paddy" (distinguished from *cutantaram* paddy) from those they served, along with cooked-food handouts from their patron houses on special occasions. For dalit laborers especially, soliciting handouts[30] was expected of them as a mark of their obligation to serve and the rights of the "lord's house" (*aiyā vīṭu*) over the dalit family's labor, as well as the reciprocal expectation from dalits of patronage and financial protection. Sebastiar Pallar remembered how after a grueling day's work on the threshing floor he was expected to plead, "Sir, my chest aches all over, please tell [give] me something" (*aiyā, neñci ellām vaḻikkitu ēṉakku colluṅka*); and a Paraiyar friend of mine, Mohan, knew well that, having accepted kalattupati rice, any family member could be called to work without wages at his "lord's house" to store grain or straw, watch irrigation ditches, or help at weddings (figure 7)—and that he was always expected to prioritize work on the "lord's" fields over his own (sharecrop) cultivation. For poor households, the value of sweepings was not insignificant, perhaps enough for two adults for a year. But Mohan was under no illusion that the more he received, the greater the extent of obligation; he also knew that building relationships with patrons was necessary to secure money at times of crisis. Although such patronage was crucial to family welfare, recent dalit feminist writing reveals the intense exploitation and vulnerability of dalit women to sexual harassment in these relationships (e.g., Bama 2005). In this context, caste-linked occupational specialization was unmistakably an idiom of domination, especially for dalits.

When staying in Alapuram in 1983–84, I mapped a pattern of hereditary interfamilial patron-client relationships of the above kind reaching back three generations between the so-called *kaḷamputikkira vīṭu*s ("house-that-take-from-the-threshing-floor"), which included most dalit households (67 percent of Pallars and 84 percent of Paraiyars), and their upper-caste *aiyā vīṭu* ("lord's house").[31] This form of patronage and dependence reflected livelihood insecurities prevalent up to the 1960s—an uncertain labor market, seasonal shortage of labor. It was enabled by, among other things, the lack of class identity among landless laborers on account of complex land-tenure arrangements that widely distributed interests in cultivation. Moreover, economic relationships were fused with caste identities through repeated ritual action and a public discourse that articulated economic dependence *as* caste inferiority while making servitude definitive of social identity. This was generalized into a public code of inferiority and untouchability.

One aspect of this was systematic separation and exclusion. Until the 1960s, Pallars and Paraiyars in Alapuram were denied any kind of honor. They were refused entry to public places such as temples, or public roles as festival donors. They were excluded from the houses of upper castes, from the services of the village barbers, washermen, or catechist, and from equal access to the village

FIGURE 7. Utaiyar wedding preparations, 1983. Photo by author.

water sources other castes used. In the 1940s Alapuram Pallars and Paraiyars were forced to draw water from separate parts of the common pond using palmyra baskets so that their mud pots did not "pollute" the water, and to bring separate boards for laundering so as not to touch the washing stones. They were barred from village teashops, being served in separate tumblers or coconut shells while standing outside in the sun. Denied drinking vessels at upper-caste houses, they received water poured into their cupped hands. Those who had to pass through upper-caste streets to reach the school and shops were forbidden to ride bicycles, wear sandals, or carry umbrellas; and earlier still (before 1906) Pallar and Paraiyar women in Alapuram were forbidden to cover their chests in public, the female body being a site of assertions of upper-caste masculine power and "degraded [dalit] female value" (Rao 2009, 67–68).

This untouchability was enacted through Christian worship. Pallar subordination was dramatized at every imaginable public moment of Catholic ritual in the village. Pallars were seated separately in church, received Communion after upper castes, and were not allowed to read lessons, lift the processional statutes, or pull the saints' chariots at festivals. Their funeral biers and graveyards were separate, and in some villages of the parish, dalits had separate churches.

Pallar and Paraiyar inferiorization was a matter of language, too. Members of these castes recalled how they were obliged to use honorific terms for *mel cāti* (upper-caste) individuals regardless of age, and likewise to be addressed in the dishonorific "tu" form. For elite Maravars and Vellalars they used religious and courtly forms of address, such as *cāmi* (lord, god) or *nācciyār* (mistress—of a servant), while in relation to others (Utaiyars, Acaris) they used kinship terms denoting more intimate forms of subordinate incorporation as "sons" or "nephews" (Mosse 1986, 166, 232–36; cf. Levinson 1982). The "habitus" (Bourdieu 1977) of subordination entailed not only the matter of clothing and unclothing, but also everyday submissive comportment, as well as extreme demonstrations such as prostration at the feet of their *aiya vitu* lords on the occasion of a death in their own families.

The elevated status of upper-caste Catholic and Hindu households was marked by the possession of dependent clients and their dramatized caste subordination. Correspondingly, dependent inferiority and the denial of autonomy ideologically constituted rather than simply described the identity of Pallars and Paraiyars, who personified subordination. They were objects of the ordering principles that defined dominance (Dirks 1987, 279; 1990), their internal organization (of clans), their codes of conduct—even the adjudication of conflicts within their communities—were all made extensions of the order of dominant groups (ibid., 274–75, 279). Where various rights and honors defined status for upper castes in themselves or in relation to the deity, a saint, or the king (Hocart 1950), dalit rights to subsist existed only in relation to service rendered to patrons (and to the wider village).

While control and order are idioms of dominance in the discourse of power, disorder, danger, and impurity are idioms of subordination. At least, such is the view of theorizing anthropologists who have sought not the outer form (as I have here) but the inner reasons of caste, especially as a system for the social management of disorder and the dangerous residues of life.

PURITY, POLLUTION, AND RITUAL SERVICE AMONG CATHOLICS

In Dumont's famous conception, castes in India separate, specialize, and rank themselves with regard to matters of purity and especially impurity, which ultimately arises from the "the irruption of the biological into social life" (1980, 61). The functional specialization of barbers, midwives, or funeral drummers extends the temporary impurity of birth or death into the massive permanent impurity of certain categories of people. This, together with the secondary concept of nonviolence (its derivatives and metaphorical associations), creates occupational distinctions around meat eating, fishing, even oil pressing, and transitive ranking through the acceptance or refusal of marriage, food and water, and other exchanges. The earlier-mentioned village-integrating system of patronage and specialist service—often named as the *jajmāni* system—for Dumont primarily allowed the management of pollution and the maintenance of purity. Raheja's (1988) reformulation shifted Dumont's focus on hierarchy and impurity to a concern with "centrality" and "sin" (or rather a cluster of negatives including inauspiciousness, evil, and impurity) in which unequal social relations are enacted through nonreciprocal transactions—gifts (*dān*) that transfer negative effects such as sin from dominant donors to recipient clients.

Raheja is an ethnographer of Rajasthani society, but the paradigm has proved influential in the Tamil south as well. Mines is thus able to describe upper-caste transactions with kutimakkal households, including the various gifts and cutantaram payments, as the exteriorization of harm. In life-crisis rites particularly, negatively valued, harmful, and "transformative substances" carrying bodily and life residues of the givers are passed onto those who are constitutively "other"—that is, the kutimakkal and dalits, who (from the "inside-ur" point of view) are part of the wild, chaotic exterior or katu, and so appropriately qualified (or constituted) to receive and imbibe (consume, digest) such dangerous residues. Life-crisis rituals in particular, Mines says, involve "exteriorizing practices" by which upper-caste "urmakkal render . . . themselves dharmic or orderly while also rendering kutimakkal and katu adharmic or chaotic" (2005, 69). Despite the shift in idiom from hierarchy to exteriority, from pollution to chaos, or purity-impurity to dharma-adharma, this analysis retains the logic of Dumont's argument. The difference and ranking among castes (from the upper-caste perspective) arises from transactions that are in all but name organized around dealing with purity and impurity as condition and effect.

These models, moreover, offer an *interactive* view in which caste rank is performatively maintained through exchanges of substances. Mines, in particular (following Marriott 1976 and Daniel 1984) explains that material transactions between peoples (and deities, places, or seasons, for that matter) are "transformative" in the sense that they have bio-moral effects. Kutimakkal take on the "gross" transforming substances of their landlords, especially those thought to carry the bodily substance of the givers such as cooked food, hair, or soiled clothing, but the patrons receive only "'subtle' non-transformative returns in the form of work, service and obedience" (Mines 2005, 57). Through transactions, all people take on the qualities of those with whom they interact, but the "intimate, yet asymmetrical connections" between urmakkal and kutimakkal inferiorize the latter, being marked by the expelled parts of their upper-caste patrons. Transition rites of puberty, and death especially, heighten and dramatize this transmission of negative residues in "poisoned gifts" (Raheja 1988) to appropriately constituted "others."

Do Tamil village Christians also articulate the social inequality of caste in such cosmological terms? The best way to answer this is to examine Catholic practices around that most crucial site of disorder, impurity, and the dangerous residues of life—the rites of death.

A CATHOLIC FUNERARY RITUAL

In the early hours of 22 November 1983 the church bell begins to toll and a distant wailing announces the death of Santanammal, an elderly Catholic Utaiyar woman. Until dawn the pounding of a sole *tappu* drum travels through the night streets of the main village. By the time I approach to pay my respects, removing my shirt and tying my *tuṇṭu* (shawl/towel) around my waist, her body has been laid out under a canopy, a lamp by her head, rosary in her hands, and crucifix above her head. In the final days of her illness, the catechist had been called to say prayers, the parish priest had performed the last rites, after which her relatives kept watch with quiet laments. The Paraiyar drummers who beat the melancholic rhythm through the night are joined by a funeral band from the neighboring village who drum out dance steps—although without the raucous sexual choreography that Clark-Decès (2006) describes—as relatives arrive with the customary gifts of cloth and rice, summoned by the family's Paraiyar servant. The village barber comes to conduct the "water garland" (*nīrmālai*) ceremony. He takes Santanammal's sons and daughters to the village tank for a purifying bath (fully clothed) and to collect water to prepare the body. The chief mourner, garlanded and wearing a reversed sacred thread, carries the water in a decorated clay pot (prepared by the barber) in procession under a white sheet provided by the village washerman and accompanied by relatives and the funeral band. The barber oversees the preparation of Santanammal's body: sealing of eyes and mouth with turmeric and betel, tying threads around limbs, the libations of oil and powder poured onto her head, and dressing her in her finery, with a coin on her forehead for the washerman. She is placed in a decorated bier (*acanti*),[32] and we wait for the Catholic priest to bless the body.

He arrives in black vestments accompanied by the Vellalar catechist and altar boys carrying crosses and lighted candles. After he has solemnly walked around the body, anticlockwise aspersing incense and holy water, the bier is taken up with a burst of sound. The church bell tolls, Paraiyar women keen (*kulavai*), and the barber sets off a clatter of firecrackers as the drummers lead the procession to the church. There suddenly the noise ceases.[33] The barber and the Paraiyars wait outside as the bier enters the church and is rotated to face away from the house and toward the altar, where the priest—now in white vestments—conducts the funeral Mass. He changes into black to sing the *Libera me Domine* and again blesses the bier. Once outside the church, the barber and band again join the cortege, which proceeds noisily to the cemetery, reaching a crescendo as the body is lowered into the grave, dug in this instance by relatives but usually by Paraiyar or Cakkiliyar servants. (Women do not usually follow to the grave, and if they do they stand apart with heads covered.) The priest completes the liturgy, asperses holy water, and is the first to shovel earth into the grave (although his presence is not essential, and other relatives often recite prayers). The barber cuts the threads and removes her jewelry. Money and betel leaf are placed on her body and collected by the Paraiyar funeral servants. The barber shaves the chief mourner's head and removes the sacred thread. Candles, incense sticks, and pots of embers are left burning at the grave as the men retire to the tank's embankment to arrange payments for the specialists (barber, washerman, Paraiyar drummers).[34] They take a purificatory bath before returning to the house. The family return to the grave on the third and sixteenth days to "wash" the grave, install a cross, and complete further ceremonies at which the Vellalar catechist officiates (see Mosse 1996).

The ritual structure of such a Tamil Catholic funeral accomplishes the transition necessary for the "good death" explained in chapter 2. A standard repertoire of symbolic materials, "reagents," and basic procedures are deployed to effect this transformation (Good 1983, 225).[35] The funeral also involves a particular structure of ritual service. The village barber officiates as "funeral priest," preparing the bodies of both mourned and the mourner; the washerman is required to provide cloth and the Paraiyar funeral servants to carry pots of burning embers, drum, keen, and sing laments. Key to this service is the obligation as a matter of custom (*vāṭikkai,* as it was put to me) to accept substances—rice kept near the body, cloth for the shroud, food prepared by relatives—equivalent to those described as "transformative" or "polluted" by the impurity (*tīṭṭu*) of death. During rites of first menstruation, too, when Christian girls in transition are considered in a vulnerable state, likely to attract evil spirits (pey-picacu), kan tirusti ("evil eye"), and other agents of misfortune, the same specialists perform procedures akin to Mines's (2005) "rituals of removal" of these harmful influences. In what is sometimes called the *vaṇṇan caṭaṅku*—"dhobi ceremony"—the washerwoman removes the steamed rice, sweet snacks, and other edibles used in the ritual that might be thus construed, prior to the auspicious part of the ceremony, where the girl is honored by her maternal uncle or *māmaṉ* (cf. Good 1991, 194–98). Catholic life-crisis ritual reveals a structure shared with Hindus. But what, if anything, do Christians have to say about such rites of removal?

THE GOOD AND THE BAD *(NALLATU-KEṬṬATU)*

For Tamil Catholics, death is the most important of the several moments of life transition, when "the good" and "the bad" have to be separated through ritual action. Consider the following.

When Xaveriamma died on 21 September 1983 after a long and fruitful life, and her body had been washed, adorned in a fine sari, hands clasped around a rosary, a picture of Our Lady of Good Health (Arokkiyamata) by her head, her younger sister placed a small pile of paddy at each corner of the mat on which her body lay. Her son and his wife knelt at her feet, the son holding a lamp and his wife a full measure of rice. The couple walked around her body anticlockwise three times, kneeling at her feet each time they passed. Her *marumakaḷ* (son's wife) gave a circular wave (*ālātti*) of the rice measure before her dead mother-in-law and touched it to her now uncovered clasped hands, before taking it into the house. The four piles of rice at the corners of the body were then removed by the dalit washerman-barber.

When later I inquired, the family told me that the full measure of rice was mixed with the seed rice for the following season; it was Cītēvi, while the four piles of rice removed by a ritual servant were Mūtēvi. They said no more; but I knew that in everyday Catholic usage Citevi and Mutevi (the goddess personifications of good and ill fortune) referred to those influences that result in worldly success or failure. Moreover, Citevi was spoken of as a property of persons or households that could be lost, leaked out, or unwittingly transferred to another through transactions—especially, it appeared, nonreciprocal transactions across boundaries—day and night, light and dark, inside and outside, this season and next season. Shopkeepers feared the loss of Citevi if they sold certain items (salt, cotton thread, needles, limes) or anything on credit at "lamp-lighting time"; landlords, having given a sharecrop tenant part of the harvest, took back a handful to prevent the departure of Citevi; and Citevi was also lost if cooked food was taken out of the house at night, if seed rice was given or sold before sowing was complete, or in any transaction taking place across a doorway.

If Citevi passed with the substance in a transaction across such boundaries, so, too, at the funeral rite marking the most significant boundary of all. The dead woman's marumakal performed alatti—an encircling action that Dumont suggests always precedes the receipt of something (1957, 224–25)—with a full rice measure in the same way that her *māmi* (mother-in-law) had many years earlier at her puberty ceremony. Here it is the positive influences of the old woman's past fertile life—her Citevi—that passed to the household through her daughter-in-law. But crossing the boundary between this world and the next also releases the negative influences/effects of the lived life—its Mutevi—trapped in the four piles of rice at the corners of the mat and then transferred to the low-status barber or the Paraiyar funeral servants.

Generally, ritual practice of this sort does not present itself as symbolic action open to exegesis, which is hazardous to attempt. Explicit statements by Alapuram Christians on matters like purity and pollution were always ambiguous or evasive. Transitions such as puberty involve vulnerability to harm, but there is wide variation in the protective practice undertaken. Many Christians told me in 1983–84 that such things were no longer important: girls were not, as earlier, secluded at first menstruation; the mud pots of the house were not broken on the thirtieth day after childbirth; and various domestic purificatory rites were much attenuated. Perhaps worries lingered most around the "virgin pollution" (*kaṉṉi tīṭṭu*) of puberty. Christian girls ought not to cook or fetch water, but the apparent "pollution" restrictions or special diets were usually glossed in quasi-medical terms as "for hygiene," or appropriate to the special bodily states (cf. McGilvray 1982b; Caplan 1987, 150–51). Later, in 2009, I found that the contemporary failure to follow these traditions had become part of a narrative of the modern weakness of the female working body.[36]

It is fair to say that Alapuram Christians emptied out life-transition rites of any specific symbolic content. Yet the rituals were still structured by meaningful opposition. They not only effected certain changes, but also communicated social differences by consistently discriminating between the positive and the negative; and dealing with the latter involved specialists appropriately different and inferior in relation to those they served. In other words, what mattered was the "oppositional idiom" (Quigley 1993, 32–33), not the symbolic content, and this repeatedly aligned dalits with service functions, "disposals," and social subordination.

This logic of ritual service and caste rank appeared in the early 1980s to be worked out in Alapuram with peculiar exactness. Village barbers, washermen, or drummers would not provide their services to those whom they regarded as socially inferior. Lower-caste Christians therefore found alternative officiants. Murukan and his son, who belonged to a dalit dhobi or Poṭera Vaṇṇar caste, served Catholic Pallars. He lived in their street, received cutantaram grain from them, and was also a Tamil Siddha medicine practitioner. But Murukan himself would not serve the Protestant Paraiyars, who for a while patronized members of a different Āmmā Potera Vannar caste living in their lane and acting as their "funeral priests."[37] By 1982 this arrangement had ceased. Unable to find suitable caste "others," Paraiyar affinal relatives or *cammantis* had assumed the specialist functions (cf. Raheja 1989, 95).[38]

"PURE" PRIESTS AND CATECHISTS

As Hocart (1950, 11) first noticed, the barber's role as "priest of the cremation ground" on the first day of a Hindu funeral is often complemented and opposed by the role of the Brahman priest in the purificatory rites of the final day. Dumont cast the distinction as the pure in relation to the impure. Catholics did not employ Brahman priests, but the role of the barber "funeral priest" was nonetheless complemented by that of the Vellalar-caste catechist or *kovilpillai*. Like the Brahman priest, the kovilpillai had a ceremonial role in "assisting" the soul on its journey and returning the mourners to normal life. He officiated at household rituals for the dead *after* the burial—for example, reciting prayers and aspersing holy water at the final funeral rite (or *kallaṟai caṭaṅku*) before mourners returned for their final purificatory bath. In earlier times, the Alapuram kovilpillai conducted a widow's rite of "purification" in the church after her marriage emblem or *tāli* had been removed by her in-laws beside the tank (or, as I witnessed it, dropped in a dish of cow's milk). Father Gnanaprakasam's diary for 7 October 1896 records that "the [Utaiyar caste] widow and relations go to the church. The kovilpillai opens the door and recites the Salve Regina. Inside he throws holy water on the widow. . . . She is clad in white and not in the kandanghi [cloth in colors]. Then she returns home. During the Salve Regina candles are lighted [in the] church."[39]

The kovilpillai was at one level associated with the honored dead in whose name food was prepared or offerings made. Like the Brahman, he was a worthy ("pure") recipient of the gifts and implicitly identified with the ancestors (*pitṛ*) (Kane 1974, 460). As well as reciting prayers for the souls of the dead and reading out their names during the "Mass for the soul's peace" at the festival of All Souls, the kovilpillai received gifts of rice referred to as *tarma cōr* (*tarumam*—a gift given in lieu of a deity or ancestors) when families cooked rice in honor of their dead—as Sebastian Utaiyar did every Wednesday in 1983–84 for his father's soul. The kovilpillai received a share of the money paid to the church for prayers and lights for the dead as well as small amounts of paddy placed on the graves along with candles and incense after they had been "washed," decorated, and blessed by the Catholic priest as part of the All Souls ritual.

Like Brahman purohits, kovilpillais were employed for household and domestic rituals. They recited prayers for the sick or dying, blessed the newlyweds and first communicants. They mediated between people and the priest, accompanying him or conducting worship in his absence. As well as teaching catechism, preparing children for their first Communion, and assisting in meetings of religious associations,[40] kovilpillais held privileged ritual roles in church ceremonies and festivals (leading morning and evening prayers, ringing the church bell) and handling sacred objects.

While themselves distinguishing sharply between religious meaning and social rank, Jesuits established the ritual office of kovilpillai in a manner that evidently reproduced in Catholic form prevailing ideals of priestly status and caste rank. Kovilpillais and their co-caste members did indeed preserve a superiority of rank. First, their exchanges with upper-caste Catholics (the urmakkal) fell outside the cutantaram patron–client relationship. Apart from a salary from the priest and grain shares accepted on behalf of the saint from royally gifted land, the various *nonwage* gifts kovilpillais received fell into the category of *tarumam*, gifts conferring merit on the giver, in contrast to the obligation-bound "threshing floor" grain handouts (kalattu nel).[41]

Second, until recent decades kovilpillais acted out caste rank by not entering the houses of inferior-ranked Catholic castes (Nadars and Pallars) to say prayers—waiting outside if accompanying the missionary priest—refusing cooked food from these castes, or rice from their graves at the festival of All Souls. Ever-pragmatic, Jesuits arranged for Pallar and Nadar Catholics to have separate catechists known as *paṇṭārams*, who, until the 1940s, "mediated" between these inferiorized castes and the missionary priest—effectively "replicating" the ritual services of the kovilpillai, at least for domestic rites including funerals. They received the same kind of gifts and a half share of "prayer cash" and St. Anthony ponkal rice.[42] The Pallar lineage who held this pantaram office were of a different, reportedly superior, Āyyā Pallar subcaste from the majority Āmmā Pallar Catholics they served, further reproducing the logic of priestly rank.

In their life-transition rites, it seems clear, Christians in Alapuram reproduced a structure of ritual service that was also used to organize church services and offices. In fact, Alapuram, as witnessed in 1983–84 or remembered by my informants, showed a double reproduction of this structure of Tamil ritual service—among Christians *and* among the excluded dalits. Caste roles and identities (such as the barber and the catechist) were systematically differentiated through rites that hierarchized services in relation to the almost universal association of transition with heat and danger (impurity) and the return to normality with coolness and purity; and which involved pan-Indian notions of the high status (if not purity) of the domestic priest and the inferiority (if not impurity) of barbering and funeral service. Moreover, the social production of the extreme inferiority of Pallar, Paraiyar, and Cakkiliyar "untouchables" made use of a cultural semantics that connected their caste-defined work (*toḻil*) to the death of higher beings, whether humans or cows (funeral service, grave digging, announcing death, watching over suicides, beating drums made of calf hide, cattle scavenging, leather work), or warding off evil spirits (by drumming) (Moffatt 1979). In 1983–84, the consumption of carrion beef was recalled as a particularly potent inferiorizing practice. But while Christians reproduced a structure of ritual service, they refused the commonly associated meanings that were indeed denied by their faith.

CASTE AND CATHOLIC RELIGION

Catholicism brought distinctive values, teachings, ritual experiences, and connections to Alapuram village. Purity and pollution and allied cosmological notions found no justification in Catholic theology, either in themselves or as the basis of essential differences between people. Jesuit missionaries sharply distinguished moral fault (sin), having salvational outcomes, from other effects and influences on Tamil lives. Only the sacraments of the Church could be personally transformative by disposing of the effects of sin that attached to the eternal soul; all other matters—*tiruṣṭi, tīṭṭu, karumam* ("evil eye, pollution, karma")—were either denigrated as superstition or secularized as matters of social convention, prestige, or pride.

Christianity can in fact be regarded as bringing about two effects on Tamil rites: one was to hollow out other meanings while retaining the ritual structure, and the social distinctions that this marked; the other was denial to these distinctions of any ultimate significance. This denial also found ritual expression. Thus, while Catholic death rites to a degree separated out the life-enhancing and the dangerous residues of life—for instance, as Citevi and Mutevi—they also relativized these distinctions as relevant only to the living, and so trivial to the essential funerary purpose. After all, for the Christian, fortune, health, and prosperity cannot be guaranteed *in this world.* Wealth and poverty, fertility and infertility, purity and impurity, like the distinctions of caste, were, in relation to transcendent goals, merely worldly concerns, represented by undifferentiated rice to be removed in the transformation of an ordinary death into the ideal sacrificial death of the saints.[43]

The arrival of the priest at a funeral marked this shift away from concern with managing life's residues and to the sin that attaches to the soul and can be destroyed only through the atoning death of Christ made present at the funeral Mass. Those who, like Xaveriamma Pallar's family, could not afford the considerable expense of a funeral Mass in church accomplished the same identification with Christ's death by chanting the text of Mary's lament as they shouldered the body in the bier in which the Corpus Christi statue was carried in the Good Friday procession (figures 8 and 9).

From a Christian point of view, there is no impurity in death. In the rites conducted by the Catholic priest, the ambivalence of death was marked by signs of sorrow, somber respect, or inauspiciousness—black vestments, anticlockwise circumambulations—not of danger or impurity,[44] and the Tamil spatial logic of center and periphery collapses when the procession from house to cemetery

FIGURE 8. A Catholic Pallar funeral procession halts while a lament is sung, 1983. Photo by author.

takes a corpse that would desecrate a temple into the sacred center of the church for Mass. While the Vellalar catechist retained caste "purity" in relation to ritual office, the Catholic missionary priest abandoned the distinctions of caste entirely. Representing values external to the distinction of pure and impure, he, unlike the catechist, attended the graveside ritual and entered houses of low castes and those exposed to the "pollution" of death. Perhaps like the Lingayat Jangama priest described by Dumont (1980, 402), the missionary priest transcended impurity, which was abolished in his presence.

Generally in Alapuram, persons in dangerous "impure" bodily states were not restricted in their contact with the Catholic sacred. As well as the bodies of the dead, women after childbirth or during menstruation freely entered the church and received Mass—although there may be exceptions in practice (see Caplan 1987, 150). For instance, some in Alapuram were hesitant about attending Communion following sexual intercourse, without appropriate delay and washing.[45] Sex, along with sin, defined inappropriate states for Catholic worship. Of course, there was no question that members of any caste could touch the statues during ordinary worship.[46]

Modeled on the missionaries, the Catholic clergy in the 1980s presided over a domain that stood apart from cultural processes of Tamil society. Formerly, priests had mostly been foreigners (Portuguese, French, Goan), whose sacerdotal

FIGURE 9. Good Friday procession of the body of Christ, Alapuram, 1983. Photo by author.

power derived from celibacy, from social apartness, and especially from ordination and office. After all, only the liturgical words of an ordained priest can allow the presence of Christ in the Eucharist (*naṟkaruṇai*), or the removal of "birth sin" (*jeṉmapāvam*) and the birth of the soul through baptism. The priests in fact presided over a parallel set of relationships that cut across caste and kinship, such as being a godmother or godfather (*ñāṉattāy, ñāṉattakappaṉ*) responsible for the spiritual development of a godchild and providing gifts at major transitions such as confirmation and first Communion or before pilgrimages.[47] And at Mass, dalits and upper castes found themselves addressed by the priest as a community of Christians in a manner that found no parallel in Hindu ritual.

As "overlord," the *cāmiyār* (priest) might have stood at the apex of Alapuram's social order, but as priest he stood outside it. In the 1980s, most Catholic priests did indeed remain apart from the mundane world of their parishioners, from whom they demanded submission as their spiritual leader. Priests charged an annual levy on parishioners of six measures of paddy (in 1983) and received tribute (cantippu) at festivals, as well as gifts taken as tarumam—money, raw food, the thighs of offered goats—given as if to God, or preceding the receipt of a blessing, whether of a married couple, a new house, the sick, or cattle at the festival of Ponkal. But there was no suggestion here that these gifts transferred inauspiciousness, as those to Hindu purohits might (Schmalz 2005, 244). Although with less certainty than in the missionary era, in the 1980s priests were still seen as belonging to a sacred sphere, and to a different class. They received parishioners at the presbytery and responded to requests mostly relating to marriage, or advice on family problems, or property disputes or assistance with finance, education, or employment rather than spiritual matters—but did so as impartial *religious* leaders and advocates. Even in 1984, only a minority made pastoral visits to villagers' houses (Houtart et al. n.d., 348).[48]

In short, the Catholic priest was (in principle) the prime actor in a ritual domain beyond the social order, the experience of which relativized without unsettling the institutions of caste society. The idea of a caste-based priesthood was anathema. However, the castelessness attributed to foreign missionaries would be hard to reproduce in the national and Tamil church. In 1980s Ramnad, the vast majority of Catholic priests were in fact upper caste, either Vellalar or Utaiyar.[49] This had become an expectation such that the few dalits who were ordained tended to be posted in far-off parishes, and on more than one occasion upper castes had boycotted Masses conducted by visiting priests known to be Pallar. I return to the hidden caste ordering of the priesthood itself and the activism that this provoked in chapter 6. But let me now draw out some general points on the Christian influence on caste.

CHRISTIAN CASTE?

What difference did Christianity make to the experience of caste in Alapuram? In 1983–84, caste remained central to the associations and negotiations of village life, and yet the notions of purity or impurity or the transmission of coded substances so key to the narrowed interpretations of structuralist or ethnosociologist scholars were quite peripheral. When Protestant Paraiyars referred to funeral service as "slave work" (*aṭimai vēlai*), they acknowledged that death work was degrading, but refused the notion that it or its effects (perhaps impurity) were the cause of their subordination. We will see that Christian Pallars and Paraiyars interpreted untouchability as an "outer" matter of historical oppression, not an inner one of substance or moral condition, and imagined funeral work or drumming as impure only *to the extent that* it was part of a relationship of servitude (*aṭimai*) (chapter 5). The cultural meaning of these acts could be redefined along with the renegotiation of relationships with patrons. Correspondingly, if Catholic landlords' tenants and workers refused threshing-floor paddy or to bury their cattle or take rice at their family functions, it was not the removal of impurity, substantialized harms, or dharmic order that was at stake, but a dent in the prestige and public honor that came from the loss of transactions that signaled the command over dalit laborers/tenants as feudal retainers (cf. McGilvray 1983).[50] Upper-caste Catholics lost no social standing among their Hindu co-caste members on account of their lax ritual practices, and none explained social standing in terms of transactionally maintained qualities of blood purity or bodily substance (McGilvray 1982a; Stirrat 1982).

Two hundred fifty years of Jesuit mission had desacralized caste. It had stripped out meanings, divorced actions from identities, and pushed dalit Christians especially toward a social symbolic understanding of the ritual transactions in which they were involved such that these represented or enacted relationships of command and servitude rather than substantially producing physical-moral conditions. The ritual roles or substances (at funerals, for example) were socially significant because they were coded with indignity rather than moral danger, and from this point of view there was little difference, for example, between the rice taken away from the threshing floor and that removed from the funeral. While Christians, like other Tamils, might materialize moral characteristics or sin (see chapter 2), Christian teaching worked against the idea of essential-substantial differences between people or the notion of moral states changed through shared/exchanged substances (cf. Mines 2005). Castes might be stereotyped as human types—Utaiyars as thrifty, Maravars as fierce—but a more common epithet was the one that asserted that "all blood is one," *irattam oṉṟu tāṉ* (cf. McGilvray 2008, 112). In short, Tamil Catholics may have materialized sin, but they did not transact sinful material. Today it is not Christians alone who are increasingly immune to the mixing of moral substances, imagining themselves compatible with more places, people, and palates, and less connected to their own. However, there can be little doubt that in missionary villages such as Alapuram, Christianization had an early, profound, and long-term influence. It marginalized priestly idioms—after all, Christianity was first incorporated on the Ramnad plains as a "cultural paradigm" of Maravar warriors—and in various ways secularized or denaturalized caste relations.

As a young researcher trained on early village studies and their tables of exchange-based caste ranking (Dumont 1980; Marriott 1955; Beck 1972), I was rather surprised by the *un*importance of interactional rank in the everyday life of Alapuram (cf. Good 1978, 38; S. Barnett 1976, 1977). But as a diligent student I tried anyway to establish a ranked caste order generated by asymmetrical exchanges in matters such as the etiquette of interdining or the use of respectful/disrespectful forms of address (Mosse 1986). As I did so, three things struck me. First, there *was* pervasive, if not marked, caste status sensibility in the village, not only in eating or speaking, but in the negotiation of deference and disrespect in the everyday use of space, seating, body posture, gesture, or demeanor that Mines notes in her examination of the practice of *mariyatai*—the "differences that make a difference" (2005, 83–87). But second, this distinction making was far too complex, contingent, and indeterminate to produce any sort of ranked order of castes (factors of wealth, education, or character being as important as caste). And third, despite this, I *was* able to construct a model of ranked castes, having solicited what turned out to be a remarkably consistent set of opinions on the relative position of different castes in terms of expected asymmetrical exchanges in interdining and in forms of address, and these were consistent with the formal ranking of public honors.[51]

This kind of discrepancy between expectation and practice has sometimes been interpreted as the informal subversion of formal caste orders through the use of alternative reckoning (e.g., purity-pollution versus master-servant in Beck 1972; Mines 2005, 92). However, in Alapuram what was socially significant was not the informal subversion of a fixed rank but rather the translation of the everyday fluid relations and pragmatic adjustments *into* a symbolically important and publicly contestable order. To put it in other terms, caste here was neither a *performative* structure nor a *prescriptive* structure (Sahlins 1985)—neither a social form produced interactively nor an underlying social form that generates appropriate acts.[52] Instead, it was a public and political representation that existed as a kind of public knowledge (such as that recorded in my survey). This was a simplified and formalized representation of power produced in ritual-spatial contexts and disembedded from actual interplays of power or economy. Life-crisis events with their ritual service and etiquette of serving food, like the grain distribution on the threshing floor, or the public presentations to king, priest, or landlord, occasioned "lines of honor" (mariyatai *varicai* [Mines 2005, 84]) that were the "fabrication mechanisms" (Latour 2005, 31) of a caste-political social-spatial order.[53]

Catholic ritual and church festivals provided the most important moments in the public manufacture of caste—especially the Santiyakappar festival, which involved both Christians and Hindus—and submerged any particular notion of caste interaction or scale of caste status in a common metaphor (cf. McGilvray 1982, 78). This was the dramatized order of royal service, honor, and rank,[54] represented as shares in worship of the saint as paradigmatic ruler and protector, endorsed, recorded, and adjudicated by outside actors, whether regional chiefs, Jesuit missionary priests, or government officers. This was probably the closest thing the village ever got to an ideology of caste. For Christians the caste order was a form of public knowledge. It was a display of honor in public rituals generating deliberative contests. Caste, as Nobili had insisted, was an outer thing, an explicit structure—something that could be objectified, named, discussed, criticized, or studied; it was an institution about which one could have an opinion, so that villagers and priests could talk about caste much as social scientists might—as an oppressive structural effect detached from moral codes for action, more about power than person. Such were the effects of the hollowing out, the denaturalization or "secularization," of caste.

As Christian influence underlined caste as a domain of power, it brought to the fore distinctions between transactions—types of work, remuneration, or substances exchanged—according to the degree of obligation or choice implied (degrees of "casteness" as a matter of power, not purity). Some were, to borrow terms from David's (1977) work among Jaffna Tamils, part of "bound mode" (*kaṭṭupāṭu*) relationships of order and control, while others involved relationships of "free choice" (*iṣtamāṉa*). For Alapuram artisans or laborers this would be the difference between caste-linked work or service involving cutantaram grain (hereditary and obligatory), and cash-remunerated "private" work. The tying of the work of carpenters, barbers, or dalits to caste made implicit reference to the order of caste articulated in public rituals (shares, honors). In recent decades, village artisans and dalits have worked to detach technical service from vestigial public models of caste by privatizing work and shrinking the realm of public order and obligation (see chapter 7). The contractual relations of what might now be presumed to be "the market" were encouraged by a Christian secularization of caste and the provision of services at agreed rates, with cash payment and mutual satisfaction (*cantōṣam*), which was conceived as an alternative and an aspiration, allowing escape from the obligation or servitude (*kuṭimai* or *aṭimai*) implied in caste-based work. This we will find in discussing forms of dalit mobility in later chapters. Economic enfranchisement, changed caste relations, and cultural renegotiation come together in a way that is summed up when the dalit dhobi's son Ravi tells me that "work paid for in cash has no pollution (tittu)."

A second model of nonservile relations enhanced the status of services rather than detaching them from caste status altogether. It was provided by high-ranking ritual specialists who were not *bound* to serve their patrons from whom they received unsolicited honorific taccanai or tarumam "gifts" for merit. To some extent modeled on the position of Brahman priests, the Alapuram catechists and carpenters (for house rituals) were engaged on these terms. In chapters 5 and 7 we will see how distinctions between "bound-mode" service, cash-contractual transactions, and honorable ritual service came into play in the 1980s and 2000s as part of the characteristic *negotiability* of Christian caste relations. Importantly, the distinctions that Alapuram Christians made concerned different forms of *relationship* rather than different types of caste person or inherent caste qualities—relationships of power, not of substance.

CONCLUSION

In this chapter, caste in Catholic Alapuram has been introduced variously as a historical identity linked to migration and settlement, as the arrangement of space and neighborhoods, and as communities of belonging and divine protectorates. Caste was also part of the collective organization of agricultural production and a set of relationships of service and obligation expressed in cutantaram and threshing-floor grain payments. As well as public dramas of rank and honor, caste relations were defined by public codes of exclusion and inferiorization expressed in transactions over food, water, use of space, or language that drew particular attention to the historical subordination of Pallars and Paraiyars in village life.

Alapuram illustrates the way in which social and economic relations took shape within a discourse of caste among Tamil Catholics. Christians participated in Indian cultural semantics in which disorder and impurity are idioms of subordination (Pfaffenberger 1982, 58–59; Deliège 1992, 279; cf. Mines 2005); however, ideas of purity or of transacted moral substances were subordinated to a public model of service and rank enacted at the palace, at the presbytery, or at the saint's festival, where local social orders and wider state systems had been symbolically interlinked (Dirks 1987). Under Jesuit influence, Christians strained away from "indexical contiguities" emphasized in recent Tamil village ethnography and toward manipulable *symbolic* associations (in the Piercian terms used by Daniel [1984] and Mines [2005, 138]), making the social meaning of ritual action or substances—drumming, barbering, or removing ritual cattle or ritual leavings—highly negotiable and open to reinterpretation as social relations changed. Divorced from dependent service relations, for example, Paraiyar drumming ceased to be ignominious or "polluting."[55] Alapuram villagers' capacity for experimentation with signs undoes the Marriott-Mines transaction of coded substances as well as Dumont's dichotomy of purity (status) and power.

The idea of caste among Catholics as a matter of outer form rather than inner reasons was brought about by the very hollowing out of religious meaning that Nobili presumed. However, caste among Christians was not simply a Hindu institution that survived conversion, "weakened and incomplete" (Dumont 1980, 210) by the absence of its Hindu ideological basis in purity and impurity or its equivalents. Nor was it a religious institution that became political with modern democratic practice. Caste was constituted or composed (Latour 2005) through Catholic ceremony as a public and political institution.

Christianity, of course, denied any spiritual sanction to the moral world of caste. Even if caste was allowed politically, the Eucharistic unity of the Communion was an explicit denial of difference and rank. This denial coexisted with an articulation of caste honor right from the moment of Communion itself. The dual moral world of Christians reconciled the demands of caste-ordered Tamil social life and their theological denial, just as it also reconciled Christian absolutism and shared popular religious culture (chapter 2). Again, Catholicism stood as a devotional "religion of choice" superimposed on the morality of caste, which was relativized and subordinated in relation to faith but never entirely denied (Dumont 1980, 211).

This structural relation of Church and caste existing at different moral levels (spaces) draws attention to the coexistence of otherwise quite incompatible practices: the funeral Mass of the priest with—but only *after*—the "purifying" rituals of the barber; the benevolent sanctity of Jesus and the saints *and* the reality of pollution in relation to the still-present Hindu divinity. While Cannell (2006, 145) describes Bicoli Catholics replacing the Church's focus on the fate of the individual soul with processes to protect the living from the harmful dead, Alapuram Catholics retained both concerns but allocated them to different ritual spaces and actions separated by boundaries on the ritual journey—in this case, marked by rotating the bier or entering the church, silencing the drumming, keening, and firecrackers for the Catholic Mass or for Mary's lament.

The dual morality of Tamil Christians has taken other forms at other times and places. Drawing on Trawick (1990), for example, Hudson (2000, 177–84) suggests that high-caste Protestant Christians in the nineteenth century rationalized the reality that those who prayed together would not eat together in distinctively Tamil terms. The Christian communion of spirit or *uyir* did not imply commensality of substance or *uṭampu* (body). Spirit was the domain of Christian love; it was unchanging, unlike the changeable substance—vulnerable to the effects of others and habituation (*paḻakkam*) to them through association and commensality. "The congregation gathered together as 'God's people' and shared a common sacrament that was ritually a festive banquet. . . . [T]he congregation was more a 'village' (*ūr*) gathered for a festival than a family of lineage (*kulam*) gathered for a meal. . . . [P]eople retained their finely graded social distinctions through their seating and eating but shared the effort to create *aṉpu* [love] amongst themselves" (ibid., 180).

Struggles over the boundary between Christian universalism and particularist caste (however conceived) shaped much of Alapuram village politics. The Catholic sacred (even the Mass itself) was invaded by caste segregation in seating arrangements, in the organization of distribution of the sacrament, in church entrances. Opportunities for the validation or contestation of caste position were found in every conceivable aspect of Catholic ritual, including funerals. The bier pointing to the symbolic identification of human death with the transcendent sacrifice of Christ was duplicated by caste into two: one for upper castes kept inside the church, the other for dalits kept outside the church. And if Catholics left caste at the church door, where the barber and dalit funeral servants also waited, this social order was reinstated at the cemetery, which remained a microcosm of the social distinctions in the village: upper-caste graves to the north, Pallars to the south (echoing the geography of caste streets and church seating); large tombs of the wealthy, decaying crosses of the poor. The human dead had not really left the social world at all. Their tombs "provide an idealised material map of the permanent social order" (Bloch and Parry 1982, 35). Even those who die away from the village have false graves made for them at a rite resembling the kallarai catanku. But the dynamic of Christian caste comes particularly from the extension of Christian universalism outward from a narrow religious equality into village society. In the next chapter we turn to the saints' festivals as key sites for this social dynamic of social reproduction and challenge.

4

Public Worship and Disputed Caste

The Santiyakappar Festival over 150 Years

The French Jesuit Edmond Favreux, who settled in Alapuram village in the 1860s, worked with a thoroughly embedded Tamil tradition of public worship. The spectacular festival for the guardian saint Santiyakappar was a meticulously scripted performance that annually mobilized and signified a Hindu-Christian social order. A century and a half later (in 2010) the festival had become a Catholic *religious* ceremony controlled by the clergy, articulating the messages of global Catholicism and delineating a community of worshipping Christians. It now excluded Hindu participants, and its material forms, roles, and gestures no longer signified social groups in relation to one another. Its communication technologies—posters, films, sound systems—had a "socially 'disembedding' effect" (Babb and Wadley 1995, 3–4, in Waghorne 2002, 33) even while offering liberating possibilities for historically subordinated groups.

Between these two moments was a remolding of religion and village society, traceable through the drama of this one village festival over 150 years. It is a story of how a Catholic religious domain was produced, how missionaries displaced kings as the key "mediators"[1] of caste relations, how non-Christians lost rights in Christian shrines—a story of the bifurcation of Christian and Hindu, church and temple, religion and society, not through the imposition of some a priori scheme, but as the result of contingent action and worked-out compromises of missionaries and villagers operating within overlapping but inconsistent frameworks (cf. Mitchell 2002). Missionary effects that were not of their own making nonetheless facilitated significant social change. So, if the Santiyakappar festival provided a context for remolding local Catholicism, it was also a site for the colonial and postcolonial renegotiation of caste. The record of festival honors and disputes, in particular, is a historical trace of the delineation of castes as interest groups and an unfolding local politics of caste in rural Ramnad.

Catholic saints (like other village deities) had annual festivals that combined the devotional form of the Catholic novena with the structure and aesthetics of Tamil temple festivals. Festival days were above all the ones on which to ask for favors or to fulfill vows, and to receive back objects (salt, grain, water candles, flowers) "transvalued" by contact with the saint, when streams of pilgrims, worshippers, and relatives converged on saint shrines in remote villages. In 1983–84, I would frequently accompany my neighbors to the festivals of their favored saints. Bringing animals and cooking utensils, family groups would encamp with bullocks and cart around the churches, where they cooked, ate, and slept for the duration of the festival. Devotees prepared animals for slaughter or sat beside long lines of ponkal rice pots marked with crosses and kunkumam to be taken into the church and blessed before food was shared and donated. If merit was gained by feeding the needy, certain punishment awaited those who took offered food away from the shrine. As the numbers swelled over the usually ten-day festivals, fruit and sweet stalls appeared, along with bangle stalls and stalls selling flowers or candles. Hawkers of statues, lithographs, and other religious memorabilia solicited pilgrims as did Nari Kuruvar "gypsies," beggars, or rosary-necklaced Christian sanniyasis clad in saffron cloth. The elderly watched over the family belongings and babies tied in makeshift hammocks, while young men in ironed "shirt and pant," slicked hair, and "cooling glasses" passed by the girls "all gossip and giggles" (Bama 2000, 83). People pressed into the small churches to have sight (*taricaṉam* or darshan) of the saint, to make offerings, to touch and receive grace from the statues. While the kovilpillais (catechists) led prayers in the church, some took advantage of stranger-priests to make their confessions on the holy day, although, Bama wonders, "how was one to confess anything in the midst of all that noise? The priest couldn't hear what we said nor could we hear what he told us to do" (2000).

The high points were the nightly processions of the saints, each in a wheeled chariot (*tēr*) or an open palanquin (*capparam*) held aloft on the shoulders of privileged devotees (figure 10). These were inaugurated by the priest walking under a ceremonial umbrella on *māttu* cloth laid on the ground by the dhobi, brought with drums and pipes to bless the statues already dressed by the catechist in silk, and carried to their vehicles by privileged persons (figures 11 and 12). Others pushed forward with flowers or cloth to garland or to touch the statues and their palanquins, which were raised as people intensified worship with upstretched hands, fingering rosaries, women drawing their saris over their heads in respect (*mukkāṭu mariyātai,* "veil respect"). In Alapuram, the daily processions of four or five saints were always led by St. Michael the Archangel, slayer of demons and Catholic counterpart to the obstacle-removing god Ganesh. The

FIGURE 10. Saint statue in decorated processional palanquin (*capparam*). Photo by author.

saints were accompanied not only by a large cross, flags, bells, and men carrying flaming torches or Petromax lamps, but also by fireworks, drumming, and the drink-fueled dancing of young men (cf. Still 2007, 79). The huge crowd jostled for position amid showers of salt, pepper, flowers, puffed rice, and other offerings. Along the processional street, rows of oil lamps were set on verandas to welcome with joy (*cantōcam*) the saint as royal visitor (or like a bride and groom) before whom families knelt to pray, offering garlands to the saint and sugar for the milling children. At each corner or crossroads of the route, the procession halted

FIGURE 11. Festival donors carry the festival images of the saints to their processional palanquins (*capparams*). Photo by author.

before an arch of fireworks blazing a message of supplication. While the clamor paused for a somber devotional song, the Paraiyar *tappu* players tightened the hide of their drums over piles of burning straw. The processions, which could last for hours, finally arrived back at the church. The saints were rotated a half turn and lowered amid a percussive crescendo as devotees rushed forward to receive blessing (*ācīrvātam*) in the form of flowers or bits of decoration "from the feet of the saint" (later placed in the roof of the house).[2] The statues were returned to the altar in the church and garlanded once more. The final night's procession, involving the great tēr chariot,[3] was followed by a popular drama drawn from a Christian repertoire lasting until daybreak (for example, on the life of Arulanandar [de Britto], or, at Easter, the *paska* or Passion play).[4] A sleepy congregation then heard the festival (Episcopal) Mass—a collective worship that marked the event and participants as Christian, even while much of the vow-fulfilling crowd was Hindu. The festival concluded with a final daytime procession of all the statues.

Saint festivals displayed a rich amalgam of Hinduized Catholic and Catholicized Hindu practices (cf. Meibohm 2004).[5] But above all, the repeated devotions and multiplied offerings, the rising piles of grain and chilies, flower garlands or the skins of sacrificed goats before the altar and statues, the moving colorful

FIGURE 12. The priest arriving in procession to bless the festival statues, Alapuram, 1983. Photo by author.

forest of flags and crosses, the decorated cattle, the piercingly amplified devotional songs and prayers, the intense light and brilliant color of decorations, candles, and incense, and the crush and heat of the crowd, all these show the saint shrines, like their Hindu counterparts, to be, in Mines's apt phrase, "centres of 'density'"—a reference to the "aggregate excess," the repeated images and saturated visual field, of such crowded places and events (2005, 157, 163). And, most important, this "density," regardless of its provenance (Hindu or Catholic), was converted into a scale of social value, of reputation or "relative bigness (*perumai*)" (2005, 157)—that is, a quality of persons and places that compares one village shrine or one donor's procession with another, and therefore the "productive capacity" of both divinity and community (2005, 157–58, 163–64). Within this are the "strategies of self-importance" found in public displays of donorship or devotion, piety or penance, in the gifts, the decoration, the performance of singers or actors, the prostrations or the endurance of knee walking while following the procession, making the body a vehicle for devotion (Clark-Decès 2008, 22; S. J. Raj 2008, 84, 90). The sheer size of the crowds made these events the mass media of their day, communicating religious imagery and social and political messages (cf. Waghorne 2002, 33).

The figure at the center of this annual drama in Alapuram was, of course, Santiyakappar, ruler of the village and its lesser gods and goddesses (chapter 2), whose inclusive *tiruviḻā* (festival) in the month of Āṭi (16–25 July) was on the scale of perumai, as preeminent in the ritual calendar as was his kovil (church) in the sacred geography. The *āṭi tiruviḻā* was a Catholic agricultural festival signaling seed sowing and the start of the growing season, marking the passage from the season of sun and heat (*uttarāyaṉam*) to the season of water and fertility and the decreasing strength of the sun on its journey southward (*takṣiṇāyana*). It stood at the opposite polar point to the Ponkal festival of St. Anthony on 17 January (Tai 3–4) (Good 1983; Beck 1972, 54; Reiniche 1979, 45),[6] and followed on from the priests' blessing of farm implements, cattle, and the ceremonial first plowing in the month of Cittirai (April–May) (details in Mosse 1986).

The special presence and power of the saint during his annual festival[7] was, as noted in chapter 2, marked by the transition of the saint from "inside" (as normally worshipped) to "outside" (among his people), effected through the inaugural raising of the kotimaram or "flag tree," a metonym of saintly power and dharmic rule (cf. Reiniche 1979, 93–95).[8] The missionaries' exposure of the saint for public veneration and the "blessing with the statue" at the entrance of the church fell within this logic. But of course the clearest enactments of Santiyakappar's "outside" sovereign presence were the daily processions of his decorated statue with saintly entourage around the processional streets (*tēr ōṭum vīti*). These traced the boundary of the church, which for the duration of the festival became coextensive with that of the village and over which the saint extended his blessing and protection (Mines 2005, 148–49). After the "flag tree" was raised, a greater moral and sexual purity was required of villagers. There was a prohibition on staying outside the village boundary overnight (*koṭitaṭai*—the impediment of the flag), as I recall from my neighbor's refusal to visit a dentist to salve a raging toothache until the festival had concluded. The presence of the saint turned the "outside" village space into an enclosed "interior" (*akam*) moral-social space, the bustle of the bazaar conceding to the saint and his processional and auditory order (Bate 2009, 79–80).

This kind of public worship has to be understood differently from the reciprocal transactions of private offerings, penances, and vow fulfilling. Worshippers still made offerings and received back some of the divine power-grace through indexical connections to the saints (ibid.). But the public worship of the Christian kovil, as Appadurai says of Hindu kovils, involved a flow of redistributive transactions "between worshippers and deity, in which resources and services are given *to* the deity and are returned *by* the deity to the worshippers in the form of 'shares' demarcated by certain kinds of honours" (1981, 18). "Honors" (*mariyātai,* Sk. *mariyāda*) in Catholic usage refer to betel nut, sandal paste, cloth, and other substances returned from the church to the people as markers of distinction, equating to the *prasad* (*piracātam*) returned to Hindu devotees from the deity. Recall that services and resources were given to the saint and honors received by persons as representatives of interdependent and ranked groups within an idealized social whole, a Hindu-Christian community of cosharers in the worship and protection of the saint, linked upward to the sovereign and state, whose power participated in that of the saint-deity. Stein's comments on the medieval Tamil temple "as a set of sharing beneficiaries in the generosity of a deity" are applicable: "What shares of village income was for the distribution and redistribution of resources in the material order of time, shares of support to deities and *prasadam* from these deities was in the moral order of time . . . there could be no complete moral order without the sharing and transactional nexus centring upon a god, whether of a family, a *jati,* a clan . . . a village, a locality or a kingdom" (Stein 1980, 452–53). Worship in turn required the existence of "complex local communities of castes" to attend to the deity, ideally arranged by the king, whose authority and preeminence were legitimated through his role as protector of the shrine (ibid.). The kovils, in other words, ideologically prefigure society; they "determine or fix boundaries of social groupings and social space reckoned to mark off the community of co-sharers in the worship of a particular god" (ibid., 454).

Catholic churches and ritual systems were, from the early 1700s, transactional centers of power in polity and village. Then in the nineteenth century, while gradually detached from the actual political and redistributive economic system, they became *the* focus of status competition. The now "commoditised" (Dirks 1987, 339) shares and honors of the Santiyakappar festival, for example, publicly enacted a "metasocial" model of Christian-Hindu caste order in which changing economic and political relations could be played out. From the 1800s, no festival went off without confrontations over its honors. The violence was preplanned, patterned by a "restricted cultural repertoire," and was as central an expressive action as worship of the saint himself (Good 1999, 53). Before turning to this history, let me first set out more fully the services and honors that constituted this idealized and contested model of social order.

CHURCH SERVICE

The worship of the saint in his kovil first involved hereditary caste-specific services (table 2) that mapped the previously discussed cutantaram grain-share rights and prestations at the palace (the worldly counterpart of the saint's royal seat). So the village carpenters (the Acari caste) had the right and duty—carried out in rotation—to repair the processional vehicles,[9] as well as the corresponding "carpenter church honor" (*taccu kōvil mariyātai*), which took the form of cloth, betel nut (and other items) received in the church from the hand of the kovilpillai.[10] These festival rights both authorized the carpenters' special part in the worship and publicly declared the standing of their caste.

Festival services differentiated caste identities and rank. The nineteenth-century Jesuit notebook on the Sarukani church Easter festival, for example, records duties around the use of processional torches that produced an order of four ranked "untouchable" castes: the "Sakkiliyan" received "honors" at the festival for holding the container for a supply of oil that was carried by the "Totti" (Paraiyar), which was poured by the "Koudoumban" (Pallar) onto the torch that was born by the "Valeyan" when the statues were carried from the church by the "upper castes."[11] Catholic festivals provided formulas for hierarchal incorporation through complementary roles in the ritual. As one Pallar man put it to me, "[W]hile they (Utaiyars) carried the *cāmis* (saints), we (Pallars) made and carried the lights," until abandoned as servile (*aṭimai*) work. The prestige roles of the Vellalar kovilpillai—reciting prayers, adorning the processional statues, removing them from the altar, and the distinctly priestly function of handing out the "church honors" (cf. McGilvray 1982a, 80–81)—were complemented by the inferior tasks of the Pallar catechist (pantaram), who decorated the processional vehicles with engraved leaves of lead (*īyam takaṭu*) and hundreds of candles, and was given the menial title of *capparamēstiri* ("*capparam* head workman").[12] Michael Moffatt (1979), as well as insisting that, when excluded, "untouchables" replicate ritual services among themselves, argued that when ritually *included,* they perform complementary but clearly inferior roles. But it would more accurate to say (with Fuller) that low and service castes were "included precisely so that they can be portrayed as excluded" (1992, 139).

TABLE 2 Church services for Santiyakappar (St. James) at Alapuram

Title	Caste, office, and function
ampaḷakārar (ampalam)	Maravar village headman: organizes the village for the final *tēr* procession
karṇam (kaṇakkupiḷḷai)	Velallar village accountant: assists the ampalam
mukkantar	Konar (shepherd caste) headman: brings a goat for the priest and brings Hindu Konars to drag the tēr
talaiyāri (kāvalkaraṉ)	Cervarar village watchman: ensures order at the festival
kōvilpiḷḷai (ōciyar)	Velallar catechist: ritual service in the church, assists the priest
kollaṉ	Acari blacksmith: repairs the *capparams* and the *tēr*
taccaṉ	Acari carpenter: repairs the capparams, and so forth
vaṇṇaṉ	Vannan washerman: provides ceremonial cloth (*māttu*), saris for the priest to walk on when going to bless the capparams and tēr, cloth for decorating the tēr, cloth for the processional torches (*tīveṭṭi*)
paṇṭāram	Pantaram caste florist: provides flower garlands
paṇṭāram	Pallar catechist: decorates the capparams and the tēr (*capparamēstiri*)
kuṭumpaṉ	Pallar measurer (and relatives): carry the torches, beat the church *tampuru* drums [French: *tambour*]
tōṭṭi	Paraiyar caste drummers: play *paṟai* (*tappu*) drums and *kompu* horns, pour oil for the torches

CHURCH DONORS

The church and its festival cycle secondly provided opportunities for notable or aspiring families, lineages, or castes to obtain the benefit of the saints' grace (*aruḷ*) and social honor through conspicuous public expenditure for religious purposes. Upper-caste notables decorated the church, paid for new statues or vestments for the priest, for a new flag post or a ceremonial umbrella. They distributed food on special occasions, as well as regularly paying for Masses, processions of the saints, or honorable gifts (cantippu) to the priest. At festivals, the principal donors had the honor of carrying the saint from the church to the processional vehicle, and received back from the church the substances that marked first respect (*mutal mariyātai*) in the order of men.[13] As well as cloth and betel nut, symbols of distinction included public blessings, sometimes graded according to donations. For example, when daily processions of the novena of the Feast of the Blessed Sacrament were sponsored by different Utaiyar families in the 1930s, Fr. Veaux recorded the following in his diary: "It is ruled that . . . those of the manthapapadikarers [donors] who give Rs.3 or more would have the benediction service of the Blessed Sacrament in the evening. Those who give less than Rs.3 will have only the benediction of the statue."[14]

At the Santiyakappar festival, donors held what were called *maṇṭakappaṭis*—that is, the right to arrange and pay for the saint to be taken out from the shrine in procession on one of the nine nights of the festival (table 3).[15] Jesuits added a tenth "day zero" mantakappati as the feast of Our Lady of Mount Carmel to honor a particularly influential and wealthy Utaiyar family who converted in the early 1900s. The caste or village involved in each mantakappati was represented by a headman (*talaivaṉ*) or elder (*mūttayaṉ*) who collected festival tax (*vari*), a fixed portion of which went to the priest to organize the festival and pay the church servants, including the Paraiyar drummers who brought each group of donors (*maṇṭakappaṭikārars*) to the church in procession. The remainder of the money covered customary services from the donor's village (e.g., of dhobis and musicians), martial-arts displays, fireworks, and other expenses, increased by intercaste and intervillage competitive pageantry. Thus the fourth day was remembered as the "horn mantakappati," so called because Maravars of Cankani village arrived for the festival accompanied by forty or so Paraiyar horn blowers, as well as the usual drummers and torches, in an expression of local power. The big men of each mantakappati brought the priest in procession to bless the saints (see figure 12) placed in their decorated chariots made to specification by Alapuram carpenters, and were first to receive flowers offered to the saintly entourage as the big men returned the statues to the church after the procession.

The last two mantakappatis were multicaste, involving the various castes of Alapuram. The penultimate *ul-ur* ("inside village") mantakappati, where the village (ur) was presented as a community of Catholic upper castes, was, as will become clear, the particular focus of contests over rank and honor played out in front of the largest festival crowd. But until the 1920s, low-caste Catholics were barred from donorship and forbidden from carrying the statues or palanquins. Older Pallar informants recalled being forbidden to touch the flag post or the rope pulling the chariot, and having to stand aside while Utaiyars took petals from the feet of the saint. They received rights and respects only as inferiorized kutimakkal village servants.[16]

The concluding night of a Tamil temple festival is commonly sponsored by political leaders, who act as temple trustees and receive first honors (Reiniche 1979, 86–87). As chief donors they represent the *yajamāna* (Sk.) or "sacrificant," paradigmatically the king (ibid.).[17] The old Jesuit mission encouraged rajas and chiefs into this role at their centers, where, as principal donors and holders of the final mantakappati, they received first honors. The new Madurai mission Jesuit fathers who settled in the Tamil countryside, however, construed *themselves* as rulers (rather than renouncer-teachers). They took over this patron role and its first respects in what became referred to as the *cāmiyār* (priest's) mantakappati. In Alapuram, the authority of the Maravar headman (ampalam)—his participation in the power of Santiyakappar and the saint's encompassment of the village

TABLE 3 *Maṇṭakappaṭi* donors for the Santiyakappar (St. James) festival, Alapuram*

Day of festival	Date in July	Village and caste or lineage of donors	Statue taken on final night
0	15	Alapuram Arulappa Utaiyar *paṅkālis* ("lineage") (Feast of Our Lady of Mount Carmel)	
1**	16	Akkavayal (Maravars and Konars) (*koṭieṟṟam* ceremony)	St. James (small statue)
2	17	Utaiyanur Utaiyars	Uttiriyamata (Virgin Mary)
3	18	Vatatirukkai Utaiyars	St. Michael
4	19	Cankani and Pancayatti Maravars	St. Sebastian
5	20	Acaris of the parish	St. Anthony of Padua
6	21	Kuriccinatu Pallars	Vanattu Cinnappar (St. Paul the Hermit)
7	22	Nadars of the parish	St. James (large statue)
8	23	ūḷ-ūr mantakappati ("inside" village Christians)	St. James
9	24	Cāmiyār (priest) mantakappati	Virgin Mary

* The festival probably had this particular form by the 1870s, although mantakappatis almost certainly existed throughout the eighteenth century.

** Before 1872, the second mantakappati (July 16) was held by the Utaiyars of three adjacent villages.

domain—was nonetheless recognized (until the 1930s) by his right to conduct a final daytime procession (on the tenth day) with the huge *cattatēr* chariot, and to receive appropriate distinction. It was here, most especially at the distribution of honors after the procession, that Christian and Hindu villagers came together as a ranked order of castes, officers, artisans, and village servants under the peculiar bicephalous authority of the Catholic priest and the Hindu headman.

CHURCH HONORS

These heightened moments of public distinction took place both at the beginning of the festival, at the raising of the banner, as well as at its end. The priest first touched the cloth, betel leaf, areca nut, and sandalwood paste, and these "honors" were then distributed by the kovilpillai in a designated order (table 4). As noted in the previous chapter, first the church and then the state, regional powers, and hereditary officers of the administrative village (kiramam) were honored—then the Catholic upper castes representing the community of worshippers incorporating those "outside" castes honored as servants.[18] A public ranking was meticulously marked by the order, quality, and location of the prestations of cloth and

TABLE 4 Order of distribution of church honors (*kōvil mariyātai*) at Alapuram

Named honor (institution or group)	Representation
kōvil (church)	the priest
carkkār (government)	any police officer present
nāṭu (region)	the *nāṭṭars,* Maravar regional headmen
kirāmam (village)	village officers: munsip/ampalam (headman), karnam (accountant), mukkantar (representative of the Konar shepherd caste), talaiyari (watchman or kaval, a Cervarar). In addition to receiving betel and sandal paste, the headman and accountant were garlanded with a dhoti (*keṇṭai veṣṭi*) and towel (*tuṇṭu*). The talaiyari received a slightly inferior dhoti (*eṭṭu mul̲a veṣṭi*).
village Christians *(ūḷḷūr maṇṭakappaṭikārars)*	first Vellalars, then Utaiyars (Only in 1924 was it agreed that Pallars should receive a share of the mantakappati betel, and even then from the Utaiyar headman *outside* the church rather than from the kovilpillai inside; see below.)
maṇṭakappaṭikārars	Each mantakappati's headman was called to receive the mariyatai.
kuṭimakkaḷ	village servants: Acari (carpenter [*taccan̲*] and blacksmith [*kollan̲*]), washerman, barber, kutumpan (Pallar paddy measurer), Totti Paraiyar (scavenger, drummer), Cakkiliyar (leatherworker)

betel. Until the 1920s, the Acari (carpenter) and all those before him received the church honors *inside* the church, as earlier noted, but the remaining kutimakkal received the betel *outside,* or standing on the steps of the church door.[19]

Such was the festival system, recorded and "stabilized" in Jesuit notebooks and in the memory of my 1980s informants; one might even say rendered inert or socially dead (Latour 2005), because the *real* story is in the history of contestation and conflict around this order, and in the way narratives were enlivened by the diverging views of upper castes lamenting the loss of custom (*māmul*) and order (*kaṭṭupāṭu*) (and the good harvests this had brought the village) and dalit outrage at the feudal injustices and caste exclusions sanctioned by the Church.

Church honors certainly did not portray a ranked order present at some more concrete level (see chapter 3). They were a public fiction, reflecting power as the capacity to shape and stage symbolically important and publicly contestable representations that were always provisional, given shifting political-economic relations.[20] Moreover, by inserting themselves into the place of kings and overlords, missionaries helped transform festival honors from emblems of a bundle of rights and political connections into signifiers of the identity of caste groups in themselves—the "festishized" object of competitive acquisition into which wealth and power could be translated (Dirks 1987, 339). As a common Hindu-Christian currency of social standing, honors subsumed claims to social position on the basis of, inter alia, royal authority (Maravars), ritual office (Vellalars), or economic power (Utaiyars) (cf. McGilvray 1982a, 81). The saint's festival became the principal context for public articulations of social ambition, and as such a significant precursor to twentieth-century caste politics.

Driven by the logic of their own evangelistic objectives—to attract and retain converts—Catholic priests (Jesuit and Goan) played an active part in constituting this symbolic language of caste. In places like Ramnad, their elaborate ritualizing and recording of schemes of caste rank and service were significant alongside the more usually cited efforts of British census takers or army recruiters (Cohn 1990; Raheja 1996). At the very least, Catholic missionaries made sure that the schemes of caste rank that were becoming the order of the day (Dirks 2001), and that made religious centers important, were built into their festival systems—not, it must be stressed, as a matter of priori design, but through contingent responses to a local culture of power. Bringing missionaries into this politics made Catholic schemes of caste uniquely responsive to shifting power relations.

Three aspects of the historical circumstances under which the elaboration of Catholic systems of caste rank took place need underlining. First, British rule enabled French Jesuits to forge Catholic religion as a separate administrative domain over which they would rule, wresting control of churches from Hindu rajas and headmen, inserting themselves as royal personages, arbitrating rank, and granting honors that were now severed from formerly bundled resource rights. (See chapter 1 and Frykenberg [2008, 350–58] for the papal decrees and ecclesiastical structures that underpinned this domain separation.) The conflicts with existing rights holders brought into play quite different conceptions of the Christian kovil/church.

Second, Jesuit "lordship" was itself compromised by the competition over shrines with sitting Padroado "Goanese" priests. Jurisdictional claims depended upon demonstrable popular support,[21] and shaping the mission's ritual system so as to articulate the local politics of caste was a sure way of popularizing Catholicism. A third circumstance was the rising wealth of Catholic Utaiyar settlers who turned colonial changes in property systems and markets into economic success through fixed-rent dryland cash-cropping or adventures into migrant-labor contracting in Burma and Ceylon. Their privatized control of land, irrigation, labor, and village service (asserted against an existing village establishment headed by Maravars [chapter 3]) was turned into public honor through church contests that involve translocal mobilization of the caste. Let me begin with the last two circumstances before returning to the emergence of the Catholic religious domain.

MISSIONARY COMPETITION AND CASTE HONOR AT THE SANTIYAKAPPAR CHURCH: 1856–62

Propaganda Fide French Jesuits claimed the authority of Rome to recover Christian villages from the "abuses and scandals" of Goan "schismatics," whose priests were considered responsible for moral and spiritual decline. These were guilty of corruption, of enriching themselves while spending nothing on the church, and in particular of allowing the "pagan authorities" to take control of Catholic shrines.[22] But in the 1840s the English magistrates privileged prior possession over papal commission and repeatedly ruled in favor of the Goanese in jurisdiction disputes. Jesuits faced embarrassing police-enforced public expulsion from more than fifty churches and presbyteries in the Madurai region (Jean 1894, 265). Their memoirs make it clear that this was more than a struggle of pope over Portugal. It concerned the missionary conquest of an indigenous clergy couched in terms of a struggle between European and "black priests" (*prêtres noirs*) (*Résumé,* 106)[23]—ironically, just as Jesuits were themselves establishing systems (seminaries and a Madurai novitiate) for the production of their own indigenous priesthood (Frykenberg 2008, 350–58). French Jesuits informed Christians in Ramnad's former Padroado parishes that *they* were the true inheritors of the tradition of St. Xavier and the Blessed de Britto, sent for their salvation. They insisted that the Goanese had no rightful claim to priesthood, and wherever Jesuits staked a pastoral claim they underlined this point by calling all Catholics by caste to have their marriages reconsecrated (*Résumé,* passim). The fate of the parishioners' souls was at stake, Jesuits insisted. Continued pastoral neglect would lead to apostasy and conversion to the Protestant "heresy," a now growing threat in rural Ramnad (Jean 1894, 248).

Embedding themselves in remote rural villages, French missionaries such as Joseph Bertrand and Edmond Favreux (below) began a twenty-year "guerrilla" struggle, village by village, church by church. Their journals describe how they "studied the terrain," developed tactics and plans before some "solemn assault on the fortress of schism" (*Résumé*). There were "preliminary advances," tactical concessions to win local support, nighttime moves, traps and ambushes, spies and intrigue; and at one point Bertrand suspects he is being poisoned by Padroado supporters who have infiltrated his entourage (Jean 1894, 260–63). In contemporary accounts the "ardour and zeal in battle" of the warrior blends with the ordeal and self-giving of the apostolic life (ibid.). But above all, the saint shrines and their festivals were the focus of this ecclesiastical warfare. The French priests gathered deputations of villagers for impressive pageants and public processions, especially, as Favreux put it, "to serve our intention of better stating our case before the English justice . . . that far from troubling the countryside we have only responded to the wishes of the people" (*Résumé,* 96). They planned impressive new churches beside dilapidated Goan ones and began by setting up ornately decorated and garlanded *pandals* (sheds) by the locked Goanese churches, making these the focus of festival celebrations (Besse 1914, 246–48; Bertrand 1865, passim; Jean 1894, 265; *Résumé*). In unmistakably martial performances, Favreux and other "warrior" missionaries traveled to important churches on horseback, accompanied by drummers and horn players, picking up groups of supporters on the way. They planted the festival flag post on their rivals' territory to open the festival "in the name of our mission," and then conducted the processions of the saints with as much pomp as possible, ensuring that reports of the great crowds of pilgrims and worshippers reached the English magistrate in Madurai.[24]

As these Jesuits began their campaign against the Goanese "schism," their journals record that the Utaiyar caste had already begun to press for public recognition of enhanced caste rank across the region. Intervillage council meetings and resolutions communicated by palm-leaf *olai* coordinated new caste-wide codes of upper-caste practice by, for example, prohibiting widow remarriage and claiming new honors at Catholic churches. In the 1810s to 1830s, the caste had acquired preeminent privileges (protected by Padroado Goan priests) at major Catholic shrines including at Oriyur, where they controlled the lucrative de Britto exorcism cult, but had yet to acquire honors commensurate with their new wealth at Alapuram's important Santiyakappar pilgrimage. Here Vellalars, office bearers (kovilpillai) within an existing order of caste rights and rank under the "pagan [Maravar] village authorities," held festival preeminence in the betel honors and carrying the statues (*Résumé*, 59).

When Favreux renewed his "assault" on Alapuram in 1857, the Utaiyar leaders of the village offered their support as a means to challenge this Padroado-backed old order. The Utaiyar dilemma was that members of their caste elsewhere, from whom they sought support, owed their privileges to the Goanese rivals. Indeed, the Utaiyar chiefs of Oriyur and Pulial had raised funds to help Padroado priests fight court cases against the Propaganda Fide Jesuits. Moreover, the Jesuits would be worth backing only if they had a realistic chance of retaining control of the church ritual system; and this was far from certain. Indeed, in 1857 a "concordat" was signed between the apostolic delegate and the Portuguese crown that established a system of "double jurisdiction" that left the Alapuram church under Goanese patronage.

Undeterred, in 1858 Favreux planned a massive ceremonial attack to "liberate" the church and acquire control de facto. He was brought on horseback together with a colleague in an imposing procession to celebrate the Santiyakappar festival. As he recorded in his journal:

> Tous deux à cheval, nous nous dirigions vers [Alapuram]. D'un commun accord par les payens aussi bien que par les Chrétiens, toutes les trompettes si éclatantes du pays qu'on avait pu réunir, annonçant notre passage et semblant donner le

> signal de l'assaut [on the shrine]—tantans, tambours de diverses formes[. . . .] C'était vraiment spectacle curieux de voir, au fur et à mesure que nous avancions, s'agglomérer le monde autour de nous par les députations des villages[. . . .] Dans le voisinage chacun nous saluait à l'envi comme les libérateurs de ce Sanctuaire dont tous voyaient avec peine les ruines s'agrandir. (*Résumé,* 96)

Goan priests then arrived with their own entourage from Sarukani to the north, halting outside the village. As tension mounted, one local Maravar chief offered Favreux four to five hundred men under his command to defend the Santiyakappar shrine. Violence broke out at the festival, escalated simultaneously by conflicts over jurisdictional claims, sectarian affiliation, and caste precedence, especially during the penultimate-night ullur mantakappati, which concluded with the expulsion of the Goanese priests by the police (*Résumé,* 105–16).

Favreux considered the adventure to have been a great success—even the Hindu Maravar village headman now offered support to the Jesuits—which he sought to consolidate the following Easter (1859) by inaugurating a procession of the image of the body of Christ and a Passion play (*paska*) "which attract[ed] an incalculable crowd," creating further symbolic resources to allocate (*Résumé,* 172). The rearrangement of rights and distinctions that Jesuit success over the Goans inevitably brought then released a veritable flood of petitions for religious privileges—claimed as customary or as rewards for allegiance—from competing groups within or between castes, "jusque dans le basse caste des Pallars" (*Résumé,* 101–2). The disappointed parties sought alliance with co-caste members in villages under Goanese control, and, building on this frustration, "les émissaires du schisme" gradually built up a following in the village until a court order in their favor brought Padroado priests back to Alapuram later in 1859 (ibid., 125, 137–38, 143–45). This time the Goanese priest (as elsewhere) offered Utaiyar leaders the honor of putting the name of their caste to new construction works at the shrine, but failed to win their allegiance because of the still-endorsed Vellalar ritual preeminence, now also championed by the Maravar headman. Eventually the high court ruled in favor of the Jesuits, returning Favreux as the first resident parish priest in Alapuram (Bertrand 1865, 439–43; *Résumé*).

The rule of "double jurisdiction," however, continued to intertwine caste and ecclesiastical contests, producing shifting allegiances up to the end of the century. Utaiyars, for example, petitioned neighboring Goanese priests or invited them to conduct ceremonies in the village, such as the "flag raising" in 1859, to win honors, while Vellalars exploited alliances with kovilpillais at Goanese churches such as Oriyur or Sarukani in order to preserve their own privileges (ibid., 248, 252, 256–57). Then, new competing sources of manipulable missionary patronage appeared. Some were Catholic, such as the infamous breakaway "schismatic" Soarez (see S. B. Bayly 1989, 316ff), whom Alapuram Utaiyars warned they would join in 1895 if they were not handed betel honors before Vellalars;[25] but more important were the Protestant Christian missions present from the 1850s to whom villagers threatened to turn if denied claimed honors.[26]

The extraordinarily elaborate systems of ritual privilege and caste rank developed at Catholic centers such as Alapuram in the nineteenth century were, we can conclude, not the result of theologically reasoned Jesuit "accommodation" to some indigenous social system, but rather the outcome of a series of immediate, tactical actions by missionary priests engaged in legal and ritual battles to secure control of popular shrines intersecting with caste conflicts, played out simultaneously to a local audience, missionary organizations, and the British courts through petitions, lawsuits, and appeals in the Madras high court (ibid., 78–79; Bertrand 1865, 431–32; cf. Bayly 1989, 424). Winning Church approval and the allegiance of locally influential actors (not to mention success in court) depended upon the manipulation of at best only partly compatible notions of Catholic devotional pomp and Tamil perumai (bigness, or *mutaṉmai*—precedence) and mariyatai (honor). These conjunctions led not only to unprecedented aggrandizement of Christian churches and festivals, but also to forging a key role for missionary priests themselves as custodians of ritual honors and arbiters of caste rank.

DISPUTING HONOR AND THE RISING POWER OF UTAIYARS: 1860S TO 1920S

Sustained efforts by Utaiyars to outrank Vellalars in the Alapuram church defined the fault lines of conflict right up to the 1920s, throughout the incumbency of some fourteen Jesuit priests whose diaries chronicle the struggles in which they were themselves implicated.[27] Utaiyar big men gradually turned from appeals to alternative missionary patrons to direct intimidation, resulting in frequent, open, and violent conflict at the heightened moments of mariyatai such as the lifting of the capparams or the betel distribution at the ul-ur mantakappati, when Utaiyars of the region gathered in imposing numbers to assert precedence over Vellalars. Since it was the signs of honor and not the religion in whose name they were allocated that mattered (Good 1999, 62), Hindu Utaiyars were equally involved. Facing such intimidation, priests would suspend processions, as Favreux did at Easter 1862. This provoked an Utaiyar caste council, which declared that refusing them the right to touch the chariots in favor of Vellalars and Maravars was an affront to their caste honor and insisted that the office of kovilpillai be withdrawn from Vellalars. When ignored, Utaiyars organized a region-wide boycott of Catholic Masses and festivals, and refused the priest entry into twenty-eight Utaiyar villages (*Résumé*, 272–77).

The boycott broke after about four weeks for reasons that suggest a weakening of Utaiyar regional caste networks, as well as the growing power of the Jesuit priest freed from Goanese competition. Favreux himself believed the boycott to have been "a grave insult to divine majesty and the sacrifice of Christ," but also that in this pagan country "these Christian children little understood the malice" of their actions (*Résumé,* 275). It was characteristically as disobedient children that priests would manipulate their parishioners with ritual rewards and penalties. When cholera broke out amid the boycott of 1862, Favreux innovated a procession of the statue of the Virgin in her month of May; and the threat of exclusion from both divine protection and caste honors played its part in breaking the Utaiyar rebellion. Their return was then rewarded with the privilege of placing a new wooden altar in the church (*Résumé,* 277–78).

After three decades of such protests and boycotts, Jesuit priests were persuaded that Utaiyars should have parity with Vellalars in the church, and from 1893 they tried alternating the order of betel distribution at the ul-ur mantakappati, and in 1895 offered the two castes separate mantakappatis on the eighth and ninth days of the festival. But mariyatai does not admit equivalence. Utaiyars refused to pay the festival tax and again signaled interest in other Christian sects, while Vellalars withdrew from the festival entirely, rejoining Utaiyars for the "inside ur" mantakappati on equal terms (rotating precedence) only thirty-six years later, in 1928.[28] Over this period, Utaiyars continued to consolidate their honor in the festival system despite occasional public snubs: in 1903 the Vellalar kovilpillai handed them the Acari (carpenter) betel; another year the priest transferred the second mantakappati to Vellalars following an internal Utaiyar dispute.[29] By 1915 Utaiyar leaders had taken over the role of representing the kiraman (village) and distributing betel honors to village officers and servants—a sure measure of the new dominance of their caste in the eyes of the long-opposed village administrative heads responsible for allocating this honor.[30] And Utaiyars relentlessly sought to weaken the office of kovilpillai as a source of Vellalar mariyatai—in 1912, for example, withholding the church tax on marriage (*kalyāṇam vari*) that paid the catechist's salary. Then in 1915 the Vellalar caste privilege of presenting their cantippu (ceremonial gifts) to the priests and visiting bishops separately from other Catholics was removed.[31]

Hyperpublic Catholic festival conflicts were the means by which wealthy Utaiyars challenged the authority of Maravars and Vellalars within the "old order" mission and village administration *and* legitimized economic power as they pushed themselves into the metaphorical and physical center of the village, building mansions and buying up core village wetland.[32] The strategy found a parallel in the way wealthy Cettiyar merchants and bankers, also empowered by colonial changes, inserted themselves as royal patrons and recipients of first honors at Hindu temples (Price 1996; Rudner 1994).[33] But what the Catholic ritual systems offered were scales of recognized distinction that were more negotiable than those at Hindu temples. They were less tied to emerging orthodoxies of rank (whether of purity or royal title) and for this reason were important to the social integration of immigrant groups of ambiguous standing such as Utaiyars (cf. Baker 1984, 91).[34] Here Tamil Catholicism echoes the innovations of medieval temple-based devotional religion, which provided a hierarchy of statuses and ranked ritual roles, enabling "powerful and populous part[s] of Hindu society [i.e., peasant elites] (formerly excluded by criteria of purity by birth) . . . to enjoy ritual rank commensurate with [their] ranking in other aspects of south Indian life" (Stein 1968, 81). How did Jesuit missionaries regard this system of caste honor interwoven with devotion to saintly power and within which they were themselves firmly planted?

JESUITS PRIESTS AND CASTE HONOR

As Favreux and his colleagues settled into the Ramnad countryside in the 1840s and 1850s, they offered their European superiors a devout vision of local Christians of different castes joining together in magnificent public worship, each making their particular contribution. And it was only "natural that the nobles of the country desire to receive honors by courtesy of the Christians and the priest whom they have a duty to help" (Jean 1894, 377; *Résumé*, 273). Jesuits were familiar with systems of patronage widely common in Europe (Molinié 1996) and did not share the Evangelical horror of public religious displays denounced as the height of licentiousness and "the epitome of all that is idolatrous and dangerous in Hinduism" (Waghorne 2002, 19). In Favreux's view, the festival racket, although "the music of hell to the European ear," was effective for the Indian (*Résumé*, 273); and worldly honors (*honneurs mondains*) that demonstrated the devotion of the faithful were a favorable sign of divine Providence. He was clear that only under the Goanese had these "our most holy external solemnities (*solennités extérieures*) been left to paganize themselves (*se paganiser*)." "If the devil under the Goanese turned this [arrangement], legitimate in itself, to ruin, it is necessary under our [Jesuit] jurisdiction to seek to turn to good instead of destroying, [even] in case that was possible—what can the Jesuit do, *Omnibus omnia factus sum*"[35] (*Résumé*, 273). They were indeed far too deeply embroiled in local political systems to denounce them.

Caste was still recognized as a benign civil order, although missionaries such as Favreux did (like the colonial masters) begin to perceive the moral capacities or deficiencies of their parishioners in terms of essentialized and ranked categories of caste: the Pallars were "simple souls" of "manageable character," faithful and with fear of God; Nadars, although "above Pallars in the honor of caste," were affected by "their almost wild habitat isolated from centers of population among the palmyra trees," while Utaiyars were compulsive and blinded by material interest (*Résumé*). Caste seemed to provide a natural arrangement for Catholic worship. But as festival-honors disputes ensnared them, Favreux and his colleagues felt that the customary honors (*honneurs d'usage*) of the feast were being confused with something altogether different—the "pride of caste" (*orgueil de caste*). This was an amoral madness, a "magical power on the spirit of the Odeages [Utaiyars] mingling with the vapor of self-pride" that "is so strong [that] it is often very difficult for the missionary to convince [them] that in this lies sin" (*Résumé,* 309).

The demands of mariyatai were thus increasingly condemned as sinful pride "impeding the work of saving souls" (ibid.). Priests would intervene to rescue true worship by suspending processions when honors conflicts erupted, or wait for the crowds to disperse before completing the necessary ceremonies for the statues quickly, at night, with a few loyal authorities and Christians (*Résumé,* 274). Missionaries would reward those who placed piety above prestige with individual honors. When amid the Utaiyar boycott of the church in 1913 "lower house" Gnani sent money for the festival, Gamon (parish priest 1900–23) sent honors to his house (15 July 1913). The sinfulness of caste pride lay in its *irrationality,* its capacity to distort individual reason and conscience. Like women possessed with spirits (chapter 2), men who suffered the "delirium of pride" had to be brought to their Christian senses. In fact, there was more than an incidental connection between the struggles of caste honor and possession-exorcism in nineteenth-century Catholic Ramnad—twin irrationalities against which Jesuits set themselves.

JESUIT MISSIONARIES AND FEMALE AUTONOMY

It will be noticed that women are largely absent from the record of honors conflicts, and yet the burden of honor associated with practices of status striving in families of cultivator castes such as Utaiyars in southern India often fell disproportionately onto women (e.g., Kapadia 1998; Still 2007). Controlling female sexuality and contracting prestige marriages were especially important among the upwardly mobile, who, in search of appropriate alliances, widened marriage circles and expanded networks beyond the safe confines of the prescribed close relatives of Dravidian kinship. In doing so, they had to establish and advertise compliance with high-status norms that involved more restrictive ideas of female chastity and domesticity, the withdrawal of women from agricultural work, and, in the case of Utaiyars in the 1850s, a new prohibition on widow remarriage, while at the same time "Sanskritizing" Catholic marriage ceremonies through, among other things, the acquisition of elaborate horoscopes. This brought leading Utaiyar families into conflict with Jesuit priests.

Not only were restrictions on widow remarriage and the use of horoscopes specifically prohibited in pontifical bulls (*Résumé*, 309), but also missionaries were opening space for prestige-threatening autonomous female agency and choice through a life in the convent. Quite the sharpest conflicts between village big men and Jesuit priests concerned the threat to family honor posed by the missionaries' support for their young women seeking vocations in defiance of family wishes. In 1917, for example, a daughter of the powerful Utaiyar "lower house" caused a scandal by running away to join a convent in order to escape family pressure. Big man Gnani Utaiyar blamed Father Gamon and immediately invited Lutherans to the village and made public death threats against the priest. "In the evening as my disciple Sebastian was closing the eastern door," writes Gamon in his diary entry for 13 April 1917,

> an old Christian woman came to tell him "Ah! tell the Father to be on his guard. The great man Gnani wants to kill him." I have been warned by two of three good souls. If his daughter has run away, I am not the cause of it. Why did he beat her several times because she wanted to become a nun? Why was she insulted and despised at home daily? She is now nineteen, exactly of age. She can choose for herself. [15 April . . .] In the sermon I spoke about the religious vocation. Toward the end I was interrupted by that beastly Appucutei alias Santiago. I only told him to shut his mouth. [18 April . . .] Gnani Odean [Utaiyar] threatened to tie [the catechist] to a tree and beat him because his daughter had run away to a convent. This evening after having lighted my cigar I went as usual to take walk in the kanmai [tank]; there I met [a group of] Christian Pallars who saluted me. "Ah, Father," said one of them, "do not go out at this time. It is not safe, I tell you," and, afraid, he followed me. I answered, "Yes I know—I have told them, every evening I would be here. Let them come." (Translated)

At the time it was not unlikely that the errant will of a young woman would have been diagnosed as spirit possession leading to exorcism at shrines such as de Britto's at Oriyur. The exteriorizing of blame for socially deviant behavior onto spirit agents allowed family honor to be preserved while reinforcing authority over women (see chapter 2). But the individual female agency, moral choice, and evasion of family control that Father Gamon encouraged here had the reverse dishonoring effect. In this context, popular Catholic exorcism cults (such as at Oriyur) and the possession narratives they involved had a double significance: first, as part of women's response to new restrictions or the demands of prestige models of matrimony; and second, in disciplining errant or rebellious women in an idiom of demonic intrusion that allowed the recovery of honor (Nabokov 1999; cf. Still 2007, 226). If by suppressing possession-exorcism and insisting on individual agency, personal choice, and morality Jesuit missionaries left upper-caste Catholic families with little room for managing family honor at times of crisis and change, their support of young women's escape into the religious life in cases such as Gnani Utaiyar's daughter heaped on insult and provoked rage.

Meanwhile, by insisting on the right of Alapuram Pallar women to cover their breasts in the presence of upper-caste men, Jesuits (from 1906) challenged the corresponding degradation of female value among subordinates.

JESUIT PRIESTS AND THE MAKING OF A CATHOLIC RELIGIOUS DOMAIN

As missionary priests gained power, the conflicts between their own pastoral project and the strategies of caste honor intensified. By the 1900s, Jesuits had taken control of disputed Catholic shrines and used the British courts to erode the rights of Hindu kings and local Maravar chiefs as well as Padroado rivals,[36] arrogating to themselves rights and royal honors. They demonstrated overlordship of an increasingly disembedded ecclesiastical domain in conventional ways by inaugurating devotions; creating, transferring, or eliminating valued privileges; allocating signs of caste honor; and arbitrating disputes. Tamil *kovils*—the focus for political rights—began to turn into Christian *churches*—domains of ecclesiastical authority. Favreux's attempt in the 1850s to erase the historical rights (of village offices or castes) in the Santiyakappar kovil by demolishing the old church building in which he imagined these rights and rivalries were rooted failed (*Résumé,* 151, 175). Yet by the end of the century, the priests' ability to exclude castes or abandon important ceremonies altogether had strengthened in relation to the ability of villagers to manipulate them through shifting sectarian affiliation, refusal of church taxes, or boycotts of Mass.[37] By this time, the church honors system provided not only a field for contesting the village social order but also one in which the Catholic priests worked to reposition their relationship to that order and to make themselves heads of the church as a separate religious realm. In the twentieth century, this authority itself began to transform the festival system from a political institution into a Catholic religious ceremony.

A critical point in this transformation came in 1936. At the inaugural raising of the Santiyakappar festival flag that year, Sousaiyamanikam, the first Vellalar Jesuit parish priest, refused to hand the betel and sandalwood paste honors to the Hindu village headman and officers *inside* the church, because, as he put it, "it is not becoming chiefly when there is the Blessed Sacrament" (APD, 17–25 July 1936). The affronted headman threatened to stop the festival, and the priest reacted by contacting the seniormost subdistrict police officers to secure protection during the festival, and sent a complaint against the headman and his brother to the collector, the subcollector, and the submagistrate. Thus backed by state authority, he set about denying the headman rights in the church. At the principal night priest's mantakappati, the Maravar headman and Vellalar accountant were purposefully not invited by the village drummers to the procession, which in the end all but Pallars boycotted. Then, on the final day,

> [a]t 5pm, as we are preparing to distribute the vetileipakkou [betel honors] before the procession, there arrives a bus bringing the Sub-magistrate of Paramagudi, the Sub-Inspector of Police, Ilayangudi, the Head Constable and some other influential men of Ilayangudi. We four fathers, the Government officials and the two men sit in a row under the pandal in front of the steps before a vast crowd. The Headman and Karnam present themselves. The distribution begins. First Kovil, then "Sicar" [government]. The Headman and Karnam are excluded from touching the *cantanam* [sandal paste] or receiving *veṟṟilaipakku* [betel honors]. Third *kirāmam* [village]. The *maṇṭappaṭi* follows.[38]

Sebastiar Utaiyar (son of the "upper house") and those of his generation interviewed in 1983–84 recalled these events clearly. The headman, forced to acknowledge the loss of rights in the Catholic shrine, yet refusing the dishonor that receipt of the "honors" *outside* the church would entail, persuaded the priest in 1937 to abolish these kovil mariyatais entirely. From that year the procession with the great cattatēr chariot, which had always been organized by the Maravar headman and semiotically produced the village as an integrated Hindu-Christian caste order, was abandoned. The village headman and officers were no longer recipients of the saint's blessing materially transferred through cloth and betel honors. Henceforward, Hindus participated in the festival as individual devotees without specific rights and honors, and their own mariyatai disputes shifted to the festival of the village god Aiyanar (Mosse 1986, 378ff).

The village festival had become a Christian festival and Santiyakappar a Christian saint rather than the village deity. The privileges that remained (paying for processions or carrying the statues) were still the focus of contest between Christian castes, but shares in the festival were to a further degree separated from other rights with which they had formerly been bundled, such as the right to office or service roles, rights to grain shares, and representation at the palace. Once shares in production and in worship—threshing-floor cutantaram and church mariyatai—were no longer interlinked, and village (kiramam) and church (kovil) were decoupled, and the saint's festival and its honors lost valence as the means symbolically to produce a local caste political order. The exclusion of secular power from the definition of the saint equally delimited and Christianized Santiyakappar. Once the ontological contiguity (Bate 2009) between Santiyakappar and the village, between saintly power and political power ("religion" and "politics"), was fractured, the power of the saint as much as the headman was diminished.

The exclusion of the Hindu headman from Catholic ritual was just one particularly important moment in a series of moves by which, over a period of a century, Jesuit priests in colonial India brought into play a European idea of religion as a "bounded domain of action separate from other domains" (Stein 1980, 452). As a Christian church under the authority of the Catholic priest, the Santiyakappar church was now a religious space whose sacredness—defined by the presence of the Eucharist—could not integrate non-Christian claims. A practice earlier considered separate and secular (handing mariyatai to the Hindu headman and karnam inside the church) now compromised the sacred. The Nobilian boundary between the religious and the civil had been relocated within what was "the social" world so as to make Christian-Hindu religious division more marked. The headman's presence in the church was not anomalous simply because it represented a social right in a religious ceremony—after all, Catholics continued to receive caste honors at the festival; it was anomalous because his was a Hindu presence in a Christian rite. In the same way, as late as 1956, the priest of Sarukani church challenged the rights of Hindu chiefs in the area to conduct the large chariot procession of the risen Christ on the grounds that this "is not part of Christian ritual" and that the only rights existing in Catholic religious observances were those granted under the code of canon law (promulgated in 1917) and administered by the bishop (Sarukani parish diaries).

The two processes that had, perhaps for 250 years, constituted the Santiyakappar shrine—one derived from the Holy Church (*tiruccapai*) and its sacraments, and the other derived from the kovil as a field of rights, services, and honor inseparable from caste—now became unstuck. With the gradual institutionalization of Tamil Catholicism as a realm of sacerdotal authority began a process of disembedding Christian practice from caste-political order. This would be of fundamental importance in opening opportunities for lower "untouchable" or dalit castes whose struggle for honor in the twentieth century dominated the next phase of the festival history.

PALLAR CHALLENGES TO HIGH-CASTE RITUAL PREEMINENCE: 1910s TO 1930s

Jesuit missionary priests in Alapuram were not social egalitarians. Up until the 1930s they had no objection to caste distinctions at festivals and even in the central rite of the Mass. Pallars received the sacrament *after* upper castes and at a separate rail at the *back* of the church, where they also sat. They used a separate church entrance and had a separate burial ground. But the equality of all before God meant that Catholics should hear the same Mass in the central parish church, and the priests upheld "the right of all castes to render honor to the saints" by contributing (*vari*) for the processions, with or without "worldly honor" (*Résumé*, 318–19).

Pallar participation in the festivals as subordinated drummers, torch bearers, and menial village servants was emphatically without such honor. However, from the 1910s missionaries gave these Catholics temporary honors, initially through fissures that opened up during upper-caste conflicts and largely as part of their efforts to discipline Utaiyar or Vellalar parishioners. During the 1913–14 dispute-driven

Utaiyar boycott, Gamon offered two Utaiyar mantakappatis to Pallars of neighboring villages, providing police protection against reprisals— although these privileges were swiftly removed once Utaiyars returned to the church in 1915.[39] Then, on 13 May 1917, amid the scandal of big man Gnani Utaiyar's daughter's escape to a convent, Gamon descended from the altar to administer the sacrament. Finding that no upper castes had come forward to the Communion rail, he went to the back of the church to serve Pallars. Two years later he removed the rail separating upper and "lower" castes, inviting Pallars to the southern transept (*maṇṭapam*) of the cruciform church, where they would be equally close to the altar.[40]

If Gamon had initially been anxious about innovation—after all, each such gesture provoked anti-Church upper-caste boycotts—so, too, were most Pallars. In 1919 he writes that they refused to move from the back of the church even when Gamon no longer served Communion there, standing outside in the sun to hear Mass or threatening to convert to Protestantism rather than move to the southern transept. This was possibly out of fear of the consequences for their relationship with landlord patrons. Certainly, "lower house" Gnani Utaiyar had offered to advance money in order to prolong this reactionary rebellion.

The way things had changed four years later, in July 1923, is indicated by a joint deputation of Vellalar and Utaiyars who arrived at the presbytery to petition against Pallar insubordination. Specifically, they demanded that Pallars receive Communion after them, that Pallars be forbidden from following the Way of the Cross, that they should not cook food during the retreat preparing children for confirmation, that there be separate axes for their use in building the church wall, and that girls of different castes should not be mixed in the convent school.[41] Priests, meanwhile, showed a new willingness to protect Pallar interests. In the same year (1923), the new parish priest, Father Veaux ("Ō-cāmi," as he was remembered), supported Pallar drummers' refusal to bring the Maravar headman in procession for the *kovil mariyatai* since the previous year he had insulted them by denying them their betel (APD, 23–25 July 1923). And Pallar leaders themselves took the further significant step of making a public claim, albeit unsuccessful, to festival donorship: the right to carry the saints and chariots, and to sing on the processional route and receive mariyatai equally as contributors to the saint's procession (as mantakappatikarars) and not as village and church servants. Despite forceful upper-caste resistance, in 1924 Veaux did manage to reach an agreement that entitled Pallars to receive a share of the ul-ur mantakappati honors (betel and cloth) for the first time, although this was less than their full share and, more important, was received indirectly from the hand of the Utaiyar headman *outside* the church beside the capparams, rather than *inside* the church from the Vellalar catechist (27 February 1924). Devotional equality still permitted social rank.

By the mid-1920s one or two Pallar families drawing wealth from outside the village (see chapter 5) found other routes to social honor. So Veaux could note, in his diary in June 1924, that "the Feast of the Sacred Heart with sapram [*capparam*] was celebrated as usual by a Pallar [from] Colombo" (APD, 12 June 1924). Four years later Pallar leaders were again pressing for proper mantakappati honors for the caste—that is, a third share of the betel or alternating receipt of the betel, giving Pallars the honor one year in three (APD, Veaux 20 July 1928)—but still with little hope of success against the combined force of upper-caste Catholics, who even in the 1940s invited co-caste Hindus from other villages to carry the capparams rather than involve Pallars (APD Mahé, 23 July 1942). It was clear that missionaries were more willing to object to the treatment of their Pallar converts as *Hindus* in fulfilling duties at temples than their treatment as "untouchables" by caste Christians. In protest, after 1936 Pallars refused servile festival services, especially drumming and bearing the processional torches, and, with little prospect of honor, in the 1940s they withdrew from the Santiyakappar festival entirely.

Disembedding kovil (church) from kiramam (village) after 1936 allowed Pallars to delink roles in the festival from village service, and so freely to appeal to parish priests for equal rights *as Christians.* In this same year, the Jesuit bishop of Tiruchirapalli, Jean-Pierre Leonard, took a series of measures to ensure the equality of Christians more widely. He began celebrating Mass in "Pariah" *cēris* (colonies), and most famously ordered the demolition of a caste-dividing wall in the cathedral.[42] He also issued a pastoral letter requiring every parish priest to "remove all barriers marking a separation between Christians of caste and outcastes wherever they exist."[43]

If Pallars and Paraiyars could now more definitely claim equal treatment *as Christians,* upper castes were just as significantly unable, as Christians, to appeal to the bishop to preserve customary exclusions. When they appealed to colonial authorities for the preservation of distinctions in church ritual, they did so as *Hindus*—the case being that it was against their established custom as converted Hindus (or "Hindu Christians of caste") to be forced to sit next to a body of Adi Dravidas ("untouchables") "composed solely of scavengers and cobblers and flayers," for the sacrament to be served to these people first, or for "Panchama" (untouchable caste) marriages to be held in the central nave of the church, "where Christians of caste sit."[44] The subdivisional magistrate, Mr. S. G. Grubb, did indeed pronounce in favor of the upper-caste Catholics on such grounds of noninterference in custom, deciding that

> although the Christian religion should not, in the strict sense, recognise any distinction of caste, as all the parishioners who frequent the church are only converted Christians who were marked by customs and manners and the ways of Hindus from time immemorial, the distinction between caste Christians and Adi-Dravidas was until now preserved like many rites, such as car processions which were not anticipated in Canon law. That the clergy has recognised and tolerated such resil-

ient distinctions is reflected in the fact that even now these separate arrangements are maintained for the European and Anglo-Indian communities in the church.[45]

While the Alapuram Pallars' claim to equality as Christians received qualified support from clerics after the bishop's reform, their mobility as Pallar "untouchables" was encouraged by a broader critique of caste gaining popularity regionally in the 1920s and 1930s. This was a result of the rise of the secular non-Brahman movement, and especially the more radical anti-Brahmanic Self-Respect Movement of E. V. Ramasamy or "Periyar" ("the great one"), M. K. Gandhi's rationalist counterpart (Washbrook 2009) whose anticaste propaganda gained force in Madras, prompting the formation of new dalit Christian associations. The Catholic clergy, meanwhile, were more vocal in opposing the antireligious Self-Respecters (who had targeted them) than in opposing caste itself (Mallampalli 2004, 175–77). Nonetheless, Jesuits had to respond to the secular movements and to anticaste Protestant missions, at least on the religious matter of opening worship to all and "the doors of the priesthood . . . to the Pariah." As the Jesuit journal *La Mission de Maduré* reported at the time, anti-Brahmanism was turning dalit Catholics against the missionaries: "[T]he hatred of the Brahmans becomes for them mistrust of the clergy; they extend to their priests that which the pagans say of caste."[46]

Very few Jesuit priests rose to condemn caste, as social reformers or Protestant missionaries had. Some, following their bishop, now said Mass in "Pariah" colonies or enlarged churches to allow them equal access (Manickam 2001, 246, 330–44). This itself was enough for upper castes to feel that they could no longer depend upon Jesuits to safeguard their privileges, and they began forming their own associations to petition to keep "Pariahs" out of churches, schools, colleges, and convents, and to organize open revolt against bishops and priests, particularly the "low Jesuits of Toulouse," seeking out Belgian or Indian clerical alternatives (Manickam 2001, 247, 325). A handful of Jesuit priests lent support to dalit Catholics struggling against the oppression of landlords, but they were weak when it came to resisting pressure from upper-caste Catholics. And it was this that perpetuated dalit exclusion, especially from the priesthood (see chapter 6).

THE FEAST OF OUR LADY OF LOURDES (LURTUMATA) AS A PALLAR FESTIVAL

Jesuits missionaries may have had little enthusiasm for anticaste social ideologies, especially radical secularist ones, but their commitment to the principle of equality in the newly redefined realm of religion allowed Alapuram Pallars to acquire formerly denied ritual privileges, and provocatively to translate these back into the language of caste honor and later political rights (chapter 5).

Having withdrawn from the Santiyakappar festival in the 1940s, Pallar leaders began to focus their campaign for respect on a secondary May festival—that of Our Lady of Lourdes (Lurtumata), whose grotto shrine stood over the spot where their ancestors had planted the miraculous tree of Santiyakappar. From 1935, Pallars of the region were the dominant presence in this three-day festival. Denied the honor of paying for the processions themselves, in 1939 Pallars organized the festival drama and in 1943 arranged the devotional singing as well as putting up flags to advertise their *own* newly formed caste society or *caṅkam*. The parish priest, Mahé, sought to resolve the now-annual conflicts over the carrying of the saints' chariots at this festival by allocating one of three mantakappatis to Pallars.[47] His plan never materialized, and it would be the next, more-militant generation of Pallar youth who would secure such honor by taking matters into their own hands. Lurtumata mariyatai conflicts in fact came to a head in 1969. Pallar men forcibly took over the novena procession, grabbing the statues from the hands of Vellalars and Utaiyars in what those I interviewed in 1982–83 still recalled as a pivotal moment in the Pallar struggle against untouchability, leading as it did to the priest handing the entire festival to Pallars and leaving the Santiyakappar festival to Utaiyars and Vellalars.

Pallar youth richly elaborated, with dramas and ceremonial stick fighting (*cilampu viḷayāṭṭu*), their Lurtumata festival, which attracted Christian and Hindu Pallars from surrounding villages. From 1972, the festival involved staged performances (undertaken with police protection) that emphasized Pallar education and empowerment, symbolically represented in the figure of the national untouchable leader Dr. B. R. Ambedkar. The new Ambedkar Club arranged the dramas, and in 1980 the festival hosted the first meeting of the Educated Dalit Youth Organization with speeches on subjects such as "the life of Ambedkar" broadcast to the whole village. At that time, under the leadership of college-educated Michael, who wrote the social and political dramas, the festival had become a forum for "consciousness raising" and education in the ideology of an emerging statewide Pallar caste association (see chapter 5). As Michael explained to me, the Mata feast was crucial to developing a positive nonservile Pallar identity, to the acquisition of skills (in oratory and acting) and mobilizing resources and connections to articulate a critique of socioritual exclusion (cf. Rao 2009, 74). It gave educated young men the freedom to shape public events and to forge cross-village caste networks. In this form, the festival was less the enactment of metonymic connections between divine and political power, and more an arena for explicit *symbolic* struggles and innovations..

Parish priests frowned on the secular and increasingly radical drama scripts, and on the way the feast was now a focus for Pallar identity formation. These parish priests were now Indian (Tamil, Vellalar) and diocesan rather than Jesuit. Pallar elders, whom Michael regarded as self-servingly submissive to the priest (particularly as holders of Roman Catholic school posts), also objected to the transformation of the festival.[48] The Lurtumata festival had become a venue for intergenerational conflict and aired long-standing interfamily feuds that divided the Pallar street and commonly broke into public fights. So, Michael explained, organizing the festival involved nifty internal political work, drawing in youth support, inviting figurehead elders to preside, and keeping factions apart, quite apart from handling upper-caste reactions.

THE DEMOCRATIZATION OF PUBLIC WORSHIP IN THE 1980s

While the Lurtumata festival incubated challenges to upper-caste Catholic ritual privilege in the 1970s, other exclusions were also broken. Pallar youth appropriated the role of altar boy previously reserved for high castes, and in 1978 they commandeered the high-caste funeral bier (acanti), usually kept separately in the church, for one of their own funerals. Thereafter, Utaiyars and Vellalars refused its use, instead bringing a bier from an adjacent hamlet where Utaiyars had preserved it for their exclusive use.

As Pallar economic mobility weakened the power of upper-caste landowners over them (chapter 5), such Catholic signifiers of caste honor became the focus of attack by Pallars, most especially those focused on Santiyakappar, the saint with whom Pallars now asserted a foundational connection through the narration of the sacred tree myth, but whose festival still remained a site of exclusion. This was a burning issue in Alapuram as I settled there in 1982–83. At the festival in 1980, a group of Pallar men had grabbed the microphone from the Utaiyar singer of processional hymns during the major camiyar (priest's) mantakappati. The priest left the procession, and infuriated Utaiyars cut the cable from the generator. Violence escalated as Pallars attempted to carry the statues from the capparams at the end of the procession. After this, the parish priest abandoned his ninth-night mantakappati, the source of so much conflict, and transferred it to the Nadars of the parish for the 1981 and 1982 festivals, effectively managing caste conflict by eliminating the mariyatai contests of multicaste mantakappatis. Catholic festival worship now involved caste-segregated rather than ranked interdependent parts. Then finally, at the All India Catholic Bishops' Conference in 1981, it was resolved to abolish the caste mantakappati festival system entirely.

I recall the Alapuram priest in May 1983 interpreting the circular letter containing the bishops' declarations to a gathering of the village's influential Catholics. The implications, he asserted, were four: (1) the saint's festival was to be celebrated without extravagance and without distinctions of caste on *only one* day; (2) on each of the nine days following the "flag hoisting" there was to be a Mass and a small capparam procession organized by representatives of the different castes of the parish; (3) the festival would be organized by a committee of representatives from each caste and former mantakappatis; and (4) if people refused to comply with these rules, the festival would be terminated. Predictably, Pallars supported the reform, but those Utaiyars consulted preferred to abandon the feast rather than agree to the abolition of customary (*māmūl*) practice. In July, only at the last moment did the priest muster enough upper-caste support to plan the festival he was expecting to abandon. The plan was this: Santiyakappar's statue was to be decorated jointly by the Vellalar kovilpillai and the Pallar pantaram, who would together place it on a "caste-neutral" tractor and trailer *before* the procession. At the end of the procession, the statue was to remain on the trailer and be returned to the church during the next day by the kovilpillai, who would also then distribute the garlands offered during the procession.

The festival went ahead as planned except that the Nadar *ratam* (festival chariot) was used for the statue instead of the tractor. The turnout for the festival was small and made smaller by torrential rain and an almost complete boycott of the procession by upper-caste Catholics. As the Paraiyar band took shelter in a school classroom, a small crowd of mostly Alapuram Pallars and parish Nadars, with a handful of Utaiyar and Vellalars, recognizable as allies of the priest, took the ropes to drag the large wheeled chariot through the plowed mud of the processional streets, passing rows of bedraggled street vendors and under an arch of less than usually spectacular fireworks. All of the other privileged roles were performed by the kovilpillai. There was murmuring disappointment when the priest capped the moment of reform by arranging the showing of a pious film on the life of Jesus in place of the usual stirring and slapstick drama.

The dismantling of this festival system and its distinctions following the 1981 bishops' conference was a decisive move against caste. This was driven by the Tamil Nadu Catholic Church's attempt latterly to bring itself into line with the anticaste position of the modern Indian state, as well as a post–Vatican II emphasis on social justice. The wavering dichotomy between religious and social action that the Alapuram priests had inherited from Nobili was now ready to be dismantled; caste was challenged, not as an affront to Christian *religion* but as a contravention of Christian social ethics. It was in this spirit that a couple of years later an ardent Alapuram priest assembled all the saints' capparams and burned them.

Following my fieldwork in the 1980s, Tamil priests set about eliminating the remaining caste distinctions.[49] Segregated seating in church and separate funeral biers were abandoned and church decision making democratized through a structure of parish councils.[50] Meanwhile, caste issues were evaded rather than resolved by a series of younger priests influenced by liberation theology (see chapter 6), who drew on Paulo Freire's ideas of "conscientization" to set up a core team of educated youth to "animate" mixed-caste youth and women's groups organized in the seventy-three villages of the parish. In 1985–86, the priest tried to rearrange the Santiyakappar festival around residential (village) rather than caste identities. He began by dividing the parish into nine "zones" (*vaṭṭāram*) comprising four or five villages, each responsible for organizing one day of the festival. Behind this formal arrangement, however, caste relationships still organized interests in the festival, reappearing in the lobbying for privileges from the priests, who themselves "played caste" by, for example, holding one vattaram in the name of a Pallar hamlet because Utaiyars refused to cooperate (while justifying the move in terms of the geographical centrality of the Pallar hamlet in question).

The saint's processions had anyway been transformed into parades for social and moral education. Themed slide shows and dramas on caste, corruption, or dowry were scripted and rehearsed for each day by the different "zones," and printed notices and banners with slogans such as "Let us be united" and "Let us eradicate caste" were produced. Viewed in terms of caste honor, these could still provoke upper-caste retaliation (not least where dramas, posters, or parades involved veiled challenges to particular individuals), and threats or physical assaults were once again directed at the parish priests (see chapter 7). Then in 1989 and 1990 upper-caste Catholics in Alapuram found support from the Hindu nationalist Rashtriya Swayamsevak Sangh (RSS) rallying public objection to the priest's erosion of customary caste honors in the church festivals. Not for the first time, upper-caste Catholics found in "Hinduness" a refuge from the erosion of their caste honor.

Finally, dismantling earlier forms of public worship also partly disembedded Catholic devotion from local forms of popular religiosity. Santiyakappar had become less a divine king and source of territorial protection and more a human exemplar. His festival was an opportunity to communicate social or spiritual messages, but the saint himself seemed less present as a source of divine power for his devotees, who could no longer touch his statue encased behind glass.

CONCLUSIONS: A CATHOLIC FESTIVAL AND ITS TRANSFORMATION

The festivals of the saints were at the center of a remarkable Hindu-Catholic synthesis in rural Ramnad, where Catholic ritual articulated a local culture of power. But Catholic churches were not simply replicas of Hindu temples. They generated their own distinctive dynamics. For one thing, in colonial India, French Jesuits missionaries were able, by stages, to produce Catholic religion as an institutional domain separate from and incompatible with the demands of caste society, shifting the boundaries that marked the distinction between "the religious" and "the social" inherited from Nobili. The understanding of what constituted Christian practice was not, however, stable. Jesuit missionaries moreover failed to appreciate the extent to which, for local actors, meaning lay as much in ritual-aesthetic form as in religious content (saint or deity, church or temple). From the point of view of Tamil villagers, the ritual of the newly separate domain of Catholic religion remained an important part of caste honor as the cultural performance of power. Between missionary and local interpretations lay a manipulable ambiguity in which Jesuit mission building and village caste politics were played out. In fact, it was the particular negotiability of ritual in Catholic kovils that made them important sites for groups such as Utaiyars (in the nineteenth century) and Pallars (in the twentieth) to dramatize their social repositioning in the context of colonial and postcolonial shifts in economic and political power.

The intersection of mission building and caste politics produced three kinds of long-term social effects. One was the fragmentation of a socially integrative festival system into competing social parts; the second was a disembedding of Catholic practice from village social relations; and the third was a sharpening of the boundary between Christian and Hindu religious identities. Let me conclude this chapter by considering each in turn.

As the gradients of socioeconomic power in Alapuram leveled somewhat, competition over symbolic resources intensified. At the same time public expressions of social rank were less tolerated. The way in which caste orders fragment under antihierarchy pressure into independent parts is captured in Dumont's conception of the shift from caste as holistic structure (hierarchical, complementary) to caste "substantialized" as separate, and competing groups (1980, 222). Certainly, it is common for groups in *mariyatai* contests to withdraw from Tamil village festivals and to establish their own independent cults. This is similar to what happened under the influence of a series of parish priests who disintegrated the Santiyakappar festival itself into caste-separate parts in attempts to manage honors disputes. In chapter 3, I noted how the array of Hindu temples in Alapuram can also be seen as the outcome of a particular history of mariyatai contests around the Aiyanar village temple (see Mosse 1986, 374–402).

In her study of Hindu cults in rural Tirunelveli, Mines (2005) shows how the assertions of independent worship give subordinated groups control over ritual and spatial processes (during space-altering processions) so as to sanction alternative social orderings that empower. The withdrawal of Pallars from the Santiyakappar festival and their capture and elaboration of the Lurtumatha festival as a venue for display, donorship, and service-free mariyatai offers a Catholic example of such a process. But Mines wants us to look beyond the structural effects to examine the cultural processes of empowerment at work. In particular, she argues that divinity itself is incorporated into assertions of low-caste social power through independent cults focused on their "fierce gods." The agency of excluded groups such as Pallars, she argues, is amplified because of their material participation in the dangerous power of these divinities—a power that is conceptualized as the cumulative effect of sin/harm displaced (by rituals of disposal) to exterior places (katu) to which subordinated people and their gods are connected.[51]

If Hindu dalits are so empowered through their gods, what of Catholic Pallars? Although Mines's analysis of materially connected divine-human power derived from exteriorized sin or harm makes no Christian sense (chapter 3), the shrines of Catholic Pallar (and other dalits) that were established after breaking away from caste-dominated parish churches did commonly focus on the "dangerous" and ambivalently powerful ascetic saints such as St. Sebastian and Vanattu Cinnappar (St. Paul the Hermit) (chapter 2). When Paulraj Pallar returned from Malaysia in the 1960s and established a new shrine as a mark of distinction, he built it for Vanattu Cinnappar in the dangerous, liminal wasteland on the tank's edge, beside a cemetery—exactly corresponding to the outside space of Mines's "fierce gods." Rather than parading the saint, the prestige of donorship here involved sacrificing goats and arranging a public feast.[52] In narrating their originary connection to Santiyakappar, Pallar neighbors likewise connected themselves materially to dangerous saintly power, informing me that when it stood, the sacred Santiyakappar tree would paralyze any goat that was allowed to wander into the church compound and eat its leaves. Only the direct descendants of those Pallars who brought the tree to the village (the *kōvilaṉ vamcam* or "church lineage") could intercede to release them.

The Catholic saints of Pallars may be dangerous, fault punishing, and linked to the exterior (chapter 2), but it would be overstretching the parallel to suggest that they embody the interests of one group over another. In the 1980s, at least, Catholic Pallars in Alapuram did not conceptualize divinity in the shape of aggressive caste ambition so much as insert themselves into a structure of public worship so as to effect a shift from subordinate service to donorship and honor. The objective of Pallar assertions was to be at the controlling *center* of public worship, not a danger from outside.[53] The particular success of the Lurtumatha cult was its centrality, its recognition by the public and the Church (while Paulraj's Vanattu Cinnappar shrine never received the priest's blessing).

That Pallars (dalits) were able to dominate the festival associated with a major shrine—to carry the statues and conduct the procession, and receive all the publicly acknowledged marks of caste honor—was unprecedented in the region.[54] This and the festival's paradoxical capacity to allow Pallar mobilization *against* caste exclusion by laying claim to markers *of* caste distinction (commensurate with their altered socioeconomic position) was reason enough for a new educated youth leadership to make the Catholic festival a vehicle for activism, aspiration, and the caste's political consciousness (see chapter 5).

As the Jesuit missionaries began to control church ritual and make it more Christian, they reduced the upper castes' share of symbolic capital (Harrison 1995, 268–69) and made it more difficult for these groups (Christian or Hindu) to secure rank through public enactments at festivals or funerals, or through seating at Mass. But they made it easier for lower-caste groups such as Pallars to lay claim to caste honor on the pretext of religious equality *as Christians*. Making public ritual more separately Catholic had opened up new political space, a new political identity, and a set of possibilities for dalits. It was as Christians that they shifted from service to donorship in the festival; as Christians that they first publicly enacted a critique of caste society. Indeed, the erosion of existing tradition (*māmūl*) and its replacement by church administration was supported by low castes. Dalits gained rights and honors through the institutionalization of Catholic religion and the exclusion of non-Christian rights bearers. The limitations of entitlements born of religious exclusivism rather than inclusive public and civil rights will become clear in chapter 5. But a more immediate dilemma was that claims to caste honor were linked to an institutional move against caste that would ultimately push the Church to dismantle the symbolic system that generated this honor in the first place, rendering obsolete the Durkheimian model of social integration with its services, donors, and ranked honors, disembedding Catholicism from the social matrix in which it first took root in the Tamil countryside, and delinking Hindu and Christian systems of public worship. The Santiyakappar festival was now a church ceremony rather than a village institution, participation had more to do with a person's relationship with the Church than their social group's place in society, and it now mattered whether this person was Catholic or Hindu.

Did this create new Hindu-Christian boundaries or enhance the social significance of religious difference? As Good (1999, 55) reminds us, "identities based on caste and religion are ideological constructs whose significance is constantly being renegotiated and reinterpreted." Chapter 7 assesses whether in the longer run the removal of shared ritual gave religious difference a new social meaning in Alapuram, and whether the events of the 1930s (excluding Hindus) or the 1980s (burning caste capparams) can be looked back on as key moments that allowed "new categories of identity and new understandings of society" (Tejani 2008, 20), and specifically whether religion now "provide[d] the most compelling basis for community" (Freitag 1989, 187–88, in Good 1999, 61). And such looking back would search colonial rule and missionary endeavor for other processes that built religious difference into ritual, government, and law as a basic premise. Chandra Mallampalli (2004) in particular has examined the way in which in the 1920s and 1930s Catholic elites, fitting with colonial assumptions of the foreignness of Christianity and the rulers' categorizations of "community," sought "Indian Catholic" entry into the public life of the emerging nation (in provincial politics and constitutional debates) as a separate electorally protected *religious* minority. But the marginality within the nation that arose from this assertion of distinct Catholic identity, culture, institutions, and interests *obedient to Rome*—hence the refusal of politics independent of religion—was not reproduced among the rural majority. Here religious difference was not social premise.

The Jesuit production of a Catholic religious domain did, however, mark its ontological separation from the domain of politics in Tamil society—Christian divinity from royal power—which could on occasion find public expression. When, for example, in February–March 1995 Tamil Catholics mobilized in public protest against posters of the Virgin Mary and child with the face of Chief Minister Jayalalitha, the still-rarely articulated "Christian community" stood against this political appropriation of religion in a manner that was distinct from Hindus at the time as well as from Catholicism in earlier centuries.[55]

The period covered in this chapter spans one in which scholars have nonetheless commonly sought to describe and explain the sudden assertion of politically significant religious difference, or "communalism." Indeed, debate on religious identity is often shaped within a telos of division and conflict (Tejani 2008). Once it became clear that in "modern" India religion would not be consigned to the private sphere, attention turned to explaining the persistence of religious divisions and conflicts as a product of colonial rule's exigencies or a failure of national identity and the secular state—as a crisis of modernity (Tejani 2008). Ramnad was not lacking in the circumstances thought to produce religious conflict and violence, such as changing structures of authority caused by the rapid modification of "local systems of compromise and bargaining" or arising from the social mobility of newly powerful groups, or the "defensive manoeuvres" of a declining elite (Bayly 1985, 202, in Good 1999, 53). However, these circumstances tended to presage caste rather than interreligious violence.

The microprocesses in Alapuram that separated "Hindu" and "Christian" in the 1930s or in the 1980s relate to those on a larger scale that might indeed have realized the imagined "Christian minority" as a political constituency, and that might later in the 1990s shape the response to a resurgent Hindu nationalism that conceived of the Christian community as an "antinational" target of aggression. But in the 1980s, Hindu and Christian identities had not become the basis upon which political and economic interests were organized or imagined locally (Good 1999, 62). Deepening religious division had not acquired social valence, even when outsiders—whether the Church, colonial courts, or the post-Independence state—gave special significance to religious identities and action, customs and sentiments, although this fact meant that competing groups might choose tactically to present themselves and their interests in religious terms. Thus dalits claimed equality as Christians, knowing that missionaries would support them on this basis; and upper castes sought to protect their customary privileges as Hindus (or "Hindu Christians"), knowing that British courts (or more recently Hindu nationalist organizations) would protect established arrangements that were "religious." Both challenged the idea of a "Christian community," making caste again the mediator of the boundary between the religious and the social.

5

Christianity and Dalit Struggle

1960s to 1980s

How in the postmissionary era was Christianity drawn into Tamil dalit struggles against caste and untouchability? What did the Church and Christian identity have to offer amid the post-Independence project of equalization, in a society that had acquired universal franchise as well as legal protection and targeted welfare programs for dalits, who were now claimed by the state as its "injured subjects" (Rao 2009, 177–78)? How did dalit Christians respond when the protections and resources available for targeted victims depended upon governmental categories that excluded Christian converts and reproduced the stigmatized identities that Christians had sought to escape, and required that they present themselves as Hindu if not actually reconvert to Hinduism?

Beginning with Alapuram village and moving outward, this chapter explores interactions of caste and religion, and the emergence of a Christian dalit politics initially growing out of the politics of festival honors. It will first become clear why the Church was especially important as a site for dalit social struggle, and second, how the rise of a discourse of civic rights gradually replaced Christian religious equality as the medium through which dalits strove against exclusion. In the process caste was "rendered public" at new sites of contest, including public amenities and educational institutions. While there was a progressive weakening of specific discriminations against dalits in the pragmatic "civic culture" of post-Independence India, dalits seemingly remained or even newly became a distinctive social grouping separated by a "hard bar" or "fault line" that ran through society as a whole, particularly evident in caste violence (Mendelsohn and Vicziany 1998).

Observing the microprocesses at the village level in the 1980s also showed a differentiation of opportunity among separate dalit castes and revealed the unequalizing effects of struggles for equality. This chapter will then highlight the different ways in which Christianity (Catholic versus Protestant) was incorporated into projects of mobility and modernity, and how being or remaining Hindu was also made available as a dalit identity choice.

From late colonial times, Christian affiliation had provided a means for dalits in rural Ramnad to claim honor or contend with subordination *within* existing orders, and Christianity was rarely a *religious* challenge to (Hindu) caste. But from the 1980s a more explicitly countercultural dalit-discourse began to construe caste as a Hindu Brahmanic imposition. This coincided with the post-Independence consolidation of the idea of the nation as Hindu that, as we will see, gave dalit religious conversion a new political significance. In this context, the identity of "dalit" itself emerged as one that explicitly rejected patronizing assimilation both to the Hindu majority as "Harijans" (children of God) and to the state welfare category of "Scheduled Caste." Toward the end of the chapter it will be seen how a dalit cultural movement that began outside politics was gradually institutionalized within party politics, while the next chapter will trace the specific Catholic contribution to this new Tamil dalit politics.

PALLAR PROTEST: FROM RELIGIOUS EQUALITY TO CIVIC RIGHTS

From the 1920s, Catholic Pallars in Alapuram had pressed for *religious* rights as Christians, although their aspirations were increasingly fostered "through the institutions and ideologies of colonial modernity" (Rao 2009, 77). Education, the military, migrant labor, or the courts extended ideas of entitlement to equal treatment and enhanced a dalit capacity for social challenge. The arrival of Catholic primary schooling in Alapuram around 1925 was particularly significant in facilitating Pallar occupational diversification and escape from agrarian servitude—for instance, though migrant labor to Burma or Ceylon[1] as well as jobs in the military, the police, the railways, or other colonial enterprises. Upper-caste villagers reacted to the leveling norms of the new primary school by trying to reproduce caste codes, passing a resolution in 1932 that "the *vāttiyār* [teacher], a Pallar, cannot sit while giving his class."[2] Economic opportunities were certainly unevenly available to Alapuram dalits. They were mostly captured by Catholic Pallars, and that, too, by families of one Konan or "kingly" lineage (*vamcam*). These families were the first educated and employed in Catholic schools, and one in particular worked tenanted rice paddies in Burma, investing profits in a grand house and dryland holdings of thirty acres (a 16 percent share of Pallar landowning, by my survey).

In the interwar years such progressive Pallars as well as their poorer neighbors had good reason to use the Catholic Church as a vehicle for status aspirations. Jesuit missionaries willingly defended Pallar rights as Christians to refuse demeaning funeral or festival service, Sunday work, and humiliating acts of physical prostration or female exposure.[3] They also intervened in agrarian relations and in the affairs of village administration to prevent injustice to Christians, while using their control of prized ritual honors to impose sanctions on oppressive landlords or village officers. As early as 1870, we find Father Favreux protecting the Pallar kutumban's grain-share entitlement (put at risk by his withdrawal from Hindu festival service) by threatening to exclude the village accountant (karnam) from Santiyakappar festival honors. By the 1920s, Pallars expected such support from Jesuits and in its absence threatened to join the Protestants.

Jesuit action for secular justice was constrained, however, first by their own sense of the specifically "religious" domain of their authority, and second by the noninterference exceptionalism with which the colonial courts to whom they appealed treated matters of religious or customary rights. In the same year (1923) that Fr. Veaux equalized access to Holy Communion, to the Way of the Cross, and extended donorship to Pallars at the Santiyakappar festival, he was quite unable to challenge their exclusion from public utilities such as the village tank. Regarding a petition to the submagistrate on the right of Pallars to place their mud pots in the tank as other castes did, rather than scoop water with palmyra-leaf baskets, the court ruled that "Pallars have the right to the *urani* [tank]. However, as they acknowledge in practice the superiority of the Maravars [and] Udeyars [sic] . . . they may not draw water with *kuṭams* [mud pots], but with *verkuṭam* or with *peṭṭi* [palmyra baskets]."[4] Even fifteen years later, in 1938, when Pallars appealed against the practice of funeral prostrations in front of upper castes, another submagistrate similarly insisted that "the parties keep the peace, [and do] not write useless petitions, the result of which will be nil . . . till the Pallars surrender or the Odeages [Utaiyars] consent to give up their claim for the observance of the custom of prostrating."[5]

In time, subaltern groups would use colonial ideas of public access to subvert colonial ideas of custom and community (Rao 2009, 82); but in the 1930s, the commons (tank or temple, water or wood) still referenced an older Tamil conception of the "public" as the space of mariyatai and differentiated rights rather than of civic access (see Mosse 2003). This made the Church—ready to equalize its own spaces of honor—particularly important to dalit emancipatory action, while building a strong commitment to Catholic identity among Pallars. The particular space that the church offered in which dalits were able to press demands for religious equality was later subsumed under a liberal paradigm of civil rights, especially once the late-colonial government began to erode its distinction between rights that were customary or religious (treated as exception) and those that were civil, and as untouchability was "secularized" as exclusion from public amenities

(Rao 2009, 82, 131, 176). The dalit leader Dr. B. R. Ambedkar had himself insisted that the pivotal issue of dalit entry to temples was not (as Gandhi maintained) a matter of reforming Hindu authorities so as to extend a religious right to dalits, but a question of dalits' universal civic right to enter public spaces or government property (ibid., 81, 107).

It was the secularization of caste rights (no longer separated out as custom or religion) that opened political space for dalits. However, their claim to equal rights as Christians—which in the 1920s preceded these civic rights—had depended upon the Jesuits' denial of civic (or secular) rights—such as those of the Alapuram headman and village officers—within the saints' festival system and insistence on the exclusively religious and Christian nature of the church space. Christian dalits gained privileges through Christian religious exclusivity long before they were able in the 1950s to struggle for equivalent rights in major Hindu temples on the basis of civic access—that is, the denial of Hindu religious exclusivity (A. M. Xavier 2006, 63). Dalit equality depended upon denial of the Santiyakappar church as *kovil*—as a village institution subject to civil authority and ranked offices and honors. Jesuit priests would nonetheless invoke the secular liberal notion of private property (behavior in, or exclusion from, Church property) to exclude the rights of others, rather as Hindu temple authorities used regimes of property to challenge demands for civic access, thereby turning dalit temple entry into an issue of trespass (Rao 2009, 82, 92). Thus in the pre-Independence period, to different ends, both Hindu and Christian religion would be materialized as property so as to legally underpin religious authority.

After Independence, a younger generation of Alapuram Catholic Pallars began more consistently to focus their protests on constitutional rights and civic access, appealing to the Indian state rather than to the missionary church. Moreover, hitherto localized protests were brought together on a larger scale and into new forms of public assertion such as Gandhian satyagraha (cf. Rao 2009, 77). Decolonization had radically changed the context of such action. The Ramnad system of Zamindari rule, with all its caste-linked roles and offices, was progressively dismantled (see Mosse 2003 on this transformation). Universal franchise and electoral competition, albeit superimposed upon enduring social inequalities, fundamentally altered the practice of caste politics.[6] Various measures of state protection, including the criminalization of practices that inferiorized social groups as "untouchable," were introduced along with the new juridical category of the "caste atrocity" (Rao 2009, 173) and a range of other state measures of positive discrimination (loans, land, job reservations) for the development of the now bureaucratically categorized "Scheduled Castes."[7]

But while dalits gained civic rights, the state disqualified *Christian* dalits from the new provisions and protections by defining Scheduled Castes as "degraded Hindus" (Rao 2009, 133), even while conceiving untouchability as civic disability and socioeconomic backwardness. State policy on caste reservation on the one hand, and on religious minorities on the other, split class and religion. Thus a presidential order of 1950 determined that "no person who professes a religion different from Hinduism shall be deemed to be a member of the Scheduled Castes."[8] This barred Christians from every dalit-targeted benefit, from loans schemes to preventative police protection, although Hindu dalits hardly fared better since the sanctions of locally dominant castes in Ramnad operated with more speed, force, and certainty against dalit claims or protests than would the caste-infused police and judiciary to protect them. In this context dalits in Alapuram realized that civic-rights assertions had to be underpinned by economic independence, and Christians took the lead both in searching out economic opportunity and in subsequent struggles for civic rights in Ramnad.

By the 1960s a growing number of Alapuram Pallar families were able to take advantage of the diversification of the regional economy, working not only as laborers but also as drivers, conductors, post-office and other skilled workers, in business and in professions including teaching. But land ownership was the best indicator of rising economic strength. Investment of small surpluses (facilitated by post-Independence land-ceiling legislation) had brought more and more village land under Pallar plows, at first sharecropped, then under securer fixed-rate and land-mortgage tenure. By 1982–84, 89 percent of Pallar households were landowners. At this time, Pallars made up 25 percent of the village population and possessed nearly 16 percent (and a decade later 20 percent) of Alapuram land (two-thirds of it unirrigated). Among the younger economically enfranchised Pallar leaders who redirected public protest for church honors to civic rights was the energetic Paulraj.[9]

In August 1968, Paulraj made a complaint to the district subinspector of police about illegal practices of untouchability in the village, including exclusion from teashops, naming upper-caste individuals as perpetrators.[10] When this appeal was ignored, he and fifteen or so Pallar strongmen barged into one of the village teashops demanding hitherto denied service. There followed a three-day public fast in front of the symbolically important shrine of Our Lady of Lourdes, which brought people from the Pallar streets of some twenty neighboring villages. Here, and later at a larger rally in a nearby market town in April 1969, an "Untouchability Eradication Order" (*tīṇṭāmai oḷippu caṭṭam*) was published and sent not only to the district collector and revenue inspector, but also to the Tamil Nadu chief minister, M. Karunanidhi. The demand was for equal treatment in teashops; access to reservoirs, wells, and temples; freedom from "servile work" (atimai velai—grave digging, etc.); respect (mariyatai) in forms of address "according to age, education, and occupation"; and a prohibition on the imposition of sanctions on those self-respecting persons who claimed these rights—and finally that "the Untouchability (Offences) Act which has been sleeping for the last 21 years be woken up."

At the rally, the police initially offered protection but later intercepted trucks bringing Pallar protestors from afar and dispersed the mass meeting. Meanwhile, non-dalits (reportedly led by cadres of the Dravida Munnetra Kazhagam—DMK—party) organized reprisals, blocking Pallars' return to their streets, where property was destroyed and the houses of leaders set alight. In the aftermath of the protest, Alapuram's Utaiyar "lower house" led other landlords in throwing Pallar sharecrop tenants off their lands. Forty dalit and caste men were arrested and imprisoned, among them Paulraj—although he was soon released to make representation to the chief minister in Madras before being called back by the district collector to quiet things down in the disturbed Alapuram locality. Here he organized another round of petitions on the upper-caste intimidation of Pallars (who now provocatively contravened exclusions by wearing sandals or carrying umbrellas in upper-caste streets) and against the retaliatory attacks on Pallar teachers and the theft of dalit crops and livestock. A minister was dispatched from Madras to chair a reconciliation meeting in Paramakudi town (where twelve years earlier Immanuel Sekaran had been murdered; see p. 309n6). In the end, Alapuram Pallar rights were publicly affirmed and police protection authorized amid official warnings against intimidation. A few weeks later, an MP from Delhi was touring Pallar villages, giving assurances of justice and state protection.

The dalit leadership and political action coming out of Alapuram in 1968–69 and its effects were something altogether new, particularly the mass mobilization around rights to public access and the successful appeal to the state for intervention and protection, even where the local-level bureaucracy was under the control of non-dalit opponents. In other respects, however, this collective action was continuous with an earlier pattern of Pallar mobilization and made use of intervillage (and, through migration, international) networks that had been established over the previous fifty years to press for Catholic festival *mantakappatis*. The discourse of Pallar emancipation had moved from the particularistic to the universal, from ritual honors to civic rights, and used newly available identities as citizens of India (rather than those of Christian or Catholic). However, this action still largely excluded non-Pallar dalits. It was also distinctly male, even though dalit women—as wives, mothers, or daughters—were those most exposed to retaliatory violence, police brutality, and economic sanctions, as Bama (2008) also vividly narrates.

From the late 1950s until the 1990s, Ramnad became well known for Pallar political-legal action of this kind, typically focused on public spaces of untouchability, whether teashops, temples, public water, or public offices (Panchayat presidentships), and equally for the violence of caste reprisals that later became a rallying call for new dalit political leadership (see Human Rights Watch 1999a). The use of anti-untouchability law was central to the strategy of local leaders and their wider networks, although the judicial process involved had the inevitable effect of individualizing and exceptionalizing social subordination, by turning structural violence into untouchability "cases" (Rao 2009, 242) (whereas struggles at festivals had clearly been a matter of *collective* caste honor). Meanwhile, the "Scheduled Caste" beneficiary label could be seen as preparing for a parallel depoliticizing effect on anti-untouchability radicalism, transforming Ambedkar's idea of a political minority (see below) into a class of disadvantaged claimants (Tejani 2008, 24; Mendelsohn and Vicziany 1998).

Christians were in principle excluded from all of these laws, rules, and schedules. The post-Independence state effected bureaucratically something that the churches had largely failed to achieve socially—namely, Christian separateness, albeit imposed upon the reality of common dalit identity and experience. The social conditions of Christian dalits were thus further depoliticized as they came to be represented as part of a religious minority for whom the key protection would be defined in terms of *religious* freedom (Tejani 2008, 24). The Christian religious equality through which Alapuram Pallars had first been able to negotiate untouchability had now been turned into a politically and economically isolating cage. No wonder many Christian dalits within reach of the "Scheduled Caste," or "SC," scholarships and job reservations sought "reconversion" and through notices published in the *District Gazette* registered themselves officially as Hindus. The Madurai Aadheenam, a Saivite religious institution located near the great Meenakshi Temple in Madurai, began to organize rituals for the reconversion of Christians to the "religion of their ancestors," more than seven thousand being effected in 1979 alone (*Hinduism Today* magazine, June 1980).

The system of state provision and reservations required the articulation of demand and therefore reflection by targeted groups on their own identity and entitlement: who they are and what they deserve (Still 2007, 280). The dilemma for Alapuram's Catholic Pallar youth was that claiming protection or achieving progress by means of state concessions meant retreat to the very untouchable and Hindu identities they had left behind, as well as unwanted association with other groups inferiorized in Tamil society. But at the same time, exclusion from the "SC" list as Christians meant the failure to acknowledge the historical oppression from which these reparative entitlements arose. The problem young Pallar men debated on my *tiṉṉai* (veranda) in 1983–84 was how to reconcile climbing up with claiming down; how to ensure legal protection and access to state benefits *with dignity* when acquiring resources meant asserting inferiority (cf. Isaacs 1965, 114; Rudolph and Rudolph 1967, 150). The most articulate of my interlocutors on this dilemma was Michael (alias Kannappan), a young man whose officially Hindu identity had landed him a local college-lecturer post. His explanations told me how, throughout the 1960s and 1970s, Alapuram Pallars had secured resources and protection from the state, but found dignity from the Church. As men like him adeptly articulated "SC" identity and registered Hindu names, the church and Catholic festivals became even more important as platforms from which to launch public assertions of Christian and Pallar distinction.[11] When the bishops abolished the mantakappati festival system in 1982–83 and erased the ritual language of Catholic caste honor that had freed Pallars from the dilemmas of proclaiming stigma, Michael and others were searching out alternative discourses of mariyatai.

Specifically, Michael encouraged the youth of his street not to think of themselves as Pallar "Harijans" or "SCs," but as Devēntira Kula Vēḷāḷars (DKV), an identity promoted by the Catholic Pallar historian R. Deva Asirvatham, whose now popularized caste histories asserted that the true identity of Pallars was Mallars—the southern Tamil rulers (or *mūvēntar*) and the original settlers of fertile river tracts (or *vēḷḷāḷar*), worshippers of Indra (Teventiran) who were expelled, robbed of their land, and reduced to serfdom by conquering Telugu (Vijayanagara) and Muslim armies in the seventeenth century.[12] The Pallar response to the historical experience of subordination was to insist that theirs was a case of mistaken identity. In 1983 Deva Asirvatham traveled to visit me in Alapuram to explain the importance of his historical researches. He carefully explained that the Telugu invaders not only scattered and subordinated the ruling Mallars, changing their name to Pallan, meaning "lower," and degrading the caste who had been the heroes of *paḷḷu* songs and literature (Kannan and Gros 2002, 44), but also promoted less-cultured marginal "forest" tribes, such as the Kallars and Maravars (the "Tevars"), as their military chiefs (*pāḷaiyakkārars*). Deva Asirvatham drew on the same anti-Brahman golden-age racial theories of caste that inspired Protestant missionaries (chapter 1) but transformed the Aryan-Dravidian theory so that the target was not Brahmans but the "Backward Castes" wielding power in the Dravidian nationalist parties (the Dravida Munnetra Kazhagam [DMK] and its rival the All India Anna DMK [AIADMK]).[13] Moreover, the mythology used a classical Tamil landscape semiotic to align Pallars with a conception of "agrarian civility" while inferiorizing their political opponents in the idiom of its opposite: the "savagery" of the katu (the uncultivated space of forest or wasteland) (Pandian 2009, 34).

Michael localized Asirvatham's ethnohistory, maintaining that ruling Pallars and founders of Alapuram's Santiyakappar shrine had been pauperized by their liberal munificence—a classical quality of the *vēḷāḷaṉ* cultivator (Pandian 2009, 43)—to socially inferior migrant settlers. Minds later dulled through poverty, skins blackened by the sun, and driven by base appetites, they lost their remaining lands. Yet Pallars, being born to rule, felt slavery to be against their nature; they knew how to work to recover rightful prosperity and to fight for themselves with valor to match their Maravar opponents as well as to protect weaker groups (including Paraiyars, who shared a "softness" with their Brahman counterparts [see below]).[14]

In 1983, Michael founded a village branch of the statewide Devēntira Kula Vēḷāḷar (DKV) association at a function where Pallar village notables welcomed the movement's state-level leaders, garlanding them where else but in front of the Santiyakappar church.[15] The association's message was that Pallar political assertion depended upon dignifying their caste identity, the present struggle against subordination being understood as recovery of a usurped preeminence (cf. Cohn 1959, 207–8; Lynch 1969, 70–74; 1972, 97–112). This meant in turn that Pallar entitlement to a proportionate share of state benefits need not be acknowledgement of shared inferiority or the receipt of charity, but claiming back a part of what was rightfully theirs.[16] The DKV association was shaped particularly around the needs of educated professional men like Michael, who keenly experienced the contradiction between personal mobility and social inferiorization. It embraced Christian religious identity and lobbied against exclusion from Scheduled Caste lists. But its practical achievements were rather limited. When in 1984 the association mobilized around the proposal for a Pallar-managed "Ambedkar higher secondary school" in the village, it was thwarted by a rival proposal backed by the archbishop (a Vellalar from the village) to establish the school under the name of St. James, managed by the De La Salle Brothers religious order. The church school opened in 1989, leaving Pallar youth pondering how, having asserted caste over Christian identity, they had been marginalized from the new Church institution and its appointments (see chapter 7).

Several scholars point out that reservation policies designed to eliminate caste in fact serve to strengthen it, but my point here is that the *way* in which they "reinforce group solidarities based on caste identity" (Dudley-Jenkins 2003, 59) is shaped by particular histories of identity formation and mediated by specific discourses. The DKV discourse was not anticaste; it was a discourse of mariyatai (distinction). At the inaugural Alapuram meeting, the DKV secretary began by saying that caste in India "cannot be eradicated" (*oḻikkamuṭiātu*) and that Pallars must therefore struggle for self-advancement. This did not involve looking for common dalit interests.[17] If anything, inequalities among dalit castes were rearticulated. In DKV mythic history, Paraiyars were advisers and officers under the ruling Mallars and, although equally subjugated by Telugu invaders, had their origins in the aboriginal periphery from which Pallar ideologues distanced themselves. For this reason, in the 1980s the DKV passed several resolutions rejecting government proposals to change the collective term for Scheduled Castes to Adi Dravida ("original Dravidians"), a label by then synonymous with Paraiyars, which would implicate Pallars in a kind of inferior proto-Tamil culture. The Pallar narrative of fallen greatness and agrarian civility was a discourse of distinction that, like the Catholic festival honors, did not preclude, indeed required, the attribution of inferiority to others.

One way in which Pallar advancement was pursued, in Alapuram too, was indeed the continued inferiorization of others, especially Paraiyars and Cakkiliyars, not least through self-distancing and "downward displacement" of their own former service roles. In the 1980s, members of the Kōṉaṉ ("king") lineage told me how they had always distanced themselves from the inferior role (*toḻil*) of the *veṭṭiyaṉ* gravediggers, performed from the 1930s by a family of Pallar migrants brought to Alapuram as paid servants of an Utaiyar landlord, while they (Konan Pallars) held the superior office of *kutumpan,* with which came the honorary title of caste headman and a *māniyam* land grant (Mosse 2003, 72). Like elite Utaiyars a century earlier, Konans had translated economic success (as landowners and teachers) into social aloofness through prestige marriages with nonkin from *outside* the village, refusing to share in non-Konan food or life-crisis celebrations. Their norms of sociality ensured recognition of their success while solidifying class differences by negating the demand to share the fruits of success with poorer kin (cf. Still 2007, 134).[18] But this Pallar elite did not just engineer social separation; they also assumed the trappings of caste dominance. They settled a Pothera Vannar (dalit dhobie/barber) family to provide life-crisis services and arranged cutantaram grain-share payments along with other asymmetrical transactions that signified caste servitude (chapter 4). They also made themselves aiya vitu masters of Cakkiliyar-tied servants, who were idiomatically their "sons" (ethnographically objectified as the "untouchables' untouchables" (cf. Moffatt 1979). Evidently, a dalit elite gained some measure of social standing by displacing markers of their own former subordination and, by becoming patrons, acquiring their own caste-ascribed services.

After the 1969 conflict and the termination of sharecrop contracts with upper-caste landlord patrons, a wider section of the Alapuram Pallar community acquired economic enfranchisement, having been forced into independent earning outside the village. Economically rational and socially prestigious marriages with nonkin outsiders followed.[19] By 1983–84, Pallars had almost universally displaced the roles and rewards of caste subordination onto Alapuram's poorer landless Paraiyars. Members of this caste had not shared in Pallar success and were absent from 1960s struggles over church honors and civic spaces alike. Even in 1983–84, Paraiyars had singularly failed to lose their status as subordinated people. At that time their forty-four households were crammed into small streets sloping away from the tank bund, so narrow that the thatched roofs almost touched each other as they stretched over the narrow verandas on which I conducted my interviews. Many of these dalits had also converted to Christianity, although their Protestant religious affiliation, I want to suggest, had a rather different social significance.

FROM STRATEGIES OF PLACE TO TACTICS OF SPACE

In his classic work *The Practice of Everyday Life,* Michel de Certeau (1984) drew a distinction between "strategies" of *place* and "tactics" of *space* (see Schmalz 2005).[20] "Place" (*lieu*) in de Certeau's (1984, 117) terms is a stable "configuration of positions" within which negotiations occur. Pallar narratives of self-improvement and strategies of mobility were precisely concerned with finding a "place" within such an order, with gaining public acceptance of changed position in a set of power relations. Through organized action and associations they struggled for place within ritual systems, ranked honors, schools, or convents. First, the Catholic Church had provided the locations and moments within which this struggle had taken place—premised on the Jesuits' own strategies of "place" that secured the Church's position in the ritual and physical order of the village—but later we see strategies of place focused on constitutional rights, civic access, and appeal to the state, backed by public recognition of mythic histories of greatness.

De Certeau's notion of "space" (*espace*) is quite different. It is "unstable and activated by the movements deployed within it" (Schmalz 2005, 218). The politics of Paraiyar households in Alapuram are best described in terms of such a realm of improvisational "tactics." Paraiyars had played little part in the dramas of place led by Catholic Pallars and were geographically removed from the equivalent intellectual and social movements of Paraiyar pride taking place in the demographic and political centers of their caste in northern Tamil Nadu (see below). Having no power of place and "only limited opportunities for movement and expression," Paraiyars asserted agency in relation to dominant orders not through direct action, but through imagination, storytelling, rumor, mythology, noncompliance, and modes of consumption (Schmalz 2005; de Certeau 1984).

In these Paraiyar tactics, Christianity was a resource quite different from that found in Pallar struggles for place through Catholic ritual. The Paraiyar turn to the Protestants was itself an outcome of the denial of place within the Jesuit mission, which hardly sought the entry of "lower," less-valued "Pariah" converts into the Church, especially where it threatened to offend upper castes to the point of defection (see chapter 1). Paraiyars participated in the ritual of the Santiyakappar festival only as low-ranking village servants and parai drummers (figure 13). Their pastoral care was left to the Protestant "heretics." The local caste-denominational politics of the 1910s to 1940s clearly aligned Pallars and Paraiyars on opposite sides of the Catholic–Protestant divide, as a long- and deep-running conflict over the use of a Christian burial ground in the 1910s showed. Jesuit priests had been supporting Catholic Pallars against Paraiyars, who were in turn backed by Maravars and the American missionary Rev. Vaughan.[21] So it was rather fancifully that Jesuit Fr. Mahé, after recording how he had gone "to the

FIGURE 13. Alapuram *paṟai* drummers, 1983. Photo by author.

house of an old Pariah (baptized lately) to take the corpse with cross and candles, a crowd follow[ing] with tambour and kulavai [keening, and] after church to the cemetery," asked himself, "Will any conversion follow among Pariahs?" (APD, 24 July 1939). In fact, within two years these Paraiyars had converted en masse to the Anglican SPG (Society for the Propagation of the Gospel in Foreign Parts) mission.

Given the caste embeddedness of the Catholic mission in Ramnad, it might seem natural that the Anglican (SPG) missionaries, with their post-1850 missiological opposition to caste, would draw converts from the area's caste periphery—from Paraiyars (and from Nadar palmyra climbers who later mostly reverted to Catholicism). As elsewhere in Madras, in the 1940s Ramnad Paraiyars suffering the injustices of servitude and caste abuse sought protection from well-connected missionary members of the ruling race (chapter 1). And for their part, the SPG missionaries, as well as sending evangelist-catechists to prepare Alapuram Paraiyars for baptism, were also willing to take a stand against what they categorized as "slavery." Menon suggests that there was in fact a Protestant understanding of the "status of lower caste converts as 'freedmen' . . . rooted in a comparative reading of Black America experience" from novels (2002, 1665). In any event, by the 1940s Protestant missionary support for Paraiyar neophytes in Ramnad interlinked with this caste's own practices of insubordination—as with Jesuits and Pallars earlier—especially the withdrawal from practices such as drumming for Hindu ceremonies, village scavenging, or the consumption of carrion, and refusal of the restrictions on using the upper "breast cloth," (cf. Arun 2007a, 61). An elderly Malliamma recalled that it was the SPG mission's emissary to Alapuram—in fact, a Maravar evangelist—who backed Paraiyar converts' right to good clothing—to shirts on their backs, "breast cloths" on their chests, *tuṇṭus* ("towels") on their heads, and sandals on their feet—contravening the sartorial codes until then imposed and tightly policed by members of the dominating castes (cf. Rao 2009, 67–68).

However, Paraiyars, unlike Pallars, were not able to deploy missionary support to alter (or find) their social place in the village, and Protestants did not offer a status-graded ritual system for such social ambition. What Paraiyars found rather was protection and patronage (cf. Bugge 1994, chap, 1). Conversion involved a kind of bargain. Neophytes converted, "expecting good things from God—a place to live, clothes, food, health and shelter," education, and protection (Wingate 1999, 97). But when good things failed to materialize, or their experiments in a new habitus brought reprisals from dominant groups, there was resentment. A recent convert, complaining about failure to acquire land security as a result of his relationship with the mission, challenges Rev. Andrew Wingate in an idiom of hospitality: "[I]f you come to my house as a guest, I will provide hospitality. So our expectation is that we have come into Christianity, and so Christ will provide for us" (ibid., 78).

The reality was that the Protestant mission fell well short of expectations. Protestant convert communities in Ramnad were on the Christian periphery, weakly linked to their mission church. They were scattered, lacked resident pastors, and were too far from mission centers to the south in Tirunelveli—and the schools, collective farms, mission settlements, or debt release they provided—to alter Paraiyar conditions in any significant way. In 1983–84, after the foreign missionaries had long gone, the infrequently visited dilapidated Protestant chapels in the poorest dalit sections of Ramnad villages had become identifying markers of the Paraiyar caste.[22] In fact, Christian Paraiyars in Alapuram lacked possession of even this sign of social place. The chapel in which they prayed was constructed in the adjacent Nadar street, and there worship was led by a Nadar catechist. "Place" for the Paraiyars remained symbolically marked by the tree shrine of their ancestral virgin goddess, Mankiliyakari, in the midst of the street. Everyday religious practice was hybrid. As the elderly Lily put it, "[O]n Sunday we worship Jesus, on Tuesday and Friday we burn *cāmpirāṇi* (incense) for Mankiliyakari," who also received offerings during the Santiyakappar festival and by whose tree shrine wedding saris were customarily laid.[23]

MAKING THE PAST UNTOUCHABLE THROUGH CHRISTIANITY

Protestant Christianity separated Alapuram Paraiyars neither from their old religion nor from their extreme poverty. In 1983–84, over 90 percent of these households were entirely landless, and three-quarters depended upon rewards as dependents of upper-caste *aiya vitu* patrons; deference was still necessary to survival (Still 2007, 270). However, subordination had lessened, and many were on a shallow trajectory toward greater economic security. This began in 1969 when, having expelled Pallar tenants, Utaiyar landlords offered sharecrop leases to their Paraiyar laborers instead, marginally increasing their independence and food security—even though sharecropping, like money lending, was also a means to secure laboring dependents (cf. Baker 1984, 156). At the same time, by toiling and stinting and through seasonal labor migration, especially in the Chennai brick kilns, Christian Paraiyars saved small sums to invest in land. When they were resurveyed in 1993–94, their average landholdings had increased from zero to 1.2 acres; and half of their sharecropping had been replaced by the more rewarding fixed-rent (*kuttakai*) and land-mortgage (*otti*) tenure (see Mosse 2003, 205–8).

When I revisited the village in the 1990s, Paraiyar households had mostly pulled away from relations of caste dependence and given up funeral service, drumming, or "disposal" duties. A decade earlier this was impossible. But more interestingly, Paraiyar men I knew had already begun the symbolic work of redefining the meaning of the service roles they could not afford to discard so as to increase their sense of dignity, and at least "warp the vectors of domination" (Schmalz 2005, 228). The coercive and obligatory aspects of work relationships were curbed. Abolition of the village office of *tōṭṭi* and its grain shares had already erased their generalized obligation as "village servants," and they now restricted their services to a small elite in the village. Paraiyar men and women tried to accept a reduced form of patronage from their lords' houses. They took less than their entitlement of "threshing-floor paddy," refused or reciprocated gifts and handouts,[24] emphasized affection and mutuality—earlier expressed in extra gifts from landlords at festivals or the indulgence of the patron's children by servants (Still 2007, 95)—over obligation as aspects of the service relationship, or demanded cash rather than grain payments, invoking the "free choice" idiom we associate with "the market."

Those whose livelihoods depended upon the conventionally lowering tasks of cattle scavenging, grave digging, or parai drumming reworked the context and performance of these duties so as to rid them of the implication of servitude (atimai). Prakash and his brother used their musical skills to negotiate a way out of humiliation. They agreed to play drums in the village, even at funerals, if paid well and in cash. In 1983 they had recently switched from playing parai drums and horns to the more prestigious *mēḷam* temple drum and *nākacuvaram* (a double-reed wind instrument) and had begun to perform at auspicious occasions such as weddings as part of a professional band rather than as village servants (at least in neighboring villages) (figure 14). And within Alapuram they expected Utaiyar or Vellalar households to solicit their drumming with the conventional signs of respect such as money wrapped in betel leaves offered on a brass tray, and being invited to sit on their clients' verandas like other musicians, in addition to payment in cash and receiving the raw foods and new cloth *taccaṇai* gifts due to nonbound experts and ritualists such as catechists or carpenters (see chapter 3). Those who offered funeral services—insisting that this was out of kindness or compassion for the bereaved patron within a relationship of mutuality—refused negatively charged substances, just as the village barber and dhobi themselves now retained only their "priestly" ritual functions and insisted on payment in cash or new cloth alone (except from a small village elite).[25] Ironically, it was the "orthoprax" Catholic elite unwilling to construe the relationship with their Paraiyar servants in nonservile terms who ended up having to dig their own graves and bury their own cattle.

Of course Paraiyar households varied in the particular trade-offs they could afford between economic security and concessions of dignity. Few Paraiyar men achieved the autonomy they aspired to, but, to use James Scott's phrase, all were looking for "patronage which is not patronising" (1990b, 197). They blunted the sharp edge of dishonor, but also to some extent found mariyatai by displacing ignominious obligations *within* their families onto the youth, who would emphasize the cash potential over the indignity of ritual work, and especially onto wives, daughters, or elderly mothers, whose transactions carried the continuing burden of caste humiliation.[26]

In the 1980s, Alapuram Paraiyar men and women would often characterize their aspirations to me in terms of the notion of *nākarīkam*—that is, civility, politeness, urbanity (Fabricius 1972, 595; Sk. *nagar* or city)—in contradistinction to a servile past that was identified as *aciṅkam* (degrading, disgusting, or shameful). Cattle scavenging, beef eating, tappu drumming, receiving threshing-floor sweepings, and extreme deference to upper castes, as well as the parai drum or the kompu horn as objects in themselves, were all acinkam, marked in contrast to signs of nākarīkam: work without servitude (*aṭimai illamai*), respectful ritual roles and taccanai gifts, contractual relations and cash wages, or objects such as temple drums and pipes or honorific terms of address. Apart from signifying a difference in caste relationships, the acinkam/nakarikam dichotomy was part of a Paraiyar narrative of change and of their own *changeability* (Vincentnathan 1993). It was within this discourse that people spoke of their conversion to Protestant Christianity.

Perhaps its greater historical proximity made conversion more readily a topic

FIGURE 14. A new generation of Paraiyar musicians with temple drum and *nākacuvaram*, 1983. Photo by author.

in interviews with Alapuram's Protestant Paraiyars than with Catholic Pallars; but perhaps it was also that Paraiyar discourse on identity was itself more culturally disjunctive, for which Christianity provided an idiom of expression. While the Catholic Pallar mythic self-recovery as Deventira Kula Velalas sought historical continuity, these Protestant Paraiyars repudiated rather than glorified their past. They worked conversion to Christianity into the separation of a shameful past from a better future.[27] While Catholic Pallar narratives of mobility invoked the classical Tamil virtue of the agrarian life, drawing a moral distinction between lowland civility and upland barbarity (above), Paraiyars used the valued notion of urbanity (nakarikam) and a modernist judgment critical of rustic coarseness and incivility to imagine progress and freedom (see Pandian 2009, 43–47). The first is a language of power; the second, of moral transformation (cf. ibid.). If the Catholic Pallar discourse affirmed their place in the agrarian order while decivilizing political others (the wild Maravars or aboriginal inferiors), the Paraiyar narrative was premised on their agrarian exclusion. Paraiyars reached beyond the present order in a language of urbanity (nakariyam) that involved a civilizing of the self drawn to the modernizing idioms of twentieth-century Protestant missions rather than the traditionalizing ones of rustic French Jesuits.

Despite its failure to sustain material or social improvement, or the freedoms first mediated by European missionaries, Protestant Christianity appeared to offer my 1980s Paraiyar interlocutors ideas, stories, or symbols with which to contend with caste-based inferiority. It neither altered material conditions nor provided a revolutionary ideology (and conversely, the "SC"-reserved jobs or higher education that Christian identity might jeopardize were anyway beyond Paraiyar reach). But Christianity did support a way of thinking about improving change, in the first instance by providing the dignity of a socioreligious identity that did "not depend on its acceptance and recognition by the higher castes" (Forrester 1980, 77) and that signified autonomy as a social possibility to people historically defined by service and subordination. The missionaries put in place a self-respect model of Christian life that demanded dignifying changes to lifestyles, leaving converts with a narrative fusion of baptism and positive self-fashioning, whether this involved giving up drink, ending consumption of carrion beef, washing with soap, or confidence in comportment and speech—that is to say, work on the self that was political and challenged stigma and exclusion, albeit in a very different manner from Catholic Pallar associationalism (cf. Wingate 1999; Still 2007, 111).[28] And today Paraiyar men and women will readily say that God has changed their condition. In short, Protestant Christianity is nakarikam. We can say that long before the Tamil churches promoted a theology of social action in the 1990s, Protestant Christianity provided a way of "imagining a different context for autonomy and agency" (Schmalz 2005), a kind of imaginative "space making," or a cultural capacity akin to what Arjun Appadurai (2004) refers to as the "capacity to aspire."

Christianity offered Paraiyars a worldview consistent with and justifying the everyday renegotiations of still-essential service identities, not least through narratives of modernity that put distance between themselves and those inferiorized objects of others' judgments. This allowed advancement through self-reform without having to accept the Hindu upper-caste moral discourse on untouchability. Here we have a way of rereading some well-know Paraiyar "origin myths" that, for example, deal with exclusion and the stigmatized practice of beef eating (Mosse 1986, 243–46; cf. Moffatt 1979; David 1977; Deliège 1992; Arun 2007a). Sitting in his cramped thatched hut, in 1983, an elderly Prakash told me the following version of one such myth:

> There were two Brahman brothers, Annan and Tampi. The elder (Annan) would conduct puja in the temple, offering ponkal rice, some of which he would bring home as piracatam for his pregnant wife. He would also worship god with a drop of blood from a cow that would reappear at each puja from Intira *lōkam* (heaven). One day, his wife, hearing a false rumor from the younger brother, Tampi, that her husband was eating beef in the temple, complained to him, "Although I'm pregnant, you only bring me ponkal rice; if you don't bring me some beef, I'll kill myself." Worried for his wife, Annan returned with some flesh cut from the temple cow. The cow died, and seeing this, his brother Tampi hid and refused the meat. The villagers told

> Annan, "Since you killed the cow, you take the dead animal away and eat it. You are untouchable, you beef eater! Go away from the village!" Asked while on his way to another place who would now look after the temple, he replied with the pun: *tampi pāppāṉ:* "Tampi will see to it" (tampi *pārppāṉ*), "Tampi is the Brahman" (tampi *pāppāṉ*). In another village, Annan was given work as village watchman and to call people to meetings and told to go house to house daily to collect cooked rice to eat. To make his work easier he took skin from a dead calf and made a tappu (parai) drum to beat, so people called him Paraiyan. At first people brought him their dead cattle; later they make him collect dead animals and avoided him because of his work.

While such a story is often described as a Paraiyar myth of origin (e.g., Deliège 1992), it is better seen as a Paraiyar commentary on someone else's myth that places Paraiyars under scrutiny and objectifies them as "untouchable" (Zene 2007, 270, citing Leslie 2003, 42).[29] The myth appears to connect the loss of Brahmanhood and enslavement with the ultrasinful acts of cow killing and beef eating. But in its retelling here, a caste Hindu *morality* of Paraiyar banishment is turned into a (Christian) *sociology* of Paraiyar inferiorization. That is to say, the myth reveals a consciousness *of,* not a concession *to,* the culture of oppression. Prakash's point (reiterated by others) is that our condition is such because *they* associate beef eating with untouchability (*tīṇṭāmai*) and that we gave up beef eating not because it was sinful but because they used it as a reason to ill-treat us. Making the link between beef eating and ill treatment quasi causal rather than moral distances Paraiyars from the reformist morality of upper-caste others who might rationalize dalit degradation as the result of stigmatized practices so as to conceal the real facts of servitude and economic exploitation that underpin untouchability (Vincentnathan 1993; Rao 2009, 74).[30]

Especially in its Christian telling, the sibling myth is a countermyth. It does not claim an original preeminence for Paraiyars as Brahmans (akin to Pallar myths of former royalty) but rather asserts the essential *sameness* of all humans, the Brahman-Paraiyar pair being the "logical minimum set" to claim the brotherhood and equality of all (Vincentnathan 1993, 67).[31] The myth portrays Paraiyars' nearness to God (Zene 2007, 261) and declares untouchability to be a matter of external causes, historical contingency (rather than inborn qualities), and the misconstrual of good intentions (although once again negativity is allocated to women). Above all, the countermyth establishes the changeability of human conditions, anticipating self-improvement and the recovery of dignity. If we regard such storytelling as "make[ing] the journey before or as the feet make it" (de Certeau 1984, 116, in Schmalz 2005, 228), then the myth allows an ironic disengagement from dominant discourses of untouchability—relativizing and secularizing untouchability as an unjust social convention—which anticipates the semantic inventiveness through which Paraiyars would begin to divorce funeral work, cattle scavenging or drumming from impurity and servitude. This employed a

Christian semiotic that strained away from "indexical contiguities" and toward manipulable symbolic associations (see Introduction) that rendered meanings around drumming or beef eating arbitrary and thus changeable.

It is evident that being Christian meant strikingly different things for Alapuram Pallars and Paraiyars in their struggle with caste subordination. Protestant Christianity did not allow Parayars to renegotiate "place" in de Certeau's terms, as the Catholic Church clearly had for Pallars, but its teaching helped Paraiyars detach their identity from signs of untouchability. Paraiyar elders would describe untouchability in terms of what their Christianization had left behind: ignorance, gullibility, dullness of mind, or the lack of hygiene—the stereotypes used of them by others now used to mark a boundary between the present and the discarded past (cf. Schmalz 2005, 220–26). Christianity offered redemption from untouchable selves (ibid.) without, however, making them any less Paraiyar in the eyes of other villagers.

REMAINING HINDU

Just over half of the Paraiyar households in Alapuram converted to Christianity; the other half remained Hindu. This was not an individual but a subcaste decision. Indeed, the conversion of all Paraiyars of the Totti subcaste to Christianity made Hindu identity for the first time a matter of choice for the rival Necavar subcaste of Paraiyars rather than the normal condition of being. "Necavar" means "weaver," and those I questioned told me that their true identity was *kōḷiyapiḷḷai* weavers given high title (*paṭṭam*) by the Kallar rulers of Pudukottai, from where they migrated to Alapuram several generations ago. When they first came to Ramnad, Necavars were successful weavers, the story goes, until the witchcraft of local silk-weaver competitors (*paṭṭunūlkārarkaḷ)* caused their looms to fall apart. They lost their skills, failed to pass them on to their children, abandoned their proper work (*taṉ toḻil*), started eating beef, and became like Paraiyars.

Necavars shared with Protestant Tottis the historical experience of servitude and untouchability in the village, and in recalling this history of abuse, their elders would also relate the Brahman sibling myth of exclusion. But they also shared with Pallars a narrative of mistaken identity by which they marked a separation from the Protestant Tottis and distanced themselves from the latter's death-related "untouchable" services. Inter-Paraiyar subcaste status rivalry was public. Apparently, one year in the 1940s Tottis challenged the hitherto acknowledged precedence of Necavars in the public distribution of sacred ash and betel festival honors outside the Aiyanar temple, on the grounds that *they* held the village office (totti or sweeper-drummer). The Maravar headman supported their claim, and at the next year's festival the priest was ordered to offer the ash simultaneously with arms crossed so neither group could claim precedence. Of course, this satisfied neither party and both withdrew from the festival. Totti Parayar Prakash's wife recalls that it was Maravar efforts, following this dispute, to force the fulfillment of Totti temple-service obligations, especially drumming, that prompted them to appeal to the SPG mission for protection. Their Necavar rivals withdrew from the village temple festival to their own independent cult to the god Muniaiyar, a troubling demon-god (see chapter 2) now settled at his tank-side temple, as their own (*contam*) source and symbol of protection, power, and honor in the village (Mosse 1986, 390–91; cf. Mines 2005).

Thereafter, Necavar status aspirations took on the flavor of Hindu orthodoxy, which placed a boundary between both their untouchable past and their Christian Paraiyar rivals. I was alerted to the distinctly Sanskritic form of Necavar nākarikam one day in July 1984 when I went with Mohan to the tank bed, where his relatives had assembled for a final funeral rite (*karumāti*). A visiting Valluvar Pantaram (low-caste purohit) performed a highly Brahmanical rite to complete and perfect an ideal sacrificial cremation with a effigy substitute of the deceased. Necavars would also seek the anonymity of regional temples to obtain the services of Brahman priests. These were "tactics of space" by a group who, although marginally better off than Protestant Paraiyars,[32] was not able to launch the public claims to "place" that Catholic Pallars so successfully had.

So, the village-level micro–religious politics of dalit dignity in the mid-1980s was complex. Alapuram Pallars claimed entitlement to resources from the state, and place and honor within the village, through imaginative connections to royal power. Protestant Paraiyars made the past untouchable while negotiating space through Christian modernity. Necavars found independence and self-respect in Brahmanic codes of ritual practice. But the households of one dalit caste in Alapuram lacked the resources either to claim "place" or to reimagine "space" for autonomy, and those were the two Cakkiliyar (cobbler) families (formerly atimai servants to Pallars) whose interests in the 1980s were bound into the system of caste inequality. These households were isolated from self-respect.[33] They were not trying to renegotiate service relations in the village, but rather to *widen* the range of people they served, retaining the generalized subordination formerly ascribed to all dalits.[34] Concessions of status and dignity still had material rewards, and Muthu and his brother maximized the returns and security that subordination and service in the village could still offer.

DALIT REPLICATION AND CONSENSUS, OR DISJUNCTURE AND COUNTERCULTURE

The divergent discourses of advancement among Alapuram's subordinated castes in the 1980s anticipated the difficulties that would later emerge in efforts to forge a common "dalit" (or "dalit Christian") identity or social-political movement in south India. Evidently, intercaste relationships among dalits in the 1980s involved religiously marked status competition. Intermarriage, interdining, or even sharecropping were also rare.[35] Those whom I questioned about the usual terms of address between members of dalit castes chose pronouns and kinship terms that denoted mutual respect but also distance, indicative of the "minimizing" strategies of status rivals (Marriott 1976; Moffatt 1979, 141; Mosse 1986 for a detailed analysis). Pallars and Paraiyars both possessed a rich repertoire of myths and proverbs, tales of mistrust and cunning, with which to stereotype the other to an outsider.[36] At times there seemed to be more social distance among dalits than among any other castes, and this separation, like that between Mala and Madiga dalit castes in Andhra Pradesh described by Still (2007, 197), was reinforced through childhood socialization and intensified by physical proximity and competition within the same local labor market.

While it is important not to overstate or hierarchize these divisions, it remains true that the century that saw markers of separation and rank abandoned among upper castes—for example, making disputes between Utaiyars and Vellalars a thing of the past—saw relationships among dalit castes become more complex and divided in ways that would later be generalized into divided political constituencies. Of course this is not to say that the boundaries of caste (and derivatively religion) defined social relations or precluded close personal and interfamily friendships, not least those built around mutual support and financial borrowing, although, as Still (2007, 197) points out, generally men crossed social boundaries into friendship and commensality—in churches, on pilgrimages, or over drink—more easily than women. What my fieldwork in 1980s Alapuram had clearly revealed was how the dalit drive for independence and honor had produced or amplified a differentiation of cultural styles and religious affiliations among the most disadvantaged and socially subordinated.

Aspirations for equality had also produced new inequalities. Where population, resources, and elite accumulation permitted, those able to do so escaped ignominious roles, which were then passed on to others; and some dalit elites acquired their own inferiorized dependents. The description of such differentiation within lower-caste orders in the 1970s and 1980s generated a rather fruitless anthropological debate on whether this indicated that those at the bottom were in consensus with a cultural system that so demonstrably inferiorized them. In his influential book *An Untouchable Community in South India: Structure and Consensus*, Michael Moffatt (1979) argued the case for consensus on the basis of a detailed description of the "replication" of ritual services among dalit castes—for example, services provided by priests or barbers dealing with impurity—from which they were excluded, and the delegation of negatively valued work (such as funeral service) to members of lower "grades" (endogamous subgroups) *within* the Paraiyar caste, who he suggested acted as "untouchables to the untouchables."

Moffatt argued that this all provided structural evidence, first, that untouchables "possess and act upon a thickly textured culture whose fundamental definitions and values are identical to those of the more global village culture" (1979, 3); second, that—following Dumont—these values centrally concern the opposition of purity and impurity; and third, that untouchables are "motivated to stay low by their fundamental agreement with the postulates of the system which requires such low actors as themselves" (ibid., 218).

Moffatt's argument has rightly been challenged on each point (e.g., Deliège 1992). His (last) derivation of human motivations from abstract structural form represented a classic error arising from structuralism's implicit and therefore inadequate theory of practice (Bourdieu 1977, 29).[37] His argument was also at odds with the almost universal view among dalits themselves that their position is the product of contingent history and forced servitude (atimai), and was blithely dismissive of dynamic Paraiyar movements against caste at his time of writing and long before, including agrarian unrest and Christian conversion movements from the late-nineteenth century. The structures of differentiation in large dalit communities such as Alapuram, or Moffatt's Endavur, might appear to be mimetic of the wider hierarchical order of caste, but as I have shown, they are in fact more likely to be the contingent effects (probably recent in origin) of strategies of place making or status striving—the downward displacement of negative services, role bifurcation, and trade-offs between dignity and resources. These arise not from "cultural consensus" but from the impulse of those with adequate means to ensure that as far as possible it was *not* they who fulfill the inferior service roles, and of those unable fully to withdraw from ritual service to abandon the most negative aspect of these roles, displacing them onto those with less power to negotiate—in particular, in the present case, onto Alapuram's poorest Paraiyar and Cakkiliyar households.[38] The increased but varying access to resources, education, and migration in the 1960s to 1980s, which allowed the rejection of ascriptions of inferiority and assertions of autonomy, paradoxically generated caste structures in dalit communities—and no less among Christians—that were more complex, internally differentiated, and ranked than those of other castes (cf. Cohn 1959; Shah 1990, 323), as well as a hardening divide between dalits and others.

On Moffatt's second point, enough has been said already in this book to throw doubt on any theory that gives centrality of the idea of impurity and its removal in discourses of caste. But his chief argument (the first) was against those who considered caste subalterns as constituting a distinct subculture within Indian society. As soon as some anthropologists began in the 1950s to theorize Indian society as a Hindu culture of differentiation—of caste and coded substance—that inferiorized "untouchables" as the constitutive outside, others turned this into an alternative proposition that dalits were not in fact, and never had been, part of this dominant tradition (e.g., Miller 1966). One strand of this opinion would imagine dalits as bearers of a non- or pre-Brahmanical "little tradition" (Cohn 1959, 207; Mahar 1960, 230–40; see Moffatt 1979), a view that Lele (1980) traces back to attempts by Indian intellectuals serving the Raj both to justify the presence within Hinduism of "primitive forms" with reference to the tolerant absorption of others into Aryan culture, and to legitimize improvement through processes of Sanskritization.

A second strand, influenced in part by Ambedkar, regarded dalits as adherents to a pervasive countercultural tradition, an egalitarian antithesis, manifest in recurring anticaste movements, including those of the caste-negating ascetic tradition (Khare 1982) or the equalizing *bhakti* devotional religion, whose saint-heroes later became the symbolic focus for political mobilization (Miller 1966; Lele 1980; Juergensmeyer 1982; Dube 1998). Ambedkar's own project was the recognition of a dalit *political minority,* a "separate element" in the nation, an identity of marginalization, and a broad community of the deprived and excluded that would merge caste and class interests and disregard religious boundaries in ways that subverted colonial and Gandhian ideas of (primordial) community. From this came the political necessity of antimajoritarian cultural difference and religious separation, and the conception of a dalit political subject—which Ambedkar would find in Buddhist identity recovered from the "deep structure of Hindu history" (Rao 2009, 150, 143, 77).

In south India, these arguments were anticipated by the historical and linguistic work of Protestant missionaries who constructed Tamils generally as prepared for Christianization by their authentic Dravidian traditions always disjoined from Brahmanism (Dirks 2001). Conversion to Protestant Christianity has indeed persistently been regarded as an expression of this radical dalit break with dominant (Brahmanical) values (Juergensmeyer 1982). Dalit Christianization is taken as part of the way in which a humanizing colonial modernity (including missionary education) was conjoined with the anti-Brahmanism of Ambedkar or E. V. Ramasamy ("Periyar") to offer hope for progress. In the twentieth century, diverging from nationalist visions, politicized dalits would come to associate "the Christian," "the Western," or more recently "the global" (especially human-rights discourses) as countervailing loci of values, culture, and power beyond the nation (cf. Still 2007, 110; H. Gorringe 2005a, 32n9). Cultural disjuncture, expressed as dalit rejection of "Hindu" identity, was in fact present even earlier in the thinking of early Paraiyar leaders such as Irattaimalai Srinivasan (b. 1860) and his brother-in-law Iyothi Thas (b. 1845), who became a Buddhist in 1898.

We will see how this intellectual work became part of popular dalit cultural politics only much later, in the 1990s (see chapter 6). In 1980s Alapuram, however, it was not possible to weave the threads of Christian religion, education, and advancement into anything like self-conscious countercultural practice. The complex culture of Tamil Christian dalits, even within this one village, shows that it makes no more sense to try to choose between consensus and dissensus prior to conversion than between continuity and discontinuity after (Appadurai 2004, 61; Robbins 2007). The evidence reminds us that perceptions, judgments, and actions, including those as Christian converts, are made within "structures of choices" that are already constituted socially and historically (Lukes 2005, 7–9). Pallars used Catholicism in their strategies of place (rather than as countercultural resistance), and in doing so appropriated key signifiers of power and dominance (the ones implicated in their own subordination) to relocate themselves from the periphery to the ritual center of the village.

Paraiyars, more deeply involved in the process of inferiorization, imaginatively separated themselves from ever-present untouchability by reworking continuing relationships of service, tying hopes of autonomy to Christian modernity, the market, and honorable service. They used myth and symbolism to make space for ideas of historical contingency and social injustice, thus prizing parai drumming, funeral work, or cattle scavenging apart from essentialized social inferiority. While not consciously countercultural, they did (unlike Pallars) use Christianity discursively to distinguish themselves from a dominant culture, making space for action within a structure of marginality (cf. Schmalz 2005). Moreover, Protestant Paraiyars did not try to hierarchize relations with the socially weaker Cakkiliyar households. Those I asked about this in 1983–84 insisted on a mutuality and commensality between Paraiyar and Cakkiliyar households, expressed in sibling kinship terms, commensality, and a reciprocity of ritual service (drumming, grave digging), in which the more economically independent Hindu Necavars or Catholic Pallars would not participate.

So one can say that Christianity could be linked implicitly to projects of either cultural continuity or disjuncture, the identities, symbolic resources, equalities, and inequalities being worked variously into strategies of "place" or tactics of "space." Being Christian offered a means to negotiate or modify, but never to substitute for, caste identity. Indeed, for Christian dalits the problem was not "caste" in the abstract but how to succeed in overcoming their particular disabilities (cf. Sharma 1976). Denominational and even Hindu or Christian religious boundaries arose out of localized fields of status competition (Caplan 1980b).[39] From this situation, in the 1980s, came a very different kind of conversion—public, political, and controversial.

A NEW POLITICS OF CONVERSION

In 1981, a small and unknown village in Tirunelveli District to the south of Alapuram suddenly became the focus of national debate on caste discrimination. In that village, Meenakshipuram, several thousand relatively prosperous and educated Hindu and Catholic Pallar families had become Muslim (Mathew 1982,

1069). At issue was not only the immediate harassment by upper-caste Maravars, discrimination in the Church, or a "crisis of expectations" as Christian education failed to materialize into jobs (Wingate 1999, 156), but also a sense of the inadequacy of the political means to social change given the marginality of dalits within the main Dravidian political parties. These Muslim conversions were not replicas of earlier Christian mass conversions in the Tamil countryside. As I have suggested, these latter had by and large taken place *within* rather than against existing social frameworks. The Meenakshipuram conversions were different. They were political acts of protest, in relation to an Indian nation-state that, in ways Tejani (2008. 14) explains, had gradually come to be understood in terms of a "democratic majority" defined broadly as upper-caste Hindu. The implicit conception of the independent nation in terms of Hindu unity gave a new force to religious conversion (a particular assertion of difference) as a tactic with which to bargain with the Indian state rather than as an idiom of caste mobility.[40]

As the case unfolded, it was indeed clear that the threat to convert could bring immediate approval of wells and loan schemes from the government as well as funds for temple repair or new public-address systems from Hindu organizations such as the Arya Samaj, galvanized into previously unseen missionary activity, including transgressive entry into dalit colonies in order to achieve reconversions (Wingate 1999, 162–63). The evidence, however, is that these conversions to Islam had more to do with the political gains from religious protest than the material gains from new patrons, despite the allegations that Middle East money was involved (ibid.). Uppermost was the fact of Islam's mullahs living in the villages, being open to dialogue with Pallar youth, eating in each of the converts' houses, clear teaching and fellowship, and equality in congregational worship, as well as religious solidarity (although rarely intermarriage) with established Islamic communities. As a convert from Christianity told Wingate, "Jesus's dream of one flock and one shepherd has been fulfilled in Islam" (1999, 158).[41]

In 1983–84, my young Pallar associates in Alapuram were well aware of the Muslim conversions to the south. Many faced similar frustrations but did not favor joining the sizable but culturally distinct local Muslim population or abandoning the Catholic or caste (Deventra Kula Velalar) identities that had hitherto provided the framework for their struggle for social recognition. Some Catholic Pallar families did, however, find a religions means to protest caste exclusion through the more socially disjunctive Pentecostal Christianity. Paulraj, who led the 1968 rebellion, and who with his brother had (on return from Malaysia) organized public feasts at their St. Paul the Hermit (Vanattu Cinnappar) shrine, now stopped this and established the (all-Pallar) "Church of God" prayer hall at the end of the tank-side Pallar street. This was later moved onto land donated by a relative near the main Catholic cemetery. A pastor from the southern Nagarcoil District was invited to stay there and lead regular worship.

In the 1980s, those who joined this congregation were some of the better-off dalit households who (like their Meenakshipuram counterparts) felt persisting caste discrimination acutely, although this was never the only reason to join Pentecostal congregations. These were radical in their rejection of caste and all vestiges of priestly and episcopal rank and authority, but they were politically conservative. They offered a faith compatible with class differentiation through personal accumulation and the consolidation of new economic gains, so that Pallar neighbors would not refrain from noting how Pentecostal women who refused to adorn themselves had sold their jewelry in order to buy land. Still, those whose poverty in jewels was genuinely economic could also use Pentecostal religion "to transform symbols of inferiority into signs of moral standing" (Still 2007, 77). The Pallar Pentecostals' failure to attend family functions or to comply with marriage expectations initially provoked anger; stones and cow dung were hurled at them during prayer meetings, and a (Pallar) caste council resolved not to speak to the converts, or to "give them fire" for their hearths, Santanam recalls. But the ostracism did not last, and the congregation began to grow, albeit slowly, through kin and caste connections.

DALIT CHRISTIANS AND CASTE HINDUS: THE CULTURAL POLITICS OF CASTE

Let me draw this chapter to a close by linking the politics of conversion to a contemporary dalit politics that revives and extends earlier countercultural dalit discourse. Although Muslim and Pentecostal "conversions" were not the outcome of the same cluster of factors, they both had something to do with a growing desire in the 1980s to express social ambitions and to make political demands in an idiom of *difference*. It was as if Alapuram's Pallar struggle for upward mobility and the Paraiyar strategies of difference had come to merge in a sociopolitically novel (though intellectually established) convention of caste struggle as the rejection of dominant culture now characterized as Brahmanic Hinduism. Drawing on Ambedkar's writing, this became part of a self-conscious articulation of *dalit* identity now constituted in opposition to that of "caste Hindus."

At this point "dalit," "the oppressed, downtrodden, or broken" (equivalent to the Tamil *tāḻttapaṭṭōr,* "those who have been put down"[42]), emerged as a collective identity of difference and protest—one that explicitly rejected the Gandhian inclusion of "untouchables" within the Hindu majority as *harijans* ("children of God"), and the socialist-communist submersion of caste in class identity. Indeed "dalit" signaled the shift away from a variety of assimilations, whether to the Catholic Church or to anti-Brahman or Dravidian politics (Lakshmanan 2004). Its use implied a conscious assertion of socioreligious and political identities that were disjoined from what was now conceived of as the dominant Brahmanic

Hindu culture, drawing on the above-mentioned "countercultural" discourses of Jyotirao Phule (1829–90) (in Maharashtra) and Ambedkar as well as Iyothi Thas and Periyar in the Tamil south. Even those whose experience of caste subordination bore little or no relation to priestly models of purity-impurity—those from regions such as Ramnad, where royal-feudal models of caste articulated poorly with the Hindu theories of caste or *varnashrama dharma* and whose experience of caste was the political and economic domination of "Backward Caste" Maravars, Kallars, or Utaiyars rather than of Brahmans (as captured in Pallar mythologizing)—were encouraged to articulate dalit dissent as the rejection of Brahmanic Hindu ideology and to reimagine caste as a Hindu religious institution. In short, dalit ideologies began to elaborate the "other" as the Hindu Brahman, and this in turn gave new significance to "dalit Christian" as a countercultural identity.[43] The point is that Christianity was *made* culturally disjunctive through a particular traceable politics of caste; it was not inherently so.

In the 1980s, this kind of religio-politics picked up on what had begun as a cultural movement *outside* the mainstream political processes—outside, that is, because of the failure of dalit political mobilization and the muting of dalit interests within the major parties: Dravidian, Congress, and Communist (see M. R. Barnett 1976). In Tamil Nadu this cultural politics occurred rather later than in some other Indian states, notably Maharashtra, where dalit intellectuals looked first to Ambedkar and his conversion to Buddhism (in 1956 along with many thousand dalits) and then to the American blacks to inform a dalit literature and a Dalit Panther movement in the 1970s (Zelliot 1996; Omvedt 1994; Mendelsohn and Vicziany 1998). A Tamil dalit literature also emerged after some delay (see Kannan and Gros 2002 for an assessment). The effervescence of dalit activism in India that was apparent by the 1990s can be regarded as "a second upsurge . . . in an era of the crisis of nationalities and of socialism," reviving radical anticaste movements that had begun and contended with the nationalist movement but that had been marginalized in post-Independence politics and by the churches (Omvedt 1994, 134).[44]

Indeed it is true that the mobilization of south Indian dalits under alternative (Christian) religious and political identities was dissipated and discouraged by a nationalist resistance to religious conversions and the activities of foreign missions (Wiebe 1970; Estborn 1961), whose welfare and educational functions were surrendered to the Indian state and its programs for Scheduled Caste welfare. The clergy (now Indian and mostly non-dalit) had themselves sought to free the Church from missionary paternalism and to develop a truly Indian form of Christian theology and organization. There was an emphasis on church consolidation rather than growth and a more positive evaluation of Indian cultural traditions, including caste (see chapter 2; Forrester 1980, chap. 7; Caplan 1980a, 228; Kim 2003). Indeed there is little to suggest that the established churches—

Protestant or Roman Catholic—had generated any distinctive political identities for dalits in Tamil Nadu before the 1990s. It was the ideological reimagination of Christianity by dalit intellectuals and activists that would provoke the idea of Christianity—or the teachings of the New Testament—as a dissident (even dalit) faith in relation to which the Church itself was in hypocritical contradiction. The dalit revolt in the Church that followed, and the emerging "dalit theology"[45] that consolidated the idea of Christianity as dalit religion, are subjects for the next chapter.

There is now a fast-growing and rapidly changing scene of dalit activism in Tamil Nadu with a multiplicity of organizations, approaches, regional bases, and social constituencies. This was triggered in part by the national celebration of Dr. Ambedkar's birth centenary in 1990, reawakening interest in his writings, which were newly available in Tamil. The Tamil unit of the Dalit Panthers, formed in 1983, took on a new life (Kannan and Gros 2002, 44), and around this time movement leaders emerged from among dalit professionals (government officials, nongovernmental-organization workers, doctors, lawyers), broadening the scope of their existing forums and caste associations. Other leaders came from the communist movement or underground Marxist-Leninist groups; and others still from a section of the Christian clergy who, the next chapter will show, proved particularly influential in shaping a new dalit cultural politics.

From this activist firmament emerged a handful of political figures who turned their movements and associations into political parties, entering the fray of Tamil elections in the late 1990s (Gorringe 2005; Wyatt 2010). However, the exigencies of constituency building, developing a mass movement, and especially the logic of electoral politics itself, ensured that movements, parties, and leadership alike consolidated around specific caste identities—Pallar, Paraiyar, Cakkiliyar (Arunthathiyar)—rather than tapping the potential for power of a large 16–20 percent unified Tamil dalit vote bank. The initial division was between Pallar and Paraiyar. The leader of the Deventira Kula Velalar Federation (DKVF), a cardiologist, Dr. Krishnaswamy, launched his political career and the Puthiya Tamizhagam party (the political front of the DKVF) out of the uprising and outrage that followed mid-1990s massacres of dalits in the (largely Pallar) southern Tamil districts, where he and his party (in various alliances) were successful in state-assembly and parliamentary elections.[46] Undoubtedly this success influenced R. Thirumavalavan, convener of the largely Paraiyar-caste Dalit Panthers of India (DPI, later named "Liberation Panthers" or Viduthalai Chiruthaigal Katchi [Viṭutalai Ciṟuttaikaḷ Kaṭci]—VCK), to contest elections in the northern districts as part of *his* fast-rising (and initially NGO-supported) political profile (see H. Gorringe 2005). Still other dalit leaders such as Christian Pallar John Pandian emerged with less ideologically or politically honed messages from caste conflict. Like others commanding regional and caste-based followings, Pandian was willing to enter into short-lived tactical political alliances.[47] More recently, dalit leaders who recognize the ultimately self-defeating nature of narrowing constituencies around caste have searched for new alliances with non-dalits or Muslims around which to consolidate subaltern support, or broader identities drawing on the more inclusive epithets of "sons of the soil" Tamil nationalism. Tamil nationalism, however, brings its own ethnic-linguistic divisions to dalit politics and a forewarned failure to be an effective vehicle of dalit interests. As dalit parties today (2010) are beset by electoral and ideological dilemmas, issues of untouchability and dalit rights have been taken up by the Communist Party (after a half century's refusal of the caste issue) and its Tamil Nadu Untouchability Eradication Front (see H. Gorringe 2009, 168). Meanwhile, other dalit movements—such as the "Martyr Immanuel Front" memorializing the Pallar leader—stand against electoral politics on the grounds that its fissions divert from the true politics of dalit liberation, insisting that "dalit" is anyway not a caste but an anticaste egalitarian identity (Front leader Chandra Bose, interview, 23 November 2004).

While these various dalit movements and parties did not consolidate around Christianity or produce "dalit Christian" as a focal identity of politicized dalits, we will see in the next chapter, first, that Christian organizations (churches, seminaries, NGOs) provided the support structures, pedagogical innovations, ideological-theological frameworks, and popular movements that underpinned the newly emerging Tamil dalit politics; and second, that it was the politics of dalitness that drove significant Christian social and theological innovation.

CONCLUSIONS

The new circumstance of Indian Independence altered the field of Christian practice and brought into existence a dalit politics. Christian ideas and practices were implicated in broad strategies of social mobility as well as micronegotiations of dignity, in public protests against the state, and in reconceptions of caste as Brahman conspiracy. In one village (Alapuram), Christianity was part of both the Pallar striving for change in relation to others, and the Paraiyar working on change *in themselves.* The first went along with emancipation through mythologizing difference (between Pallars and others), the other through unity (the Brahman-Paraiyar siblings). These alternative ideas of person and society arose under different objective possibilities for mobility and meaning-making given by the particular context of power.

Christianity has often provided a language of change and changeability premised on the claim to more universal and emancipatory identities—as Christians—although for south Indian dalits its place came to be overtaken by the competing discourse of citizenship and, more recently, of dalit human rights.

But freedom from the particularities of caste claimed in the name of any universal principle has always been constrained by relations of power. Though dalits were addressed by their priests and pastors as communities of Christians, and might identify themselves as such, the churches had no power to insist that their dalit converts be recognized by others as Christians rather than as Pallars or Paraiyars. Rather than displacing caste, Christianity was drawn into the strategies of place and tactics of space through which dalits contended with subordination in Tamil society. Christianity has been "the basis for [dalit] self-worth as well as the medium through which they express this" (Still 2007, 81); but this has by no means always engendered social critique. Alongside the firebrand young Catholic Pallar activist, there is the Protestant Paraiyar widow who still survives through loyal deference to Utaiyar patrons or the Pallar neighbor, supported by her upper-caste lover.[48] In places like Alapuram, Christianity was not present as a gathering critique of Hindu caste, but remained woven into dalit forms of social adaptation, negotiation, and protest, providing ritual and symbolic means for the making of self and community.

Then in the 1990s, the ideological work of dalit activists and intellectuals began to construe Christian identity and Christian conversion in terms of a more global dalit revolt against the Brahmanic Hindu system of caste. In the next chapter we will see how this gained further momentum with the rise of Hindu nationalism. At the same time, it will be clear that the identity "dalit Christian" did not in fact acquire political salience as a Christian critique of Hindu caste society so much as within a politics generated by the contradictions that erupted as changed circumstances in the 1990s brought the collapse of Catholicism's old mechanisms of reconciliation of Christian faith and the culture of caste.

6

Hindu Religious Nationalism and Dalit Christian Activism

In the summer of 2008, as I began preparing this book, two events brought international attention to Christians in India. Both involved violence against dalit Christians by their neighbors, who in the first case were people mobilized by Hindu nationalist organizations in a rural locality in Orissa, and in the second case upper-caste Catholics in a village in northern Tamil Nadu. These confrontations signaled two phenomena of critical importance to Indian Catholicism at the turn of the new millennium: the rise of Hindu nationalism, and the eruption of the politics of caste within the Church. Simultaneously attacked by politically assertive Brahmanism as an antinational intrusion and ruptured by dalit protest against its Brahmanical accommodations, the Catholic Church is now challenged to reframe its relationship with Indian society. Above all, in Tamil Nadu this has involved engagement with the experience of "dalitness" and the demands of dalit Christians in ways that this chapter will explain.

The assertive "Hinduness" of the 1990s coincided with moves to define Christianity as "dalit religion" and the Bible as "dalit literature," which were themselves part of a broader revitalized south Indian dalit cultural politics. Although we find the Church looking to its dalit social base and its representational organizations—the dalit movements—as a means of political protection against the incursions of a Hindu nationalist state, the proximate condition that drove a radical dalitization of Tamil Catholicism was an *internal* movement of protest against the incongruity of Christian universalism and the persistence of caste. In other words, out of its own deep contradictions, Tamil Catholicism provided an institutional and symbolic milieu for a language and practice of protest.

HINDU NATIONALISM AND THE TURN AGAINST CHRISTIANITY IN INDIA

The idea of India as a primordial composite Hindu nation, and the notion of "Hinduness" or *Hindutva,* emerged in the 1920s when late-nineteenth-century German and Italian ideas of the nation and ethnic nationalism joined Hindu revival and reform movements.[1] But the development of a homogenizing, some say "Semitized," Hinduism with unified creed and cult was above all a mimetic reaction to the Christian missionary "other." In broad terms it is often argued that in colonial times, missionary practices such as conversion and education were adopted, along with practices from scouting organizations and the British police, in advancing a parallel Hindu reform project to "civilize" backward communities of dalits and tribals who were to be recruited by the Sangh Parivar—the "family" of Hindu nationalist organizations.[2] As Clarke (2002, 201) points out, "[U]nder the banner of Hindutva, [an Indian elite] joined in the enterprise of representing themselves (the East) within the already established representational discourse of the West." Here was a strand of anti-British nationalism whose activist front, the Rashtriya Swayamsevak Sangh or RSS (the National Volunteer Corps), became notorious and temporarily banned after alleged involvement in the assassination of M. K. Gandhi in 1948.

This of course is a complex field of scholarship; suffice it to say that the Hindutva agenda was revived in the 1990s when religious identity along with caste was enhanced as an instrument of political-electoral manipulation in the competition that followed the disintegration of the post-Independence "rule" of the Congress Party (see Corbridge and Harriss 2000). Critics argue that a parochial neotraditional elite worked to make their (Brahmanic) worldview and religious practice hegemonic (Lobo 2002, 47–51); and the peculiarity of this "syndicated Hinduism"—a form that encapsulated or subjugated all other localized non-Brahmanic traditions—was captured in Kancha Ilaiah's polemical book, *Why I Am Not a Hindu* (1998; Lobo 2002, 50). Of course, making one tradition hegemonic required effort: the use of the mass media (especially television) and symbolic and political action. Above all, an imagined Hindu community required the idea of vulnerability to a threatening outsider enemy.

The Muslim minority was Hindu nationalism's principal "threatening other."[3] However, the move to national office (in a coalition) of the pro-Hindutva Bharatiya Janata Party (BJP) in 1997 coincided with a rise in anti-Christian rhetoric of a kind that had hitherto been reserved for Muslims. Representatives of Sangh Parivar organizations began to insist that Christianity was a serious threat to national integrity. The Vishva Hindu Parishad (VHP) general secretary, Giriraj Kishore, claimed that "[t]oday the Christians constitute a greater threat than the collective threat from separatist Muslim elements."[4] There was a concerted campaign against Christians and the spread of anti-Christian propaganda in the media, through polemical literature (see Goel 1994; Shourie 1994) and political speeches. These called for a "national debate" and a ban on religious conversion, for the expulsion of all missionaries, and for Indian churches to sever all foreign links and "set up a swadeshi church on the lines of [the] orthodox Syrian and Marthoma Church of Kerala."[5] In the "Hindutva script," Christians in India were an antinational presence with extraterritorial loyalty. They were a threat to national security and corrosive of Hindu values and traditions—a reference to anything from "Western" school uniforms to Valentine's Day cards.[6] Their missionaries used foreign money for Christian education, health, and other programs cynically to induce vulnerable dalits and adivasis (tribals) to convert and augment their numbers, seeding conflict and feeding separatism (Lobo 2002; Suresh and Gopalakrishnan 2003; Zavos 2001).[7] And in Hindutva terms, conversion itself was not just a humiliating attack on Hinduism and a threat to national unity; rather, it amounted to the change of a person's nationality (Lobo 2002, 71).

This anti-Christian rhetoric was accompanied by a flood of reports on violence against Christians by people associated with the Sangh Parivar: the murder of missionaries (most notably, the arson attack that killed the Australian medic Graham Staines and his two sons in Orissa), the rape of nuns, attacks on Christian social workers, the destruction of churches and statues, the desecration of graves, threats, and false cases. One Catholic compilation recorded 130 atrocities against Christians in 1998 and 177 in 2000. Significantly, these mostly took place within adivasi or dalit communities in areas of Orissa or Uttar Pradesh, and especially in BJP-governed Gujarat.[8] As we will see, Christians in Tamil Nadu experienced distinctive, if less marked, effects of Hindutva.

Explanations offered for the recent anti-Christian turn drew attention to the shifting grounds of BJP politics while also taking analysts deep into the contradictions of contemporary Hindu nationalism and surfacing historical confrontations between Brahmanical Hinduism and Christian missionaries (Sarkar 1999; Suresh and Gopakakrishnan 2003; M. S. S. Pandian 2002). Certainly for a BJP government in power, the small and scattered Christian minority, steadily declining as a proportion of the country's officially recorded population,[9] was a softer and less politically risky target for Hindutva "othering" than the Muslim population,[10] but more importantly Lobo, among others, argued that it was through the vilification of Christians that significant dilemmas, contradictions, and opportunities of the Hindu nationalist movement in the late 1990s were being worked out (2002). In order to survive, the movement's political wing (the BJP) needed to continue a program of economic liberalization begun in 1991 under the Congress government that encouraged foreign direct investment, integration into global markets, and the removal of regulatory barriers; and yet its cultural-ideological wing (the RSS) mobilized a base of support on the back of a xenophobic campaign rejecting new economic policies, Western patterns of consumption, and the entry of multinationals into India, at times supporting violent direct action against foreign companies such as KFC (Assadi 1996) while invoking *swadeshi* or "own-country-self-sufficiency." According to this argument, the anti-Christian posture linked the present cultural invasions of globalization to the specter of a persisting colonial presence (Lobo 2002; Zavos 2001; Hansen 1999). The "Christian threat" to the honor of Hindu national culture was a useful surrogate onto which anxieties about liberalization could be displaced without derailing neoliberal economic policy; and targeting the Christian minority as representatives of Western imperialism was a better alternative than targeting the multinational companies themselves (Froerer 2007, 11).

The Christians onto whom these negative identifications were projected were in large majority from groups such as dalits and adivasis, whose values, cultural practice, lifestyles, and patterns of consumption were in fact *least* influenced by economic growth linked to global markets—while the upper-caste/upper-class Hindu nationalists who objected to the cultural threat implied by church schools opened in such communities were themselves competing to take advantage of higher education in Jesuit colleges and convent schools so as to best prepare their own children to take advantage of the economic opportunities of globalization (Lobo 2002).

The anti-Christian ideology of vulnerable "Hinduness," critics concluded, was primarily a construct for transmission to a poorer majority. Its objectives were political—namely, to win party political allegiance of a majority while protecting the interests of an upper-caste class (the same group that had earlier in 1989 mobilized against the state implementation of the so-called Mandal commission to extend reservations to an additional category of "Other Backward Castes")[11] from the gathering threat of subaltern political aspirations in the name of preserving a Hindu social order. And in the countryside, the real but unspoken grievance of the Sangh Parivar was not that Christian organizations were converting subaltern dalits and tribals, or destroying their culture, but that they were "spreading awareness of human rights and dignity through education" (Lobo 2002, 95). Targeting Christian mission became, then, the means to contain political resistance from the margins in the name of an external threat to the nation, making the bearers of this threat the tiny Christian population. Then further, as enthusiasm for an evidently inconsistent and potentially destabilizing Hindutva agenda declined among an important section of the BJP-supporting urban middle class, who were by 2000 themselves reaping benefits from economic liberalization and service-sector-driven growth, the antiminority RSS redirected its focus to peripheralized rural dalits and adivasis—now the critical terrain for political incorporation (see Corbridge and Harriss 2000; Froerer 2007, 7). This shift would produce the most deadly anti-Christian violence.

In rural regions of persisting poverty, Lobo (2002, 89, 128) and other analysts argue, Hindu nationalists were in part able to appropriate the aspirations of the subordinated, using the specter of Christian conversion to divert attention from the real problems dalits and adivasis faced, not least dispossession of their land, water, or forest resources to Indian capitalism's primitive accumulation; adverse economic incorporation as unskilled migrant laborers; or continuing usury, low wages, and exploitation by landlords, officials, and contractors, who were mostly from the upper-caste sections of society close to the Sangh Parivar (see Mosse 2010). Moreover, RSS- or VHP-connected activists were seen as playing a key role in turning local tensions inherent in transactions around land use, jobs, common resource use, or trade (perhaps of liquor) between rivalrous castes or ethnic groups (but having no basis in religion) into violent but politically productive confrontations between Hindus and Christians (Froerer 2007). In regions spread across the country, convert groups known as "Oroans," "Bhils," or other caste-tribe titles were newly identified as "Christian" and transformed into a "threatening Other," Froerer explains (2007, 20). The vernacular media meanwhile linked these conflicts back to the wider discourse on the Christian destruction of Hindu culture. The violence in Orissa's Kandhamal District, which led to the massacre of dalit Christians in August 2008, is an instance of these processes (Kanungo 2008; also Froerer 2007; Lobo 2002).[12] In Tambiah's (1996) terms, generalized and violent conflict arose as Hindutva activists facilitated processes of "focalization" (denuding local incidents of their particulars of context) and "transvaluation" (assimilating the particular to larger, enduring, less context-bound causes and interests). In political terms, the production of singular antagonistic religious identities—that is, "communal" identities—not only victimized Christian minorities but also produced constituencies that reliably turned in votes for BJP candidates in old Congress areas (Froerer 2007; Kanungo 2008). In broad terms, while missionary churches were construed as a threat to the Hindu nation, the presence of Christian groups was absolutely necessary to the politics of Hindutva.

TAMIL NADU: ANTICONVERSION LAW AND DALIT REACTIONS

This nationally projected agenda, which gave Christianity a new political profile, was, through political alliances in the late 1990s, brought to the more Christian south, a region with no recent history of "communalized" Hindu-Christian relations. As shown in previous chapters, social tensions in this region were not easily translated into religious conflict, and Hindus and Christians did not generally imagine themselves as members of communities with conflicting interests (Sarkar 1999). Nonetheless, by the year 2000, Hindu nationalist ideologies had acquired popular acceptance in urban and rural Tamil Nadu, where "changes to the public space . . . encourage[d] Hindus to become more conscious, demonstrative, and assertive about their religion" (Fuller 2003, 137). The openness of Tamil Nadu to Hindu revivalism, as well as an escalation in caste conflict in the state, certainly appeared to belie the view that Dravidian nationalism and its populism would "temper the potential of ethnicity to generate conflict" and "ensure a pluralist democracy" (Subramanium 1999, 31, as discussed in Harriss 2002). The Hindu Munnani (or Hindu Front), an activist Hindu organization formed following the mass conversions in Meenakshipuram in 1981 (chapter 5), was successful in "normalizing" Hindu revivalism, inter alia through processions for the popular pan-Hindu deity Vinayakkar (Ganesh) (Fuller 2001). Hindu revivalism was led by Brahmans but also incorporated economically successful and locally dominant "backward castes" such as Tevars (Maravars, Kallars), Goundars, and Nadars keen to project themselves culturally onto the wider pan-Indian stage through identifying with the Hindutva agenda and (in places) Sanskritizing their religious practice (see Harriss 2002; Fuller 2003; Wyatt 2010).

Consolidating support from these groups (having displaced its rival the DMK as the southern ally of the ruling BJP in Delhi), Ms. Jayalalitha's All India Anna DMK (AIADMK) government (2001–6) adopted an overtly anti-Christian stance. This administration eroded the autonomy and privilege accorded to Catholic schools, colleges, and medical and social missions as minority community institutions, curtailing their freedom to admit or appoint their own people (Christians) and subjecting them to close surveillance, to obstructive scrutiny of FCRA (foreign contributions regulation) accounts, and to harassment by means of bureaucratic lethargy. But most significant was the anticonversion legislation prepared in October 2002—a measure against minorities that went further than the pro-Hindutva BJP itself.

The Tamil Nadu Prohibition of Forcible Conversion of Religion Bill (2002) imposed three- to four-year prison sentences and fines on those who "convert or attempt to convert . . . by use of force or by allurement or by any fraudulent means."[13] The main threat to the churches lay in the ambiguity of the language of "allurement" or "force." The former included any temptation such as a gift, gratification, or material benefit; and the latter, a threat of any kind, including "divine displeasure or social excommunication." "Anything a Christian does—whether it is teaching in schools or working in hospitals or slums," said the Protestant Bishop Devasagayam, "could be considered an 'allurement' to convert."[14] This provided an opportunity for agents of the state seriously to constrain the work of the Church, priests argued, and to intimidate and suppress it through selective use and motivated prosecution.

The Tamil Nadu government justified the legislation by interlinking highly evangelistic churches such as the Seventh Day Adventists (whose program for growth, "Go one million," received widespread critical publicity) and some high-profile mass conversions by dalits to Buddhism, Islam, and Christianity that were explicitly protests against continuing *caste* exclusion.[15] In this way the anticonversion legislation won strong support from religious leaders of Hindu mutts (monastic establishments) and temples who had at the time acquired a new role in the political field, as well as from Hindutva organizations (the Hindu Munnani, RSS, VHP), while curtailing (anti-Hindutva) dalit social protest in the interest of the AIADMK's core Backward Caste supporters who backed the law.

The key point is that Hindu nationalism found its place in Tamil society through *caste* rather than religious politics. It largely failed to exteriorize Tamil Christians as *Christians*.[16] Even when nationally anti-Christian violence was at its height, in Tamil Nadu direct intimidation of Christians and priests was rare and limited to certain localities such as Kannyakumari, where the BJP gained some support. In the southern districts such as Ramnad, Hindutva become integrated into the caste identity of Tevars (Kallars, Maravars, Cervarars), who offered the greatest resistance to dalit social mobility (and backed the anticonversion legislation), while in Catholic villages such as Alapuram, Hindutva organizations were even able to recruit support from upper-caste Christians in order to resist dalit assertions. At the same time the anticonversion law reflected a battle for dalit constituencies. Hindutva sympathizers hoped first that dalits would be enrolled *as Hindus* (encouraged by the widespread but as it turned out short-lived participation of slum-dwelling dalits in RSS night schools, devotional groups, Vinayaka processions, Hindutva rallies, and antiminority graffiti or pamphleteering),[17] and second, that pro-dalit social activism could be delegitimized by equating it with Christian proselytism.

It is the *consequences* as well as the causes of the anticonversion bill that are of interest here. The bill was widely condemned by human-rights groups, dalit movements, and opposition parties—on several grounds. It was judged as belittling converts as passive respondents to the inducements of others and as unfairly attributing this motivation to all Christian clergy. Because the law stipulated that a conversion ceremony could take place only with the permission of (intimation to) the district magistrate, it involved intrusion of the state into the personal domain, removing the right to privacy, and "passing judgement on people's subjective reasons for choosing to change their religion" (Suresh and Gopalakrishnan 2003). By criminalizing conversion, the law contravened the "the right freely to profess, practise and propagate religion" guaranteed under the Indian Constitution.

Most significantly, although the anticonversion bill was ostensibly an attack on Christians, it was not Church leaders but dalit organizations and dalit politicians (regardless of religion) who led the objections. True, on 24 October 2002 the churches closed their educational institutions and joined fifty thousand people on a one-day fast in Chennai, which included Christian revivalists, Muslims, dalits, and opposition parties; and the bishops went to meet the chief minister under the banner of the Tamil Nadu United Minorities Forum. But the institutional response of the established churches on the issue of conversion was muted, decidedly defensive, and socially conservative (mindful of the need to protect their *minority* privileges). While the mainline churches were insisting that they neither practiced not encouraged conversion, dalit activists were organizing mass conversions in public, enacting the dalit struggle as the rejection of Hinduism. Dalit leaders such as Udjit Raj, R. Thirumavalavan, and Dr. Krishnaswamy, among others, declared that they would lead the conversion of some twenty-five thousand dalits to non-casteist faiths in defiance of the law, beginning with a ceremony in Chennai on 6 December 2002, the anniversary of Dr. Ambedkar's death. This was the culmination of agitation against the legislation by dalit rights activists, NGOs, dalit Panchayat presidents, and dalit political parties that built on a movement launched by some sixteen dalit organizations invoking Ambedkar's call to "quit Hinduism," as well as the ideas of writers such as Kancha Ilaiah, and before him the Paraiyar leader Irattaimali Srinivasan (b. 1860), who insisted that dalits had never been Hindus (Thirumaavalavan, 2003, 2004). In the event, a few hundred (some claim five hundred) converted amid police pickets and the arrest of ten of the organizers. It was expected that other conversions would follow in rural areas.[18]

Unsurprisingly, the effect of the Hindutva anticonversion legislation was not to diminish but to enhance the significance of conversion, or its threat, as an idiom of dalit protest. Even upper castes threatened conversion to or from Christianity in reaction to various dalit demands.[19] This was Tamil caste politics projected in the religious idiom of Hindu nationalism and Christian conversion. The dalit politician-led mass protest against the bill was not a pro-Christian stance against Hindu religion, but an expression of dalit opposition to the casteism implicit in Hindutva; that is to say, it involved the enrollment of Christian conversion onto the dalit political agenda (not vice versa). Nonetheless, it was a demonstration to Christian leaders—newly vulnerable to the intimidations of a Hindutva-sympathetic state, which could impose on if not outlaw their work (or have the effect of licensing attacks on Christians by caste Hindus who made themselves custodians of the new law [Sudhakar 2003])—that the Church now depended politically upon dalits and their movements. So, while in the Hindutva heartlands such as Gujarat the Church response to attack was to stress post–Vatican II interreligious dialogue (Lobo 2002), the Tamil Church began to see the assertion of "dalitness" as a way of standing against Hindutva. Radicalizing the Church's message, making itself "more dalit," claiming a mass support base, and so enhancing its political significance offered a safeguard against the incursions of a pro-Hindutva state. As one dalit Catholic priest put it to me, with a full sense of the historical irony, Church leaders "are using the dalit community as their savior." Thus, if the Church's social agenda—its educational and social work among subordinated communities—was the putative cause of the Hindutva anti-Christian campaign, it can also be seen as its consequence.

This supposed alignment of the Tamil Catholic Church with dalit movements (apparently reversing and repenting the original Nobilian alignment with Brahmans) was in fact rather more complicated (see below)—and dalit leaders' political support for the Church a good deal more tactical. In speeches, the Liberation Panther and Paraiyar leader Thirumavalavan insisted on the right to religious conversion in order to resist historical oppression and Hindu assertion, but equally during an election campaign (in 2004) he did not flinch from accepting temple honors from conservative (pro-bill) Brahman priests in his constituency to win their support. Meanwhile, the Pallar leader Dr. Krishnaswamy appealed to pro-Hindutva religious leaders to protect dalit rights to temple honors (at the Kandadevi temple in Sivagangai) as an anticonversion measure.[20] Here, from a dalit political point of view, the issue was not whether dalits should become Christian or Hindu (authentic dalit religion being neither; see below), but that when called "Hindus," dalits were refused entry to temples; when called "Christians" they were denied honor in churches; and both temples and churches accumulated resources from which they were excluded.[21]

In May 2004, the BJP-led government was replaced by a Congress-led coalition. Jayalalitha withdrew the anticonversion legislation (under which no cases had in fact been registered) along with other pro-Hindutva Sanskritizing measures such as a ban on animal sacrifices[22] (see M. S. S. Pandian 2005). "This is fresh air," commented one dalit priest. "We were able to breath freely after Congress." The new prime minister, Manmohan Singh, reassuringly appointed an independent commission on minority rights (the Justice Ranganath Misra Commission), and Christian leaders could shift from defending conversion back to lobbying in Delhi against the exclusion of dalit Christians from Scheduled Caste status on the grounds that this, too, was unconstitutional religious discrimination.

THE CHRISTIAN DALIT CLAIM TO SCHEDULED CASTE STATUS

The campaign to have Christian dalits included in the list of Scheduled Castes (SC) and so eligible for state benefits and protections alongside Hindu dalits precisely contradicted the conversion discourse of dalit struggle against caste as a *Hindu* institution. The report of the above-mentioned Ranganath Misra Commission in 2009 concluded that "the caste system should be recognised as a general social characteristic of the Indian society as a whole, without questioning whether the philosophy and teachings of any particular religion recognise it or not," and that Christians of equivalent caste should be included in the SC list (Ministry of Minority Affairs 2009, 153–54).

The recent dalit Christian campaign for the implementation of this recommendation is only the latest in a series of representations from 1950 onward to presidents and prime ministers to include Christians in the SC list. Perhaps best known was the legal case against the state that went to the supreme court, arising from the instance in 1983 of a Christian dalit, Soosai, in Chennai denied assistance from a central government scheme allocating bunks (work stations) to street cobblers.[23] But the bishops' promotion of the Christian dalit cause had always been constrained by a dilemma that was summed up in the supreme court's judgment in this case. If Christian dalits were to have the same compensatory privileges as Hindus, "it must be shown that they suffer from a comparable depth of social and economic disabilities and cultural and educational backwardness and similar levels of degradation *within* the Christian community, necessitating intervention of the state under the provisions of the constitution" (quoted in A. Raj 1992, 2–3 [my emphasis]). Bureaucrats in Delhi could turn to Christian leaders and say, "You proclaim there is no caste in Christianity; but now that you are asking for reservations, you say that you practice untouchability" (Fr. Antony Raj, interview, November 2004). The bishops had to either accept that Christianity perpetuated caste or deny dalit Christians state support. And the dilemma was deepened by the fact that the Church's primary interest in relation to the state had always been to preserve the privileges of its distinct minority status (the right to independence in appointments and admissions in its institutions).

The judgment in the Soosai case, like the Constitution Assembly, took as real an "imagined community" of Christians (outside of caste) within the nation that the Church claimed to be; and that rendered the category "dalit Christian" meaningless.[24] Those who represented the "Christian community" at the 1947 Constitution Assembly took it as a matter of principle that Christians would *not* accept special privileges related to caste and that the Church would see to it that the Christian principle of equality was realized in community.[25] But of course Christian dalits, even when they struggled to this end, were never able to join or constitute a community outside of caste.

By the 1990s, some broad political changes had in fact created space for the assertion of "dalit Christian" identity and interests. Among them were the communalizing of Indian politics (indicative of the failure of Nehruvian secularism), the rising power of lower castes, and a new era of coalition politics (Wyatt 1996). Dalit Christian activism on the reservations question became increasingly well organized, taking the form of dharnas (picket-protest), rallies, long marches, use of the media, and lobbying MPs with the partial and reluctant support of international figures such as Mother Teresa. However, supporting dalit Christians' claims served no party's political interest, and there was strong resistance from Hindu nationalists, who probably regarded exclusion of Christians from the Scheduled Caste list as a good disincentive to religious conversion (ibid.). The passing of legislation in favor of scheduling Christian dalits (introduced as private members' bills) seemed unlikely, and remains so even under the Congress-led government and despite the unequivocal findings of the Ranganath Misra Commission on the equivalence of Christian and Hindu dalit discrimination and disadvantage.

CATHOLIC ACTIVISM AND MASS DALIT PROTEST

The campaign for state recognition of dalit Christians as Scheduled Caste is important, not just for its own sake, but also for what it says about the contradictions of caste and Christianity and the roots of a new form of Catholic activism to which I now turn. Catholic bishops had generally argued that it was the historical and continuing reality of caste oppression in society that made the denial of state recognition and protection to Christian dalits a matter of unconstitutional religious discrimination. The Church in Tamil Nadu had itself become more conscious of the injustices of caste from the late 1970s. The generation of Catholic priests who are now prominent in the various movements, campaigns, legal cells, or commissions for dalit rights found inspiration in the anticaste ideologies of the Communist movement, from the work of Ambedkar and from Periyar—although it was their formation in seminaries in the 1970s and early 1980s, and their reading of liberation theology and inspiration taken from the work and sacrifice of radical Latin American priests such as Rutilio Grande and Gustavo Guttierez, that especially led these priests to rethink their ministry in Tamil parishes (A. M. Xavier 2006, 53–54, 56).[26] The core theme of "social justice" challenged the deep social conservatism inherited from three hundred years of Jesuit "cultural accommodation."

I have elsewhere narrated examples of the various action-reflection experiments that resulted from these influences, including the "Working People's Liberation Movement" (WPLM) started out of Alapuram village by a radical parish priest in the late 1980s (Mosse 2009, 179–81). The point that I want to emphasize here is that the leftist movements started by such priests in their parishes were soon mired in caste-based identities and interests. Some priests tried to lift social action out of this caste form through class- or occupation-based movements (the WPLM brought together laborers, palmyra tappers, fish workers, and others). Meanwhile others such as the Jesuits who formed nearby People's Action for Liberation Movement in Eastern Ramnad (PALMERA),[27] found that the cross-caste solidarities of their movement were ruptured by local temple-honors-related caste violence. As dalit membership of village-level associations expanded, the Jesuit intervention took on the form of a local dalit movement, whose members were encouraged to enter Assembly elections (ibid.). By the late 1980s it was clear that a *dalit* caste-focused rather than class-based approach to Catholic social activism would become the predominant form.

Following Rome's approval of the Province Congregation's Postulate in 1987, the Jesuit "preferential option for the poor" was recast as an "option for dalits." The Madurai Jesuit counter-Nobilian policy was to "reach out in a special way to the most marginalized and discriminated in Tamilnad society, namely Dalits" (JMP, 2002, 64, 66; A.M. Xavier 2006, 31). Following the PALMERA experiment, "mass-based" dalit organizations were promoted in other districts, creating institutions owned by and under the control of dalits. Jesuit regional centers coordinated and extended the scope of this work through the provision of legal services, support for dalit victims of violence, training, legal awareness, education, and the documentation of human-rights violations, with media support for clergy, dalit NGOs, and the youth cadres of dalit movements and political parties. Meanwhile, AICUF (the Jesuit-led All India Catholic Universities Federation) acquired a largely dalit student membership and, together with the Dalit Youth Christian Movement and the International Dr. Ambedkar Centenary Movement, provided further means by which Jesuits advanced their "dalit option," both in villages and within Catholic institutions.[28]

Even before the Hindutva threat, the Church had found reason to support pro-dalit social-action ministry. Among other things, there was fear of a dalit exit from the Church, not through (rare) reconversion to Hinduism in response to Hindutva activism (or to Islam), but from the readiness of dalits to adopt Hindu names and to change their religious identity to access state benefits, making the campaign for Scheduled Caste reservations pastorally important. Moreover, some priests felt that the middle classes were already turning away from mainstream churches to evangelical groups, "so the only ones they can keep are the dalits" (interview, Fr. Manu Alphonse, November 2004).[29] Then, in the 1990s, Catholic clergy sought to resolve the stark paradox that their own premier educational institutions were serving the children of the very pro-Hindutva middle class who were attacking them, while excluding dalit Christians (interview, Fr. "S," October 2004).

More powerful and more immediate as a drive for the dalit option, however, were the exposed contradictions of Tamil Catholicism itself erupting as protest *from within*. Dalit leaders, particularly dalit Catholic priests including those lobbying for "SC" status, insisted that it was not their exclusion *as Christians* that was significant, but their identity and discrimination *as dalits*; and discrimination not in (Hindu) society at large, but most immediately within the Church itself—that is to say, as "dalit Christians" rather than as "Christian dalits". Growing awareness of "dalitness" within the Church made the situation of dalit Christians the central missiological and theological concern of south Indian Christianity in the 1990s. Although "dalit Christian" and "caste Hindu" became dichotomized labels, dalitness was not expressed primarily in Christian terms. Indeed, the Catholic Church became a crucible for anticaste radicalism not as a result of any countercultural rejection of resurgent Brahmanism, but because of its own embodiment of the antagonism between universal values and the particularity of caste culture.

While the mostly upper-caste activist priests inspired by liberation theology grappled with the class-or-caste dilemma, the small minority of Catholic priests who were themselves dalit had a different perspective. For them, caste was an immediate and *experiential* phenomenon. The Church was a dalit church, they argued, but ruled by non-dalits; and they demanded religious equality as Christians, concretized sociopolitically through proportionate access to resources and appointments (Antony Raj, interview, 16 November 2004).[30]

Returning from the United States with a sociology PhD, the dalit Jesuit Antony Raj undertook a survey, *Discrimination against Dalit Christians in Tamil Nadu* (1992), not so much to establish that caste was a social phenomenon affecting Christians as well as Hindus as to expose caste discrimination in the Church itself. His study documented the everyday exclusion of dalits from upper-caste churches, the separation of cemeteries and funeral biers, seating, and Communion, and the disallowing of dalit funeral processions to pass through upper-caste streets. Dalits were still refused the role of lectors or prevented from assisting in the Eucharistic celebration, from teaching catechism, serving Mass, joining the choir, acting in Passion plays, or washing the feet of the priest on Maundy Thursday. Dalit Christians were not asked for contributions to festival processions that avoided their streets.[31] Dalit Christians were poorly represented among Church leaders, on parish or pastoral councils, on finance committees, or in social-service societies.

Raj recorded that Christian dalits did not regard discrimination by "caste Christians" (in public or private domains) as significantly different from that by "caste Hindus" (A. Raj 1992, 202). In fact, he concluded that they experienced discrimination more intensely than Hindu dalits in that they were "twice discriminated"—in society and as a *majority* in the Church—and as well as excluded from state protection and privileges. Raj used sociological awareness as an instrument for popular mobilization around the idea that dalits had not received from the Church compensation for societal oppression, and that it was *within* the Church itself that dalits experienced the most intimate (if disguised) discrimination: priests (and even more so nuns) not only lent tacit support to the exclusions imposed by upper-caste parishioners but were themselves discriminatory in relations with dalits, in speech, in social etiquette—offering seats or accepting cooked food—and in the appointment of catechists or teachers (A. Raj 1992; ex-nun Bama's testimony 2000). It was priests who failed to celebrate Mass in dalit villages and chapels or to extend honors at dalit funerals (A. Raj, 1992). In some respects, such as the use of pejorative caste names and stereotypes, priests and nuns were regarded by the dalit men and women questioned as more discriminatory than laypeople—in particular, younger non-dalit priests, scholastics, and seminarians (Thangaraj 2003, 20). When interviewed, dalit activists like Antony Raj insisted that priests and nuns were not acting under pressure from their high-caste parishioners. They themselves were guilty of enacting a "self-deification before the voiceless" (A. Raj 1992, 345).

Within Catholic institutions, prejudice against dalits was systematic, Raj reported, in reference letters, in admissions, in the exercise of discipline in schools, in neglect and denial of opportunity, in the stereotyping of dalit students as lazy, distracted, or lacking potential; or indirectly in the prohibitive costs and entry requirements that restricted access to Church education for poor dalits and caused high dropout rates (ibid., 347, 349–51).[32] In Raj's survey of 120 Catholic schools, colleges, seminaries, and orphanages, these institutions were found to reproduce a caste order in which upper castes predominated in teaching and clerical posts while dalits were found in menial or "scavenging" (toilet-cleaning) work. In religious orders dalit nuns experienced subordination and were "given insignificant roles . . . whereas the upper caste nuns adorn powerful posts" (Thangaraj, 2003, 56; Bama 2008, 89).

Dalit priests (whom I interviewed in 2004 and in 2009) were quite explicit on the mechanisms that reproduced caste power in the Church. As one put it, "[I]f a Vanniyar [upper-caste] priest is rector of a particular seminary for five years, you will see only Vanniyars recruited" (cf. Thangaraj 2003, 56). Where Vellalars and Utaiyars dominate Catholic parishes, they promote their own into the priesthood and religious orders to the exclusion of dalits.[33] The fact that very few vocation promoters were dalit meant that in the 1980s a largely dalit Church had very few dalit priests and (until 1991) not a single dalit bishop. "Is God casteist?" one critic rhetorically asked. "Does He also practice untouchability?" (Arulraja in Thangaraj 2003, 57). Even a decade later, dalits accounted for as few as 4 percent of priestly and religious vocations in Tamil Nadu.[34] And despite its "dalit option," in 2003 only eighteen of the three-hundred-odd Jesuit priests were dalit (Thangaraj 2003).

Dalit priests who raised these issues were angrily critical of a Church system producing instance upon instance of normalized caste prejudice: an upper-caste parish priest replies to a dalit girl's request for a recommendation to a teachers' training school saying, "I cannot even find jobs for my people, and you people can go for some tailoring or other jobs"; a priest headmaster says, "[B]eef-eating Paraiyars are not good for studies but only fit for taking care of cattle"; "[T]he induction of dalit teachers," comments an institution head meeting the archbishop, "would bring down the standards of the students" (A. Raj 1992, 355).

Above all, however, it was the reflection upon their *own experience* and position in the Church that fueled dalit priests' activism. They disclosed personal experiences of discrimination that marked their own route through school, college, seminary, or formation house. Several I interviewed from rural backgrounds began the journey to priesthood because apostolic schools (with boarding) were a means to otherwise unaffordable higher education; the vocation came later. In seminaries, their common experience was of institutions ruled by upper castes where, without patronage and protection from co-caste supporters among teachers and senior priests, they (as dalit students) were exposed to criticism, disciplinary action, or dismissal for small failings that their non-dalit peers could cover up with the collusion of co-caste seniors.

Dalits lacked the social networks necessary to build and protect confidence within the seminary. They explained how anxiety of exposure or prejudice made them cautious and self-contained, vigilant in observing rules, guarded in their behavior and in the expression of opinion in relation to teachers, and withdrawn from peers (lest closer relationships reveal their identity). As students and novices, these dalits sometimes faced caste-based ribbing, hate mail, social isolation, or change in behavior toward them if their caste identity was revealed, perhaps inadvertently in the public announcement of scholarships or a discovered SSLC book (a school-leaving certificate that identifies caste)—but equally they feared the negative rebound that might follow their reports of discrimination.[35] Others faced the internal struggle that went along with the successful concealment of their dalit identity. Fr. "X" spoke to me about his guilt in being mistaken as upper caste by his speech, manner, and academic achievement; but also of how his "passing" made him aware of the dress, speech, and body language that revealed other students as dalit, *and* that in making these judgments he was himself perpetuating the self-fulfilling negative stereotypes of others. Some dalits appealed to their bishops to send them to more distant seminaries in metropolitan centers (Bangalore or Pune), where social divisions among students would be linguistic—Tamil, Telugu, Malayalam—rather than caste based. Some dalit priests disclosed traumatic childhood experiences of untouchability; for others awareness of caste discrimination came with entry into secondary schools or colleges or seminaries themselves: regardless, the initial reaction to the experience of caste prejudice was often confusion and guilt accompanied by intense anxiety and distress associated with social rejection and the discovery of something wrong or defective about themselves.

Some dalit priests from urban backgrounds who had not grown up in the context of caste inequality, or had attended metropolitan seminaries, were astonished to witness discrimination against their own caste when they began their appointments in rural parishes. There were new dilemmas. When pressed by their parishioners, should they conceal their caste identity, or declare and forge solidarity with dalit parishioners (with the implication of distance from upper-caste Catholics)?[36] For dalit priests, struggles in village and diocese were interlinked. Those who chose to identify themselves as and with dalits described being marginalized from diocesan opportunities or promotions acquired through caste networks (Thangaraj 2003, 19). It was not unusual for dalit clergy to objectify the experience of discrimination as an essential quality, describing the affinities and prejudices of caste as "natural," as "in the genes," or as "an inner compulsion," a "deep stream" that shapes thoughts and influences actions, overlain by a surface stream of Christian ethics and anticaste ideology.[37] And this latter duality was also a common theme: "As a priest you profess Christian values whereas you act on the basis of caste," says Father "T." There is a public morality of unity and brotherhood from the pulpit, "but your private morality is determined by your social origins, by your prescriptive role . . . you are socializing the faithful into a life of hypocrisy" (interview, November 2004); or, as Bama writes of the convent world, "There seemed to be one God within the church and another outside" (2000, 93).

Many dalit priests and ex-nuns I interviewed offered a sharp distinction between the prejudice, piety, and sacerdotal practices of institutional religion and their individual discovery of the person of Jesus as a primary source of inspiration and radicalism, particularly directed against the hypocritical religious authorities of his day, who they say were equivalently "Brahmanical" (e.g., Bama 2000). That is to say, the dalit critique of the Church is made in Christian terms with reference to the spirituality of Jesus. "The life of Jesus as revealed in the Gospels is the touchstone," one dalit Jesuit says to me; another that "the New Testament is a manual to lead the [dalit] movement." It is *religion*—Christian as much as Hindu—that has oppressed dalits, insists the dalit lawyer Fr. L. Yesumarian, who sees the dalit struggles within the Church as being against the first of a triad of Dalit exclusion: the denial of God, the denial of land, and the denial of education. It is the frustration with institutional religion that has turned several dalit Christian activists to Buddhism as a personal religious practice, linked to a wider Ambedkarite discourse.

The intensely personal and emotional nature of their experiences of caste discrimination made all dalit nuns and priests I spoke with clear on the point that, as Fr. "T," a Jesuit dalit leader, put it to me, "only a dalit can understand a dalit; for you [a non-dalit] atrocity is only an observation; for me it is my existence." Identification (of non-dalits with the cause) is not the same as *identity.* There is a stark experiential divide:

> You build the temple but you are not allowed to enter. When your sister is raped, how must you feel? If a dalit is raped will you feel the same? When a dalit is forced to eat human excrement, for you it is news, for me it is a question: how can a human being treat another like that? For me it is feeling; emotion not intellect [it cannot be] neatly analyzed. My blood boils . . . I become hypertensive when I hear such things; but others are able to rationalize and analyze and come up with beautiful conclusions. In Jesuit meetings my language comes from emotion; it will be

> scathing . . . but if it is a neutral theological issue, I can outwit them. (Interview, November 2004)

These narrations confound and challenge theoretical abstractions of caste (M. S. S Pandian 2008; Sarukkai 2007). Caste is a lived reality whose truth is in experience, and in emotion (fear, anger, outrage, shame).[38] Moreover, caste is the everyday and ordinary, repeated and ever present. It is the unsanctioned behavior among novitiates, the informal comment, the intimidating note pushed under a dormitory door, the abusive graffiti, the obscene message left on a classroom blackboard, the counterauthority hate mail sent to a dalit provincial. These narratives involve a "depletion of past-ness"; they contradict the teleology of Christian modernity and equality (or of citizenship) that leaves caste behind in the village, in the past, among Hindus or the uneducated (M. S. S. Pandian 2008, 38), and that allows caste among Christians to be regarded as of a different time, the residue of a Hindu past, syncretic folk tradition, as incomprehensible or irrational. The presentness of caste makes it out of place, beyond "the *ūr*," and makes the ethics of caste more urgent. Caste is where it ought not to be: in Catholic institutions of learning, among priests and nuns, in the very spaces that should represent the Christian negation of caste.

In the same year that Antony Raj produced his survey (1992), the former Catholic nun Bama's Tamil autobiographical *Karukku* ("serrated leaves," "blades") was published, offering another window onto dalit experience of the institutional Church, and starting a genre of dalit women's writing.[39] Bama narrates her growing sense of anger at the Church. First, she becomes infuriated by the way in which nuns treat poor dalit children in the convent school where she teaches: "injustice that dances like a demon in the convents" (2000, 92). Then she reveals a deeper anger at the manner in which the convent, far from opening these children's eyes to injustice, prepares them to accept "that this is the way it was meant to be for Dalits." And she is disturbed by the effect of the convent world on herself: how it dulled her social conscience, trapped her in comfort, isolated her from life, stripped her courage and her independence of thought, so that "we become strangers even to ourselves" (2000, 103). She then forces herself to escape a "counterfeit existence," but "with all their words and rules in the convent, they cut me down, sculpted me, damaged me. Today I blunder and stumble about in the world outside" (2000, 103–4). Like the dalit priests I interviewed, Bama is shocked by the contradiction between the religion of obedience, patience, and daily pieties put on show, and the God she discovers for herself in reading the Bible, "who is just, righteous, is angered by injustices, opposes falsehood, never countenances inequality," and the Jesus hidden by the Church who associates with the poor and with compassion for the oppressed, who is not meek and mild but a revolutionary (2000, 90; interview, 22 April 2009).

DALIT CHRISTIAN ACTIVISM

Activist dalit priests drew on and fostered a groundswell of resentment among dalit Catholics. They not only laid claim to the Church's social agenda, but also turned it into a mass movement. Fr. Antony Raj was one of the first to give public expression to this dalit Christian anger. Outspoken, eloquent, and powerful, at Jesuit and diocesan conventions he laid out the contradictions of "a Church with outcasts." Dalit seminarians and novices facing their own crises of identity recall being "empowered" by a dalit standing before the intellectual might of four hundred Jesuits, declaring that a continuation of discrimination would see the formation of a breakaway dalit Church (Fr. "S"). Although not all Christian dalits saw a solution in ecclesiastical division, Antony Raj's message, inspired by the American black movement, about overcoming fear and shame, dalit self-acceptance, and the confident assertion of identity and rights found a ready audience. Together with the lawyer Fr. L. Yesumarian and other dalit Jesuits and a group of dalit-led NGOs (or social action groups), he promoted the agitative Dalit Christian Liberation Movement (DCLM) in order to politicize the issue of caste discrimination in the Catholic Church.[40] Through village-level cells and the skilled oratory of second-line leaders, the DCLM undertook a campaign on local issues such as appointments, admissions, and dismissals while using statistics to support the slogan that "the Tamil Church is a Dalit Church." Young priests also found inspiration in the Dalit Panther leader Thirumavalavan, whose slogans (*aṭanka maṟu*—"rebel"; *tiruppi aṭi*—"hit back") put their feelings into words (see Gorringe 2005a). The movement submitted memoranda and consolidated its determination and militancy through mass action—public meetings, *dharna*s, black-flag demonstrations, "ambushes"—which brought thousands of dalits into confrontation with Church authorities. Dalit Jesuit priests led protests at bishops' houses, at superiors' meetings, and at the Jesuit Province Congregations (in 1989), and on one occasion threatened to hold the participants of the Tamil Nadu Bishops' Council (TNBC) and the Tamil Nadu Conference of the Religious of India (TNCRI) in the meeting venue until their demands were met (for proportional representation for dalits in Church governance, the priesthood, appointments, admissions, employment, and for action against untouchability).

Support for the movement grew among Catholic dalits. It received the tacit backing of certain liberal bishops (and the Jesuit archbishop of Madras) and focused its protests on dioceses with a poor record of dalit rights. The movement used public action to reject Church patronage and the politics of the gift, and its leaders had contempt for the paternalistic voluntarism of a "preferential *option*," insisting instead on dalit *rights* (Fr. Yesumarian, interview, 18 March 2009; A. Raj 1992, 399). Dalits stood up to bishops. They refused to kneel and receive their blessing, saying, "We don't want your blessing, we want our rights" (Fr.

Paul Mike, interview, November 2004). Meanwhile, bishops wrote to the Jesuit General and to the Vatican warning of these "Marxist or communist" priests leading a movement against the Church; or they turned to upper-caste police, officials, and politicians to contain DCLM protests.[41]

Dalit priests gained support from a number of upper-caste Catholics, but they commonly perceived upper-class clergy as preferring to extend patronage and guidance to them than to see dalits in charge of prestigious institutions. It remains the case that dalits have rarely headed Jesuit institutions, and the only dalit Jesuit provincial is known to have faced obstacles and resentment. Unsympathetic clergy complain that the dalit Christian movement has been diverted into a politics of institutional control. But others acknowledge their historical complicity in dalit oppression and now challenge the prejudice and practices of their own caste community (perhaps refusing to bless their relatives' own-caste marriages or renouncing caste-acquired postings [Stephen 2008])—the model for such action often being Jesus's chastisement of his own Jewish community.

Dalit priests I have come to know well understand that undoing the deep and penetrating negativity of untouchability involves hard social and cultural work: confronting the wasted energy of dalit fear, as Fr. Yesumarian explains, and developing dalit personality, and even confronting stereotypes of dalits in his movement by insisting on neat dress, clean, organized office space, and the aura of professionalism (interview, 18 March 2009). In the opinion of many of these dalit priests, social action weighs greater than the ministering of the sacraments. But while valuing the life of Jesus over the magisterium in their religious lives, these priests also stressed that the outer work of action needs its inner counterpart in a life of prayer; daytime engagement with the "multitude" needs nighttime withdrawal to the "mount." Several Jesuit activists found disciplined guidance and direction specifically through the "Spiritual Exercises" of St. Ignatius—that is, the imaginative participation in scenes of the New Testament, and self-critical recursive reflection on the interior movements of the self (Clooney 2004). Other dalit Jesuits turned to the Bible, "full of the poor and the marginalised," and use scripture to challenge the Church to "initiate atonement for the past social and religious sins" (F. Xavier 2009, 1).

Because caste in the Catholic Church is characterized by its *public denial,* the task of "outing" caste has been challenging. Even in his Church-commissioned study, Thangaraj (2003) had serious problems getting responses on caste questions from priests and heads of institutions (rectors of seminaries, heads of congregations, even bishops): letters were unanswered, questionnaires unreturned, meetings refused, and enquiries subverted by unusable, inaccurate estimates. They refused the questions and reprimanded the questioner for the un-Christian fostering of caste consciousness, saying, "We are not working on [a] caste basis, caste is un-Christian" (ibid., 49). They denied knowledge or records of caste in parishes, institutions, or in relation to admissions or appointments when, Antony Raj claimed, "[i]n reality the religious authorities use every conceivable method to identify a candidate's caste" (1992, 383).

CHURCH RESPONSES TO DALIT CHRISTIAN ACTIVISM

It is fair to say that in the early 1990s the sudden appearance of a dalit protest movement took Church authorities by surprise. It "opened [the lid] and laid bare the contradictions in us," wrote the Jesuit provincial at the time. The "genie of caste" was out of the bottle (JMP 2002, 65). Until then, the Catholic bishops' response to the post–Vatican II emphases on social justice and the need to bring the Church into line with the anticaste stance of the modern Indian state was limited to festival reform (chapter 4) and lobbying the state for the rights of the Christian minority, including reservations for Christian dalits. The DCLM had brought an "insurrection of the prohibited language of caste" (M. S. S. Pandian 2002, 1739) into the realm of Catholic religion "beyond caste." This social movement had arisen among Jesuits (generally more permissive of dissent), and Jesuit leaders effectively appointed themselves as mediators between the bishops and the DCLM. They introduced measures into the Society of Jesus, including targets for dalit appointments to posts in Jesuit institutions and a coordinating "Dalit Commission" (JMP 2002, 65), which were then reproduced in the dioceses. The Tamil Nadu Catholic bishops announced the years 1990 to 2000 as the "decade of Dalit development" and drew up a "10-point programme" to eliminate everyday caste discrimination, promote vocations, and encourage dalit appointments, admissions, and leadership in Church organizations (Thangaraj 2003, 6–7).

When these measures were independently evaluated in 2001–2, however, the widespread dalit skepticism about their effectiveness was rather confirmed (see Thangaraj 2003). Resistance to dalit interests seemed still to pervade everyday work in Catholic parishes. The caste-based system of recommendation and sanctioning of jobs, loans, or admissions was perhaps even strengthened by upper-caste associations and networks that appeared to have been encouraged as countermeasures to dalit assertions, making representations, pressing counterdemands, or lobbying over matters such as bishops' appointments.[42] DCLM activism had enhanced caste-based associationalism among Catholics.

The survey's conclusions about persisting and institutionalized caste discrimination were not welcome news for the bishops, especially given the rising profile of caste questions. In November 1999 an open memorandum had been issued by the DCLM president to Pope John Paul II on the occasion of his visit to India, noting that "since the powers, authority, official posts, organizations and financial resources are all in the absolute hold of the caste-Priests, Nuns, Bishops and religious, the Dalit Christians are not able to get an equal share for them in education, employment opportunities, welfare and development schemes available in the Church."[43]

And in November 2003, during their visit to Rome, the Tamil Nadu bishops received from the pope a letter specifically drawing their attention to "the unjust system of caste division which denies the human dignity of entire groups of people," saying that they must "continue to make certain that special attention is given to those belonging to the lowest castes, especially the Dalits" (letter from the Vatican, 17 November 2003). Following a closed-door review of the study findings in 2004, the bishops issued a statement acknowledging the fact of continued caste discrimination, reasserting the opposition of Christianity to casteism, and setting out an "[a]ction plan for the integrated development of Dalit Catholics in Tamil Nadu." A restated ten-point program now included teaching against untouchability in prayer and catechism texts, making proportionate reservations in admissions and appointments in a diocese compulsory, and ensuring data collection for monitoring.

By late 2004, dalit Christian activism had lost much of its militancy. Skeptics spoke of appeasement, co-option, and the use of institutional processes and concessions to "break the movement," and the theft of "dalit-deprivation" for use as a foreign fund-raising slogan. A new non-dalit Jesuit provincial less sympathetic to the DCLM was unable to resist demands from the wider Church. Meanwhile, the movement's leader, Antony Raj, was under pressure from Rome to transfer the DCLM to lay leadership. He decided to withdraw and devote his energies to Jesuit–dalit institution building. As with many social movements, the effect of the Dalit Christian Liberation Movement had been less to alter fundamental social processes (of Church and caste) than to change the terms in which society debates change and legitimates policy options (Mitlin and Bebbington 2006, 1). By the mid-2000s, the issue of caste and dalits had become prominent—if not *the* top item—on the agenda of the Catholic Church in Tamil Nadu. Dalit Christians, seminarians, novices, and others could to some degree articulate caste identities that a decade back it would always have been strategic to conceal (although open knowledge of caste brought other problems such as disparaging individual achievements under the rubric of the "dalit quota"). While caste identities, networks, and associations had become, to a new degree, the medium of Church politics, those dalit Christian activists radicalized through the DCLM had, by the time of my interviews in 2009, become more closely involved in the secular dalit movements. Meanwhile, there was a growing reaction against the pro-dalit Church policy. Some non-dalit clergy I interviewed (including bishops) sought to discredit dalit Christian activism, suggesting that dalit priests exaggerated the proportion of dalits in the Church and indulged in "vicarious thinking" by narrating the suffering of their forefathers as if it were their own, obtaining overseas funding on this basis from uninformed European and American Christian congregations and charities.

ERAIYUR—2008

The new dynamics of Christian caste were played out dramatically in a violent confrontation between dalits, upper-caste Catholics, the bishops, and dalit political parties in the large and ancient Catholic village of Eraiyur (Pondicherry diocese) and in the rapid-feedback media coverage, pamphlet and poster campaigns, websites, and streams of internet blogging that connected local events to wider processes of Church and state.[44]

As the Introduction noted, Eraiyur's dalit Catholics had protested against persisting practices of untouchability, focusing on the demand for "place" in church and streets for wedding and funeral processions. On 7 March 2008 they sat in hunger strike, demanding from the archbishop a separate parish centered on their own chapel so as to turn exclusion into honorable independence.[45] Angered by this defiance, a crowd of Vanniyars attacked the dalits, burning and ransacking their homes, property, and livestock. When armed police intervened, two Vanniyars were killed. In the recriminations that followed, the DCLM and dalit priests held the Vanniyar archbishop responsible for protecting members of his caste and indulging their claim that they were merely preserving "age-old custom and tradition." At least twenty dalit priests then locked churches and boycotted the Holy Week Chrism Masses, raised black flags, and organized their own hunger strike. In the aftermath of these events a compromise was reached.[46]

What was distinctive about this protest was, first, the lead taken by dalit political parties, especially the Liberation Panthers—Viduthalai Chiruthaigal Katchi (VCK)—who now challenged the Church hierarchy as surely as they had earlier supported it on the anticonversion issue. Dalit Christian mobilization in the state, weakened in itself, now took place within a space opened up by the dalit politics within which dalit priests negotiated solutions. As VCK leader Thirumavalavan said during the *dharna* outside the archbishop's Pondicherry house, "[T]he bishop is the shepherd of the sheep, [but] not of the panthers" (in Arulnathan 2010). Second, there was a new attempt by the hierarchy to isolate Catholic religion from relations of caste. Amid the conflict, an (upper-caste) bishop wrote a memo withdrawing Church responsibility for the secular sociocultural phenomenon of caste over which it could exercise only limited moral authority. Dalit priests, the bishop implied, had strayed into the curved, manipulating, and devious arena of "politics" (Latour 2003). They were reprimanded for the promotion of caste division, using the media in disloyal alliance with electorally motivated dalit parties.[47] Standing with dalits against the authority of the apostolic successors was a failure of *faith*.

The Episcopal attempt to separate Christian religion from a subordinate moral realm of caste neutralized in Nobilian fashion as "politics" received its retort. Fr. Francis Xavier, the former Jesuit principal and himself a dalit, in a paper presented to the Tamilnadu Bishops' Conference in 2009, wrote of a village where "there is a wall separating the Dalit houses from other houses. One wonders [on] which side of the wall the Catholic Church and the hierarchy stand. . . . [They] have not taken any efforts to break-down this social evil since they claim they have only spiritual power. The hierarchy cannot offer [a] spiritual solution to human rights violations. In other words, the spiritualistic (superficial) model of the Church has failed. If one is truly spiritual he/she cannot but play the prophetic role in denouncing whatever is unjust" (2009, 3). The view that, far from being irrelevant to Christian spirituality, the experience of caste—of "dalitness" and the struggle with caste oppression—is constitutive of Indian Christianity stands at the center of the new theological and cultural move of "dalit theology," which began to gain ground in the mainline churches in the 1990s. When "*dalitness* . . . is what is 'Christian' about Dalit theology," as one prominent theologian wrote (Nirmal 1990, 129), and when "the broken Christ whom they [dalits] can identify themselves with, follow behind and minister to, is for the most part non-Christian!" (Pieris 1993, 38), the boundary between the religious and the social had, despite the bishop's objection, been radically redrawn.[48]

FROM CHRISTIAN TO DALIT: DALIT LIBERATION, DALIT THEOLOGY, DALIT ANTHROPOLOGY

Within dalit theology, the anti-Brahmanical social critique—of Ambedkar, of the rationalist reformer Periyar, or of the Paraiyar intellectual Iyothi Thas (b. 1845)—was given theological expression, enabling Christian converts to be identified with the wider dalit movement through a discourse of shared origin, experience, and interests *beyond* the Church. The theological starting point was not abstract soteriology but the concrete experience of oppression and dalit protest. As Antony Raj put it, "[T]he act of disobedience [was] the sociological foundation for a Dalit theology" (1990, 17).

Like liberation theologians, dalit writers refused to see sin as a purely personal matter divorced from social injustice. They sought an authentically Indian motif of liberation grounded in the dalit experience of oppression, to replace the "salvation theology" of sin and redemption. Dalit theologians also discovered the cross as a symbol of dalit brokenness—and the Bible as "a Dalit book [w]ritten for an oppressed people . . . truly part of a Dalit literature" (Soares-Prabhu 1992, 94, cited in Wyatt 1996, 127) exemplified by the words of the Old Testament prophets, and the liberation paradigm provided by Exodus. When Jesus identifies with the poor and when (in Luke 4:18) he uses the prophet Isaiah to describe his work for the poor in terms of freedom for prisoners and release for the oppressed, the latter term is taken as precisely synonymous with "dalit." Indeed, these theologians write of the Christian God as a dalit god, of Jesus the dalit, God incarnated as a dalit, the servant-god, the broken-bodied, whose achieved deviance made him an outsider, an outcast—the "Dalit Christ" refused a place in the Brahmanized church—"who restores 'humanness' and community to Dalits" (Nirmal 1990). At the same time, dalit theology is a project of "decolonization" that involves reclaiming the Bible through dalit commentaries that represent an authentically Indian exegesis unmediated by Western theologians.[49]

Dalit theology is also a matter of cultural politics involving an anthropology of "outcaste culture" (cf. T. Gorringe 2004, 171). This is founded on an idea of the kind of disjunctive tradition noted in the previous chapter, rooted in missionary Aryan invasion theory, influenced by the Paraiyar intellectual tradition of Iyothi Thas and Dravidianism, and developed by Ambedkar's anti-Brahmanism (Jaffrelot 2003). It locates caste oppression in the historical set of relations that gave hegemony to a denigrating Brahmanic ideology (*varnashrama dharma, karma* theory, etc.) and sees dalit theology as the cultural work of *recovery* of an autochthonous, pre-Aryan, non-Sanskritic culture and identity.[50] Cultural *disjuncture* itself becomes the basis of liberation, just as cultural unity is the basis of hegemonic caste power; and the shared history of oppression and memory of rejection provides the charter for a new "imagined community" (Wyatt 1996, 119). In this way, dalit theologians rejected both the Hindu unity of Hindutva *and* the exclusionary "Brahmanic" accommodations of the Indian Church—the reliance on Sanskritic religious/philosophical vocabulary, and the work of "Sanskritizing" theologians, architects, or artists (including the 1970s Christian ashram movement), now specifically delegitimized by the rise of Hindutva. It was through a "Hinduizing" of Christianity, dalit theologians maintain, that caste thrived in the Church. As the status of Hinduism is "caught within a debate about the location of power within the structure of Indian society" (ibid., 122), dalit theology defines itself in opposition to the transcendentalism of classical Indian Christian theology (such as Nobili's) by emphasizing the incarnation as a historical act of solidarity.[51] It also takes up the theme that dalits have never been Hindu, claiming that Christian conversion movements of the late nineteenth century were public acts of cultural protest through which the modern dalit movement began.

Current trends in dalit theology move from biblical exegesis to dalit historical experience; from texts to songs, stories, and proverbs; from Christian to preexisting dalit religious traditions; from an emphasis on suffering and pathos to a celebration of dalit cultural traditions; and from church dialogue to popular religious synthesis. This involves the liberative work of shaping a subjugated dalit "folk" religious tradition construed as pre-Hindu rather than pre-Christian, and identifying those oral, collective, and egalitarian elements excluded by textual Indian-Christian theology (Clarke 1999, 157ff).[52]

Tamil Protestant Christian centers,[53] in particular, had a key role in articulating, honoring, and theologizing an "outcaste culture" through symbolic reversal, remythologizing, and performatively reinterpreting dalit cultural practice.[54] The Protestant theologian-composer James Theophilius Appavoo, or "Parattai" (at the Tamilnadu Theological Seminary, or TTS), ran stories in the magazine *Tamukku* (drum) to positively redefine markers of untouchability. He also brought *paṟai* drumming into Christian liturgy and the Eucharist (Sherinian 2002, 237). In Sathianathan Clarke's theological elaboration, the drum becomes "a theological interpretant through which alternatives of the Divine can be experienced and reflected upon" (1999, 169). The drum is a symbol of suffering and emancipation, captured in the notion of "Christ as drum" (an extension of the idea of "Jesus as Dalit"), which is presented as a counterpart to Christ as the Word. In this new field of Christian cultural signification, the aim is no longer the "inculturation" of Christianity to Indian semiotic forms. This is a project of dalit social recognition requiring the assemblage of semiotic elements (artifacts, music, dance, mythologies) in reconfigured settings—special events and new audiences—so as to decontextualize them from relationships of subordination and thus produce dalit culture and art. As "art" (*kalai*) these performances break the nexus of social relationships and ritual structure (chapter 3) so as both to generate new meanings *and* to change the semiotic process (from index to symbol, ritual effect to interpreted meaning). Dalit art then becomes a field of meaning, authorship, and political intent partly within the domain of Christian religion, which, as already argued, is characterized by such semiotic possibility.[55]

Thus from 1994 TTS began organizing annual dalit arts festivals (Dalit Kalai Vizha) that celebrated dalit songs, poetry, drumming, and dance forms. Here, for example, parai drumming was recoded as a core symbol of dalit honor instead of indexing servitude. This public celebration of dalit art cued further decontextualizations as dalit performances traveled as part of national and international cultural programs, or accompanied political rallies. It also lent support to new professional Tamil dalit performing troupes, including those, such as "Sakti," composed entirely of dalit women (Arun 2007a; Karunambaram 2002).

However, dalit art and theology thus assembled have an uncertain relationship with the heterogeneous world of dalit politics. Catholic and especially Jesuit dalit activists whom I interviewed tended to regard dalit theology's "new talk" as ideologically significant in setting up the idea of a "dalit culture," but as sociologically naive (e.g., Fr. "S," interview, 16 April 2009). This dalit culture is, in particular, either insufficiently or excessively socially decontextualized. In the first case, establishing dalit cultural festivals and forming professional troupes for the promotion of dalit arts and the like opens up new possibilities of symbolization, but such redefinition is unlikely to be accepted by all dalits, let alone by dominant castes; its separation (decontextualization) from caste power is incomplete. As Friedman points out, "culture" may be "supremely negotiable for professional culture experts, but for those whose identity depends upon a particular configuration this is not the case. Identity is not negotiable. Otherwise it has no existence" (1992, 852).

In the second case, the social decontextualization of dalit "art" limits its political significance. "Dalit arts are weapons for liberation" (*talit kalaikaḷ viṭutalaiyiṉ karuvikaḷ*), the slogan goes, but hardly, Fr. "S" insists, when they are confined to the stage once a year as a "showpiece." Only after funeral drumming has been erased from villages can the drum be reworked as a celebration of difference freed from stigma, he suggests. Until then, "are medical students going to take to the stage to beat tappu drums?" he asks. Despite its staged celebration, for many, parai dance-drumming (*tappāṭṭam*) remains ambivalent or degrading.

For such dalit Jesuits, resignification has to be a matter of social protest and action beyond the seminary. Antony Raj insists that being dalit "presumes a protest culture . . . it has to start with a process of *inversion* . . . whatever the dominant castes consider as respectful and sacrosanct the Dalits should learn to disrespect and desacralise" (1992, 399). He regards dalit liberation as a dual process, first of *negating* or "decoding" existing cultural values as a means to remove fear, pain, and enslavement from hearts and minds; and second, of *affirming* liberative values and identities. The Dr. Ambedkar Centenary Movement (from 1991), led by Fr. Yesumarian in the northern Chengalpattu District, demonstrates how such appropriation of the stigma—whether of drumming or of beef eating—acquires political meaning as part of social struggle. When at night movement members reoccupied some *panchama* land—that is, land allocated to dalits in perpetuity by the British government, but alienated by non-dalits—they erected an Ambedkar statue as a proclamation of dalit ownership and as a political symbol, which also, being a potential source of caste clashes if damaged or desecrated by non-dalits, acquired state protection.[56] Then in the morning, Fr. "S" recalls with pride, they would arrive with parai drums, shouting slogans, and then slaughter a cow on the occupied land and cook and share beef as an assertion of victory and identity.

Under the influence of Jesuit activists, beef was also a weapon in claims over water resources; for example, in 1989 dalit women of Pappanallur who had been denied water facilities by the village authorities cooked meat and washed their hands by the village well and threw beef into it, thereby "polluting" the water for upper castes (Arun 2007a, 164–66). And when the consumption of beef in villages also involved carrying the flesh on a wooden pole though upper-caste streets, followed by public cooking and eating on Sundays or festival days, beef eating by Christian dalits became a provocative, conflict-generating, dramatic act of protest and a denial of shame (Arun 2007a).

The Jesuit priests of Madurai Province who took over several predominantly dalit (Paraiyar) parishes in northern Tamil Nadu incorporated such countercultural affirmative messages into their pedagogy in order to shape a positive dalit subjectivity among the students of their residential high school. "Moral instruction" focused on the history of dalit oppression and the lives of dalit leaders, and pupils were encouraged to celebrate their dalit/Paraiyar identity in oaths of pride, assertions of the moral-medical benefits of beef eating, and the like, which Arun (2007a) describes as processes of "resocialization." These symbolic manipulations once again work against the kind of south Indian indexical connections between objects and meanings, actions and persons, that constituted earlier experiences of untouchability. But such semiotic rupture, Arun implies, depends upon social rupture, the point being that Jesuit activists staged conflicts precisely in order to disrupt old meanings, just as they used education to instill new ones (2007a, 131–37).

Jesuit dalit priests insisted that such public acts of resignification were also personal acts of self-acceptance. The lawyer-priest Fr. Yesumarian, remembering the time after he first joined the Society of Jesus when a senior Jesuit father asked him if he was a "Harijan" and he broke out into a shivering sweat, realizes that "to accept myself as a dalit, that is a project of years . . . to be successful, all the insult and humiliation that I have experienced has been changed into positive steppingstones for me to organize people; that is my strength" (interview, March 2009).

Despite this "dalitization" of the Catholic Church, it is not clear that the rural majority of dalit Catholics any more regard the Church or its clergy as a solution to their social and political disadvantage, even while they actively press for equal treatment and opportunities (see chapter 7). This does not at all mean that dalit Catholics consider leaving the Church. Quite apart from their religious commitment, the Church still projects itself as a "big power" through its educational institutions, disproportionate influence, and international connections (Mosse 2009, 199). What is significant, though, is that the struggle for rights and resources is now *as dalits,* not as Christians, and this means that the wider dalit movements and political parties play an increasingly central role in caste struggles within as well as beyond the Church.

DALIT CHRISTIAN ACTIVISM, TAMIL DALIT POLITICS, AND CONTESTED "DALIT" IDENTITY

It was noted in the previous chapter that the 1990s witnessed an upsurge of dalit social movements and cultural politics, inaugurated by Dr. Ambedkar's birth centenary. In this chapter I have argued that dalit Christian activism, especially that led by Tamil Jesuits, was impelled by the internal contradictions of the

Catholic Church. In Tamil Nadu, Jesuit activists and Christian centers (Catholic and Protestant) went on to play an important, though underrecognized, role in promoting dalit leadership and shaping dalit social movements, as well as being centers of dalit cultural production.

Father Antony Raj, the DCLM firebrand already known for his activism during caste clashes in Villipuram (northern Tamil Nadu) in the early 1980s, was a focal point for emerging leaders from the different dalit caste constituencies—Pallar, Paraiyar, and Arunthathiyar (Cakkiliyar)—whose movements for dalit respect and rights themselves originated from the context of shocking episodes of anti-dalit violence. For three years (1992–5) Antony Raj lead a Dalit Integration Federation attempting to bring different dalit movements together onto a common platform to shore up "the moral authority to fight against caste" (interview, 18 November 2004). While it proved impossible to sustain the common platform, leaders of the different dalit castes made use of the institutional momentum and resources generated by Christian activists and the DCLM in order to access financial and logistical support as well as intellectual leadership from Jesuit centers, Protestant seminaries, and dalit Christian–led NGOs. These same institutions later offered *indirect* support to dalit leaders through free training for their youth cadres, dalit night schools and education centers in remote villages, and legal support or relief (channeled through leaders) when agitation led to retaliatory violence and loss.

The subsequent shift of dalit social movements into electoral politics—with its calculated compromises with the non-dalit leadership of the major parties and the corrupting chemistry of money, dispute settlement, and *katta panchayats*,[57]and the caste fragmentation of dalit constituencies—left dalit Jesuits like Antony Raj and Yesumarian profoundly disappointed. Raj contrasts contemporary dalit politics with black-power and antiapartheid movements, and laments the lack of a "proper intellectual formation for the cadres," the absence of agenda setting or a dalit manifesto, and the weakness of ideological commitment (interview, 19 November 2004), while Fr. Yesumarian, arrested and beaten for his activism, decries the cowardice and compromise involved in turning away from the risks of a radical social movement to the perks of party politics (including media recognition, police protection). Dalit political parties, he insists, are the first to dilute and abandon the dalit agenda, losing the radicalism of Periyar, Ambedkar, or Jesus; the political party is a platform for compromise, nowhere capable of dealing with the issue of untouchability (interview, 18 March 2009). These dalit Jesuit leaders express the need to keep dalit movements apart from formal structures whether of the party, state, or Church: they will not accept too many invitations to tea! Meanwhile, as Jesuit priests they do not cease to see the struggle for dalit liberation in terms of a "religious" formation, which like their own ultimately has to be founded upon intellectual discipline and personal and ideological commitment.

Saddened by the unbridged divide between the personal, the intellectual, and the political, Antony Raj gradually withdrew from the dalit movements. Pursuing the "character forming," "intellectual molding," and "capacity building" (skill formation, vocation training) of dalit youth, he built up the Dr. Ambedkar Cultural Academy (DACA) in Madurai. Such ideological "formation" of dalit cadres is a Jesuit ideal, regarded as a counterpart to the reality of untutored dalit youth forming shallow emotional bonds with dalit leaders in the manner of film-star fan clubs. Influenced by figures like Augusto Boal, Raj recently described his turn from the explicit ideology of politics, speeches, or religious protest to forging new emancipatory social practice, perhaps organizing several thousand dalit women to gather to sing, dance, cook ponkal rice, and share food—the creation of a festival around which hawkers and stalls will also spring up (interview, April 2009).

Other Christian centers also tried to facilitate a broadening of the dalit agenda beyond the electoral caste politics—for example, by supporting the position taken by dalit movement leaders such as Chandra Bose, and by certain dalit NGO networks, against "globalization" manifest as state-backed privatization of land and water commons, health, and education, the compulsory acquisition of land for new Special Economic Zones, or the outsourcing of government functions, all of which are seen to dispossess dalits while undermining their constitutional rights and their gains through reservations.[58] At the same time, Jesuit priests (especially through policy research and advocacy groups such as Social Watch–Tamil Nadu) have taken dalit rights into the realm of state planning and budgeting, shaping a civil-society campaign for the implementation of the routinely disregarded state commitment to proportional budgeting for dalit development under what is known as the Special Component Plan.

The Protestant churches, meanwhile, encouraged the growth of independent dalit-led NGOs, often intervening in villages (as missionaries had before them) to shift the balance of power so as to bring constitutional protections, provisions, and laws on untouchability within grasp. In the late 1980s, while I was still Oxfam's representative in south India, dalit-led local NGOs, supported by European Church donor agencies, were the first to turn the prevailing Marxian (or Freirean) class perspective on poverty into an explicitly caste- and dalit-focused analysis (Mosse 2011). By the mid-1990s, new NGOs emerged around the dalit self-respect agenda; many were led by Christian dalits. European development donor agencies had become major sponsors of dalit centers and cultural initiatives (such as the Dalit Resource Centre at the Tamilnadu Theological Seminary), which in turn supported emerging dalit leaders. By the time I returned to south India in 2004, a significant part of the NGO sector (including the NGO network that inherited Oxfam's program) had constituted itself around the theme of dalit human rights. This trajectory of NGO activism and its links to transnational advocacy on dalit rights and development (below) are the subjects of separate and ongoing research. All these initiatives followed secular trends in rights-based development and were entirely devoid of evangelistic intention. Nonetheless, they have to contend with a persistent Hindu nationalist delegitimation of dalit activism as a Western-inspired antinational vehicle for Christian proselytism and cultural appropriation.

While dalit Christian activism works to unify and expand the dalit agenda, it is also caught up in processes of separation and division. By the late 1990s, the social identity "dalit," whose culture and theology Christian thinkers had been shaping, had become a focus of contestation. What began as a dissent category expressing the condition of the oppressed (Gorringe 2005b) existed alongside clearly distinct caste identities. The three major Tamil caste groupings of Pallar (Deventira Kula Velalar), Paraiyar (Adi Dravidar), and Cakkiliyar (Arunthathiyar) were rooted in distinct regional cultural traditions, respectively of the south, north, and west of the state, and had developed historically in dynamic relation with the predominant groups of those regions (respectively, Tevars, Vanniyars, and Kavuntars [Goundars]). Paradoxically, the effort to claim a common emancipatory cultural space as "dalit," and to make explicit a *shared* subaltern experience of caste oppression and subordination, has enhanced the significance of these divisions.[59]

Theological centers and seminaries active in defining "dalit culture" now find this labeled as "Paraiyar culture" (because of the influence of this the largest and most influential dalit caste group in the churches and in state politics).[60] Pallar leaders, for example, insist that their people have no connection to *parai* drumming or beef eating. Their intellectuals and historians trace a lineage from Mallar Tamil kings displaced by Nayakkars under Vijayanagara (see chapter 5), not from ancient Buddhists suppressed by Brahmanism (as Paraiyar intellectuals argued). They are now joined by Arunthathiyars (Cakkilyars), who equally distinguish their history, their conflicts, their warrior heroes, and their traditions from those of Paraiyars. The various cultural markers—the title Adi-Dravida (original Dravidians), the symbol of Ambedkar, even the identity "dalit"—have all been regarded as captured by Paraiyars; dalit arts are Paraiyar arts, dalit music is Paraiyar music, dalit literature is Paraiyar literature, dalit theology is Paraiyar theology, dalit politics is the Paraiyar politics of the Liberation Panthers. At the extreme, non-Paraiyar critics narrate a progressive Paraiyar capture of the liberative discourses and identities of anti-untouchability, Adi Dravida, Ambedkarism, dalitness, human rights—and Christianity.

If a vocal section among Pallar activists has now begun to exclude themselves from the category "dalit" itself (insisting that as Deventira Kula Velalars their identification as untouchables was mistaken in the first place), and if Paraiyar activists are increasingly caught in the field of Liberation Panther (VCK) politics—they are in both cases distanced from the now significantly Church- and

NGO-supported activism of the politically weaker and predominantly Hindu Arunthathiyars.

Jesuit social-action programs recently targeted their support to this group subordinated *within* dalit politics and social action, who are openly represented as "dalits of the dalits." Aruthanthiyar leaders themselves acknowledge the role of Jesuit priests and centers in providing the ideological ground, education, and cadre training for their movements (partly through their youth hostels),[61] as well as the role of Protestants in creating a platform bringing together the many separate Arunthathiyar movements into a "confederation" in 2004–5 (although these are again fragmented). However, the "subcaste" politics of social action is fraught. By focusing on the subordinated among dalit castes, non-dalit Jesuits or NGO leaders face reprimands from dalit colleagues for fostering division and fragmentation; or they are accused of reinstating forms of patronage in relation to weaker clients, in preference to having to give space for dalit leadership within their own institutions (Yesumarian, interview, 18 March 2009).

FROM CHRISTIAN DALIT MOVEMENTS TO INTERNATIONAL HUMAN-RIGHTS CAMPAIGNS

Today, the interface between Christian activism and dalit politics in Tamil Nadu is clearly complex. Many Christian priests see quite definite limits to their role in the political field. Some argue that their focus has to be on dalit *Christians;* others (non-dalit Jesuits), that their role is to follow Jesus in launching a critique of their own casteist practices. But if they are now a diminishing influence within the dalit party politics of Tamil Nadu, a Christian dalit elite has found other avenues for secular activism outside the churches, not only through development NGOs but also, and most recently, through national policy campaigns and transnational advocacy.

Christian dalit networks are now international in their reach. Instead of the political party, the social movement, or the development NGO, they take the looser form of solidarity networks and campaigns on dalit rights. Dalit Christians happen to have taken the lead in what are, and have to be seen to be, secular processes. Prompted by the fiftieth anniversary of the Universal Declaration of Human Rights, which in 1948 spawned various UN commissions and several human-rights organizations (among them Amnesty International and Human Rights Watch), in 1998 a group of dalit activists (mostly Christian) launched the National Campaign for Dalit Human Rights (NCDHR) as a step to a wider international campaign to have discrimination on the basis of caste recognized as a separate agenda alongside the violation of human rights based on race, gender, place of birth, child labor, and the like. The initial campaign brought a resolution from the Committee for Elimination of Racial

Discrimination (CERD) to include discrimination on the basis of "work and descent" (i.e., caste) along with race. Now, with the claim that worldwide nearly 260 million people experience caste discrimination as dalits, the NCDHR and affiliated dalit solidarity groups in Europe (linked through the International Dalit Solidarity Network—IDSN) are pressing for a separate UN agenda on caste. As mentioned, this is the subject of separate inquiry. My point here is that Christian dalits, decreasingly prominent in dalit movements and political parties in the state, have been able to access the United Nations in association with, among others, the international churches (e.g., the World Council of Churches, the Lutheran World Federation), and at one moment provided a means for dalit leaders such as Thirumavalavan to enter this stage and to internationalize dalit politics (Vincent Manoharan, interview, October 2004). Christian dalits from south India have in different ways long found the means to deprovincialize their social experience and introduce a cultural critique, and are now involved in *de-Christianized* (secular) scale-jumping and "globalizing" dalit concerns. The specifically Christian (and south Indian) roots of this dalit activism are, however, a difficult heritage for those now involved in dalit rights organizations at the national level and in mediating links to the international sphere of the United Nations—especially when Hindu nationalist sympathizers seek to discredit the whole dalit agenda as inspired by foreign-backed Christian proselytism and the political intention to undermine the unity of the Indian nation (sometimes through academically untrustworthy but well-disseminated "research" [e.g., Malhotra and Neelakandan 2011]).

Nonetheless, for some dalit priests internationalization is also a *religious* imperative. As Antony Raj put it: "Sociologically speaking, the broken people or the excluded people [dalits] should have a network by which they can create a pan-world consciousness of excluded people . . . and theologically speaking, . . . we dalit Christians are [also] part of the mystical body of Christ, so if one part is affected . . . I think you also could feel the pain . . . therefore you are under moral obligation to take up the issue [through] advocacy and lobbying" (interview, October 2004).

CONCLUSION

The twenty years between my first fieldwork in 1984 and my return in 2004 proved to be one of significant change in the context of Tamil Catholicism. In the 1990s resurgent Hindu nationalism nurtured a "communalization" of religious identities throughout the country. In the Tamil south, however, Hindutva politics were translated into the politics of caste. Rather than consolidating socially the imagined "Christian community," communal politics brought into play "dalit Christian" as a politically "composed" identity performed in a variety of different ways (Latour 2005). First, within the anti-Hindutva discourse, "dalit Christian" was forged as a category opposed to "caste Hindu" and marking the difference produced by religious conversion (actual or potential). "Dalit Christian" was, second, a constituency mobilized by the claim against the state for exclusion from statutory protections and reservations. "Dalit Christian" was, third, a protest identity enunciating the outrage of caste discrimination within the Church.

These were to some extent independent articulations. By arguing that it was the latter that was most critical to south Indian dalit activism, my point is that the Catholic contribution to dalit politics did not come out of a Christian critique of Hindu caste society (the conversion narrative), but from the contradiction, *within* Tamil Catholicism, between the universal demands of faith and the particularistic interests of caste, long present but having surfaced politically by the circumstances of the 1990s, and experienced intensely by the dalit clergy (especially Jesuits) who lead the dalit Christian movement. The tension between Christian religion and caste society, faith and culture, had been culturally resolved over centuries in ways examined in earlier chapters. The collapse of these mechanisms in contemporary political conditions drove a mode of social activism that made an important and distinctive contribution to the political organization of dalits in the state more generally. And Christian activism, which itself began with a focus on ritual exclusion, expanded and merged with other streams of activism focused on land and human rights in a fast-changing world of dalit politics.

The street protests of "dalit Christians" were returned to the seminaries as the impetus to frame a "dalit Christianity" and a dalit theology. This deployed Christian modes of thought, action, and signification to rework and manufacture dalit "art," "culture," or the theology of the parai drum. These were enacted at village sites of struggle over resources such as land or churches. Meanwhile, reworking Christianity meant "recovering" dalitness from the assimilations of Brahmanic Hinduism and Brahmanized Christianity so as to discover the Bible as dalit literature and Christianity as dalit religion. In various ways, then, the late-twentieth-century dalit experience of Tamil Christianity was politically productive, providing an institutional and symbolic milieu in which to develop a language and practice of protest that proved highly influential within the wider south Indian dalit movement. This was not because Christianity provided a universal social ethic, but because of its deeply embedded and unresolved contradictions between religion and culture.

The intersection of religious nationalism, caste politics, and dalit social activism has unpredictable implications both for the Catholic Church and for social relations in the Tamil countryside. My recent round of interviews with clerics in early 2009 revealed the Church—headed by a new pope—to be more assertive of its Roman identity and its demands as a minority in the nation. It had set aside experiments in inculturation but remained vigilant in relation to still-present

Hindu nationalist threats. At the same time, the dalit critique exposed in ever starker ways the caste loyalties and divisions of the so-challenged "Hinduized" Church, its institutions, and its clergy. As the post–Vatican II engagement with liberation theology was transformed into dalit theology, the Church had been forced, in Nancy Fraser's (1997) terms, to engage with its dalit members' demand for sociocultural *recognition* along with socioeconomic *redistribution*. But those who work for dalit recognition, symbolic justice, and resignification have to contend with the unstable and contested nature of the dalitness itself, which mires such cultural work in further processes of caste-identity differentiation.

It seems indisputable that the cultural politics of the Church and the state has in recent decades produced a sharpening of religious and caste identities in Tamil Nadu. From the late 1980s rural Tamil Nadu seemed to have become an increasingly violent place. Reports of a social dynamic of growing competition and conflict between politicized caste-interest blocks, rising caste tension, polarization, and violence—between dalits/Backward Castes, caste Hindus/dalit Christians, dalit/non-dalit Christians—became commonplace. Renewed dalit assertions provoked violent retaliation in what some began to call "caste wars" (Human Rights Watch 1999a), and out of these confrontations were born new human-rights activism and movements, and dalit political parties. Those subject to violence were radicalized into violence. An "intertwining of collective violence and collective identity" (H. Gorringe 2006, 247) became pervasive in slogans, posters, murals, or speeches (for example, those of the Liberation Panthers, who prior to the moderating influence of party politics regarded themselves as "guerrillas engaged in violent protest as a means of self-defence and retaliation" [ibid., 241]).

It appeared that in the 1990s the caste-religious mix of Tamil society had lost some of its historical resilience, flexibility, and negotiability in ways that found parallels in other fundamentalist or culturalist settings (Hastrup 2006), becoming subject to processes of "focalization" and "transvaluation" (Tambiah 1996; see above). The "ethicized" caste and religious politics of the nation began to reappear in studies of Tamil villages (for example, Mines 2005). These described villages as arenas of competitive identity formation, involving increasingly violent confrontations as caste groups carved out spaces of influence and forged new solidarities.

Regional, national, and global arenas of identity formation coincided with a village-level dismantling of earlier religious integration in places like Alapuram. The various interlinked moves against syncretism, whether from dalit Christian movements, from Rome, now suspicious of inculturation, or from the growing influence of charismatic and Pentecostal religious forms, combined with the effects of Hindu nationalism to encourage the further defining and dividing of "Hindu" and "Christian," upper caste and dalit. And because identity formation is relational, this also involved new subordinating or violently excluding alterities (to use terms of Baumann and Gingrich's [2005] "grammars of alterity").

In this analytical mode, the caste-religious politics of the village and of the state were easily read into one another while being tightly interconnected through the work of caste movements, activists, churches, Hindu organizations, NGOs, or those producing media representations of "communalized" social relationships. It was in this political and analytical context that I returned to Alapuram village in 2004.

7

A Return Visit to Alapuram

Religion and Caste in the 2000s

My journey to Alapuram in October 2004 anticipated the new public profile of "ethicized" identity and caste honor. It was the anniversary of the execution in 1801 by the British of the ruler-rebel and Tevar (Backward Caste) hero Marudu Pandiyan (royal patron of Sarukani church), and Tevar youth in yellow T-shirts, accompanied by trails of flags and loud film songs celebrating Tevar caste pride, amassed at key centers of Sivagangai District amid roadblocks and police traffic controls—a precaution that recollected the recent history of violent Tevar-dalit confrontations in the district. As I reached Alapuram, a worrying sense persisted that differences of religion and caste had become a source of new tension and conflict. By the bus stop and tea stalls a crowd of party flags and billboards of caste societies and dalit movements advertised an outbreak of competitive associationalism. I soon heard of the growing reach of caste-based political parties, dalit movements, forums, and fronts. And news, too, of local religious revivalism leading to Hindu–Christian tension, attacks on priests, conflicts over new temple building, over the raising of flags and the pasting of posters in public places, of youth martial-arts training by local Hindu nationalist (RSS) activists and by radical Jesuits, and the appearance of new fundamentalist Pentecostal churches. Had Alapuram become a colorful microcosm of Tamil Nadu's violent identity politics? Did religious division and caste competition now feed each other? Was there a truly new dynamic to village life? And if not, what was going on? How had the dynamics of caste and Christianity changed in a quarter century?

A closer encounter with contemporary Alapuram, in fact, questioned the telos of division and conflict (Tejani 2008) while highlighting a disjuncture between the "dominant" discourse of ethicized caste and communalized religion—pervasive in ideologies of movements, theologies of activists, or media representations—and a "demotic" village-level discourse on religion and caste (to borrow Baumann's term).[1] The broad aim of this chapter is to explore these "demotic" discourses and their mode of articulation with dominant ones. First, I look into cases of Hindu-Christian conflict that suggested a significant redrawing of religious boundaries in the village as the Church is further disembedded locally to become a democratized domain of global Christian practice.

Second, I turn to the central paradox of caste—namely, that while declining in significance in everyday social relations, caste is more than ever asserted through caste fronts, forums, and political parties. This will involve explaining a shift from caste as a public discourse of distinction or rank (enacted in Catholic ritual) to caste as a discourse of equal rights. Successively, I will then explore change in the public space of caste, the "interiorization" of caste prejudice, and the altered relationship between service, work, and caste in agrarian relations. How and in what idioms do villagers themselves represent such social change? Finally, I will turn to local forms of dalit activism in Alapuram that interlink (or intertranslate between) local conflicts and the wider movements to show both how today caste is the basis of rights claims and how the dangerous implications of caste or religious politicking are diffused locally in a multicaste and religiously plural community.

HINDU AND CHRISTIAN AS RELIGIOUS COMMUNITIES?

It was not difficult in 2004 to imagine that religious tension driven by state-backed aggressive Hindu nationalism and Christian assertiveness had found roots in Alapuram. The signs of Hindu revivalism were everywhere. The main village temples had been renovated through local contributions, city remittances, and state grants including stipends for priests conducting regular pujas. The formerly inconspicuous stones, trees, or tridents of caste or lineage temples had become "pucca" structures with statues and elaborately molded towers (gopura), all indicative of an intensification of religious patronage in Tamil politics and a public reassertion of Brahmanical Hinduism begun in the 1990s (Harriss 2003; Fuller 2003). The renovation of churches, the installation of bright statues for veneration, modern public-address systems, and new Pentecostal congregations in the village seemed to mark a rivalrous Christian revivalism.

Hindu and Catholic systems of public worship began to disengage from each other back in the 1930s with the transformation of the caste-embedded Santiyakappar village festival (chapter 4). In 2004, even though privately Hindus continued devotions to the saints, and Catholics made offerings to Hindu deities, where necessary, the public worship of the two religions was not only markedly separate, but also subject to opposite trends. On the one hand, there was a fragmentation of village Hindu temple worship into separate caste or lineage cults. This began in the 1970s with defections following honors disputes, and was furthered by state aid for separate temple building by Utaiyar, Tevar, Pallar, or Paraiyar groups, whose celebrations now vied to make claims on the central public spaces of the village.[2] On the other hand, Catholic public worship in the village was increasingly unified and restricted to the realm of the church's compound and its canon (the liturgy and sacraments), minimizing or eliminating family and lineage saint shrines and caste-based festival days.

This division of Christian from Hindu in Alapuram appeared to coincide with unprecedented interreligious antagonism. Catholic sacred space was directly threatened when village members of the Hindu nationalist RSS planted a trident and constructed a Hindu shrine against the St. James church wall, provoking an instant and angry response from those alerted by the untimely tolling of the church bell. Intergroup violence again broke out when, just before my visit, RSS supporters removed a wedding announcement that Catholic Pallar youth had pasted over an RSS poster carrying pictures of prominent BJP figures near the bus stop. Then Hindutva legislation banning animal sacrifice brought Hindus into conflict with Catholics at saint shrines where this took place. Potentially yet more serious was the dispute during which members of a Pentecostal group buried a dead calf in front of a newly built Hindu goddess temple. In each instance, in expectation of a "communal clash," scores of police had arrived to arrest the key protagonists.

During my visit, there was also fresh memory of the incident a decade earlier when a Catholic priest accompanying pilgrims to de Britto's shrine at Oriyur had been hospitalized following an assault by upper-caste Hindus under the auspices of the RSS. Manikkam—a retired soldier, the son of the old village accountant, and the principal RSS activist—had brought the specter of militant Hindu nationalism still closer when, together with others, he organized early-morning martial-arts training for khaki-uniformed Hindu boys outside the Aiyanar village temple, which some regarded as a response to the instruction of Jesuit novices in the *cilampu* Tamil martial art, a form of "inculturation" mistakable as a projection of militant Christianity in the village. There seemed reason enough to imagine that Hindu and Christian religious identities were sharpening into mutual antagonism in ways quite at odds with Alapuram's long history of religious synthesis. Even village politics seemed realigned by religious affiliation. A Catholic Panchayat president had ousted the virtually hereditary Hindu Maravar family from office by mobilizing dalit Protestant votes after building a new church in the Paraiyar street. (This contest between *men* was for a position reserved in 2004 for women, held in name alone by the wife of the winner.)

As I looked into the details of these conflicts, however, it became clear that they were not in fact *religious* at all. They arose instead from attempts to take strategic advantage of a wider communal discourse in order to mobilize support for specific interests. RSS-backed attacks on the Church were a response to its developing anticaste stance. The assault on the Catholic priest's pilgrim procession was triggered by personalized chants by dalits against practices of untouchability. This was the latest in a series of Catholic platforms—sermons, slogans, banners—used to challenge caste that began with Fr. "X"'s dismantling of the Santiyakappar festival mantakappatis and his burning of the capparams. RSS rallies against this destruction of customary (*māmūl*) privileges were backed by upper-caste Catholics (chapter 4), who were also among those arrested following the later RSS-Catholic Pallar poster dispute. Other religious conflicts (such as that over animal sacrifices) were provoked by factional divisions; and the standoff over the buried calf and the goddess temple was widely understood as resulting from a long-standing dispute between two branches of a Pallar family over a plot of land. One (the Hindu branch) built a lineage temple on this land, responding, family member Rajesh maintained, to an instruction the goddess gave him in a dream. This implicit land claim was then consolidated with an application for money to the government's temple-renovation fund, on receipt of which (net of bribes to department officials) there was a grand inauguration ceremony with RSS invitees. The other (Pentecostal) branch of the family ignored the implications of this (that is, the presence of the goddess) by asserting their own claim to the land and to its prior use for storing firewood, straw, dung, and—to make the point forcefully—the burial of a dead calf. In the event, the police intervened with a compromise that gave the temple the right to the space during festivals but allowed common usage at other times.

During the short period of BJP rule (1998–2003) and the media-led discourse of communal tension it provoked, protagonists in disputes found that making a conflict "religious" by invoking Hindu identity and anti-Christian sentiment and exploiting Hindu nationalist connections or convictions could serve their interests. Indeed, by 2004 there was a firm view in the village that these efforts, and the appeal to Hindu nationalism in general (its symbols and practices—flags, posters, temple building, martial-arts training), were opportunistic. And since these tactics depended upon categories and narratives manufactured by the political process (Bourdieu 1991), they quickly lost salience once the pro-Hindutva BJP lost hold of national government in 2004. In fact, whenever relations between Hindus and Christians as members of different *religious* groups were in jeopardy, there was quick reparation. Following the attack on the priest, a court case was dropped after the Hindu headman made a public apology at the bishop's house. He was also believed privately to have made offerings to St. James and to have paid for church Masses for three weeks, not least (according to gossip still circulating in 2004) because following his ill-advised action his daughter had disappeared (she was later found) and one of his prize cows had died. Similarly, when the church bell alerted villagers to the RSS-inspired temple construction, it was Hindus (even before Christians) who mobilized to dismantle the construction in advance of the arrival of the police on the scene.

Regardless of religious nationalist discourse or anticonversion or Hindutva rhetoric, and despite the deafening early-morning competition between Hindu and Christian devotional hymns brought by ever-louder public-address systems, there had been strong resistance in Alapuram to making religious affiliation a basis of social division. Of course, religious difference was a subject of comment. Catholics such as Antonymuttu would suggest that whereas "Hindus worship with fear, with Jesus it is not like that, . . . there is compassion, a compassionate and loving God." Meanwhile, Hindus—who of course hold a different view of their own gods and continue devotions to Catholic saints—puzzled at the fact that Christians were not permitted to worship Hindu deities even while in all other regards they follow "Hindu culture" (*intu kalāccāram*), as Manikkam, who has now given up RSS activism, pointed out. Yes, Pentecostals are different in this, but he dismissed the idea that anyone would try to stop them preaching or converting, saying that "if we interfere they will say we are terrorists" (*nāma talaiyiṭṭāl tīviravāti eṉṟu colvārkaḷ*).

The appearance of new Pentecostal churches does not in fact mean that Christianity is experienced (or resisted) as a proselytizing religion. Nor do evangelistic Christians demonize Hindu religion. Contemporary charismatic cults of healing and exorcism align Satan and his demon underlings firmly in the category of *pēy*, distinct from the world of Hindu gods (cf. Bergunder 2008, 147). Catholics are likely to recognize and relativize non-Christian divinity, saying, as devout Antonymuttu did of Hindus, that "their gods are important for them" (*avar avarkaḷ cāmi avarkaḷukku peritu*). Even Prakash, a member of the most radical new Pentecostal group, did not endorse the dualist view of Hinduism as demonic, but said that Hindus were people who did not know the truth and that *picācus* (demons) change people's minds so they do not hear and cannot understand the Bible; its message is secret, revealed by the Spirit. In other words, Alapuram villagers quickly isolate themselves from the implications of a "communalist" discourse and its tactical use in specific conflicts. For them, religious change and revivalism are not about the formation of new political or social identities, but about "discovering consciously the salience of religious ideas and practices in their private and public lives" (Starrett 1998, 91). So, what changes have there been in the last quarter century in Christian practice and in the social negotiation of religion in Alapuram?

DISEMBEDDING CHRISTIAN WORSHIP

First, there has been a continued social disembedding of Christian worship (see chapter 4). In the long history of Alapuram that has been traced in this book, Christian worship and congregations were significantly structured by caste. The Catholic accommodations of caste; the emergence of a separate Paraiyar Protestant congregation; the arrival of Pentecostal churches in the 1970s as a mode of Pallar mobility—are all instances of this. But by 2004, it is fair to say, Christian assembly and worship was no longer caste structured. Instead, denominational differences and individual preferences reflected choice in religious styles.

In 2004, caste honor was no more articulated in public Catholic worship. Instead of a caste pattern of seating, women now occupied the nave, men the transepts, and Communion was administered by priests or nuns moving among the congregation. No single caste could claim the honor of carrying the statues at festivals or having their feet washed by the priest on Maundy Thursday, or of laying the first cloth (tuntu) on the body of Christ at the Good Friday procession, or of singing the processional songs or any other of the many markers of mariyatai. All such roles were now allocated to office bearers or elected members of the parish council or to catechists. The office of kovilpillai itself was no more a Vellalar caste position. In 2004, an Utaiyar man held the post; but the parish priest had so diminished the status of this ritual office (which instead of focusing on prayer, assisting at Mass, ringing the church bell, issuing marriage certificates, and the like now included the menial duties of church-compound maintenance, kitchen cleaning, and gardening alongside the priest himself as a mark of humility and service) that this man resigned, unwilling to be treated as *kūli* (hired laborer). None in Alapuram would replace him, so Susaiarul came from a neighboring village, the first dalit (Pallar) occupant of a ritual office now depleted of honor. The old "dalit catechist" or *pantaram* had left the village, although each year his nephew comes from Karaikudi town to decorate Santiyakappar's chariot at the festival as cappara meistri. But the caste-ranked festival honors that this function recalled, and that preoccupied the experience of those I interviewed in the early 1980s, were now a reluctant memory of the older generation, or lost in that undifferentiated "time before" (*muṇpu*).[3] For the many working elsewhere, the annual festival for which they return is now about connection to place, not a fount of caste honor (Dirks 1987).

If Christian worship was socially disembedded, paradoxically, the priesthood was more socially engaged. Priests had, without question, lost much of their social apartness and their (spiritual) power. They were more involved in the delivery of worldly development assistance, in organizing public demands for amenities (water, roads, or crop-insurance payments), or mediating village conflicts; and of course they were men of caste and the subjects of speculation or accusation in diocesan caste politics. Over twenty-five years, Alapuram villagers had experienced different styles of priesthood—socially radical, conservative, and pietistic. Priests had left legacies ranging from social movements to beautified churches. Regardless of the approach to ministry, villagers in 2004 were not slow to pass judgment on their ministers, perhaps most evidently through reduced attendance at Mass, now visibly slanted toward women and the older generation. The old catechist tells me that people have become selfish, concerned with their family affairs and without fear of God; it's a question of *nākarīkam* (urbanity, modernity). But it would be impossible to say that confession and Communion were any less powerful and transforming in the minds of Alapuram's Catholics, and even those who were least often seen at Sunday Mass maintained personal and household devotions. Indeed, in early 2009 a far greater number of men and women than in the 1980s were fasting in preparation for a Lenten (*tavucukālam*) pilgrimage to the Virgin at Velankanni, wearing cloth of saffron or blue hue, garlanding themselves with rosaries blessed by the priest, and attending special Masses. One dalit priest was convinced that it was dalits who swelled the numbers because as pilgrims "for forty days they are honored and respected," while his bishop insisted that pilgrim devotionalism was mimicry of popular Hindu styles, especially by the youth, inadvisably promoted by priests, who made pilgrimage shrines out of their churches (interviews in Sivagangai, February 2009). One of the many pilgrims, Michael Acari, tells a more enduring story about how, by fasting for thirty days and traveling to Velankanni every year, he finds satisfaction "if my heart (*maṉam*) is troubled," and how the Virgin appears amid his worries about his two daughters, calling him to her shrine; and perhaps if he listens with faith (*nampikkai*), he hears her beckoning him in the call of lizards or birds.

Despite two decades of teaching from the pulpit on saints as great personages and human exemplars, saints remain for many power divinities transmitting grace through the mediation of presence, touch, salt, soil, or water and, in the case of male saints, receive the life of the devotees' animals in return—although some I spoke with regarded (or thought others might judge) "cutting goats" as a rather uncouth form of devotion. Rayappan, for example, used to make vows to St. Sebastian and offered a goat at the local Kokkurani shrine after his son got a job in the military. But now in his midsixties, looking for peace (*amaiti*) after a self-confessed life of drink and bad habits, he spoke about turning instead to Velankanni in terms of progressing from a "small" to a "big" deity (and a more refined style of worship). The possessed still gather in similar numbers to confront their demons with St. Anthony at his "forest" shrine (chapter 2), but the catechist-exorcist's manner of dealing with them had mellowed in twenty-five years, and he told me that the *pey* themselves are not dancing as much as they used to when confronting the saint, but would instead (in Pentecostal idiom) cry that their body is burning.

If worship in the village seemed to conform to a more standardized practice of "global" Christianity, this was produced through the Church's specific adaptations to its environment, including borrowing from Pentecostal (alongside Hindu) devotionalism. Charismatic and healing conventions were introduced into worship (especially during Lent). Neighborhood groups (*anbium*) for Bible reading, prayer, and support, modeled on the idea of Basic Ecclesiastical Communities, became part of the parochial structure. Good Friday Mass in 2009 interwove distinctive Tamil performances of the Washing the Feet, the Way of the Cross, and the Corpus Christi procession in the village streets with preaching on the fate of Tamils in Sri Lanka, screen-projected excepts from Mel Gibson's *The Passion of the Christ,* and slide-show moral lessons on personal Christian living.

What of Alapuram's other congregations? When the old Paraiyar street was dismantled and relocated to the western edge of the new dalit colony, the Nadar family took over the original church, effecting a caste-street division of the Church of South India (CSI) congregation. Patronage of the Utaiyar Panchayat president provided Christian Paraiyars with the important and long-denied honor of a church of their own. The worship had changed little. The liturgy now led by the catechist Israel, or the still-rare visiting pastor, was heard mostly by women and young children. It was complemented by family prayers and devotions infused with Catholicism, especially focused on the Virgin and the saints. However, the most significant change in village congregations was the arrival of new Pentecostal churches.

The broad contours of south Indian Pentecostalism were explained in chapter 2, and the first appearance of the Church of God as a form of Pallar separatism was mentioned in chapter 5. By 2004, an additional two self-labeled Pentecostal congregations had established themselves in the village, clearly demarcated from the established churches from which they mostly drew their membership. In 2001, the Prayer Garden Fellowship, arising from the healing ministry of the charismatic ex-Catholic priest Fr. S. J. Berchmans (chapter 2), moved its meetings to Alapuram, and in 2003 "The Pentecostal Mission" (Ceylon Pentecostal Mission) established a prayer hall on land donated by Martin Pallar.[4]

These churches are small, each with fewer than a hundred listed members, of whom a third or less (mostly women) attend regular weekly prayer meetings, although the leaders admitted that numbers are swelled by the anxieties of health or imminent exams. While initial recruitment followed caste networks of an original sponsor, membership is caste diverse and widely spread across villages. As one pastor proclaimed, there is "no place for caste" (*cātikke iṭamē illai*). While dalit Pentecostals decry discrimination in the Catholic Church, their end-time ethics repudiates the gospel of social justice or dalit theology. The Church of God pastor's wife, Daisy, insisted, "We do soul winning; they [Catholic priests] do social work." The Pentecostal churches may aim to disjoin their members from the relationships and preoccupations of this world in order to pursue their relationship with God (Robbins 2004b, 128), and it is true that women and men participate as individual "believers" and emphasize personal transformation; but the break with social obligations is far from complete. As noted (chapter 2), involvement in Pentecostal churches often falls short of baptism, which would jeopardize family relations, marriage prospects, or entitlement to Church or state benefits and may even be entirely concealed from Catholic or Hindu families.[5] Among the male Pallar youth, Pentecostal spiritual individualism has been no bar to engagement in village-level dalit-rights activism.

These churches are locally oriented, low cost, and congregation supported; and while theologically connected to international Pentecostal churches, they remain far from the centralizing foreign influence and crusades that characterize Pentecostal expansion in urban south India (Bergunder 2005, 199; Thomas 2008). The Church of God and the Prayer Garden Fellowship share a theology and style of worship and support married pastors. who describe their separate projects without interest in collaboration. Both emphasize sacrifice and suffering for God, exemplified by their own movement from richer areas to simple living in remote and water-scarce Alapuram. However, it is "The Pentecost Mission" that retains the "ascetic moralism of the classical Pentecostal churches" (Robbins 2004b, 121). In the prayer hall built on wasteland at the village's edge, the two resident white-clad unmarried "sisters" explain to me the importance of celibate service and "living by faith"—a principle that not only prohibits soliciting resources but extends to the refusal of medical treatment in favor of "divine healing" (a position rejected by the other pastors). Helped by a local young woman healed of fainting fits (*mayakkam*), and under a branch church in Paramakudi town, "The Pentecost" sisters live without wages (relying on tithes and gifts) within a disciplined cycle of daily prayer—differentiated as "supplication" (*viṇṇappam*), "praise" (*tōttiram*), and so forth. A strict church authority insists that the "sisters" deny family (referring to Luke 14:26) and refuse contact with relatives, even for funerals. As Robbins puts it "The asceticism these codes enjoin provides people with guides for living with the ruptures P/c [Pentecostal/ charismatic] ritual and dualism create" (Robbins 2004b, 127). But in Alapuram of 2009, there was a widening gap between the sisters' codes and the congregation's desires. The sisters, who discouraged prayer for worldly matters—for family, work, or possessions that corrupt the main churches—complained that people were leaving the congregation once their problems were solved. Other Pentecostal leaders have found it hard to insist on injunctions such as against wearing jewelry or marriages to nonbelievers—not, it should be said, because these churches promote a class-protecting "prosperity gospel" for the better off (as elsewhere [Robbins 2004b, 123, cf. Caplan 1987a]). On the contrary, today these congregations mostly attract people who are poorer, less educated, or suffering. Where Pentecostalism demands radical rupture, not just with caste but with social life, it is rarely successful in such rural areas. "The Pentecostal Mission," the most demanding of the churches, found its core membership in the village, falling from twenty-seven to fifteen people in just five years (2004–9).

As noted in chapter 2, even though the intensity of worship and pastoral care—focused on personal health, relationships, and emotional problems—brings people back to prayer meetings, Pentecostalism is not sweeping aside participation in mainline churches in rural Tamil Nadu. For one thing, even long-term converts to Pentecostalism might say, as Ramesh did, "I remain Roman Catholic in name; I will be buried in the RC cemetery." But more significantly, charismatic worship, healing prayer, devotional fervor, and Bible study are now also part of contemporary mainstream Catholic practice in the village. Unlike their missionary forebears, present-day parish priests do not try to impose, constrain, or determine forms of worship. As noted, the Church accommodated and expanded a range of religious styles, and it is according to these, rather than ascribed roles or claims to social honor, that worship is today differentiated.

The exclusion of Hindus and the burning of the capparams marked steps in Alapuram's erasure of localized ritual forms to produce an ever more separate Christian religious identity. But this has not centralized religion as a mode of identification in the village (or elsewhere) or brought Christians into a media-facilitated global Christian *umma* (Thomas 2008). Alapuram may not be isolated from the "cyber-contestations" or "web-wars" between Hindu and Christian extremists (ibid.), but there is still no sign that religious divisions register other kinds of social differences except in short-term tactical and immediately reversible ways. The failure of increasingly distinct religious attachments to become socially salient as categories of identity in places like Alapuram has something to do with a secularizing modernization ethos in the village, where Christian religious practice is increasingly regarded as a matter for individual choice and social coexistence. But it also has much to do with the still-overriding significance of caste as a mode of identification in rural Tamil society, which raises the question of how the relationships of caste had changed in this same quarter century.

THE PARADOX OF CASTE

As idea, attitude, or practice, caste in Alapuram in the 2000s has become extremely difficult to pin down. In the simplest terms there is a paradox: caste inequality among Christians and Hindus is evidently receding as an aspect of village life (less practiced, less spoken), and yet caste is asserted and more visible than ever. The question is, How is the decline in the significance of caste in everyday life *and* the growing presence of a public discourse of caste and the proliferation of caste fronts, forums, and parties to be explained? Here I need to return to social practice in the village as encountered in recent visits to explain the way in which markers of caste inequality have disappeared, been suppressed, or been evaded, and to discern the local commentary on such social change; and then to explain the way in which caste reappears in part as a discourse of rights.

It will be recalled that caste as a mode of power and interrelationship (rather than as an aspect of belonging or kinship) was best understood as a set of services, offices, and honors, grounded in agrarian relations and enacted through public ritual (chapter 3). This involved the exclusion and othering of subordinated groups that alluded to notions of order/disorder and in some analyses the "exteriorisation of harm" (Mines 2005) as well as rank and royalty (Dirks 1987). The relationship between caste and Christianity was a cultural complex of social ordering and social critique, which through the twentieth century was increasingly organized into a coherent dalit challenge (chapters 4, 5 and 6). In the village, caste inequality was most immediately challenged in the public realm, in Christian worship, and in sacred space. By 2009, a history of contests and conflicts over precedence (*mutaṉmai*) or first respect (*mutal mariyātai*)—focused on festival processions, teashop entry, or access to water—appeared to have worked these concerns out of the public space of the village. Public enactments of caste exclusion and rank had been virtually erased. Under the interlinked influence of a secular democratic state, economic change, and the social interventions of activists and the Church, the "yearning to outrank"—such a mainstay of analyses of rural Tamil society (Clark-Decès 2007, 21)—had been transformed into a preoccupation with having an equal share or equal access (to opportunity or resources).

By 2004, Catholic Pallars in Alapuram, representing an advanced guard of dalit mobility, held high office (as Panchayat vice president) and power equivalence, and in many cases shared a class position with upper castes. Their "strategies of place" (chapter 5) had brought them to the commercial center of the village, where they ran provisions shops and other businesses. Government officers, police constables, and other significant outsiders could often be seen around the Pallar-owned tea stall by the bus stop. Rather than a space of honor, the village public—public space, institutions or ceremonies—was now a space marked by the principle of equal rights (*cama urimai*), which strongly reprimanded acts of discrimination. When Perumal Konar (a Shepherd caste) shouts at Paraiyar boys playing cricket near the temple, saying, "This is not your people's place," their instant reply is that he has no right to object to their use of a public place. If the village barber hesitates when dalit boys come to his salon for a haircut, or anyone passes comment on dalits entering the village temple, there is embarrassment or the threat of petitions or police cases on acts of "untouchability" that are offences under Protection of Civil Rights ("PCR") and SC/ST Prevention of Atrocities ("PA") acts. Of course, the fact that dalits tend not to go to the village barber or to enter certain temples (most dalits are anyway Christians) allows a degree of interpretive flexibility around claims to rights and equality; but the very fact that the public space is now indirectly policed by the state gives heightened salience to caste discrimination. This makes public but also "recontextualizes" everyday actions into crimes that individualize and exceptionalize caste discrimination (Rao 2009; see chapter 5). Well-publicized local incidents in which dalits, supported by human-rights groups, lodged "PCR cases" leading to plainclothes-police investigations into exclusion from temples, teashops, or water (etc.), even without convictions, acted as a threat, noticeably restraining behavior and language in public. While dalits do refer to the empowering effect of the PCR (or PA) act, upper-caste interviewees commonly complain of manipulation of the law, either by dalits who they maintain make spurious allegations of casteist motivations to press their interests in disputes over water, land, and grazing, or by their caste adversaries who use (or bribe) dalits to put "PCR" cases against them.

In the decades since I first visited Alapuram, caste has become a "hidden transcript" concealed behind a "public transcript" of equality (Scott 1990a). The physical space of the village is also being reorganized so as to preclude caste arrangements. By 2009, wealthy Pallar individuals had made themselves "central" by building "terraced" houses along the roadside—the new social-commercial center—where they interspersed with those of upper castes. This, plus the style of houses (set in fenced compounds), breaks with the social geography of the "caste street." In this context, the ubiquitous dalit lobbying for approach roads, electricity connections, street lights, piped water supplies, or ration shops involves important symbolic acts—claims against marginality expressed as spatial differentiation.[6] The fact is, today no caste group has the capacity to make itself spatially or ritually central in the village because space, like ritual, is losing the capacity to symbolize inequality. Even powerful symbols of caste difference such as beef eating are eroded by a thriving market for this butchered meat that would have been unimaginable in the early 1980s. Moreover, dalits do not feel the need to hide their caste identity in unknown places to the extent that they used to (although evasive identifications such as "Christian," "weaver," and "SC" are common).[7] Dalit caste names are for the first time proudly added to some wedding announcements.

Negotiating the signs of distinction and equality in the village is ever more complex and requires innovations. When the village teashop was forced open to dalits, a powerful upper-caste elite had insisted on being themselves served outside across the street in separate tumblers, thus turning a mark of stigma into one of distinction. New artifacts and technologies were also used to negotiate (or rationalize) equalized caste social relations. I was told in 1983–84 that it was of less consequence who was invited to sit on a veranda made of cement than of plastered cow dung, and water carried in a plastic pot apparently did not confer the pollution of a "mud" pot.[8] Today, the ubiquitous plastic chairs further evade seating protocols and allow code invention. They displace the ritualized role of supplying *mattu* seating cloth by the dhobi, who in turn narrates the caste democratization of access to her laundry services with reference to the use of detergent powder in place of the earlier process of boiling and sun-drying/bleaching clothing. More easily negotiated spaces are also created by relocating marriages from homes to caste-run marriage halls (*kalyana maṇṭapam*). Intercaste dining is itself regarded as a sign of civility and a way of building social networks. Nadars eat in the houses of Konars (shepherds), who help them buy goats or assist in police cases arising from illegal palm wine (toddy) brewing, for example. But a Pallar woman who knows that most Nadars would not accept dalit hospitality—in a way that it would be noticed—sneers at this social climbing by telling me how Nadars are trying to become "like kin" (*contakāramatiri*) with Konars. And my Paraiyar friend Mohan illustrates the point with the case of his roadside Nadar neighbor, Xavier, who used to visit his house and exchange gifts of food and festival snacks until, that is, a Konar family built a house in the vicinity, thus making this commensality too public. Ambiguities abound. When an Utaiyar teacher comes to Mohan's house to ask a favor, he is invited to sit in a chair on the veranda; but Mohan is constrained from offering him tea for fear of a demeaning refusal (or the delicately untouched glass).

THE "INTERIORIZATION" OF CASTE

One clear concomitant of the equalized public space is a privatization of caste distinction.[9] By this I mean not only restricting exclusions to the realm of the home, family, and food (which remain political even if not public), but also the notion, or more often the accusation, that publicly evaded acts of discrimination have "gone inside" and exist invisibly as a residual state of mind. While caste is less publicly enacted or spoken, Christian villagers I talked with often stated that, as the (Utaiyar) catechist put it, there is a "feeling [affliction] inside the mind/heart" (*manattukuḷḷē vētaṉai irukkum—maṉatu* or *maṉacu,* meaning the mind, heart, or will [Fabricius 1972, 783]). There it exists as the widely disparaged "caste feeling" or *cāti veṟi,* which might also be rendered as the "drunkenness," "anger," "confusion," "possession," or "madness" of caste (ibid., 897). Like the equivalent view of caste among the clergy (chapter 6), attention to caste as an inner attitude can be linked to what Ram (1995, 312) argues is a form of Christian reform involving "a transition from more traditional forms of subjectivity which locate causality and agency outside the subject to one which is located in the interior world of the subject"—a contrast that is itself part of the classical Tamil tradition of "internal critique"—and which makes caste a sin. "Caste feeling" is an accusation against others. It is the residue of discrimination that, for dalits, explains stifled but persisting concern with purity and status (as in the persistent avoidance of food from their kitchens, or the keenly noticed practice at their weddings of making gifts, drinking "cola," and then leaving before food is served). It is revealed at moments when the line between "outer modernity" and "inner tradition" blurs (Tanabe 2007).[10]

"Caste feeling" is taken to account for the awkwardness or resentment of upper castes having to ask favors or make requests from dalit professionals—such as headmasters or doctors—those, as they might say, "whose fathers worked our land." It is that persisting sense of distinction or difference in kind (*iṉavēṟṟumai*) sometimes glossed as "race." "Caste feeling" is an inner attitude that rarely escapes expression without sanction, ridicule, or mockery from dalits. Indeed, among my dalit interlocutors (male and female), expressions of caste feeling invoked a sense of pity as much as anger. Caste feeling is a weakness of the old, the uneducated, or the uncivilized. It comes close to Ambedkar's notion of caste as a "disease of mind" (1982, 38). Significantly dissociated from power, caste feeling is an affliction that affects Hindus more than Christians, Konars (Shepherds) more than Utaiyars. The habit of caste can even be invoked to excuse bad behavior and avoid conflict. Mary (a Nadar) explained how if a Shepherd woman shouts at her she doesn't bother to react; instead, she tells herself, "She's just a Konar, that's how she'll behave." When asked to explain their own casteist attitudes, upper-caste individuals might also point to the wayward desires of the unrestrained heart (*maṉacu*). As Sebastian Utaiyar said, when pressed on exactly why he would avoid food from dalit houses, simply, "The heart does not desire [it]" (*maṉa viruppam illai*).[11]

Less relevant to social interaction than formerly, caste is further muted by the many caste-crossing connections or divisions of residence or religion, work, or wealth. Caste has always been an idiom intersecting with other idioms of respect or disrespect that attach to wealth and poverty, power and powerlessness; it is even more so today, when, as a matter of status, caste is dispersed as individual strategies of "gentrification" or pulling rank—for example, in the complex etiquette of interdining, especially in new caste-mixed neighborhoods or the "Basic Ecclesiastical Communities." While these strategies may still converge to highlight broader social divisions, these are not the ones of twenty-five years ago, and are now as likely to reveal divisions among dalit castes as between them and upper castes. True, the idiom of caste can still deepen discrimination against the poor, who have to find ways to evade humiliation and spaces of discrimination, but in Alapuram at least, questions of caste rank or exclusion do not provoke collective action as they did in the 1980s. In the earlier-used terms (chapter 4), caste fails to be mounted as an overarching simulation of power, a kind of public knowledge, political representation, or "spin."

Caste may be regarded as a weakened presence, an internalized attribute, but it is also a resistant residuum. Baskaran Utaiyar is not alone in thinking that "only when the world ends will caste cease [*oḻiyum*]." But the reasons given for this resistance are quite different. Opposing those who emphasize the inner compulsions of the caste mind are those who find *external* causes of the persistence of caste, especially the state and its policies. The most common point is that, as Baskaran put it, "the government says that it will get rid of caste, but when we go for admission in the school they ask what is your caste; then how will caste be eradicated?" However, dalits—at least those adopting Hindu identities who turn to the state, its law, and concessions for advancement—would more likely evade the contractions of affirmative action and agree with Pallar Perumal's assertion that it is from the government that our equal rights (*cama urimai*) come. Either way, the state is implicated in the local discourse on caste, simultaneously the means to civilize, equalize, and modernize, *and* the reason for the perpetuation of narrow caste interests (cf. Tanabe 2007, 660). But I doubt that villagers' views divide sharply caste-wise in this kind of debate. I remember provoking a lively argument among a group of middle-aged Pallar men, between those who felt strongly that without taking account of caste through reservations the rich would grab all the opportunities, and those who agreed with the businessman beside whose general stores we sat that "when we come up through merit (*meriṭṭilē*), we do not need caste."

Life in the village today seems to require performative and discursive competence in the evasion of caste, perhaps most especially among Christians. Intercaste relations have to be carefully negotiated; rules emerge in practice, the frame with the act (Hastrup 2006). With the need for concealment, muting, and euphemism or with new rituals for greeting or avoiding, matters of caste today demand finesse (and more descriptive explanation than I have space for here). The effect is to dissolve both old hierarchies and new essentialisms. There is, however, one peculiar fact: while caste separations are muted among the living, they seem to persist in matters of the dead.

Soon after I returned to Alapuram in November 2004, I found myself in the cemetery amid the throng and the colorful, incense-filled smoky haze of the festival of All Souls, sharing the intimate family moments and remembering the many friends (and informants) who lay beneath. The washed and decorated graves retained the structure of the old order—upper castes to the north, dalits to the inauspicious south—but the caste logic of this arrangement of space was now explicitly denied. Then the two priests came to bless the graves with aspersions of holy water after prayers. In a deliberate gesture—silently noted by all who watched—the upper-caste (Acari) priest moved among the Pallar graves, while his dalit assistant (a Paraiyar man) blessed the grander garlanded tombs of the Utaiyar and Vellalar caste elite of former times. Comment on such expressions/transgressions of rank between Christian castes was of course censored;

but still an unspoken but unmistakable tension pervaded the act. In parallel, the upper-caste Catholics still insisted on using a separate funeral bier (acanti) brought from the Kiliyur hamlet. The refusal to share the church acanti with Pallars was sometimes rationalized by saying that it is old, or heavy, or "We prefer to use coffins" (another caste-evading technology). But Pallar interlocutors readily explained upper-caste refusal to use an acanti that has carried a Pallar body in terms of their lingering ideas about rank, impurity, or the respect due to their dead. Not only in Alapuram; funeral routes and graveyard divisions all remain public arenas for highly charged caste conflict, as the violence of Eraiyur discussed in the previous chapter testifies.

In Alapuram, these are practices without actor vocabularies, which evade the attribution of motivation (a counterpart *negation* of interiority or intention or motivation, among those who avoid giving reasons for continued caste practice).[12] If upper-caste actors "exteriorize" practices of distinction as insignificant acts or habits so as to evade responsibility, public practices of caste can also be seen as persisting where intention can in some way be displaced away from the living onto the dead (who though socially alive cannot speak), whose wishes and spaces carry the last vestiges of caste purity or pollution or bring the past back into the present.

SERVICE, INDEPENDENCE, AND MARKET TRANSACTIONS: "WE HAVE BECOME SOCIAL"

Unlike much of rural India (cf. Jeffrey, Jeffery, and Jeffery 2008a), and in striking contrast to some nearby villages, Alapuram could be said to have actually experienced structural change in which dalits have, through land acquisition, education, and independent earning outside the village (sometimes far afield in brick kilns or as hotel workers or musicians), genuinely raised their political and economic position—not all dalits and not all of a sudden, but over a period of more than fifty years. The economic mobility began with Catholic Pallars in the 1960s. Today, Protestant Paraiyars have acquired place in the village symbolized by a church in their street, although in several ways they remain far from the village center. Even with widespread education up to year twelve, they still find themselves excluded from the best opportunities for want of social and financial capital. Some, when interviewed, complained that Pallar economic success still involved asserting status over them—denying association or commensality. But Paraiyar men will nonetheless readily admit that their own challenge to social exclusion has been achieved behind the historical struggle and mobility of Catholic Pallars, which can be said to have altered the field of power in which other dalits live and so to have weakened caste as a frame for relations of economic dominance and dependence in the village.

In 2009, service relationships in Alapuram were much altered. Those between dalit laboring clients and their upper-caste aiya vitu (lord's houses) that I mapped in 1983–84 were scarcely remembered. Independent earning, including locally from the state National Rural Employment Guarantee Act (NREGA) scheme (the "100 days' work"), prevented upper-caste landowners from asserting economic power over formerly permanent dalit labor—a fact lamented by many of them; and none could command from dalits the range of ritual services that earlier so clearly signified social subordination. The village washerman had become a minor official in the water board, and his wife only collected clean clothes for ironing (from all, irrespective of caste), although a relative had set up shop washing clothes for cash. The upper-caste and dalit barbers and washermen still fulfilled their parts at funerals and puberty ceremonies, but, stripped of their "impure" tasks (such as washing polluted cloth), these were now cash-remunerated petty jobs. Puspam, the dhobi, was not happy to dwell on her role as recipient of ritually charged items at puberty rites, which she said she simply threw away. Paraiyar men now avoided drumming and funeral service entirely, although they are the ones approached to arrange outsider funeral bands, while Paraiyar women no longer perform laments (cf. Clark-Decès 2005). Mobile phones have made the ignominious caste-typed function of death announcement (*ketam*) redundant, and it is rare for anyone but the family themselves to dig graves.

There is profound and continuing change, not so much in what people actually do—laboring, barbering, drumming—but in the terms of the transactions involved. Relations of "bound-mode" agrarian service symbolized by hereditary cutantaram grain payments (chapter 3) are rare and repudiated, replaced by a now universal emphasis on socioeconomic "independence" (another meaning for *cutantaram*), choice, friendship, mutual respect, and market-mediated contractual relations (the "market" in this context being a specific moral space rather than a universal institution). When I used the term *kaḷamputikkiṟa vīṭu* ("house-that-takes-from-the-threshing-floor") when talking with Nallappan Utaiyar in relation to his former Paraiyar dependents, three of whom now borrow money from him as their former aiya vitu and irrigate and work his fields, he looked surprised and laughed, saying, "Nowadays you can't speak like that. They think it offensive (acinkam). If there is affection (*aṉpu*) they'll come [and work if asked]; they won't come in servitude (aṭimai)." And when I asked a village carpenter, Michael Acari, if he still received cutantaram for repairing farmers' implements, he immediately replied, "[I'm] not going for slave work (atimai velai) nowadays; if [we] work, [we] get wages (*kūli*)." He went on to explain that for cutantaram he had to work for everyone; that farmers would come at five o'clock in the morning demanding that their plows be sharpened. "For kindness (*aṉpukku*) we will fall at the feet, but [we] will not submit to power (*atikāram*)," he said, adding, "We've become social (*cōcalāyirucci*)." Ceremonial work, too, is stripped of idioms of service. Michael will repair Santiyakappar's chariot as individual waged work, no longer as the hereditary church right of the Carpenter caste (*taccu kōvil mariyātai*); and he insists that he conducts door-frame ceremonies (*nilai vaikkiṟatu*) because he has the experience and possesses an almanac, not because he is member of the Acari caste. Baskaran Utaiyar, one of his many would-be house-building clients, makes the same point when he says of this ritual (using *ācāri* in the generic sense of "carpenter") that it can be done by "an Alapuram acari, another village acari, an Indian acari, American acari, any acari!"

The disconnection of work from caste (and status), continuing from the 1980s, is of course especially important for dalits. In 2009, Alapuram Paraiyar drummers had transformed themselves from ignoble village servants given demeaning handouts into professional performers negotiating prices in advance as members of registered societies of artists whose instruments, rhythms, and performances had changed. "They used to say the drum (tappu) and horn (kompu) were uncouth and ugly (acinkam), but now there is no slavery (atimai); this is an honorable art (*kalai*)," says Mani, who performs far away from the village in Thanjavur at life-crisis rituals, at political rallies, election tours, government arts and education programs, most recently on AIDS awareness, and has traveled as far as Delhi and Calcutta. "Others can think what they like," he continues. "This is an art . . . [and] for art they give respect. . . . In those days [they shouted] 'Hey you! Come and beat the drum'; now, 'Please come, father, beat the drum.'" Nonetheless, neither he or anyone else in the Protestant Paraiyar street expressed any interest in reviving parai (tappu) drumming or *karakāṭṭam* dances (with pots) as symbols of dalit power, preferring to play the standard temple drum and wind instruments (melam and nakacuvaram). Making the parai drum a core Christian symbol remained a remote idea for those who (as I overheard in a side discussion between women) still wondered whether the drum of public performance was really made of the same stigmatized cowhide. And the all-night "folk art" entertainment of village-based Paraiyar troupes has anyway given way to *āṭal paṭal*—filmy song and dance routines, leaving karakattam, *oyilāṭṭam,* and the like as arts of the urban stage, the convention, or the arts festival (and discredited as such by some dalit activists).

Alapuram specialists (carpenters, drummers, washermen, etc.) and their patrons each proffered narratives of "becoming social"—that is, being unbound by social conventions, having choice, and providing services "according to will or conscience" (*maṉaccāṭci*), respectful kindness being the expected relational basis of transactions.[13] Here, free will, individual agency, and intention come to be emphasized in place of notions of obligation or natural propensity. Christian dalits, carpenters, and others continue the effort to separate the actor and the act, freeing occupation from caste identity in what looks like a Protestant "work of purification" (Keane 2007; see chapter 1), further confounding the "nonduality" celebrated by ethnosociological models.[14]

"Being social" implies, most broadly, a separation of self from social roles and substance, and thus a reflective awareness of "society" as a discursive subject of free individuals (Keane 2007, 185). But more concretely it referenced an accelerating shift toward "unbound" relations of the "mercantile schema" (David 1977) with negotiated "rates" (*reṭṭū pēci*) and "independent money" *(tāṉikkācu)* (chapter 3), whether for laundering, barbering, or carpentering. This involved a corresponding spatial relocation from person-centered transactions at the house and village lane to the impersonal transactions of the shop, stall, and salon in Alapuram's expanding commercial center—an "outside" space where unknowing and unknown outsiders mingle and are served. Only a tiny elite still had the power to retain a home-based personalized service (from barbers and others) for yearly payments. This expansion of the market as a physical and moral space has no single source; neither is it recent. The Catholic Church not only created ritual spaces of relative castelessness, but also supported the expansion of commercial space in the village, building shops currently leased to twenty-two different businesses, including a salon for the dalit barber, whose clientele gradually expanded to include non-dalits.[15]

The replacement of a "moral economy" of service with market-based integration, education, independence, and individual free will is a pervasive narrative of social change among those I have known over twenty-five years. Of course, this narrative is accented by caste, class, and gender positions. Take the question of the attribution of agency for social change. My dalits interlocutors (Pallars especially) tended to regard change as a consequence of their own active efforts, their education, hard work, the acquisition of land, and the history of their own struggle against oppression. This made repeated reference to the paradigmatic caste conflict of 1969 (chapter 5). Upper-caste informants were more typically resigned to change as a passive effect, commenting that "times have changed" (*kālam māṟirucci*), that this is the "computer age," in which "the village had now *become social,*" "without upper and lower." Among dalits, only the most powerless—the Cakkilyar Muthu—who had substituted village servitude for paid employment as the high-school toilet cleaner (work so noxious that only drink made it bearable), saw change as a passive effect of time. He insisted that he had not tried to reject oppressive (aṭimai) village work, but that this had "automatically stopped" (*āṭṭamēṭṭikkā niṉṭukirucci*): his Maravar patrons did not call him, and he did not refuse to go for work; it is just that, as he put it, "civility (nākarikam) grows and grows." Publicly, some upper-caste individuals expressed a patronizing pride, exaggerating the progress of the "colony people," as Utaiyar and Maravar big men did when invited to inaugurate the Paraiyar temple drama in 2009 (cf. Jeffrey, Jeffery, and Jeffery 2008a, 1388). Others bemoaned the loss of mutual dependence or village "unity" (*oṟṟumai*)—a veiled reference to long-gone public order of caste—accusing dalits of creating division and seeking separate honor for themselves, as Velu Maravar put it. Meanwhile, the idea that all were now equal (*ellām camam*) was invoked to challenge the legitimacy of concessions (*calukai*) to dalits, accused of exaggerating their disadvantage, of becoming lazy with abundant state benefits including TVs, cookers, and now "100 days' work."

The divergence of these narratives of active versus passive social change should not be exaggerated. Social, material, and religious change—equality, improved facilities, and new temples—were commonly described in terms of civility (*nākarikam*) and progress (*muṉṉeṟṟam*). While one group of Maravar men spoke of nākarikam bringing a loss of order or discipline (*kaṭṭupāṭu*), I did not find the kind of moral critique of modernity as "love's decline" or the growth of selfish profiteering that Gold (2009) describes among her Rajasthani rural informants. If like Gold's informants mine noted the decline of grain in relation to money in the village economy, it was not as a moral-ecological lament—a longing for subsistence and local varieties—but a comment on the disappearance of old grain-share dependencies or the replacement of subsistence with cash purchases, or agriculture with business, as a viable means of livelihood. The successful village businessman Baskaran Utaiyar admits that his new roadside bungalow in which we sit and talk is built from previously impossible profiteering, but also that the independent living it allows is an escape from the competitive jealousies, the "[despair] that others were doing better" (Clark-Decès 2007, 34), that attended communal living in the past. If in 2009 the passing of the rural order was generally unlamented in Alapuram, this was of course markedly so among dalits.

NEW ECONOMY, NEW CASTE: EDUCATION, EMPLOYMENT, AND ACTIVISM

What these discourses of equality and civility, freedom and market choice, concealed were the ways in which, in the context of agrarian change, access to economic opportunities—now found outside the village in nonagricultural employment—were in new ways shaped by the social and cultural capital of caste (cf. Jeffrey, Jeffery, and Jeffery 2008b), not by means of servitude but indirectly through the mechanisms of "opportunity hoarding" and structural exclusion (Tilly 1998; Mosse 2010).

By 2009, the agrarian economy had entered a period of stagnation and decline, especially in ecologically vulnerable industry-scarce places like Ramnad and Sivagangai. Staying in Alapuram in the season of chili cultivation after yet another failed paddy harvest was an opportunity to experience the effects of this. With rising costs, low returns, usurious credit, and the uncertain fluctuation of rains and of prices, farming had become a most unreliable source of livelihood. Farmers were more visibly dependent upon the state for livelihoods than for many years. Crop-insurance payouts (in 2009 secured through public agitation organized by the Catholic priest) were a better bet than careful tillage, although it was owners, not tenants, who stood to benefit, and "ration rice" available for one rupee per kilo from the state's public distribution shop was cheap and labor saving compared to parboiling, husking, and storing home-grown paddy. The year-round cost of keeping cattle and the availability of rental tractors meant that whereas in 1983 some two hundred houses owned a pair of plowing bullocks, in 2009 there were only six.[16] And without need for fodder, farmers were doing the previously unthinkable: burning straw in remoter fields to save the cost of carrying it to the streets, or laying fields down long-term to thorny bush *proscopis* as a firewood cash crop.

The view of many Utaiyars and Vellalars (among others) I spoke with was that today farming is only for those who cannot escape the village economy into permanent employment. In several families land was cultivated in rotation by family members while others worked away from home. These upper castes, especially Catholics, have seen their numbers in the village decline as the next generation establishes itself in towns, returning only for festivals or for the dead.[17] They have leased out more of their land and now prioritize "cultivating" their children for salaried jobs. Poorer families also seek out non-farm work—turning, if not to migrant labor, to cutting brushwood and burning charcoal, laboring on the new houses being built by their commercially successful neighbors or working on the National Rural Employment Guarantee Act schemes. Village-based livelihoods have become marginal; some productive activities like Nadar toddy brewing are now criminalized. Poorer people's hope, too, is that their children will get higher education and salaried jobs. But access to these is far from easy.

Alapuram Christians for long gave importance to education. The establishment of the St. James higher secondary school in the village has considerably equalized access to education up to year twelve, and school attendance to this level is almost universal in the village.[18] Dalits (especially Paraiyars) may be overrepresented among those who fail and drop out at earlier grades or are prevented from continuing education by the crippling direct costs of college studies (or the indirect loss of earning opportunity) unmitigated by scholarships, from which Christian dalits are excluded and which Hindus rarely fully receive (cf. Jeffrey, Jeffery, and Jeffery 2008b, 56), but high enrolment is a testament to their consistent view that education is the most necessary of investments for their economic future. "Progress through education" is a hegemonic discourse of Church and state, linking education to social capabilities (ibid., 63; Dreze and Sen 1995). In interview after interview, I found education woven into narratives of Pallar independence, progress, and mobility.[19] Indeed, education is an obligation as well as an opportunity. It is a "civilising resource" (Ciotti 2006, 900) that eradicates untouchability (especially conceived of as exclusion from knowledge), and consigns casteism to the uneducated and uncouth, in a way that stresses educated/

uneducated as a noncaste form of differentiation for upwardly mobile dalits. First marked among Christians, education as progress is now a general outlook. But there is an opportunities crunch.

Sivagangai District suffers a common postliberalization problem of shrinking public-sector employment and economic growth that is "not generating jobs in the private sector at anything like the rate needed to allow people to leave the land" (Jeffrey, Jeffery, and Jeffery 2008b, 36, citing Jha 2004). The emphasis on study that gives almost magical power to marks and qualifications mistakes the range of attributes needed for "young people [to] negotiate the post-educational terrains" (ibid., 31). Payback on investment in higher education (fees and expenses, "donations," and bribes amounting to hundreds of thousands of rupees for private engineering and other popular colleges) is uncertain, and high-risk, high-cost shortcut alternatives to salaried jobs, such as overseas labor migration mediated by often fraudulent agents, became a closing window in recession-hit Dubai or Malaysia in 2009.[20] Still, as Jeffrey, Jeffery, and Jeffery (2008b) found in western Uttar Pradesh, the uncertain route from schooling to jobs, or the failure to gain permanent employment, does not lead to disillusionment with mainstream school and college education.

Securing employment of any kind depends upon connections and capital—well-positioned relatives, places to stay in the city, social networking and external contacts, and money for college fees, down payments, broker fees, and bribes—that give continuing importance to the historical privileges of caste: inherited wealth (land) and productive social networks, including those in the Church. Although no longer unchallenged, upper-caste households benefit from better representation on college campuses, in companies, and amid mediating agents, among them the priests and bishops, vocation promoters and heads of institutions, through whose recommendations college places, training, and jobs are acquired (chapter 6). Their larger landholdings can be mortgaged or sold to raise funds for college or agents' fees. Meanwhile, marriage into job opportunities also depends upon mobilizing large dowries for daughters. It now impresses upon Alapuram's dalits that "emancipation" is not being "'free from bonds' but *well*-attached" (Latour 2005, 218 [original emphasis]). Failing to materialize the necessary resources for jobs leaves a significant proportion of young men in a condition of chronic waiting (Jeffrey 2010a, 2010b).[21]

So, while caste recedes as the framework for socioeconomic relations within the village, it remains important to income earning in the worlds beyond. Moreover, the Church has reacquired its centrality in the local politics of opportunity as a key mediator of access to new social rewards, at the center of competition for qualifications and employment, and as the route to college places or posts as teachers, trainers, or caretakers in the very large number of Catholic institutions. As dalit Christian activists point out, competition for opportunities has enhanced rather than eroded the significance of caste in parish, diocese, and state. Indeed, it was caste-Catholic "opportunity hoarding" that impelled dalit Christian (DCLM) activism (see chapter 6) along with the persisting categorical exclusions that educated dalits faced in the wider world of work brought about through various mechanisms including recruitment practices existing alongside explicit meritocratic commitments (see discussion in Mosse 2010; Thorat and Newman 2007).

In their study in rural Uttar Pradesh, Jeffrey, Jeffery, and Jeffery (2008b, 33) found that while upper castes tended to respond to the challenges of unemployment/underemployment by mobilizing capital and connections externally and investing in village-based business, dalits responded by "becoming lobbyists and social animators for their community." To some extent the same is true of Alapuram. Upper-caste Catholics found openings through urban and Church connections, and 80 percent of the ninety-three businesses in the village center are today (2010) run by upper-caste or Muslim (10 percent) families. However, another 13 percent of village enterprises are run by Pallars. Their patterns of consumption—housing, education, dowry payments—demonstrate their class convergence with upper castes while raising the costs of participation in opportunity-generating networks that increasingly exclude poorer households concentrated in the Paraiyar section of the village (who run only one provision shop and a cycle-repair stall). Nonetheless, the relative deprivation of aspiring dalit youth has also been a spur to renewed Catholic Pallar activism in the village.

In the 1990s young unemployed/underemployed Pallar men holding college degrees of uncertain value revived the Deventira Kula Velalar (DKV) organization, which had offered a "non-untouchable" narrative for Pallar mobility in the 1980s (chapter 5). The DKV Federation, recall, had produced Tamil Nadu's first dalit (Pallar) political party, but it was the radical end of the movement that appealed to the young Catholic university-educated men, who not untypically had become exposed to militant dalit discourses and consciousness of caste identity through student politics,[22] and whose educated aspiration grew frustrated amid rustic joblessness.[23] Bringing activism back to the village, these youth came together as a cell of the John Pandian Youth Front, identifying with a Pallar leader (John Pandian—JP) who was a symbol of caste power, conflict, and violent retaliation—everything, in fact, that no longer characterized *actual* caste relations in the village. Stephen, the branch leader, shows me a picture of tall John Pandian—whose "macho" bearded image these men emulated—eating at his house after a mass meeting in Alapuram in 1997. He boasts about JP's inflammatory speeches, which provoked conflict and brought devastation (even when replayed on PA systems),[24] and about the one thousand court cases against him. Invoking the past of untouchability and intercaste conflict, he describes the actions of the local JP group as a struggle to "finish the fight started in the village teashop in 1969."[25]

FIGURE 15. Billboard of the "All India Devēntira Kula Vēḷāḷar Progress Association," Alapuram, 2009. Photo by author.

In 2009, Pallar youth still gathered around John Pandian's billboard figure, centrally located by the bus stop and church (see figure 15). It advertised a potential collective power and a warning of violent retaliation.[26] The JP Front represented itself as a force against untouchability and caste exclusion. Earlier this would have focused on churches, temples, or teashops, but now it was educational institutions, the gatekeepers of aspiration, that were at the center of local antidiscrimination activism. These institutions had become the symbolic focus of assertions of caste honor in the state as castes competed to found, sponsor, and name schools and colleges. The fathers of these educated Pallar youth had failed to win managerial control of the new village high school (see chapter 5), and they saw this as an arena for JP activism to expose upper-caste privilege and dalit exclusion, not least their own exclusion from prized permanent posts almost exclusively held by non-dalits.[27] Meanwhile, they were pushed into unemployment or precarious jobs as shop assistants, mechanics, or rickshaw drivers—a condition now understood as representative of wider dalit exclusions in Tamil society. The JP group drew the village school into the politicized field of Catholic education in ways that linked to the strategies of the Dalit Christian Liberation Movement, taking the school as a public institution whose smallest transactions were surrounded with suspicion—part- or full-time appointments, promotions, exam marks, scholarships, pay, fees, or foreign funds all presenting themselves as occasions for contest over symbols of caste exclusion.

In the 1950s to 1980s, Catholic Pallar youth had mobilized protests to claim the honor of carrying statues of the saints at festivals and public rituals, capturing symbols of resource access and power within a caste discourse of hierarchy. In the 2000s, the next generation organized leafleting, petitioning, and public protest against discriminatory entrance requirements, the allotment of low marks, or the unfair disciplining or dismissal of dalit students (allegedly to maintain position in results leagues) in Catholic schools and colleges that had emerged as the new centers for the allocation of privileges, tickets, or chits of access to wider resources (Ciotti 2006, 900), and did so now within a caste *discourse of equal rights*. So, when the non-dalit headmaster without just cause expelled a Paraiyar boy who has been sick, "JP" youth approached the headmaster, petitioned the district collector, prompted a visit by officers of the district department of education, and printed and distributed leaflets about the case. They exposed this as a caste problem—as the way in which dalit failure was manufactured in Catholic institutions. The boy was readmitted, although he allegedly left after persisting harassment. Another dispute concerned the marks given to a JP Front member's sister in her science practical (marks not subject to verification). Again, when a dalit headmaster of the school was assaulted by Konar parents for expelling a pupil twice caught cheating in an exam, the John Pandian group apparently organized more than fifty Pallars to go to the boy's village to ask why the headmaster was beaten. The Konar men were forced to back down and to make a public apology to the head during one morning assembly.[28] Then, during my visit in 2004, the JP group were planning to erect a protest board against the discriminatory entry standards that they considered worked against poor dalits in favor of non-dalits with "recommendations."

The point is not just that Catholic educational institutions (schools, technical colleges, teacher or nursing training centers) had replaced religious ones as critical "public arenas" (Freitag 1989), but that the discourse of caste had itself significantly changed from rank to equal rights, from honor to opportunity. What the school as a public institution offered Pallar youth was an arena for the "microcosmic" enactment of a wider state and Church politics of caste, and for caste group re-formation locally. Other local conflicts, too—over land, water, loan repayment, sexual harassment, or elopement, as well as school marks or dismissals—got translated into reportable acts of "untouchability." Like political animators elsewhere, the JP boys found "trigger events" that could "speak to the underlying anxieties" about their social standing and future (Jeffrey 2010b). They were brokers turning personal disputes that happened to cross caste lines into collective protests, using *public* institutions (the school as a focus of symbolic contests around equality of opportunity) to link individual struggles with struggles of the wider group and to remanufacture "dalit" as a rights-bearing identity. They worked to produce the most efficacious representations—reports of untouchability or caste violence that brought police presence, state support, and judicial process under Scheduled Castes antiatrocities legislation. But these were efficacious only because of a wider state-level, media-sustained discourse of caste conflict and communal violence that allowed links to wider coalitions of support (the dalit Christian movement, associations, fronts, and parties) or signaled this possibility locally—a discourse that was reproduced in the stereotypes deployed in bureaucracies or the police, as well as being built into political processes and administrative structures, primed to respond to "ethicized" caste. Everyday caste discrimination acquired "publicity" as it was "recontextualized" for wider audiences (the Church, NGOs, media, politicians), as in PCR/PA cases (Rao 2009, 220); and as with these, responsibility for discrimination was individualized (as law requires) in ways that ultimately avoided provoking actual intergroup conflicts.

It is partly *because* these dalit youth had weaker social networks into the Church and local bureaucracy or police (so that discrimination was real) that they had a special need to represent their disputes over resources in the arresting language of caste conflict in order to alert attention, press for rights, and mobilize support (cf. Jeffrey, Jeffery, and Jeffery 2008a). However, the JP group proved to have limited capacity to sustain itself and gradually collapsed. It was not buttressed by a wider caste organization (after 2000, John Pandian was himself in jail serving a life sentence) and had failed to operate through the formal structures of village government (the Panchayat), in which leaders of the older Pallar generation now held office alongside upper castes. Its public action became sporadic, incident focused, and it failed to take on a broader range of cross-caste public issues to do with mobilizing state resources for water, roads, or crop-insurance claims (as the parish-priest-led Working People's Liberation Movement [chapter 6] had, drawing on the cross-caste collectivities of village Catholic women).

In 2004, a lightheartedness, "mischief, irony and humour" ran through the narration of JP protests (Jeffrey 2010b). By 2009, the group's members had somehow found work, got married, had young children, or left the village. Stephen himself now worked as one of the very few dalit contractors in the Panchayat Union, successfully building links across caste to negotiate local works. Today there is little sustained interest in activism among Alapuram's dalit youth (Christian or Hindu, Pallar or Paraiyar), partly because the historical struggle of the 1960s has made this unnecessary. The fact that dalit youth in the village are able to disregard collective action and focus on getting jobs and moving forward as individuals is itself an indication of a change in the field of power, achieved by Catholic Pallars but also experienced by the still-disadvantaged Paraiyar youth. As the Paraiyar leader Israel recently complained, people in his street say, "We earn, we develop and stand on our own legs. Why do we go for struggle and why [bother] to unite?" (interviewed by A. Selvaraj, November 2009).[29] John Pandian Front activism many not have been sustained, but it did for a short while produce a new kind of caste politics locally in the context of the declining significance of caste discrimination, sometimes out of disputes that did not originate in and were not initially experienced in caste terms. To borrow Baumann's (1997, 209, 212) terms, the dominant discourse of caste on which the JP youth drew was not "'false' or 'plain reificatory,' for it formed part of the 'discursive competence'" of these dalit youth in contesting rights and negotiating political representation and access to support/resources. This highlights the need for a "dual discursive competence," in villages such as Alapuram—one that both emphasizes and deemphasizes caste identity and conflict, *and* that selects the appropriate contexts for each, such that (at least in Alapuram) real and wider social conflict is not generated. Such dual discursive competence (also apparent in the micropolitical use of *religious* identities, as above) both allows local conflicts to retain their context and restrains the processes of amplification that are played with.

DALIT MOVEMENTS, VILLAGE CONFLICTS, AND CASTE "SETS"

For a while, dalit youth activists (the JP boys) translated the fragmentary experience of dispute, especially over the school as allocator of opportunity, into the collective caste politics of Church and state in the absence of a polarizing caste politics in the village. Elsewhere (Mosse n.d.) I have explored the way in which a regional dalit movement trying to establish itself in the village traveled in the opposite direction, translating a unified discourse of dalit rights into fragmentary village-level conflicts over such matters as land, water, or marital relations. Using dispute-mediation skills to embed itself in the matrix of local conflict resolution, the movement builds its following without recruiting on the basis of disseminated ideology.

The key protagonist in this case is Palanisami, a local leader with the Pallar Martyr Immanuel Front, the Pallar left-wing movement named after the murdered Christian Pallar political leader Immanuel Sekaran. Typical of local political leaders, he extends and sustains the wider movement by using village-level conflicts and offering resolution to dalits and upper castes alike through katta panchayats ("kangaroo courts") outside police stations or subdistrict courts. While few of these conflicts or problems are primarily represented in caste terms, it does not escape notice that Palanisami has power and influence with the police and departments *because* he is a leader with a mass following, and that this following has a caste basis. And because of this following, such dalit movements then reappear as caste players at the macroplane of state politics.[30] Meanwhile, potential recruitment to the dalit movement is shaped by existing social divisions defined, in Alapuram, by opposition between Catholic Pallars and Protestant/Hindu Paraiyars.

The point is that caste issues and "dalit rights" appear quite incidental to the recruitment of supporters for a dalit social movement that can expand mass support in the countryside beyond the orbit of ideological influence and without any deepening of identity politics or local caste antagonism. As Hugo Gorringe in his recent study of the Liberation Panthers observes, the influence of movement ideology falls off sharply with distance from the movement's urban strongholds (2005a, 70). Movement leaders forgo recruitment along ideological grounds—whether the communal politics of caste pride or the radical politics of caste abolition—and concede to the logic of reputation building that attracts local followings along preexisting (residual) lines of caste group membership. Perhaps unsurprisingly, *katta panchayat*—the Tamil term that captures this logic—is also the term through which urban ideologues (including dalit Jesuit activists introduced in chapter 6) question the integrity of movement leaders. Radical politics does not (or at least need not) spread through the generation of commitment to any particular ideological discourse—in this case, that of dalit rights—but exactly the same point can be made in relation to Christian conversion movements and the work of nineteenth-century missionaries.

The role of caste in caste politics (or social movements) is *not* premised on the *politicization* of (local) caste identity, and correspondingly the presence of dalit movements and caste associations in a village like Alapuram does not indicate a new radical politics of caste. Indeed, in Alapuram caste continued to recede as an everyday frame for local interests amid multiplying dalit associations.[31] And because of the brokerage involved, recruitment to dalit movements may not increase the political power of dalits per se. Despite being by far the largest voting block in Alapuram, dalits have never managed to return a dalit Panchayat president. Put another way, the point would be that the mechanisms of village-level brokerage that underpin the rise of dalit leaders limit the potential for democratic empowerment, which remains "contingent and reversible" (Jeffrey, Jeffery, and Jeffery 2008a, 1374).

Pallar associations may have been the first in the village, but a number of caste cankams linked to wider associations have now gained visibility. The Utaiyar cankam, Yadavar Front, Nadar Front, and Tevar Front are among those whose boards and flags pepper the Ramnad countryside, each simultaneously invoking ancient history in kingly figures, the recent political past with political leaders or martyrs and sometimes present-day film stars. The attention of their subscription-collecting monthly meetings, taking the Alapuram Utaiyar example, is on the advancement of caste members within the opportunity-generating nexus of qualifications and matrimony—giving scholarships to needy students and rewarding the marks "toppers" with prizes, and progressing plans for an Utaiyar marriage hall, as well as linking and lobbying politicians. If politicized caste identity does not lie behind the village-level caste associations, what does?

Some explain Alapuram's burgeoning caste societies, forums, or associations as a response to Pallar organization in the village and beyond. Others point to another trend. As we stand by a Pallar-owned tea stall by the bus stop, Michaelraj, a retired school headmaster, complains that the village is becoming more and more caste ridden. "Now everybody has a cankam" (association) he says.

> As a minority group I feel I also need to form a *caṅkam*. You see, if he [pointing to a Pallar teacher] does something wrong nobody will blame him. They will make excuses. . . . [But] I am a Kammalar (carpenter caste), a minority. If I am attacked they will say, "Oh dear, the *vāttiyār* (teacher) is attacked," giving lip sympathy, and go away. There is nobody there. So it has come to this: minorities need a cankam to survive. I have made enquiries, we are about 150 houses—Kammalar, Cettiyar, some Nadar. I will not be the leader, but will advise.

His point is that village society is such that any dispute can escalate, and without group support a person is vulnerable. It is this desire for protection in conflicts that opens up spaces for political actors such as Martyr Immanuel Front leader Palanicami. Of course, everyday disputes over water, land, love affairs, or inheritance are nothing new in the life of villages like Alapuram; but the village-level mechanisms that routinely dealt with these things during the period of my first fieldwork in the 1980s—informal panchayats with mediation by invited big men—are the victim of changes in authority in rural areas (see Vincentnathan and Vincentnathan 2007). Impaired local mediation means that any dispute can escalate, and even trivial conflicts are routinely taken to the police station eleven kilometers away, where without support or backing a person is vulnerable. This is how the desire for associations was commonly explained. The pragmatic need that ordinary people have for backing in conflicts and the political ambitions of association leaders coincide with the paradoxical result of the local extension of dalit associationalism (for example) in the documented absence of knowledge of dalit issues or movement ideology. Of course the periodic need for backing in disputes is unlikely to sustain commitment to collective action in the long term.[32]

Caste encountered in this form is less a matter of *substance,* in Dumontian, ethnosociological, or "ethnicized" identity terms, and more of *set*—that is, intentional, strategic, reflexive association, to draw on a distinction deployed by Kirsten Hastrup (2006). These caste "sets," linked across religious affiliation, have tended to involve competition over the use of public space in the village—the placing of posters, loudspeakers, flag posts. Those are all intensified by new technology, whether amplified sound or massive digitally generated poster boards, and aimed at the caste association- or party-affiliated announcement of weddings or puberty ceremonies. The public representation of caste offered here is far from the "sacrificial cooperation" (Tanabe 2007) earlier enacted at Santiyakappar's festivals. It is, rather, caste as loose interest sets ordered by the principle of equal shares in the public realm. It is on this basis that the Catholic priest now makes his intervention in village affairs—for example, organizing a "peace committee" (*amaiti kuḻu*) to which he calls representatives of the main caste groups of the village to set out rules to deal with an escalation of petty conflicts over common resources and public space.

CONCLUSIONS

My return visits to Alapuram after 2004 revealed an intricate reworking of the relationship between Christian religion and caste society. No longer structured by caste, Christian worship in the village is disembedded from social relations and diversified into a variety of religious styles, denominational affiliations, and congregational "sets." The affiliations, attachments, and associations around religion are loose and flexible, and do not congeal into religious community, not least because the continued primacy of associations of caste makes belonging through religion unnecessary or difficult. Caste itself is paradoxical: caste distinction is evaded and erased from public space, and yet as a basis of claims to equal rights, caste is more visible than ever. Erased as village service and rank, caste reappears as a portable form of belonging and connectedness structuring opportunity.

The Catholic Church, which played a central part in both constituting and erasing hierarchies of honor in the earlier agrarian order, has acquired a similarly contradictory role as the source of opportunity and expectation in a postagrarian economy of caste. The grain shares and church honors that defined social success in rural Ramnad for over two centuries find their counterpart in the admissions, scholarships, and positions that make up the material and symbolic resources now dispensed by the Church. But there is skepticism about the Church's ability to address the disadvantage of dalits who might most need or use its support. "Earlier, we converted to Christianity for independence (*cutantiram*)," says Manuel (a Pallar man), "but religion only increases caste. Now if dalits get anything [from the Church] it is only by fighting for it. Or coming like a beggar, . . . [the Church] gets [money/resources] in the name of dalits but gives to upper castes . . . only now are we thinking about this."

I have shown that the public appearance of conflictive caste and religious politics can be misread. There is no question about the seriousness of the communal conflicts that erupted in Tamil Nadu the late 1990s and early 2000s; and it is clear that this contributed to consolidating a public discourse on the "politicization" of identity and the threat of communal riots, which challenged the way in which caste and Christianity had been experienced over centuries. This discourse, moreover, established an interpretive framework within which local conflicts came to be registered in the state's media, its bureaucracy, and its policing systems, as well as in the Church, feeding back into increasingly competitive caste politics. This itself lends power to caste-based movements as representatives of interest groups that have now to be taken seriously in multipolar party competition. And it was this that encouraged the late-1990s entry of dalit movements into electoral politics and ensures that caste remains the defining issue of Tamil Catholicism. As Tanabe points out, caste is not annihilated by local democracy, but made its moral basis (2007, 568). The arrangement of groups competing for resources, often from the state or the Church, is generated by what Tanabe (2007) calls "the politics of demand." It is on this basis that external agencies engage with Alapuram villagers, especially dalits, using caste to gain space in democratic settings by asserting equal share-based rights (ibid., 568). Ultimately, this caste-based assertion of rights, Tanabe argues, is a critical moment between hierarchy and democracy in which caste is re-formed. "a pivot between the ontology of caste and a moral basis of democracy in rural India that recognised difference" (ibid.).

At a certain level of political aggregation, Tanabe and others who posit the consolidation of identity-based politics are undoubtedly right. But if this chapter has shown anything, it is the provisional and contingent nature of political and religious identity formation. A framework that imagines a shift from caste hierarchy to caste democracy has to look closely into these processes and the disjunctures between political discourses and local social relations involved. As a "regime of enunciation" (Latour 2003, 143) "caste" unifies and represents various events, individuals, and conflicts. This translation of "the many" (events, individuals, etc.) into "the one" (a category such as "dalit" in a regime of enunciation) is the precondition for politics; but it also involves brokerage that brings distortion and imposture (Latour 2003). The categories "Christian" and "dalit," formed in the "enveloping . . . curve of political talk without which enunciation they would not be thinkable, visible, viable" (ibid., 148), are invoked strategically in village disputes, without taking root as social aggregates. Correspondingly, despite a wider politics of caste polarization, it is not necessarily the case that locally dalit "political engagement [. . .] has served to exacerbate caste tensions and cohesion," as Hugo Gorringe puts it (2005a, 324). The categories of "political talk" do not return unchanged to those who have conceded to be represented as "dalit," "Christian," "dalit Christian," or holders of "human rights" or other universalizing categories. Behind these categories are paradoxical processes.

The micropolitical logic and social arrangements in Alapuram are such that, despite the active presence of Christian revivals and vibrant caste associationalism, neither religious nor caste affiliations get consolidated as antagonistic identities, despite engagement with the wider communalized politics of state or nation. And the mediating work of priests and evangelical pastors, caste-front leaders or youth activists, that produces the impression of a communal politics in the village also isolates actual social relations from the tension of politicized caste or religion. A dual discursive competence intertranslates between local disputes and movement politics so as to keep both apart. The polarization of interests is resisted and diffused, such that caste and religious affiliation does *not* reappear in politicized form (its media representation) in the everyday—so that representations of "community" do not shape actual disputes.

There is, then, a significant disjuncture between a public or media discourse of "communalized" caste and religious identity that sets dalits and non-dalits, Hindus and Christians, against each other, and the everyday, local, or demotic discourse that erodes bounded identities. Dealing with a range of pragmatic interests demands competence in both discourses—whether dealing with conflicts (around land or water or sexual relations) or in building local support for mass organizations. In this light, youth activists and dalit leaders, and at times religious fundamentalists, intertranslate local conflicts and the categories of communal identity not only so as to engage with a caste or religious politics, but also so as to *diffuse* its effects (turning generalized identity politics back into particularized conflicts over land or water as conflict mediators) while nonetheless contributing to the reproduction of a public discourse of communalism.

These observations do not deny the significance of politics and politicians in generating religious or caste communal conflicts (especially at the state or town level), or in the appearance or (post-BJP) disappearance of communalist discourse (Wilkinson 2005); indeed, it is "political talk" (Latour 2003) that offers the frame for local action. What they do is suggest that conflicts manifest at one level do not emerge from local identity politics at another. To reiterate a repeating theme of this book, public discourses of caste and religion do not produce their own reality. Local events and relations are autonomous from the categories in which they are represented and whose potential for conflict is diffused locally, perhaps through theatrical displays of rivalry.

Unsurprisingly, people are well aware of the risks associated with a political logic of conflict and social strife (as well as its efficacy at times) and are careful to ensure distance (or to preserve autonomy) from the destructive language of communalism—diffusing conflict, suppressing talk of caste and religious difference, and insisting on its irrelevance in the everyday. Of course, graphic reports of violent caste or religious conflict may themselves directly contribute to the suppression of caste or religion as idioms of everyday dispute.

Considerable intellectual energy currently goes into trying to explain the causes of ethicized conflict and violence, but perhaps rather less into understanding the normal processes that refuse orientalizing alterity, prevent polarization, and inhibit the aggregation and amplification of local conflicts; into examining the historically acquired social capacity to retain flexibility and context (resisting Tambiah's "focalisation and transvaluation" [1996]), and explaining, against the trend, why India's religious diversity is not always fragile. Fundamentalist, racist, or culturalist processes may then be understood not in terms of root causes but in terms of the disruption of other mechanisms and social competences. The broader argument is that the dual discursive competencies to which this chapter points have antecedents in the ways Tamil villagers have negotiated between absolutist discourses and the demands of everyday life in communities divided by caste and religion. In particular, there is an echo of the way that villagers reconciled the absolutist missionary teaching that polarized Christian and pagan with the social reality of coexisting with Hindus, avoiding the dangerous disruption of relationships implied in demonizing the gods of neighbors or allowing the battle between good and evil to be conceived as a battle between Christian and Hindu divinity. Dalit Christian activism in the 1990s may have been driven by a specific rejection of the earlier "dual morality" in which the particularities of caste coexisted with its Christian denial. Yet when the oppositional discourses of dalit activism or Christian fundamentalism return to the village, they are again prevented from disrupting social relations. My point is that the dual discursive competencies that now allow engagement with polarizing absolutist, communalist, caste, and religious discourses while preserving flexibility and negotiability in social life are embedded in the long history of reconciling Christian universalism and the particularism of caste that this book has traced.

Conclusion

Let me recall and draw together some of the main themes from this social history of Catholicism in Tamil south India. This will return to the recurring question of the relationship between the Christian faith and its cultural setting, to the manner in which the very categories of "religion" and "culture" were themselves formed and negotiated in missionary encounters, and to the mediating role of caste.

THE PRODUCTION OF CATHOLIC RELIGION IN SOUTH INDIA

In common with several other early modern European missionary encounters overseas, the Jesuit Madurai mission in the seventeenth-century Tamil country involved, first, a conception of Christian truth apart from the cultures and languages in which it would be expressed; and second, engagement with people, the Tamils, on the basis of a separation of their social world into the "idolatrous" and the purely "civil" (long before colonial rulers and reformers in the nineteenth century set about describing aspects of indigenous life as "religion" in the sense equivalent to Protestant Christianity). Given the cultural vilification of Christianity by elite groups as "Parangi" practice, Nobili's mission tried to clothe the faith in what he regarded as the hegemonic semiotic forms of the time, which would signal wisdom, cultural acceptability, and above all caste rank to the benefit of the mission. Early Jesuits required a particular contingent idea of "culture" to "de-Parangify Christianity," to "de-paganise Indian customs," and to "Indianise Christianity" (Pelkmans 2007, 885). The initial secularizing of Brahmanic caste practice was necessary so that it could accommodate Christian faith rather than be rejected as paganism, effectively Brahmanizing Christianity. Tamil Catholicism would become embedded in distinctions, discriminations, and public orderings of caste, which were accepted as morally indifferent things—*adiaphora*. This, at least, was the one aspect of Jesuit "accommodation" that survived the transition of the Jesuit mission from the Tamil cultural "center," where it mostly failed to recruit converts, to the peripheral plains (such as Ramnad) where its following grew significantly in the eighteenth century. Here adopting Christian "religion" (*mārkkam*—path; *camayam*—faith or sect) never marked converts out as socially separate, nor did it involve a break with full participation in Tamil society. While missions had limited success in the strategic appropriation of local "culture" (often a "folklorized" version [cf. Pelkmans 2007]), Catholic religion was itself culturally appropriated in locally varied ways.

The key to mission success in the Tamil countryside lay in the way in which Catholic churches became the target of political-economic investments, along with temples and other pilgrim centers, and especially as the object of royal patronage within a particular indigenous mode of statecraft. Christian affiliation was thus an element in seventeenth- and eighteenth-century political relations. Systems of rights, services, and schemes of honor were elaborated at Catholic churches as kovils so as to assemble and integrate communities of Christians and Hindus through the shared worship of protector-saints whose powerful shrines had acquired recognition within the existing pantheon and sacred geography. As heads of such religious centers, Jesuit missionaries found themselves unwittingly playing a critical part in local ritual-political systems, especially through their control of access to festival honors. These represented political power and a wider bundle of graded socioeconomic rights. Such Tamil forms of Catholic worship were elaborated not as a matter of theologically rationalized design but through contingent adaptations by Jesuit missionaries to the caste-political exigencies of the kovil.

Initially, the circumstances of British rule, especially the intersection of competition between missionary groups for jurisdiction and between castes for honor, involved further elaboration of ranked caste orders around Catholic worship so as to secure for the Jesuit mission the affiliation of upper-caste members of Tamil society. This affiliation was won at the expense of the exclusion or systematic subordination of others, specifically "Pariahs"—that is, the dalits. Honors disputes were unleashed by new economic opportunities under colonial arrangements of property and market, but the caste orders they described were increasingly reified. Subsequently, British rule supported missionary ambitions by facilitating the institutionalization of religion apart from politics, which, paradoxically, allowed Jesuits to transition from spiritual teachers and ritualists to become overlords and "kings" of the newly separate domain of Catholic religion. Missionary efforts to put this domain of Christian religion in place underpin a particular village-level social dynamic unfolding over a hundred years (c. 1850–1950). Among the aspects of this that have been tracked are the tension between priestly authority and royal power; the imposition of control over heterodox religious practice; the progressive exclusion of Hindu rights; and the de-exclusion of dalits in Christian churches. Several of these processes are evident from a history of the Alapuram Santiyakappar festival, whose disputes offer a record of societal changes such as the rise of missionary authority under colonialism, the rearrangement of social and economic power brought by migration and new regimes of property and production (the effect of Catholic Utaiyar cash-cropping or Pallar labor migration), the changed relationship of church and village, and the incubation of dalit politics within a Catholic festival system. The conjunctions and incompatible logics (Catholic/Hindu, religious/political, Christian worship/caste honor) at work in such rural Catholic churches made them politically fruitful. The political role of Catholic priests was central, whether this was through engaging in caste disputes by intervening in the arrangements of worship, or through using the presence of the Eucharist to deny social honor to Hindu heads; but it was also concealed behind sacerdotal functions. Missionary agency was through rather than over this hybridized ritual system. However, by using the indigenous symbolism of royalty and kingship, and through interventions that were strategic within the logic of caste power, Jesuit missionaries during the nineteenth and twentieth centuries also gradually undermined Christian *kovils* as loci of general political rights, transforming them into Catholic *churches* as the domain of ecclesiastical authority progressively disembedded from village society.

What can be described, therefore, is the production of Catholic religion as a distinctive domain in a particular social context. *The Saint in the Banyan Tree* is an examination of the events, conflicts, compromises, and missionary exigencies that go into the making of localized Christianity in this sense, and the responses and effects that this brings. It is an instantiation of the argument that Catholic religion is not a transhistorical global phenomenon introduced into "local cultures" by missionary agents, but a contingent and at times unstable category of thought and action—wrought in ways that need to be discovered—that does not, however, fail to point beyond itself to transcendent truth.

Alongside the making of distinctively Tamil forms of Christian public worship was the constitution (also within existing representational systems) of processes and objects of worship—Catholic divinity and saintly power. Saints took on the character of royal personages, virgin goddesses, or tortured sages turning bloody history into divine power. And this cultural traffic was not just one-way. Some of the Virgin Mary's benevolence rubbed off onto the usually fierce local virgin goddesses, and Hindus brought to bear distinctively Christian notions of embattled forces of good and evil when turning to Catholic saints to deal with malevolent manifestations of fierce gods by exorcising them as demonic intrusions. Tamil semiotic forms infused with personal significances and inferences from missionary teaching were central to the invention and elaboration of a localized Catholic imaginary through which divine power could be drawn to human anxieties and needs. A recognizable Tamil symbolic logic ordered a complex (and confusing) array of divine beings and relationships across religious boundaries so as, importantly, to allow continued relationships with neighboring people and their gods, isolating social relations from the implications of the antipagan absolutism of the nineteenth-century missionaries. Catholic imaginaries mapped onto social relations in locally relevant ways. Thus a shared social and symbolic space in villages such as Alapuram produced hierarchical royal metaphors for the Catholic inclusion of Hindu divinity rather than the rivalrous sibling ones common in Kerala (Dempsey 2001) or the exclusionary demonization of Hindu divinity found in socially segregated coastal Catholic communities (Ram 1991) or among certain excluded dalit Catholic ones (Deliège 1988).

Some elements of Catholic practice were forged in the context of still-relevant tensions between the Catholic Church and Tamil society, such as the prohibition on involvement in non-Christian worship; some were the sediments of historical encounters between Hindu kings and missionaries, priests and their parishioners, lineages and their land. In this sense, Catholic practice in Ramnad can be regarded as a palimpsest of a series of critical moments always available for reinterpretation. Certainly my fieldwork in Tamil villages in the 1980s did not record a stable religious synthesis, still less global Tamil Catholicism, but rather a dynamic social field, or a series of assemblages animated by encounters across the boundaries between inconsistent frameworks of Hindu and Catholic, of missionary and missionized.

Although clearly beyond the control of missionaries, the popular Catholic religiosity so vibrantly evident at shrines, feasts, and festivals was also influenced by distinctive Jesuit doctrine including teaching on interiority, personal sin, and confession. Sometimes popular religiosity was shaped in mimetic response to this, doubling and disturbing Church sacraments (Bhabha 1994), which is how I suggested we might view nineteenth-century exorcisms at forest saint shrines (or even more recent Pentecostal centers), which dramatized the removal (expiation) of the effects of sin in material and exteriorized form. In any event, the nature of festivals and funerals, dreams and devotions, pilgrimage and exorcisms, are the outcome of a Tamil negotiation of missionary Catholicism in the context both of existing notions of worship and its objects, and of existing social relations (intercaste and interreligious). Jesuit Catholicism was in various ways worked into a socially viable form. But popular Catholic religiosity also incorporated the missionary teaching on the substantially different nature of Christian divinity as well as the priests' transcendent claims and absolutist conceptions.

THE SOCIAL EFFECT OF CHRISTIANITY

The hierarchical orderings of caste were crucial to the way Catholicism was integrated into rural Tamil society. This Catholic ritual system did not just adapt to an existing order; in the honoring of saints at their kovils, for example, it became itself a key "fabrication mechanism" (Latour 2005) of the institution of caste. Social power was produced distinctively through Catholic festivals. This is rather different from saying that Catholicism "accommodated" caste. Alongside the more usually recognized effects of colonial census, army recruitment, or domestic service (S. B. Bayly 1999), Christian centers elaborated, formalized, hierarchized, and negotiated orders of caste in colonial India. Catholicism also had disjunctive social effects of its own. Catholic caste was distinctive in its translations between the private and public aspects of belonging, between economic relations and public honor, and in the way that the exclusions and subordinations of "untouchability" were enacted through Catholic ritual. One particular historical effect of Catholicism was the tendency to forge widening kinship circles and more universal forms of caste belonging through regional associations, inclusive church institutions, or saint festivals, which also meant losing touch with territorial and clan-based identities. Another effect was the (re-)constituting of caste through Catholic ceremony as emphatically a public and political institution.

While the ritual practices of village Catholics (festivals, arrangements in church or at life-crisis rites) enacted exploitative economic relations and dramatized given patterns of social dominance in ways that paralleled Hindu contexts, Catholicism placed significant limits on the naturalization of inequality. Christians reproduced the *form* of caste service and interdependence (for example, at life-crisis rites), but this was hollowed out of any particular meaning. For example, under Jesuit influence, Christians strained away from the "indexical contiguities" emphasized in recent ethnographies of Tamil villages (Daniel 1984; Mines 2005; both using C. S. Pierce's terms) and toward manipulable symbolic associations and negotiable meanings. Christian "untouchables" (dalits) who entered the church and received the sacraments were able to treat their exclusion as "polluted" persons as arbitrary and *symbolic* of their inferiorization as laborers and servants, rather than as substantially connected to—an "index of"—their persons. Signs of untouchability could be detached from the identity of the persons they related to. There was a certain refusal of indexicality. The same would be true of the delinking of occupations and caste identity, performance, diet, and caste status. Catholic religion taught that code and substance, the actor and the act, were separable and that the exchange of substances was unimportant in the making of moral persons, confounding the "nonduality" celebrated by ethnosociological models (cf. Good 1982). For Catholics, caste could not be a transactional system of codes and "sinful" substances, and ritualized exchanges were more evidently about power in the minds of Alapuram actors I knew, especially dalits. Or to put it differently, caste inequality might be experienced interactively but not *produced* interactively.

Since, in matters of caste, explicit meanings became emphasized over implicit conditions, the procedures, objects, and actions involved (including ritual service, dalit drumming, or beef eating) were open to symbolic reinterpretation or reversal. Indeed, the experience of Catholic religion as a realm of meaning making or symbolization (cf. Daniel 2000) could be applied elsewhere, permitting new (self-) understandings and supporting a creative manipulation of social transactions. New interpretations came along with changes in economic relations such that, as Alapuram's dalit dhobi's son said in 1983, "services paid for in cash have no pollution (tittu)."For dalits especially, contractual relations of the market became a model of respect that disconnected technical services from vestigial hierarchical models and public enactments of caste. This capacity for resignification becomes especially evident in contemporary dalit cultural politics, dalit theology, and dalit anthropology that honors an "outcast" culture.

Two hundred years of Catholicism had desacralized caste for Christian actors, making it an outer thing, an explicit structure, a public form of knowledge, a display of honor in public rituals that offered a model of society subject to deliberate contest, something that could be objectified, named, discussed, criticized, or studied. Caste was denaturalized and more about power than person—enacting control, not maintaining moral condition. And as a matter of public order and symbolically important public performance, Catholic caste orders were especially open to contest and subject to change. Here there is more than a little of Nobili's "secularized" notion of caste stripped of "incantations" and "superstitious rights"—outer form without inner reason—which could then "harmlessly" migrate into church institutions. Of course, Christianity was not the only influence in what might be argued is a more general characteristic of caste relations in regions where royal rather than priestly models of social relations are strong (Dirks 1987). But there can be little doubt that by signaling a transcendent Christian truth, the Jesuit missionaries did introduce a relativizing self-awareness into social forms in Tamil villages such as Alapuram, a reflexive capacity or sociological awareness and self-distancing from conventions captured in the notion that "we have become *social*" (chapter 7). Missionaries also relativized and subordinated the codes of caste by introducing alternative ones: the Eucharistic unity of the Communion, congregational worship, being addressed by the priest as a Christian collective, caste-free interactions with the missionary priests, or in the godparent–child relationship. Participating in the church pointed to a different order within the realm of Catholic religion, which ultimately denied difference and rank and gave no reality to matters of purity and pollution. An elderly Paraiyar man recalls the significant experience of sitting on a bench in front of the priest along with other castes when "we are all the same with equal rights." In short, four hundred years of Catholic missionization had an impact on the construction of caste in certain areas of the Tamil countryside such as Ramnad, and on the character and dynamic of change, which was at least as significant as that of the colonial state.

STRUCTURES OF RECONCILIATION

The Catholic secularization or denial of caste difference was, however, deeply conservative. It stabilized an existing order and failed to generate radical critique. From Nobili's times until very recently, caste was secularized *in order* that it could be tolerated among Christians. There was no sin in caste discrimination per se. Caste and Church were different moral discourses, generating actions that were allocated to different spaces, allowing the coexistence of otherwise incompatible practices. Indeed, village Christians not only enacted distinctions of caste rank, ritual roles, purity, and impurity, but also the abolition of these distinctions in certain Christian contexts: the funeral rite that first discriminates "the good" and "the bad"; pure and impure; catechist, barber, and untouchable; and second, abolishes all such distinctions in the priest's funeral Mass over the body in the church.

For much of Tamil Catholic history the caste-abolishing transcendence had the "otherness" marked by the foreign priest. Catholic religion was institutionalized as a domain apart from life in the village through a European-Indian cultural-racial division that mapped the noncaste asociality of foreignness onto that of otherworldly detachment. More particularly, the absolute demands of missionary religion were managed and separated from an existing set of obligations, whether to humans divided by caste or the differentiated powers of divinity (village saints and gods), through various "structures of reconciliation." A dual moral world allowed space for absolutism and universalism, but this was space set apart from the world of everyday society and religiosity. And this separation was itself an effect of power and missionary detachment. Catholicism was introduced into Tamil society by Jesuit "renouncers" as a faith beyond society, relativizing but permitting complex forms of hybrid and hierarchical relationships to exist in the everyday. This Brahmanic (and later Dumontian) conception of the relationship between transcendent absolutism and the relativity of socioreligious order, which found indigenous metaphorical expression as the relationship between the moral spaces of the "forest" (katu) and the "village" (ur), was also deeply conservative in religious and social terms. A Christian space *apart* protected Catholicism from both syncretic merging and social challenge. And until the later part of the twentieth century, Jesuit missionary action was more directed at managing the boundary between religion and society, purifying the agency and moral responsibility of their parishioners as they approached the Christian domain, than at encouraging transformation in the everyday social order.

The festivals of the saints were especially dynamic because they bridged the divide between Catholic religion and caste, or between church and kovil; or rather, they were a space in which contests over the boundary between the two took place and were drawn to disputes over caste honor. Through such contests missionaries gradually consolidated their ecclesiastical authority, expanded the Catholic religious domain, unbundled rights in worship from rights in production, and separated church and village, and St. James the Catholic saint from *Santiyākappar* the village deity. By excluding Hindus in the 1930s, Catholic festivals became more Christian. The most important effect of the disembedding of church from village after 1936 was not, however, to sharpen religious boundaries or to set Christian and Hindu against each other, but rather to create the space within which dalit public protest would develop (traced in chapters 4 and 5).

CHRISTIANITY AND THE RISE OF DALIT POLITICS

The consolidation of a domain of Christian religion was crucial to the emergence of dalit politics locally. The separating out of Christian ritual and the dismantling of the Catholic synthesis with caste social order was of course supported by dalits themselves. After all, it was only *as Christians* (in now religiously separate festivals) that subordinated Catholic Pallars gained access to the public domain and first acquired a political voice and, with missionary backing, pressed claims to equal rights and honors. In Alapuram, the Catholic religious system provided the first arena for a dalit (Pallar) politics of dignity from the 1910s. Indeed, before Independence, when denied legal support for claims to equal access to public amenities because of the colonial policy of noninterference in customs and religion, the rights and honors of the church were centrally important to dalits, not least as a context in which they acquired organizational skills for public action that were later used in civil-rights activism.

Christianity become part of a dalit politics of dignity; but as the case of Alapuram shows, this could take very different forms. Catholicism provided the Pallar caste with a discourse of honor and distinction with which to secure a recognized place within the structures of agrarian caste society. This was later developed into imaginative connections to royal power and a mythic recovery of lost history and lost power. By contrast, Paraiyars (dependent, and excluded from the Jesuit mission) used idioms of urbanity and Christian modernity to break with a shameful past. Conversion to Protestant Christianity was for them part of a disjunctive narrative of changeability and moral transformation. Untouchability was what their Christianization had left behind, allowing them ironic disengagement from dominant tropes of dalit subordination, and invoking human sameness (as in the Brahman-Paraiyar sibling myth) rather than distinction as a basis for new aspiration.

Christianity has evidently had significant effects on the dynamics of social change in Tamil south India, of course through the educational and employment opportunities it provided, through its institutions and power-brokering capabilities, but *also* I suggest through its cultural effects—its secularizing, its symbolizing, and its demand that the absolute and the everyday be reconciled (and so that people have a facility for moving between "representational economies" [Keane 2007])—which influence social processes in nondeterministic but important ways. The fact that caste-based relations of service and servitude became negotiable in 1980s Ramnad was a consequence of economic changes, but the manner in which this negotiability was expressed drew on experience of the sacraments and public rituals, the moral codes and modes of signification, that came to dalits as Christians. Even system-preserving Catholic rituals organized things so that certain transactions or boundaries were disrupted: the differences of humans or their condition (pure or polluted) were abolished; people were detached from their caste identities, even from their lineage deities, who could be exorcised as demons (as well by Hindus). But if Christian experience opened up such alternatives, the deployment of these in social struggle was dependent upon other social and political changes that occurred in Tamil society only in the twentieth century. Religious change has rarely (if ever) been an independent source of social transformation. Becoming Christian was certainly never sufficient to free dalits from the subordination they experienced in village society.

In the post-Independence, postmissionary period, Christianity weakened as a vehicle for dalit advancement. Struggles for religious rights were subsumed under a more liberal paradigm of civil rights, and pressing claims as Christians actually became a barrier to now important state-mediated resources and protections available as (Hindu) Scheduled Castes—facilities that in fact far surpassed the provisions of the Church. But to become claimants from the state, Christian dalits had to retreat to the very stigmatized untouchable and Hindu identities they had left behind, and as *individual* beneficiaries or litigants they could not produce the collective identity and honor that they (at least Pallars) had found through saint festivals. Christianity thus remained a touchstone for dalits engaged in the local politics of dignity.

Then, in the 1980s, across denominations Christianity began to be incorporated into an emerging dalit cultural politics that differed significantly from antecedent local struggles. This was enlivened by Ambedkar's wider vision for dalits and included an important ideological stream that set up Brahmanic Hinduism as the root of caste oppression. This gave a new significance to Christianity, especially against the background of the solidifying idea of the nation defined by its democratic majority as *Hindu*. In the particular circumstances of the 1990s,

Christianity came to be explained by dalit intellectuals as a liberative countercultural space (in ways that were quite at odds with earlier mission histories) within a new religious politics of caste that produced "caste-Hindu" and "dalit-Christian" as an oppositional pair. Caste was simplified as a Hindu religious institution resting on *varnasharma dharma,* which had to be challenged in ideological terms—for instance, through religious conversion rather than socioeconomic struggle. In this context religious conversion was now an idiom of protest, not against dominant castes of the locality, but against a state and a civilization that, despite affirmative action, failed to address persisting dalit disadvantage (and historical conversion movements were now reinterpreted in these terms). Christianity was then incorporated into an ideological construction of "dalit" superimposed upon the actuality of caste power, which was often based on royal-feudal arrangements and the economics of discrimination characteristic of places such as Alapuram.

With the deepening of a Hindu nationalist stream in Indian politics, and the election of pro-Hindutva parties to state and national governments from the late 1990s, this political-oppositional notion of dalit Christianity was deepened but also confronted with the Hindutva conception of Christianity as an antinational threatening "other." When linked by Hindu activists to local conflicts or to regional party-political strategies, this anti-Christian sentiment turned into deadly violence or into restrictive state interventions such as Tamil Nadu's 2002 anticonversion legislation. The latter provoked public protest, less as a show of support for Christian resistance to the Hindutva threat and more to underline the symbolic significance of conversion within the rising dalit political agenda. Indeed in the Tamil south a politics of religion never emerged separate from caste. Neither the local disembedding of Catholicism from shared ritual in villages such as Alapuram, nor the communalizing discourses provoked by Hindu nationalism, produced widespread interreligious Hindu–Christian tension in the 1990s. As missionaries of all denominations well understood, being Christian or threatening conversion offered a means to negotiate or modify but never to substitute for caste belonging.

Although the various dalit movements and political parties to emerge in the 1990s did not consolidate Christianity or produce Christian (or "dalit Christian") as a focal political identity in Tamil Nadu, Christian institutions (churches, seminaries, NGOs) did provide the organizational and pedagogical resources, the mass mobilization, and the ideological-theological and cultural work that underpinned this dalit renaissance. The Catholic Church in particular had a crucial role. But this was not driven, as might have been imagined, by a post–Vatican II Christian critique of caste society (although priests' support for local dalit activism played its part), but by the far older and deeper internal contradictions *within* south Indian Catholicism, between its claimed universal ethics and its caste particularism. In the 1990s this contradiction broke out as a radical movement for dalit Christian liberation led, significantly, by dalit Jesuits of the Madurai mission. From the tradition that had created the conditions for a dual ethics—the retention of civil distinctions of caste and a domain of religion beyond—came an angry response from humiliated dalit Jesuits who found that Catholic religion was far from being free from caste and was in fact the persistent source of caste discrimination, systematically organized and propelled by caste divisions that excluded and abused them. A forceful dalit social movement arose not from Christian ethics per se, but from their negation in the life of the Church—that is, from the experience of *dalitness* rather than of Christianity. Thus the campaign for state reservations that began by asserting the rights of the Christian minority to Scheduled Caste status came to be driven by a movement of shared dalitness. While wider forces in the past twenty years in Tamil Nadu have both consolidated Catholicism—opposed by Hindu nationalism and disembedded from rural society—and broken it apart through divisions of caste, it is the latter—the politics of caste rather than of religion—that most forcefully shapes contemporary Tamil Catholicism.

It was a struggle against discrimination *within* the Church and its institutions (religious or educational) that provided the crucible for dalit activism in the 1990s, rather as it had in village festivals from the 1930s. In other words, it was dalit claims to equal treatment as Christians that was translated into the wider dalit movement. The dalit critique indicated the failure of Nobilian distinctions. Caste was not subordinated to faith; it was not an indifferent, external thing (consigned to the secular, the village, the past, the uneducated, the non-Christian). It had become an "idolatry" (as Protestant missionaries earlier maintained) of Tamil Catholicism and a sinful state of mind-heart. As foreign missionaries were replaced by men of caste, Catholic religion was evidently less a domain of religion beyond the social: taking Catholic religion out of caste no longer took caste out of Catholic religion. There were continuing but failed attempts by some bishops to return caste to the realm of the secular, and so protect the Christian-spiritual. But in seminaries if not in parishes, facing the sin of caste was now a spiritual obligation. Dalitness had become definitive of Indian Christianity in the mainstream churches. Caste oppression pointed to the very meaning and purpose of the Gospel. The route to universal Christian truth would now have to pass through the suffering of the dalits. Any Christian theology of transcendence that ignored this reality (including earlier forms of Sanskritic Hindu–Christian dialogue) was deeply suspect (as indeed were Marxian and other universalist frameworks). The dalit Christian message was that rather than caste being rendered trivial and inauthentic by the Christian faith, Christian faith was made inauthentic by oppressive tolerance and the eruption of caste in the Church.

As "dalitness" was centralized in theology by a section of the clergy, Christian seminaries became centers for the production of a distinctive dalit culture, celebrated in festivals of dalit arts, often through exercises in resignification, symbolic reversal, or honoring the stigma (in order to destigmatize) applied, for instance, to parai drumming or beef eating, and involving changed semiotic processes. Meanwhile Jesuit dalit activists incorporated such cultural assertions in the pedagogy of their schools for dalit children, and in their social struggle. Thus cooking beef along with planting statues of Ambedkar became part of actions reclaiming land alienated to upper castes in a Jesuit-led dalit movement, and "polluting" water with beef food waste an assertion over disputed drinking water. As postcolonial Indian Christianity is caught between "inculturation" and cultural critique, one (still minority) response has therefore been the alignment of cultural expressions of Tamil Christianity, liturgical forms, and social ethics to a historically excluded group, assembling subaltern, non-Sanskritic "culture" and dalit Bible interpretations as a basis for Indianization. But today the Church is embattled as a significant part of the hierarchy resists, rejects, and reverses the dalit effort to subsume universal Christian ethics within the particularistic ethics of (anti-)caste or dalitness.

The anticaste tradition that was sought through dalit Christianity has, anyway, been hard to sustain when drawn into Tamil Nadu's cultural politics of caste, which involves contestation among different castes over the category and liberative space of "dalit" that subsumes their identities and has become open to competitive claims. Thus the early "colonization" of this space by Christians (who were in majority Paraiyars) was challenged by Deventira Kula Velalars (Pallars) or Arunthathiyars (Cakkiliyars) with their own ideological projects, who would say that in promoting Christianity as dalit religion shaped by dalit culture, it was Paraiyar religion and culture that was privileged.

Despite such provincializing of dalit Christian liberation within Tamil caste politics, dalit Christians have been prominent in globalizing their concerns through scale-jumping participation in transnational forums that represent caste oppression in ever more universal terms—for example, within the United Nations discourse on racism, slavery, and international human rights. If for Nobili in the seventeenth century caste was a vehicle for the intercultural transmission of Christian faith, today Christianity is a vehicle for the internationalization of dalit human rights. On the one hand, as M. S. S. Pandian pointed out at a recent workshop, for dalits, being Christian and participating in the universalist language of Christianity allowed a collaboration with other universalist languages in politics or human rights within which caste discrimination could be understood and acted upon; on the other hand, the Christian churches and organizations offer the institutional structures and audiences necessary to "globalize" dalit rights and the problem of untouchability. This has provoked resistance not only from Hindu organizations, who delegitimize dalit campaigns against "Indian racism" as a form of Western Christian aggression, proselytism, and cultural appropriation, but also from the Indian state, which has taken a stand against the internationalization of caste, which it regards as an "internal" matter to be handled through existing instruments of affirmative action. In both cases, the situation of dalit Christians acquires publicity and symbolic importance as India negotiates is cultural representation in a global space still dominated by the Christian United States.

How have such broad trends in the profile of Indian Christianity impinged upon Tamil village communities like Alapuram? It is fair to say that while Christianity is "dalitized" in the seminary, it appears "globalized" in the village. Christian practice is disembedded from structures of caste or separated (like the newly glass-encased statues) from the grime of cultic worship, and diversified into religious styles reflecting various streams of global Christianity, whether Catholic or Pentecostal. These are more universal, personal, Christian, and, in principle, othering of Hinduism. But the increasing separation of spheres of Christian and Hindu religion does not mean that religious identity has become the basis of social division, even if communalist connections and discourses are manipulated in local disputes. The environment of Hindu nationalism or Christian fundamentalism has not fostered Christian political identification, not least because caste identity remains the structural basis of religious coexistence.

As for caste, in Alapuram today there is a legally backed social prohibition on claims to caste distinction or exclusion in any public space—the street, the shop, the temple, or the water tank, as well as the church, which was the first space of equalization. But the Christian ethics of caste remains highly ambiguous: caste distinction persists as an "internalized" state of mind or an "externalized" effect of state policy; its weakening is the result of active struggle or the passive effect of modern times; caste is lamented as the loss of village community or dismissed as politics. Also generalized is what I suggested might have been at first a Christian "secularization" of caste relations, a reflexive awareness of social conventions ("becoming social"), and the reinscription of various roles and technical services in the idiom of the market disconnected from vestigial public models of caste. Regardless of its erasure as a scheme of service and public order, caste reappears in village life as private social capital essential to negotiating access to higher education and employment or to "opportunity hoarding." This turn of the social form in fact reinvents the Catholic Church as mediator and allocator of chits for today's honors and aspirations—school admissions or posts, discipline or exam marking—on which focus dalit youth activism and caste competition comparable to the honors at saints' festivals that were in former times the signifiers of opportunity.

But these struggles rarely produce violence in Alapuram, despite articulating a "communalizing" language of caste division. In fact, a dominant mediated state-level discourse of caste and religious division, and the "demotic" discourse through which everyday relations are negotiated, are kept apart by adept inter-translation (cf. Baumann 1997). Dalit youth translate everyday local conflicts into the antagonistic language of caste discrimination, just as regional dalit movements translate their political-ideological discourses into everyday matters, gaining a village foothold for movements or political parties by entering a range of local conflicts (which are not based on caste) as brokers and mediators. This means that a new caste and religious associationalism (including new religious congregations) appears in villages in the absence of any more general politicization of caste or religion, enhanced tension, or conflict.

The hierarchical incorporation (or "sacrificial cooperation") that was brought into existence through the Catholic mission and festivals such as Santiyakappar's at Alapuram, has not then been replaced by castes or religions "ethicized" into conflicting interest groups, as so often represented, but rather by loose, strategic associations or "sets" (Hastrup 2006) claiming equal shares in the public realm, mobilizing support for individuals in dispute, or securing the rewards of healing and renewal from religious association.

Social life in south Indian villages divided by religion and caste requires this capacity to manage the threat of antagonistic social difference by negotiating between absolutist religious or caste discourses and the demands of everyday life in community, so as to avoid a disconcerting sense of rupture or social conflict with neighbors or kin. I have suggested that the capacities that are key to social adaptations in the context of disruptions of the new politics of caste and religious extremism in India require particular discursive competences. In places such as Alapuram, these have their historical root in the way in which generations of Catholics living in caste society worked out the means to reconcile everyday social life with the potentially perilous demands of an uncompromising missionary Christian exclusivism that polarized Christian and "pagan." This required moving between incompatible meanings, morals, and modes of signification and contexts of practice: between the demands of a Tamil "being in the world" and of Catholic religion, between village and church, headman and priest, and the relational world of saint and deities and Christian divinity conceived in absolute and transcendent terms. Neither the violence of the "forest"-shrine exorcism nor the violence of communal conflict was allowed back into the village.

CHRISTIANIZATION AND ETHICS

The way in which missionary Catholicism for much of its history "encompassed" (Dumont 1980) the inequality and relationality of Tamil social life, producing a "dual moral world," as well as the forceful collapse of this into the radicalism of those oppressed by it in the Church, invites comparative reflection on Christianization and ethics. Let me do this by turning to a recent contribution by

Joel Robbins (2004a) and his fruitful deployment of Michel Foucault's thought on ethics (1990, 1997). Central to Robbins's ethnography of the Christianization of a tiny Papua New Guinean society, the Urapmin, is his idea that these people began to experience themselves as sinners because the "techniques of self-formation" newly brought by Christianity and oriented toward salvation (a new "telos") made control of the inner life the sole ethical goal (2004a, 224), and yet their continuing pre-Christian moral codes and ethics, oriented toward living as "good people" (which ought to but could not be abandoned) brought repeated moral failure in these terms. Christianization brought "moral torment" through the contradictions of a dual moral world. Setting aside the question of whether this intolerable situation is transitory in historical terms (Keane 2006b), Catholic south India is strikingly different. Here one could say that Christian ethics and techniques of the self relativized but did not require the abolition of caste self-formation. The moral Catholic person attentive to the fate of the soul—and the target of missionary preaching, confession, and the sacraments—always existed alongside a different kind of person, even if not one permeable to the influences of place, soil, food, and other people through transactions, and oriented to maintaining equilibrium and balance in the flows of substance (Daniel 1984), at least a person concerned with caste-marked relational identity and distinction. This coexistence did not generate "moral torment" in communities of Tamil Catholics, although it did generate increasingly intense moral outrage among discriminated and humiliated dalit Christians. Two moralities coexisted involving different "technologies of self," the one through attention to relations, transactions, and public orderings; the other through prayer, confession, and the Eucharist.

Unlike Urapmin converts, until very recently Tamil Catholics were never told that regulating interactions, enforcing distinctions, separation, and ranking, or even the extreme subordination of coreligionists as "untouchables" was sinful. Indeed, the processes of differentiation and inequality were incorporated into Catholic ritual. Even though Jesuits raised the fate of the individual soul (the salvation *telos*) above the ethics of living in caste society, they accepted caste as a condition of Tamil sociality and tolerated the existence of this other mode of self-formation, which required its own rites of birth, puberty, death, the house, land, and attentiveness to the status-coded management of bodily states, life transitions, and caste interaction. Here was a dual moral system in which practices of caste distinction did not draw Catholics into sin or produce moral failure—until recently (Robbins 2004a, 254). Indeed, one measure of the power of this arrangement is the force of its current collapse, which propels dalit Christian activism and theology. But what is striking in the longer history of Tamil Catholicism (in contrast to the Urapmin) is the stability of this Tamil Catholic dual morality, which for at least two hundred years kept the religious and ethical ideals of Christianity apart from the practices and obligations of caste.

The inequalities of caste were underpinned by relations of power and by Jesuit complicity with the social dominance of their privileged "upper"-caste converts and the oppression of dalits. But Eucharistic unity and oneness in Christ were not trivial notions. The question then is, Were continuing practices of untouchability over long periods of time stabilized additionally by some "structural disposition" (see Hefner 1993, 37n13, citing Sahlins) mediating the mission's response to Tamil society and the local response to the Catholic Church? These might indeed be evident in what I have referred to as structures of reconciliation. Without confusing descriptive form with historical cause, it is possible at least to suggest that the relationship between Catholic faith and Tamil society (and the ethical dilemmas involved) could be conceived in indigenous as much as missionary terms. Beyond the fact that the category of *sanniyasi* or *bhakti* devotional order was explicitly used by Jesuits to allow Christian faith and caste society to coexist, there are also the more general indeterminacies in Tamil moral tradition between universalistic and particularistic-relational tendencies (see A. Pandian 2008) evident in locally significant spatial metaphors of "forest" (*katu*) and "village" (*ur*) that allow for such dilemmas.

In his ethnography of Melanesian Christianization, Robbins (2004a, drawing on Sahlins 1985) suggests that such *assimilation* of what missionaries bring to existing categories of understanding (which also govern their conversion [Peel 2007, 27]) can be regarded as the first part of a two-stage model of conversion as cultural change. The assimilation of missionary teaching leads to an expansion of the range of referents of those categories without changing the relationships between them. Catholicism introduced new conceptions of divinity, forms of interiority, religiosity, and devotionalism, new institutional arrangements, and the resignification of a range of social and ritual processes. Yet the relationships between religious devotion and caste society, between universalism and particularism—even the exogenous distinction between "religion" and "culture"—was accommodated to an existing structure of representations that distinguished the transcendent from the world and separated Catholic religion as a kind of devotional sect or order. This structure was evident in the distinctive ways in which Tamil Catholics managed the tensions between the demands of Jesuit missionary Catholicism and the obligations of pre- or non- Christian lives so as to avoid rupture and conflict, moving between contexts with incompatible meanings, morals, and modes of signification (village/church; ur/katu; relational/absolute divinity). In doing so, they defined and separated contexts of Catholic practice and moral worlds, implicitly drawing on indigenous categories.

However, Robbins explains, in time efforts to reconcile new experiences or teachings leads to changes in the *relations between* categories. This *transformative* reproduction, he argues, is a precursor for engagement with a new religious tradition entirely in its own terms—that is to say, *adoption* (2004a, 6–15). In the

Tamil countryside, the assimilation of Catholic practice unfolding over centuries certainly had unforeseen "ramifications—moral, aesthetic, cognitive, social, or organisational" and semiotic (Peel 2007, 27) that intersected with other historical processes so as to bring significant "transformations." But what is remarkable in this case is the stability and resilience of assimilations that preserved existing categorizations and stabilized modes of reconciliation of Catholic religion and the continuing human discriminations of caste. Robbins (following Peel [1968, 288]) suggests that the "localization" of Christian authority in the form of locally held "stable clerical roles" protects Christianity from being modified to "traditional ends" (2004a, 123). But while indigenous clergy did assume the missionary control of Catholicism as a domain distinct from Tamil cultural forms in the twentieth century, the native clerical roles were to an important degree "localized" *into* rather than against the traditional ends of caste in ways that were both perpetuated and concealed by the cultural logic that secularized and subordinated caste in relation to Catholic religion. The argument here would be that relations of power underpinning caste orders allowed the persistence of socially conservative categorical relationships.

For these structural reasons (that is, the caste reproduction of clerical roles) Tamil Catholicism per se did not provoke the kind of cultural critique or "cultural debasement" that Robbins (drawing on Sahlins) sees as driving a "second-stage conversion" (Robbins 2004a, 9). Instead, it was the continuing categorical exclusion of some Christians by others as "untouchable" that would eventually precipitate a heightened "countercultural" awareness, and the demand from its own humiliated priesthood that the Church repent the production of caste and outcaste within and be converted (as the archbishop proclaimed in the words that opened this book's introduction). In doing so, dalit Christians contributed to wider movements of cultural critique, not simply drawing upon "key tropes of Tamil regionalist discourse" (Ram 1995, 311), but developing and spreading a distinctive culture of protest in the Tamil region. "Localization" in Peel's and Robbins's sense has not so much driven a Christian revivalism—despite the appearance of Pentecostal and charismatic forms of Tamil Christianity—as drawn Christianity into a regional politics of caste and a new social ethics increasingly definitive of Tamil Catholicism. In some villages such as Alapuram, dalit protest took place earlier (from the 1940s) and largely within a discourse of Catholic caste distinction, such that today village Catholicism has dropped its marks of caste; but in others Catholic religiosity is now drawn to the social project of dalit liberation—a dalit Christianity, dalit parishes, and dalit festivals invariably focusing on the tortured figure of St. Sebastian. A few years ago dalit priests addressed the Papal Nuncio in Delhi with an appeal for an Indo Dalit Christian Rite within the Roman Catholic Church but separate from the Latin Rite, having its own liturgy, sacraments, and administration that recognized the distinctiveness of dalit

Christian life and culture. With south Indian Christianity, the form of cultural continuity and that of disjuncture—incorporation and resistance—have both been shaped by the indigenous institution of caste and its continuing structural effects.

These dynamic shifts of south Indian Catholicism point to a serious limitation in anthropological debates on Christian cultural "continuity" or "discontinuity," especially the dependence on models that presume stability or integration either of "local culture" or of "Christianity." Tamil ethical tradition is characterized by fragmentation and an "irregular mosaic of moral possibility" (A. Pandian 2008, 472), and the values that come to be attributed to Christian or Catholic tradition in any specific context arise from a complex intercultural space, even though (as Graeber points out) later authors "tend to represent matters as if the ideas emerged from that tradition rather than the spaces in between" (2006, 24). I hope that this book has shown the value of looking at the "tradition-making," interactive, in-between space that Tamil Catholicism represents.

NOTES

PREFACE

1. Estimates of the number of Christians in India are controversial and vary widely—from the official 24 million (2001 Census of India) to the 68.2 million recorded in the World Christian Database (Frykenberg 2008, vii). Informal Christian religious practice eludes official statistics, which are also distorted by the fact that the declaration of Christian identity bars certain categories of converts from state welfare and protections as Scheduled Castes.

INTRODUCTION

1. In the last two decades, *dalit* has become the preferred umbrella term of identification for numerous formerly untouchable castes throughout India. In the rural locality of my fieldwork in the 1980s, however, the term was unknown and remains little used today. Originally a socially inclusive anticaste protest term, *dalit* has become used as a sociological category, even a shorthand caste title. In this book, I will use *dalit* as a transhistorical social category of castes historically subject to inferiorization-exclusion as "untouchables," but I will try to avoid the confusing use of the label as a caste name, and to underline this usage I will not capitalize *dalit*. Note that in referring to "upper caste" and "lower caste" I reflect the local usage—*mēl cāti, kīḻ cāti*—and not some accepted social rank and distinction.

2. Of course, historically speaking in Catholicism, Latin was privileged in the Tridentine Church in relation to the Bible and the Order of the Mass, and strictly so in the Eucharistic Prayer. The linguistic autonomy of Catholic rites that were not Latin, such as the one of St. Thomas Christians in Kerala, was secondary to the rule of *preminentia ritus Latini* (prominence of the Latin Rite). I am grateful to the historian Paolo Aranha for clarifying this for me (personal communication).

3. Another early modern idea was that Christianity in fact *preceded* all other religions but that the faith preached in apostolic times had been perverted (Paolo Aranha, personal communication)

4. The Jesuit mission in Madurai, on which I focus, was not singular in this respect. The study of Jesuit missions elsewhere in India, and in Japan or China (Fontana 2011), offers equivalent insights.

5. For a general overview of the Goa Inquisition, see Priolkar 1961; although Paolo Aranha (working on a research project entitled "Between Repression and Collaboration: Indian Christians, Hindus and the Goa Inquisition") warns that this book should be read in the context of the propaganda war that preceded the armed annexation of the Portuguese colonies to the Indian Union.

6. While I will describe this Jesuit presence as "precolonial," being in some respects autonomous from the coastal trading power, it should not be forgotten that the Madurai mission was, through the Padroado Real (royal patronage), "part of the global strategy of the Portuguese thalassocracy" that had ambition for both spiritual and temporal conquest (Paolo Aranha, personal communication).

7. While in the seventeenth century Jesuits did not have a concept of "Hinduism," the notion of "Brahmanism" expressed the close connection between gentile religion and the Brahmans (Rubiés 2005, 256). It is beyond my present purpose to debate the problematic category "Hindu" (and "Hinduism"), which for centuries meant only native or indigenous to India. The question of whether the category "Hinduism" is a Western explanatory construct derived from colonial, missionary or orientalist interventions, or whether it is rooted in an older sense of Hindu religious identity especially in opposition to Muslims, has been much debated (see essays in Sontheimer and Kulke 1989, King 1999, Lorenzen 1999, Oddie 2006, and Pennington 2005). Historiographical concerns notwithstanding, contemporary usage allows "Hindu" (as religious identity) to be used in ethnographic description and social analysis.

8. The Saiva Siddhanta was perhaps the most important Tamil theological tradition in which Nobili grounded his arguments about the truth of Christianity and the wisdom of Indian philosophy. See Dhavamony 1971 for a contemporary Jesuit engagement. In the following paragraphs, I draw on Amaladass and Clooney 2005, Amaladoss 2007, Arokiasamy 2007, Arun 2007b, Clooney 2007, Rubiés 2005, and Županov 1999.

9. Of course, Nobili used a particular framework to discern the way in which Tamil words were used in Brahmanic religion, and their appropriateness for signifying Christian truth, having for example preference for *carvēcuraṉ* (supreme being), to convey the "supreme personhood" of God, over *deva* (Tam. *teyvam,* deity), with its polytheistic connotations. While Nobili regarded Sanskrit as the "Indian Latin" and the preferred "receptor language" for Christian spirituality (Županov 2005, 28), later Jesuit missionaries such as Fr. C. J. Beschi (d. 1764), produced a rich Christian devotional literature and became inscribed in the canon of Tamil literature. For further discussion on the derivation of Tamil Christian theological terms in different traditions (Catholic, Protestant, Lutheran), see Tiliander 1974, Clothey 1976, and Bergunder 2002.

10. These distinctions can be discerned from several of Nobili's texts, in particular "The Report on Certain Customs of the Indian Nation" (Nobili 2005), and from the

tūṣaṇa tikkāram ("Refutation of Accusations/Abuse"), written in 1641 while Nobili was imprisoned (analyzed in Clooney 2007).

11. *Poṅkal* can refer to either the act of overboiling rice or the specially prepared rice dish. Both signify productivity and abundance.

12. In general it is necessary to be wary of a certain hagiographic approach to Nobili that underplays the fact that he was still a Padroado agent (albeit Italian), incompletely isolated from Portuguese empire; that his representation of Indian customs and culture was framed in the context of a European religious controversy (specifically for the Roman Inquisition, which would approve or condemn his method); and that in his Tamil works Nobili clearly denounces heathenism and offers a polemic against textually expressed indigenous theological ideas (Paolo Aranha, personal communication).

13. In section 9.6 of his Tamil *Dialogue on Eternal* Life (9.6), headed, "The proper understanding of images as symbols," Nobili's master explains to his student the distinction between "visible form" (*rūpa*) and "symbolic form" (*lakṣaṇa*), the latter understood as "pertaining to several kinds of indirect and implied meaning and representation" (Amaladass and Clooney 2005, 295).

14. Nobili drew on Aquinas's linking of reason and morality—the path from wrong reasoning to immorality, and the weakening of human reasoning by sin—as well as on his critique of idolatry in *Summa Theologiae* (see Amaladass and Clooney 2005, 10–15). The distinction between the rational and the irrational in human culture would reappear (albeit in reversed form) in the Victorian evolutionary schemes, such as Edward Tyler's, that influenced Protestant missionaries and marked irrational "primitive survivals" for destruction (Keane 2007, 95).

15. For arguments that Jesuit attempts to divide the sacred, the rational, and the demonic in approaching indigenous traditions (both in India and in pre-Hispanic South America) paved the way for the modern religion-secular distinction by relativizing faith, in a manner extended by eighteenth-century Enlightenment philosophies, and so created a "new social space ready to accommodate modernity," see Županov 1999, 35; Rubiés 2005; and Stack 2007.

16. Robert de Nobili's letter to Pope Paul V (c. A.D. 1610). In Kuriakose 1982, 50–52.

17. Robert de Nobili's manifesto, 1611, reproduced in Kuriakose 1982, 49.

18. Nobili confided as much in a letter to his cousin Constantia, Duchess of Sora, dated December 1606, cited in Amaladass and Clooney 2005, 19n24.

19. Here it is necessary to distinguish "Orientalism," the late-eighteenth-, early-nineteenth-century study of Indian antiquity through its languages and literatures, from "orientalization," the construction of India as Europe's radical "other" for hegemonic, colonial purposes. (Young 2009, 60)

20. Mohan 2004 begins to distinguish French from British constructions of India, a difference that lost definition in the unified category of imperial power deployed by writers such as Cohn (1987, 1996), Dirks (2001), and Inden (1990). These are linked to separate and competing colonizing projects—the French preoccupation with Brahmanical India drawing directly on the Jesuit tradition. See Trautmann 2009 on the relationship between Orientalist and missionary knowledge, and the qualified (sometimes limited) influence of the latter on the former, which was vastly expanded by empire.

21. Protestant missionaries evaluated Brahmans quite differently. In the seventeenth and eighteenth centuries Danish missionaries such as Bartholomäus Ziegenbalg (d. 1719) sought the "fundamentals" of culture in Tamil aphoristic literature that rejected Brahmanical privilege, ritualism, and caste hierarchy. Then in the nineteenth century, British Protestants developed a critique of the corrupting Brahmanical influence on Tamil culture, using scholarly arguments to retrieve works such as the philosophical system of Saiva Siddantha as a distinctly Tamil (non-Aryan) achievement. Twentieth-century non-Brahman and Dravidian movements would later borrow from this missionary work. See Dirks 2001, Frykenberg 2008, Hudson 2000, Irschick 2003, Pandian 2007, and Ram 1995.

22. Coeurdoux's detailed description of Brahman social life was, Murr (1987) argues, later plagiarized as Abbé Dubois's (1906) *Hindu Manners Customs and Ceremonies* (Dirks 2001, 21). Margherita Trento at the École des Hautes Études en Sciences Sociales in Paris is currently exploring how Dubois's book and Coeurdoux's urtext (among other writings) both drew an inherited wealth of knowledge and manuscripts collected by missionaries in the previous century (personal communication).

23. In the seventeenth century, Brahmans were already a rising power (Bayly 1998) offering an ideological integration of Indian society that prefigured the unquestioned primacy of Brahman social models of Indian civilization, and whose texts were codified into colonial systems of native law and administration (Dirks 2001).

24. These Protestant traditions have been the principal focus of recent anthropologies of Christianity that turn fruitfully to the study of semiotics to grasp underlying ideas about "what words and things can or cannot do, and how they facilitate or impinge on the capacities of human and divine agents" (Keane 2007, 59; Engelke 2007).

25. Catholic theologians distinguish metaphor and "analogy," saying, for example, not that God is like human love, but that human love is an analogy for God: "there is a reality in human love which God is like and in which in some fashion human love participates" (Greeley 2001, 7).

26. The Eucharist liturgy also enables "presence" through effecting a suspension of *time* (and space) that makes the passion and death of Christ present so that communicants can receive its benefits. This contrasts the Protestant Eucharist as a memorial that accommodates secular time (Killingly 2004).

27. For a related discussion on the trust/mistrust of ritual versus language—indexical signs versus words—see Robbins 2001.

28. The doctrine of transubstantiation and the "real presence" declared in the Council of Trent (1545–1563), holding that Christ is "truly, really, and substantially present" (ascended, whole and divine) in the changed *substance* of consecrated bread and wine, which nonetheless retain their unchanged *species* (appearances) as bread and wine (Council of Trent, 13th session; http://history.hanover.edu/early/trent/ct13ce.htm) derives from an Aristotelian distinction between a substance and the properties it possesses (Keane 2007, 133–34).

29. See Bate (2009, 100) for an explanation of the primacy of contiguous and indexical relations (i.e., metonymy—"the master trope of Tamil thought") over analogy and iconicity (i.e., metaphor) in the Tamil "semiosocial" world.

30. According to its proponents, this theory of Indian social life (an "ethnosociology")

implies a view of persons as protean *dividuals*, "divisible into separate [coded] particles that may be shared or exchanged with others" (Marriott and Inden 1977, 232). For other scholars, "[t]alk of the transfer of substances or of fluidity hovers uneasily on the borderlines between the literal and the metaphoric" (Busby 2006, 86).

31. While van de Veer (1988, chap. 3) and Dube (1998, 7–13) offer well-advised caution in using the term "sect" to describe religious groupings or orders in arguments against Dumont's (1960) now classic categorization, we will see that Dumont's formulation has a relevance here precisely because of its kinship with Jesuit-Brahmanical conceptions (see also Pocock 1973).

32. Nobili and his contemporaries in the early seventeenth century arrived from a Europe in which the "inworldly individual," the notion of a self-contained, self-experiencing separate person in society, was only just developing (Hunt 2007).

33. Dumont's (1980) structuralist notion that the individual does not exist except as constituted by the relations of the system developed from de Saussurean linguistics and the anthropology of Evans-Pritchard, and amounted to saying that what goes on inside individuals is not different from what goes on between them. His nonindividualist view of Hindu society finds its parallel in the earlier-mentioned ethnosociological idea of the relationally constituted "dividual" (Marriott and Inden 1977, 232–33).

34. There is a large literature on this. See Davis 1976, Mines and Gourishankar 1990, Burghart 1983, Das 1977, Denton 2004, Khare 1984, and van der Veer 1988.

35. Dumont (1980) himself regarded Indian society as accommodating Western individualism by merging this with the renouncer category.

36. In fact the merging implication of this language led Nobili initially to reject *markkam* as a term for religion (Tiliander 1974).

37. This is how Dumont (and others: Pocock 1973, Holmström 1971, Hopkins 1966) analyzed the devotional sect or "religion of choice." Some, like Swaminarayan devotionalism "demonstrate . . . very clearly how *bhakti* can be accommodated to institutionalised inequality in . . . Indian society" (Fuller 1992, 174), while other sects have separated themselves as a "caste," or are internally differentiated into caste groups. (Dumont [1980] cites the case of Lingayats in southern India.) Clearly comparison between affiliation to the Roman Catholic Church and any of the many devotional sects is conceptually approximate and empirically tenuous.

38. Mosko, from a Melanesian context of Christianization, suggests that "the ["outworldly"] individuality at issue concerns only a single, detachable element of an otherwise composite agent." Rather than exemplifying the modern bounded possessive *in*dividual, Christian individuals detached their inwordly parts to receive outworldly religious gifts (2010, 219–20).

39. It was the definition of "religion" in these terms that was so clearly rejected by Talal Asad (1993).

40. While the notion that belief is a state of mind somehow prior to cultural practice is no longer tenable (Ditchfield 2009, 560–61), it is possible to qualify Needham's (1972) skeptical dismissal of the concept of belief with Harré's argument that "belief is a mental state, a grounded disposition, but it is confined to people who have certain social institutions and practices" (1981, 82, cited in Asad 2002, 123). By emphasizing the grounding

of belief in practices and bodily techniques, Asad (2008) in fact departs from Charles Taylor's (2004) notion of belief as a matter of the construal of experience—that is, as a frame of interpretation.

41. Gombrich (1971) alludes to something similar when he draws a distinction between "cognitive belief" (that which people say they believe and do) and "affective belief" (people behaving as if they held a particular belief).

42. One could follow Mosko and suggest that the Christianization of Tamils produced "two cultural orientations . . . closely approximating the profane and the sacred respectively—i.e., having desacralized their traditional culture while sacralizing Christianity—and it is the intrinsically oppositional character of *this* relation as posited by Durkheim which has inhibited their synthesis" (2010, 232–33).

43. While this is generally the case, Paolo Aranha has pointed out that in the context of the controversies over their adaptations to caste known as the Malabar Rites (see chapter 1), "the Jesuit representatives in Rome did not hesitate to list all possible scriptural and theological sanctions of social hierarchies, including justifications of slavery" (personal communication).

44. Among anthropologists of Melanesia, there has been some debate on the displacement of indigenous cultures of "nonduality" and "dividuals" (with parallels to India; see Busby 1997) through Christianization and its individualized conception of sin and salvation and dualist thinking. A contrary argument is that a conception of partible persons and divinity persist within Christian devotion (Catholic or charismatic) in which penitents transact parts of themselves, detaching offerings, sins, or sacrificed animals, and attaching absolution, divine grace, or spiritual gifts (see Mosko 2010, and responses in the same issue of *JRAI* 2010). The evidence in this study suggests that such "elicitive detachments and attachments" (Mosco 2010, 217) may persist in devotion, even while being explicitly refused in a now separated realm of the social.

45. The Protestant Church, which had long resisted caste as an aspect of paganism and consequently acquired a more uniformly "low" caste membership, did not generate the same social radicalism.

46. Arrupe 1981 [1978], cited in Keane 2007, 91.

47. Among the several hazards of a generalized wedding of Christianity to narratives of modernity is the effect of locating non-Christian traditions in a nonmodern domain (Soares and Osella 2009, S5).

CHAPTER 1

1. For general debates and definitions on Christian conversion and proselytism in India, see Frykenberg 2003 and Kim 2003.

2. For a historical overview of Christianity and south Indian missions (which this book is not intended to be), see Frykenberg 2008, Neill 1984, Hambye 1997, and Grafè 1990.

3. For a later parallel, but minority, position among Protestants, viewing Christianity as the "Crown of Hinduism," see Farquhar 1913 and Sharpe 1965.

4. This elitist innovation developed by Jesuit successors such as C. J. Beschi (d. 1747)

into a high Tamil literary tradition (and much criticized by colloquial-oriented Protestant evangelicals) carefully avoided biblical reference to the lower-caste occupations of carpenters and fishermen (Županov 1999, 28; Bugge 1994, 58; cf. Dubois 1977 [1815], 18–19).

5. Note the parallel with Louis Dumont's (1980) structuralism (see Introduction)—not only his conception of reality made meaningful by the inner template of ideology (the "pure" and the "impure"), but also his opposition to 1960s empiricism in the sociology of India (cf. Županov 1999, 208). It should be noted that some doubt has been expressed concerning both the degree of Nobili's anti-Portuguese elitism and Fernandes's subalternity. Portuguese interests and trade presence in Madurai may have been more pervasive, and Nobili's perspective less "emic," than later Jesuit representations care to admit (see the Introduction, note 9) (Paolo Aranha, personal communication)

6. As in the sources, in this chapter "Pariah" refers generically to "untouchable" castes (today's dalits) rather than to the Paraiyar caste from which the term derived.

7. Historical background on statecraft and temples in this section draws on Appadurai 1981, Dirks 1987, Kadhirvel 1977, Ludden 1985, Mosse 2003, Price 1996, Rajaram Row 1891, Rajayyan 1974, and Stein 1980; and the de Britto narrative draws on Kadhirvel 1977, Houtart n.d., Nevett 1980, and Saulière 1947.

8. One pantaracami, Laynez, claimed to have converted ten thousand people in 1693–94 (Ponnad 1983, 137; Bertrand 1865, 442). By 1714, there were around twenty thousand Christians, and by 1780 some thirty-five thousand, in the Ramnad region (Hambye 1997, 162). On the earlier repression of Christians, see Nevett 1980 and sources cited in Manickam 2001, 202–6.

9. From the 1730s, Jesuit annual letters (A.L.) record the increasing popularity and miraculous power of this shrine—e.g., A.L., J. Vieyra 1734 (14 July 1735); A.L., Salvador dos Reys 1735 (27 June 1736); A.L., F. M. Orti 1743 (4 September 1744). See *Lettres Annuelles du Maduré,* no. 17 (1708–1756) (Trans. F. L. Besse). Since the annual letters available at the Jesuit Madurai Mission Archives (JMMA, Shembaganur, Tamil Nadu) are often available only in translated typescript, they have to be treated with some caution.

10. The Italian Jesuit Costanzo Giuseppe Beschi (Virāmuni Swami) (1680–1747) was perhaps an exemplar, awarded an *iṉām* (see below) of four villages, a serving *diwan* (royal minister), and a regal entourage (Frykenberg 2008, 139–40).

11. A.L., J. Vieyra 1734; A.L., M. Orti, 1734; A.L., J. Khrening 1745; A.L., Felix 1749, JMMA.

12. Kadhirvel 1977, 61; A.L., J. Vieyra 1730; A.L., C. J. Beschi 1731; Besse 1914, 246.

13. A.L., C. J. Beschi 1731; A.L., J. Vieyra 1733.

14. On the role and importance of natu structures and chiefs in precolonial Ramnad, see Mosse 2003, 53–70.

15. This is recorded in palm-leaf manuscripts (*ōlai*) found by the Jesuit missionary Edmond Favreux c. 1858, inscribed when the church was built (c. 1778).

16. Issued on 23 Markali in 'Salivahana kala 1723 (c. 1801) by Vallava Periya Utaiya Tevar—taken from a translation of the original Tamil copperplate, JMMA.

17. While the prevailing arrangement of shares and honors was recorded in distinctly nineteenth-century systematic detail in the 1880s by the Jesuit inamtar, it articulated a model of village resource rights and social ranking that was ancient and pervasive on

the Tamil plains (see chapter 3). The Jesuit record, *Cramam de Sarougani* (henceforth *Cramam*), is a handwritten unpaginated notebook in French, c. 1880 (JMMA). It will be referenced by section headings.

18. *Cramam,* "Usages des Fêtes." For a full listing of the twenty-eight caste-ranked honors, see Mosse 1997, 111–12.

19. Paolo Aranha's (2012b) doctoral research suggests that the Malabar Rites controversy was more complex than is conventionally understood. Its immediate cause was a local dispute over pastoral responsibility for Indian Christians between French Jesuits and Capuchins in Pondicherry. Tournon settled this in favor of the Jesuits, but was seemingly unaware of the negative reception his decree *Inter graviores* (23 June 1704), forbidding practice of the Malabar rites, would have among Jesuit missionaries. What Aranha's thesis does more generally is to challenge the hagiographic and anachronistic celebration of Nobili's *accommodatio* as a project of "inculturation" with its post–Vatican II meaning as a correction to missionary European ethnocentrism. A historical reading has to take proper account of power relations within missions, including within the newly established Christian community. In arguing that *accommodatio* was above all a means to official recognition of caste hierarchies among Christian converts, Aranha shows that the "Malabar Rites were primarily Christianized Hindu *saṃskāras*, i.e., 'sacramental' rituals functional to the reproduction and distinction of caste hierarchies rather than mere cultural traits that should be accepted in order to make Christianity more palatable to non-European peoples" (Aranha 2010, and personal communication). Despite its representation for Europeans, what Nobili's mission was doing in practice in Madurai in the seventeenth century was little different from the tactical embedding of Catholicism in a culture of power in Ramnad a century later.

20. Aranha (2011) finds an apologetic work by Fr. Broglia Antonio Brandolini (c. 1729) with a diagram portraying a physical arrangement that confines the congregation of the "Parreas" (Paraiyars) to a space that is separate from the church of the "nobles." The "Parreas," Aranha points out, do not have an independent church but a place in which they gather as an audience for the "theatre" of worship in the "nobles'" church, having sight not of the altar itself, but of the priest celebrating the Eucharist in front of it—a sort of *darśana* or auspicious vision of the divine presence.

21. Madras District Records, Madurai District, vol. 4682, Tamil Nadu State Archives, Chennai. The Congregatio de Propaganda Fide was established in 1622 by Rome to coordinate missionary efforts in Asia and regain some influence in the face of rights to ecclesiastical patronage held by the Spanish and Portuguese kings (Wright 2004, 99).

22. See Dirks (1987, 380–83) on the new bureaucratic conception of religion among Brahman administrators of temples.

23. The fear of contamination from European lifestyles (stripped of the power of rule) was evident in the Church. In the 1840s upper-caste Tamil Catholics apparently refused to confess to the first three Indian priests trained in Europe, since they had become degraded by beef eating while outside India. A similar logic lay behind the rebellion against the desegregation of the dining rooms of (upper-caste) Indian seminarians and European clergy that in 1848 temporary closed the MEP (Société des Missions Etrangères de Paris) seminary in Pondicherry (Manickam 2001, 293–94).

24. E.g., the exchange between Superior General Roothan and mission Superior Bertrand in 1841 (Manikam 2001, 285–86).

25. “Thomas Babington (Lord Macaulay)'s Minute on Education,” 2 February 1835 (reprinted in *Thomas Babington Macaulay: Prose and Poetry*, ed. G.M. Young [Cambridge, MA: Harvard University Press, 1952]; reproduced in Kuriakose 1982, 122–25).

26. The literature on mass conversion movements is too extensive to cite here; see bibliographies in Frykenberg 2008 and Webster 1992. Recent work includes Bugge 1994, Cederlöf 1997 and 2003, Forrester 1980, Kooiman 1989, and Viswanath 2010.

27. Undoubtedly the nineteenth century saw an intensification of agrestic servitude as well as a deepening stigmatization of “the Pariah,” inferiorized by Brahmanic theories of impurity that thrived in British India's civil society (S. B. Bayly 1989; Dirks 2001; Viswanath 2008, 4; Washbrook 1993).

28. While a visit by an English missionary to a Pariah settlement contending with an injustice from upper castes sent a powerful signal (Viswanath 2008, 12), even Jesuit priests (who still maintained some distance from government) were perceived as influential sources of support.

29. Cederlöf (1997, 2003) provides a parallel contrast from 1930s–1940s western Tamil Nadu.

30. On the development of the Protestant critique of caste during the nineteenth century, see Forrester 1980, Warren 1967, and Oddie 1979.

31. Mission societies would, however, later adapt their strategies to the process of mass conversion (Cederlöf 2003).

32. Dayanandan's (2002) account of the Free Church of Scotland missionary Rev. Adam Andrew is a case in point.

33. *The Harvest Field*, 1863–64, “Our Native Christians,” p. 203m, cited in Viswanath 2008, 12.

34. Mgr. Alexis Canoz, bishop of Tiruchirappalli, 1888, quoted in Manickam 2001, 309.

CHAPTER 2

1. Doctrinal distinctions detailed by Thomas Aquinas in his *Summa Theologica* (1270, II-II, Q. 103), between “worship” (Gk. *latrīa*) due to God, honor or “servitude” (Gk. *dulia*) due to the saints, and the special veneration (Gk. *hyperdulia* “higher servitude”) due to the Virgin Mary as mother of Christ, or between divine intervention and saintly intercession (for the living and the dead), became blurred in Tamil vocabularies of worship.

2. Alapuram Parish Diaries (APD) Gnanaprakasam, 24 January 1895. These diaries (in French or English with Tamil) were either archived in Shembagaur (JMMA) or stored in parish presbyteries. Translations are my own.

3. Cholera epidemics occurred almost yearly in Alapuram village—for example, in 1895, 1898, 1900, June 1903, and 1904; and smallpox in 1906 (APD passim).

4. APD Gnanaprakasam, 28 February 1896, 4 March 1896, 6 March 1896, 25 August 1896.

5. The priest noted that when one Santiago arranged ceremonies and sacrifices in his house for his sick son, “God punished witchcraft by sending a double death,” and

that recourse by a Christian family to a *pattunūḷ* (spirit intermediary) resulted in three deaths.

6. APD Mahé, 14 August 1936; Sarukani parish diary, 9–10 July 1926.

7. As Pope Gregory the Great said in his message to Augustine of Canterbury in relation to allowing sacrifices at the shrines of the pagan Angles to be redirected to the praise of God (Bede 1969, cited in Greeley 2001, 11).

8. APD Gnanaprakasam, 11 February 1896, 6 May 1896.

9. While Hindus adopted Christian holy figures as divinities, Christians adopted Hindu forms of worship; but never vice versa.

10. Not as indigenous penitents, as the earlier Jesuit pantaracamis had been.

11. APD Gamon, 7 June 1907; APD Veaux, 2 February 1924.

12. A centralized church structure and the lack of an indigenous clergy "rising from the popular ranks"—until the mid-twentieth century almost all Catholic clergy in Tamil Nadu were foreign—in fact sharpened a distinction between salvation-oriented and practical religion, as well as making "it more difficult to identify the faith as indigenous" (Hefner 1993, 33).

13. "Diableries, extrait d'une lettre du P. Fasenille. *Lettres de Vals,* 1896–1880, 13–14, JMMA.

14. See the published letters of Fathers Larmey (1876), Pouget (1890), and Lacombe (1892), APD Favreux, 1873; APD Gnanaprakasam, 24 November 1896. On seventeenth-century missionary conversion healing and Jesuit admiration for the bodily suffering and sensuous devotion of the pagan redirected to Christian worship, see Županov 2003, 2005, 2008.

15. APD Favreux, 25 July 1873, 8 September 1872.

16. Something similar is alluded to by Schmalz (1998, 105–6), writing that a north Indian lay Catholic healer implies an Ayurvedic conception of the body in terms of channels of vital fluids, and the effect of sin that "occludes the flow of grace as it ripens or hardens in the body" (cited in Csordas 2007, 299). Bloomer's informants in a present-day Chennai Marian healing cult also describe evil released as substance (2008, 105–6). Such externalizing materialization of sin or evil is a kind of resistance to Catholic interiorization giving rise to complex interpretations of healing events and agents (see Schmalz 1999).

17. When my close neighbor Savariyammal (I give all villagers pseudonyms) was talking to me about her relationship with the Virgin Mary, she recalled a sin she could not confess to the priest, meaning that she dare not take Communion. Amid her anxiety she dreamed that when passing the reservoir carrying cow dung to the manure pit, Mary with child, crowned and in golden jewels, seemed to come close from above and touch her head, telling her she was forgiven. When she woke, she felt that her sin had gone, and went to confession and Mass.

18. Bloomer relates the exteriorization of emotion to properties of the Tamil language (2008, 124).

19. Father Gnanpragrakasam was one of a handful of Tamil Jesuits serving in the French mission at the time as an assistant parish priest.

20. Out of 153 cases of possession recorded at St. Anthony's shrine in 1984, 90 percent were women, and of these 65.7 percent were between the ages of sixteen and twenty-five.

21. See Stirrat 1992, 107; 1977; Kapferer 1983; Boddy 1994; Stoller 1995. The collective nature of the process challenges not only the missionaries' insistence on *individual* morality, but also anthropological models of possession as female protest (e.g., Lewis 1971) that privilege one (the victim) of the many actors involved. See also Nabokov (1997) on how women victims find their problems (and their persons) refigured in *public* idioms of possession that discipline them and reproduce a "demonological interpretation of the ordinary female reproductive cycle" characteristic of Tamil Catholic and European traditions (Ram 1991, 90–91).

22. On the bodily conditions associated with pey possession at St. Anthony's shrine and related humeral imbalances, see Mosse 1986, 574–75.

23. Which is why for feminist Tamil Catholic writer Bama (2005, 59), the rejection of possession discourse is a means of empowerment.

24. Michael, an educated and successful Pallar (dalit) college teacher (whom we meet again in chapter 5) explains how when he arrived home to Alapuram with town grooming and finely dressed, his mother stopped him, walked around him, sat him facing east by the hearth, and then thrice encircled his head with a mixture of sand (taken from a crossroads or the footprint of an envious person), salt, and chilies, with the recitation, "Remove the eyes [the gaze] of friends and relatives and throw the eyes in the fire" (*uṟṟār uraviṉar kaṇkaḷaippiṭuṅki tīyil pōṭu* [*uṟavu* is glossed as both relationship (kin) and "worldly attachment" or "desire" in Fabricius 1972, 128, although the latter meanings are irregular/archaic]) (Rajan Krishnan, pers. com.).

25. The lotus (a symbol of perfection and purity) links the Virgin to the goddess Lakshmi or Saraswathi (Meibohm 2004, 161). Matted hair is a sign of divine communication (Obeyesekere 1981).

26. Notes such as: "To Punita Antoniyar (St. Anthony) from Sebastiammal. I am sincerely writing this letter, swami, [because of] our family difficulty [. . .] if we succeed, I will. . . ."

27. We might say that the majority of vows to the saints are what Raj and Harman call "mundane vows" ("getting what you want") rather than "soteriological vows" ("getting what you need"); most are "fulfilment vows" (payment for benefits delivered arising from a pledge) rather than "down-payment vows" (payment in anticipation of benefits); some—more often collective than individual—are "tribute" vows that, like "dedication vows," involve regular insurance or thanksgiving payments (for example, at each anniversary or festival) in anticipation of the long-term protection and blessing of the saint, or "dedication vows" (2006, 250–51).

28. When offered (paid for) for worldly success (in exams or jobs) or for the souls of the dead, the sacrament of the Mass is itself turned into a reciprocal transaction (cf. Harris 2006, 55–56).

29. Christian pilgrimages in the West have been voluntary acts of devotion and have also formed part of a penitential system (Turner 1973, 198–200). The Tamil Catholic pilgrimages appear to emphasize the former while illustrating the interdependence of renunciation and its earthly rewards.

30. From Hubert and Mauss (1964) onward, the ritual offering of a life has been understood as an "individually transformative" experience—self-negating, cathartic,

vitalizing—as well as a public statement of a personal answer to prayer (Nabokov 2000, 162–64, 171).

31. On the necessary complementarity of performative and symbolic analyses of ritual, see Good 2003. Nabokov in particular finds the power of Tamil ritual in its suspension between public prescriptions and personal performances, and in the constant infusing of shared symbols with "felt significances created out of existential predicaments so as to . . . resolve them" (2000, 12).

32. Given that moral and natural orders are not clearly separable, and that salvation may itself be imagined in material terms as protection or healing, or a reharmonizing of the material and the transcendent (Bloomer 2008, 501 et seq.), any global separation of transcendent and pragmatic religion would be meaningless (Mandelbaum 1966; Stirrat 1984, 207).

33. On the need for a culturally specific understanding of the "saint" category, see Dempsey 2001, 115 et seq.

34. The importance of tombs as ritual sites may have been influenced by the move of the Madurai mission to integrate the practice of interment, and to move moved away from cremation, which had been permitted in the funeral rite of Christians from 1625 (Aranha 2012b, 263–67).

35. APD Favreux, 24 February 1873, 22 April 1874, 26 April 1874, 27 April 1874, May 1874.

36. APD Favreux, 2 November 1872, 23–25 December 1872.

37. See Dempsey (2001, 115–31) for a discussion of the divergence and mirroring of Hindu and Christian traditions of female saintliness—respectively, devoted wife and virginal ascetic.

38. On the paradoxes of female power (*sakti*) derived from the suffering subservience, self-restraint, and chastity (*kaṟpu*) of married women on the one hand, and their simultaneous consent to, and critique of, patriarchy on the other see Dempsey (2001, 139–42); Egnor (1991). One hot afternoon in Alapuram, Arokia Mary had been telling me of the misery caused her by the unkindness of her son's wife. Suddenly she stopped herself, saying that all she wanted was a "good death" and that for this she would bear it all. She then continued with a story of the great ascetic saint Vanattu Cinnappar (St. Paul the first hermit). Once, he was praying in the wilderness, living off fruit brought him by wild animals (a typical prelapsarian image), when Jesus, appearing as a young boy, told him that there was a person living at home whose asceticism was even greater than his own. The saint searched until he eventually found a woman ruthlessly beaten by her husband, whom she continued to serve devotedly.

39. On bodily decay and saintliness, see Bloch and Parry (1982, 22–27), Pina-Cabral (1980), Wilson (1983, 10), and Warner (1978, 97–102).

40. The emphasis on immaturity here perhaps reflects the absence of socially acceptable social models of virginal asceticism in Tamil society as well as the natural connection of women to Eve and original sin in Christian tradition (see Dempsey 2001, 131–32). See Dempsey (2001, chap. 4) for a discussion of female Christian sanctity in the different Kerala context.

41. This alongside cures for strange human and animal abnormalities (Annual Letter [A.L.] Salvador dos Reys, 1735 [27 June 1736]; A.L. F. M. Orti, 1743 [4 September 1744]).

42. In 1735, Jesuit Father Vieyra writes of "a gentile" who committed the "sin of perjury" at Oriyur: "All at once his legs and arms became horribly swollen. He became blind and within eight days was dead. Nobody dare now take false oath . . . that is why the gentile judge declared guilty a pagan who refused to swear in this place that he was innocent of a crime of which he was accused, whilst he declared that he was ready to do it in the temples of idols" (A.L. J. Vieyra, 1734 [14 July 1735]). In 1896, Father Gnanaprakasam notes that "[t]he revenue inspector of Mangalam sent two litigants . . . each of whom charged the other with having felled a certain number of trees . . . to take oath at St. James's church [Alapuram]" (APD, 10 February1896). There were many further cases in Alapuram where vacant house sites and land donated to the church are testimony to unresolved disputes taken to oath (no party risking saintly punishment) (APD Gnanaprakasam, 8 November 1894; APD Gamon, 24 October 1902, 11 November 1906, 21 July 1909; APD Mahé, 11 December 1930). For other oath-taking practices, see Mosse 2006a, 132n37.

43. While always nonviolent, the Virgin is sometimes the focus of exorcism cults. The Virgin may be imagined as protecting Christians against Hindu deities as malevolent demons, particularly if taking on the role of village guardian where, as in the dalit Christian village Deliège (1988) describes, opposition to/by "caste Hindus" is a social reality.

44. One of several versions (Mosse 1986) of the myth related in Alapuram village: a shepherd boy carrying milk from his village to his master's house in Nagappattnam town used to pass through a wilderness (katu) and rest under a particular banyan tree beside a tank (reservoir). Once, a mother approached and asked for some milk for her young child. While the shepherd boy was explaining that his master would be furious should any milk be lost, unnoticed her child drank half the milk. The woman and child disappeared. The shepherd boy was distressed and feared a beating, but when he reached his master's house he found that the milk pot was full and "boiling over" (*poṅkiṟatu*). When he returned with his master to pray at the place by the tank (*mātā kuḷam*), Mata came to them as in a vision (*kaṭci*), telling them to build a church on this spot. (See Meibohm 2004 for further analysis of Our Lady of Health [Arokkiyamata] Velankanni origin myths.)

45. The negative attitude is not marked; as the saying goes, *koṉṟāl pāvam tiṉṟāl pōccu* ("[in] killing there is sin, [in] eating it is gone").

46. While Ramnad villagers organize relationships of Catholic divinity according to political relations of subordination and superordination, in a Kerala fishing community "it is the connections of Dravidian kinship that offer the model for the Trinity/Holy Family as divine Mother, Father, and Son . . . at some level the two [God and Joseph] become identified as one" (Busby 2006, 83).

47. In some narrations the Muni was installed in the dome of the church, rather like the "fierce" guardian Pandi Muni installed in a tower of the great Madurai Minakshi temple.

48. The relationship between Santiyakappar and the village goddess is less clear. As earlier mentioned, he is sometimes said to protect the village from the ravages of smallpox that the goddess manifests.

49. Doniger suggests that the willing sacrifice of, rather than for, God is without Hindu parallel (1987, 183, cited in Meibohm 2004, 164).

50. Note that the hierarchical-royal metaphors for Catholic inclusion of Hindu divin-

ity in Ramnad are distinctive in comparison with the sibling metaphors of saint–deity relations in Kerala, where Christians and Hindus live parallel but separate lives (Dempsey 2001), or the exclusory demonization of Hindu divinity (including the goddess) characteristic of the more socially segregated coastal Catholic fishing communities (Ram 1991) or of "outcaste" Catholic Paraiyars (Deliège 1999).

51. The imported "forest" grottos of Our Lady of Lourdes (in Alapuram set beside the tombs of Jesuit missionaries) remind us that this idea is as much European as Tamil. However, in bringing the European calendar to India, the Marian feasts of May—European celebrations of the spring green season of fertility and growth—were transferred into the Tamil season of scorching heat already associated with the ascetic goddess.

52. In drought-stricken 1983, Mata was invoked by Alapuram women preparing ponkal rice and performing circle (*kummi*) dances in the dried-up tank bed while the (Hindu) washerwomen sang a drought-related lament.

53. Alapuram villagers spoke to me about the Holy Family in ways that constantly stripped out the biological: Mata was conceived immaculately, born from a flower consumed by the elderly St. Anne, and the birth of Jesus was itself more "as in a dream" (*piṟappu vaḷarppu*). Untouched by birth pollution, free from original sin (*jenma pāvam*), untainted by sexuality, the Virgin is the divine midwife, and queen who conquers and subjugates demonic disorderly forces attached to human biology (cf. McGilvray 1982; Warner 1978, 92–94, 116).

54. In associating sex (especially illegitimate female sexuality) with sin, and sin with death (the narrative of the Fall), missionary Catholicism echoed and reformulated themes already present within the Tamil countryside (cf. McGilvray 1982a, 1982b; Daniel 1984, chap. 4; Shulman 1980). The punishment imposed on women caught in adultery made explicit the link between illegitimate sex and death. Such women were made to wear black saris and a crown of thorns (*muḷmuṭi*—the emblem of Christ's humiliation and death) and to walk around the church seven times, and, I was told, the priest might conduct a rite called *kallaṟai pūcai,* a simultaneous reference to a the grave (*kallaṟai*) and "false Mass" (*kaḷḷam*—falsehood).

55. See Fuller (1988) on relational versus substantialized divinity in popular Hinduism.

56. Pilgrims at Velankanni imagine the Virgin Mary according to their different backgrounds (Sébastia 2002). If Alapuram pilgrims identify a cosmopolitan Mary, others find Mata as a lineage deity (kula teyvam), or as the goddess who fled the Brahmans to make herself available to low castes (ibid.). Researching at Velankanni itself, Sébastia finds a Virgin who *does* retain the ambivalence of the goddess (Mariayammal), who is angered by impiety and unfaithfulness and requires care (attention to purity) when approaching, touching, or dressing her statue. The spatial arrangement of this pilgrimage center itself allows a differentiation of the Virgin into forest goddess (by the tank), healing mother (in the basilica), and exorcist virgin (Viyākula mātā, Our Lady of Dolores, whose shrine between the basilica and the ocean is the site of countersorcery as well as a barrier to the entry of evil spirits) (Sébastia 2002; Bloomer 2007).

57. In one version I heard, a shepherdess passing daily through the wilderness (katu) beside a tank to sell milk finds herself repeatedly tripping on a particular stone and spilling some of the milk. Men of the village unearth a statue at the spot but accidentally cut

its arm, from which blood pours. They built a temple for the goddess there. In another, a pregnant shepherdess passing by the same place falls into labor and is approached by an old woman in white (or saffron) who delivers her child (in some versions, in the inner sanctum of the temple). Compare to note 44 above.

58. Arrival from "outside" in the form of a tree (Cantiyakkappar) or soil (Arulanandar) is a common motif for "fierce" Hindu gods as well (Mines 2005).

59. Here the Tamil katu merges with the wilderness legacy of Christian asceticism. The wilderness is both a prelapsarian or redemptive space apart from the sinful city, and the sanctuary to which the demons fled, weakened by the advance of Christianity (Adler 2006). It is the site of Christ's own struggle with the tempter, and the place to which the demonic, no longer working through human social relations, engages the saints directly in "hand-to-hand combat" (ibid., 25).

60. Vannatu Cinnappar is the exemplar of asceticism, worshipped outside the settlement in the paddy fields, which he protects from pests and where he is represented by a simple cross. In the 1960s a migrant returning to Alapuram from Malaysia built a Cinnappar shrine in the asocial wasteland by the cemetery, beside the village tank—a classic location for demons (Mines 2005). Another family found that even the tree under which the saint was once worshipped fell down, since it compromised his extreme asceticism. Recall that Vanattu Cinnappar's crucifix (the focus of a nineteenth-century exorcism cult) refused the shelter of a St. Xavier chapel (see above). Indeed, in Alapuram, Vanattu Cinnappar and Santiyakappar stood as the renunciation of the forest in relation to the ordered rule of the village. Then, in addition to the liminal *space,* the forest saint Anthony the hermit (Vanan Antoniar) is connected with transitional *times,* and worshipped at the festival of Poṅkal, a major Tamil festival of socioeconomic transition in the month of Tai that marks the move from one agricultural cycle to the next, from the season of water and fertility to that of sun and heat (Reiniche 1979, 43, 65ff; Good 1983).

61. MacKendrick (2010) offers insight into how dismemberment of medieval saints' bodies involved a divine *multiplication*—the saint whole in every relic part—and how (at Tamil shrines, too) pilgrims who are restored to wholeness leave as tribute their own parts (metal images of ailing body parts).

62. On possession by St. Anthony, see Mosse 1986, 481, 576–77; by the Virgin Mary, see Bloomer 2008.

63. Villagers also spoke of becoming Christian following an episode of unjust affliction from their deities, articulating the missionary idea of Christian freedom from the fear of capricious demon gods.

64. Županov (2007, 2008) argues that in the sixteenth-century Portuguese Jesuit mission, the ecstatic "confession mode" was a kind of possession involving priests as shamans and scenes of fervent mortification by flogging and "neophytes [speaking] about their most intimate desires, fears and angers." These theatrical performances were guided by the *Confessionario*—a codification of emotion, sin, and penance. The great demand for this confession from Tamil women was hugely beyond the capacity of missions to hear them.

65. Caroline Osella raised the issue of mimesis in possession for me.

66. See useful recent accounts by Collins (2007) and Kim (2003, 109–22) as well as by Boyd (1975) and Sharpe (1965).

67. On the rise of Tamil Pentecostal Christianity in the 1970s, see George 1981; Caplan 1983, 1987, 1991; and Nelson 1975. Bergunder 2008 provides an authoritative overview.

68. On the distinctively Indian (rather than American) roots of Tamil Pentecostalism, see Bergunder 2005.

69. Although he still presents himself as a cassocked priest, Berchmans effectively separated from the Catholic Church in 1991 to join the Pentecostal movement and is now well known as a gifted composer and performer of hymns (Bergunder 2008).

70. Urban Pentecostal congregations are evidently more stable and more permanent, and their focus is on social identity and relationships (Caplan 1983, 1987, 1991).

CHAPTER 3

1. Among these processes were those of census making (reifying rank [Cohn 1987]), domestic and military recruitment (standardizing caste as a division of labor [e.g., Raheja 1996; S. B. Bayly 1999]), and Protestant missionizing (rendering caste religious and subject to conversion and theologizing [Viswanath 2010]).

2. S. B. Bayly 1999 and Dirks 2001 provide overviews of the colonial transformations of caste. See also Fuller 1996, Inden 1990, and Gupta 2000 and 2004.

3. Bruno Latour's (2005, 63) "sociology of association" would examine how caste groups are "'constantly' being performed" and would focus not on taken-for-granted social aggregates but on caste as a local project or practice shaped by debates and controversies in agencies such as churches, associations, political parties, or social movements.

4. For references on the studies of caste organization among Christians in south India up to the 1990s, see Mosse 1996, 478.

5. Although religious affiliation was subordinate to caste in matters of kinship, Christian identity did have some independent effect on the prevailing Dravidian cross-cousin marriage practice. According to my survey of 1983, Christian members of each caste (compared with Hindu members) contracted a smaller proportion of marriages with close cousins, and a greater proportion with nonrelatives (*aṉṉiyam*). In other words, Christians had somewhat wider marriage circles, so that, for example, 52 percent of Catholic Pallars married nonrelatives as against 6 percent of Hindus, and the equivalent figures for Vellalars were 43 and 15.4 percent, and for Utaiyars 47 and 33.3 percent. However, this difference between Christian and Hindus almost disappeared among the lower-caste Paraiyars in the village who were more recent converts to Protestant Christianity (Mosse 1986, 75–78). The Church also forbade otherwise common uncle–niece marriage.

6. When Rani, daughter of my Hindu Paraiyar friend Mohan, married into a co-caste Catholic family she was baptized and settled into her husband's Catholic hamlet. As it happened, Rani was not happy in her married village and, rather untypically, persuaded her husband to move with her back to Alapuram. Here she readopted Hindu rituals, joined by her husband as a marginal Catholic. Their two sons are religiously Hindu although disqualified from state concessions as Scheduled Castes by their father's Christian name, which reverses the more common adoption by Christian dalits of Hindu names for these entitlements.

7. Taking the lead from Cohn (1987), anthropologists began to see that what had

been discovered as "traditional" village India was in large measure a product of colonial knowledge practices as well as historical processes of sedentarization and settlement under British colonial rule. These reified as the "traditional Indian village" what were in fact truncated remnants of earlier forms of state, decapitated by colonial rule (Dewey 1972; Dirks 1987; Fuller 1989; Inden 1990; Mayer 1993; Mosse 2003).

8. In 1982 the church still had an income from landholdings granted by the raja, and that income increased as the saint acquired disputed property subject to oath taking.

9. By the nineteenth century most Maravars had abandoned Christian affiliation, while some still held Arulanandar (St. John de Britto) as their family or lineage deity.

10. Today Pallar intellectuals would argue that the influence was the other way around—Pallars over the culturally backward Maravars (see chapter 5). In 1980s Alapuram there were eight Maravar kiḷai in the village but (because of wider marriage networks) as many as twenty-three Pallar kiḷai.

11. Thus Necavar (weaver) Paraiyars from Pudukottai to the north were given title to clear and cultivate land (*kāṭuveṭṭi paṭṭam*) as clients of the Vellalar village accountants and their kin, with whom in 1983 they still used fictive affinal kin terms (*māmā-maccāṉ*).

12. Jesuit histories record the land grants made to four Catholic Utaiyar chiefs by the Cetupati of Ramnad at the behest of his finance minister (Periya Annan Pillai Mandiri) on the grounds of their superior cultivation skills. The chiefs were Michael Utaiyar of Andavoorani, Rayappan Utaiyar of Nedumaram, Cinnappar Utaiyar of Kilyur, Mutappa Utaiyar of Kookudy, and the Hindu Utaiyar chief of Pulial (Annual Letters vol. 8, p. 263, to Castets from Fr. Leveil, 17 January 1929 (JMMA); also "Notes on the Parishes—Calladitidel (JMMA); and Leveil 1937, 442; Mahé 1939, 14.

13. Utaiyars stereotyped Pallars' putative rude appetites and ignorance of the true value of their land in moral tales about the exchange of fields for trivia such as alcohol, meat, or the proverbial chicken's head.

14. Sources: Rajaram Row 1891, 187; Census of India 1961, 1971; my own census in 1983. These figures mask significant further population movements. A large proportion of Maravars from the village migrated south to Tirunelveli (in the nineteenth century), while Vellalars, like other upper castes (especially Brahmans), sought mobility through professions and business in urban centers.

15. There has also been an upward trend in the proportion of households with members temporarily or permanently living and working outside the village—a quarter in 1983, a third in 1994 (my surveys in 1983–84 and 1993–94.). A similar proportion of households derived supplementary incomes from off-farm work in the village: as unskilled labor, from salaried employment as teachers, drivers, bus conductors, employees on government schemes, from businesses such as provisions shops, teashops, grain commission shops, tailoring and, by 2009, photocopy, phone, and medical shops as well.

16. Before the Second World War cheap land leases from the (British) government opened up virgin delta land for rice growing for the European market. Profits were invested in extensive dryland landholdings in Alapuram and neighboring villages as well as in mansions.

17. Holding the hereditary office of headman had allowed the small minority of Maravars to maintain a certain political domination in the village. Even after the abolition of

this office, a Maravar was returned to the elected post of president of the local council (Panchayat) up until 2004.

18. Cervarar (or Akamuṭaiyār) is the third of the three warrior castes adopting the honorific title Tēvar (sons of Indra), besides Maravar and Kaḷḷar.

19. Castes also brought their clan names from their origin region's socioterritorial units: Paraiyar *nāṭus* from Pudukottai region, Utaiyar *kāṇis* from Thanjavur, and so on. Clan names encoded rules of patrilineal descent and exogamy but, being disperse, do not now identify corporate groups (Burkhart 1976). The socioterritorial organization of the kind described elsewhere (Dumont 1957; Beck 1972) was weakly developed on the later-settled Ramnad plains, where social forms were more influenced by hierarchies of political-military control (Baker 1984, 45; Mosse 2003).

20. These are the terms in which Reiniche (1979, 182–84) explains the cult of Sasta (Aiyanar) in a Tirunelveli village similarly lacking territorially organized lineage cults.

21. Farmers did not sow seed until after this festival.

22. The term *kuṭi,* is the polysemantic root of various words. It may refer variously to "house," "inhabitant," or "subject." With reference to kutimakan (village servant), Mines (2005, 56) references kutimai as the condition of being in kuti, which "connotate[s] personal attachment[,]" dependency, and subordination.

23. I have elsewhere (Mosse 2003) described this system and its transformation under colonial and indirect Zamindari rule (after 1800). Grain shares (and the *māniyam* service tenures they replaced) were a "burdened form of property" (Rao 2009, 109) implying labor obligation and signifying social status.

24. This was an echo of the "old regime" transactional system "decapitated" by British rule, and ethnographically reinvented as the village "jajmani system" in 1950s and 1960s village studies (see Dirks 1987, 125–26; Fuller 1989; Mosse 2003).

25. I have summarized the economic history of the village from research over a decade elsewhere (Mosse 2003, 204ff).

26. The palimpsest of village-level dyadic relations of service and an older redistributive system is what Fuller (1989) argues produced confusion in the ethnographic literature on the so-called Indian jajmani system. My point, however, is that the "confusion" of patron-client relations and village service is not an analytical error, but a social fact: the enactment of the former as the latter. A public hierarchy of village service was invoked as an idiom of subordination within dyadic relations. And the "public" that is referred to in these events is not an anonymous, open-to-everyone outside, but the social space of the "inner" order of village or kingdom (see Bate 2009, 79–80).

27. Good (1982) explains how (in rural Tirunelveli) this distinction between technical skill and caste qualification was marked by different sorts of payments.

28. Rayappar told me that for the inauguration of his own new house he had traveled to the Virgin at Velankannni and brought holy water to add to the ponkal rice that was by convention prepared.

29. Alternatively, *kalapiccai*—"alms at the threshing floor" (Rajaram Row 1891, 318; *Cramam* op. cit., pp. 13–14, 26–32).

30. Sometimes described as *viṉiyōkam,* "giving in expectation of return" (Fabricius 1972, 891).

31. In 1983–84, no Pallar household had served as a client for some time. In fact, only households of the Protestant Totti Paraiyar and Cakkiliyar castes (but almost all of them) had aiya vitus in the full sense (see Mosse 1994, 1986). By 2004 such relationships were hardly remembered at all.

32. The bier, which Hindus dismantle and discard at the cemetery, is kept by Catholics inside the church and used as well to carry the image of the body of Christ at the Good Friday procession.

33. Jesuits brought a culturally specific notion of noise and the sacredness of silence, and insisted that all processions (including Hindu ones) were silent as they passed the St. James church (e.g., APD Gamon, 1 November 1916).

34. See Mosse 1996, 478n5, for the specific funeral services and payments.

35. Water, turmeric, cow's milk, and gingili oil are substances that "cool" and purify. Basic procedures include those to create boundaries or offer magical protection (circumambulation, rotating the bier, tying threads around things, lighting lamps, keening, drumming, firecrackers), those that protect from pollution (sealing orifices), or separate (cutting threads), or cool (pouring water, bathing, shaving), or remove faults, evil, or envious gazes (Good 1983, 225; cf. Mines 2005, 72–73). These substances and procedures effect change through the indexical qualities of the signs, regardless of the particular meanings or interpretations given to them (which in this Christian and Hindu context would be unreliable; see Robbins 2001). But in "constructing" funerary and other rituals, Christians also follow Nobili's model by making *substitutions*, adding symbolic substances: candles for camphor, the sign of the cross for the smearing of sacred ash, as well as certain *additions* (rosaries, holy pictures, the use of incense or holy water, or the sounding of the church bell). These do not, however, alter the underlying structure of the ritual.

36. This all fits within a spectrum of evidence from south Indian Christians. Some studies insist on the persistence of ideas of pollution among convert groups (Estborn 1961; Diehl 1965; Caplan 1980), while others suggested that such ideas are either absent or vestigial (Fuller 1976; Caplan 1987; Ferro-Luzzi 1974; Ram 1991).

37. The same logic of refusal and replication meant that in the 1980s Protestant Paraiyars would not take on, for Pallar funerals, the roles they performed for upper castes (drumming, carrying "fire-pots," singing laments, or removing death-marked food and cloth), and instead it was Muthu and his brother, members of the lower-ranking Cakkiliyar caste, who took on these tasks (except drumming, for which professional bands were hired).

38. Moffatt (1979), analyzing the situation of Paraiyars in a northern Tamil village similarly without such specialists in the 1970s, found the "necessary" service roles provided through an internal differentiation of the caste into endogamous subgroups or "grades," with the assignment of "polluting" functions to the lowest grades.

39. Twenty years earlier, the priest had been approached for the honor of conducting a Mass for "the final detachment of the tali" of a young Utaiyar widow, a request he refused (Alapuram Parish Diary, Fr. Favreux, 3 June 1870).

40. For a survey catechist roles, see Houtart et al. n.d., 386–88.

41. Between these were the honorific *taccanai* payments to ritualists such as Acari carpenters at house-building rituals. For a parallel tripartite classification of prestations for services, ritualists, and divinity, see Parry (1979, 62–63). Significantly, as a recipient of

tarumam gifts, the catechist did not, as a Brahman purohit might, "eat" the evils or sins of his patrons, and there was no sense that he was an endangered remover of faults or spiritual impurities. No more was the taccanai-receiving carpenter (cf. Mines 2005, 70; Raheja 1988; Quigley 1993).

42. APD Gnanaprakasam, 17 January 1896, 6 October 1896; APD Gamon, 24 December 1904; Sarukani parish diary, 2 November 1916. Arguably, the pantaram catechist stood in the same relation to the Pallars he served as Moffatt's (1979) Hindu Valluvar serving dalits excluded from Brahman ritualists (see Moffatt 1979).

43. Rice and its processing has a widespread significance in symbolizing female fertility, sexuality, and reproductive processes more generally (e.g., Fuller 1992, 192).

44. Christian explanations of rites of purification are in fact often glossed in terms of mourning and sadness rather than impurity. For Hindus, acts of purification are also acts of worship, and the logical status of the deceased is, as Good puts it, the "sacred in transition," decorated, honored, and eulogized (1980, 170; Clark-Decès 2007, 2005). Tamil Christians share this sentiment. Even when coffins rather than open biers are used, the deceased is exposed or laid on top of the coffin to be honored (Diehl 1965, 119; also see Moffatt 1968, 98–103; Dumont 1957, 222).

45. While there was no pollution in relation to the Catholic sacred, many Christians had not ceased to recognize or interact (directly or indirectly) with Hindu deities known to be particular about such matters. Indeed, for Christians states of pollution had relevance *primarily* in relation to fierce village gods, and women's ambivalent attitudes to menstrual pollution reflect a continuing awareness of the dangers of inadvertently walking past a shrine in an inappropriate state, perhaps while collecting water from the village tank, or attracting maleficent ghosts and demon. The relevant distinction, then, is not between attitudes to pollution of Hindus and Christians, but *of relations to Hindu and Christian divinity*.

46. However, on special occasions and festivals, codes of caste honor forbade dalits from handling the processional statues. Moreover, it is not entirely exceptional to read of churches such as the one in Thanjavur District, where there are two statues of Our Lady of Perpetual Succor, one for veneration by high castes and another for dalits (Singarayar 1978, 391).

47. Nonetheless, the godparent relationship seemed to create a "parallel" kin link between families that precluded marriage. For this reason, in practice "cross relations" did not tend to become godparents, although there were certainly cross-caste godparent relations, including between Utaiyars and Pallars, although in 1983–84 this spiritual kinship did not imply social exchanges such as sharing cooked food between those households.

48. Only three priests out of forty-two interviewed in a 1980s Ramnad survey made pastoral visits to parishioners' houses, chiefly to conduct some blessing (for example, to receive the first-boiled milk in a new house) or to collect funds. Most priests reported that villagers would consider household visits (involving informal conversation or the company of women) undesirable from persons who were expected to emulate the apartness of their missionary forebears, and whom it would anyway be awkward to host, especially for the poor, who would not have facilities to receive them (Houtart et al., n.d., 344–47).

49. A survey in 1976 recorded twenty-one of the forty-nine parish priests in the East

Ramnad region as Vellalar (43 per cent), seven as Utaiyar (14 per cent), and only two as dalit (4 percent) (Houtart et al. n.d., 283).

50. Commanding high-status ritualists was also about such public honor; hence the disturbance in 1896 when the Vellalar kovilpillai refused to perform purificatory rituals for Catholics Utaiyar widows (APD Gnanaprakasam, 6 October 1896).

51. Using a card-sorting-based opinion poll of representatives of all castes, surveying reported habits of interdining and norms for the use of respectful and disrespectful terms of address, I mapped intercaste relations in terms of vertical rank (and horizontal social distance) (see Mosse 1986, 62–65, 228–36).

52. The everyday etiquette of interdining or forms of address was neither a "competitive game" nor a "passive scoreboard" (Levinson 1982, 149ff).

53. Bate (2009, 76–78) makes a similar point in describing how the spatial politics of Madurai temple festivals and political events alike temporarily impose a singular meaning—a "simplex," single "spin"—onto normally diverse, complex experiences of the cityscape.

54. The Easter festival cycle also produced such public display with its order of garlanding and the quality of cloth used at the Maundy Thursday foot-washing ritual, in the order of the laying of cloth on the dead Christ during the Good Friday procession, and in the allocation of honorable or dishonorable roles in the Passion plays. This was especially so in the village of Sarukani.

55. Pushed further, this argument suggests that in the absence of structures of dependence and subordination, ideas of pollution would disappear. This is in fact how Ram understands the absence of "pollution" among Catholic Mukkuvar fishing communities on the Coromandel coast, who live separately and are not in relations of servitude with upper castes (1991, 82). The form of the ritual roles of removal and "impurity" are retained in Catholic Ramnad, along with the caste organization of agrarian society.

CHAPTER 4

1. I use the term "mediator" in Latour's sense of those who "transform, translate, distort, and modify the meaning of the elements they are supposed to carry," as distinct from an "intermediary" who "transports meaning or force without transformation" (2005, 39).

2. Like the flowers placed in the roofs after village processions, fragments of Velankanni Mata's silk sari obtained by her devotees are treated as protection against harmful forces rather than (as in the Christian West) relics for veneration in the quest for miracles—a notion that, Sébasita (2002, 31) points out, is not familiar in India.

3. See Waghorne (2002) on the structural and artistic characteristics of the multistoried carved *tēr* chariots—"mobile architecture" that takes its form from the *gōpura* or temple gate towers (ibid., 29; Michell 1992).

4. This play on the life, temptation, and passion of Christ is performed over three days by villagers who compete caste-wise to take the prestige roles. On the first night (as I witnessed in Sarukani in 1983), the drama turns to sacred ritual as the body of Christ is taken in mournful street procession, preceded by *paṟai* drummers, a large cross draped in a white sheet (later auctioned), and followed by the (male) actor singing Mary's lament.

Devotees press forward to touch and lay cloth, flowers, and coins on Christ's body (a statue), to throw water and puffed rice (as at a funeral). In some villages this leads on to the *pēy paska* (demon paska) staging Jesus's decent into hell, a sharply costumed and caricatured battle between Jesus and the devil, good and evil. The next day the pyrotechnically risen Christ is taken in procession, "God from heaven appearing to the people" (Bama 2000, 86; cf. Waghorne 2002).

5. Labeling practices by geocultural origin is purposeless. There are cross-cultural shifts in the significance of even familiar practices such as lighting candles. Candles, which in Western Christianity perhaps symbolize the longing of the heart or the sacrifice of Christ, or express light against darkness, are in this Tamil context treated as an offering made in large bundles (Meibohm 2004, 176). Nonetheless, processions are clearly marked as Christian (by symbol, substance, and color) in ways that allow similarities of ritual form to stress rather than blur religious difference (Waghorne 2002, 16, 25).

6. St. Anthony's feast—already an ancient European agricultural festival—was superimposed on the Tamil festival of new-year productivity, Ponkal, named by the swelling and boiling over (*poṅkal*) of rice pots and the transitional act of cooking rice on open fires fed with the dead refuse of the old year (leaves and straw) at liminal places (thresholds, the veranda, the street or tank bed, or the "forest shrine" of St. Anthony—guardian of transitions and defeater of demons) (Mines 2005, 151). The ritual process "both enacts and helps terminate the main events of the agricultural year" (Good 1983, 237). Alapuram Catholics took their rice pots, and the following day their cattle, to be blessed in the church from a large vat of holy water. This water was also aspersed over homes and cattle so as to prepare for the new year with the removal of the evils of the old.

7. For similar ideas in the cult of saints elsewhere, see Wilson 1983; Brown 1981, chap. 5.

8. One story in the village was that Santiyakappar himself struck down with cholera the Hindu Vellalar family who once blocked erection of the flag post on land they owned, after which this family made reparation through regular offerings to the saint, including at their weddings. The festival flag was blessed by the priest and raised by the kovilpillai catechist. Any hitch in its ascent forebode ill for the coming season. Atop the flagpole was placed a straw rope entwining mango leaves, later mixed with seed rice to ensure pest-free crops.

9. These are the palanquins and chariots, including the largest decorated chariot or cattatēr, used for the final procession and assembled from its parts after a special rite (*Cramam,* Usages des Fêtes: Décoration de tēr).

10. The term used for church rights-duties was *kovil mirācu* (mirācu—an Arabic term referring to hereditary rights to landholding or service).

11. *Cramam,* Usages des Fêtes, c. 1876. Details in Mosse 1997.

12. By the 1980s, palanquins and chariots were decorated with colored paper and "tube lights" powered by portable generators accompanying processions on bicycles or bullock carts.

13. APD Gnanaprakasam, 3 October 1896, 22 November 1986; APD Veaux, 18 March 1928; Sarukani parish diary, 10 March 1911.

14. APD Veaux, 6 June 1935.

15. The term "mantakappati" equates to *maṇṭaka-paṭi* (or *maṇṭapappaṭi*), "the expenses

of the *maṇṭapam*"—that is, the special costs for one day of the ritual required for the passage of the deity/saint from inside the shrine outside onto the mantapam (a raised platform in front of the sanctuary) to be exposed to view and devotion during the festival (Reiniche 1979, 87n7).

16. Palmyra-tapping Nadars, included as donors in their own caste mantakappati on the seventh day of the festival, did not face the same indignity.

17. Reiniche (1979) contrasts this role to that of the Brahman priest who never acts as a donor at major village festivals.

18. The Sarukani church honors before the final procession of the risen Christ at the Easter festival (as recorded in 1876; listed in Mosse 1997) show how the royal palace was still incorporated into the church festival system, with the king as the principal donor and protector of the shrine.

19. See, for example, APD Gnanaprakasam, 25 July 1896; APD Gamon, 25 July 1896; APD Veaux, 25 July 1925. One Paraiyar informant insisted that serving castes divided themselves into an (elsewhere described—Beck 1972) left/right classification according to the side of the east door at which they stood.

20. They were Latourian "political talk," an "enunciation regime" that brought particular castes as status groups or political entities into existence (Latour 2003).

21. As early as 1839, the Madurai collector received petitions from Roman Catholics in Ramnad pressing the case for one or another of the competing missions. Board of Revenue, 22 July, back no. 75, 9050; 15 August, back nos. 59, 60, 16887–90.

22. The most detailed account of events in this period comes from Fr. Favreux's two-volume Latin *Diarium Maravae* (summarized in the French *Résumé*) covering the effort of his ministry in inaccessible villages of "the Marava" between 1854 and 1865 to "bring the ancient Christians under the authority of the Vicar Apostle." I reference the *Résumé du Diarium Maravae* (original and typescript pages at the JMMA) as *Résumé*. Translations are my own.

23. Reminiscent of sixteenth-century Portuguese assertions over west Asian (Nestorian) clerics and their patronage of Syrian Christians in Malabar (S. B. Bayly 1989, 258–60).

24. Besse 1914, 246–48; Bertrand 1865; *Résumé*.

25. APD Gnanaprakasam, 23 June 1895, 7 July 1895.

26. Maravar Christians also secured their mantakappati rights through threatening defection in the context of their dalliance with "schism" and "heresy." S. B. Bayly (1989, 420–52) describes parallel shifting ecclesiastical-caste rivalry involving Goan and Jesuit priests, as well as Vellalars and members of the commercially successful Nadar caste.

27. Alapuram parish diaries, passim. See Mosse 1986, 317–47, and Mosse 1997 for more detailed accounts based on these sources.

28. APD Gnanaprakasam, 23 June 1983, 7 July 1895; APD Veaux, 20 July 1928.

29. APD Gamon, 25 July 1903. It has not been the emphasis of this narrative, but church honors were also the focus of recurring intracaste, interfamily disputes over local or regional caste headship or the holding of offices such as village catechist and accountant.

30. APD Gamon, 24 July 1914, 24 July 1915, 11 November 1915.

31. APD Gamon, 24 July 1915, 18 June 1912, 8 July 1912.

32. Alapuram Maravars tried legally to contest these land acquisitions, or withheld communally controlled irrigation water from them (see Mosse 2003, 216).

33. The colonial empowerment of Vellalar village accountants vis-à-vis Maravar headmen (Baker 1984, 447) was equally worked out in contests over precedence in honors at the St. James festival from 1871.

34. *Uṭaiyār* ("wealthy, landowner, lord") was an honorific title for a group of castes whose origin myths, in some telling, conveyed an ambiguous social standing as descendants of union between the god-king Pārkkulateyvīkarāja and a mystically empowered Paraiyar woman (see Mosse 1986). The Catholic Church thus both added solidity to a nebulous caste category, uniting diverse subgroups (as it had for Nadars to the south [Hardgrave 1969; Good 1999, 56]), and allowed this category to establish its position in regional schemes of public ranking.

35. "*Omnibus omnia factus sum, ut omnes facerem salvos*" (1 Cor. 9:22)—"I became all things to all men that I might save all."

36. In Sarukani, continuing Padroado administration allowed the remnants of royal houses to retain rights in the shrine.

37. APD Favreux, April 1872, 16–25 July 1872.

38. APD Sousaiyamanikam, 26 July 1936.

39. APD Gamon, 18 June 1912, 8 and 13 July 1912, 14 July 1913, 18 July 1913, 17–25 July, 15 July 1915.

40. APD Gamon, 13 May 1917, 21–28 March 1919. See Mosse 1986, 333.

41. APD Gamon, 7 July 1923.

42. Vellalar Catholic opposition to this took a variety of bizarre forms: disrupting Mass by releasing a pig and then a snake into the cathedral, stoning the bishop's car, writing to the pope, and threatening to join the Jacobean church, as well as taking their objections to court (Manickam 2001, 365–67).

43. J.-P. Leonard, pastoral letter, Diocese of Tiruchirappalli, 1936, cited in Manickam 2001, 364.

44. Report of the trial "Plaint of a Parishioner against the Bishop," July 1936, Tiruchirappalli. Jesuit Archives, Vanves, France. Cited in Manickam 2001, 366.

45. Report of the trial "Plaint of a Parishioner against the Bishop," July 1936, Tiruchirappalli. Jesuit Archives, Vanves, France. Cited in Manickam 2001, 366. Mallampalli (2004) shows how, on a larger scale, the colonial judiciary was in fact used not only to resist but often to assert (or impose) Christian difference among native converts, to construct the "India Christian" against the social stream.

46. Les Missions des Jésuites de France, *La Mission du Maduré: L'Année apostolique 1931–1932* (Paris, n.d.), 34, cited in Manickam 2001, 325.

47. APD Mahé, 19–25 May 1939, 29 May 1943, 28 May 1948.

48. A common theme in recent scholarship, educatedness does not always promote the public demonstration of dalitness.

49. Visits to the village between 1987 and 1991, and interviews with the three parish priests in office, 1985–1991.

50. Apparently the priest who abolished separate seating (in 1986) began by revers-

ing the usual manner of aspersing holy water during the Mass (from upper castes in the northern transept to Pallars in the south).

51. Reiniche (1979, 183–86) offers a structural rather than culturalist way of putting the same point. In offering a cult to a "fierce" god, a group accepts subordination (*aṭimai*) in return for the right to protection (from, among other things, attack by other violent deities).

52. The meal was prepared in brass pots by an upper-caste cook to allow the participation of all castes.

53. A self-essentializing, self-exteriorizing notion of Christian dalits as "outcastes" does indeed emerge, but only much later in the 1990s with dalit theology (see chapter 6).

54. Even ten years later, in 1979, Hindu Pallar attempts similarly to exercise their legal right to receive festival honors at the Aiyanar temple of Unjanai village, and to have joint ownership of the drama stage, led to a massacre in which Kallar caste opponents killed five, injured twenty-nine, and caused mass destruction of Pallar property (Mosse 2009).

55. The contiguity of divine and political power and the elision of the god-human personalities (implicit in the practice of Christian *kovils*) was still unremarkable to Hindus. Hindu nationalist organizations responded to the Jayalalitha superimpositions of the Hindu goddess only *after* and in response to the Christian action (Bate 2009, 136–44).

CHAPTER 5

1. Nineteenth-century droughts and famines precipitated migration, and from the 1860s until the 1930s the government actively encouraged migration to Burma. The "upper house" landlord Sebastian, whose father handsomely profited from labor contracting, estimated that a quarter of the village had labored overseas in rice paddies, plantations, or domestic service. On regional patterns of labor migration, see Kumar 1965, 128–30; Mosse 2003, 120.

2. APD Veaux, 20 August 1932.

3. Parish diaries, passim. On the moral-religious framing of missionary support to low castes in conflict, see also Viswanath 2007; Oddie 1975,74; Fishman 1941, 12–14; Hardgrave 1968.

4. Quoted in APD Veaux, 18 July 1923.

5. Quoted in APD Mahé, 10 December 1938.

6. Because connected to a preexisting politics of honor, caste/party-based electoral competition produced violent confrontations, including the notorious 1957 Ramnad riots, sparked by election contests between "Backward Caste" Maravars and "Scheduled Caste" Pallars. Widespread killing and arson followed the murder of the young ex-army Pallar Congress delegate Immanuel Sekaran amid state-arranged "peace" meetings. Martyr Immanuel remains today a powerful popular symbol of Pallar struggle against the "Backward Castes" who came to capture a dalit-marginalizing Dravidian politics (M. R. Barnett 1976). On 11 September 2011 an ill-judged police firing on a dalit mass gathering to commemorate Sekaran at his Paramakudi tomb killed six mostly laborer dalits, old and young.

7. The increasingly rigorous and comprehensive pieces of legislation arising from the

Indian constitutional ban on the practice of untouchability (and the reasons for their ineffectiveness) are too complex to detail here (see Ramaiah 2007; NCS 2010). Rao (2009, 174–78) makes the point that the new legal discourse of untouchability (heralded by the 1955 Untouchability [Offenses] Act) that described and delimited caste relations had a social effect of its own. Antiatrocity laws and reported caste crimes were not only preventative but also *productive,* reorganizing social life around new governmental categories, both entrenching stigmatized identities as subjects at risk and heightening the salience of anti-dalit violence. Similarly, post-Independence politics would develop around the eligibility categories of welfare provision ("Scheduled" or "Backward" Castes, etc.) that were initially intended as temporary and reversible (ibid., 168).

8. Since the passing of the Government of India (Scheduled Castes) Order in 1936, the state had implicitly held a *religious* theory of caste as a Hindu institution (Kannanaikal 1983, 12–15). The Indian Constitutional (Scheduled Castes) Order of 1950 that excluded non-Hindus was amended in 1956 and in 1990 to include Sikhs and Buddhists respectively, and remains the object of campaigning by dalit Christians (see chapter 6) who are placed in the less prioritized, broad Backward Caste category, where they have to compete with regionally dominant caste groupings.

9. This shift in emphasis from Church ritual to state rights in fact evolved out of a complex dynamic of factional and intergenerational conflict among Alapuram Pallars.

10. This was the year of the deliberate massacre of forty-four dalit (Pallar and Paraiyar) farmworker women and children of Kilavenmani village in Thanjavur District, burned alive in a locked building following a labor dispute with landlords. It became a point of reference in dalit struggles in many respects, not least for the way it signaled the failure of Dravidian politics to take into account dalit interests (see M. R. Barnett 1976).

11. The predicament dalits face in concealing their Christianity to obtain caste certificates for employment registration (etc.), under the gaze of skeptical and aggressive officials, is the subject of much anguished personal commentary and novelistic description.

12. Deva Asirvatham's key texts are *Mūvēntar Yār?* [Who were/are the three great Tamil kings?] (1977) and *Vēḷāḷar Yār?* [Who were/are the Velalars?] (1981).

13. There is a parallel here with Ambedkar's adaptation of Jyotirao Phule's racial-conquest narrative, but an alternative valuation of agrarian settlement is involved (Rao 2009, 151).

14. Michael's narrative typically oscillated between historicizing and naturalizing the character-conditions of Pallars. He emphasized Pallar laboring inferiority, racialized by upper castes as "blackness." Then, while using a "black is beautiful" trope, he attributed his own ability to mediate with upper castes in the village to his fair skin. On politicized blackness among dalits, see Still 2007, 145.

15. By 2004 the society was holding regular meetings in the Alapuram area, advertised with leaflets that brought past and present politics together, proclaiming: "Our leader," Mavīraṉ Cuntaraliṅkam (the sword-wielding horse-backed Tamil king); "Our ancestors," Cera, Cola, Pantiyar (the three great Tamil royal seats); and "Our guide" (*valikāṭṭi*), the martyr Immanuel Sekaran.

16. Deva Asirvatham, personal communication, and letter to the *Indian Express,* 16 April 1980.

17. In the 1990s, the statewide Devēntira Kula Vēḷāḷar Federation allied with the Pattali Makkal Katchi (PMK), a "Backward Caste" political party at one time organized in opposition to Paraiyars in caste-violence-prone northern districts of the state.

18. Michael remembers his own (Konan) childhood isolated from the Pallar majority, being expected to play with Utaiyar and Vellalar children, warned about closeness to his "unclean" co-caste neighbors. His father, who unusually had married into the Konan lineage from a "lower status" Muṇṭamuḻi lineage (the first such marriage for two generations), was expected to separate himself from his kinsmen. Michael's own transgressive dowry-free "love marriage" to a woman from the disapproved of "tamarind tree" lineage brought an end to Konan claims to distinction. But he recalled his family contending with jibes, theft, fear of sorcery, and legal challenges to their property from neighbors resentful of their conceit; and how, unable to get co-caste people to work their landholdings, Konan Pallars depended upon Paraiyar laborers.

19. The widened marriage circles of Christians noted in chapter 3 (note 5) partly relate to this mobility (cf. Gough 1993; Kapadia 1993; Still 2007).

20. See de Certeau (1984, xix) on his distinction between a *strategy* of power and place, and a *tactic* that "insinuates itself into the other's place, fragmentarily, without taking it over in its entirety, without being able to keep it at a distance."

21. APD Gamon, 14–30 May 1913, 18 April 1914, 15 September 1915. At one point Paraiyars turned up to destroy the cross that Pallars had put up for prayer in their burial ground.

22. On the desperate situation of dalit Protestant converts post-Independence, see also Luke and Carmen (1968), Diehl (1965), Wiebe (1970), Koshy (1968), and Shiri (1977).

23. While Lily expressed a closeness to the goddess as much as to Jesus, and made vows and cut roosters for St. Anthony to protect the family's health, others like Roseamma were clear that joining the "mission church" meant giving up offerings to their lineage gods.

24. When his Catholic Utaiyar patron sent three measures of coriander and two and a half kilos of onions to his house, my Paraiyar friend Mohan preserved the relationship *and* his dignity by reciprocating with half a kilo of meat and vegetables at the next festival.

25. Upper-caste Catholic households washed and kept the menstrual "polluted sari," and gave the dhobi a new one.

26. Different responses to the continuing demands of patronage could lead to tensions across generations as well as genders within households. The personal independence of the vulnerable elderly with fragile entitlements rested upon continued servitude. Interestingly, a recent "National Rural Employment Guarantee Act" scheme, which makes the elderly income earners once again, may have begun to change this (Sri Raman 2009).

27. On the sharp contrast between future and past in forms of dalit modernity, see Still (2007, 107) and Ciotti (2006, 899).

28. Others, too, point out that Protestant Christian identity never displaces dalitness but rather marks difference *among* dalits through distinct forms of consumption, artifacts, habits, and forms of linguistic expression. The importance of education stands out, as does Bible reading identified as a source of articulate and confident speech (Rajan Krishnan, personal communication), although Alapuram Paraiyars in the 1980s could afford few tokens of Christian difference.

29. Zene (2007) suggests that such untouchable "origin myths" were indeed authored by others. But the point, as Vincentnathan (1993) notes, is that these caste Hindu motifs are given a Bakhtinian "second context." The myth contains a hidden dialogue or polemic.

30. In the 1980s, beef eating was indeed widely abandoned for its social rather than its moral effects, especially (I was told) after encouragement from visiting Congress Party minister P. Kakkan (a dalit himself). But an elderly Roseamma remembered the mission evangelist arriving many years earlier to find an empty church and people butchering a cow. When he furiously sprayed the carcass with mud and told them never to eat beef, it was not because the people were acting immorally, but because they had turned their back on the modernizing promise of Christianity. In 2004, Ragappan's negative reaction to his son-in-law's plans to start a beef-butchering business in the village came from a recollection of the time when other castes refused to enter their street because Paraiyars hung the meat to dry for storage. During my 1983–84 fieldwork, few considered beef eating morally wrong, polluting, or, in ethnosociological terms, "superheating" or stupefying (Still 2007, 156, 160); but neither was there any discourse on the rebellious virtues of beef eating (see chapter 6). Most were happy to eat beef with relatives in Paraiyar-only hamlets. Beef eating was part of the public discourse of caste rank, as in the myth one Paraiyar man used to sum up the relative power and rank of the three dalit castes: "Pallan and Paraiyan were sharing beef one day, but Pallan gave his beef to Cakkiliyan, who worked for him, saying, "We don't want to eat this. Cakkiliyan is like our son. Let him eat."

31. Likewise, some claimed a continuing relationship with Paraiyars, recognized in the Brahman wedding ceremony by leaving betel for Paraiyars under an *erukku* tree.

32. In 1983–84, an average Necavar household owned half an acre of dry land. They had been able to invest in the more secure (than sharecropping) land-mortgage tenure (otti), only a minority (30 percent) were landless, and none were still bound to aiya vitu servitude.

33. One day, I arranged to eat in Muthu's house. I turned up to find the house locked, discovering later that he had disappeared, fearing retribution for having the cheek to think he could entertain the *veḷḷaikkārar* (white man).

34. On the state-level intellectual mythmaking that later turned the humiliated Cakkiliyar into the dignified Arunthathiyar with high Tamil ancestry and royal lineage, see Kannan and Gros (2002, 45).

35. Unlike the more contractual relationships involved in otti land mortgage tenancy agreements, sharecropping carried a symbolic burden of obligation, and Paraiyar cultivators tended to avoid relationships of dependence with Pallar households. In all but 5 percent of cases, they sharecropped upper-caste land, yet Pallars were their most significant source of otti leases (16 percent).

36. If Pallar tales celebrated their martial bravery over Paraiyars' Brahman-like timidity, Paraiyars stereotyped the brutish stupidity of Pallars in contrast to their wit. But then many of these tales also conveyed the notion of the original unity and closeness of the two castes as brothers or cousins, often alluding to the practice of eating beef that divided and (in Pallar telling) ranked them.

37. Moffatt conflated both Dumont's own distinction between the structural form of society and its empirical causes, and Quine's distinction between rules that fit in a purely descriptive way and those that guide behavior (cf. Bourdieu 1977, 29).

38. This is what is meant by "role bifurcation." For example, in 1983–84 the dalit dhobi (Pothera Vannar) provided "priestly functions" but refused "death-polluted" substances at Pallar funerals (a Cakkiliyar woman came to take them away), just as at a Nadar girl's puberty ceremony that I attended, a Totti Paraiyar woman removed the charged items that the village dhobi refused.

39. Still (2007, 194) also notes that in Andhra Pradesh, "Baptists became known as Madiga religion, the Lutherans the Mala religion" and that "[Lutheran] Malas and [Catholic] Madigas maintained more distance from each other than they do with any other caste," working, worshipping, eating, and being educated separately (ibid.).

40. Tejani (2008) further explains how questions of class/caste that had been part of pre-Independence debates on minorities, communities, and nationalism became framed in terms of "secularism" understood in relation to *religion.* Ideas of community and the politics of religions minorities (constituencies of religion) after 1935 became antinational "communalism." Communalism and nationalism came to be defined together. This points to important changes in the way in which society negotiated religion.

41. Wingate reports that converts initially regarded Islam as religiously close to Christianity and continued their devotion to Christ, but that there was a gradual hardening of religious boundaries, with stronger connections to Muslim brothers in the towns (1999, 158).

42. Vincentnathan (1993, 76) points out that the causative form here—"he who has been made to go down"—differs from the caste Hindu label of dalits as *tāḻnta cāti,* "the caste that has gone down." The term *dalit* was used by Bharathi Desai in the 1930s when working for the self-respect movement (Holmström in Bama 2000).

43. Rajan Krishnan traces the articulation of this framework though a reading of the south Indian journal *Dalit Voice,* launched in the 1970s under the editorship of V.T. Rajshekar Shetty. His point is that emphasis on the ideational over the historical overplays the importance of ideological challenge (including religious conversion) without regard to the actuality of caste power and the economics of discrimination (2011, and personal communication).

44. Ambedkar's own idea of a political Buddhism with a close alliance between new Buddhists and an all-India untouchable party, the Republican Party, founded in 1958, failed. While the figure of Ambedkar grew in importance as a national dalit symbol, in political terms dalits tended to be incorporated into regional electoral coalitions (Mendelsohn and Vicziany 1998), and the Buddhist movement increasingly focused on a self-respect identity and a new *religious* culture unrelated to the wider political field (Zelliot 1966, 207ff).

45. The phrase was first used following the initial National Conference of Christian Dalits in 1985, organized by the Christian Dalit Liberation Movement (Prabhaker 1989, 35).

46. Some intellectuals within the orbit of Krishnaswamy argue that Pallars, already successfully upwardly mobile, should entirely reject the identity of "dalit," from which they have little to gain.

47. See Wyatt (2010) for an analysis of the shifting alignments of Tamil Nadu's party system within which dalit politics finds its place, and H. Gorringe (2005) for an account of the shift from Dalit Panther movement to political party.

48. A growing biographical and fictional literature now captures the diversity of Tamil

dalit Christian experience in the rich contradictions of everyday life, "its fears, its spirits and sensuality, and laughter" (Kannan and Gros 2002, 60). See novels by Bama (2000, 2008), Imayam (2001), and Gowthaman (2002) and commentary by Krishnan (2011).

CHAPTER 6

1. This short account, primarily drawing out the Indian Christian perspective, cannot but oversimplify the complexity of Hindu nationalism. I draw especially on Froerer 2007, Hansen 1999, Lobo 2002, Ludden 2005, van der Veer 1994, Sarkar 1999, and Suresh and Gopalakrishnan 2003.

2. See note 1 above. The Hindu reform Arya Samaj introduced rituals of purification (*shuddhi*) that "reconverted" dalit Christians as "twice born" Hindus (Jordens 1977).

3. Perhaps the most significant act setting this agenda was the 1992 demolition of the Babri Masjid (mosque) at Ayodhya claimed as the birthplace of the Hindu god Ram now recovered from oppressive Muslim rulers. The demolition was preceded by chariot processions (*yath rathra*) mobilizing religion-based support across the country organized by Bharatiya Janata Party (BJP) politician L. K. Advani (later home minister), which provoked large-scale violent clashes (see van der Veer 1994) .

4. Quoted in A. Xavier Arul Raj, "Hindutva and Our Response—An Outline," paper presented at the Tamil Nadu Bishops Council (TNBC), n.d. [ca. 2002].

5. Rashtriya Swayamsevak Sangh (RSS) chief K.S. Sudarshan ("Set Up Swadeshi Church: RSS," *The Hindu,* 8 October 2000). Sudarshan also claimed that the Church "is an arm of the West's defence forces" (Ramakrishnan 2000). The threat to Indian cultural identity of conversion to non-Hindu religions has been a repeating post-Independence theme since the Madhya Pradesh government's 1956 Niyogi inquiry on the conversion of tribals. There is an underlying Hindu antipathy to the project of Christian conversion. As M.K. Gandhi put it, "India's religions are adequate for her people. We need no converting spiritually" (*Collected Works* 45:320, in Claerhout and De Roover 2005). Different Hindu/Christian viewpoints and notions of "religion" apply. "While it is obvious to one party that belonging to a religion implies the need and the right to convert others to that religion, the other party shows nothing but incomprehension towards this professed link between religion and conversion"; and the universal freedom of conscience can be argued both ways (freedom to convert; freedom from conversion) (ibid.).

6. My Jesuit interlocutors here point to the way in which films reproduce othering stereotypes of Christians as evildoers, thugs, or licentious women who lead heroes astray (Fr. Paul Mike, personal communication). But see Jain (2009) on expectations of fair representations of Christians in current Indian filmmaking.

7. In this context, the pope's visit to India in 1999 and the attendant theological language of "planting the church" or "opening wide to Christ the doors of Asia" became a focus of protest (Lobo 2002, 28–29).

8. "Incidents of Atrocities [against] Christians: A Brief"; "Atrocities against Christians: 2000": reports supplied by the secretary of the Legal Cell of the Tamil Nadu Bishops' Conference. See Human Rights Watch 1999b; Lobo 2002.

9. Officially, from 2.8 percent in 1951 to 2.3 percent in 1991 and 2001.

10. The anti-Christian campaign also served to embarrass the Congress Party, whose party leader was Sonia Gandhi, the Italian Christian wife of assassinated Rajiv Gandhi.

11. For a discussion of the violence in north Indian states that followed the retabling of the Mandal Commission, see Engineer 1991.

12. One aspect of the conflict here between tribal (adivasi) and Christian dalits was that the latter had begun to claim tribal status so as to be eligible for Scheduled Tribe reservations denied to them as dalit Christians.

13. Tamil Nadu Ordinance no. 9 of 2002 (www.tn.gov.in/acts-rules/ord9–2002.htm) was promulgated by the governor on 5 October 2002 and replaced by a bill passed in the Assembly on 31 October 2002 amid strong protest from the opposition, including the DMK, Congress, and Communist parties.

14. Quoted in Scott Baldauf, "Religious Rights Take a Hit." Accessed 15 March 2005. www.hrwf.net/html/india2002.HTM#MadrasHighCo.

15. While the Sangh Parivar used the boasts of evangelistic American churches as support for its case that Christians were a threat to national security, Fernandes (1999) notes that closer scrutiny of claims of hundreds of thousands of new churches "reveals that by planting a church, these groups mean no more than that they have held prayer meetings in so many families. Most such families have not changed religions."

16. Mallampalli argues that in portraying Christian conversion as denationalizing, the Parivar merely adopts the British Raj's "image of the apostate convert's severance from Hindu family" and society (2004, 195). Mallampalli then researches the colonial origin of the political marginality of Tamil Catholics and Protestants. But the more important sociological point is that it is not primarily *as Christians* that their social-political identity has been forged. Christians are not isolated from indigenous institutions, and the marginality of Christians as an imagined religious community is the effect of their prior enrollment through caste identities.

17. See Fuller, 2001; Anandhi 1995; Rajadurai and Geetha 2002, 123.

18. "Conversion to Counter- Ordinance" *The Hindu,* 23 October 2002; Rajesh Chandramouli, "Dalits Warn of a Mega Conversion Drive," *Times of India,* Times News Network, 25 October 2002 (accessed 15 March 2005), http://timesofindia.indiatimes.com/articleshow/26292215.cms; Jill McGivering, "India Conversion Goes Ahead," BBC, 6 December 2002, http://news.bbc.co.uk/2/hi/south_asia/2549817.stm.

19. *Indian Express,* 10 June 2003.

20. *New Indian Express,* 3 July 2003; *Indian Express,* 30 June 2004.

21. Interview with the dalit lawyer and movement leader L. Yesumarian, 18 March 2009.

22. This ban was generally unpopular (among non-Brahman Hindus and Christians) and was lifted as a pre-poll gesture in February 2004 (accessed 15 June 2006; www.telegraphindia.com/1040221/asp/nation/story_2920345.asp).

23. Soosai v. UOI 1985 (Supp) S.C.C. 590 (Ministry of Minority Affairs 2009, 140). The latest demonstration on the Christian Scheduled Caste issue was a "Long March for Equal Rights to Dalit Christians" from Kanyakumari to Chennai, 10 February to 5 March 2010 (see http://dalitmarch.blogspot.com).

24. Rajan Krishnan's work on "the problem of the primacy accorded to the Hindu ontology of caste," whether framed by colonial orientalists, the state, or in the opposi-

tional discourse of dalit intellectuals, has helped clarify my thinking on this issue (personal communication, 2011).

25. James Massey notes that the three Christian leaders consulted—H. C. Mookerjee, Amrit Kaur, and Jerome D'Sousa—were respectively high caste, royal, and Jesuit by background (in Wingate 1999, 21).

26. In the mid-1970s, Jesuit superior general Pedro Arrupe gave leadership to the justice movement.

27. So named to invoke the ubiquitous palmyra trees that punctuate the Ramnad plains.

28. For a recent account of the history and range of Jesuit social action in the Madurai Province, see A.M. Xavier 2006. Dalit orientation within the Protestant Church was influenced by the parallel action-research of the Christian Institute of Religion and Society (CISRS) in Bangalore and the Madurai Tamilnadu Theological Seminary (TTS) and its Rural Theological Institute (RTI) under the leadership of Rev. Dayananda Carr.

29. Fr. Aloysius Irudayam recalls that when he went for his "account of conscience" at the congregation of Provincials in Loyola, the father general "observed that if the Church in Europe has lost the labour class at one point of time in history; and if the Society in USA has been losing the Blacks in recent times, the same situation should not happen in the Church/Society in India/Tamilnadu with regard to Dalits. For me these were prophetic statements which, deeply etched within me, influenced and energised me in my thinking and actions" (JMP 2002, 66–67).

30. Dalit priests were also encouraged by individual non-dalits such as Jesuit writer Mark Stephen, who trained dalit youth to agitate against Church discrimination, which he also exposed in Tamil Catholic magazines. It was Fr. Mark Stephen who drafted the Postulate, which was adopted as the Dalit Option, he says, before the still-conservative Society of Jesus had woken up to the implications of opening its institution to dalits (interview, 31 March 2009).

31. Further evidence appears in Sivasubramaniyan 2002; Thangaraj 2003; and Tamil Nadu Bishops' Council (TNBC) SC/ST/OBC Commission reports (available from the Commission Secretary, Udaya Deepam, Karumandapam, Tiruchirappalli, Tamil Nadu).

32. Bama, interviewed on her life as a teacher, 22 April 2009.

33. The dominant castes of a few villages contributed disproportionately to vocations, and a regional pattern ensured that, for example, Tutukudi was a Paravar diocese, Madurai a Vellalar diocese, Sivagangai an Utaiyar diocese (A. Raj 1992, 385)—a caste pattern entrenched by the selective bifurcation of dioceses.

34. Report of the TNBC Commission for SC/ST/BC 1998–99, in Thangaraj 2003, 57. Marginal increases mean that the Sivagangai diocese (in which Alapuram parish sits) had 1 dalit priest in 1990, but in 1999 still only 7 out of a total of 113, and that of 382 priests ordained in 1991–2001, 70 were dalits. But still, overall only 1 in 10 priests in the state were dalit, very few of them in positions of leadership.

35. The humiliation of publicly announced SC scholarships is a painful moment in the personal narratives of dalit writers (e.g., Bama [2002]).

36. Fr. "P," the first dalit (assistant) priest in Alapuram, faced not only this but the added dilemma that members of his own Paraiyar caste were discriminated against by

his Pallar parishioners and their "Brahmanical mentality," as he put it, and excluded from Pallar youth activism. He decided therefore to revive the *class*-based "Working People's Liberation Movement" founded by his predecessor. This was de facto dalit (since upper castes largely absented themselves from its social agenda) and allowed him to work equally with Protestant Paraiyars (see Mosse 2009, 186–87).

37. For some priests, caste is "an evil force that takes possession of thinking," as Jesuit Fr. "S" put it, echoing his nineteenth-century French forebears (chapter 4).

38. One could alternatively (M. S. S. Pandian 2008, 40) view experience and theory as distinct—akin to Tambiah's (1990) separation of the "discourse of causality" and the "discourse of participation," analytical reason and sympathetic performance—and being related through a process of multiple distancing.

39. Encouraged by Fr. Mark Stephen, but quite without the intention of publishing, Bama began writing as a means of coping with the trauma following her departure from her religious order. *Karukku* was later used in Jesuit formation houses, but Bama's own religious order dismissed the reference to casteism as fabrication, and to her surprise, the most intensely negative reactions initially came from her own people, claiming to be dishonored by her candid account (Bama, interview, 22 April 2009; Mark Stephen, interview, 31 March 2009).

40. There had been earlier (1940s and 1960s) and parallel Protestant agitations against casteism in the Church, but nothing so militant or sustained (see Thangaraj 2003).

41. While dalit women were active in the protests and agitation organized by the DCLM, Bama explained the absence of activist dalit nuns in terms of their subjection to an authority backed by caste *within*, and to the enormous social cost of *exit from*, religious orders. To live as an ex-nun, as a single woman in Tamil society, as Bama struggles to do, is hard. (Interview, 22 April 2009.)

42. See JMP 2002, 65; interviews with Fr. Jabamalairaja and Dr. Mary John; see Mosse 2009.

43. Letter to Apostolic Pro-Nuncio. Subject : "Request for an appointment with our Holy Father Pope John Paul II for our delegation during his visit to India in November 1999 to make a representation on Dalit Christians' problems."

44. Interviews in 2008–9 with dalit priests who were involved; compiled sources at the now-expired site http://eraiyurdalits.org; also S. Viswanathan (2008b); Anandhi (2008); Ragunathan (2008).

45. Dalit opinions are divided on such caste separation, some in favor and others insisting that this compromises the "Church free of caste," or that self-respect without respect of the other is meaningless and even reinscribes exclusion.

46. Dalits and Vanniyars would use the same bier (*tūmpā*) and church street for funeral processions (without percussive accompaniment); any new cemetery would be common; dalits would make festival contributions; but the processional route would not extend to their streets (*The Hindu*, 4 April 2008).

47. In strikingly Dumontian manner, this bishop further distinguished dangerous conflictual "class society" from a "caste society" that values harmony and hierarchy.

48. Dalit theology is a complex, diverse, and fast-growing field inspired by the Dalit Panther movement in Maharashtra and the dalit literature of the 1960s (itself drawing on

black American literature). Dalit theology was introduced, first, as a *historical* project to reclaim the history of the Church from its captivity in European mission narratives by beginning with the experience of the dalit majority (Webster 1992); second, as a *theological* project to reject the Brahmanical orientation of Indian Christian theology in favor of the lived reality of the dalit majority; and third, as a *sociological* project to confront the marginalization and ill treatment of dalits in the Church and to develop a new basis for ecclesiastical life. These different agendas are captured in the publications of the mid-1980s, especially Prabhakar 1989 and Irudayaraj 1988, which launched this ecumenical intellectual project. My brief account here also draws on Ayrookuzhiel 1990, 2006; Clarke 1999; Devasahayam 1992; Massey 1991, 1995, 1998; Nirmal 1990, 1998; A. Raj 1992; and Wilson 1982. For overviews see Wyatt 1996, 110 et seq.; and Oommen 2000. Clarke, Manchala, and Peacock 2010 is a recent collection written amid a more confident dalit movement and politics, amid a critique of the framework of "pain and pathos," but equally amid anxiety concerning "dalit" as a narrowing identity-bound discourse.

49. Leading practitioner James Massey insists that dalit Bible commentary involves reading scripture through dalit experience and context, directly and unmediated by other commentaries: "[W]ith only Bible and the notebook in my hand . . . I am in the text and in the [dalit] context . . . coming and going" (interview, Delhi, 29 June 2010; Massey 2010).

50. In some cases this is the recovery of a lost historical identity as ancient Buddhists suppressed by Brahmanism (Aloysius 1998; T. Dharmaraj, interview, Tirunelveli, 9 November 2009).

51. Dalit theology itself has a secular social "ontology of power and conflict," force and counterforce (Robbins 2006, with reference to Milbank 1991). It is as suspicious of the theological ontology of unity and peace as of the integration and holism of Jesuit-Brahmanical anthropology.

52. Such religiosity "reinstates" as dalit deities those popular heroes who were believed to have been persecuted by Brahmanic religionists (and incorporated as forms of Siva) or the land-earth and ancestor figures. Wounded hero figures are aligned iconographically to Christian saints such as St. Sebastian installed in dalit churches, and theologically to Jesus the suffering God as dalit. A well-known ex-Catholic priest recently established a "dalit ashram" figuring "booshakti"—symbolized earth as source of energy—as a central symbol in dalit religion (Jyoti and Raj 2005), while the ex-nun Bama spoke to me of a personal dalit spirituality in terms of the caring presence of ancestors (interview, April 2009).

53. The earlier-mentioned CISRS and the Tamilnadu Theological Seminary (TTS), along with Jesuit centers such as the Folklore Resources and Research Centre at Palayamkottai.

54. The exemplar of resignification was perhaps the cross—a symbol of shame, criminality, and punishment turned into a symbol of liberation.

55. See Tilche 2011 for a parallel exploration of the social making of *adivasi* art and culture drawing on the work of Gell (1998) and of Webb Keane.

56. Fr. Yesumarian, who faced repeated harassment, arrest, and imprisonment in this struggle, explains that for this effect the statues should be *breakable* (interview, 18 March 2009).

57. A ubiquitous criticism of dalit political leaders is that they are involved in lucrative dispute settlement and informal deals outside local courts and police stations known as

kaṭṭā pañcāyattu or "kangaroo courts." The trajectory of dalit parties and the complex dilemmas of dalit identity politics are beyond the scope of the present discussion. (See Gorringe 2005a, 2005b.)

58. Chandra Bose, interview, 23 November 2004; *The Hindu,* 24 May 2002, in *Thamukku* 3, no. 11 (May–June 2002); Athiyaman 2003.

59. I draw these views from a series of interviews with Pallar and Aruthathyar activists conducted in Tirunelveli, Madurai, and Tiruppur in autumn 2009. I am grateful to T. Dharmaraj for his explanations of contemporary dalit cultural politics.

60. Although, interestingly, early leadership in both the DCLM and the DPI was with Pallar individuals. The prominence of Paraiyars may have to do with the greater mobility and urbanization of Paraiyars predominating in districts close to Chennai—the political and media center from which dalit movements have been communicated (T. Dharmaraj, personal communication; Kannan and Gros 2002, 42 ff.; Barnett and Barnett 1973).

61. The Jesuit "Karisal" program started in Viruthunagar District among Hindu Arunthathiyars by Fr. Mark Stephen and Fr. Michaelraj—priests who initially concealed their Catholic identity in order to emphasize solidarity with a subjugated and stigmatized group—in particular was the crucible forming several important Arunthathiyar leaders.

CHAPTER 7

1. Francis Jayapathy, SJ (personal communication), first pointed out to me a significant change in south Indian public discourse on identity politics in the past twenty years, especially as a result of the media, including television, which is present in virtually every village. Through instant communication of events using the same words and statements (interpretations), and the same commentary on repeating stories, a statewide discourse of dramatic communal politics is produced. However, the use of a common language has not actually influenced social practices, even as it continually represents local conflicts (of all kinds) in communal terms. I am grateful to Hugo Gorringe for suggesting the relevance of Bauman's theorization here.

2. For example, in 2009 the bus conductor Velu arranged a drama to follow the festival of his Necavar Paraiyar caste deity Munisvarar in the formerly excluding space in front of the Aiyanar temple.

3. As Littlewood argues, "[A] new dispensation demands that details, indeed memories, of the old ways be forgotten as fresh ideals and modes of action become paramount" (2009, 113); meanwhile dalit Christian activists actively perpetuate the mobilizing memory of caste discrimination in Catholic worship.

4. This non-American church, founded in the 1920s, with fifteen thousand members in Tamil Nadu by 1994, has a reputation for separatism, an exclusive doctrine, and refusing contact with other Pentecostal churches (Bergunder 2005, 193–95; 2008, 309).

5. In two cases where Hindu women were baptized, they had been brought to the Pentecostal Mission by their families after suffering from spirit attack or mental illness (interviews, March 2009).

6. Elsewhere, aggressive assertions of caste spatial politics involve the substitution of private property and trespass for caste as a basis of exclusion, through building walls or

barriers, or extending buildings, enclosing space, or blocking routes (Rao 2009). See the infamous case of Uthapuram village, Madurai (S. Viswanathan 2008a).

7. Dalits are also less likely than in the past to be asked about their caste directly, and more often by older people. The different effects and perceptions of dalit caste identification are the subject of current research.

8. This I discovered when replacing household clay pots with plastic ones, which halved the time for the task of the young Cakkilyar woman who brought water to my house, since upper-caste women were now willing to help lift the full vessel onto her head, whereas she previously waited for a dalit woman to cross the tank to assist her.

9. Following Bate (2009, 79–80), one could say that the "public" space has become socially unenclosed (*puṟam*, "outer"), having been denuded of its "interior" (*akam*) moral-social-caste character.

10. An example of this inner-outer blurring was given to me by Sebastian Pallar. At the St. Anthony festival in 2009, ponkal rice prepared in the private space of residential-caste devotional groups was then mixed in the church for distribution to all. The Catholic priest, suspecting that some of his congregation might try to avoid rice from the common pot, announced that "people following old habits (*paḻaiyakālattu paḻakkavaḻakkam pākupāṭu pākkira ālkaḷ*) can leave the church now."

11. Let me be clear: I am here referring to the "hidden" casteism attributed to others. I am not speculating on the history of the interiority of caste per se, which would for several reasons be hazardous. See A. Pandian 2009 for an extended discussion of mind-heart and the cultivation of affect and virtue in a Tamil setting.

12. The pervasive public discourse of communalism may itself discourage speaking openly of caste amid continued caste practice (Francis Jayapathy, personal communication).

13. Use of the phrase "being social" to convey a modern departure from conventional social roles and obligations has been popularized through movies. It is a reference to certain permissive changes from social norms or hierarchies in caste, gender, parent–child, or interreligious relations (Sundara Babu, personal communication).

14. Today, too many are caught in the broad sweep of this moral narrative of modernity for this to be an account of specifically Christian influence (cf. Keane 2007, 73), although the historical influence of missionization remains significant.

15. By 2009 there were as many as 105 small businesses in the village center, four times the number in 1984: provisions stores, photocopying and telephone shops, a sawmill, butchers, ironmongers, medical shops, barber salons, clothes shops and tailors, blacksmiths and electrical shops, bicycle-repair, vegetable, or fertilizer stores.

16. Tractors and plastic pots contributed to the disappearance of cutantaram relationships with village carpenters and potters.

17. "They come for festivals, worship the dead, and go" (*tiruviḻāviṟku varuvārkaḷ iṟantavarkaḷai kumpiṭa varuvarkaḷ pōvarkaḷ*), as Lurtucami Vellalar put it.

18. In 2009, the headmaster's records suggested that 80 percent of students continued in the school after tenth year and that in the "plus two" (eleventh and twelfth) years, girls outnumbered boys by five to four.

19. On the high perceived returns from investment in human capital (education and

health) by south Indian dalits given relatively inferior extended family networks, see Luke and Munshi (2007) and Ayres and Simon (2003, 216–17).

20. Advances to agents of sixty-five to eighty-five thousand rupees for these opportunities are as expensive as college "donations" and fees, and riskier given fraudsters, fake work permits, and unskilled wages that fall well short of expectations, as recent returnees to Alapuram explained in their tales of hardship and exploitation.

21. In 2009–10, my assistant M. Sivan revisited some sixty families of different castes to ask about the route to work of their sons and daughters. The importance of both kin networks and finance—connections and capital—to entry into higher education or employment in public or private sectors was clear. Relatively few dalit families were able to substitute reliance on SC quotas, district employment offices, or SC loan schemes, and scholarships were a small contribution to the overall costs of usable professional qualifications. Raising capital for jobs or business required land to sell or mortgage, or jewelry to pawn. It was also clear how the circulation of capital through dowry payments and receipts was linked to income and employment so as to reproduce the caste-class differentiation of opportunity. One hundred sixty grams of gold jewelry, household goods, and a moped costing another thirty thousand rupees were common as a "bridegroom price" (Caplan 1984) for well-employed (non-kin, aṉṉiyam) spouses; and incoming dowries raise essential job-finding capital. Narratives of employment, of course, also included the importance of good qualifications and the connection of college friends, work colleagues, and the Church as well as unmediated application processes and personal talent and drive.

22. The All India Catholic University Federation (AICUF) played a particularly important role in shaping ideologies, fostering dalit activism, and providing resources for Christian dalit university students in ways that are being explored in current research.

23. Educated youth who bring ideas of the city to the village with fashionably cut "shirt and pant" are ambiguous figures. Those who fail to negotiate the boundary between urban life and village home—appropriately interchanging jeans and lungis—become the object of ridicule from their peers. For example, Bama's character Jayaraju, who "land[s] up at the [village] bus stop with shirt all tucked in, and wearing dark glasses," clothes his dalit identity with a feigned urban outsider's ignorance of his village, and asks the way to the "R.C. [Roman Catholic] street" (2008, 23). The humor is in the misjudgment of a regularly negotiated social-spatial transition—a joke on the one who fails deftly to interchange urban and village ways.

24. Stephen says that the Maravar–Pallar conflict that erupted at one nearby John Pandian meeting he attended held up forty buses, burned fifteen haystacks, and damaged one thousand banana trees. Comparing John Pandian and the party leader Dr. Krishnaswamy, another commented, "Krishnaswamy is for voting; John Pandian is for fighting." But it was barring Pandian's participation in the 11 September 2011 commemoration of the dalit martyr Immanuel Sekaran that preceded the protest and lethal police firing on dalits noted earlier (p. 309n6).

25. In terms of current debates on youth and masculinity, it could be said that the presentational strategies of this group brought together the often divided cultural styles of "educated moderns" and "violent hypermasculinity," the latter captured in the epithet

"rowdy"—a category acted out with reference to the "street-wise, quick witted, educated rowdy" of film fight scenes (Still 2007, 120) and officialized by a "rowdy list" kept by the local police on which Stephen's name apparently appeared— but without the sexual harassment of upper-caste women reported by Anandhi, Jeyaranjan, and Krishnan (2002) and Rogers (2008) (see "Rowdy-Sheeted Element," *The Hindu,* 17 February 2005). The question of how Tamil dalit assertions are linked to "emergent forms of caste masculinity" (Rao 2009, 68) and whether these take aggressive forms of "hypermasculinity" (linked to drinking, martial arts, bodybuilding, or the sexual conquest or instrumental harassment of non-dalit women), and the connection of this to the historical emasculation of dalit men in upper-caste practice (for example, ensuring the failure of dalit men to protect the sexuality of their women), has been the subject of continuing and controversial academic debate (see Lakshmanan 2004; Rogers 2005; and Osella and Osella 2006). Still (2007, 104) rightly argues for doubt and uncertainty regarding dalit masculine models and strikes the right note by concluding, "Dalit men negotiate the dilemmas of how to be respectful yet not obsequious, manly yet moral, aggressive but not mindless, often with slightly different outcomes."

26. Commonly, as Hugo Gorringe (2005a) notes, dalit-movement flags mark the residential territory of dalit castes—a domain delimited rather as that of a lineage or "watcher" (kaval) deity. Placing the "JP" billboard in the public (or church) space did provoke complaint, but village leaders agreed to keep the peace by letting it stand.

27. In 2004, all but three of the higher secondary school's twenty-seven teachers were non-dalit.

28. Interviews, Alapuram, November 2004.

29. In the Paraiyar street, youth-led collective activism had always been weaker, and brokerage styles of leadership mediating state and NGO benefits predominated. Israel, a CSI catechist and Paraiyar street prominent, built his political reputation and stood for Panchayat Union election by mediating NGO and CSI Church welfare and service delivery including brokering scholarships, training, literacy programs, jobs in church institutions, roads to the dalit colony, and the like.

30. Despite boycotting state elections (as an ineffective means to break the feudal relations of caste), the Martyr Immanuel movement has contributed to the success of Pallar-caste-based political parties.

31. Ongoing research on attitudes to associations and conflict resolution (differentiated by gender, caste, age, education, employment, etc) gives little evidence of caste "politicization" among Alapuram's dalits. "Dalit" remains an unfamiliar concept, and links to wider caste politics are weak.

32. There are in fact different associational forms in the village. Others arise from the interventions of especially dalit-led NGOs. These are commonly gendered: male youth are enrolled onto fronts or movements around land or common property, while women are brought together street- or caste-wise into savings and credit groups. The intersection of these activities with village-level politics and caste relations is a subject of separate study.

GLOSSARY

This glossary only includes terms that are used repeatedly in the book. For caste names, the respectful and currently used "-ar" ending is employed rather than the formerly common and disrespectful "-an" (i.e., Paḷḷar *or* Uṭaiyār, *rather than* Paḷḷan *or* Uṭaiyān*). Diacritics on proper names are omitted after their first appearance in the text.*

ampalam	Maravar village headman (or *ampaḷakkārar*)
acanti	a Catholic funeral bier
Ācāri	carpenter caste
aciṅkam	degrading, uncivilized, or shameful
aiyā vīṭu	house of the landlord patron
Āṭi	the Tamil month July–August
aṭimai	slavery, servitude
bhakti	devotion
Cakkiliyar	leather-worker caste (Arunthathiyar)
cāmi	a deity; honorific term of address
cāmiyār	Catholic priest
cantippu	honorific gift to an important person (king or Catholic priest)
capparam	processional platform on which statues of saints/deities ride
cāti	caste
cattatēr	large wheeled processional chariot or "car"
Cētupati	Maravar monarch of the Ramnad kingdom
Cītēvi	good fortune, the goddess Lakshmi

cutantaram	(or *cuvantiram*) caste-linked grain-share payment to a village officer or servant
Devēntira Kula Vēḷāḷar	Pallar caste
iṉām	(Arabic) a gift; tax-free grants of land and water by rulers; i.e., a gift of the ruler's revenue share of village produce
iṉāmtār	holder of an inam
kaipiccai	"hand alms"
kaḷam	threshing floor
kaḷampuṭikkira vīṭu	"house that takes from the threshing floor"; a dependent servant
kaṇakkupiḷḷai	Vellalar-caste village accountant
kaṉṉi	virgin
karṇam	Vellalar-caste village accountant
kāṭu	forest; uncultivated wasteland
kirāmam	village (*kirāma teyvam*—village deity)
Kōṉār	pastoralist; shepherd caste
koṭimaram	ceremonial flag post
kōvil	church or temple
kōvil mariyātai	temple/church honors distributed at festivals
kōvilpiḷḷai	Vellalar Catholic catechist
kuṭi	resident, inhabitant, villager
kuṭimakkaḷ	village servants
kuṭumpaṉ	Pallar caste measurer of "shares" (*varam*) on the threshing floor
Lūrtūmātā	Our Lady of Lourdes
maṇṭakappaṭi	payment for the saint or deity to be taken in procession on one of the nights of a festival
maṇṭakappaṭikārar	family, caste, or village group holding a mantakappati
Maṟavar	warrior caste
Maṟavarnāṭu	"Maravar country" or Ramnad and Sivagangai
mariyātai	respect, honor, distinction
mātā	mother; the Virgin Mary
mēḷam	temple drum
mēlvīṭu /kīḻvīṭu	upper house/ lower house
mutal mariyātai	first respect/honor
Nāṭār (Nadar)	caste associated with tapping palm wine or toddy
nākarīkam	civility, urbanity
nāṭṭampaḷam	Maravar chief of a *natu*

nāṭṭār	chiefs of the *natu*
nāṭu	region, tract, division of the country
ōlai	palm leaf (manuscript)
Paḷḷar	dalit cultivators/laborer caste (Deventira Kula Velalar)
panchayat; Panchayat	a council; statutory body of local government
paṅku	share, sharecropping; a parish
paṇṭāram	Pallar Catholic catechist
paṇṭāracāmi	(pantaracuvami) Jesuit missionary serving non-Brahman castes
paṟai	frame drum of Paraiyars (see *tappu*)
pēy-picācu	evil spirit, demon, ghost
poṅkal	ceremonial overboiling of rice; the harvest festival
pūcai	Catholic Mass (*puja*)
pūcari	a temple priest
purohit	classically trained Brahman domestic priest
sanniyāsi	(*canniyāci*) a renouncer or mendicant
Santiyākappar	St. James the Greater
taccaṇai	(*taṭcaṇai*, Sk. *daksina*) a gift to a ritual specialist
tappu	(*paṟai*) Paraiyar frame drum made from calf skin
tēr	processional car
tīṭṭu	impurity, pollution
tōṭṭi	Paraiyar village servant
Tōṭṭi Paṟaiyar	Protestant Christian Paraiyar subcaste
ūḷḷūr	inside village; *ūrmakkaḷ*—upper-caste villagers
ūr	place, village
Uṭaiyār	agricultural caste
Vaṇṇan	washerman caste
Veḷḷāḷar	high-status non-Brahman caste acting as village accountants and holding catechist offices

REFERENCES

ARCHIVES CONSULTED

India Office Collections, British Library, London.

Jesuit Madurai Mission Archives (JMMA), Shembaganur, Tamil Nadu. Missionary correspondence, parish diaries, notebooks.

Parish Records, Sarukani Parish, "Alapuram" Parish. Diaries, notebooks, parish records.

Sivagangai Samasthanam Record Office (SSRO). Miscellaneous revenue and administrative records and surveys; district-court cases.

Tamil Nadu State Archives (TNA). Madurai District records (including settlement reports); Court of Wards, Board of Revenue.

BOOKS, ARTICLES, AND OTHER REFERENCES

Adler, Judith. 2006. Cultivating Wilderness: Environmentalism and Legacies of Early Christian Asceticism. *Comparative Studies of History and Society* 48 (1): 4–37.

Aloysius, G. 1998. *Religion as Emancipatory Identity: A Buddhist Movement Among the Tamils Under Colonialism.* New Delhi: New Age International Publishers for the Christian Institute for the Study of Religion and Society.

Amaladass, Anand, and Francis X. Clooney. 2005. *Preaching Wisdom to the Wise: Three Treatises by Roberto de Nobili in Dialogue with the Learned Hindus of South India.* St. Louis: Institute of Jesuit Sources.

Amaladoss, M. 2007. Roberto de Nobili's Attitude to Other Religions. In *Interculturation of Religion: Critical Perspectives on Robert de Nobili's Mission in India,* edited by C. J. Arun, 42–52. Bangalore: Asian Trading Corporation.

Ambedkar, B. R. 1982. What Path Salvation. In *Thus Spoke Ambedkar,* vol. 4, edited by Bhagwan Das. Bangalore: Ambedkar Sahithya Prakashana.

Anandhi, S. 1995. *Contending Identities: Dalits and Secular Politics in Madras Slums.* Delhi: Indian Social Institute.

———. 2008. The Elusive Peace at Eraiyur: Dalit Christians Demand Justice. Unpublished paper.

Anandhi, S., J. Jeyaranjan, and Rajan Krishnan. 2002. Work, Caste and Competing Masculinities: Notes from a Tamil Village. *Economic and Political Weekly* 37 (43): 4397–4406.

Anderson, Benedict. 1991. *Imagined Communities: Reflections on the Origin and Spread of Nationalism.* Rev. ed. London and New York: Verso.

Appadurai, Arjun. 1981. *Worship and Conflict under Colonial Rule.* Cambridge: Cambridge University Press.

———. 2004. The Capacity to Aspire: Culture and the Terms of Recognition. In *Culture and Public Action,* edited by V. Rao and M. Walton, 59–84. Stanford, CA: Stanford University Press.

Aranha, Paolo. 2010. Sacramenti o saṃskārāḥ? L'illusione dell'accommodatio nella controversia dei riti malabarici. *Cristianesimo nella Storia* 31:621–46.

———. 2011. The Social and Physical Spaces of the Malabar Rites Controversy, 17th–18th Centuries. Paper presented at the international workshop "Space and Conversion: Urban Stages, Institutions and Interiority (16th–20th Centuries)," Scuola Normale Superiore, Pisa, Italy, December.

———. 2012. Malabar Rites: An Eighteenth-Century Conflict on the Catholic Missions in South India. PhD thesis, European University Institute, Florence, Italy.

Armstrong, Karen. 2009. *The Case for God: What Religion Really Means.* London: Bodley Head.

Arokiasamy, S. 2007. Development of Theological Languages in the Context of Encounter with Cultures and Religions. In *Interculturation of Religion: Critical Perspectives on Robert de Nobili's Mission in India,* edited by C. J. Arun, 68–82. Bangalore: Asian Trading Corporation.

Arrupe, Pedro. 1981 [1978]. Letter to the Whole Society on Inculturation. In *Other Apostolates Today: Selected Letters and Addresses of Pedro Arrupe,* vol. 3, edited by J. Aixala, 172–81. St. Louis: Institute of Jesuit Sources.

Arulnathan, Selvaraj. 2010. A Philosophical Reading of Social Consciousness with Special Reference to Dalit and Black Identity. PhD thesis, Madurai Kamaraj University, Madurai, India.

Arulraja, M. R. 1996. *Jesus the Dalit.* Hyderabad: Volunteer Centre.

Arun, C. Joe. 2007a. *Constructing Dalit Identity.* Jaipur and New Delhi: Rawat Publications.

———. 2007b. Introduction: Revisiting de Nobili's Mission to Tamil Nadu. In *Interculturation of Religion: Critical Perspectives on Robert de Nobili's Mission in India,* edited by C. J. Arun, 1–18. Bangalore: Asian Trading Corporation.

Asad, Talal. 1993. *Genealogies of Religion: Discipline and Reasons of Power in Christianity and Islam.* Baltimore: Johns Hopkins University Press.

———. 2002. The Construction of Religion as an Anthropological Category. In *A Reader in the Anthropology of Religion,* edited by Michael Lambek, 114–32. Oxford: Blackwell Publishing.

———. 2008. Thinking about Religion, Belief and Politics: Exploration of Religion and "Belief." Foerster lecture, 22 June 2009. First air date: 8 December 2008. www.uctv.tv/search-moreresults.aspx?contactID = 103030.

Asirvatham, R. Deva. 1977. *Mūvēntar Yār?* [Who were/are the three great Tamil kings?] Thanjavur: Irama Tevan Padippakam.

———. 1981. *Vēḷāḷar Yār?* [Who were/are the Velalars?] Thanjavur: Irama Tevan Padippakam.

Assadi, Muzaffar. 1996. Attack on Multinationals: Re-enactment of Gandhian Violence. *Economic and Political Weekly* 31 (20): 1184–86.

Athiyaman. 2003. Interview with Mr Athiyaman. *Thamukku* 5 (15): 1–2.

Ayres, Ron, and Manuela Torrijos Simon. 2003. Education, Poverty and Sustainable Livelihoods in Tamil Nadu: Inequalities, Opportunities and Constraints. *Review of Political Economy* 15 (2): 211–29.

Ayrookuzhiel, A. M. Abraham. 1990. Towards a Creation of Counter-Culture: Problems and Possibilities. In *Emerging Dalit Theology*, edited by Xavier Irudayaraj, 64–70. Madras and Madurai: Jesuit Theological Secretariat and Tamilnadu Theological Seminary.

———. 2006. *Essays on Dalits, Religion and Liberation*. Bangalore: Christian Institute for the Study of Religion and Society, Asian Trading Corporation.

Babb, Lawrence A., and Susan S. Wadley, eds. 1995. *Media and the Transformation of Religion in South Asia*. Philadelphia: University of Pennsylvania Press.

Baker, Christopher John. 1984. *An Indian Rural Economy, 1880–1955: The Tamilnad Countryside*. Oxford: Clarendon Press.

Balaganghadara, S. N. 2010. The Dark Side of the Secular: Defining "Religions" in Colonial India. Paper presented at the conference "Religious-Secular Distinctions," British Academy, London, 14–16 January.

Ballhatchet, Kenneth. 1998. *Caste, Class and Catholicism in India, 1789–1914*. Richmond, Surrey: Curzon Press.

Bama. 2000. *Karukku*. Translated by Lakshmi Holmström. Chennai: Macmillan.

———. 2005. *Sangati*. Translated by Lakshmi Holmström. New Delhi: Oxford University Press.

———. 2008. *Vanmam: Vendetta*. Translated by Malini Seshadri. New Delhi: Oxford University Press.

Barnes, R. H. 1982. A Catholic Mission and the Purification of Culture: Experiences in an Indonesian Community. *Journal of the Anthropological Society of Oxford* 23 (2): 169–80.

Barnett, Marguerite Ross, and Steve Barnett. 1973. Contemporary Peasant and Post-Peasant Alternatives in South India: The Ideas of a Militant Untouchable. *Annals of the New York Academy of Sciences* 220 (6): 385–410.

Barnett, Marguerite Ross. 1976. *The Politics of Cultural Nationalism in South India*. Princeton, NJ: Princeton University Press.

Barnett, Steve. 1976. Coconuts and Gold: Relational Identity in a South Indian Caste. *Contributions to Indian Sociology*, n.s., 10 (1): 133–56

———. 1977. Identity, Choice and Caste Ideology in Contemporary South India. In *The*

New Wind: Changing Identities in South Asia, edited by Kenneth David, 393–441. The Hague and Paris: Mouton.

Bate, Bernard. 2005. Arumuga Navalar, Saivite Sermons and the Delimitation of Religion, c. 1850. *Indian Economic Social History Review* 42 (4): 469–84.

———. 2009. *Tamil Oratory and the Dravidian Aesthetic.* New York: Columbia University Press.

Baumann, Gerd. 1997. Dominant and Demotic Discourses of Culture: Their Relevance to Multi-Ethnic Alliances. In *Debating Cultural Hybridity: Multi-Cultural Identities and the Politics of Anti-Racism,* edited by R. Werbner and T. Modood, 209–25. London: Zed Books.

Baumann, Gerd, and André Gingrich, eds. 2005. *Grammars of Identity/Alterity: A Structural Approach.* Oxford and New York: Berghahn Books.

Bayly, C. A. 1985. The Pre-History of "Communalism"? Religious Conflict in India, 1700–1860. *Modern Asian Studies* 19 (2): 177–203.

Bayly (née Kaufmann), S. B. 1981. A Christian Caste in Hindu Society: Religious Leadership and Social Conflict among the Paravars of Southern Tamilnadu. *Modern Asian Studies* 15 (2): 203–34.

———. 1989. *Saints, Goddesses and Kings: Muslims and Christians in South Indian Society, 1700–1900.* Cambridge: Cambridge University Press.

———. 1999. *Caste, Society and Politics in India from the Eighteenth Century to the Modern Age.* Cambridge: Cambridge University Press.

Beck, B. E. F. 1972. *Peasant Society in Konku: A Study of Right and Left Subcastes in South India.* Vancouver: University of British Columbia Press.

———. 1981. The Goddess and the Demon: A Local South Indian Festival and Its Wider Context. *Puruṣārtha* 5:83–136.

Bede, the Venerable Saint, 1969. *Ecclesiastical History of the English People I,* xxx, *Bede's Ecclesiastical History.* Edited and translated by Bertram Colgrave and R. A. B. Mynors. Oxford: Clarendon Press.

Beidelman, Thomas O. 1982. *Colonial Evangelism: A Socio-Historical Study of an East African Mission at the Grassroots.* Bloomington: Indiana University Press.

Bellah, Robert N. 1964. Religious Evolution. *American Sociological Review* 29 (3): 358–74.

Bergunder, Michael. 2002. The "Pure Tamil Movement" and Bible Translation: The Ecumenical Thiruviviliam of 1995. In *Christians, Cultural Interactions and India's Religious Traditions,* edited by Judith M. Brown, Robert E. Frykenberg, and Alain E. Low, 212–31. Grand Rapids, MI, and Cambridge: William B. Eerdmans Publishing Company; London: Routledge Curzon.

———. 2005. Constructing Indian Pentecostalism: On Issues of Methodology and Representation. In *Asian and Pentecostal: The Charismatic Face of Christianity in Asia,* edited by Allan Anderson and Edmond Tang, 177–213. Oxford: OCMS.

———. 2008. *The South Indian Pentecostal Movement in the Twentieth Century.* Grand Rapids, MI, and Cambridge: William B. Eerdmans Publishing Company.

Bertrand, Joseph. 1848. *La Mission du Maduré: D'après des Documents Inédits.* Vol. 2. Paris: Librairie de Poussielgue-Rusand.

———, ed. 1865. *Lettres édifiantes et curieuses de la nouvelle mission du Maduré.* 2 vols. Paris: J. B. Pélagaud.

Besse, Leon. 1914. *La Mission du Maduré: Historique de ses Pangous.* Tiruchinapoly: Mission Catholique.

Bhabha, Homi. 1994. *The Location of Culture.* London and New York: Routledge.

Bialecki, Jon, Naomi Haynes, and Joel Robbins. 2008. The Anthropology of Christianity. *Religion Compass* 2 (6): 1139–58.

Biardeau, Madeleine. 1965. Ahamkara, the Ego Principle in the Upanishads. *Contributions to Indian Sociology* 8:62–84.

———. 1976. Le Sacrifice dans l'Hindouisme. In *Le Sacrifice dans l'Inde ancienne,* edited by M. Biardeau and C. Malamoud. Paris: Presses Université de France.

———. 1989. *Hinduism: The Anthropology of a Civilisation.* Delhi: Oxford University Press.

Blackburn, Stuart H. 1985. Death and Deification: Folk Cults in Hinduism. *History of Religions* 24 (3): 255–274.

Bloch, Maurice, and Jonathan Parry, eds. 1982. *Death and the Regeneration of Life.* Cambridge: Cambridge University Press.

Bloomer, Kristin. 2008. Making Mary: Hinduism, Roman Catholicism and Spirit Possession in Tamil Nadu, South India. PhD thesis, University of Chicago.

Boddy, Janice. 1994. Spirit Possession Revisited: Beyond Instrumentality. *Annual Review of Anthropology* 23:407–34.

Bourdieu, Pierre. 1977. *Outline of a Theory of Practice.* Translated by R. Nice. Cambridge: Cambridge University Press.

———. 1991. *Language and Symbolic Power.* Cambridge: Polity Press.

Boyd, Robin H.S. 1975. *An Introduction to Indian Christian Theology.* Madras: Christian Literature Society.

Breckenridge, Carol A. 1985. Social Storage and the Extension of Agriculture in South India, 1350–1750. In *Vijayanagara—City and Empire: New Currents of Research,* edited by A.L. Dallapiccola, 41–72. Stuttgart: Steiner Verlag Wiesbaden.

Brown, Leslie. 1982 [1956]. *The Indian Christians of St. Thomas: An Account of the Ancient Syrian Church of Malabar.* Cambridge: Cambridge University Press.

Brown, Peter. 1981. *The Cult of Saints: Its Rise and Function in Latin Christianity.* Chicago: University of Chicago Press.

Bugge, Henrietta. 1994. *Mission and Tamil Society.* Richmond: Curzon Press.

Burghart, Richard. 1983. Renunciation in the Religious Tradition of South Asia. *Man,* n.s., 18 (4): 635–53.

———. 1990. Ethnographers and Their Local Counterparts in India. In *Localising Strategies: Regional Traditions of Ethnographic Writing,* edited by R. Fardon, 260–78. Edinburgh: Scottish Academic Press.

Burkhart, G. 1976. On the Absence of Descent Groups among Some Udaiyars of South India. *Contributions to Indian Sociology,* n.s., 10 (1): 31–61.

Burridge, Kenelm. 1973. *Encountering Aborigines, a Case Study: Anthropology and the Australian Aboriginal.* New York: Pergamon Press.

———. 1979. *Someone, No One: Essays on Individuality.* Princeton, NJ: Princeton University Press.

Busby, Cecilia. 1997. Permeable and Partible Persons: A Comparative Analysis of Gender and Body in South India and Melanesia. *Journal of the Royal Anthropological Institute* 3 (2): 261–78.

———. 2006. Renewable Icons: Concepts of Religious Power in a Fishing Village in South India. In *The Anthropology of Christianity,* edited by Fenella Cannell, 77–98. Durham, NC, and London: Duke University Press.

Cannell, Fenella. 1995. The Imitation of Christ in Bicol, Philippines. *Journal of the Royal Anthropological Institute,* n.s., 1 (2): 377–94.

———. 2005. The Christianity of Anthropology. *Journal of the Royal Anthropological Institute,* n.s., 11 (2): 335–56.

———, ed. 2006. *The Anthropology of Christianity.* Durham, NC: Duke University Press.

———. 2007. Comment on Joel Robbins's "Continuity Thinking and the Problem of Christian Culture: Belief, Time and the Anthropology of Christianity." *Current Anthropology* 48 (1): 3–38.

Caplan, Lionel. 1980a. Caste and Castelessness among South Indian Christians. *Contributions to Indian Sociology,* n.s., 14:213–38.

———. 1980b. Class and Christianity in South India: Indigenous Responses to Western Denominationalism. *Modern Asian Studies* 14 (4): 645–71.

———. 1983. Popular Christianity in Urban South India. *Religion and Society* 30 (2): 28–44.

———. 1984. Bridegroom Price in Urban India. Class, Caste, and "Dowry Evil" among Christians in Madras. *Man* 19 (2): 216–33.

———. 1987. *Class and Culture in Urban India: Fundamentalism in a Christian Community.* Oxford: Clarendon Press.

———. 1989. *Religion and Power: Essays on the Christian Community in Madras.* Madras: Christian Literature Society.

———. 1991. Christian Fundamentalism as Counter-Culture. In *Religion in India,* edited by T. N. Madan, 366–81. Delhi: Oxford University Press.

Cederlöf, Gunnel. 1997. *Bonds Lost: Subordination, Conflict and Mobilisation in Rural South India, c. 1900–1970.* Delhi: Manohar.

———. 2003. Social Mobilization among People Competing at the Bottom Level of Society: The Presence of Missions in Rural South India, ca. 1900–1950. In *Christians and Missionaries in India: Cross-Cultural Communication since 1500,* edited by R. E. Frykenberg, 336–56. London: Routledge Curzon.

Christian, William A. 1972. *Person and God in a Spanish Valley.* New York: Seminar.

———. 1981. *Local Religion in Sixteenth-Century Spain.* Princeton, NJ: Princeton University Press

Ciotti, Manuela. 2006. In the Past We Were a Bit "Chamar": Education as a Self and Community Engineering Process in Northern India. *Journal of the Royal Anthropological Institute,* n.s., 12 (4): 899–916.

Claerhout, Sarah, and Jakob De Roover. 2005. Challenge of Religious Conversion and Hindu Response. *Economic and Political Weekly* 50 (28): 3048–55.

Clark-Decès, Isabelle (Nabokov). 2005. *No One Cries for the Dead: Tamil Dirges, Rowdy Songs, and Graveyard Petitions.* Berkeley: University of California Press.

———. 2007. *The Encounter Never Ends: A Return to the Field of Tamil Rituals.* New York: State University of New York Press.

Clarke, Sathianathan. 1999. *Dalits and Christianity: Subaltern Religion and Liberation Theology in India.* New Delhi: Oxford University Press.

———. 2002. Hindutva, Religious and Ethnocultural Minorities, and Indian-Christian Theology. *Harvard Theological Review* 95 (2): 197–226.

Clarke, Sathianathan, Deenabandhu Manchala, and Philip Vinod Peacock, eds. 2010. *Dalit Theology in the Twenty-First Century: Discordant Voices, Discerning Pathways.* New Delhi: Oxford University Press.

Clémentin-Ojha, C. 1997. Des Indiens et quête de leur Indianité: L'Inculturation personnelle des Jésuites de Patna (Bihar). In *Altérité et identité: Islam et christianisme en Inde,* edited by J. Assayag and G. Tarabout, 249–64. Collection Puruṣārtha no. 19. Paris: Editions de L'Ecole des Hautes Etudes en Sciences Sociales.

Clooney, Francis X. 1999. Roberto de Nobili's *Dialogue on Eternal Life* and an Early Jesuit Evaluation of Religion in South India. In *The Jesuits: Cultures, Sciences, and the Arts, 1540–1773,* vol. 1, edited by John W. O'Malley, G.A. Bailey, S.J. Harris, and T.F. Kennedy, 402–17. Toronto: University of Toronto Press.

———. 2004. Jesuits and Brahmins in 16th-18th century India. Lecture series. "Relating to the Other: Hindu and Christian Perspectives." Oxford Centre for Hindu Studies. 19 February 2004. http://ochs.org.uk/node/371.

———. 2005. *Divine Mother, Blessed Mother: Hindu Goddesses and the Virgin Mary.* Oxford and New York: Oxford University Press.

———. 2006. Francis Xavier and the World/s We (Don't Quite) Share. In *Jesuit Postmodern: Scholarship, Vocation, and Identity in the 21st Century,* edited by Francis X. Clooney, 157–180. Lanham, MD: Exington Books.

———. 2007. Yes to Caste, No to Religion? Or Perhaps the Reverse: Re-Using Roberto de Nobili's Distinctions among Morality, Caste and Religion. In *Interculturation of Religion: Critical Perspectives on Robert de Nobili's Mission in India,* edited by C. Joe Arun, 158–74. Bangalore: Asian Trading Corporation.

Clothey, Fred W. 1976. Review of *Christian and Hindu Terminology: A Study of Their Mutual Relations with Special Reference to the Tamil Area,* by Bror Tiliander. *History of Religions* 16 (2): 185–88.

Cohn, Bernard S. 1959. Changing Traditions of a Low Caste. In *Traditional India: Structure and Change,* edited by M. Singer, 207–15. Philadelphia: American Folklore Society.

———. 1987. *An Anthropologist among the Historians and Other Essays.* Oxford: Oxford University Press.

———. 1996. *Colonialism and Its Forms of Knowledge.* Princeton, NJ: Princeton University Press.

Coleman, Simon. 2006 . Studying "Global" Pentecostalism: Tensions, Representations and Opportunities. *Penteco Studies* 5 (1): 1–17.

Collins, Paul M. 2007. *Christian Inculturation in India.* Aldershot, UK: Ashgate Publishing, Ltd.

Comaroff, Jean. 1985. *The Body of Power, Spirit of Resistance.* Chicago: University of Chicago Press.

Contributions to Indian Sociology. 1990. Special issue: vol. 24, no. 2 (June).

Corbridge, Stuart, and John Harriss. 2000. *Reinventing India: Liberalization, Hindu Nationalism and Popular Democracy*. Malden, MA: Polity Press.

Correia-Afonso, John. 1997. *The Jesuits in India, 1542–1773: A Short History*. Anand, Gujarat, India: Gujarat Sahitya Prakash.

Cramam de Sarougani. [c. 1880]. Manuscript. Jesuit Madurai Mission Archives, Shembaganur, India.

Csordas, Thomas J. 2007. Global Religion and the Re-enchantment of the World: The Case of the Catholic Charismatic Renewal. *Anthropological Theory* 7 (3): 295–314.

Daniel, E. Valentine. 1984. *Fluid Signs: Being a Person the Tamil Way*. Berkeley: University California Press.

———. 2000. The Arrogation of Being: Revisiting the Anthropology of Religion. *Macalester International* 8 (17): 171–91. http://digitalcommons.macalester.edu/macintl/vol8/iss1/17.

Darrieutort, Fr. 1876. Diableries. In *Scholasticat de Vals, 1876–1880*, 1–6. Shembaganur: Jesuit Madurai Mission Archives.

Das, Veena. 1977. *Structure and Cognition*. New Delhi: Oxford University Press.

———. 1995. *Critical Events: Anthropological Perspectives on Contemporary India*. New Delhi: Oxford University Press.

David, Kenneth. 1977. Hierarchy and Equivalence in Jaffna, North Sri Lanka: Normative Codes as Mediator. In *The New Wind: Changing Identities in South Asia*, edited by Kenneth David, 179–226. The Hague and Paris: Mouton.

Davis, M. 1976. The Individual among Bengali Hindus. *Man in India* 56 (1): 189–214.

Dayanandan, P. 2002. Dalit Christians of Chengalpattu Area and the Church of Scotland. In *Local Dalit Christian History*, edited by George Oommen and John C. B. Webster, 18–64. Delhi: ISPCK.

de Certeau, Michel. 1984. *The Practice of Everyday Life*. Translated by Steven Rendall. Berkeley: University of California Press.

———. 2000. *The Possession at Loudun*. Translated by Michael B. Smith. Chicago: University of Chicago Press.

Deliège, Robert. 1988. *Les Paraiyars du Tamil Nadu*. Nettetal, Germany: Steyer Verlag.

———. 1992. Replication and Consensus: Untouchability, Caste and Ideology in India. *Man* 27 (1): 155–73.

———. 1999. *The Untouchables of India*. Oxford: Berg.

Dempsey, Corinne. 2001. *Kerala Christian Sainthood: Collisions of Culture and Worldview in South India*. New Delhi: Oxford University Press.

Denton, Lynn Teskey. 2004. *Female Ascetics in Hinduism*. Albany: State University of New York Press.

Devasahayam, D. V. 1992. *Outside the Camp: Bible Studies in Dalit Perspective*. Madras: Gurukul Theological College and Research Institute.

Dewey, Clive. 1972. Images of the Village Community: A Study in Anglo-Indian Thought. *Modern Asian Studies* 6 (3): 291–328.

Dhavamony, Mariasusai. 1971. *Love of God according to Śaiva Sidddhānta: A Study in the Mysticism and Theology of Śaivism*. Oxford: Clarendon Press.

Diehl, Carl Gustav. 1965. *Church and Shrine: Intermingling Patterns of Culture in the Life of Some Christian Groups in South India.* Acta Universitatis Uppsaliensis Historia Religionum 2. Uppsala.

Dirks, Nicholas. 1986. From Little King to Landlord: Property, Law and Gift under the Madras Permanent Settlement. *Comparative Studies in Society and History* 28 (2): 307–33.

———. 1987. *The Hollow Crown: Ethnohistory of an Indian Kingdom.* Cambridge: Cambridge University Press.

———. 2001. *Castes of Mind: Colonialism and the Making of Modern India.* Princeton, NJ: Princeton University Press.

Ditchfield, Simon. 2009. Thinking with Saints: Sanctity and Society in the Early Modern World. *Critical Inquiry* 35 (3): 552–84.

Doniger (O'Flaherty), Wendy. 1987. The Good and the Evil Shepherd. In *Gilgul: Essays on Transformation, Revolution and Permanence in the History of Religions,* edited by S. Shaked, D. Shulman, and G. Stroumsa. Leiden: Brill.

Douglas, Mary. 1966. *Purity and Danger: An Analysis of Concepts of Pollution and Taboo.* London: Routledge and Kegan Paul.

Drèze, Jean, and Amartya Sen. 1995. *India: Economic Development and Social Opportunity.* Delhi: Oxford University Press.

Dube, Saurabh. 1998. *Untouchable Pasts: Religion, Identity and Power among a Central India Community, 1780–1950.* New York: SUNY Press.

DuBois, Abbé. 1906 [1897]. *Hindu Manners, Customs and Ceremonies.* Translated, annotated, and revised by Henry K. Beauchamp. Oxford: Clarendon Press.

———. 1977 [1815]. *Letters on the State of Christianity in India.* New Delhi: Associated Publishing House.

Dudley-Jenkins, Laura. 2003. *Identity and Identification in India: Defining the Disadvantaged.* London: Routledge Curzon.

Dumont, Louis. 1957. *Une Sous-caste de l'Inde du Sud: Organisation sociale et religion des Pramalai Kallar.* Paris: Mouton.

———. 1959. Structural Definition of a Folk Deity. *Contributions to Indian Sociology* 3:75–87.

———. 1960. World Renunciation in Indian Religions. *Contributions to Indian Sociology* 4:33–62.

———. 1965a. Functional Equivalents of the Individual in Caste Society. *Contributions to Indian Sociology* 8:85–99.

———. 1965b. The Modern Conception of the Individual: Notes on Its Genesis and Concomitant Institutions. *Contributions to Indian Sociology* 8:13–61.

———. 1980 [1972]. *Homo Hierarchicus: The Caste System and Its Implications.* Translated by M. Sainsbury. Chicago: University of Chicago Press; London: Paladin.

———. 1982. A Modified View of Our Origins: The Christian Beginnings of Modern Individualism. *Religion* 12:1–27.

———. 1992. *Essays on Individualism: Modern Ideology in Anthropological Perspective.* Chicago: University of Chicago Press.

Dumont, Louis, and David F. Pocock. 1959. On the Different Aspects or Levels in Hinduism. *Contributions to Indian Sociology* 3:40–54.

Eagleton, Terry. 2009. *Reason, Faith, and Revolution: Reflections on the God Debate.* New Haven, CT: Yale University Press.

Eck, Diane. 1981. *Darsan: Seeing the Divine Image in India.* New York: Columbia University Press.

Engineer, Asghar Ali, ed. 1991. *Mandal Commission Controversy.* Delhi: Ajanta Publications.

Egnor, Margaret. 1980. On the Meaning of *Sakti* to Women in Tamil Nadu. In *The Powers of Tamil Women,* edited by S. Wadley, 1–34. Foreign and Comparative Studies/South Asian Series, no. 6. Syracuse, NY: Maxwell School of Citizenship and Public Affairs, Syracuse University.

Endean, Philip. 2008. The Spiritual Exercises. In *The Cambridge Companion to the Jesuits,* edited by Thomas Worcester, 52–67. Cambridge: Cambridge 'University Press.

Engelke, Matthew. 2007. *A Problem of Presence: Beyond Scripture in an African Church.* Berkeley: University of California Press.

Estborn, Sigfrid.1961. *The Church among Tamils and Telugus.* Nagpur: National Christian Council of India.

Evans-Pritchard, E.E. 1937. *Witchcraft, Oracles and Magic among the Azande.* Oxford: Clarendon Press.

Fabricius, Johann Philip. 1972. [1779]. *Tamil and English Dictionary.* 4th ed. Tranquebar: Evangelical Lutheran Mission Publishing House.

Farquhar, J.N. 1913. *The Crown of Hinduism.* Oxford: Oxford University Press.

Fernandes, Walter. 1991. Jesuit Contribution to Social Change in India: Sixteenth to Twentieth Century. *Vidyajyoti Journal of Theological Reflection* 55:309–26.

———. 1999. A Conversion Debate. *The Hindu,* 19 November 1999.

Ferro-Luzzi, Eichinger G. 1974. Women's Pollution Periods in Tamilnadu (India). *Anthropos* 69:113–61.

Fishman, Alvin Texas. 1941. *Culture, Change and the Underprivileged: A Study of the Madigas in South India under Christian Guidance.* Madras: Christian Literature Crusade.

Fitzgerald, Timothy, ed. 2007. *Religion and the Secular: Historical and Colonial Formations.* London: Equinox.

Fontana, Michela. 2011. *Matteo Ricci: A Jesuit in the Ming Court.* Lanham, MD: Rowman & Littlefield Publishers.

Forrester, Duncan B. 1980. *Caste and Christianity: Attitudes and Policies on Caste of Anglo-Saxon Protestant Missionaries in India.* London: Curzon Press.

Foucault, Michel. 1976. *A History of Sexuality.* Harmondsworth, UK: Penguin Books.

———. 1990. *The Use of Pleasure.* Translated by Robert Hurley. New York: Vintage Books.

———. 1997. *Ethics: Subjectivity and Truth.* Vol. 1. New York: New Press.

Fraser, Nancy. 1997. *Justice Interruptus: Critical Reflections on the "Postsocialist" Condition.* New York: Routledge.

Freitag, Sandria B. 1989. *Collective Action and Community: Public Arenas and the Emergence of Communalism in North India.* Berkeley: University of California Press.

Friedman, Jonathan. 1992. The Past in the Future: History and the Politics of Identity. *American Anthropologist* 94 (4): 837–59.

Froerer, Peggy. 2007. *Religious Division and Social Conflict: The Emergence of Hindu Nationalism in Rural India.* New Delhi: Social Science Press.

Frykenberg, Robert Eric. 2003. Introduction: Dealing with Contested Definitions and Controversial Perspectives. In *Christians and Missionaries in India: Cross-Cultural Communication since 1500,* edited by R. E. Frykenberg, 1–32. Richmond: Routledge Curzon.

———. 2008. *Christianity in India: From Beginnings to the Present.* Oxford: Oxford University Press.

Fuller, Christopher John. 1976. Kerala Christians and the Caste System. *Man,* n.s., 11 (1): 53–70.

———. 1988. The Hindu Pantheon and the Legitimation of Hierarchy. *Man* 23 (1): 19–29.

———. 1989. Misconceiving the Grain Heap: A Critique of the Concept of the Indian Jajmani System. In *Money and the Morality of Exchange,* edited by J. Parry and M. Bloch, 33–63. Cambridge: Cambridge University Press.

———. 1992. *The Camphor Flame: Popular Hinduism in India.* Princeton, NJ: Princeton University Press.

———. 2001. The "Vinayaka Chaturthi" Festival and Hindutva in Tamil Nadu. *Economic and Political Weekly* 36 (19): 1607–16.

———. 2003. *The Renewal of the Priesthood: Modernity and Traditionalism in a South Indian Temple.* Princeton, NJ: Princeton University Press.

Gandhi, M. K. *Collected Works.* Vol. 45.

Geertz, Clifford. 1973. Religion as a Cultural System. In *The Interpretation of Cultures: Selected Essays.* New York: Basic Books.

Gell, Alfred. 1998. *Art and Agency: An Anthropological Theory.* Oxford: Oxford University Press.

George, T. C. 1981. Pentecostal Movement in South India. *Indian Church Growth Quarterly* 3:135–39.

Goel, Sita Ram. 1994. *Jesus Christ: An Artifice of Aggression.* New Delhi: Voice of India.

Gold, Ann Grodzins. 2009. Tasteless Profits and Vexed Moralities: Assessments of the Present in Rural Rajasthan. *Journal of the Royal Anthropological Institute* 15 (2): 365–85.

Gombrich, Richard F. 1971. *Precept and Practice: Traditional Buddhism in the Rural Highlands of Ceylon.* Oxford: Clarendon Press.

Good, Anthony. 1978. Kinship and Ritual in a South Indian Micro-Region. PhD thesis, Durham University.

———. 1980. Only Siva Is in the Cemetery: Death and Its Consequences in a Tamil Micro-Region. In *Hindu Death and the Ritual Journey,* edited by B. Quayle, P. Phillimore, and A. Good. Issue 4 of Working Papers in Social Anthropology. Durham, UK: Dept. of Anthropology, Durham University.

———. 1981. Prescription, Preference and Practice: Marriage Patterns among the Kondaiyankottai Maravar of South India. *Man,* n.s., 16 (1): 108–29.

———. 1982. The Actor and the Act: Categories of Prestation in South India. *Man,* n.s., 17 (1): 23–41.

———. 1983. A Symbolic Type and Its Transformation: The Case of South Indian Ponkal. *Contributions to Indian Sociology,* n.s., 17 (2): 223–44.

———. 1991. *The Female Bridegroom.* Oxford: Oxford University Press.

———. 1999. The Car and the Palanquin: Rival Accounts of the 1895 Riot in Kalugumalai, South India. *Modern Asian Studies* 33 (1): 23–65.

———. 2003. Review of *Religion Against the Self: An Ethnography of Tamil Rituals,* by Isabelle Nabokov (New York: Oxford University Press, 2000). *American Anthropologist* 105 (2): 447–48.

Gorringe, Hugo. 2005a. *Untouchable Citizens: Dalit Movements and Democratisation in Tamil Nadu.* New Delhi: Sage.

———. 2005b. "You Build Your House, We'll Build Ours": The Attractions and Pitfalls of Dalit Identity Politics. *Social Identities* 11 (6): 653–72.

———. 2006. Banal Violence? The Everyday Underpinnings of Collective Violence. *Identities: Global Studies in Power and Culture* 13 (2): 237–60.

———. 2008a. The Caste of the Nation: Untouchability and Citizenship in South India. *Contributions to Indian Sociology,* n.s., 42 (1): 123–49.

———. 2008b. From Panthers to Pussy-Cats? Replication and Consensus in Tamil Dalit Politics. Paper presented at the Dalit Studies Conference, Center for the Advanced Study of India (CASI), University of Pennsylvania, Philadelphia, 3–5 December.

———. 2009. Becoming a Dalit Panther: Caste-Based Activism in South India. In *Ethnic Activism and Civil Society in South Asia,* edited by David N. Gellner, 145–74. New Delhi: Sage.

Gorringe, Timothy. 2004. *Furthering Humanity: A Theology of Culture.* Aldershot: Ashgate.

Gough, Kathleen E. 1993. Brahman Kinship in a Tamil Village. In *Family, Kinship and Marriage in India,* edited by P. Uberoi, 146–75. Delhi: Oxford University Press.

Gowthaman, Raj. 2002. *Ciluvairāj Carittiram.* Chennai: Thamizhini.

Graeber, David. 2006. There Never Was a West: Or Democracy Emerges from the Spaces in Between. Paper presented at the Cosmopolitanism and Anthropology Conference of the Association of Social Anthropologists, Keele, UK.

Grafè, Hugald. 1990. *History of Christianity in India.* Vol. 4, pt. 2, *Tamilnadu in the Nineteenth and Twentieth Centuries.* Bangalore: Church History Association of India.

Greeley, Andrew. 2001. *The Catholic Imagination.* Berkeley: University of California Press.

Gupta, Dipankar. 2000. *Interrogating Caste: Understanding Hierarchy and Difference in Indian Society.* New Delhi: Penguin Books.

———, ed. 2004. *Caste in Question: Identity or Hierarchy?* London and New Delhi: Sage.

———. 2005. Whither the Indian Village: Culture and Agriculture in "Rural" India. *Economic and Political Weekly* 40 (8): 751–58.

Hambye, E. R. 1997. *History of Christianity in India.* Vol. 3, *Eighteenth Century.* Bangalore: Church History Association of India.

Hann, Chris 2007. The Anthropology of Christianity *per se. European Journal of Sociology* 48 (3): 383–410.

Hanretta, Sean. 2005. Review Article: Muslim Histories, African Societies: The Venture of Islamic Studies in Africa. *Journal of African History* 46 (3): 479–91.

Hansen, Thomas Blom. 1999. *The Saffron Wave: Democracy and Hindu Nationalism in Modern India*. Princeton, NJ: Princeton University Press.

Hardgrave, Robert L. J. 1968. The Breast Cloth Controversy. *Indian Economic and Social History Review* 5 (2): 171–87.

———. 1969. *The Nadars of Tamilnad*. Berkeley: University of California Press.

Harré, Rom. 1981. Psychological Variety. In *Indigenous Psychologies*, edited by P. Heelas and A. Lock, 79–104. London: Academic Press.

Harris, Olivia. 2006. The Eternal Return of Conversion: Christianity as Contested Domain in Highland Bolivia. In *The Anthropology of Christianity*, edited by Fenella Cannell, 51–76. Durham, NC, and London: Duke University Press.

Harrison, Simon, 1995. Four Types of Symbolic Conflict. *Journal of the Royal Anthropological Institute*, n.s., 1 (2): 255–72.

Harriss, John. 2002. Whatever Happened to Cultural Nationalism in Tamil Nadu? A Reading of Current Events and the Recent Literature on Tamil Politics. *Commonwealth and Comparative Politics* 40 (3): 97–117.

———. 2003. The Great Tradition Globalizes: Reflections on Two Studies of "Industrial Leaders" of Madras. *Modern Asian Studies* 37 (2): 327–62.

Hastrup, Kirsten. 2006. Closing Ranks: Fundamentals in History, Politics and Anthropology. *Australian Journal of Anthropology* 17 (2): 147–60.

Hayden, Robert. 2002. Antagonistic Tolerance: Competitive Sharing of Religious Sites in South Asia and the Balkans. *Current Anthropology* 43 (2): 205–31.

Hefner, Robert W., ed. 1993. *Conversion to Christianity: Historical and Anthropological Perspectives on a Great Transformation*. Berkeley: University of California Press.

Heimsath, Charles Herman. 1964. *Indian Nationalism and Hindu Social Reform*. Princeton, NJ: Princeton University Press.

Hjejle, Benedicte. 1967. Slavery and Agricultural Bondage in South India in the Nineteenth Century. *Scandinavian Economic History Review* 15 (1–2): 77–87.

Hocart, Arthur Maurice. 1950. *Caste: A Comparative Study*. London: Methuen.

Holmström, Mark. 1971. Religious Change in an Industrial City of South India. *Journal of the Royal Asiatic Society of Great Britain and Ireland* 1:28–40.

Hopkins, Thomas J. 1966. The Social Teachings of the Bhagavata Purana. In *Krishna: Myths, Rites and Attitudes*, edited by M. Singer, 1–23. Honolulu: East West Canto Press.

Horton, Robin. 1971. African Conversion. *Africa* 41 (2): 85–108.

———. 1975. On the Rationality of Conversion. Pts. 1 and 2. *Africa* 45 (3–4): 219–35; 373–99.

Houtart, F., et al. N.d. A Socio-Religious Analysis of East-Ramnad District. Unpublished report prepared for the Madurai Archdiocese.

Hubert, Henri, and Marcel Mauss. 1964. *Sacrifice: Its Nature and Function*. Chicago: University of Chicago Press.

Hudson, Dennis. 2000. *Protestant Origins in India: Tamil Evangelical Christians, 1706–1835*. Grand Rapids, MI, and Cambridge: William B. Eerdmans; Richmond: Curzon.

———. 2004. The First Protestant Mission to India: Its Social and Religious Developments. In *Sociology of Religion in India*, edited by Rowena Robinson, 119–230. New Delhi and London: Sage Publications.

Human Rights Watch. 1999a. *Broken People: Caste Violence against India's "Untouchables."* New York: Human Rights Watch.

———. 1999b. *Politics by Other Means: Attacks against Christians in India. Human Rights Watch Report* 11, no. 6 (C).

Hunt, Lynn. 2007. *Inventing Human Rights: A History.* London and New York: Norton and Co. Ltd.

Hwa, Yung. 2005. Pentecostalism and the Asian Church. In *Asian and Pentecostal: The Charismatic Face of Christianity in Asia,* edited by Allan Anderson and Edmond Tang, 37–57. Oxford: OCMS.

Ilaiah, Kancha. 1998. *Why I Am Not a Hindu: A Sudra Critique of Hindutva Philosophy, Culture and Political Economy.* Calcutta: Mandira Sen for Samya.

Imayam. 2001. *Beasts of Burden.* Translated by Lakshmi Homström. Chennai: Manas/East West Books.

Inden, Ronald. 1990. *Imagining India.* Oxford: Basil Blackwell.

Irschick, Eugene F. 2003. Conversations in Tarangambadi: Caring for the Self in Early Eighteenth Century South India. *Comparative Studies of South Asia and the Middle East* 21 (1–2): 3–20.

Irudayaraj, Xavier, ed. 1990. *Emerging Dalit Theology.* Madras and Madurai: Jesuit Theological Secretariat and Tamilnadu Theological Seminary.

Isaacs, Harold Robert. 1965. *India's Ex-Untouchables.* New York: John Day Co.

Jackson, Michael. 1998. *Minima Ethnographica; Intersubjectivity and the Anthropological Project.* Chicago: University of Chicago Press.

Jaffrelot, Christophe. 2003. *India's Silent Revolution: The Rise of the Lower Castes in North India.* London: C. Hurst and Co.

Jain, Pankaj. 2009. From Kil-Arni to Anthony: The Portrayal of Christians in Indian Films. *Visual Anthropology* 23 (1): 13–19.

Jeffrey, Craig. 2010a. *Timepass: Youth, Class, and the Politics of Waiting in India.* Stanford, CA: Stanford University Press.

———. 2010b. Waiting for Change: Young Men, Caste and Politics in India. Paper presented at the conference "Mobility or Marginalisation: Dalits in Neoliberal India," Oxford, September.

Jeffrey, Craig, Patricia Jeffery, and Roger Jeffery. 2008a. Dalit Revolution? New Politicians in Uttar Pradesh. *Journal of Asian Studies* 67(4): 1365–96.

———. 2008b. *Degrees without Freedom? Education, Masculinities and Unemployment in North India.* Stanford, CA: Stanford University Press.

Jean, Auguste. 1894. *Le Maduré: l'Ancienne et la Nouvelle Mission.* Vol. 1. Bruges: Desclée, de Brouwer and Co. Société de Saint Augustin.

Jha, Raghbendra. 2004. The Political Economy of Recent Economic Growth in India. Australian National University ASARC Working Paper. Canberra.

JMP (Jesuit Madurai Province). 2002. *Golden Jubilee 1952–2002 Souvenir.* Dindigul: Provincial Superior.

Jordens, J. T. F. 1977. Reconversion to Hinduism: The Shuddhi of the Arya Samaj. In *Religion in South-Asia: Religious Conversion and Revival Movements in South Asia in Medieval and Modern Times,* edited by Geoffrey A. Oddie, 215–30. London: Curzon Press.

Juergensmeyer, Mark. 1982. *Religion as Social Vision: The Movement against Untouchability in Twentieth Century Punjab.* Berkeley: University of California Press.

Jyoti and M.C. Raj. 2005. *Cosmosity: A Cultural Discourse of the Unbroken People.* Tumkur, Karnataka: Ambedkar Resource Center, Rural Education for Development Society (REDS).

Kadhirvel, S. 1977. *A History of the Maravars, 1700–1802.* Madras: Madras Publishing House.

Kane, Pandurang Vaman. 1974. *History of Dharmasastra (Ancient and Medieval Religious and Civil Law).* 2nd ed. Poona: Bhandarkar Oriental Research Institute.

Kannan, M., and François Gros. 2002. Tamil Dalits in Search of a Literature. *South Asia Research* 22 (1): 21–66.

Kannanaikal, Jose. 1983. *Christians of Scheduled Caste Origin.* Indian Social Institute Monograph Series no. 10. New Delhi.

Kanungo, Pralang. 2008. Hindutva's Fury against Christians in Orissa. *Economic and Political Weekly* 43 (37): 16–19.

Kapadia, Karin. 1993. Marrying Money: Changing Preference and Practice in Tamil Marriage. *Contributions to Indian Sociology* 27 (1): 25–51.

———. 1998. *Siva and Her Sisters: Gender, Caste, and Class in Rural South India:* Boulder, CO: Westview Press.

Kapferer, Bruce. 1983. *A Celebration of Demons: Exorcism and the Aesthetics of Healing in Sri Lanka.* Bloomington: Indiana University Press.

Karunambaram, Charles. 2002. Tuning the War Drum: The Reconstruction of "Parai" towards Dalit Empowerment in Tamil Nadu. PhD thesis, College of Mass Communication, University of the Philippines.

Keane, Webb. 1996. Materialism, Missionaries, and Modern Subjects in Colonial Indonesia. In *Conversion to Modernities: The Globalization of Christianity,* edited by Peter van der Veer, 137–70. New York: Routledge.

———. 2006a. Anxious Transcendence. In *The Anthropology of Christianity,* edited by Fenella Cannell, 308–24. Durham, NC, and London: Duke University Press.

———. 2006b. Review of Robbins 2004a. *Comparative Studies in Society and History* 48 (1): 233–35.

———. 2007. *Christian Moderns: Freedom and Fetish in the Mission Encounter.* Berkeley: University of California Press.

———. 2008. Religion as Linguistic Practice. Lecture at the Centre for the Study of Religion and Culture (CSRC), Vanderbilt University, Nashville, Tennessee, 4 April. http://discoverarchive.vanderbilt.edu/jspui/handle/1803/144.

Khare, R.S. 1984. *The Untouchable as Himself: Ideology, Identity and Pragmatism among the Lucknow Chamars.* Cambridge: Cambridge University Press.

Killingly, D. 2004. Christian and Indian Traditions in Historical Perspective. Lecture given at Oxford Centre for Hindu Studies and the Centre for Christianity and Culture, Regent's Park College, 29 January 2004.

Kim, Sebastian, C.H. 2003. *In Search of Identity: Debates on Religious Conversion.* New Delhi: Oxford University Press.

King, Richard. 1999. *Orientalism and Religion: Postcolonial Theory, India and "the Mythic East."* London and New York: Routledge.

Kooiman, Dick. 1989. *Conversion and Social Equality in India: The London Missionary Society in South Travancore in the 19th Century.* New Delhi: Manohar Publications.

Koshy, Ninan. 1968. *Caste in the Kerala Churches.* Bangalore: Christian Institute for the Study of Religion and Society.

Krishnan, Rajan. 2011. Caste and Religion in the Age of the Nation-State: Certain Polemical Blinders and Dalit Situations. Paper presented at the conference "Caste Out of Development," Chennai, December.

Kumar, Dharma. 1965. *Land and Caste in South India: Agricultural Labour in the Madras Presidency during the Nineteenth Century.* Cambridge: Cambridge University Press.

Kuriakose, M. K., ed. 1982. *History of Christianity in India: Source Materials.* Madras: Christian Literature Society.

Lacombe, P. 1892. Extract d'une Lettre du P. Lacombe S.J. In *Lettres des Scholastiques d'Ucles* 2 (2nd ser.), 284–85. Shembagamur: Jesuit Madurai Mission Archives.

Lakshmanan, L. C. 2004. Dalit Masculinities in Social Science Research: Revisiting a Tamil Village. *Economic and Political Weekly* 39 (10): 1088–92.

Lambert, Helen. 1996. Caste, Gender and Locality in Rural Rajasthan. In *Caste Today,* edited by C. J. Fuller, 93–123. New Delhi: Oxford University Press.

Larmey, P. 1876. La Danse du Diable. *Scholastical de Vals* 6–7. Shembagamur: Jesuit Madurai Mission Archives.

Latour, Bruno. 1993. *We Have Never Been Modern.* Translated by Catherine Porter. Cambridge: Harvard University Press.

———. 2003. What If We *Talked* Politics a Little? *Contemporary Political Theory* 2 (2): 143–64.

———. 2005. *Reassembling the Social: An Introduction to Actor-Network-Theory.* Oxford: Oxford University Press.

Leach, Edmund. 1983. Mechisedeck and the Emperor: Icons of Subversion and Orthodoxy. In *Structuralist Interpretation of Biblical Myth,* edited by Edmund Leach and D. Alan Aycock, 67–88. Cambridge: Cambridge University Press.

Lele, Jayant. 1980. The "Bhakti" Movement in India: A Critical Introduction. *Journal of Asian and African Studies* 15 (1–2): 1–15.

Leslie, Julia. 2003. *Authority and Meaning in Indian Religions: Hinduism and the Case of Vālmīki.* Aldershot, Hants.: Ashgate Publishing, Ltd.

Leveil, L. M. 1937. Le Maravar. *Nuntii de Missionibus* 7:441–46.

Levinson, Stephen C. 1982. Caste Rank and Verbal Interactions in Western Tamilnadu. In *Caste Ideology and Interaction,* edited by D. B. McGilvray, 98–203. Cambridge: Cambridge University Press.

Lewis, I. M. 1971. *Ecstatic Religion: An Anthropological Study of Spirit Possession and Shamanism.* Harmondsworth, UK: Penguin.

Ling, Trevor Oswald. 1980. *Buddhist Revival in India: Aspects of the Sociology of Buddhism.* London: Macmillan.

Linton, Bruce. 2003. *Holy Terrors: Thinking about Religion after September 11.* Chicago: University of Chicago Press.

Lipner, Julius J. 2006. The Rise of "Hinduism"; or, How to Invent a World Religion with Only Moderate Success. *International Journal of Hindu Studies* 10 (1): 91–104.

Littlewood, Roland. 2009. Neglect as Project: How Two Societies Forget. *Journal of the Royal Anthropological Institute,* n.s., 15 (1): 113–30.
Lobo, Lancy. 2002. *Globalisation, Hindu Nationalism, and Christians in India.* Jaipur and New Delhi: Rawat Publications.
Lorenzen, David N. 1999. Who Invented Hinduism? *Comparative Studies in Society and History* 41 (4): 630–59.
Ludden, David. 1985. *Peasant History in South India.* Princeton, NJ: Princeton University Press.
———, ed. 2005. *Making India Hindu: Religion, Community and the Politics of Democracy in India.* New Delhi: Oxford University Press.
Luke, Nancy, and Kaivan Munshi. 2007. Social Affiliation and the Demand for Health Services: Caste and Child Health in South India. *Journal of Development Economics* 83 (2): 256–79.
Luke, P. Y., and J. B. Carmen. 1968. *Village Christians and Hindu Culture: Study of a Rural Church in Andhra Pradesh, South India.* London: Lutterworth Press.
Lukes, Steven. 2005. *Power: A Radical View.* 2nd ed. Basingstoke: Palgrave Macmillan.
Lynch, Owen M. 1969. *The Politics of Untouchability.* New York: Columbia University Press.
———. 1972. Dr. B. R. Ambedkar: Myth and Charisma. In *The Untouchables in Contemporary India,* edited by J. M. Mahar, 97–112. Tucson: University of Arizona Press.
MacKendrick, Karmen. 2010. The Multipliable Body. *Postmedieval* 1 (1/2): 108–14.
Mahar, Pauline M. 1960. The Changing Religious Practices of an Untouchable Caste. *Economic Development and Cultural Change* 8 (3): 279–87.
Mahé. 1939. Letter "Alapuram." *Caritas* 23:14–17.
Malamoud, Charles. 1976. Village et forêt dans l'idéologie de L'Inde brâhmanique. *European Journal of Sociology* 17 (1): 3–20.
Malhotra, Rajiv, and A. Neelakandan. 2011. *Breaking India: Western Interventions in Dravidian and Dalit Faultlines.* New Delhi: Amaryllis.
Mallampalli, Chandra. 2004. *Christians and Public Life in Colonial South India, 1863–1937.* London and New York: Routledge Curzon.
Mandelbaum, David Goodman. 1966. Transcendental and Pragmatic Aspects of Religion. *American Anthropologist* 68 (5): 1174–91.
Manickam, Alphonse. 2001. Les Jésuites et l'intouchabilité au Tamil Nadu: Études historiques et anthropologiques sur des approches longtemps différées. PhD thesis, Ecole Pratique des Hautes Etudes, Paris.
Marriott, McKim. ed. 1955. *Village India: Studies in the Little Community.* Chicago: University of Chicago Press.
———. 1976. Hindu Transactions: Diversity without Dualism. In *Transaction and Meaning,* edited by B. Kapferer, 109–10. Philadelphia: Institute for the Study of Human Issues.
———, ed. 1990. *India through Hindu Categories.* New Delhi: Sage Publications.
Marriott, McKim, and Ronald Inden. 1977. Toward an Ethnosociology of South Asian Caste Systems. In *The New Wind: Changing Identities in South Asia,* edited by K. David, 227–38. The Hague and Paris: Mouton.

Massey, James. 1991. Ingredients for a Dalit Theology. In *A Reader in Dalit Theology*, edited by A. P. Nirmal, 145–68. Madras: Gurukul Lutheran Theological College

———. 1995. *Dalits in India: Religion as a Source of Bondage or Liberation with Special Reference to Christians*. New Delhi: Manohar.

———, ed. 1998. *Indigenous People: Dalits. Dalit Issues in Today's Theological Debate*. New Delhi: Indian Society for Promoting Christian Knowledge.

———, ed. 2010. *One Volume Dalit Bible Commentary*. New Delhi: Centre for Dalit, Subaltern Studies.

Mathew, George. 1982. Politicisation of Religion: Conversion to Islam in Tamil Nadu (Parts 1–2). *Economic and Political Weekly* 17 (25–26): 1027–34, 1068–72.

Mauss, Marcel. 1973 [1934]. Techniques of the Body. *Economy and Society* 2 (1): 70–88.

———. 1985 [1938]. A Category of the Human Mind: The Notion of Person, the Notion of Self. In *The Category of the Person: Anthropology, Philosophy, History*, edited by Michael Carrithers, Steven Collins, and Steven Lukes, 1–25. Cambridge: Cambridge University Press.

Mayer, Peter. 1993. Inventing Village Tradition: The Late 19th Century Origins of the North Indian Jajmani System. *Modern Asian Studies* 27 (2): 357–95.

McGilvray, Dennis B. 1982a. Mukkuvar Vannimai: Tamil Caste and Matriclan Ideology in Batticaloa, Sri Lanka. In *Caste Ideology and Interaction*, edited by Dennis McGilvray, 34–97. Cambridge: Cambridge University Press.

———. 1982b. Sexual Power and Fertility in Sri Lanka: Batticaloa Tamils and Moors. In *Ethnography of Fertility and Birth*, edited by C. P. MacCormack, 25–73. London: Academic Press.

———. 1983. Paraiyar Drummers of Sri Lanka: Consensus and Constraint in an Untouchable Caste. *American Ethnologist* 10 (1): 97–115.

———. 2008. *Crucible of Conflict: Tamil and Muslim Society on the East Coast of Sri Lanka*. Durham, NC, and London: Duke University Press.

Meibohm, Margaret. 2004. Cultural Complexity in South India: Hindu and Catholic in Marian Pilgrimage. PhD thesis, University of Pennsylvania.

Mendelsohn, Oliver, and Marika Vicziany. 1998. *The Untouchables: Subordination, Poverty and the State in Modern India*. Cambridge: Cambridge University Press.

Menon, D. M. 2002. Religion and Colonial Modernity: Rethinking Belief and Identity. *Economic and Political Weekly* 37 (17): 1662–67.

Michell, George, ed. 1992. *Living Wood: Sculptural Traditions in Southern India*. Bombay: Marg Publications.

Milbank, John. 1991. *Theology and Social Theory*. London: Blackwell.

Miller, Robert. 1966. Button, Button . . . Great Tradition, Little Tradition, Whose Tradition? *Anthropological Quarterly* 39 (1): 26–42.

Mines, Diane. 2005. *Fierce Gods: Inequality, Ritual, and the Politics of Dignity in a South Indian Village*. Bloomington: Indiana University Press.

Mines, Mattison, and Vijayalakshmi Gourishankar. 1990. Leadership and Individuality in South Asia: The Case of the South Indian Big-Man. *Journal of Asian Studies* 49 (4): 761–86.

Ministry of Minority Affairs. 2009. *Report on the National Commission for Religious and Linguistic Minorities.* New Delhi: NCRLM.

Mitchell, Timothy. 2002. *Rule of Experts: Egypt, Techno-Politics, Modernity.* Berkeley: University of California Press.

Mitlin, D., and A. Bebbington. 2006. Social Movements and Chronic Poverty across the Urban–Rural Divide: Concepts and Experiences. CPRC Working Paper 65. Manchester, UK: Chronic Poverty Research Centre, University of Manchester.

Moffatt, Michael. 1968. The Funeral Ritual in South India. B. Litt. thesis, Oxford University.

———. 1979. *An Untouchable Community in South India: Structure and Consensus.* Princeton, NJ: Princeton University Press.

Mohan, Jyoti. 2004. British and French Ethnographies of India: Dubois and His English Commentators. *French Colonial History* 5:229–46.

Molinié, Antoinette. 1996. *Le corps de Dieu en fêtes.* Paris: Les Editions du Cerf.

Morris, B. 1978. Are There Any Individuals in India? *Eastern Anthropologist* 3:365–79.

Mosko, Mark. 2010. Partible Penitents: Dividual Personhood and Christian Practice in Melanesia and the West. *Journal of the Royal Anthropological Institute* 16 (2): 215–40.

Mosse, David. 1986. *Caste, Christianity and Hinduism: A Study of Social Organisation and Religion in Rural Ramnad.* DPhil thesis, University of Oxford.

———. 1994. Idioms of Subordination and Styles of Protest among Christian and Hindu Harijan Castes in Tamil Nadu. *Contributions to Indian Sociology,* n.s., 28 (1): 67–106.

———. 1996. South Indian Christians, Purity/Impurity, and the Caste System: Death Ritual in a Tamil Roman Catholic Community. *Journal of the Royal Anthropological Institute* 2 (3): 461–83.

———. 1997. Honour, Caste and Conflict: The Ethnohistory of a Catholic Festival in Rural Tamil Nadu (1730–1990). In *Altérité et identité: Islam et christianisme en Inde,* edited by J. Assayag and G. Tarabout, 71–120. Collection Puruṣārtha no. 19. Paris: Editions de L'Ecole des Hautes Etudes en Sciences Sociales.

———. 2003. *The Rule of Water: Statecraft, Ecology and Collective Action in South India.* New Delhi: Oxford University Press.

———. 2005. *Cultivating Development: An Ethnography of Aid Policy and Practice.* London and Ann Arbor, MI: Pluto Press.

———. 2006a. Possession and Confession: Affliction and Sacred Power in Colonial and Contemporary Catholic South India. In *The Anthropology of Christianity,* edited by Fenella Cannell, 99–133. Durham, NC: Duke University Press.

———. 2006b. Rule and Representation: Transformations in the Governance of the Water Commons in British South India. *Journal of Asian Studies* 65 (1): 61–90.

———. 2009. Dalit Christian Activism in Contemporary Tamil Nadu. In *Ethnic Activism and Civil Society in South Asia,* edited by David N. Gellner, 175–214. New Delhi: Sage.

———. 2010. A Relational Approach to Durable Poverty, Inequality and Power. *Journal of Development Studies* 46 (7): 1156–78.

———. 2011. Dalit Rights and the Development Agenda: The Promise, Progress and Pitfalls of Dalit NGO Networking in South India. Paper presented at the conference "Caste Out of Development," Chennai, December.

———. N.d. The Appearance of Caste Politics in a Tamil Village. Unpublished paper.

Murr, Sylvia. 1987. *L'Inde philosophique entre Bosuet et Voltaire.* 2 vols. Paris: Ecole Française d'Extrême-Orient.

Nabokov, Isabelle. 1997. Expel the Lover, Recover the Wife: Symbolic Analysis of a South Indian Exorcism. *Journal of the Royal Anthropological Institute,* n.s., 3 (2): 297–316.

———. 2000. *Religion against the Self: An Ethnography of Tamil Rituals.* New York: Oxford University Press.

Napolitano, Valentina, and David Pratten. 2007. Michel de Certeau: Ethnography and the Challenge of Plurality. *Social Anthropology* 15 (1): 1–12.

NCS. 2010. 20 Years Scheduled Castes & Scheduled Tribes (Prevention of Atrocities) Act: Report Card. New Delhi: National Coalition for Strengthening SCs & STs [Prevention of Atrocities] Act.

Needham, Rodney. 1967. Percussion and Transition. *Man,* n.s., 2 (4): 606–14.

———. 1972. *Belief, Language, and Experience.* Oxford: Basil Blackwell.

Neill, Stephen. 1984. *A History of Christianity in India: The Beginnings to A.D. 1707.* Cambridge: Cambridge University Press.

Nelson, Amirtharaj. 1975. *A New Day in Madras: A Study of Protestant Churches in Madras.* Pasadena, CA: William Carey Library.

Nevett, Albert M. 1980. *John de Britto and His Times.* Delhi: Gujerat Sahitya Prakash Ananad.

Nirmal, Arvind P. 1990. Towards a Christian Dalit Theology. In *Emerging Dalit Theology,* edited by Xavier Irudayaraj, 123–42. Madras and Madurai: Jesuit Theological Secretariat and Tamilnadu Theological Seminary.

———. 1998: Towards a Christian Dalit Theology. In *Indigenous People: Dalits. Dalit Issues in Today's Theological Debate,* edited by James Massey, 214–30. New Delhi: Indian Society for Promoting Christian Knowledge

Nobili, Roberto. 2005 [1613]. The Report on Certain Customs of the Indian Nation. In *Preaching Wisdom to the Wise: Three Treatises by Roberto de Nobili in Dialogue with the Learned Hindus of South India,* edited by A. Amaladass and F. X. Clooney, 51–222. St. Louis: Institute of Jesuit Sources.

Obeyesekere, Gananath. 1981. *Medusa's Hair: An Essay on Personal Symbols and Religious Experience.* Chicago: University of Chicago Press.

Oddie, Geoffery A. 1975. Christian Conversion in Telugu Country, 1860–1900: A Case Study of One Protestant Movement in the Godavery-Krishna Delta. *Indian Economic and Social History Review* 12:61–79.

———. 1979. *Social Protest in India: British Protestant Missionaries and Social Reforms, 1850–1900.* New Delhi: Manohar.

———. 1991. *Hindu and Christian in South-East India.* London: Curzon Press.

———. 2006. *Imagined Hinduism: British Protestant Missionary Constructions of Hinduism, 1793–1900.* Delhi, Thousand Oaks, CA, and London: Sage.

Omvedt, Gail. 1994. *Dalits and the Democratic Revolution: Dr. Ambedkar and the Dalit Movement in Colonial India.* New Delhi: Sage Publications.

Oommen, George. 2000. Emerging Dalit Theology: A Historical Appraisal. *Indian Church History Review* 34 (1): 19–37.

Ortner, S. 2005. Subjectivity and Cultural Critique. *Anthropological Theory* 5 (1): 31–52.

Osella, Caroline. 1993. Making Hierarchy Natural: The Cultural Construction of Gender and Maturity in Kerala, India. PhD thesis, University of London.

Osella, Caroline, and Filippo Osella. 1996. Articulation of Physical and Social Bodies in Kerala. *Contributions to Indian Sociology*, n.s., 30 (1): 37–68.

———. 1999. Seepage of Divinised Power through Social, Spiritual and Bodily Boundaries: Some Aspects of Possession in Kerala. In *La Possession en Asie du Sud: Parole, corps, territoire*, edited by J. Assayag and G. Tarabout, 183–210. Collection Puruṣārtha no. 21. Paris: Editions de L'Ecole des Hautes Etudes en Sciences Sociales.

———. 2006. *Men and Masculinities in South India*. London: Anthem Press.

Pandian, Anand. 2008. Tradition in Fragments: Inherited Forms and Fractures in the Ethics of South India. *American Ethnologist* 35 (3): 466–80.

———. 2009. *Crooked Stalks: Cultivating Virtue in South India*. Durham, NC, and London: Duke University Press.

Pandian, M.S.S. 2002. One Step Outside Modernity: Caste, Identity Politics and Public Sphere. *Economic and Political Weekly* 37 (18): 1735–41.

———. 2005. Dilemmas of Public Reason: Secularism and Religious Violence in Contemporary India. *Economic and Political Weekly* 40 (22): 2313–20.

———. 2007. *Brahmin and non-Brahmin: Genealogies of the Tamil Political Present*. Delhi: Permanent Black.

———. 2008. Writing Ordinary Lives. *Economic and Political Weekly* 43 (38): 34–40.

Panikkar, Raymond. 1964. *The Unknown Christ of Hinduism*. London: Darton, Longman and Todd.

Parry, Jonathan P. 1979. *Caste and Kinship in Kangra*. London: Routledge and Kegan Paul.

———. 1982. Sacrificial Death and the Necrophagous Ascetic. In *Death and the Regeneration of Life*, edited by M. Bloch and J. Parry, 74–110. Cambridge: Cambridge University Press.

Peel, John D.Y. 1968. *Aladura: A Religious Movement among the Yoruba*. London: International African Institute.

———. 2000. *Religious Encounters and the Making of the Yoruba*. Bloomington: Indiana University Press.

———. 2007. Comment on Joel Robbins's "Continuity Thinking and the Problem of Christian Culture: Belief, Time and the Anthropology of Christianity." *Current Anthropology* 48 (1): 3–38.

Pelkmans, Mathijs. 2007. "Culture" as a Tool and an Obstacle: Missionary Encounters in Post-Soviet Kyrgystan. *Journal of the Royal Anthropological Institute* 13 (4): 881–99.

Pennington, Brian K. 2005. *Was Hinduism Invented? Britons, Indians, and the Colonial Construction of Religion*. Oxford: Oxford University Press

Pfaffenberger, Bryan. 1982. *Caste in Tamil Culture: The Religious Foundation of Vellalar Dominance*. New York: Maxwell School of Citizenship and Public Affairs, Syracuse University.

Pickett, Jarrel Waskom. 1933. *Christian Mass Movements in India: A Study with Recommendations*. Lucknow: Lucknow Publishing House.

Pieris, Aloysius. 1993. Does Christ Have a Place in Asia? A Panoramic View. In *Any Room for Christ in Asia?* edited by L. Boff and V. Elizondo, 33–47. London: SCM Press.

Pina-Cabral, J. 1980. Cults of Death in Northwestern Portugal. *Journal of the Anthropological Society of Oxford* 6 (1): 1–14.

Pinney, C. 1992. Underneath the Banyan Tree: William Crooke and Photographic Depictions of Caste. In *Anthropology and Photography, 1860–1920,* edited by E. Edwards, 165–73. New Haven, CT: Yale University Press.

Pocock, David Francis. 1962. Notes on *Jajmani* Relationships. *Contributions to Indian Sociology* 6:78–95.

———. 1964. The Anthropology of Time Reckoning. *Contributions to Indian Sociology* 7:18–29.

———. 1973. *Mind, Body and Wealth.* Oxford: Basil Blackwell.

Ponnad, S., ed. 1983. *Archdiocese of Madurai: Origins Development.* Madurai: Nobili Pastoral Centre.

Pouget, P. G. 1890. Un Oracle du Demon. *Lettres des Scholastiques d'Ucles,* 2nd ser., 1:283–84. Shembagamur: Jesuit Madurai Mission Archives.

Prabhaker, M. E., ed. 1989. *Towards a Dalit Theology.* Published for the Christian Institute for the Study of Religion and Society (CISSRS) and Christian Dalit Liberation Movement (CDLM). Delhi: Indian Society for Promoting Christian Knowledge.

Presler, Frank. 1988. *Religion under Bureaucracy: Policy and Administration for Hindu Temples in South India.* Cambridge: Cambridge University Press.

Price, Pamela G. 1996. *Kingship and Political Practice in Colonial India.* Cambridge: Cambridge University Press.

Priolkar, Anant Kabka 1961. *The Goa Inquisition: Being a Quatercentenary Commemoration Study of the Inquisition in India.* Bombay: Bombay University Press.

Quigley, Declan. 1993. *The Interpretation of Caste.* Oxford: Clarendon Press.

Ragunathan A. V. 2008. Call to End "Poster Culture" That Creates Communal Tension. *The Hindu,* 13 October. www.thehindu.com/2008/10/13/stories/2008101359050800.htm.

Raheja, Gloria Goodwin. 1988. *The Poison in the Gift: Ritual, Prestation, and the Dominant Caste in a North Indian Village.* Chicago and London: University of Chicago Press.

———. 1989. Centrality, Mutuality and Hierarchy: Shifting Aspects of Inter-Caste Relationships in North India. *Contribution to Indian Sociology,* n.s., 23 (1): 79–101.

———. 1996. Caste, Colonialism and the Speech of the Colonized: Entextualization and Disciplinary Control in India. *American Ethnologist* 23 (3): 494–513.

Raheja, Gloria Goodwin, and Ann Grodzins Gold. 1994. *Listen to the Heron's Words: Reimagining Gender and Kinship in North India.* Berkeley: University of California Press.

Raj, Antony, SJ. 1990. Sociological Foundations for a Dalit Theology. In *Emerging Dalit Theology,* edited by X. Irudayaraj, 7–17. Madras and Madurai: Jesuit Theological Secretariat and Tamilnadu Theological Seminary.

———. 1992. *Discrimination against Dalit Christians in Tamil Nadu.* Madurai: IDEAS Centre.

Raj, Selva J. 2002. Transgressing Boundaries, Transcending Turner: The Pilgrimage Tradition at the Shrine of St. John de Britto. In *Popular Christianity in India: Riting between the Lines,* edited by Selva J. Raj and Corinne G. Dempsey, 85–113. Albany: State University of New York Press.

———. 2008. Public Display, Communal Devotion: Procession at a South Indian Catholic Festival. In *South Asian Religions on Display: Religious Processions in South Asia and in the Diaspora,* edited by Knut A. Jacobsen, 77–91. London: Routledge.

Raj, Selva J., and William P. Harman. 2006. *Dealing with Deities: The Ritual Vow in South Asia.* New York: SUNY Press.

Rajadurai, S. V., and V. Geetha. 2002. A Response to John Harriss. *Commonwealth and Comparative Politics* 40 (3): 118–24.

Rajamanickam, S. 1972 *The First Oriental Scholar,* Tirunelveli: De Nobili Research Institute.

———. 1987. The Old Madura Mission: A Chronological Table. *Indian Church History Review* 21 (2): 130–35.

Rajaram Row, T. 1891. *Manual of the Ramnad Samastanam.* Madurai: Cleghorn Press, Tamil Nadu State Archives, Madras.

Rajawat, Mamta, ed. 2004. *Encyclopaedia of Dalits in India.* New Delhi: Anmol Publications.

Rajayyan, K. 1974. *Rise and Fall of the Poligars of Tamilnadu.* Madras: Madras University Press.

Ram, Kalpana. 1991. *Mukkuvar Women: Gender, Hegemony and Capitalist Transformation in a South Indian Fishing Community.* Sydney: Allen and Unwin.

———. 1995. Rationalism, Cultural Nationalism and the Reform of Body Politics: Minority Intellectuals of the Tamil Catholic Community. *Contributions to Indian Sociology* 1 (29): 291–318.

Ramaiah, A. 2007. *Laws for Dalit Rights and Dignity: Experiences and Responses from Tamil Nadu.* Jaipur and New Delhi: Rawat Publications.

Ramakrishnan, Venkatesh. 2000. An Agenda of Indianisation. *Frontline* 17, no. 22 (28 October–10 November).

Rao, Anupama. 2009. *The Caste Question: Dalits and the Politics of Modern India.* Berkeley: University of California Press.

Ratzinger, Joseph Cardinal. 2004. *Truth and Toleration: Christian Belief and World Religions.* San Francisco: Ignatius Press.

Reiniche, Marie-Louise. 1979. *Les dieux et les hommes: Etude des cultes d'un village du Tirunelveli, Inde du Sud.* Paris: Mouton.

Résumé du Diarium Maravae [c. 1866]. Manuscript. Jesuit Madurai Mission Archives, Shembaganar, India.

Richter, Julius. 1908. *A History of Missions in India.* Translated by S. H. Moore. Edinburgh: Oliphant Anderson and Ferrier.

Robbins, Joel. 2001. Ritual Communication and Linguistic Ideology: A Reading and Partial Reformulation of Rappaport's Theory of Ritual. *Current Anthropology* 42 (5): 591–614.

———. 2003. On the Paradoxes of Global Pentecostalism and the Perils of Continuity Thinking. *Religion* 33 (3): 221–31.

———. 2004a. *Becoming Sinners: Christianity and Moral Torment in a Papua New Guinea Society.* Berkeley: University of California Press.

———. 2004b. The Globalization of Pentecostal and Charismatic Christianity. *Annual Review of Anthropology* 33:117–43.

———. 2006. Anthropology and Theology: An Awkward Relationship? *Anthropological Quarterly* 79 (2): 285–94.

———. 2007. Continuity Thinking and the Problem of Christian Culture: Belief, Time and the Anthropology of Christianity. *Current Anthropology* 48 (1): 3–38.

———. 2010. Anthropology, Pentecostalism and the New Paul: Conversion, Event, and Social Transformation. Seminar, Department of Anthropology, University College London, London, 12 May.

Robinson, Rowena. 2003. Fluid Boundaries: Christian Communities in India. In *Communal Identity in India,* edited by Bidyut Chakrabarty, 287–305. New Delhi and New York: Oxford University Press.

Rogers, Martyn. 2008. Modernity, "Authenticity," and Ambivalence: Subaltern Masculinities on a South Indian College Campus. *Journal of the Royal Anthropological Institute,* n.s., 14 (1): 79–95.

Rothfork, John. 2006. Review of *Modern Social Imaginaries,* by Charles Taylor (Durham, NC: Duke University Press, 2004). *Rocky Mountain E- Review of Language and Literature* 60 (1), 1–7. Accessed 13 July 2009. http://rmmla.wsu.edu/ereview/60.1/reviews/rothfork.asp.

Rubiés, Joan-Pau. 2005. The Concept of Cultural Dialogue and the Jesuit Method of Accommodation: Between Idolatry and Civilization. *Archivium Historicum Societatis Iesu* 74 (147): 237–80.

Rudner, David West. 1994. *Caste and Capitalism in Colonial India: The Nattukottai Chettiars.* Berkeley: University of California Press.

Rudolph, Lloyd I., and Susanne Hoeber Rudolph. 1967. *The Modernity of Tradition: Political Development in India.* Chicago: University of Chicago Press.

Sahlins, Marshall. 1985. *Islands of History.* Chicago: University of Chicago Press.

———. 1996. The Sadness of Sweetness: Native Anthropology of Western Cosmology. *Current Anthropology* 37 (3): 395–428.

Sarkar, Sumit. 1999. Conversions and Politics of Hindu Right. *Economic and Political Weekly* 34 (26): 1691–1700.

Sarukkai, Sundar. 2007. Dalit Experience and Theory. *Economic and Political Weekly* 42 (40): 4043–48.

Saulière, A. 1947. *Red Sand: A Life of St. John de Britto S. J., Martyr of the Madura Mission.* Madurai: De Nobili.

Schmalz, Matthew N. 1998. A Space for Redemption: Catholic Tactics in Hindu North India. PhD thesis, University of Chicago.

———. 1999. Images of the Body in the Life and Death of a North Indian Catholic Catechist. *History of Religions* 39 (2): 177–201.

———. 2005. Dalit Catholic Tactics of Marginality at a North Indian Mission. *History of Religions* 44 (3): 216–51.

Scott, James. 1990a. *Domination and the Arts of Resistance: Hidden Transcripts.* New Haven, CT: Yale University Press.

———. 1990b. *Weapons of the Weak: Everyday Forms of Peasant Resistance.* Delhi: Oxford University Press.

Seager, Charles. 1847. *The Spiritual Exercises of St. Ignatius of Loyola Translated from the Authorised Latin.* (With extracts from the literal version and notes of Father [Joannes] Rothaan.) London: C. Doleman.

Sébastia, Brigitte. 2002. Māriyamman-Mariyamman: Catholic Practices and the Image of [the] Virgin in Velankanni (Tamil Nadu). Pondy Paper in Social Sciences 27. Pondicherry: French Institute of Pondicherry.

———. 2007. *Les rondes de saint Antoine: Culte, possession et troubles psychiques en Inde du Sud.* Paris: Aux Lieux d'Etre.

———. 2008. A Protective Fortress: Psychic Disorders and Therapy at the Catholic Shrine of Puliyampatti (South India). *Indian Anthropologist* 37 (1): 1–18.

Shah, Ghanshyam. 1990. Dalit Movements and the Search for Identity. *Social Action* 40 (4): 317–35.

Sharma, Ursula M. 1976. Status Striving and Striving to Abolish Status: The Arya Samaj and the Low Castes. *Social Action* 26:215–36.

Sharpe, Eric E. 1965. *Not to Destroy but to Fulfil: The Contribution of J. N. Farquhar to Protestant Missionary Thought in India before 1914.* Uppsala: Gleerup.

Sherinian, Zoe C. 2002. Dalit Theology in Tamil Christian Folk Music: A Transformative Liturgy by James Theophilius Appavoo. In *Popular Christianity in India: Riting between the Lines,* edited by Selva J. Raj and Corinne G. Dempsey, 11–38. Albany: State University of New York Press.

Shiri, G. 1977. *Karnataka Christians and Politics.* Madras: Christian Literature Society.

Shourie, Arun. 1994. *Missionaries in India: Continuities, Changes, Dilemmas.* New Delhi: ASA Publications.

Shulman, David Dean. 1980. *Tamil Temple Myths: Sacrifice and Divine Marriage in the South Indian Saiva Tradition.* Princeton, NJ: Princeton University Press.

Singarayar, J. 1978. A Survey of Christians of Scheduled Caste Origin: Discrimination in Society and Church. *National Christians Council Review* 98:389–391.

Sivasubramaniyan, S. 2002. *Kirittavamum cātiyum* [Christianity and caste]. Nagercoil: Kalachuvdu Pathippagam.

Soares, Benjamin, and Filippo Osella. 2009. Islam, Politics, Anthropology. *Journal of the Royal Anthropological Institute,* n.s., 15 (supp. 1): S1–S23.

Soares-Prabhu, G. 1992. Editorial: Biblical Reflections on Christian Dalits. *Jeevadhara* 22 (128): 92–94.

Sontheimer, G. D., and Hermann Kulke, eds. 1989. *Hinduism Reconsidered.* New Delhi: Manohar.

Spencer, Jonathan. 1990. *A Sinhala Village in a Time of Trouble: Politics and Change in Rural Sri Lanka.* New Delhi: Oxford University Press.

———. 1997. Fatima and the Enchanted Toffees: An Essay on Contingency, Narrative and Therapy. *Journal of the Royal Anthropological Institute* 3 (4): 693–710.

Sri Raman, Papri. 2009. NREGA Promises 100 Days of Employment for the Elderly. *News Blaze,* 14 October. http://newsblaze.com/story/20091014054028iwfs.nb/topstory.html.

Stack, Trevor, 2007. A Higher Ground: The Secular Knowledge of Objects of Religious Devotion. In *Religion and the Secular: Historical and Colonial Formations,* edited by T. Fitzgerald, 47–70. London: Equinox.

Starrett, Gregory. 1998. *Putting Islam to Work: Education, Politics, and Religious Transformation in Egypt.* Berkeley: University of California Press.

Stein, Burton. 1968. Social Mobility and Medieval South Indian Hindu Sects. In *Social Mobility in the Caste System in India,* edited by J. Silverberg, 79–94. The Hague: Mouton.

———. 1980. *Peasant State and Society in Medieval South India.* New Delhi: Oxford University Press.

Stephen, Mark. 2008. Repudiating Caste as My Spiritual Quest. *Caritas* 1–2 (January and July), 21–38.

Stewart, Charles, and Rosalind Shaw, eds. 1994. *Syncretism/Anti-Syncretism: The Politics of Religious Synthesis.* London: Routledge.

Still, Clarinda. 2007. Gender, Education and Status in a Dalit Community in Andhra Pradesh, South India. PhD thesis, London School of Economics and Political Science.

Stirrat, R. L. 1977. Demonic Possession in Catholic Sri Lanka. *Journal of Anthropological Research* 33 (2): 133–57.

———. 1979. A Catholic Shrine in Its Social Context. *Sri Lanka Journal of Social Science* 2:77–108.

———. 1982. Caste Conundrums: Views of Caste in a Sinhalese Catholic Fishing Village. In *Caste Ideology and Interaction,* edited by D. B. McGilvray, 8–33. Cambridge: Cambridge University Press.

———. 1984. Sacred Models. *Man* 19 (2): 199–215.

———. 1992. *Power and Religiosity in a Post-Colonial Setting: Sinhala Catholics in Contemporary Sri Lanka.* Cambridge: Cambridge University Press.

Stoller, Paul. 1995. *Embodying Colonial Memories: Spirit Possession, Power and the Hauka in West Africa.* London: Routledge.

Strickland, William. 1852. *The Jesuit in India.* London: Burns and Lambert.

Strickland, William, and Thomas William M. Marshall. 1865. *Catholic Missions in Southern India to 1865.* London: Longmans, Green and Co.

Subramanium, Narendra. 1999. *Ethnicity and Populist Mobilization: Political Parties, Citizens and Democracy in South India.* Delhi: Oxford University Press.

Sudhakar, P. 2003. Conversion Law Causes Caste Polarisation. *The Hindu,* 5 January. Accessed 4 May 2010. www.hindu.com/thehindu/2003/01/05/stories/2003010504750100.htm.

Suresh, V., and S. Gopalakrishnan. 2003. Convert, and Be Damned! *Combat Law* 7. Accessed 15 March 2005. http://indiatogether.org/combatlaw/issue7/damned.htm.

Tambiah, Stanley J. 1990. *Magic, Science, Religion, and the Scope of Rationality.* Cambridge: Cambridge University Press.

———. 1996. *Leveling Crowds: Ethnonationalist Conflicts and Collective Violence in South Asia.* Berkeley: University of California Press.

Tamil Lexicon. 1936. Published under the authority of the University of Madras. 6 vols. and supplement. Reprint 1982.

Tanabe, Akio. 2007. Toward Vernacular Democracy: Moral Society and Post-Postcolonial Transformation in Rural Orissa, India. *American Ethnologist* 34 (3): 558–74.

Taussig, Michael. 1993. *Mimesis and Alterity: A Particular History of the Senses.* London: Routledge.
Taylor, Charles. 2004. *Modern Social Imaginaries.* Durham, NC: Duke University Press.
Taylor, D. 1985. Some Theological Thoughts about Evil. In *The Anthropology of Evil,* edited by D. Parkin, 26–41. Oxford: Basil Blackwell.
Taylor, Isaac. 1849. *Loyola and Jesuitism in Its Rudiments.* London: Longman, Brown, Green, and Longmans.
Tejani, Shabnum. 2008. *Indian Secularism: A Social and Intellectual History, 1890–1950.* Bloomington: Indiana University Press.
Thangaraj, M. 2003. *Evaluation of the Ten Point Programme for the Development of Dalit Christians in Tamil Nadu.* Chennai: Madras Institute of Development Studies.
Thirumaavalavan, R. 2003. *Talisman: Extreme Emotions of Dalit Liberation.* Translated by Meena Kandasamy. Calcutta: Samya.
———. 2004. *Uproot Hindutva: The Fiery Voice of the Liberation Panthers.* Translated and with an introduction by Meena Kandasamy. Kolkata: Samya.
Thomas, Pradib Ninian. 2008. *Strong Religion, Zealous Media: Christian Fundamentalism and Communication in India.* Los Angeles, London, New Delhi, and Singapore: Sage Publications.
Thorat, Sukhadeo, and Katherine S. Newman. 2007. Caste and Economic Discrimination: Causes, Consequences and Remedies. *Economic and Political Weekly* 42 (41): 4121–24.
Tilche, Alice, 2011. Struggling with Culture in an Adivasi Museum of Western India. PhD thesis. University of London
Tiliander, Bror. 1974. *Christian and Hindu Terminology: A Study of Their Mutual Relations with Special Reference to the Tamil Area.* Uppsala: Almqvista and Wiksell Tryckeri Ab.
Tilly, Charles. 1998. *Durable Inequality.* Berkeley: University of California Press.
Tracy, David. 1981. *The Analogical Imagination: Christian Theology and the Culture of Pluralism.* London: SCM Press.
Trautmann, Thomas R. 1997. *Aryans and British India.* Berkeley: University of California Press.
———. 2009. The Missionary and the Orientalist. In *Ancient to Modern: Religion, Power and Community in India,* edited by Ishita Banerjee-Dube and Saurabh Dube, 236–58. New Delhi: Oxford University Press.
Trawick, Margaret. 1990. *Notes on Love in a Tamil Family.* Berkeley: University of California Press.
Turner, Victor W. 1973. The Center Out There: Pilgrim's Goal. *History of Religions* 12 (3): 191–230.
Turner, V., and E. Turner. 1978. *Image and Pilgrimage in Christian Culture: Anthropological Perspectives.* Oxford: Basil Blackwell.
van der Veer, Peter. 1988. *Gods on Earth: The Management of Religious Experience and Identity in a North Indian Pilgrimage Centre.* London: Althone Press.
———. 1994. *Religious Nationalism: Hindus and Muslims in India.* Berkeley: University of California Press.
———. 2002. Religion in South Asia. *Annual Review of Anthropology* 31:173–87.

Vincentnathan, Lynn. 1993. Untouchable Concepts of Person and Society. In *Contributions to Indian Sociology,* n.s., 27 (1): 53–82.

Vincentnathan, Lynn, and George S. Vincentnathan. 2007. Village Courts and the Police: Cooperation and Conflict in Modernizing India. *Police Practice and Research* 8 (5): 445–59.

Viswanath, Rupa. 2008. Religion, Secularism, Solicitude: Ways of Speaking about Pariah Conversion in Colonial Madras. Paper presented at the London School of Economics, January.

———. 2010. Spiritual Slavery, Material Malaise: "Untouchables" and Religious Neutrality in Colonial South India. *Historical Research* 83 (219): 124–45.

Viswanathan, Gauri. 1998. *Outside the Fold: Conversion, Modernity, and Belief.* Princeton, NJ: Princeton University Press.

Viswanathan, S. 2008a. The Fall of a Wall. *Frontline* 25 (11). www.frontlineonnet.com/fl2511/stories/20080606251112300.htm.

———. 2008b. A House Divided. *Frontline* 25 (08). www.flonnet.com/fl2508/stories/20080425250804100.htm.

Waghorne, Joanne Punzo. 2002. Chariots of the God/s: Riding the Line between Hindu and Christian. In *Popular Christianity in India: Riting between the Lines,* edited by Selva J. Raj and Corinne G. Dempsey, 11–38. Albany: State University of New York Press.

———. 2004. *Diaspora of the Gods: Modern Hindu Temples in an Urban Middle-Class World.* Oxford: Oxford University Press.

Warner, Marina. 1978. *Alone of All Her Sex: The Myth and the Cult of the Virgin Mary.* London: Quartet Books.

Warren, Max Alexander Cunningham. 1967. *Social History and Christian Mission.* London: S.C.M. Press.

Washbrook, David. 1993. Land and Labour in Late Eighteenth-Century South India: The Golden Age of the Pariah? In *Dalit Movements and the Meanings of Labour in India,* edited by P. Robb, 68–86. New Delhi: Oxford University Press.

———. 2009. The Majewski Lecture: Rationalism, Atheism and Hinduism in Dravidian India, c. 1920–90. *Oxford Centre for Hindu Studies.* www.ochs.org.uk/node/444.

Weber, Max. 1956. *The Sociology of Religion.* Translated by Ephraim Fischoff. Boston: Beacon Press.

Webster, John. 1992. *A History of Dalit Christians in India.* Delhi: ISPCK Press.

Wiebe, Paul C. 1970. Protestant Missions in India, a Sociological Review. *Journal of Asian and African Studies* 5 (4): 293–301.

Wilkinson, Steven. 2005. Communal Riots in India. *Economic and Political Weekly* 40 (44/45): 4768–70.

Williams, Rowan. 2008. Religious Faith and Human Rights. Public lecture, London School of Economics and Political Science, 1 May. www2.lse.ac.uk/PublicEvents/pdf/20080501_RowanWilliams.pdf.

Wilson, K. 1982. *The Twice Alienated: Culture of Dalit Christians.* Hyderabad: Booklinks Corporation.

Wilson, Stephen, ed. 1983. *Saints and Their Cults: Studies in Religious Sociology, Folklore and History.* Cambridge: Cambridge University Press.

Wingate, Andrew. 1999. *The Church and Conversion: A Study of Recent Conversions to and from Christianity in the Tamil Area of South India.* Delhi: Indian Society for Promoting Christian Knowledge (ISPCK).

Wright, Jonathan. 2004. *The Jesuits: Missions, Myths and Histories.* London: HarperCollins.

———. 2008. *The Suppression and Restoration.* In *The Cambridge Companion to the Jesuits,* edited by Thomas Worcester, 263–77. Cambridge: Cambridge University Press.

Wyatt, Andrew. 1996. The Politics of Caste in India with Special Reference to the Dalit Christian Campaign for Scheduled Caste Reservations. PhD thesis, University of Bristol.

———. 2010. *Party System Change in South India: Political Entrepreneurs, Patterns and Processes.* London and New York: Routledge.

Xavier, Arockiasamy M. 2006. Contribution of the Jesuits to Social Awakening in Tamil Nadu. PhD thesis, St. Joseph's College (Bharathidasan University), Tiruchirappalli, Tamil Nadu.

Xavier, Francis, SJ. 2009. The Rights of the Marginalized Are the Rights of God. Paper presented at the Tamilnadu Bishops' Conference, July.

Young, Richard Fox. 2009. Empire and Misinformation: Christianity and Colonial Knowledge from a South Indian Hindu Perspective (ca. 1804). In *India and the Indianness of Christianity,* edited by R. Fox Young, 59–81. Richmond, UK: Routledge Curzon.

Zavos, John. 2001. Conversion and the Assertive Margins: An Analysis of Hindu Nationalist Discourse and the Recent Attacks on Indian Christians. *South Asia* 34 (2): 73–89.

Zelliot, Eleanor. 1966. Buddhism and Politics in Maharashtra. In *South Asian Politics and Religion,* edited by D. E. Smith, 191–212. Princeton, NJ: Princeton University Press.

———. 1992. *From Untouchable to Dalit: Essays on the Ambedkar Movement.* New Delhi: Manohar.

Zene, Cosimo. 2007. Myth, Identity and Belonging: The Rishi of Bengal/Bangladesh. *Religion* 37:257–81.

Županov, Ines G. 1996. Le repli du religieux: Les missionnaires jésuites du 17e siècle entre la théologie chrétienne et une éthique païenne. *Annales: Histoire, Sciences Sociales* 6:1201–23.

———. 1999. *Disputed Mission: Jesuit Experiments and Brahmanical Knowledge in Seventeenth-Century India.* New Delhi: Oxford University Press.

———. 2005. *Missionary Tropics: The Catholic Frontier in India (16th–17th Centuries).* Ann Arbor: University of Michigan Press.

———. 2007. Language and Culture of the Jesuit "Early Modernity" in India during the Sixteenth Century. *Itinerario* 32 (2): 87–110.

———. 2008. Conversion, Illness and Possession: Catholic Missionary Healing in Early Modern South Asia. In *Divins remèdes: Médecine et religion en Inde,* edited by Ines G. Županov and Caterina Guenzi, 263–300. Collection Puruṣārtha 27. Paris: Editions de L'Ecole des Hautes Etudes en Sciences Sociales.

INDEX

jajmāni, 116, 302nn24,26
James, St. *See* Santiyakappar
Jayalalitha, J., 167, 203, 206, 309n55
Jeffery, Patricia, 254, 255
Jeffery, Roger, 254, 255
Jeffrey, Craig, 254, 255
Jesuits, ix, xv, 4, 58; "big men," 38; blood associated with, 78; Brahmanized accommodations, 4–16, 98, 149, 198, 208, 221, 267–68, 271, 292n19; Brahmanizing Catholicism, 7–9, 15–18, 22, 24, 28–36, 43, 49–52, 206, 286nn8,9, 287n20, 292n19, 318n51; caste distinctions abandoned by, 124; caste divisions among, 34–35, 50; caste rank schemes, 145–52; caste-segregated church, 34, 45, 51, 131, 156–59, 162, 240, 292n20; Christian influence on caste experience, 98, 126–30; conception of religiosity, 17; *dalit,* 2, 24, 217, 223–29, 277–78, 316n30; death rate, 48; diaries, xiv, 110–11; dress, 64; dual morality established by, 5–6, 18–19, 23, 271–73, 277, 280–84; education method, 52–53; festival honors, 42, 144, 146–59, 164, 268; French, 8, 23, 46–53, 61, 62–67, 146–67, 292n19; gurus, 15, 18, 33, 37; honors and, 42, 144, 146–59; itinerant, 13; Madurai Mission, xiv, 4–9, 14–15, 23, 32–35, 46, 49–53, 59, 62–67, 91, 142, 146–52, 209, 224, 267–68, 277, 286nn4,6; Malabar rites controversy, 44–46, 290n43, 292n19; Malayali, 53; "mediators" of caste relations, 133, 305n1; as miraculous power sources, 76, 77–78; New Madurai Mission, 46, 49–53, 62–67, 91, 142; not renouncers, 21; as overlords and "kings," 18, 42, 47–48, 145, 154–56, 268–69, 291n17; political role, 38–39, 274; and possession, 65–70; "preferential option for the poor," 209, 215; Propaganda Fide, 46, 146–49, 292n21; Protestant criticized by, 50, 52, 53; Ramnad, 15–16, 28, 36–46, 47–48, 62, 64, 77–78; religious authority, 14, 23, 38–39, 46, 47–49, 62–67, 143, 146, 154–56, 170, 171, 269, 274; royal rule transacted by, 18; *sanniyāsis* (renouncers), 17–18, 21, 33, 34, 91, 273, 282; secular category produced by, xi–xii, 7; secularization of Brahmans, 7–10; secularizing caste, 7–9, 15, 22, 58, 59, 127–29, 267–68, 272, 273, 279; separating religion and culture, 4–9, 12–24, 33–34, 90, 97, 98, 124–26, 156, 162, 267–68; and sin, 123, 127; social action programs, xiii, 208–14, 228, 319n61; social apartness, 64–65, 273–74, 304n48; sorcerous powers attributed to, 62; "spiritual entrepreneurship," 9; "strategies of place," 178; substitution strategy, 5–16, 267, 270, 303n35; Tamil, 53, 294n19. *See also* Christianity and caste; Nobili, Roberto; Society of Jesus
Jesus, 25, 237; birth of, 298n53; Catholic lineage, 25; "Christ as drum," 222; as *dalit,* 24, 213–14, 216, 220–21, 222, 225, 228, 318n52; decent into hell, 306n4; divine power, 82; dual morality and, 90, 131, 180, 311n23; exorcism focus, 93; healing power, 93, 95; image in village homes, 71, 71*fig;* Islam and, 192; life of, 213, 216; miracle-working, 95; as outcast, 24; Passion plays, 136, 148, 305–6nn54,4; Pentecostal "personal relationship" with, 94; protection of, 67; as social revolutionary, 25
John Pandian (JP) Youth Front, 255–59, 322n26
Joseph, St., 64
JP. *See* John Pandian (JP) Youth Front; Pandian, John

kaipiccai (handouts), 112–13
kaḷamputikkira vīṭus ("houses that take from the threshing floor"), 113, 249
kaḷattupaṭi nellu ("threshing floor measure rice"), 109, 113, 121, 181
Kali, 74, 84, 87–88
Kaḷḷars, 175, 186, 204, 309n54; Backward Castes, 194, 203; warrior caste, 302n18
kaṇṇi. See virgin
Kapferer, Bruce, 83
karṇam (accountant), Veḷḷāḷar, 100, 104, 111, 154–56, 170, 301n11, 308n33
Karukku (Bama), 214, 317n39, 321n23
katta panchayat, dispute mediation, 225, 259–62
Kattaya Tevar, 37–38, 39
kaṭṭupāṭu (order), 129, 144, 252
kāṭu, 86–87; caste and, 164, 175; evil disposed to, 71, 87, 164; life-crisis rituals, 116; moral spaces, 273, 282; origin of Virgin Mary and ascetic goddess, 84; saints, 86–88; tombs, 77; *ūr* and, 90, 116, 273, 282; wilderness, 77, 86–88, 297n44, 298n57, 299n59. *See also* forest saints and shrines
Keane, Webb, 5, 7, 11, 68
Kerala, ix, 32, 97–98
Kilavan, 36, 37
kīḻ cāti, 111, 285n1. *See also* lower castes
kings: claims over Christian shrines, 47, 145–56; Hindu, 44, 145, 154; Jesuits as overlords and,

Menon, D.M., 179
MEP (French Catholic Société des Missions Etrangères de Paris), 54–55, 292n23
Michael the Archangel, St., 134
migration: to Alapuram, 42, 100, 106, 130, 151, 175, 177, 186, 254; droughts and famines precipitating, 309n1; international networks established through, 173; labor, 41, 145, 169, 177, 181, 202, 253, 269, 309n1; Maṟavar, 301n14; "native village," 99; Necavar, 186
militant activism, *dalit,* xiv–xv, 2, 24, 215–18, 277–78
milk, Virgin Mary/goddess and, 81, 84, 85, 297n44, 298–99n57
mimesis, 189; Catholic-pagan, 61, 89, 270; Hindu-Christian, 199; Jesuit-Brahman, 9, 43
Mines, Diane, 164; *cāti,* 97; "centres of density," 138; "fierce gods," 164, 165; *kāṭu,* 87; *kuṭi-makkaḷ,* 108, 116–17, 302n22; *mariyātai,* 128, 130; "rituals of removal," 118
miracles: banyan tree of St. James, ix–xi, 12, 13, 40, 160, 161; de Britto, 77, 78; missionaries as sources of, 76, 77–78, 94–95; relics for protection vs., 305n2; tombs' healing powers, 76–78, 77*fig. See also* healing
misfortune: Catholic rituals of removal, 118–21; charismatic Christian and Pentecostal responses, 92; Jesuit missionary attitudes toward, 62–67, 75; popular responses to, 65–67, 73, 75, 79, 88–89. *See also* death; drought; famine; possession
missionaries, ix, xi–xii; anthropology and, xii–xiii; anti-Christian campaign vs., 199–206; assimilation of teachings, 31, 32, 282–83; and categories of religion and secular, xi–xii, 3–5, 7–9; Christian "part-cultures," 3; competition over jurisdiction, 146–49; discipline, 14, 48, 60–64, 89, 94, 156–57; era after, 29, 168, 275; mass conversions and social welfare, 54–59; miracle-working, 76, 77–78, 94–95; "mission history" separated from "economic history," 59; "part-cultures," 3. *See also* Jesuits; Protestants
La Mission de Maduré, 159
mobility. *See* social mobility
modernity, 320n14; "being social," 250–51, 272, 279, 320n13; Catholic Church and, 45, 49, 242, 287n15; Christian, 3–8, 91–95, 290n47, 320n14; contemporary Alapuram, 233–65; crisis of, 167; secular, 45, 242, 287n15; "theory of," 27. *See also* technology
Moffatt, Michael, 140, 303n38, 304n42, 312n37; *An Untouchable Community in South India: Structure and Consensus,* 188–89
Moguls, 35
monsoon, 76, 106
Moors, St. James as slayer of, 40, 80, 81
morality: caste as *adiaphora* (morally indifferent thing), xii, 7–8, 129–30, 268, 277; Hindu caste system, 57, 130–31; missionary codes, 61–69; Tamil, 18, 282, 284. *See also* dual morality; impurity/pollution; sin
Müller, Max, 9
Muniaiyar, 82, 83, 87–88, 187
Muslims: Babri Masjid (mosque) at Ayodhya, 314n3; conversions, 191–92, 193, 203, 204, 313n41; cult centers, 42; *dalit* political alliances with, 196; Hindu nationalism vs., 199–200, 314n3; SC barring, 97
Mūtēvi, goddess of ill fortune, 119–20, 123
Muthupattanam, St. Anthony's shrine, 68, 70, 80, 87, 88
myths: Paṟaiyar, 184–87, 191, 274–75. *See also* origin myths

Nabokov, Isabelle, 79, 296n31; "Expel the Lover, Recover the Wife," 70. *See also* Clark-Decès, Isabelle (Nabokov)
Nadars, 308n34; "caste feeling," 246; catechists for, 122; contemporary Alapuram, 240, 245, 246, 260; Hindu revivalism, 203; intercaste relationship negotiation, 245; Jesuit view of, 151; Nadar Front, 260; palmyra workers, 41, 51, 100, 179, 307n16; Santiyakappar festival, 161, 162; tomb, 76, 77
nākarīkam, 182–84, 187, 239, 251, 252. *See also* urbanity
nallatu-keṭṭatu (the good and the bad) lifecycle rites, 119–21, 273
Nallukkotai Utaiyan Tevar, 39
Nari ("fox") Kuṟuvar "gypsies," 105, 134
National Campaign for Dalit Human Rights (NCDHR), 228–29
National Conference of Christian Dalits, 313n45
nationalism, 199; Dravidian, 173, 175, 203; Tamil, 196. *See also* Hindu nationalism
National Rural Employment Guarantee Act (NREGA), 249, 311n26
natural reason: Brahman, 5, 9, 10; idolatry distinguished from, 5, 6–7, 9
Navarattiri festival, 110
Nayakkars, 35–40, 227

vices for, 120; servitude, 108, 112–13, 140, 144, 156, 157, 159, 164, 169–78, 251; sharecropping tenancy, 172, 173, 177, 181, 312n35; social mobility, 110, 111, 156–61, 164, 183, 191–93, 243, 248, 253–54, 255, 313n46; "strategies of place," 178, 186, 191, 243; youth activism, 160–61, 165, 174, 175, 176, 192, 235, 241, 255–59, 317n36, 322n26. See also *dalits;* Devēntira Kula Vēḷāḷar (DKV)
PALMERA (People's Action for Liberation Movement in Eastern Ramnad), xiii, 208, 209
panchayats, 238; *katta panchayat* dispute mediation, 225, 259–62; Maṟavar, 104, 301n17; presidentships, 173, 205, 235, 240, 260, 261; vice president, 243
Panchayat Union, 258, 322n29
Pandian, John, 195–96, 255–56, 256*fig*, 258, 321n24
Pandian, M. S. S., 9, 278
Pandiyan, Marudu, 41, 233
Pandyan kingdom, 32–33
Panikkar, Raymond, *The Unknown Christ of Hinduism*, 91
paṇṭāracāmis, missionaries for *dalits*, 34, 35, 43, 48, 291n8
paṟai. *See* drumming
Paṟaiyars, 101, 105*fig*, 108, 189, 227, 278, 291n6; *aiyā vīṭu*, 113, 302–3n31; autonomy denied to, 115, 182–84, 191; beef eating, 184, 185, 223–24, 312nn30,36; caste interpretations by, 126–27; Christian communities, 53, 54; claims on public spaces, 235; clan name, 302n19; contemporary Alapuram, 235, 240, 245, 248, 255, 258–59; conversion to Protestantism, 179–84, 274; exclusions, 113–15, 183–85, 186, 248, 292n20; Hindus, 186–87, 190, 260; intercaste relationship negotiation, 188, 245; Necavars, 105, 186–87, 191, 301n11, 312n32; origin myths, 184–85, 191; Paḷḷars and, 176, 177, 227, 259–60, 310nn18,21, 312nn35,36, 316–17n36; political leaders, 195, 205, 206, 215, 219, 221, 225, 227–29; political prominence, 227, 319n60; redefining service roles, 181–82, 191; religious equality, 158; services for, 120–21; servitude, 109, 118, 140, 142, 178, 179–89, 249, 303nn37,38; sibling myth, 185–87, 191, 275; subcastes, 186; "tactics of space," 178–80, 186, 187, 191, 196–97; Tōṭṭis, 105, 110, 111, 140, 186–87; urbanity, 182–84, 187, 274, 319n60; youth activism, 258–59, 317n36, 322n29. See also *dalits;* drumming
Parangis, 33, 37, 49, 267
Paravars, 34, 39, 316n33
Pariahs, 34, 35, 45, 50–58, 158–9, 178, 268, 291n6. See also *dalits*; Paṟaiyars
Paschal Lamb, Catholicism, 84
Passion plays, 136, 148, 305–6nn54,4
passions: struggles against, 61, 63, 70, 89. *See also* desires; sexuality
patronage, 101, 112–13, 181, 302n26, 311nn24,26; conversion hopes, 54; by Jesuit priests, 142–43, 151. *See also* gifting; landlords; royal patronage
Paul the Hermit, St./Vannattu Cinnappar, 65–66, 87, 106–7, 165, 299n60
"PCR" (Protection of Civil Rights), 243–44
Peel, John D. Y., 26, 283
penances, 67, 73
Pentecostalism, 3, 28, 62, 92–95, 283; Alapuram, xiv, 92–94, 192–93, 233–42, 319nn4,5; asceticism, 94, 241; and caste politics, 192–93, 231, 233, 240–41; conversion, 2, 193, 300n69; globalized form, xv, 240, 241, 279; healing, 94, 240, 241, 319n5; Paḷḷar, 192–93, 238, 240–41; "The Pentecostal Mission" (Ceylon Pentecostal Mission), 240, 319nn4,5; possession and exorcism, 93, 239; prosperity gospel, 241–42; short-time-frame ethnographies, 27; urban, 300n70
Periyar (E. V. Ramasamy), 159, 190, 194, 208, 220, 225
Periya Vodaya Tevar, 41
persecution: of Christians, 38. *See also* anti-Christian campaign
person, category of, 17
person-body, with fluid boundaries, 61, 69, 70
personhood: Christian, 17, 19–21; possession and, 69, 70; saint of exorcism, 87
perumai ("relative bigness"), 138, 149
pēy-picācu, exorcism of, 70, 88, 93, 239
Phule, Jyotirao, 194, 310n14
pilgrimages, 39, 73, 92, 295n29; continuing importance of, 239; de Britto shrine, 37–38, 87; hermit saints of the forest, 87; Hindu, 92; pilgrim rest houses, 38; Rameswaram, x*map*, 35, 37; Velankanni shrine, 298n56
place: de Certeau and, 178, 186, 311n20; prior to religious identification, 21, 98; "strategies of," 178–80, 186, 189, 191, 197, 243, 311n20. *See also* sacred geography; space; *ūr*
"poligars," 35, 36

Scott, James, 182
seating: caste-segregated, 51, 131; at church, 51, 131, 238; etiquette at ceremonies, 245; plastic chairs, 245
Sebastian, St., 2, 64, 78, 80, 165, 239, 318n52
sect, 289n31; *bhakti* devotional order, 17–18, 21, 90, 190, 282, 289n37; Christian, 15
secular: as category, xi–xii, 3–4, 7; and religion category, xi–xii, 3–5, 7, 43–44. *See also* culture; politics and governance
secularism, Nehruvian, 207
secularization, 7; Anglo-Protestant education, 53; of Brahmans, 7–9; of caste, 7–9, 15, 22, 58, 59, 127–29, 171, 267–68, 272, 273, 279; Catholic Church within secular modernity, 45, 242, 287n15; of untouchability, 170–71, 185
segregation. *See* caste segregation
Sekaran, Immanuel, 173, 196, 259, 309n6, 310n15, 321n24
self-formation, 67, 281
self-improvement, 178, 184–85
Self-Respect Movement, 159, 313nn42,44
seminaries, 53; caste discrimination, 211; *dalit* activism, 227, 276–77, 279; *dalit* cultural production, 22, 211–12, 222, 227; Tamilnadu Theological Seminary (TTS), 222, 226, 316n28
semiotic forms, 13–14; anthropologies of Christianity, 288n24; *dalit* theology and, 24, 222; Jesuit substitution strategy, 5–16, 267, 270, 303n35
service: caste defined by, 108–9, 243; caste-linked, 101, 104, 108, 112–23, 140, 141*table*, 172, 181–82, 248–50; caste rank and, 120–23, 129, 140; church, 140–41; contemporary Alapuram, 248–50; enhanced status of, 129–30; festival, 140, 141*table*, 142, 156, 157, 178; funeral, 75, 109, 111, 117–23, 126–27, 131–32, 249, 303n37; paid for, 129; redefining roles, 181–82, 191; replication of, 122, 140, 187–91, 303n37; ritual, 116–23, 303n37. *See also* employment; occupations; servitude
servitude, 57, 112–15, 189, 275, 293nn27,1, 309n51; agrarian, 101, 169; *aṭimai vēlai* ("slave work"), 126, 172, 249; British servants, 49, 50; Cakkiliyar, 118, 177, 187, 189, 251; conversion and, 54–59; elderly and, 311n26; European campaigns vs., 59; Mukkuvars and, 305n55; Necavar, 186, 312n32; Nobili and, 22; Paḷḷar, 108, 112–13, 140, 144, 156, 157, 159, 164, 169–78, 251; Paṟaiyar, 109, 118, 140, 142, 178, 179–89, 249, 303nn37,38; social activism vs., 169–78, 183; spiritual (caste as), 55–59; Tōṭṭis, 186; United Nations discourse on, 278; Vatican history of conservative views on, 51; work status and, 22, 126–27, 129, 181, 222, 249–51; work without, 181–82. *See also* caste politics; drumming; emancipation, *dalit; kuṭimakkaḷ;* service
sets, caste, 261–62, 280
Seventh Day Adventists, 203–4
sexuality: female, 79, 85, 152, 298nn53,54; male control over, 152; possession and, 69, 70; pounding sound of rice mortars, 84; purity and impurity, 79, 124
sharecropping tenancy, Paḷḷar, 172, 173, 177, 181, 312n35
shares, 109, 110, 291n17; priests overseeing, 41–42, 47–48; symbolic, 42; upper share, 41, 47. *See also* grain shares
Shaw, Rosalind, 14
shrines: goddess, 79; Jesuits wresting control of, 47, 145–56; Our Lady of Lourdes, 160; royal patronage, 38, 40, 100; Virgin Mary, 73, 81, 85, 92, 239, 298n56. *See also* churches; Hindu temples; saint shrines
Shulman, David, 81
sibling myth, Paṟaiyar, 185–87, 191, 275
signification, 22; caste as living sign, 97; *dalit* culture, 222–23, 272, 278; festival honors, 144, 161, 279; Jesuit substitution, 5–16, 267, 270, 303n35; Paḷḷar strategies of place, 191; resignification, 22, 222–24, 231, 272, 278. *See also* rituals; semiotic forms; substitution; symbolic associations
sin, 123, 127, 294n17; caste as, 1, 24, 281–2, 317n37; caste pride, 152; impurity and, 116, 294n16; misfortune related to, 66–67; possession not a matter of, 69; sexuality and, 298n54; unconfessed, 67. *See also* demonic
Singh, Manmohan, 206
Siva, 74–75, 81–84, 88, 318n52
Sivagangai, x*map*, 35; British colonialism changing, 47–48; economics, 254; Nallukkotai Utaiyan Tevar, 39; "rituals of unity," 42; Tevar celebration, 233
Sivan, M., xiv, 321n21
slavery. *See* servitude
smallpox, 62, 73, 293n3, 297n48
social justice, xv; Catholic Church and, 59, 92, 170, 198–232, 261, 274–75, 316n26; Pentecos-

tals and, 240–41. *See also* equality; liberation theology; rights; state protection
social mobility, 54–55, 145; *dalit,* 29, 110, 111, 129, 156–61, 164, 183, 191–93, 204, 243, 248, 253–54, 255; Maṟavar and, Veḷḷāḷar, 301n14; Paḷḷar, 110, 111, 156–61, 164, 183, 191–93, 243, 248, 253–54, 255, 313n46; Uṭaiyār, 149–53, 164. *See also* equality
social order: apartness of priests, 64–65, 238, 273–74, 304n48; "being social" and, 250–51, 272, 279, 320n13; desacralized by missionaries, xii, 22, 290n42; civic custom, xii, 4–9; hierarchical, 42, 59, 97, 108–9, 263; in cemetery, 132, 247. *See also* caste; culture; economics; equality; politics and governance; social mobility; village society
Social Watch–Tamil Nadu, 226
social welfare: conversion and, 54–58; liberation theology, 24, 92, 162, 208, 210. *See also* state reservations
Society of Jesus: reinstated, 46, 47, 49, 58; suppressed, 32, 44–46, 58. *See also* Jesuits
Soosai case, 207
space: de Certeau and, 178, 311n20; Protestant "capacity to aspire," 184; "strategies of place," 178–80, 186, 189, 191, 197, 243, 311n20; "tactics of," 178–80, 186, 187, 191, 196–97, 311n20. *See also* caste segregation; place; public spaces
SPG (Society for the Propagation of the Gospel in Foreign Parts), Anglican, 101, 179–80, 187
spirit possession. *See* possession
Spiritual Exercises (Ignatius of Loyola), 16, 62–63, 216
Srinivasan, Irattaimalai, 190, 205
ST (Scheduled Tribe), 243–44, 315n12
Staines, Graham, 200
statecraft: conversion as act of, 36; gifting, 41; intertwining of religious centers and rule, 32, 40, 268. *See also* politics and governance
state protection: vs. caste-based discrimination, 171, 173. *See also* law; state reservations
state reservations, 97, 176, 226, 247; Christian activism, 206–14, 217–19, 230, 277; for "Other Backward Castes," 201; ST, 243–44, 315n12; untouchable status required for, 174–75, 275. *See also* Backward Castes; Scheduled Castes (SC)
statues: Ambedkar, 278; castes forbidden from handling, 304n46; Santiyakappar, 72*fig,* 86, 100, 162
status competition: 139–163, 187–90; Catholic churches and ritual systems, 139–40; intercaste, 142, 177, 188, 191, 255
Stein, Burton, 139
Stewart, Charles, 14
Still, Clarinda, 188, 313n39, 322n25
"structures of reconciliation," 273–74, 282
subordination: *dalits* representing, 22, 185–86, 191; idioms of, 115–17, 130, 243. *See also* lower castes; servitude
substantialization, 67; caste, 164; nonrelational divinity, 85–90
substitution: Jesuit strategy, 5–16, 267, 270, 303n35. *See also* Indianization
superstition, 5–6, 9, 69. *See also* paganism
symbolic associations, 130; church honors, 48, 144–45; cross, 318n54; festival, 160; "fetishism," 6, 48, 74, 144–45; pollution, 22, 130; rice, 304n43; untouchability, 22, 185–86, 191, 271–72. *See also* rituals; semiotic forms; signification; substitution
syncretism, religious, xi, 14, 214, 231, 273–74
synthesis. *See* religious synthesis
Syriac Church, 4
Syrian Christians, 4, 36
taccaṇai, 112, 303–4n41

Tadaiya Tevar, 37
Tambiah, Stanley J., 202, 265, 317n38
Tamil "being in the world," 20, 21, 26, 99, 280. *See also* culture
Tamil Catholicism, xi, xv; Alapuram, xiii–xiv, 39–40, 66, 72*fig,* 73, 82; aligning with anti-caste position of modern Indian state, 162; anthropology of, 24–29; caste within, 23, 96; Christianity embedded in Tamil forms, xii, 19, 25, 43, 153, 179, 230, 268, 292n19, 295n25; Christian worship disembedded from village culture, 23, 29, 133, 155–58, 163–66, 234, 238–42, 262, 269, 274–77, 279; cultural identity as socially prior to, 21, 98; culturally appropriated, 268; and *dalit* entitlement to state reservations, 207; "dalitness" vs. Hindutva, 205–6; and *dalit* political identity, 194–95; delinking from Hinduism, 29, 133, 154–56, 164–67, 231, 234–36, 242, 274, 279; democratization of public worship, 161–63, 234; "Hinduized," 231; in-between space, 284; institutionalized, 23–24, 29, 90–91, 156, 268–69, 273; Jesuits Brahmanizing, 7–9, 15–18, 22, 24, 28–36, 43, 49–52, 206, 286nn8,9, 287n20, 292n19, 318n51; *kōvil* overruled by,

56–59; public spaces, 173–74; secularization of, 170–71, 185; state reservations based on assertion of, 174–75, 275; symbolic associations, 22, 185–86, 191, 271–72. *See also* caste politics; discrimination; exclusion, caste-based; inferiorization
untouchables, 2, 285n1; Gandhian inclusion within the Hindu majority, 193; "untouchables to," 177, 188–89. See also *dalits*
Upadhyay, Brahmabandhab, 91
upper castes, 188, 285n1; *aiyā vīṭu* (lord's house), 113, 181, 248–49, 302–3n31; Alapuram streets, xiii, xiv, 104, 114–15; "caste feeling," 246, 247; Catholic priests, 126; Catholic social standing with Hindus, 127, 158; Catholic support for *dalit* activism, 216; Ceṭṭiyārs, 101, 111, 150, 261; change as a passive effect of time, 251; church roles, 51, 100–101, 161; church segregation, 45, 156–59; contemporary economics, 254–55; and education, 254; Europeans judged socially inferior by, 50; festival donors, 108; French priests linking with, 50, 52–53; funeral rites, 131–32, 247–48; Hindu, 167, 192; Jesuit education for, 52–53; landlords of lower castes, 58–59, 101, 104, 110–11, 157, 159, 161, 173, 177, 181; mass conversions and, 55, 56; patrons of lower castes, 101; Protestant attitude toward, 52; Protestant Christians, 131; protests vs. lower castes, 2, 45, 157, 161, 163, 169; purity and impurity in transactions with lower castes, 116–17; RSS-Catholic Paḷḷar poster dispute, 236; Syrian Christians, 4; Vanniyars, 211, 219, 227, 317n46; and women, 115, 152–54, 322n25. *See also* Ācāri; Brahmans; Tevars; Uṭaiyārs; Veḷḷāḷars; warrior castes
"upper house," Alapuram, 104*fig*
urbanity, 239; Paṟaiyar, 182–84, 187, 274, 319n60. See also *nākarīkam*
ūr, 99; Alapuram as, 107, 108; Christian Tamil, 99–108; and *kāṭu*, 90, 116, 273, 282; as social identification, 98, 99. *See also* Alapuram; *ūḷḷūr* ("inside-ur"); village society
Uṭaiyārs, 194, 308n34; "big men," 66, 149, 153, 157, 251; boycott of Catholic masses and festivals, 149–50, 152, 156–57; caste associations, 260–61; caste discrimination, 211; "caste feeling," 246, 247; caste-segregated festival, 108, 162, 163; Catholic priests, 126, 305n49; claims on public spaces, 235; clan names, 302n19; contemporary Alapuram, 240, 246, 253; cultivators, 41, 101, 106, 110–11, 301n12; ecclesiastical conflict and, 147–49; festival honors, 145, 147, 149; festival service, 140, 142, 160, 161; funeral rites, 161, 247; Hindu, 149; intercaste relationship negotiation, 188; Jesuit view of, 151–52; land ownership, 101, 104, 110–11, 145, 150, 157, 173, 177, 181, 301nn12,13; Mandalacotei exorcist, 65, 66; Nallukkotai Utaiyan Tevar, 39; social mobility, 149–53, 164; wedding preparations, 114*fig*; and women's autonomy, 152–53

Vannattu Cinnappar (St. Paul the Hermit), 65–66, 87, 106–7, 165, 299n60
Vanniyars, 211, 219, 227, 317n46
vāram. *See* shares
varna, fifth, 55
varnashrama dharma, 194, 221, 276
Vatican: conservative views on race or slavery, 51; Vatican II, 24, 90–91, 92, 162, 205, 217, 231, 276, 292n19. *See also* Catholicism; popes
Veaux, Father, 141, 157–58, 170
Veda, Christian, 5, 10
Velankanni, Virgin Mary shrine, 73, 81, 85, 92, 239, 298n56, 305n2
Veḷḷāḷars: vs. caste desegregation, 308n42; caste discrimination by, 211, 305n50; Catholic priests, 126, 154, 304–5n49; choristers, 51; contemporary Alapuram, 243; ecclesiastical conflict and, 148–49; funeral rites, 161, 247; *karṇam* (accountant), 100, 104, 111, 154–56, 170, 301n11, 308n33; *kōvilpiḷḷai* (catechists), 82, 100–101, 108, 111, 118, 121–24, 147–50, 157, 162, 305n50; *kōvilpiḷḷai* no longer, 238; mobility strategies, 301n14; Santiyakappar festival, 140, 148–50, 161, 162; terms of address, 115; Uṭaiyār vs., 149, 150, 188
Victorian evolutionary schemes, 287n14
Vijayanagara, 35, 227
village area. *See* Alapuram; *ūr*
village gods and goddesses: Aiyanar, 80, 81, 82, 87–88, 106, 155; Alapuram, 79, 84, 85, 106–7, 270, 311n23; "common deities," 77; Conaiyar, 82; goddess cooling, 79, 81, 84, 85; goddess festivals, 76, 84; goddess and milk, 81, 84, 85, 297n44, 298–99n57; guardian deities, 81, 82, 106–7, 297n43; hierarchy of, 82–84, 88; Hindu-Christian links, 74–91; inferior/superior, 82–84; Karumeni, 85–86;

"Working People's Liberation Movement" (WPLM), 208, 317n36
worship: Christians adopting Hindu forms of, 294n9; contemporary Alapuram, 240; healing in, 240, 242; material/immaterial, 6; private, 79, 139; and servitude, 293n1. *See also* Christian worship; cults; public worship; saint veneration
Wright, Jonathan, 45, 49

Xavier, Francis, 1–2, 33, 220
Xavier, St., 146; chapel, 65, 299n60

Yadavar Front, 260
Yesumarian, L., 213, 215, 216, 223, 224, 318n56
youth activism, 162, 209, 225, 226, 264, 279–80; Arunthathiyar, 228; associational forms, 322n32; against Church discrimination, 316n30; fall in, 258–59; Paḷḷar, 160–61, 165, 174, 175, 176, 192, 235, 241, 255–59, 317n36, 322n26; Paṟaiyar, 258–59, 317n36, 322n29; Tevar, 233; and village school, 256–59

Zamindars, 46, 50–51, 109, 110, 117, 302n23. *See also* landlords
Županov, Ines G.: "confession mode," 299n64; festivals of the saints, 1; Nobili, 7, 33, 34; proto-etic approach, 34; Ramnad missions, 39; tropicality, 13